CW01547768

The Archaeology of
Medieval Europe

TWELFTH TO SIXTEENTH CENTURIES

The Archaeology of Medieval Europe

Edited by Martin Carver and Jan Klápště

Acta Jutlandica
Humanities Series 2011/9

Aarhus University Press |

The Archaeology of Medieval Europe, vol. 2
© Aarhus University Press and the Authors

Designed and typeset by Anne Marie Kaad
Cover design by Jørgen Sparre
Cover illustration: Sir John Mandeville Sets Out on His Journey,
from The *Travels of Sir John Mandeville*, British Library, Ms. 24189, folio 3v.
Printed by Narayana Press, Denmark

Printed in Denmark 2011

ISSN 0065-1354 (Acta Jutlandica)
ISSN 0901-0556 (Humanities Series 9)

ISBN 978 87 7934 289 7 (Hb)
ISBN 978 87 7934 291 0 (Pb)

Aarhus University Press
Langelandsgade 177
DK-8200 Aarhus N
www.unipress.dk

White Cross Mills
Hightown, Lancaster, LA1 4XS
United Kingdom
www.gazellebookservices.co.uk

ISBC
70 Enterprise Drive
Bristol, CT 06010
USA

Published with the financial support of

Medieval and Renaissance Archaeology, University of Aarhus
National University of Ireland, Galway
The Aarhus University Research Foundation
The Learned Society, University of Aarhus
The Charles University, Prague
The University of Bologna
The University of Granada: Laboratory of Archaeology and Architecture of the City (LAAC)
The University of Reading
The University of Tromsø
The University of York

CONTENTS

189   CHAPTER 5

MATERIAL CULTURE – ARTEFACTS AND DAILY LIFE

Else Roesdahl and Frans Verhaeghe

228   POWER

Introduction *Martin Carver*

230   CHAPTER 6

ARCHAEOLOGIES OF COERCION

In 1999, in Seville, at the 'Fourth European Symposium for Teachers of Medieval Archaeology' (ESTMA), I proposed the idea of a collaborative textbook on the archaeology of medieval Europe. This was met with acclamation – we all felt the need for a greater focus in the teaching of our discipline's European dimensions, a focus difficult to provide without a textbook. A series of meetings followed, an advisory committee was set up, the form and contents of the proposed textbook was much discussed and finally agreed. Editors were appointed, and writing started.

It was decided that for practical reasons the geographical scope would be that part of Europe which was or would become dominated by western Christendom –Roman Catholic Europe. There would be two volumes, the first covering the eighth to twelfth centuries and the second covering the twelfth to sixteenth centuries. The volumes would be independent, but the subjects treated in each would be largely comparable. There would be no theoretical or methodical straight-jacket – rather the contents would mirror the diversities of European medieval archaeology. In order to strengthen such diversities and secure a broad approach, the individual chapters should preferably be written by at least two authors from different parts of Europe and there would be additional 'Box texts' on select topics.

As was made clear in the foreword to volume 1 there has been some distance between initial planning and the final product. Volume 1, edited by James Graham-Campbell with Magdalena Valor, was published in 2007 and we are extremely pleased that the project is now fulfilled with the publication of volume 2. The vastly increasing source material and the consequent growing diversity and complexity of the archaeology of later medieval Europe, as compared with the earlier period treated in the first volume will be apparent in this volume. On the other hand its contents also demonstrate that the cultures of Europe were increasingly interlinked, and show a series of new approaches and new methods within our fast-moving subject. We hope that the two volumes of *The Archaeology of Medieval Europe* will be a useful tool for continued teaching of this discipline and related subjects.

In 2008 Martin Carver joined the project with enthusiasm and vigour. We are immensely grateful to him and to his joint editor, Jan Klápště, and to all the contributors (some of whom were with us from the beginning) for making this volume possible. We also wish to thank Philip Dixon and David M. Wilson for invaluable help and advice during its long pregnancy. It is a great sadness that Johnny de Meulemeester, vice-chairman of the Advisory committee, whose enthusiastic support provided considerable impetus in its early stages, did not live to see its completion.

Aarhus University Press accepted our publication proposal with keen alacrity, and Sanne Lind Hansen saw both volumes through the press with patient perspicacity. A number of universities helped by contributing towards the cost of production. To all these institutions we express our warmest gratitude.

Else Roesdahl
Aarhus University, Denmark
Chairman, ESTMA Advisory Committee

ESTMA Advisory Committee for 'The Medieval Archaeology of Europe'

Terry Barry, Trinity College Dublin, Ireland
Reidar Bertelsen, University of Tromsø, Norway
James Graham-Campbell, University College London, England
Anne Nissen Jaubert, University of Tours, France
Jan Klápště, Charles University, Prague, Czech Republic
Johnny De Meulemeester, Ghent University, Belgium (Vice Chair) †
Tadhg O'Keeffe, University College Dublin, Ireland
Else Roesdahl, University of Aarhus, Denmark (Chair)
Barbara Scholkmann, University of Tübingen, Germany
Magdalena Valor, University of Seville, Spain

CHAPTER 1

AIMS AND METHODS

PART 1:   SCOPE AND AGENDA *by Martin Carver*

Introduction

The purpose of this book is to show what archaeology can do for the understanding of the later Middle Ages. It is already doing so much, there are so many expert practitioners at work and the period is so rich in material that we can hardly pretend to offer a total coverage: this is therefore a book of examples – examples of overviews, examples of projects, examples of methods. There is an additional factor, important at the start of the third millennium, and that is the accelerating pace of change in our subject. Some of the changes are intellectual, the arrival of new ways of interrogating and interpreting the past, while others are practical, the discovery of numerous new sites and new methods for investigating them. Since more than 80% of all archaeological research is now undertaken in advance of losses to the heritage (*l'archéologie préventive* or *mitigation archaeology*, formerly *rescue archaeology*), we need more reliable and flexible ways of profiting from research opportunities, in government agencies and commercial companies as well as in universities and museums. This book is therefore intended as a point of departure, both for those studying medieval archaeology and those needing to establish its value in the public sphere. And not least of our objectives is to present the work of archaeologists in many different European countries, who may be writing in different languages and following different agendas, so that we may learn from each other to the greater benefit of a European discipline.

The present volume is the sequel to *The Archaeology of Medieval Europe, Eighth to Twelfth Centuries* (Graham-Campbell & Valor 2007, cited here as AME 1) and follows a similar structure, presenting each class of evidence under simple accessible headings. However, the copious documentation and surviving architectural repertoire of this later period can make it daunting to navigate. We have therefore attempted to aid the reader by grouping our numerous contributions into associated topics within their chapters, and by presenting the chapters under three general themes.

Organisation of the volume

The titles of the three parts, like three gateways, announce broad areas of medieval action. *Habitat* (Part 1) refers to the place and circumstances in which people lived, and tries to make the connections between the environment (Ch 2), rural settlement (Ch 3), housing (Ch 4) and the material repertoire at the disposal of medieval people (Ch 5). *Power* (Part 2) focuses on the prime movers, the aristocracy (Ch 6), the manufacturers (Ch 7), the merchants (Ch 8) and the town (Ch 9), this order reflecting, in a general sense, a gradual net transfer of power in this period. *Spirituality* (Part 3), the belief in another world, suffuses medieval Europe and finds its archaeological expression primarily in objects (Ch 10), buildings (Ch 11) and burials (Ch 12).

These headings are intended to provide the reader with convenient pathways, but there are frequent cross-overs between them. Environment and the role of water ('hydraulic archaeology') is pursued at the scale of landscape (Ch 2), but implies power and affects settlement (Ch 3) and building (Ch 4). Artefacts may define something as discreet as a family (Ch 4, 5) or as broad as a town or region (Ch 2, 3, 9). Aspirations to power are manifested by quite small social groups in their buildings (Ch 4), as well as by the aristocracy in their castles and palaces (Ch 6), and by the rising industrial classes (Ch 7), merchants (Ch 8), burghers (Ch 9) and religious movements (Ch 10) in investments of increasing grandeur. This can blur the distinction between the traditional types of medieval monuments: for example, churches were fortified as well as towns and castles, and monasteries were centres of industrial production (Box 1.3 and Ch 11). Similarly, we can offer examples of spiritual expression in objects (Ch 5), houses (Ch 4), trade (Ch 8) and the layout of towns (Ch 9), as well as in places of worship (Ch 11) and burial (Ch 12).

As well as having to live, work, fight and pray, each medieval person had a nested set of identities, referred to home, to community and locality, and to wider areas of allegiance: religion, folk and nation. Archaeology allows us to report at each of these levels. Current opportunities for the study of medieval landscapes, sites, buildings, things and people offer many thousands of small stories, which we can be confident will eventually help to enrich, enliven and explain the medieval processes that formed the basis of modern Europe.

Scope of the volume

As a starting point for the present two-volume work, the eighth century was recognised as a watershed, notable in northern Europe in particular for the rebirth of towns, the widespread adoption of Christianity and the formation of the Carolingian Empire. The later twelfth century offers another watershed, with a major surge in agriculture, industry, urban life and institutionalised religion (AME 1, 15; see also e.g. Astill 2010). The authors of Volume 1 addressed the period eighth to twelfth century, while those of Volume 2 embrace the twelfth to the sixteenth centuries, while exercising licence to stray into earlier or later periods when the argument demands it. The pivotal twelfth century is thus shared by both volumes. For shorthand purposes, the period of this book is referred to by its authors as the 'later Middle Ages' and we have avoided the unfortunate term 'High Middle Age' which, in countries other than Britain, means the fourth to eleventh century rather than the mid-eleventh to mid-fourteenth (cf. AME 1, 17).

The area studied here is roughly from the Atlantic to the lower Danube and the Mediterranean to the Arctic (AME 1, 70; fig 2.7). This follows the defining concept of the project as used in Volume 1, that Medieval Europe should be taken as the geographical extent of western Christendom, or the area dominated by the Catholic Church (AME 1, 13). Because of the importance of the overall physical geography, and for the convenience of the reader, we offer another version of the map, showing the main rivers and the principal ecological zones (Fig 1.1). The evolving medieval polities are shown in Fig 1.2, but the countries we refer to in the chapters are mainly those we have today.

Physical geography

Fig 1.1

Aims and Methods   17

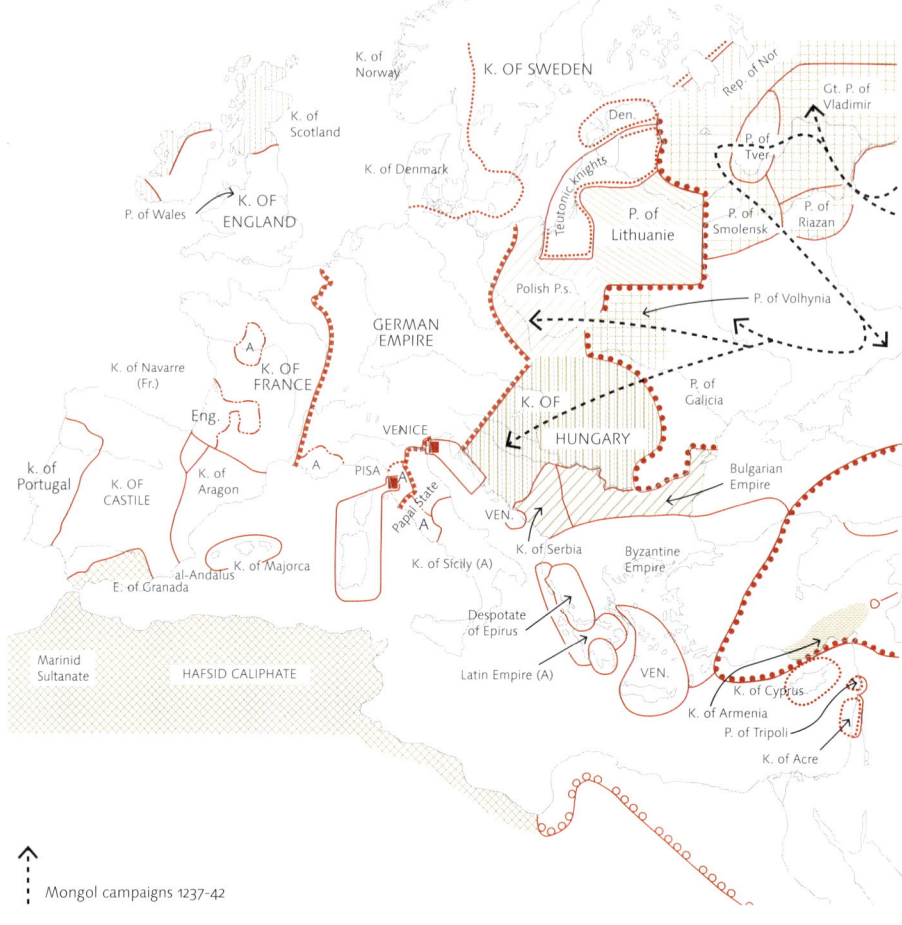

Mongol campaigns 1237-42

Fig 1.2   *Political geography of Europe in the mid 13th century, showing regions and kingdoms (adapted from McEvedy 1961, 77).*

The nucleus of Medieval Europe enlarged its knowledge of the world through belligerent crusades, against pagan nations in the north and east (Turnbull 2004), and against Islam in the south and east (Boas 1999). As a consequence, the experience of these invasions also provided a reflux of influence, as shown from contributions about Latvia and Estonia (Ch 6 and 10; p 265, p 430), and from the cultural zones dominated by Islam. Although the latter were frequently referred to in the earlier volume (see e.g. AME 1, 68-9, 157, 389-91), we have thought it useful in this one to include in-depth studies of houses and gardens (Ch 4), pottery and glass (Ch 7), religious sites (Ch 11) and burials (Ch 12), and here present a brief guide to the period terminology (Table 1). Islamic influence in Europe began at the same time as Islam itself in the early seventh century, with the settlement of Jerusalem and the East Mediterranean by the Umayyad dynasty and the invasion and settlement of the Maghreb (the north coast of Africa), culminating in the arrival of Muslims in the Iberian peninsula in AD 711. The Islamic empire was controlled in the eighth century by the Abbasid dynasty based in Baghdad, and from the tenth century by the Fatimids based at Cairo. In the early twelfth century al-Andalus became part of the Almoravid empire which stretched from Algeria to Senegal, and in the later twelfth century part of the Almohad empire which included most of the Maghreb. The principal city of al-Andalus was then Seville. In the early thirteenth century, Muslim rule was reduced to the small kingdom of Granada, governed by the Nasrid emirs. In 1492, this kingdom was conquered by the Christian nations of Spain led by Castile. The archaeology divides conveniently into an early period (eighth-ninth century) in which continuing Roman influence is evident, a middle period (tenth-thirteenth century) when al-Andalus is part of the cultural region of North African Islam, and a late period (thirteenth-fifteenth century) when it flourishes mainly within the Kingdom of Granada.

TABLE 1.1 TIMELINE FOR ISLAMIC SPAIN	
711-756	Part of the Umayyad Caliphate
756-929	Independent Emirate
929-1031	Caliphate of Córdoba
1031-c1091	First Taifa (independent kingdom)
c1091-c1145	Almoravid rule
c1145-c1151	Second Taifa
c1031-1212	Almohad rule
1228-1238	Third Taifa
1238-1492	Nasrid kingdom of Granada
1492	Castilian conquest

Even though the territory under Islam on the European continent diminished between the twelfth and sixteenth century, its buildings and cultural material continued to be actively used, emulated and adapted, and the leaders, merchants and manufacturers of the Maghreb and Islamic west Asia remained major players in the Mediterranean. Although pioneering Christians from Syria had already reached Ethiopia and China (MacCulloch 2010, 231-269), it was Islam that western European travellers mainly encountered as they pushed east into Asia and south into Africa (Ch 8). Thus Islamic practice in agriculture, architecture, urbanism, industry and religion is of rising interest to European medieval archaeologists. This can be seen, for example, in recent studies of twelfth-thirteenth century agriculture in Morocco and al-Andalus (De Meulemeester 2005), rural settlement in thirteenth century Jordan (McQuitty 2005) or the medieval cities of Merv on the silk road, their fortification and response to the invention of gunpowder (Brun 2005).

Even where no direct contact is supposed, archaeological studies of analogous periods in distant places may strengthen the interpretations of medieval archaeology and enlarge understanding of our home regions. Examples of recent studies are the relationship between the monumental centre of fourteenth century Tonga and its expanding maritime influence (Clark *et al.* 2008) or the distribution of copper ingots in fifteenth century Zimbabwe, and their connection to early kingdoms (Swann 2007). The sixteenth century tomb of Eung Tae in Korea, containing the preserved body of the dead man in a wooden coffin with intimate letters from his wife and father, offers a heart-rending encounter with the realities of medieval bereavement (Eun-Joo Lee *et al.* 2009). Increasingly rich information from medieval Mongolia (Rogers *et al.* 2005; Crubézy *et al.* 2006) and West Africa in the same period (Wynne-Jones 2007) is surely destined to lead well beyond analogy into increasing evidence of direct involvement between medieval Europe and the rest of the world (Ch 8).

Medieval Archaeology in theory and practice

Some of the achievements and objectives of medieval archaeology over the past fifty years were presented in Volume 1 (AME 1, Ch 1) and have been reviewed since its appearance for France (in Burnouf 2008), and for Britain and parts of Europe (in Gilchrist & Reynolds 2009). These two new accounts present an interesting contrast in emphasis. The first stresses the changes to the agenda of medieval archaeology brought about through the huge quantity of new information coming from mitigation or rescue archaeology (*l'archéologie preventive)*. The second, in alignment with north American archaeology, feels that the driver of the subject lies not in historical curiosity or the exigencies of the day, but in archaeological theory, portrayed as the backbone of the discipline with its own intellectual impetus. Drawing on considerable advances in the understanding of how the past is interpreted today, theory is thought to provide the principal foundation for the way archaeology is researched and taught in some European countries today (Johnson 1999; Gilchrist 2009).

In brief, theory has been championed in three main frameworks: *culture history* focuses on material remains (settlements, cemeteries, buildings and artefacts) and chronicles their significance for understanding the past. *Processualism* (equated with modernism) focuses on communities, and defines the systems governing societies and their relationship with the environment. *Post-processualism* (equated with post-modernism) focuses on individuals, their intentions and aspirations, hopes, fears, experiences of the world and their attempts to influence each other (collectively their 'agency'). The realisation that archaeologists too are in the business of influencing each other has raised a fourth area of theory, *reflexivity*, which purports to examine why we say what we say about the past.

There is an important difference in the way that processualists and post-processualists claim authority for their interpretations; the former, like social scientists, require the collection of large amounts of data and its resolution into models of events or behaviour by means of statistically supported *analysis*. Post-processualists make extensive use of *analogy* from living societies along with imaginative leaps that can be justified – a transparent intuition. Not unnaturally, this has led to an arts-science divide between theorists, but it is one that is being closed by modern fieldwork (see below).

Post-processual archaeology, it has been claimed, has "changed the questions we ask about the Middle Ages" (Gilchrist 2009, 397). This is both true, and not true. Medievalists have always wanted to know the purpose of material culture and what it tells us about the way people thought and how they treated each other in terms of age, gender and other forms of social identity. What has changed is the degree of confidence we bring to the task of interpretation, relying less on the personal prestige of scholars, more on the transparency of documented argument. We are equipped with a much greater ability to discover and record the remains of the past and a greater intellectual confidence to create and justify the pictures they evoke. This means that arts and science, and cultural historical, processual and post-processual champions need not be at war with each other (cf. Gilchrist 2009, 397).

Many medieval archaeologists are happy to treat all aspects of theory proselytised over the last 50 years as part of an intellectual toolbox, still current and available to all (Carver 2002; Gerrard 2003a). The truth is that the agenda is what each generation says it is, and it can and should make use of all the thinking that has gone before, not just the latest fashion. Some contemporary shared mood-music is inevitable, but perhaps the next generation needs to be released from over-commitment to current paradigms and allow its individual creativity to run free. The secret of this lies in evaluative design, an approach of particular importance now that the bulk of archaeological fieldwork takes place outside universities and museums and in the commercial sector.

Whether in the academic sector, driven by research, or in the commercial sector, aimed at mitigating damage to the heritage, modern archaeological investigation has a number of characteristic procedures. It is generally conducted in projects, each of which is designed to answer selected questions from a current *research agenda*. Our ability to address such questions depends on how the material evidence has survived, the nature of the *archaeological resource*. Since the materials of our research are so vulnerable to destruction, the need for preservation is also a determinant factor. A modern archaeological project is therefore designed in such a way as to match what we want to know (the agenda), with what we can know (the resource on offer) and what we desire to leave for the future (conservation). Balancing these three factors produces the *project design*, the basis of archaeological inquiry and its funding (Carver 2009). Some of these ideas will be briefly considered, insofar as they relate to the current and future programming of medieval archaeology in Europe.

The nature of the resource

Students and practitioners of later medieval archaeology are often attracted initially by Europe's many grand monuments. Castles, abbeys, cathedrals and churches of stone, together with timber-framed houses, form a prominent part of Europe's cultural heritage (Fig 1.3). Some of these buildings are ruinous, some were once ruinous and are now conserved and displayed as ruins, while others have been restored so as to echo or imitate the Middle Ages (Fig 1.4). Even where most of the materials have been replaced or conjectured, the effect of a walled citadel like Carcassonne (Ch 6) or the timber-framed

Fig 1 .3   *The castle of Sinclair-Girnigoe in Caithness, north-east Scotland, in course of a programme of making safe, investigation, conservation, restoration and display (FAS-Heritage Ltd).*

Fig 1.4   *Medieval lineaments: the bakery at 17, Pfarrgasse in Linz, Austria in continuous ownership of bakers since 1570 and home of the legendary Linzertorte. The timber façade renewed in 1870 is an evocation of the medieval shopfront (M. Carver).*

Restored timber-framed buildings at Place de la République, Bar-sur-Seine, France (M. Carver).

Fig 1.5

town of Bar-sur-Seine is still evocative (Fig 1.5). Other monuments peep out from later fabric still in use, or emerge when old buildings are demolished to make way for the new (for an example, see AME 1, 158).

Such respect for the medieval heritage is relatively new to a continent long obsessed with its Classical past. The fate of the medieval Acropolis offers a parable, in which more than a thousand years of medieval and more recent settlement were cleared away in the nineteenth century, without record, in order to create an epitome of Classical Greece (McNeal 1991). Elsewhere in Europe, and particularly in the north where the hand of Roman heritage lay lighter, the nineteenth and early twentieth century saw a rise of interest in things medieval, expressed in terms of the classification of architecture into Romanesque, Gothic and its subdivisions. This typology, sequenced by artistic analysis and dated by written records, helped to create a chronology for illuminated manuscripts, fine metalwork and the numerous churches and grand houses of medieval origin surviving in town and country throughout the length and breadth of Europe (for a handy guide to architectural terminology see Lever & Harris 1993). The fundamental groundwork also raised, and continues to raise, public appreciation of the value of these things (e.g. Alexander & Binksi 1987). Tourists are now routinely directed to medieval buildings and sculpture, and museums often include a display of late medieval suits of armour, pottery, metal buckles, pilgrim badges and so on, to accompany a table-top model of the medieval town. Medieval history, and even more so medieval fiction, sells well, and a ground swell of passion for the trappings of the era, termed *medievalism*, has continued to build until today, marked by the success of *The Lord of the Rings,* enactment societies and numerous films making references to the period with an authenticity that ranges from mildly credible to total caricature (Hall 2009).

While the received Middle Ages depends largely for its inspiration on upstanding cultural properties, these represent little more than the tip of the iceberg. The world of medieval archaeology is a very much larger one, concerning itself with everything that lies beneath: behind the façade of modern buildings and under the surface of the ground – and not only what is physically hidden from view, but what lies inside the experience of real individuals who lived in the period we study: the landscape they looked on, the houses they lived in, the furniture they used, their hygiene, their calls to war, the wounds they sustained, the objects they crafted and traded, the journeys they undertook, the rituals they performed – and, by means of all these rediscoveries, the hopes and fears that drove them.

It is apparent, however, that beneath the surface of the ground, material survival has been uneven, due in part to the original materials used, and in part to what happened to them since burial. Much of the south of Europe built in stone, but stone buildings are easily repaired and recycled to make new ones. In the northern parts of Europe, building was primarily in timber, readily burnt or rotted away. One special area, the 'organic crescent', crossing roughly from Finland to Ireland, is notable for its outstanding preservation of wood, leather, textiles and other organic materials, providing a window into life that is unusually comprehensive – Novgorod, Bergen, York and Dublin being among the most notable examples (Brisbane 1992; Carver 1993 and AME 1, *passim*).

In its more commonly encountered form, the archaeology of peasant life is notoriously ephemeral. Fields often survive as sinuous earthworks (selions) on the surface of land that was not ploughed later (Ch 3). The exploitation of resources is usually indirect – the fragments of timber, plants and animals found on sites show which species were being brought in and by implication the local habitat (Ch 3, p 66). The traces of houses of timber, turf or cob (dried mud) sometimes show up from the air, but what remains is insubstantial. A rare exception was small twelfth-thirteenth century building excavated at Wallingford Castle, England, which proved to be constructed entirely in cob (dried mud). It was preserved to a height of 1.8m, and had various internal features including wall plaster and the impressions of door-jambs (Chapelot & Fossier 1985, 256). More normally, excavators work with stubs of walls and patches of floor and may struggle even to make a complete plan. Turf and cob may disappear completely, and posts and stakes may not have reached far enough into the ground to survive later ploughing (Fig 1.6).

The archaeological target varies in size from a cathedral to a seed and from a seed to the signature of organic molecules and inorganic elements left by plants, animals and artefacts (see below, p 35; and part 2). The responses of archaeologists therefore need to be creative, not to be fixed or applied routinely; every intervention is a unique opportunity that must be adjusted to the great variety of survival in different terrain and the long list of questions posed by archaeologists, anthropologists, historians and art historians.

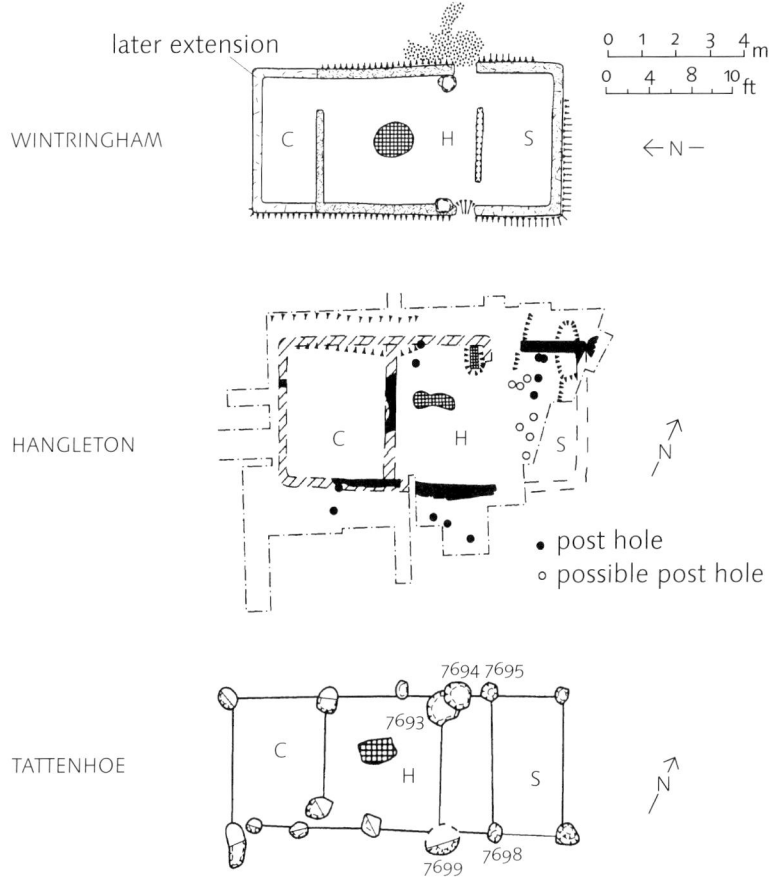

What's left: Mark Gardiner (2000, fig. 5) describes the 'standard' building plan of vernacular houses of the 12-13th century in England, consisting of a cross entry, service, hall and chamber. The plan must often be reconstructed from many different kinds of ephemeral traces, not easy to see: post-holes, stake-holes, dwarf walls of stone, walls of mud and stud construction.

Fig 1.6

Field method

In general, archaeological investigation in the field follows a simple itinerary: *reconnaissance*, which uses landscape survey to find sites, *evaluation* which uses site survey to assign them a current research value, *project design*, which sets out the research and conservation programmes, *fieldwork* in which data is gathered by survey and excavation, *analysis* where the results are studied and *publication* where they are archived and disseminated. These are professional procedures necessary for successful interaction with modern systems of heritage management of the type encountered in most European countries.

Several important consequences follow. In the first place, reconnaissance and evaluation surveys precede excavation even in towns; it is rare that an archaeologist now starts digging without a previously defined and publicised plan of research. It also follows that the techniques and methods of recording will vary with each design, depending on the questions, the nature of the resource and the amount of access permitted. Thirdly, most medieval projects will combine landscape survey, site survey, excavation and the archaeological recording of buildings, and their subsequent analyses, into an integrated and co-ordinated programme. These methods underlie many of our contributions, but often lack the space to describe what was done. Accordingly there follow some brief sketches intended to help new readers to appreciate what is involved in archaeological research in and out of the field.

Landscape survey

The study of landscape is a powerful area of research, and a necessary precursor to any major development project. Satellite photography is used in the reconnaissance and evaluation stages, for example to show up areas of buried wetland. Aerial survey at a lower height has provided striking images of medieval landscape (Fig 1.7), and methods now include Lidar, which records very small variations in the land-surface, as for example flattened rig and furrow fields.

Fig 1.7   *Aerial photograph showing the earthworks of rig and furrow fields surrounding the deserted medieval village of Olney Grounds, Buckinghamshire southeast England (Buckinghamshire). (Klápště, after H. Clarke 1984).*

The landscape is a large-scale archaeological site, which has the capacity to report the nature of the environment (Ch 2) and the location of settlements (Ch 3) and the interactions between them. Survey begins with a reconnaissance phase: for example, a recent *extensive* survey in Greenland in the core area of Norse settlement had the aim of mapping all settlements with a view to the selection of sites for more detailed investigation (Guldager *et al.* 2002). *Intensive* surveys move on to harder questions, such as how and why the settlement pattern changed between the thirteenth and sixteenth century in Brittany (Ch 3; Astill & Davies 1997, ch. 7). Ideally our agenda includes what natural resources there were, what people did with them and how these things changed: to chronicle the pulse of agricultural exploitation, as land is taken into cultivation and lost again. The Ystad project (1999-2000) selected three small regions (up to 10km across) and examined all the evidence for their ecology over the last 6000 years, with the help of excavated material and pollen trapped in a number of lakes (Berglund 1991). The size of human and domestic animal populations, plant variety, plant resources (areas of forest and grazing), plant exploitation and the use of manure were all estimated in this way. The base line was established by the rich eighteenth-century data. These highly structured inquiries address questions about human synergy with the environment and how it differs from place to place through time. It was not assumed to be a 'normative' relationship, since both the environment and the human response were subject to change.

The later medieval period features a range of evidence that gives it a high potential for this kind of investigation. Pottery is often plentiful, so that its distribution on the surface of ploughland offers a detailed map of the distribution and character of settlements and their extent (Box 1.1). Other methods include documentary survey and environmental sequences (from pollen and plant remains, see part 2). A recent study of a 'wetland' used topographical survey, placenames, environmental sampling, standing buildings and the results of excavation to formulate a basis for research into an estate managed for Glastonbury Abbey by the manor of Meare (Rippon 2004). The principal tool here was *Historic Landscape Characterisation* (HLC), a map that shows the different kinds of terrain on the estate today, and what was known about its use in the Middle Ages (Fig 1.8). This provided a template for further research, which in turn showed that there was a vast extent of wetland incorporated into the abbey's property. Initially it was very wet with occasional islands, and its value appeared to lie mainly in its sacred character, used to attract pilgrims. Some wetland was subsequently drained to create pasture that by 1300 was the abbey's most successful earner. The remainder was also economically productive from fish, wildfowl, reeds and withies.

There is no doubt that current land use and traditional farming practices are necessary parts of the study of landscape, since what can be grown is so closely linked to soil and climate. This has tended to encourage the idea of the medieval countryside as exhibiting a *longue durée* (Braudel 1972), an enduring arena on which communal and individual events impinge. But targeted, localised surveys are challenging this model, seeing a relationship between humans and their environment in which first one then the other has the upper hand (Ch 2). A recent example of landscape survey in central

BOX 1.1   SHAPWICK: INTENSIVE INVESTIGATION OF AN ENGLISH VILLAGE

The modern parish of Shapwick in Somerset, southwest England, is an economic and religious unit at least as old as the Middle Ages and covering 1284 ha (3172 acres). Investigations by Mick Aston and Chris Gerrard, with a large team of volunteer helpers, treated the whole parish as one large archaeological site, in which the buried information was accessed using different field methods in different places. The aim was to investigate the use of the land, the way it was managed, and the type of social control that was exercised, thus offering a window on the wider history of England. Geological, topographical, archaeological, and documentary methods were all used, and the survey was designed first to assess and study the sources that were richest for each period and then to use archaeology – the principal source of new evidence – to explore periods for which there was least information.

Shapwick is well documented and mapped from the nineteenth century when tithe (tax) maps were drawn up but there are eight earlier maps and good documentation from the later Middle Ages thanks to the monks of Glastonbury Abbey to whom the village belonged. 'Retrogressive analysis' or deconstruction of the maps was achieved by correlating them with the names of fields, watercourses, and routes mentioned in medieval surveys of 1327 and 1515. This enabled a map of 'medieval Shapwick' to be drawn up for testing.

The archaeological inventory held in the *County Sites and Monuments Record* was searched for finds that had been made before the survey started. One result of this archive work was to prepare a 'biography' of every field of the parish, cataloguing all that was known about it, particularly its ownership and land-use, into the Middle Ages and beyond (Fig 1). All historic buildings within and beyond the village were visited and surveyed and samples taken for dating by dendrochronology. The story of individual enclosures was enhanced by counting species of plants in hedgerow, which provided a likely minimum age for the field boundary (the more species, the older the hedgerow). Crop-marks seen and photographed from the air were plotted on the field maps. Artefact scatters were mapped where they showed on ploughsoil. All arable fields were walked at 25 m spacings (giving a 7-10% sample) and "finds of all periods collected, from prehistoric to the very recent, from flint to plastic." This total collection was to facilitate the use of voluntary labour of varying expertise; everything could be picked up and then later sorted, assigned to period. By 1996 some 70,612 artefacts had been bagged and sorted from 302 ha (746 acres), representing a coverage to that time of 40% of the walkable area.

Promising concentrations were then re-walked on 10 m grids. Details noted in field records included the conditions obtaining at the time and the identity of the collectors, so that visibility and retrieval could later be monitored. The record also included the condition of the sherds – especially whether they were abraded, i.e. worn from movement in the spoil, a condition which was equated with deposition in medieval ploughed fields. The researchers felt that most of the surface material in fact reflected not the locations of settlement but patterns of agriculture.

Shovel testing was used on unploughed land, in woods and on pasture, with 5 equally spaced 30 litre samples being taken from each 50 m². In built-up areas, 1 m² test pits were

Fig 1

Area of investigations at Shapwick, Somerset.

sunk through gardens and open spaces, and half the upturned spoil was screened. These assemblages and their sherd size were then compared with the assemblages from surface collection and shovel testing. Subterranean features in likely areas of sites, as suggested for example by placenames, were mapped by geophysical survey. Magnetometry and resistivity were used after validation by excavation of a test area to see what kinds of feature were being detected. Geochemical survey was especially effective, not only for phosphates, but carbon, lead, and zinc also proved sensitive for locating settlement areas, raising some excitement about the potential of 'multi-element signatures' as an evaluation tool. The

mapping of heavy metal concentrations, for example, indicated the extent of the medieval churchyard around the abandoned church (Fig 2). Numerous exploratory trenches were dug to help characterize the deposit by its depth and survival of artefacts and ecological and environmental evidence. Three large open areas were then excavated to investigate early medieval structures, with a fourth large sample being taken from a medieval moat to recover ecological data.

The intimate contact with the past offered by this intensive deconstruction of a single parish prompts interpretation at new levels of confidence (Fig 3). The periods of major investment and social organization were

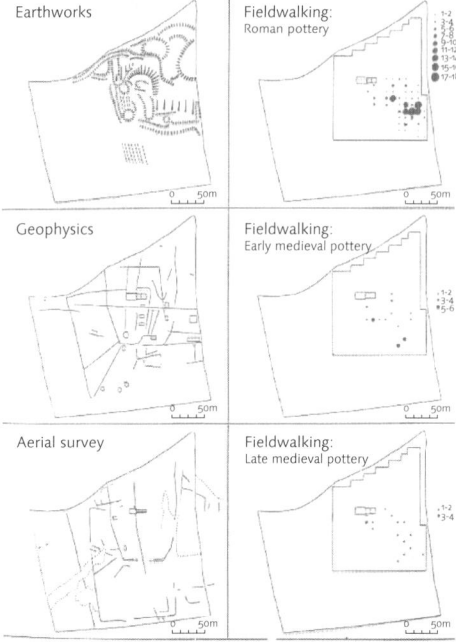

Earthworks

Geophysics

Aerial survey

Fieldwalking:
Roman pottery

Fieldwalking:
Early medieval pottery

Fieldwalking:
Late medieval pottery

Fig 2

The Shapwick Project, southern England (Somerset). The site of a buried medieval church and churchyard characterized by surface finds of pottery, topography and geophysics (after Aston and Gerrard 1999).

clearly identifiable. The persistent norm of dispersed farmsteads as a way of exploiting the natural resources was interrupted by three 'dynamic' periods: in the third-fourth centuries, the late Roman population operated from a tiered settlement hierarchy centred on a villa. In the thirteenth century, the dispersed population was rehoused in a nucleated village by the authorities at Glastonbury Abbey. Most of the families who lived in medieval Shapwick between 1200 and 1600 were tenants of the Abbey and lived in

houses which were long and low in their proportions, with thatched roofs and no chimneys. One of these houses, of fourteenth or fifteenth century date, still stands – a three-room plan with a central hall, services and inner room or chamber. Remarkably, part of its thatched roof of rivet wheat is preserved too, blackened by the smoke that once swirled upwards from the central hearth in the hall. Lesser dwellings in the village may have been built of cob with roofs supported by cruck trusses. They stood within plots, or tofts, separated by drystone walls and drainage ditches. Excavation revealed examples in which ditches had been filled, indicating the amalgamation of tofts.

The administrative centre of the abbey's lands, its *curia*, was moved into the village at the end of the thirteenth century. Excavations here identified a platform 55m wide and 120m long surrounded by a moat 6m wide and 2m deep. Written evidence suggests that there was a hall with a chapel, an ox-house, cider press, a Great Barn (which stood until the late eighteenth century), stable, granary among other buildings, as well as two gardens and a dovecote. Waterlogged contexts, sampled for insect remains, plant macrofossils, molluscs and pollen, established that the moat contained stagnant muddy water overhung with vegetation. Whipworm eggs probably indicate faecal contamination but the ditch was a dumping ground for all kinds of waste from burnt scraps of animal bone to sweepings of peat presumably stacked for fuel. At the heart of the complex lay a first floor hall and an adjacent kitchen, both of which still stand encased within later alterations. Timbers of the hall, hidden behind a nineteenth century façade, were dated by

Legend:

- ▢ Wetland
- ◦ Woodland (grazing, coppice with standards)
- ⚐ Marsh meadow
- ⋯ Stream
- ✝ Church up 1329
- ▦ Ridge and furrow
- ✶ Spring
- Field names as for 1515 survey

— N —

minor reclamation new ditches, banks

medieval pottery

digging peat turves

seasonal pasture and meadow

northern limit of common fields

approximate edge of Levels

Mill Brook

Withymere

New Mead

Catewood Close

water mill

Messewell

stream diverted to mill

Verysway

Shoote Brook

SHAPWICK

Cats Drove Stream

Eastfield by Northbrook

Harepath

Halgebroke

Stonequarrie

Verysway

✝ 4016

Foulepytt

La Hurste

WEST FIELD

EAST FIELD

windmill

Furches

Lokkesleigh

Gallows

Old Downe

Harepath

0   1 km

Fig 3

Shapwick: the Medieval village, as deduced by the investigations.

dendrochronology to 1428 and 1489. Artefacts and ecofacts hint at the lifestyle of those who lived here, including delicacies such as milk-fed lamb, fallow deer, hare, rabbit, goose and duck. Peacock, a medieval symbol of vanity as well as being valued for its brilliant plumage, was also identified and is documented at Shapwick in the early fourteenth century account rolls. Here, as elsewhere, the combination of documentary evidence, archaeology and architecture combines to give a rich picture of medieval life (Source: Aston *et al.* 1998; Aston & Gerrard 1999; Gerrard & Aston 2007)

M. Carver after Aston & Gerrard 1999, Gerrard & Aston 2007

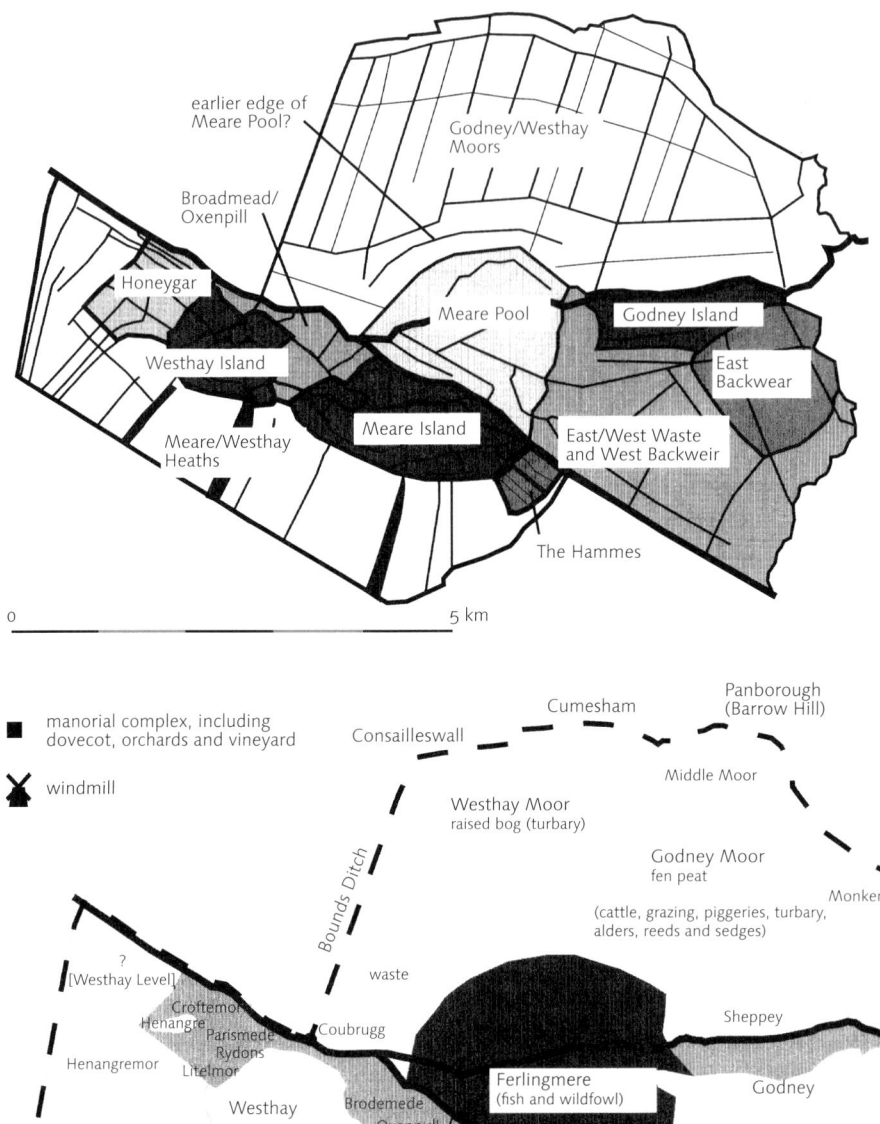

Fig 1.8 *Investigations of the wetland around Meare owned by Glastonbury Abbey. (Above): Historic Landscape Characterisation. (Below): Interpretation of the manor in c 1350 (Rippon 2004, Fig 11, 12).*

Italy examined the medieval management of sheep through transhumance. Comparing environmental, survey and settlement evidence showed that transhumance was not conditional on the terrain or climate but coincident with control by new lords, the imposition of castles and emergence of nucleated villages from the late twelfth century (Christie 2008, 117).

Site survey

A 'site' is simply a place where archaeologists work, but it is often used more specifically to mean an unnamed settlement or cemetery. Site study begins with evaluation, a stage in which the extent and character of the site, its likely contribution to research and its current value to the community are all assessed. Documentation, aerial survey, surface survey, geophysical survey and trial excavation are all methods used to predict the character of a buried deposit in advance.

'Deposit modelling' helps to formulate strategies both for excavation and for conservation and uses a number of powerful techniques. Ground survey has improved greatly in speed and precision. For example, inspecting the surface of the ground in the precinct of the ruined Gilbertine Priory of Watton in East Yorkshire, Chapman and Fenwick (2002) used a Global Positioning System (GPS) that provides increasingly precise three-dimensional co-ordinates to generate thousands of points. These were then entered into a Geographic Information System (GIS) in order to create Digital Terrain Models (DTM). This non-destructive methodology revealed previously unrecorded buildings and an enclosure to the west of the Nun's cloister. In site investigations, improvements in precision and penetration by geophysical methods such as Ground Penetrating Radar and Caesium Magnetometry, mean that the detection of ephemeral structures (such as abound in rural settlement) are now more feasible without excavation.

In towns especially, planning decisions, whether to excavate or conserve, are based on the deposit model – what is likely to be found and its context. Urban deposit modelling on the macro scale was pioneered by France's *Centre National d'Archéologie Urbaine* at Tours, which set out to map the historic towns of France and their archaeological potential (Fig 1.9; see also Carver 1983). Documentary sources and records of observations underground, archaeological or not, are combined to map the quality and distribution of *les archives du sol* – or archaeological deposits. This results not only in a series of maps setting out the evolution of the town site, but a map of where deposits have survived. The exercise brings rewards for both the protection of deposits through planning controls and for the guidance of researchers seeking to maximise research opportunities.

In the countryside, the construction of detailed deposit models makes use of place-names, topographical survey, geophysical survey, pottery surface scatters and test pits to predict the extent of a medieval site and its survival (for example Shapwick, see Box 1.1). In England, where treasure-hunting is legal, the mapping of objects discovered by metal-detectorists can theoretically locate settlements, and also more elusive and ephemeral sites like seasonal fairs. In the vineyards and olive groves of southern Europe, the pottery may need to be unearthed by shovel-testing – where shallow pits are dug at regular intervals to reveal the distribution of artefacts now buried in previously cultivated soil. Where a depth

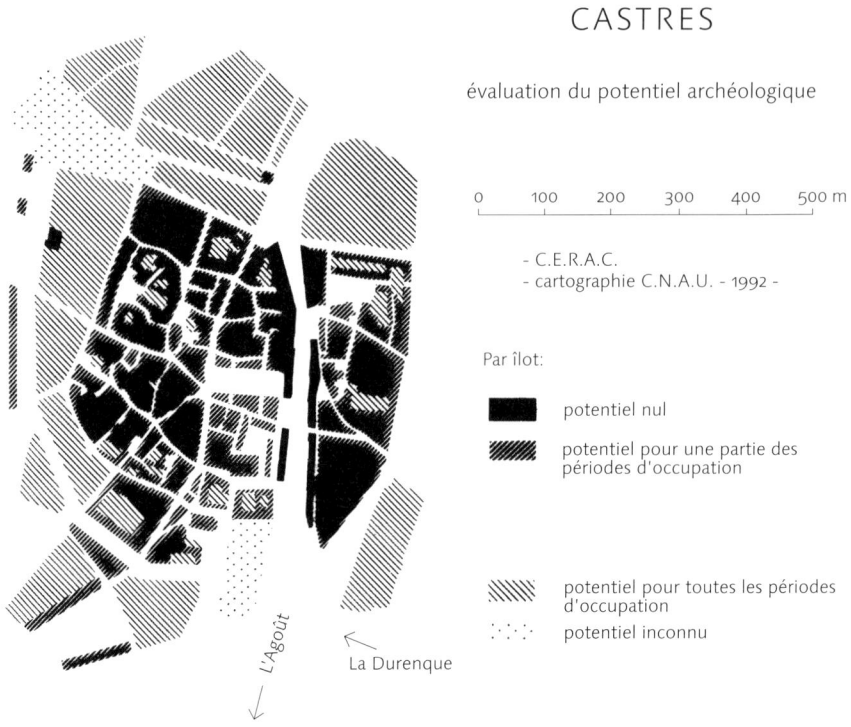

CASTRES

évaluation du potentiel archéologique

0   100   200   300   400   500 m

- C.E.R.A.C.
- cartographie C.N.A.U. - 1992 -

Par îlot:

potentiel nul

potentiel pour une partie des
périodes d'occupation

potentiel pour toutes les périodes
d'occupation

potentiel inconnu

L'Agoût

La Durenque

Fig 1.9   *Urban survey. An assessment of archaeological deposits and their potential at Castres in southern France (Cambon 1993, overlay 9).*

of strata is suspected, for example a settlement buried by river silt, the area is explored using test pits, usually measuring 1 x 1 m and taken down to the undisturbed subsoil. A concentration of medieval materials indicates a medieval deposit and the wall of the pit (section) can indicate the type of deposit – that is whether it belongs to a settlement, a cemetery or a ploughed field. Large areas are explored using long trenches (transects) cut by machine. Where a motorway or a railway line is to be laid, the area to be destroyed may be seen laced by hundreds of parallel trenches, used by archaeologists attempting to ensure that no site stays hidden to be destroyed without record (see Ch 3, p 119).

Excavation

Excavation, whether of buildings, settlements or cemeteries, brings us face to face with the Middle Ages as nothing else can (Fig 1.10). The aim is to define the strata and use them to construct a sequence of dated activity. Wherever possible, this is achieved by lifting the strata in reverse order and recording each 'context' (i.e. layer or deposit) and its contents and its relationships with the rest of the site. Traditionally these records have taken the form of measured drawings of plans (horizontal) and sections (vertical), which act as a permanent record of what was actually seen; walls, which form and integral part of the archaeological deposit, are also recorded in plan (horizontal) and elevation (vertical) (Fig 1.11). Sections have the advantage of showing the relationships between layers as they appeared on site, but the disadvantage of only showing the sequence in one place. Modern excavations generate stratification diagrams, which set out to show all the relationships between stratigraphic units, including those that were uncertain. The simplest methods use a single type of stratigraphic unit (the context, e.g. the Harris matrix, AME 1, 38-9), but more sophisticated sequence diagrams use multi-concept stratigraphic units, i.e. contexts, features and structures (Fig 1.12). These diagrams are designed to offer models for a dated sequence of events.

Excavators battle to match their questions to their opportunities. In many urban mitigation projects, access is extremely limited, but archaeological information can still be won. An archaeological opportunity in Dean's Yard at Westminster Abbey, London offered only shafts 1 m² and 4m deep dug to found underpinning columns – but archaeologists using the sections in the sides of the shafts were able to report the rise and fall of the adjacent River Thames (Fig 1.13). At other sites, the strata are so hard to distinguish that excavators work from scrupulously clean horizontal and vertical sections (the 'Schnitt' method), recording and surveying visible anomalies with high precision (see for example the excavation at Starigard/Oldenburg, Müller-Wille 1991). It is important to note that all these methods are valid in certain circumstances and a project design may adopt any or all of them.

Many medieval sites are particularly hard to define, having ephemeral structures of turf and stones now ploughed away, leaving little imprint in the ground. The sites of medieval villages are notoriously bereft of material, which can lead to their misinterpretation (see Ch 3, p 106). Even such pottery and bone as there is may be scattered on the fields with the midden, away from the settlements (see Ch 3, pt 2 Rattray). The poor survival of structures and materials on rural sites has led archaeologists to a low opinion of peasant life (Astill 1988b, 40), and yet buildings of turf and timber, so easily dispersed after their abandonment, may constitute major investments; and now elusive materials such as textiles and carved wood were among the most influential of their day (Ch 5, p 194; Ch 7, pt 3). Even a very slight assemblage may prove revealing, if plotted and collected with care. Archaeologists in Scotland used the distribution of small pebbles, smooth stones, cow metatarsals and seaweed ash to deduce the making of parchment, although there was only one diagnostic artefact (Carver & Spall 2004; cf Fig 2.13). Bioarchaeologists have proposed that some crafts, such as weaving, can be detected from 'indicator packages', a signature group of the remains of certain insects, animals, and plants, as well as artefacts (Hall & Kenward 2003).

The modern agenda requires us to do more than take opaque strata at face value. Scandinavinian archaeologists working on Viking period sites have been at the forefront of this 'nano-excavation' which uses chemical and physical trackers on clean excavated surfaces to detect the use and storage of vanished materials, such as food, salt and textiles (Hjulstro & Isaakson 2009; Oonk et al. 2009; Wilson et al. 2009). This kind of 'CSI' archaeology can also be indirect. A recent project in Greenland argued

Fig 1.10   *Excavation in progress at the cemetery of St. Catherine's Church in Eindhoven, Holland. Photograph by Laurens Mulkens, Archaeology Section, Eindhoven. Reproduced with permission.*

Fig 1.11   *Recording: Extract from the graphic records of excavated features and layers in the south transept and eastern chapels of Bordesley Abbey by Philip Rahtz. (upper) Section E-W through side-chapel C; (centre) Plan; (lower) elevation of west-facing walls (Rahtz & Hirst 1976, fig 44, 50, 56; and see Ch. 11, p 460).*

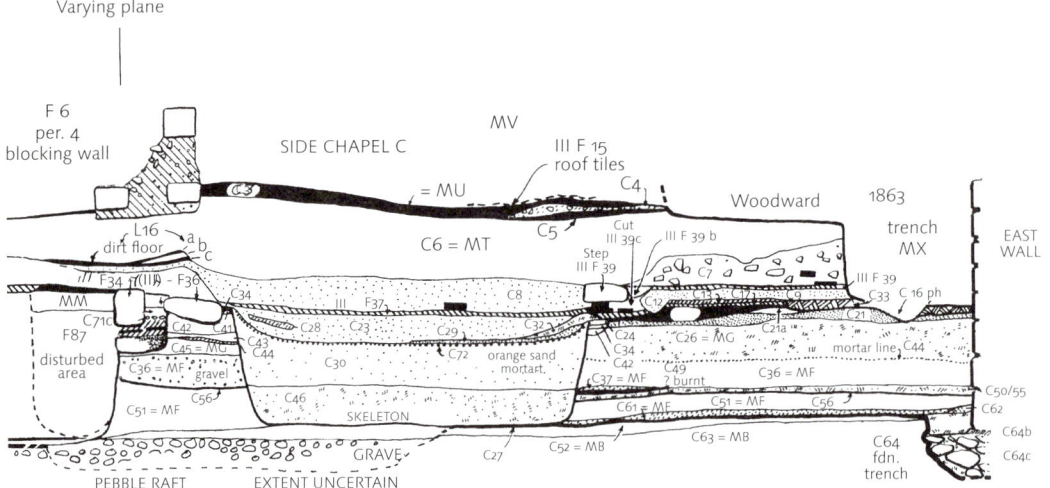

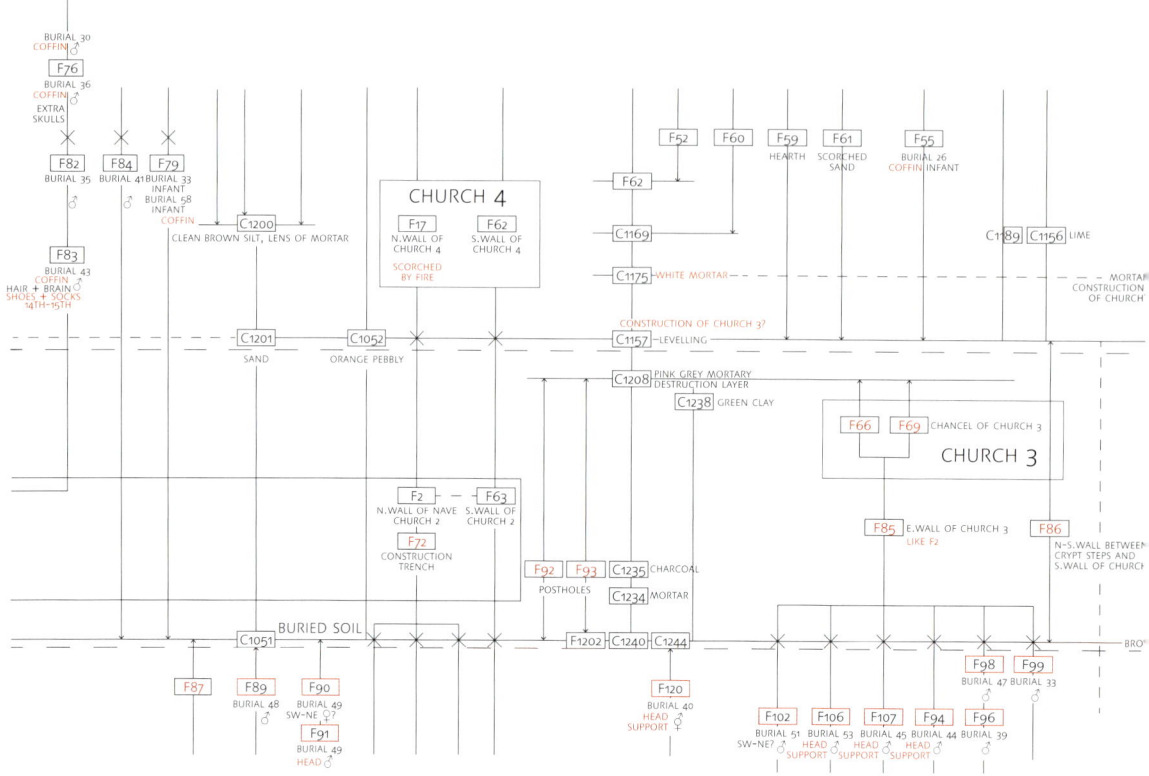

Fig 1.12 *Extract from a stratification diagram for a sequence of medieval churches and burials from an excavation in north-east Scotland, using multi-conceptual units (context, feature, structure) (M. Carver – FAS Heritage).*

that the adDNA (ancient dirt DNA) sequence of passing animals had been successfully captured in a soil column, thus chronicling the coming and going of sheep and cattle between AD 1040 and 1450 (Hebsgaard *et al.* 2009). Such 'white coat' archaeology has a high potential to address some of history's questions at sites that have almost disappeared, and suggests that medieval archaeologists will need to demand more from every research opportunity (for a recent review, see Carver 2011).

Studying buildings

In an earlier generation, medieval buildings were the province of the architectural historian, who made used of written documents in combination with observations on the ground to create a narrative for a building and place it in its artistic and historical context. In a recent study of the Bishop's Palace at St David's (Turner 2000), the emphasis of the project was on the analysis of the standing fabric. Plans and elevations were drawn and the palace 'deconstructed' into sixteen consecutive phases of building. This

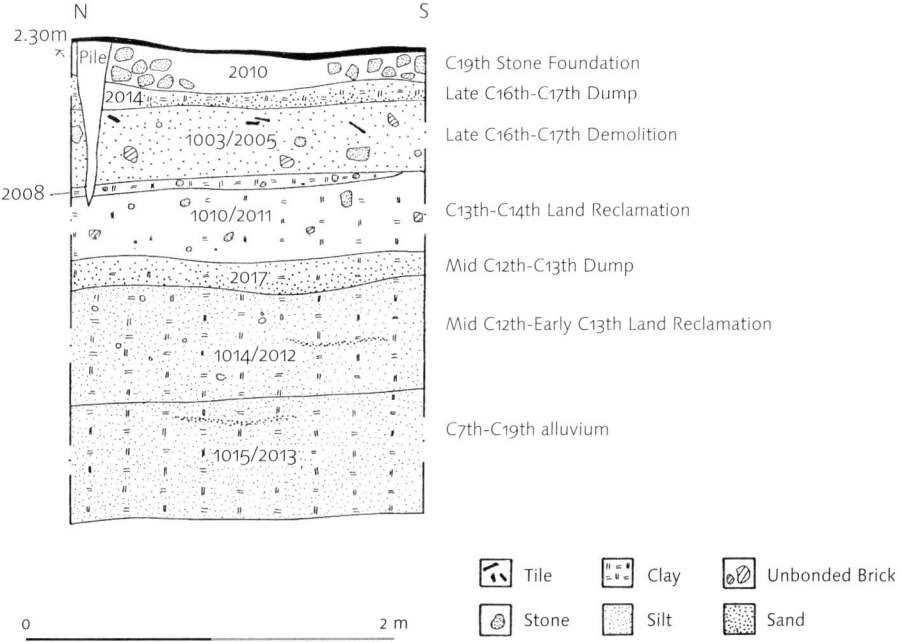

N   S

2.30m

Pile   2010

2014

1003/2005

2008

1010/2011

2017

1014/2012

1015/2013

C19th Stone Foundation
Late C16th-C17th Dump

Late C16th-C17th Demolition

C13th-C14th Land Reclamation

Mid C12th-C13th Dump

Mid C12th-Early C13th Land Reclamation

C7th-C19th alluvium

Tile   Clay   Unbonded Brick

Stone   Silt   Sand

0   2 m

Commercial excavation of a test pit in the yard of Westminster Abbey, London. The abbey was built **Fig 1.13**
on Thorney Island and the interventions in Dean's Yard showed how the modern city had developed
on land reclaimed from the flood plain of the river Thames, mainly in the middle ages, beginning in
the mid 12th century (Murray 2003, Fig. 2).

also established a context for the 130 stone corbels that had once adorned the unusual arcaded parapets of the main ranges of the palace, and allowed the author to reconstruct the form of the great hall and to imagine it in action (Fig 1.14).

What then distinguishes the methods of the archaeologist from those of the architectural historian? Superficially, it may be the selection of a particular method; for example Sally Badham (2007) used Ground Penetrating Radar (GPR) to locate lost tombs in Edward the Confessor's Chapel at Westminster Abbey, London. The subterranean stone-lined tombs enclose an air gap, which the GPR reports as an elongated smudge, and she was able to propose that five of Edward I's children had been buried there (in the thirteenth century) (for radar, see Conyers & Goodman 1997; Conyers 2010). However there is also a difference of approach between the archaeologist and the architectural historian that has led, not without some travail, to the introduction of the particular type of inquiry known as 'the archaeology of buildings' (see Box 1.2). This basically approaches the building not as a single conception but as an archaeological site, or as an artefact with a long biography (for an example of the investigation of a medieval town house, see Fig 9.4). It tends to prioritise the sequence of activities before, during and after a building was erected, and to try to elucidate a complete narrative and social meaning from them (see Box 1.3 for an example).

The 'rebirth' of Italian medieval archaeology in the '70s took place against a shift from neo-Marxism, promoted by Polish scholars from the Institute of Material Culture in Warsaw, to a more empirical neo-Positivism, of which the British archaeologists were most representative. Within the new subject area, architectural analysis was first applied to the study of the more humble residential buildings, an approach epitomised in ethnographic and geographical studies of the beginning of the twentieth century as 'vernacular archaeology' (Brunskill 2000; Schweizer 1983).

In 1974 Tiziano Mannoni suggested using archaeometric analyses for the study of wall fabric (Mannoni 1976; D'Ulizia 2005), and this was followed by the adaptation of stratigraphic methods developed for excavation (Harris, EC 1989 & 2003; Carver 1990) to the study of upstanding structures. The new direction was exemplified by work carried out in Lombardia in 1978-80, on buildings in the historic centres of Erbanno and Gorzone in Valcamonica, on the western shore of Lake Garda, and especially the buildings of Brescia, on which the students at the professional Botticino School were trained (Brogiolo 1988). While archaeological method was being refined for studying individual important buildings, such as those of the early medieval monastery of Santa Giulia at Brescia or the tower at Montarrenti (Parenti 1985), other approaches sprung from the needs of restoration, as in the method elaborated by Doglioni (1987) in the middle of the '80s for several buildings in Verona, consisting basically of a stratigraphic analysis represented by graphic conventions.

A first convergence between the research and conservation missions was hosted in 1985 in a special edition of the review *Restauro e città* dedicated to 'Archeologia urbana e restauro' (Urban archaeology and restoration). While addressing research in building works linked to restoration and rescue in Lombardia, Brogiolo and his colleagues realized that stratigraphic analysis on individual walls produced only segments of a complex sequence, giving an incomplete understanding of the monument as a whole. The response was the development of a package known as *Archeologia dell'edilizia storica* (*Historic buildings archaeology*; Brogiolo 1988).

During the 1990s, the development of medieval archaeology in Italy, and of buildings archaeology in particular, was advanced and given official status at Ricardo Francovich's celebrated professional summer schools at Pontignano, near Siena. Here, for the first time, archaeologists and architects sat around the same table to discuss integrated methods of research applied to historic buildings (Francovich & Parenti 1988). The debate became essentially one between those who analysed buildings using primarily the stylistic attributes, those who relied only on stratigraphic sequences, and those who recognised a more comprehensive approach integrating both methods. It continued not only at seminars and symposia (Tagliabue 1993; Cavada & Gentilini 2000 & 2002) but also in the pages of *Archeologia dell'Architettura*, the first number of which appeared in 1996, as a supplement to *Archeologia Medievale*. With the aim of unifying practice, some of the participants met again in Monte Barro, where the different schools (Siena, Genoa, Venice, Milan and Padua) exposed their positions, apparently incompatible. In 2002 at Vitoria-Gasteiz (Spain) representatives of the differ-

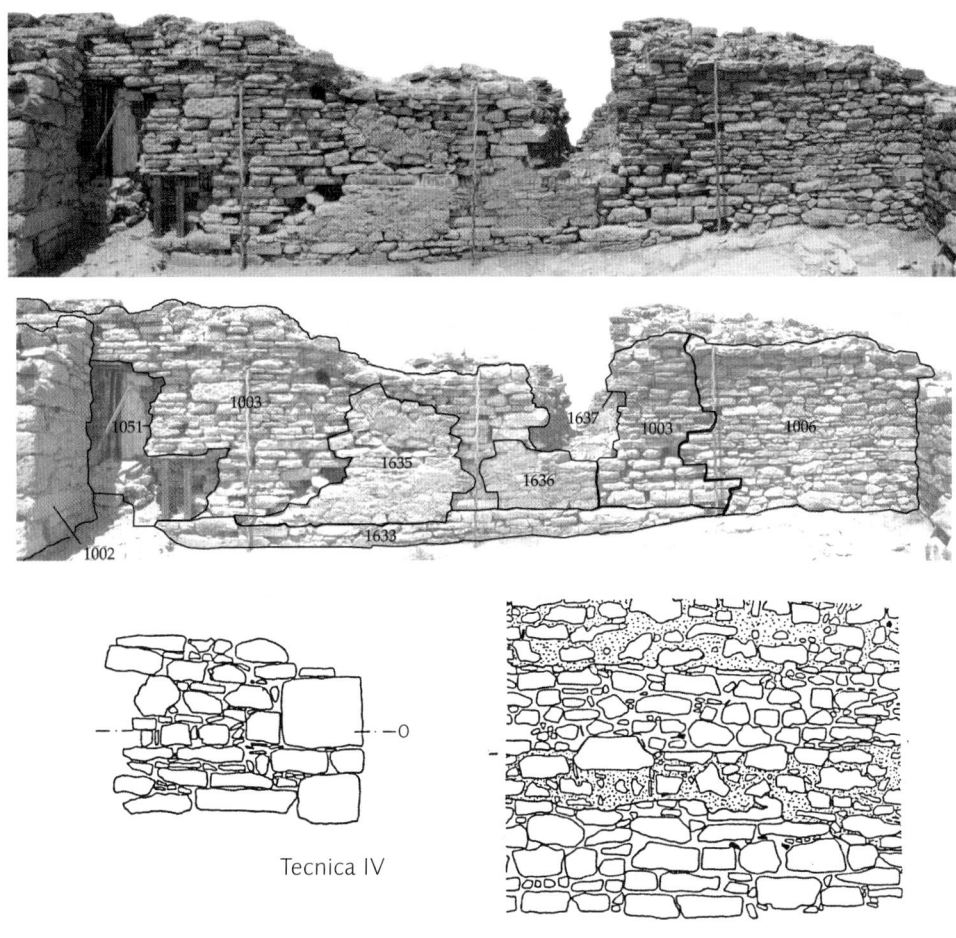

Fig 1

Recording walls at the 13th-century castle at Calatabarbaro, Segesta, Sicily. Top: Elevation of south wall. Centre: Allocation of contexts: 1003 is Period 1 (pre-12th century); 1006 is Period III.1 (12-13th century) and 1635 and 1636 are Period III.2 (1220-1250). As can be seen, the walls of different periods are not in vertical sequence. Bottom: Types of wall fabric (Molinari 1997).

ent Italian schools met again to witness the birth of *Arquelogía de la Arquitectura*.

During the last ten years, new approaches have emerged, but without finding a common basis in the different Italian research centres. If the diversity of research paths could be seen as evidence for the vitality of a subject that is still evolving, there is also a risk of being misunderstood and ignored by those who restore monuments without involving archaeological stratigraphy. For example, in a recent handbook about architectural restoration (Giusti 2000), the archaeology of architecture is not even cited, and a recent 'carta del rischio' (risk map) (Sessa 2000), ignored stratigraphic methods altogether. Thus the battle to incorporate archaeological study into the conservation and restoration of historic buildings is far from won (Brogiolo 1997, 2002 & 2006).

Buildings archaeologists often find their only opportunity to investigate when a building is being restored, and some restorers see the archaeologists as over-eager to disrupt the fabric in order to find out more about it (Pertot & Treccani 2002). But modern partnerships are possible in which archaeological recording is closely integrated with repair and restoration programmes. In these projects, archaeological recording is applied both before, during and if necessary after restoration.

To profit from these opportunities it is essential to apply a holistic approach. It is now generally accepted that in addition to the fabric sequence incorporated in walls, a building retains information about matters relating to the modification and decay of its fabric through time, such that it behaves less like a sequence of strata, and more like an artefact with its own biography. Thus, in addition to the stratigraphic order of the build, we will need to broaden and deepen our study to include at least four other important attributes relating to a building's biography (Figs 1 and 2).

First, *techniques of construction* (Rockwell 1989), including walls, openings, carpentry, the sources of materials, brick and ashlar and timber, their manufacture and treatment in the workshops, as well as fitting and finishing (e.g. Cagnana 2000). Apart from the precious archaeometric research carried out by Mannoni and the group from Liguria,

science-based studies have too often been funded independently of historical objectives, resulting only in projects of 'marginal research' in chemistry departments (Francovich 2006, 12). Given the high number of surviving monuments, the scientific study of building technology ought to play a more central role in archaeological training.

Second, the history of *building forms and materials* is an essential, not an optional, component of the archaeological study of buildings; it includes not only architectural styles but the form and metrics of bricks, tool marks, and the signs of masons. Third, *architectural design and the arrangement of space* are also concerns of the buildings archaeologist, whether rooted in long tradition or individual great architects (from Apollodoro to Palladio), or due to political sponsorship, ideology or social change. Fourth, our research should extend to *sites associated with the construction industry*, for example the masons' yard, where we are still too dependent on written sources, in order to reconstruct technical choices and imperatives (Mannoni & Boato 2002).

This type of integrated research employs both precise practical methods and a sharpened intellectual agenda. As an essential preliminary, the detailed records of fabric character, such as patches of mortar, plaster and areas of brick and stone, can be placed within a Geographic Information System (GIS) (cf. Mannoni 1994, Vecchiattini 2001), and modern researchers therefore can anticipate having a three-dimensional model of a historic building as their point of departure. Such digital models can be manipulated by computer software to provide a full biography of the building, making use of strati-

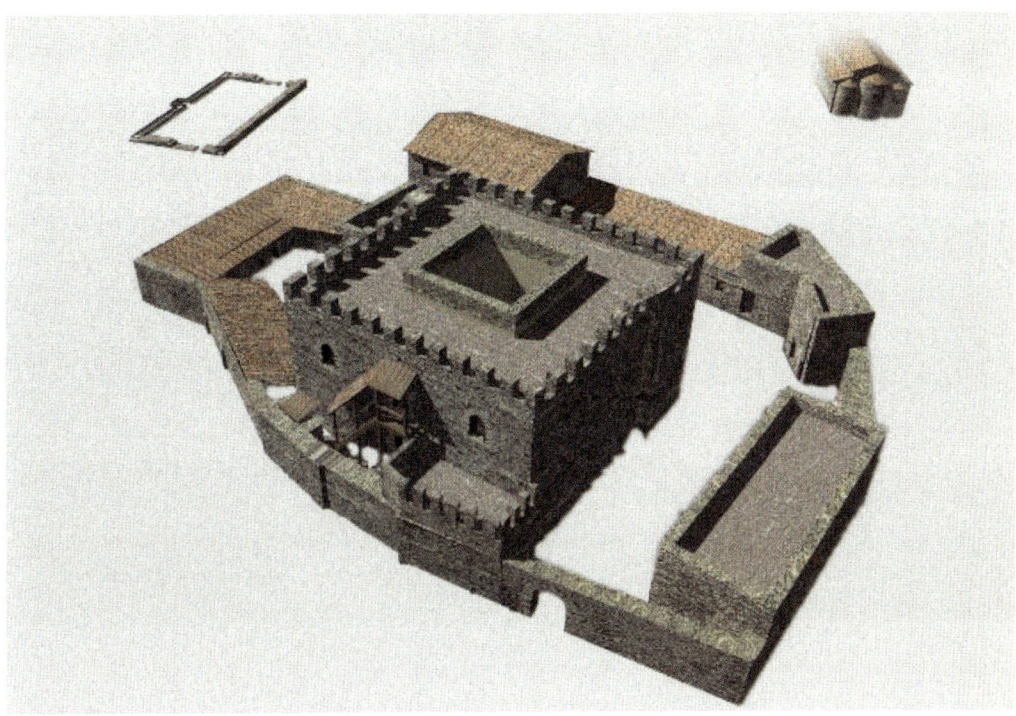

Fig 2

Digital reconstruction of the castle at Catalabarbaro at the beginning of the 13th century. At the top right is the church, and at the top left the demolished mosque discussed in Box 11.5 (Molinari 1997).

graphic and numerous other kinds of data, historical, architectural and ethnographic. The rewards can be seen in the work of Fabio Gabbrielli, who has studied the façade of the public palace in Siena (1996) and the arches of the monastic church of San Galgano (2000). Here we see the benefits of a convergence between historical, art-historical and archaeological approaches, showing a rich, deep structural sequence in which different artisans with different abilities and technical knowledge participated.

It may be that the next step should be to broaden our remit, and develop the *archaeology of architecture* into an *archaeology of architectures*, placing the sequences of buildings within a more general history (Brogiolo 2007). Different architectures are a part of a complex system. They include environmental, economic, social and ideological pressures that influenced choices of location and design. Architecture can be considered a mirror of all such variables, documented in masonry techniques and building types, and reflecting the activities and social classes that manage buildings and use them to display status and culture.

by Gian Pietro Brogiolo

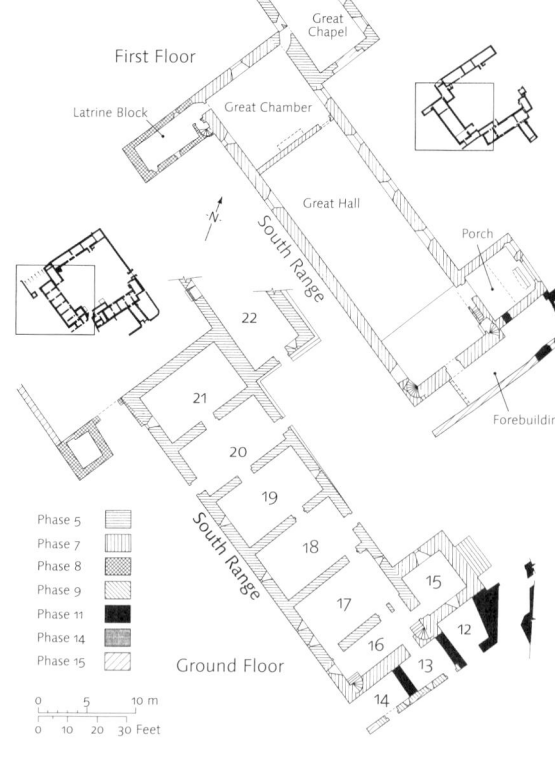

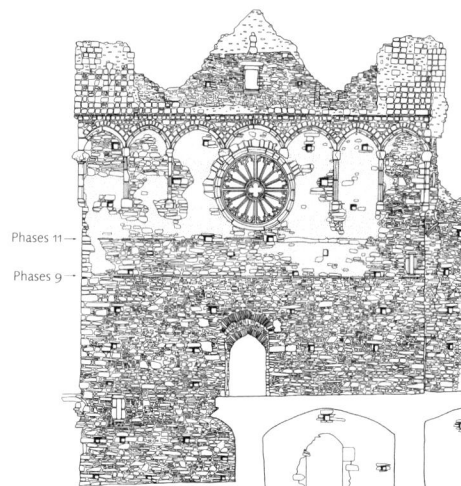

Fig 1.14 *The Bishop's Palace at St David's, Wales, recorded and studied by Rick Turner: (lower right): Phased plan of the south Range (Turner 2000, 114); (lower left): Elevation drawing of the exterior east gable of the first floor Great Hall in the south range (John Godbert) (Turner 2000, 120); (upper): Artist's impression of a feast in the Great Hall (Terry Ball) (Turner 2000, 135).*

Making sense of discoveries in the field includes the three principal tasks of defining activities, examining the use of space, and determining the chronology, with the aim of combining them into a detailed narrative. The detection of activities draws on the *assemblage*, that is the artefacts, bones, seeds, insects and samples of soil and every other kind of material that are recovered from fieldwork. Scientific applications here are legion, and every year brings new techniques and results. Technical accounts of how the procedures work will be found in the compendious Brothwell & Pollard 2001 (and see Roberts, CA, 2009b, Müldner & Richards 2005 & 2007, Sykes, 2007a, & 2009 and Bayley & Watson in Gilchrist & Reynolds 2009 for examples of medieval applications). In part 2 of this chapter we present a review of environmental, biological, microbiological and metallurgical applications to materials of medieval date.

In *artefact studies*, scientists have successfully located the place of manufacture of pots (from the clay and its inclusions) (Ch 7, p 279). The type of minerals used to make a pot can be determined by thin-sectioning (identifying the minerals under a microscope) or XRF (x-rays identifying the elements). The late Alan Vince examined over 6000 thin section analyses of early and later medieval pottery fabrics in England and concluded that pottery was being distributed through markets from the tenth century onwards – even coarse pottery seemed to be following targeted paths of distribution rather than just serving a local community. From the mid-twelfth century, new industries were producing mainly wheel thrown glazed jugs. He also found that pottery imported from the continent was being used mainly in their port of arrival (Vince 2005). One can readily imagine the powerful image of networks that would emerge were such an analysis to be applied over medieval Europe as whole. Archaeological chemists are also narrowing down the likely contents of pots (from the lipids trapped in the pot walls) (Evershed *et al.* 2001).

In another example of chemical tracking, Neutron Activation Analysis (NAA) was used to track sculptures removed from the site of Parthenay in the early twentieth century and dispersed through the art market. The twelfth century citadel church of Notre-Dame-de-le-Coudre at Parthenay was in ruins by 1834, with sculptural fragments lying about the church grounds. The exceptional sculpture (dated art-historically to the later twelfth century) was part of the west façade. NAA analysis determined the relative quantities of up to 24 chemical elements in the limestone, so providing a 'chemical signature'. Good matches were found between surviving sculpture at the church and examples now on display in museums in France, Scotland, England and the USA (Maxwell *et al.* 2005).

Material culture studies address how raw material was extracted and refined, and how objects were made, used and distributed (Ch 5,7,8). Interest also extends to what became of individual artefacts, how they were conserved re-used or recycled. Such *biographies* are particularly interesting in the case of prestigious objects such as books, brooches or stone crosses, which like standing buildings may have a long and eventful life above ground (see Box 8.3, Box 10.4; Gosden & Marshall 1999).

Human remains provide the archaeologist with their most immediate contact with medieval people, whose childhood home, diet, medical history, appearance and sex are all embodied in their bones (Uberlaker 1989; Roberts 2009a & b; and for summaries see Part 2 below; Ch 12, p 494; and AME 1, 420-30). The potential of *animal remains* to reflect on human society is also in the process of headlong development, reaching beyond what people ate to interpretations of about social structure and belief (Part 2; Sykes 2009; O'Connor 2000a; Ashby 2002). The analysis of *plant remains* also sees beyond indications of diet, into processes of procurement and preparation, which in turn reflect the social organisation of those who collect, store, cook and eat them (Part 2; Ch 3, p 137; Hastorf & Popper 1988).

Examining the *use of space* has been advanced through the use of precision plottin, and GPS on site and GIS for analysing the results. Mapping of the ancient landscape shows large-scale changes over time, as in the river valleys of the Lez delta (Burnouf 2008, 36-42) and of the Loire (Ch 2). At the level of the settlement, the exposure of large areas exposed by research or mitigation archaeology allows the whole of a village to be seen, with its houses, gardens, fields and routeways (Ch 3). With the aid of geophysics, the overall plan of even quite small scale excavations can be amplified without further destruction. Even where there is little stratification, settlement plans have the power to chronicle social change over long periods, since the building stock available and the use of the interior and the exterior reflects indirectly on the number of inhabitants and their rank.

Larger houses and their gardens may reveal their intimate use through documentation (Ch 4), but archaeological access analysis offers an independent report on how space was used (Fig 4.4; Richardson 2003a & b). Smaller, less well documented dwellings may also reveal their social geography through analysis (Ch 4, p 159). While a public role was expected of the grander buildings, privacy was valued all the more, and seems to indicate something more than the wish not to be overlooked (Ch 4, p 176).

The final part of the analytical triad is *chronology*, since without good dating the discoveries of archaeologists cannot enter the historical debate. In the later Middle Ages these dates need to be unusually precise. Traditionally, medieval archaeologists depended on their historian colleagues for a chronological framework, but the need to produce independent information, independently dated, has led to improved applications of radiocarbon dating and dendrochronology, the two principal scientific methods. Radiocarbon dating has routinely offered dates with an error range of 100 years – not especially useful for the Middle Ages (AME 1, 43), but now offers new hope of precision on two fronts (Taylor 2001). First, AMS (Accelerator Mass Spectrometry) can be applied to very small samples, so that instead of dating a handful of charcoal from a fireplace, likely to originate from wood of very different ages and thus giving dates that are crude and broad, the date can be referred to a distinct organism relevant to the event: for example an insect burnt in a burning roof. This requires very precise excavation and careful pre-sorting of samples. AMS dating requires such a small sample that it is becoming acceptable to date organic objects in museums, wood, shoes, even manuscripts, with the minimum of attrition.

A second development is the Bayesian procedure, in which a known sequence of features (for example graves that cut each other) is radiocarbon dated, and the range of error greatly reduced because the order of deposition is already known (Buck *et al.* 1991). Radiocarbon dates as precise as ±20 years have been achieved in this way. Other dating methods, such as OSL (Optically Stimulated Luminescence) which dates the last exposure of a layer to sunlight, or TL (thermoluminescence) which dates the baking of a clay layer or structure, have yet to be refined to the accuracy (within 20 years) that medieval archaeologists need – but it should come (Grün 2001).

Dendrochronology is by far the most precise method of dating we have, and has revolutionised medieval archaeology, particularly as applied to the dating of timbers in buildings. It uses the pattern of tree-rings in a timber to locate it in time, since all trees growing in a region experienced the same annual growth and should thus exhibit the same pattern (Baillie 1991; Kuniholm 2001; Burnouf 2008, 33; Schöfbeck & Heussner 2005). There is clearly a major problem with sampling timber in buildings, in that timbers may have been shaved, re-used or cut for later repair and restoration. However, these problems are being addressed (see, e.g. http://www.dendrochronology.net/).

Since the tree-ring sequence is characteristic of the region as well as the period, some timber has also been provenanced to a distant place, demonstrating a supply. For example, Dutch panel paintings were found to be framed by Polish oak (Kuniholm 2001, 41). Such dendro-provenancing has enormous possibilities for future research, applied for example to tracking the place of origin of ships, barrels and other wooden objects, found in wrecks and waterlogged deposits.

Agendas and rewards

As we can see, the archaeological agenda for later medieval Europe is stepping beyond the collection and classification of buildings, sites and artefacts, although these will remain important duties in regions that are still little known. Archaeology is good at mapping the arrival of technical innovations, and there are certainly general trends to be detected: the late twelfth-early thirteenth century saw the introduction of the windmill, rabbit farming, the mouldboard plough and examples of widespread land reclamation (Dyer 1997b, 295-304). Alongside this 'significant shift in agricultural methods' (ibid., 300) we note a new landscape of castles, churches, compact territories, planned villages and hamlets and subdivided regulated field systems and coppices. The growth of the market attracted varied produce to settlements, and allowed reliance on a single product, such as livestock in the uplands and wine in the south.

Following famines around 1300, the surge in productivity has been thought to drop, but it may alternatively have moved elsewhere. Welsh forests, for example, were farmed for *vert* (coppiced wood and berries) and venison under the supervision of foresters from the twelfth century, but from the thirteenth century efforts shifted to the production of timber and charcoal to supply the shipbuilders and iron founders (Linnard 1982, 30-86). The arts of horticulture, beekeeping, making cheese and ale are likely to have been improved and transmitted through villagers; such low technology output is hard to track but may have been significant (Dyer 1997b, 308).

The more we see of later medieval Europe, the more varied it appears to be. Reliance on the ard, and hand-digging, continued long after the introduction of the plough (Dyer 1997b, 295). Different systems of agricultural production were practised by different territories or even by neighbouring farms (Campbell 1997, 230-1). There are strong regional variations in house-form caused by social as well as ecological factors (Astill 1988b, 60). There is a diversity of religious practice in late medieval towns (Ch 10, p 412; Astill 2009, 267), and variations in identity were signalled in dress (Ch 5, p 218; Rosser 1998). These material variations offer a means of chronicling expressions of individual identity inside the ethnic or religious geographical blocks, and so begin mapping the allegiance of peoples and the distribution of ideas.

We seem to be dealing with long periods of change punctuated with moments of great acceleration, such as the eighth and later twelfth centuries (Astill 2010), but within these periods the explanations of change lie in regional and personal diversity. The detection, dating and mapping of diversity is one of archaeology's strong points: it does not rely on the survival of certain records or archives, but can apply its searches anywhere and everywhere. In this, it has a special opportunity to recreate the palimpsest of past centuries in a manner that prehistorians too may find helpful. It should also be of increasing value to the historian, aware of the many forces operating beneath the surface of society. The goal of medieval archaeology is to give every medieval person a voice.

PART 2:   MEDIEVAL ARCHAEOLOGY AND THE SCIENCES
         by Aleks Pluskowski

Multi-disciplinarity

Multi-disciplinarity has always characterised the practice of medieval archaeology, and it is virtually impossible to find a site report or synthesis that does not include some discussion of relevant written and artistic sources (see Part 1 above). Major projects continue to involve multi-disciplinary teams, and medieval archaeologists – traditionally specialists of ceramics, standing buildings or settlements – are increasingly collaborating not only with historians and art historians, but with scientists. The future of multi-disciplinarity within medieval archaeology is likely to be dominated by such partnerships, and will increasingly involve teams drawn from across Europe.

Environmental archaeology

The application of environmental archaeological techniques to medieval contexts is well established in north-western Europe, and is expanding in the southern and eastern parts of the Continent. In the Baltic region, for example, palaeobotanical investiga-

BOX 1.3 INVESTIGATING A HOUSE OF THE MILITARY ORDERS AT AMBEL, SPAIN

Fig 1

The Ambel preceptory. A largely 16th-century exterior concealing a medieval core.

A recent case study of buildings archaeology is the investigation of the religious house at Ambel in north-east Spain, a complex of medieval and later buildings which first belonged to the Templars from the mid-twelfth to the early fourteenth century and thereafter to the Hospitallers until the mid-nineteenth century (Gerrard 2003b) (Fig 1).

The upstanding building at Ambel had always been considered to be sixteenth century and later, dating apparently placed beyond doubt by the stone shields on its facade. Once inside, however, a more complex story is revealed. The use of stone, brick and rammed earth hints at more than one phase of construction, cracks in the walls beneath plaster suggest joins between structural units. The mind quickly begins to run on how the complex as a whole might 'fit' together. But the exercise is not quite the same as sequencing archaeological strata. The latest phases of construction are not necessarily at the tops of the walls, new floor levels have been in-serted and buildings that once stood apart are now joined together. This is a giant three-dimensional puzzle which requires unpicking. Among the clues on offer are some fittings such as doors which can be dated by their design (but are easily replaced and not necessarily original), certain architectural features (though few are diagnostic), shields which can be dated (but which can be moved and may not equate to the date of the wall), and documents which describe some interventions (but not others). None of this evidence can be completely trusted in its own right.

The methods used at Ambel are familiar to the archaeologist: the drawing of façades and sections through the building, the establishing of an accurate plan (1:500), the more detailed stone-by-stone recording of some elevations and datable features (1:20), shields (1:10) and the tracing of graffiti (1:1 with subsequent reductions). Rectified photography was employed for some simple elevations but mostly the survey was manual, with scaf-

Fig 2

Medieval graffiti depicting a castellated building, knights in chainmail with swords and shields and a variety of other symbols.

folding being mounted to gain access to the walls. Today the drawings would be produced digitally so that they could be edited and added to (for an example of recording standards see English Heritage 2006). A photographic collection was also established and, as a second phase of fieldwork, the plans were annotated with construction materials and features such as blocked openings, putlog holes, wall thickness, realignments, occupation scars and evidence of re-use (in roof timbers, for example). Thereafter, the different phases of construction were established and to help with this a large number of historical documents were consulted and transcribed from four different archives. Although no antiquarian accounts or illustrations survive, a vital tool

in this case proved to be *procesos de mejoramientos*, contemporary assessments of architectural and other improvements carried out at the site. Gathering background information of this kind is essential but often partial, as it was here (for other examples see Wood 1994). The *procesos*, for example, while useful, do not describe each building in turn but focus only on what has changed. Nor is the sequence complete, there are only eleven between 1601 and 1797. Lastly, as a final stage in the investigation, excavation was undertaken, partly to establish the existence of previous buildings but also to recover cultural material and develop our understanding of daily life.

The oldest structure on the site is that inherited by the Templars in the twelfth century as a *castillo*. In origin this is an Islamic tower, 11m by 7m in plan, whose base is constructed in large stone blocks in a style paralleled in the mid-tenth century. Large-scale excavation inside the adjacent church produced evidence of storage pits and an encircling perimeter wall. To this tower and its associated features the Templars added two parallel but unconnected blocks to either side, possibly a dormitory and refectory, or possibly intended as separate blocks for the monks and their servants. Parts of windows and the main exterior doorway also survive, one window having medieval graffiti incised on one of its jambs (Fig 2).

When the Hospitallers took charge of the building from the beginning of the fourteenth century, they proceeded to fortify the complex, adding towers with arrow loops to the corners of existing buildings (Fig 3). They also added a fortified church in brick with crenellations and arrow loops at roof height. This relatively austere cluster of buildings, solid with small windows, was

Fig 3

Ambel as it would have appeared in c. 1340. The early tower flies the flag with residential units to either side and the polygonal apse of the Hospitaller church behind. The construction of corner towers is underway (reconstruction by Nick Watson).

again transformed in the sixteenth century. To do this the exterior walls were maintained to their full height but all the interior floor levels were gutted and replaced at different heights. Rejecting the introspection that had gone before, the aim now was to introduce more light and present the building in a different way, as a fashionable residence suitable for its educated occupants. The changes to the building therefore tell us about the nature of patronage and influences at play.

While the preceptory at Ambel has an interesting story to tell of re-cycling, alteration, structural failures of walls and floors, military tendencies and social ambition, to give full context to this study the buildings must be placed alongside the developing medieval settlement form, which itself radically expanded in the sixteenth century, and also wider changes in the landscape beyond. In Ambel, for example, there are associated monuments such as watermills, flax-retting tanks and irrigation networks in which the Military Orders also invested. Buildings are part of our material culture; a lesson which medieval archaeologists ignore at their peril, but integrating landscape with building histories makes for an even more powerful study if the aim is to grasp the social and economic evolution of a region as a whole.

by Christopher Gerrard

tions of the later medieval period represent an invaluable tool for assessing the impact of colonisation on the landscape, as demonstrated through the vegetation changes resulting from the increasing exploitation of the interior of the Scandinavian Peninsula (e.g. Mogren 1998; Regnéll & Olsson 1998) and pilot projects associated with castles of the Teutonic Order in northern Poland (Brown & Pluskowski 2011). This can be compared with the impact of land clearance in analogous situations, such as the European colonisation of America (Pederson *et al.* 2005). The opposite effect has also been demonstrated, such as the regeneration of woodland following the abandonment of cultivated land between AD 1350 and 1440 in the south-eastern Netherlands (Van Hoof *et al.* 2006). The topic of climate change is particularly prominent in modern global-based research (featuring, for example, within the European Commission's 'Framework Programmes'). Knowledge of the Medieval Warm Period (which ended *c.* 1300) continues to be developed, for example a recent palaeobotanical study suggested its regional impact extended beyond Europe to north-western Russia (Kremenetski *et al.* 2004). A great deal of work has also been done on plant remains extracted from occupation layers. For example, a waterlogged pit from Ferrara dating from the mid-fourteenth-fifteenth century yielded 256,000 well-preserved seeds and fruits belonging to 98 species, used to provide new information on the diet and diversity of domestic activities associated with the later medieval north Italian urban elite (Mazzanti *et al.* 2005). Moving beyond the individual household, it has also been possible to model lo-

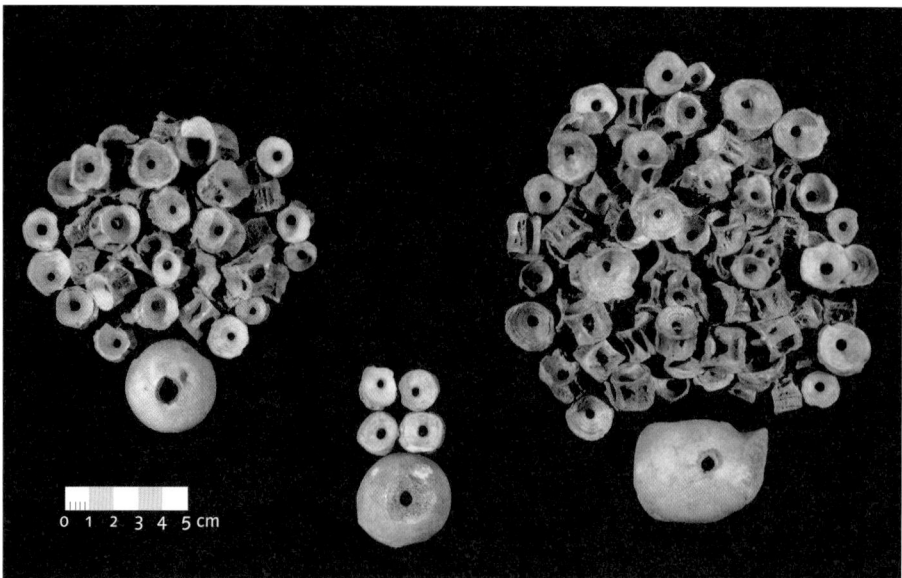

Fig 1.15   *Three sets of a perforated cattle bone fragment in association with several perforated and trimmed fish vertebrae (mostly ling), excavated from pits inside Chevington Chapel, Northumberland, England. They have been interpreted as rosaries or paternosters (Stallibrass 2007; by kind permission of Sue Stallibrass).*

cal ecology from plant macrofossils, such as those recovered from the medieval latrines in Überlingen, southern Germany (Märkle 2005).

The increasingly recognised value of palaeobotanical studies is paralleled, and complemented, by developments in the study of animal remains. Animal bones form one of the largest and most frequently occurring categories of material from any medieval site. Zooarchaeology or archaeozoology, which traditionally focused on reconstructing the diet and economy of individual communities, has significantly expanded in recent decades to include inter-regional syntheses and incorporate other strands of data within the growing sub-field of medieval animal studies (see Ch 2, p 357, Ch 8, p 80). Historians and art historians are becoming increasingly aware of the value of zooarchaeological studies, and with the growing number of multi-disciplinary, pan-European fora and networks, there is also an increasing sense of discourse and awareness, bridging the gap between scholars in different disciplines and regions of Europe. With so much data analysed and published, it has become possible to predict the faunal assemblage of different categories of site (e.g. Ervynck 2004), and this has facilitated comparisons to be made between different environmental and social contexts.

In the last decade, the study of fish remains has yielded impressive results, from the micro-scale, such as the identification of Jewish dietary signatures in medieval Budapest (Bartosiewicz 2003) and their role in religious material culture (Fig 1.15) (Stallibrass 2007), to mapping the development of international commercial fishing (see below; Barrett *et al.* 2004). Birds too have been used not just as habitat proxies, but also to illuminate material practices, such as flute production (Gál 2005; Leaf 2008), representing a growing tendency to break the barriers between the study of animal remains and artefacts (see Pluskowski 2007b). The 'Medieval Animals Database', developed at the Central European University in Budapest, recently launched a pilot project focusing on the pig in medieval Hungary; a synthesis of written, artistic and zooarchaeological data. The current study of the medieval environment represents an unlikely but wholly stimulating mixture of humanities influences such as post-processualism and the Annales School of historiography, dovetailing with scientific paradigms, particularly ecology and ethology (animal behaviour). Whilst the bulk of scientific applications in archaeology remain focused on the study of prehistoric periods, they are being increasingly used to further and consolidate our understanding of later medieval society.

Biomolecular archaeology

Osteoarchaeological analysis is being refined by the study of *ancient DNA* (aDNA), for example DNA can determine the sex of an adult skeleton. Moreover DNA is becoming increasingly used to answer fundamental questions about the later medieval period, especially concerning the spread of diseases. In 1998, a group of French scientists published their findings of DNA recovered in dental pulp taken from un-erupted teeth from human skeletons in two documented plague cemeteries in Provence dating to 1590 and 1722 (Drancourt *et al.* 1998). In seven out of eight cases they discovered DNA of ordinary strains of *Yersinia pestis*, the bacterium which causes Bubonic plague.

This was shortly followed by a second study of dental pulp from three skeletons buried in a mass grave in Montpellier, dating to 1348-1400: the era of the 'Black Death', which hit the town particularly hard in multiple episodes from 1348-1397 (Raoult *et al.* 2000). Again, the study uncovered the DNA of *Y. pestis* in the teeth of all the sampled individuals. A further study of early eighteenth-century mass graves in Provence also confirmed the presence of *Y. pestis* (Signoli *et al.* 2002). Although these findings were disputed on methodological grounds (Gilbert *et al.* 2004), evidence of the plague bacterium (specifically the *Orientalis* biotype) has been found in subsequent studies, including material attributed to the sixth-century pandemic referred to as ' The Plague of Justinian' (Drancourt *et al.* 2007). At present, a bio-molecular study is seeking to extract DNA and proteins from 750 skeletons from the cemetery of St Catherine's Church in Eindhoven (Holland), exploring the link between the genetic variant that increases resistance to HIV and genetic resistance to the Black Death (see Fig 1.10) (Pringle 2007). These studies have significantly contributed to the debate concerning the identity of the mid-fourteenth century pandemic, which had otherwise depended on extrapolation from contemporary documents and epidemiological modelling. Whilst Bubonic Plague was clearly an agent in the pandemic, future developments in the reconstruction of ancient DNA may identify the presence of additional bacteria (Piers Mitchell *pers. comm.*). However, the contributions of zooarchaeological and palaeobiological research are already being incorporated into syntheses of the vast quantities of documentary sources in defining our understanding of the Black Death (Benedictow 2010).

Fig 1.16   *The primary sources of grain, wine, cattle, salt, fish and wood used for provisioning late medieval Paris (after Spufford 2002, 103).*

Livestock could also be moved considerable distances, and the provisioning requirements of the largest European cities in the fourteenth and fifteenth centuries saw economic hinterlands extending over entire provinces (Fig 1.16) (Spufford 2002, 99-106). The analysis of this movement, using the latest biomolecular archaeological techniques, is only just beginning to be applied to the study of medieval society. Mapping of mitochondrial and nuclear DNA extracted from medieval manuscript parchment (made from calf, sheep or goat skins) at North Carolina State University, is being used to determine genetic relationships between the animals that provided the multiple skins for each manuscript. This in turn should enable the sources of manuscript materials to be pinpointed. In the future it may be possible to reconstruct the provenance and trade of parchment at an international level, and thus contribute to our understanding of the development of European book production in the Middle Ages (Stinson 2009). At the micro-scale it should be increasingly possible to map the complexity of medieval ecosystems and how they changed in relation to human activity; this is exemplified by new research targeting a range of aquatic vertebrates in order to shed light on the developing complexity of urban ecosystems – the quintessential expression of the human 'ecological niche' (Grupe *et al.* 2009).

The study of chemical isotopes has also begun to contribute to our understanding of medieval European society in terms of diet and migration (Ch 3, p 139; Mundee 2009). An extensive study of isotopic signatures identified on fish bones from sites in the North Sea region illustrated the vast distances over which fish were transported (Barrett *et al.* 2004). Stable isotope measurements have also been used in dietary reconstruction, demonstrating a peak in marine protein consumption from the eleventh to the fourteenth centuries among the male population of Orkney (Barrett & Richards 2004), which can be tied in with broader trends in the exploitation of the marine environment. The implications of this have been detected in the Mediterranean through isotopic studies, where increased fish consumption is evident from the fourteenth century (Salamon *et al.* 2008), as well as on medieval society as a whole. It has been possible to distinguish between coastal and interior populations in medieval Norway on the basis of strontium isotope ratios measured in teeth (Aberg *et al.* 1998), and to demonstrate that the composition of the crew of the Mary Rose was perhaps as much as 60% non-native; this may even have contributed to the capsizing of the ship due to poor communication (Bell *et al.* 2009). The diversity of biomolecular archaeological applications is growing at an exponential rate, and its impact on the field of medieval archaeology is likely to be revolutionary.

Archaeometallurgy

The study of later medieval technology has also benefited from the application of scientific techniques combined with critical reviews of other types of evidence (cf Whitney 2004). A major area of interest has been medieval metallurgy (Rehren 1997) and its role in the development of armour (Williams 2003). Metallographic studies, supported by experimental archaeology, have focused on the quality of armour; its composition, hardness, thickness and re-use (Jones 1992, Edge 2002). The number of journals on the subject is growing, with the most recent series – *The Journal of the Armour Research Society* – launched in 2005. The quantitative determination of the presence of specific metals has also been central to archeometallurgical studies of alchemy, which involved practitioners of both 'chymistry' and metallurgy before the seventeenth century. The largest assemblage ever recovered, consisting of over a thousand artefacts dating to *c.* 1540-1580/90 from the waste dump of a church in Oberstockstall, Austria, represents a 'state-of-the-art Renaissance laboratory.' The metallurgic techniques identified from this assemblage were combined with a review of written sources, and situated within broader historical contexts such as the early modern expansion of mining (Martinón-Torres & Rehren 2005). Indeed, our understanding of mining and sourcing of materials is likely to expand with the increasing application of new techniques; studies of ore sourcing in relation to smelting sites within the French Mont-Lozère Massif have relied on lead isotope studies (e.g. Baron *et al.* 2006). The scientific study of medieval technology is no longer exclusively concerned with the technical aspects of composition and manufacturing, but with the cultural contexts of sources of raw materials, processes and artefacts.

Conclusion

Medieval archaeology is therefore embracing a diversity of scientific applications, and approaching the use of multiple sources with increasing awareness of the limits and possibilities of each dataset, as well as the methodological challenges posed by the study of written and artistic sources (Dyer 1988; Carver 2002; and see Box 5.1). Conversely, excavations of medieval sites yield a diverse range of material which can be used to fill significant gaps in the historical record, but more importantly to further our understanding of the inter-play between physical and conceptual realities in medieval society, i.e. the differences between what people experienced and what they imagined. For example, the ideology of hunting was central to the identity of the high medieval European aristocracies, yet the nutritional contribution of game to their diets was virtually insignificant (Fig 1.17), even in regions with plentiful wild mammals such as the Ardennes and Livonia (Ervynck 1992; Mugurēvičs 2002).

Medieval archaeology can also illuminate longue durée trends in the use of material culture and the human impact on the environment, stretching from prehistory through to the modern era, thereby situating the Middle Ages in a more meaningful context. Whilst individual sites remain a key focus for research programmes, large, inter-regional projects involving multi-disciplinary teams, targeting key research questions, are an increasingly important requisite for successful funding applications. With the sense of increasing communication between scholars across Europe in terms of collaborative projects, networks and conferences, the future of medieval archaeology can be envisaged as truly 'European'.

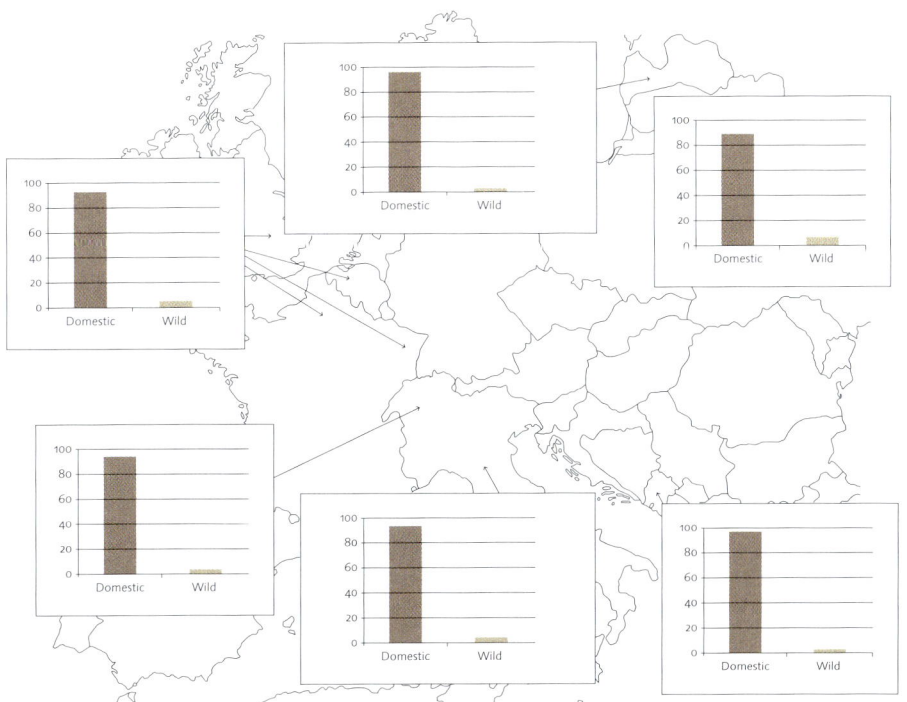

The relative representation of domestic and wild mammals from aristocratic sites in select regions across Europe: England, north France and Belgium, Switzerland, North Italy, Latvia, Moldova, Montenegro (sources: various, see Chapter 2, part 3). The assemblages are not statistically comparable, but suggest the role of game at aristocratic sites across medieval Europe was similar.

Fig 1.17

HABITAT

Introduction *by Martin Carver*

This first section of the book presents four chapters concerned with the environment, settlement, housing and everyday material culture, collectively termed the habitat (Fig 2.1).

We begin by introducing the environment and resources of medieval people (Ch 2), their fields, woods and rivers and how these changed, how land was reclaimed, the challenges of survival in marginal places and the changing perceptions of the tame and the wild. Life in rural places was lived out in settlements (Ch 3) that might range in social character from dispersed farmsteads and hamlets (Skramle in Sweden, Tårnby in Denmark, Beaume in southern France) to a laid-out nucleated township at the foot of a castle (Rattray in Scotland). Work in rural places was mainly about growing food – grain, cattle, sheep – inferred from animal bones and plant remains found on archaeological sites, or from the isotope signatures in the bones of buried people. For some archaeologists, the initial attraction of rural settlements lay in their desertion; now we see that 'desertion' is a relative stage in a constant process of shrinking, shifting and adaption, in which environment, epidemic, war, religious intolerance and especially economic demand played a role. The stability of some settlements and their growth into the villages and towns that often survive today is no less remarkable than the abandonment of those that failed.

Within the landscape and within the settlement in which a person was born, grew up and worked, the household, the *domus* was the centre point in the circles of social action. Our discussion of housing (Ch 4) begins with visit to the more palatial establishments in the north, their estates and accoutrements, and follows with an overview of some of

Hinterland of Orvieto, Italy, on the road between Rome and Florence. The town owed part of its 13th-century wealth to a papal residence in the city as well as to its famous vineyards (Peter Forster, Creative Commons).

the most interesting questions relating to housing in England between *c.* 1200-1600. The Boxes consider the new standards of heating and hygiene adopted in the homes of the medieval northerners. Then by way of contrast we go south to Spain and inspect the factors governing the development of the grander stone houses of Andalusia, and their gardens. Readers will also encounter houses in many different guises in other chapters: simple rural dwellings in Chapter 3, palaces and fortified houses in Chapter 6, town houses and guildhalls in Chapter 9, and residences of the clergy in Chapter 11.

The rounded, varied and often brilliant life of the increasingly prosperous medieval middle-class was written in detail in their artefacts, in the vocabulary of things (Ch 5). The repertoire of objects available to medieval people, portable artefacts and interior furnishings, tell us how they cooked, how they ate, what they wore and how they kept themselves amused. Here is a guide to the astonishing range of objects that have survived from the later Middle Ages, and at the same time this chapter offers a translation of the language of cultural material, its role in creating identity, cementing alliances with fellow humans and divine spirits and transforming a house into a home.

CHAPTER 2

THE MEDIEVAL LANDSCAPE

PART 1: INVESTIGATING THE MEDIEVAL ENVIRONMENT IN FRANCE
by Joëlle Burnouf

Development of the study

The subject to be introduced in this chapter is the medieval landscape, that is the natural environment at the time of the Middle Ages, and the way that contemporary people related with it. My concern is to show how the study of the medieval environment has progressed, review the questions we ask and how they are answered. By way of an example, I will consider the recent evolution and direction of the subject in France.

The environment, or in our case the *palaeoenvironment*, is an aspect of our study that has only taken root slowly. The pioneers of research in the medieval and modern environment were prompted by global reflections on environmental change some forty years ago. Le Roy Ladurie's work on climate history (1983), first published in 1967 and reissued ever since, is an essential point of departure for the understanding of climate at a global scale. Since then, the application of environmental research has transformed our understanding of early society, and revised earlier reductive and determinist views. It has allowed us to enlarge the range of questions we pose about agricultural and industrial activity. Our general explanatory models are also being revised, revisiting the fundamental questions raised by the eighteenth century enlightenment after its break with the Christian ideological framework (Cosmopolitiques 2001). The consequent division of nature and culture into two separate worlds is again under scrutiny today, when we are more ready to see humans as just another element contributing to the biodiversity of the planet.

Environmental archaeology was first developed in the nineteenth century at a European level by specialists in prehistory, at a time when the archaeology of human origins grew in tandem with geology. But it is mainly in the second half of the twentieth century that it has begun to take shape in medieval archaeology. It was pioneered mostly in the countries of northern and north-western Europe: Scandinavia, Holland, Great Britain. In France and the Mediterranean zone in general it is the last twenty years that has seen the growth of this type of research. While the natural sciences, in a general sense, had featured in prehistoric and protohistoric research from their inception in the nineteenth century, it was not so for the medieval period. For many years, medieval archaeologists devoted their energy to clearing away the debris and detaching structures and artefacts from their matrix of sediments. Even when it was collected, environmental evidence was treated in a narrow and descriptive sense (Chouquer 2006a & b). For a long period, the only project in France that had seriously concerned itself with ecological data was the underwater investigation at Charavines (Isère), begun in the early 1970s (Colardelle & Verdele 1993).

This project clearly provoked a change of thought amongst the community of medieval archaeologists, but the inclusion of environmental programmes was not straightforward. Prehistorians had been reading the environmental sequence as part of the *longue durée,* and had learnt to study the changing interactions between peoples and the environment, often framed as a series of interacting and interdependent systems. Archaeologists of the Medieval and Modern periods have only recently begun to address questions about the relations between people and landscape, and to do so in the framework of their own research questions. An important step forward was taken in 1993 with a pivotal conference at Grenoble entitled *Man and Nature in the Middle Ages. Palaeoenvironment and Medieval European society,* when the results of the PIREN (*Programme Interdisciplinaire de Recherches en Environnement*) research programme were presented. Here, for the first time, historians of written sources and archaeologists, the 'historians of the soil,' were invited to reflect on the environment and the concept of the *longue durée* as promoted by Fernand Braudel (1980).

But the real motor driving the development of the subject has been rescue archaeology (*archéologie préventive*) (Ch 1, p 20). Rescue archaeology's relatively well-funded *mitigation projects,* carried out in large numbers in the 1980s, began to appear in print during the 1990s, and they reaped the rewards of having on-site specialists competent in the natural sciences. As a result of this work, our understanding of the interconnections between societies and their milieu has evolved dramatically. The size of the areas excavated and the extent of the sedimentary and stratigraphic sequences uncovered have opened an entirely new corpus, not only for vast areas but also over long tracts of time. While some these studies informed environmental change in a global manner, it also became possible to examine different spatial and temporal scales. A mass of data, notably on sediments and on biota, are now available, giving new insights into relationships between communities and their landscapes, at a local and regional level. Major advances have been achieved on the relationship between communities and valley environments, on communities and the terrain, on the archaeology of agrarian exploitation, on societies and biodiversity, on the soil as an archaeological entity of its own, as well as on the *chaîne opératoire* involved in the treatment of resources and materials.

New objectives

French archaeologists are now engaged in the construction of a comprehensive agenda designed to address fundamental questions about the relations between medieval environment and society. The objectives are to investigate the dynamics and transformations at work in the varied environments and to understand the processes of modification, exploitation and management of the landscape by their communities. In principle, this requires an understanding of how climate, and the available natural resources of soils, fauna and flora, all change through time; how humans respond to these changes in the environment, and how their responses cause the environment to change in turn. In practice, environment and human response are so enmeshed that it is often difficult to distinguish natural from anthropogenic causes. Similarly, the evidence for the environment and for environmental change is observable both at general points of reference, such as the pollen in a bog and the tree-rings on a tree, and in particular localities, such as may be retrieved in the form of plant remains, animal bones, insects and sediments during the excavation of archaeological sites.

Modern environmental archaeology is therefore not a separate discipline reporting the operation of a separate system, but is intimately incorporated into every archaeological project, whether instigated by mitigation or research. Environmental archaeology is one form of archaeological practice (buildings archaeology is another) which considers that communities are in constant co-evolution with the milieu in which they live and which they transform; environmental archaeology thus opens an interdisciplinary dialogue with the natural sciences in order to understand and explain the different stages of socio-environmental systems during the Middle Ages.

Fig 2.1   *The church of St Mary and St Lawrence in the village of Ellerton, East Riding of Yorkshire, England, seen from across the 'ings' (water meadows) beside the River Derwent. The church stands on the site of a Gilbertine Priory dissolved in 1538. Like all the medieval settlements beside the Derwent, Ellerton was sited on a promontory above the level of the floods that submerge the ings every winter and refresh the land with silt carried from the high moorland to the north.*

Scales of inquiry

Environmental archaeologists are aware that they work at a set of different scales, both temporal and spatial. The question of scales is relevant not just for the gathering of data, that is, observation and recording, but also for its interpretation. A medieval community may not itself comprehend the genesis of the environment it has inherited. To track the formation and inherent perils of each local environmental inheritance, a long temporal overview is needed (Magny 1995; Bravard & Magny 2002). In this way we can better understand the interaction between a community and the risks, hazards and rewards potentially present in their landscape.

Another question of scale concerns space, that is, what affects communities at a micro-local scale, at a regional scale and at a global scale. Medieval communities will not have been aware of the global conditions that affect climate, but they still felt the effects of 'le temps qu'il fait' (in Alain Corbins's phrase). Although archaeology mainly observes and measures practices and natural conditions that are locally focused, the number and quality of these observations now allows us to study variations over wider regions with greater confidence. The use of the local environment by different communities is not simply reactive: it has social implications and is a major item on the agenda of modern research (Chouquer 2003, 2005, 2006 a-c). The use of space can be seen as a result of the interaction of social and environmental imperatives, as in the case of the Alpine communities studied by Estelle Herrscher (see Ch 3, 139).

Methods

Working both on site and off site, archaeological teams now routinely contain natural scientists (archaeozoologists, archaeobotanists, geoarchaeologists), archaeologists (prehistorians, Romanists, medievalists) and historians. Environmental archaeologists of the historical periods draw on written sources, measured surveys, maps and photographs of all types. By combining these sources, it is possible to conduct comprehensive analyses similar to those carried out by social geographers. Environmental archaeology is one of the oldest interdisciplinary bridges (Butzer 1982), in part because it has always been an explicit concern of archaeologists, and in part because its 'specialists' have long been associated with archaeology one way or another.

Specialist expertise is required to capture the primary environmental data – soils, fauna and flora – identify them in the laboratory and determine their significance. Soil scientists examine *sediments* using micromorphology (Goldberg & Macphail 2006) or X-rays of soil blocks taken in the field (Denham *et al.* 2009). From these blocks, and the presence within them of certain *peds* or soil relics, they can write a soil history (pedogenesis), showing whether and when it has supported forest or crops or heathland. Chemical and biological analyses are also applied increasingly to anthropogenic deposits, such as strata inside houses or in yards, to detect traces of earlier activities (see Ch 1, 35). *Animal bones* are now routinely analysed for species, age, health and husbandry practices (O'Connor 2005). The animal population exploited by a community leaves its remains on site, and may also be implied by the type of landscape, and by the isotopic evidence for human diet (see Ch 3, 139). Small mammals, such as mice and rats that cohabit with humans, also report on the micro-environment – the local conditions within a settlement. *Insects*, extracted from particular contexts by paraffin flotation, also reflect local conditions, since they are specific feeders and their presence will distinguish between cold and warm, outdoor and indoor settings (Robinson 2001). *Plants* leave their traces in a number of different forms: their pollen collects in bogs and, when analysed indicates the dominant plants and trees over a radius of several kilometres, and how this changes through time. Episodes of clearance and the rise of agriculture are particularly evident. On site, contexts may contain pollen, or phytoliths from crops, or more specific to local use, burnt wood and grain (Evans & O'Connor 1999).

All these analyses lead to a better comprehension of the way land was used by medieval communities. This new understanding extends over a wide spectrum of activities related to land use and the way it functioned, be it at the scale of a settlement or living unit or at the scale of exploited hinterlands (for example, the cultivation of arable, pasture, meadow and forest). The data are recorded as specific signals observable at different scales, within a context, within a site and over a region. These markers constitute an essential source for the reconstruction of socio-economic behaviour patterns and for the understanding of the relationships medieval communities had with their environment.

For example, as well as reporting local medieval procurement and diet, faunal remains also offer information about the animal populations over thousands of years, information still important today. In the basin of the Loire, one of the most extensive in France, there remains an enormously diverse fish and bird population. In the sustainable management of this biological heritage, it is necessary to understand the role communities have played over the last two millennia in the maintenance, protection, introduction or reduction of species, some of which, such as salmon, eel or carp, have close bonds with human communities. Different types of exploitation (hunting for food, skins, furs, eradication of 'vermin', procurement of birds of prey for use as 'hunting auxiliaries' in the Middle Ages) have a – direct or indirect – impact on the wild fauna. The thirteenth to fifteenth centuries may well have been a crucial period for animal diversity, when we witness the elimination of certain species (see part 3, below). For example, taking into account their predatory activity and management politics, it is possible to detect the impact of the Dukes of Valois on the water and forest resources, and thus the habitat of their domain.

Bees are one of the rare insects to have been domesticated. Beekeeping implies an indirect use of the local vegetation, and bees seem to be at the centre of a network of links between vegetable and animal realms on the one hand, and between nature and culture on the other. The bond between humans and bees goes back to at least the Neolithic and the products of the hive – honey and wax – played a not insignificant role in the daily lives of people: beekeeping is described in certain medieval texts as 'flying stock'. Beekeeping has long suffered from a lack of interest on the part of the historic disciplines (Crane 1983).

Many pollen studies, including doctoral dissertations have addressed, or are in the course of examining, long time spans that include the medieval period. The dialogue between pollen specialists and archaeologists includes the discussion of diagrams displaying pollen sequences that allow us to propose new historical interpretations of the relationship between medieval communities and their landscape. Charcoal analyses have revealed modes of extraction from the plant realm by communities and, combined with the analysis of phytoliths contained within the same stratigraphic contexts, they build up a picture of the interaction with plants, whether trees, shrubs, grasses and fruits. The study of tree-rings, apart from its use for dating (dendrochronology, see Ch 1, p 28), enables us to measure, through the analysis of stress on wood, the amount of pressure put on forests by society.

Geoarchaeology has employed the methods and techniques of geophysics, geochemistry, geology, soil science and micromorphology to build a palaeoenvironmental framework for different areas such as the Rhône valley (excavations at Lyon, archaeological investigations on the route of the TGV Méditerranée), eastern France (investigations on the route of the TGV-Est), in the Loire valley (archaeological interventions on the routes of the motorways A85, A28, Val d'Orléans and Val Triple in the programme 'Zone Atelier Bassin versant de la Loire), in the valley of the Meuse in Belgium and on the route of a European gas pipeline in the Netherlands.

Environmental archaeologists use the methods of archaeology to collect their samples, and the methods of the earth and life sciences to analyse them. This double affiliation means that researchers have specific constraints and need to respect the protocols of each discipline. Research in environmental archaeology can only be relevant and fruitful if it is conducted under permanent interdisciplinary dialogue. It requires us to know the possibilities and limitations of the sources: they are often unpredictable, partial and, since excavation is irreversible, we cannot exactly replicate our investigations. The protocols which must be respected are those dealing with the recording of field data, of survey data and of interpretation, since archaeological sources are silent: it is the archaeologists who make them speak, who construct an interpretative discourse of history.

The study of relationships between human need and natural resources has led to a complete re-evaluation of medieval society and the advance of new explanatory models. The aim is to bring to light the choices and the decisions made at every stage in the exploitation of a given resource. Spatial analysis (of land plots, tracks and roads, of soil cover, hydrography, and network dynamics) allows us to understand how geographic units worked within relatively short time spans. The consequences of choices made by medieval societies, the constraints and the legacy from the *longue durée* can now be apprehended thanks to this paradigm shift. There follow some recent examples of investigations with a strong environmental slant, and the reader will find others in the remaining contributions to this chapter.

Rivers and ponds

The increased opportunities for study provided by rescue archaeology have completely changed our view of valley-community relationships during the Middle Ages in many areas – the Rhône valley (Burnouf *et al.* 1997), the Loire valley (Burnouf & Carcaud 2000; Garcin *et al.* 2006), the valley of the Moselle in Luxemburg, the valley of the Meuse in Belgium and also in the valleys of small coastal rivers: the valley of the Lez, the small river valleys of the Dives and Seulles on the Calvados coast. It has been possible to construct a history of rivers from investigations carried out in the valleys (Bravard & Magny 2002, Burnouf & Leveau 2004) and to situate the inherent risks to them over the long term. This requires an understanding of the hydrosystem, the bioclimate and social context of the late Pleistocene and Holocene, and the study of questions of sustainability, the ability of the system to resist change, and the thresholds, which, once crossed, result in catastrophe. From the study of formation processes, as well as from observing the rhythms and ruptures that occurred, there emerges a diachronic view of the morphological-sedimentary basis of the alluvial plain (see p 68-77 below).

Amongst environments favourable to the preservation of ecological evidence are zones of wetland, which constitute veritable archives of human-environment relationships. Studies being conducted on the dynamics of the historical landscape of the Brenne (Indre) were designed to investigate over a long time span (from protohistoric times to the present day) a marginal wetland anthropic system (Burnouf 2008, 100-101). They have brought to light an economy based on agriculture, husbandry and fish rearing and a history of water management (including the creation of an artificial wetland) and biological and mineral resource management (including the exploitation of iron ore). A previous interpretation, which saw the origins of the Brenne as a marsh, was discarded in the light of the new evidence: it is now seen as a landscape of ponds, developed to serve an increasing demand for fish. The results highlight the 'artificial' character of the landscapes created by medieval communities, particularly for the rearing of carp. In the Middle Ages, such spatial transformations take place in a cultural context that includes religious constraints and the medieval urban boom, and takes into account the distance from the coast and therefore the likelihood of procuring fresh sea fish. The increase in the number of ponds, now dated not only by documentary sources but also by radiocarbon dating and dendrochronology, reflects a choice by medieval communities spurred on by technical progress, by a socio-economic context and by the introduction of the Danubian carp. The landscape of these artificial wetlands and the aquatic biodiversity which they harbour represent the determining role played by people and the new species that they introduced. In Burgundy also, it is research on water and forests that forms the basis for a renewed understanding of the relationships that medieval communities had with their environment.

The Little Ice Age

Second millennium Europe has experienced climatic events, including major deteriorations in the climate which affected the entire European peninsula. They occurred during the sixth century, at the very beginning of the ninth century, and from the first quarter of the fourteenth century, in what is commonly called the Little Ice Age ('Petit Age Glaciaire' or PAG). Between the ninth and fourteenth century a period of climatic improvement occurred, the Little Medieval Optimum ('Petit Optimum Medieval' or POM). These events put constraints on society. Even in the Optimum period, which is considered stable, extreme phenomena such as the flooding of some rivers are not excluded. This well documented and well-dated climatic sequence has attracted interest from global climate historians, but is not thought to be general: the Little Ice Age has in fact been revisited as a 'Euro-centric' perception (Ogilvie & Jónsson 2001). However, we are currently some way from knowing how such variations in climate actually impacted on local communities.

Environment and builders

A completely different aspect of the relationship between people and environment lies in building practice. The built fabric rests upon the exploitation of the immediate environment (constraints in the choice of site, organisation of access), which the built environment will affect in turn. It also rests upon material resources that need to be considered in their entirety and the types of exploitation that they have occasioned. For the medieval urban fabric we can list the stone to be quarried, sculpted or cut into blocks, the mineral materials used in composite materials for making mortar and plaster, paint, clay for manufacturing tiles or bricks; wood in its diverse cuts and sizes; the different kinds of metal (iron, tinplate, lead, copper, tin); window glass. These resources have been managed and exploited in order to provide materials; we would like to know how modified these were prior to arrival on site. The industrial network in place ahead of a construction site is not just punctuated by extraction sites but also by sites where the materials were made and fashioned in a way that we still need to explore (for cut stone, prefabrication on order or standardisation anticipating demand). The analysis of the built environment, all categories included, lets us detect different types of economy in the building trade that are differentiated but linked by the know-how of the builders themselves. The value attached to materials depends on factors related to access and transport, as well as to management and exploitation methods that channel demand (culminating by of the end of the Middle Ages in the capitalist system). It is the entire process of the *chaînes opératoires* in their relationship with the environment and the management of resources that are now being studied.

The notion of legacy

Medieval communities have managed and created their surroundings, causing irreversible changes in all domains: wetlands, forests and chases, wood resources, minerals and industry, artificial constructions such as dykes, the closing off of estuarine and interior marshes and lagoons. The impacts on what is commonly known as the landscape are dynamic and enormously varied; the dynamics introduce their own chronology and pivots of change, which are as yet little known. The changes may result from haphazard initiatives with unintended consequences. The resulting landscape contains the memory of what was done to it, something researchers are in the process of defining under the concept of 'legacy'.

This notion of legacy invites us to consider the 'nature-culture' package as an 'anthropic system' (Burnouf 2003, Lévêque & van der Leeuw 2003), i.e. an ensemble of dynamics, interactions, adaptations, choices and decisions in constant co-evolution. In France, the layout of the present landscape is thought to be largely owed to protohistory, particularly the Iron Age (Chouquer 2006c). The organisation of the landscape is therefore a phenomenon that we must consider since protohistoric times, i.e. the first millennium BC. Medieval people inherited the topographical consequences of earlier actions, adopted them, transformed them, re-created them and produced another state of synergy between their needs and their resources (Garcin *et al.* 2006, Burnouf 2003, Burnouf 2008).

The idea of 'legacy' in landscape leads us to propose replacing the notion of *degradation* with the concept of *dynamics*. Several colloquia have debated the matter and, based on the results, showcased new ways of interpreting the records (for example Van der Leeuw 1995). Here the emphasis was still on the role humans played in the degradation of the environment, but increasingly dynamics take first place (Burnouf *et al.* 1997). Space is constantly being reconfigured, at the scale of settlements, just as at the scale of the agrarian landscape.

The study of the environment offers us a model or *scenario* of the landscape made by humans and inherited from them, at a given moment in time, described according to the current concept of medieval life (Burnouf 2003). We can never describe exactly what happened, since the evidence always increases and evolves and our ability to define and retrieve it improves. We must be content to provide an image of the complexity of medieval landscape appropriate to our times.

PART 2:   MANAGING THE ENVIRONMENT: EXAMPLES FROM FRANCE, HOLLAND AND GREENLAND

River management in the middle ages: taming the Loire *by Cyril Castanet*

A gradual increase in the vulnerability of settlements to flooding can be observed during the Middle Ages. Overflow of rivers was caused by new agricultural practices, the urban boom and episodes of increasing hydraulic energy (Burnouf *et al.* 2003; and see Part 1 above). In periods of flooding, the flow of water on the surface and underground is controlled by dykes and banks and the cutting of bypasses for the river bed. These were measures taken by the inhabitants confronting a vulnerable situation during the Middle Ages. Here we consider an area of the Loire east of Orléans where the medieval river was extensively managed to prevent flooding and maintain productivity.

In the valley of Orléans, the Loire today is contained by two lines of banks (Fig 2.2). The later of these (the *levées*), which contain the main narrow river bed, are high and continuous, and can be dated to the sixteenth century. The earlier riverbed was wider and marked by now discontinuous banks; these are the remains of the works of medieval hydraulic works or *turcies*. Numerous breaches are apparent in these banks, caused by major episodes of flooding. The oldest embankment of the Loire was probably not (or not exclusively) carried out downstream in Anjou, but on this stretch of the Loire in the Orléans region (Castanet 2008).

At Jargeau, the River Loire flowed in a broad southerly meander, from at least the fourth century AD (Fig 2.3 left). The southern banks were reinforced by medieval dykes intended to protect the medieval village and its fields from flooding. Following a rise in the water level in the river bed and probably at the time of a major flood, the meander was cut off at the neck by a new channel. This rise in water level had been provoked by the embankment, which had also facilitated the recut. The episode must have taken place before the beginning of the thirteenth century, the date of the bridge at Jargeau (Fig 2.3 right). This implies in turn that the embankment of the Loire in the central Orléans plain had already begun during the twelfth century (and probably much earlier).

Risks of flooding increased during the Little Ice Age that followed the creation of the short cut, and a new bed for the Loire was created in the sixteenth century, using a new type of bank (levée). This was aimed at protecting the village of Jargeau and its land,

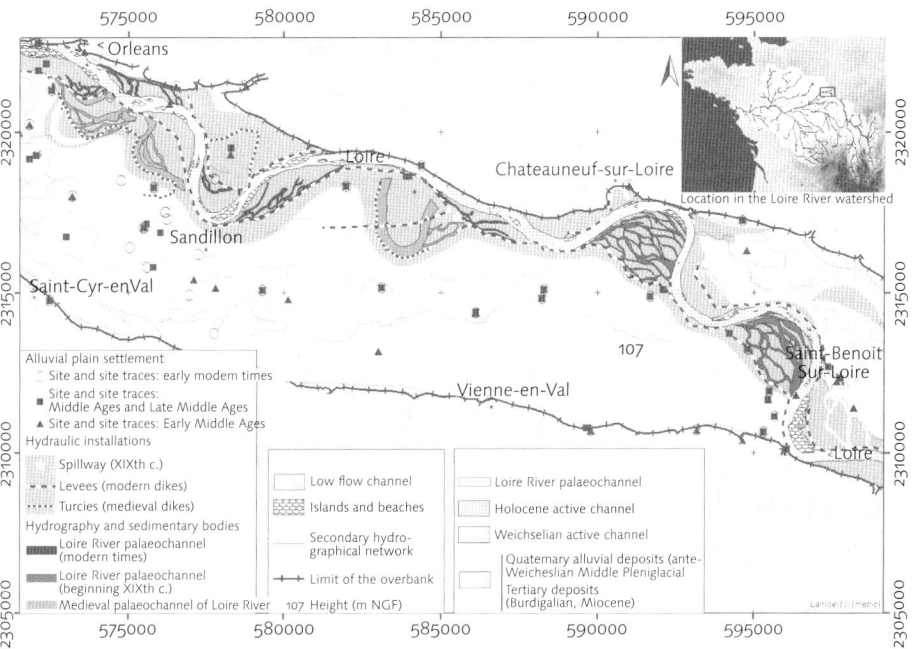

Occupation of the alluvial plain and hydraulic installations of the middle Loire in the valley of Orléans (France) in medieval and modern times. (Base: hydrography, palaeohydrography and strip of the Loire active over the last 30 000 years).   **Fig 2.2**

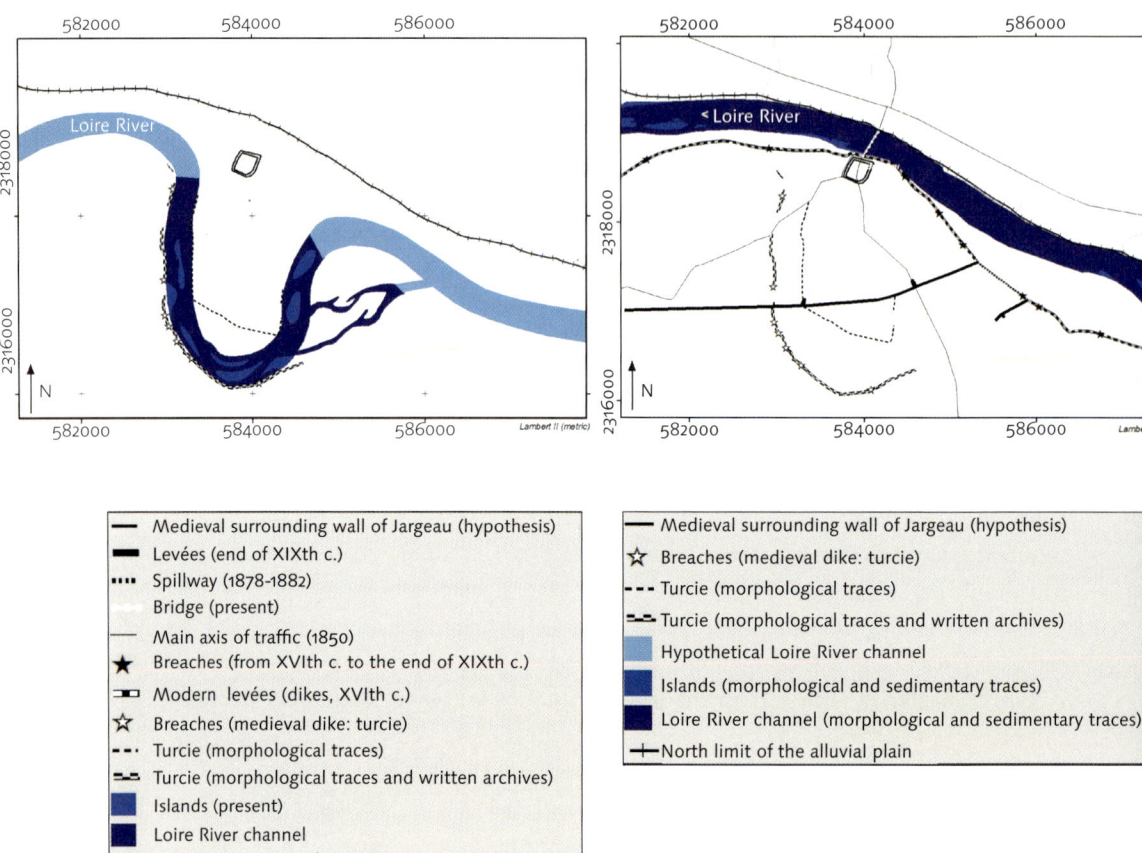

582000   584000   586000   582000   584000   586000

Fig 2.3   *The Loire at Jargeau, upstream from Orléans: (left) before the early 13th century, with the meander embanked during the 12th century; (right) After the early 13th century, showing the new channel, across the neck, the Medieval bridge and the location of the levées of the 16th century and later.*

still situated on the left bank of the river, although now someway downstream from the previous site. A high risk of flooding inherited from the medieval centuries continued all through the modern period. Written sources and observations on the ground bear witness to numerous breaches in the levées, the most severe upstream from Jargeau.

After the last great flood of the mid-nineteenth century, and the realisation that the sixteenth century levées could not contain the river, two weirs were built in the valley of the Loire in the Orléans area. These interactions between communities and their environment in the Orléanais during the Middle Ages and in modern times illustrate the changing perils and responses of those living near the river.

Communities and rivers in the Roussillon:
confronting environmental change *by Jean-Michel Carozza and Carole Puig*

The plain of the Roussillon is a vast triangular sedimentary basin more than 850 km² in extent opening onto the Mediterranean coast, which was densely populated during the Middle Ages (Fig 2.4). The drainage consists of four main rivers, their courses roughly parallel but with different hydraulic regimes. These rivers have been subject to management and exploitation from at least the ninth century AD (Caucanas 1995). In the north, the Agly, which starts in part from the limestone massifs of the Corbières, has a fairly regular flow linked to the influence of a karstic aquifer. Further south, the Têt represents the main drainage and communications axis with the mountainous region of the Pyrénées which determines its rain- and melt-water regime. The centre of the plain is home to the basin of the Réart whose regime is like that of a *wadi* with frequent dry episodes. Finally the south is drained by the Tech whose autumn floods (*aiguats*) are particularly destructive and lethal. This geographical configuration, at the junction of uplands and lowland coastal plains means that this basin contains the record of hydro-sedimentary events that occurred over millennia.

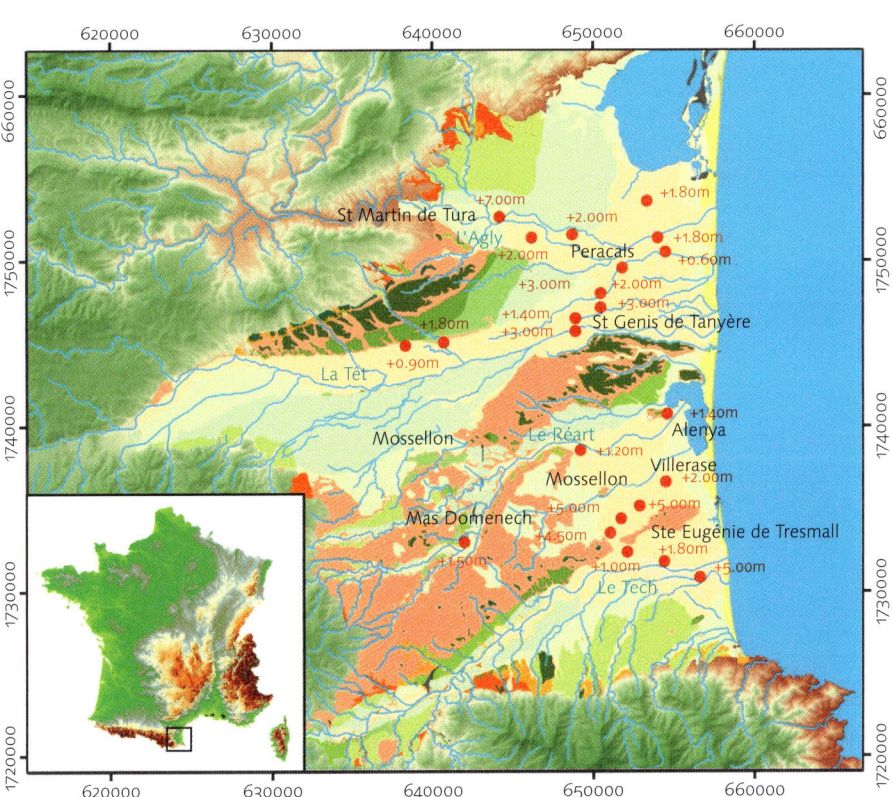

The Roussillon flood plain, showing the locations of evidence for flooding, and the depth of flood deposits recorded in metres.   **Fig 2.4**

Work carried out on these river courses since the mid-2000s demonstrates that the riverine environments have been subject to modification since around AD 1250-1280. Up to then the indications, though still sparse, are that the lowland zones were stable, as shown notably by the beds of the major rivers between the end of the ninth century and the middle of the thirteenth. Thick alluvial soils developed, indicating a phase of low fluvial activity. Numerous villages and religious establishments occupy these lowland zones and participate in a settlement network that largely survives today. From the second half of the thirteenth century, however, a series of events radically transformed the river system in the lowlands, its exploitation and integration into land boundaries.

Geoarchaeological investigations have shown that many sites on the alluvial plain, some of which contain Roman and medieval occupation on the same level, were abruptly sealed by thick deposits of sand brought by the rivers. These deposits are sometimes spectacularly deep: more than 7m at Saint Martin de Tura where they completely buried the village and its church, 5m at Mossellon, around 2m on average on some twenty sites (Fig 2.5). The shape of the rivers and of the major river beds is also subject to change. Water courses that were previously linear or meandering tended to become wider and develop multiple channels that are not very sinuous and deposit considerable amounts of sand and gravel. The section from the site of Mas Domenech close to the Canterrane illustrates this. This change in the configuration of the rivers results in a change in their dynamics, notably in an increase in the occurrence of major episodes of flooding. The heightening of the river beds led to rivers bursting their banks and permanently following new courses as their major stream. Such displacements can reach some 10km. The Tech, which once flowed south of the Elne, flowed along two

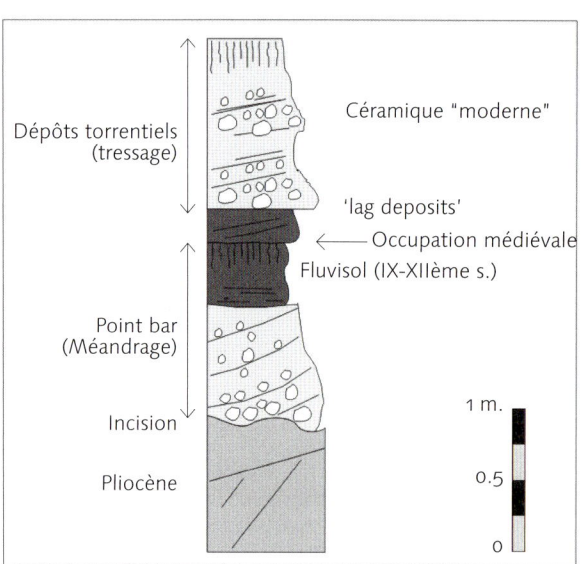

Fig 2.5   *Flood deposits seen in section at Mas Domenech in the Canterrane basin.*

new passages to the north that ran over a former wetland zone with its associated settlements (Mossellon, Villerasse). In the north of the basin, the Agly has gradually moved to its current location from an earlier south-north course that debouched in the pond of Salse-Leucate. The increase in place names *Agly Vell* or *Tech Vell* in documents dating from 1350 onwards is a further indicator of such movement.

Faced with such transformations, communities did not remain passive but adopted several strategies of adaptation. It is worth noting that the floods in themselves did not seem to pose direct problems to the riverine communities. They sometimes took more than a century to vacate regularly flooded areas, as at Saint Martin de Tura, Mossellon or Peracals. On the other hand, flooding events on agricultural land were a greater source of preoccupation and perhaps caused the decline or abandonment of some settlements. Changes in the dynamics of rivers and the generalised heightening of the level of the plain caused arable land to be covered in sterile sandy deposits. This phenomenon is illustrated by the field system of Alenya, which was buried in nearly 1m of sand between the thirteenth century and the end of the fifteenth century. The determination to maintain land ownership in mobile environments is shown by the care taken to preserve field boundaries. Thus boundary markers are doubly marked, using a system of high posts which would allow land divisions to be retraced in case of major silting. Such practices, known from the area of Perpignan, would explain why the land boundaries of Alenya were preserved up to modern times, after a period when the ground level was raised considerably (Fig 2.6).

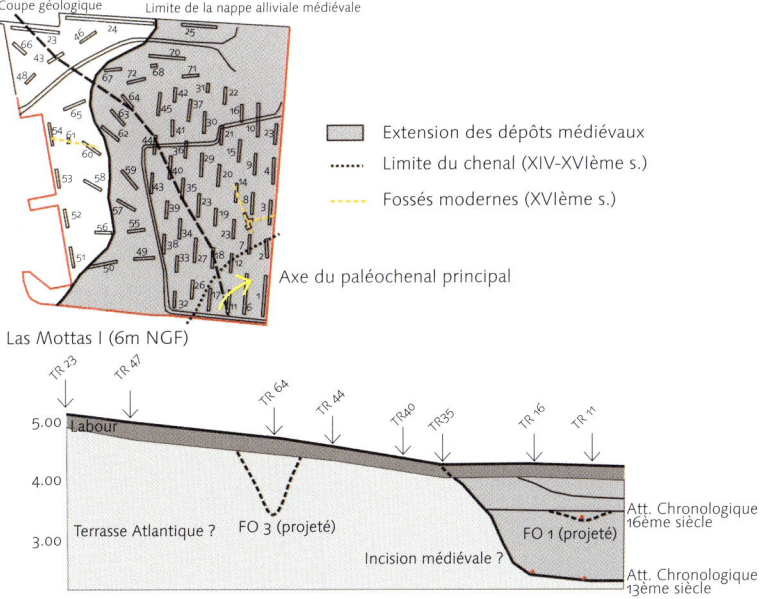

Medieval deposits beside the river channel at Alenya, showing the maintenance of property boundaries over areas of flooding.

Fig 2.6

Land exchanges between neighbouring communities began to take place, probably in order to compensate for the decrease in soil quality and to maintain the population. It may also indicate a practice made necessary by the rapid transformation of the natural limits between land parcels in relation to the movement of water courses. The first response to transformations in the environment consists therefore of partially re-organising the land boundaries. Conversely, the abandonment of settlements and their re-grouping in areas above the high water mark is rare, at least until the beginning of the fifteenth century.

Hydraulic engineering was a second type of response. From the first third of the fourteenth century direct interventions on the river courses increased: banks or dams (*reclausa*) were built on the Têt in 1327, the Agly was embanked around 1380. But other measures, which appear very modern, were also employed: destruction of any obstacles obstructing the flow of water at Perpignan in order to maintain the width of the minor bed at 40 poles (around 80m), and, above all, obliging the riverside population to plant copses or palisades 10 poles wide (or 19.7m wide) to fix the riverbanks and limit erosion and overflow.

The data obtained by geoarchaeology and the documentation in archives combine to allow a reading of the evolution of communities and their environment which integrates climatic variability and its effects as a significant component. Synchronising the chronological sequences remains difficult however. While the geoarchaeological data allow us to detect trends on specific sites, they remain imprecise in terms of chronology. Radiocarbon dates are widely bracketed (between 100 and 140 calibrated years) and dating from archaeological assemblages, though more precise, only gives a precision in the order of several decades, notably after the fourteenth century. Conversely, documentary sources give precise dates but the exact location, and the spatial extent of the phenomena they refer to, are difficult to pinpoint. It is nevertheless possible to propose a chronological sequence, which combines both approaches in order to throw light on the climatic tipping point that occurred at the end of the twelfth century.

The oldest mention of floods during the last millennium dates to 1224 (Mengel 1909) and perhaps they constitute the first indications of this episode of climate deterioration. As for the years 1256-1258, these were clearly cold and wet in southern Europe, as were the years 1276-1278. The floods of the rivers Aude and Roussillon in 1289-1290 continue this trend. On the other hand, the last decade of the thirteenth century and the first quarter of the fourteenth appear to be characterised by a period of hydrological calm. It is mainly after 1333 that indications of a climate change begin to increase again, to the point that this year was dubbed '*Mal any primer*' in the territories belonging to the kings of Aragon, a period that must probably be extended to the year 1346-1347. The great flood (*aiguat*) of 1421 marks an interruption in a dry phase that continued at least until the first decades of the sixteenth century. From 1522 onwards and up to 1598 repeated flooding shows that the greatest impact of this climatic deterioration happened during the sixteenth century, to reach another peak in the second half of the eighteenth century and the nineteenth century.

The sequence elicited reveals that there is a direct relationship between the fluctuations of the climate during the last millennium, as reconstructed by palaeoclimatologists (Jones & Mann 2004, Mayewski *et al.* 2004) and the changes experienced in the plain. However, and despite the record showing the magnitude of such changes, society seems to have responded by making adjustments within its margins. The multiplicity of responses, rather than inertia or passivity, is one explanatory model that would account for apparent stability in a heartland riven by major environmental crises.

Medieval reclamation and land use in the Netherlands
by Jan van Doesburg & Bert Groenewoudt

During the Middle Ages, especially between *c.* AD 800 and 1500, the foundation of the present-day landscape of the Netherlands was laid. Even in the most distant corners of the country human influence became visible in many different ways, resulting in the emergence of a wide variety of cultural landscapes. Partly these developments are related to the incorporation of the Netherlands into the Frankish Empire, bringing about new rights of ownership, domainial structures (manorialization) and major socio-economical changes (e.g. Theuws 1990 & 2008). Christianisation followed the Frankish conquest (seventh-eighth centuries). By the twelfth century the whole country was covered by a dense network of churches and parishes. Around that time too, depositions on 'pagan' open-air cult sites in the eastern Netherlands came to an end (Van Beek 2009), although depositions in peat bogs continued until the sixteenth-seventeenth centuries. This seems to demonstrate the continuity of some pre-Christian ideas and practices, and the migration of these practices into the realm of witchcraft (Van der Sanden 2004).

After the earlier deforestation and reclamation of most of the higher parts of the landscape, low-lying areas also began to be reclaimed, often systematically and on a large scale. Between *c.* 950 and 1300 the large scale reclamations of raised bogs were carried out in the west and north (e.g. Van der Linden 1984; Hendrikx 1989; Groenendijk & Schwarz 1991; Borger 1992; De Bont 2008). In the north, these reclamations were initiated by monasteries. In the west, the Count of Holland and the Bishop of Utrecht played leading roles. The peat areas were systematically divided into large units and given to groups of colonists who carried out the reclamations. Mutual rights and obligations, such as tax rates and the legal position of the colonists, were written down in a contract or '*cope*'. *Cope* reclamations consist of many very narrow, parallel fields (Fig 2.7).

In most cases the reclamations started from a central axis. This may have been a natural stream or a newly dug canal, road or dyke. In some areas peat domes served as starting points for reclamations. At right angles to the starting line, narrow ditches were dug bordering each individual strip of reclaimed land. In most cases all such plots had more or less the same size. Farmsteads were mostly situated at the front of the individual plots, making up long linear settlements. Arable farming seems to have played a minor role compared to animal husbandry. In some areas successful colonists started to built brick tower-keeps surrounded by a moat. This new elite gradually integrated into the ranks of the lower nobility. Quite often settlements shifted at some stage towards a new reclamation axis. This may have occurred repeatedly.

The large-scale reclamation of raised bogs and other 'wildernesses', and the digging of dykes to gain new land in the coastal districts were all part of a wave of agricultural expansion affecting the whole of north-west Europe. The *cope*-reclamation technique was later exported to other wetland areas. In the beginning of the twelfth century inhabitants of the western Netherlands peat area were invited by the Bishop of Bremen (Germany) to help reclaiming the peat areas in his bishopric.

From the eleventh and twelfth century onwards in the sandy 'uplands' in the east and south already existing fields on raised ground were joined to create open fields: '*essen*' (Spek 2004, 2006). Farms were moved to the very edge of these *essen*. In some cases, settlements clustered together, elsewhere dispersed settlement remained usual. Prior to recent re-allotment many *essen* had an intricate structure consisting of a large number of narrow, parallel fields. This pattern was the result of sub-dividing large reclamation 'blocks' of different ages and with different orientations. Irregular and small-scale allotment in the oldest core of some *essen* probably mark the sites of abandoned (early medieval) settlements (Fig 2.8). On many *essen* from the late fourteenth century onwards thick *plaggen* soils developed (see Ch 3, p 101). This was a consequence of the introduction of a new manuring technique, aimed at maintaining soil fertility. The surface covered by *plaggen* soils shows marked regional differences, probably caused by differences in local habitation density and distance to population concentrations (cities). Due to over-exploitation and soil degradation much of the sandy areas in the south and east gradually turned into 'marginal' landscapes (Groenewoudt 2009). Sand drifts expanded, especially after the fifteenth century, when sheep farming intensified (e.g. Koster 1978; Van Doesburg 2009).

Hydraulic works were carried out from the eleventh-twelfth century onwards at an accelerated pace. Often such activities were instigated by monasteries, after the thirteenth century also by district water-boards ('*waterschappen*'), public organizations that were established to improve drainage and prevent flooding (Van der Ven 2004). Along the coast and rivers dykes were constructed or improved. Numerous canals and ditches

Fig 2.7 *Aerial view of the starting point of a 'cope' reclamation near the village of Loosdrecht (Province of Noord Holland) (Photo: Paul Paris Les Images).*

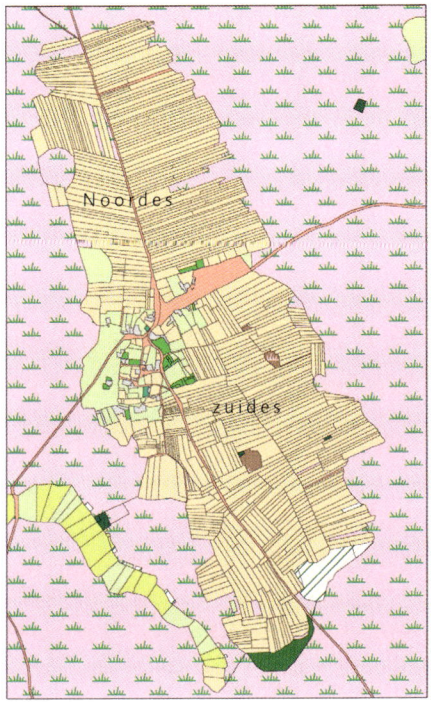

The two 'essen' (north and south) belonging to the village of Grollo (Province of Drenthe). The small square fields ('Kreuzgewannflur') in the west go back to the Early Middle Ages. The larger and more regular reclamation 'blocks' are Late- and Post- Medieval extensions. Source: land register 1832 (Research data Th. Spek).

Fig 2.8

were dug to drain and improve low-lying areas. In some cases natural waterways were canalized or connected to improve transport facilities. From the twelfth-thirteenth centuries onwards many wind- and watermills appeared in the Dutch landscape. They served as pumping-engines (drainage), to process foodstuffs and for the benefit of crafts (like paper-making).

Especially between the eighth and tenth centuries the production of iron was a major economic activity in the central and eastern Netherlands (e.g. Heidinga 1987; Van Nie 1995). The ore was extracted in marshy areas (bog iron ore) as well as on some ice-heaved ridges. Charcoal was used as fuel. Not only iron production, but also (large-scale) charcoal burning may have been organized by the Frankish authorities. Along the coast the cutting and dredging of turf for heating and salt production *('moernering'* and *'selnering')* expanded. This made the coastal area vulnerable to erosion and flooding. Much agricultural land was lost to the sea and expanding lakes.

Around the ninth century settlements became increasingly fixed. In this period in many areas the foundation was laid for the present-day settlement pattern. Along rivers the first pre-urban centres appeared (e.g. Dorestat, Utrecht, Maastricht, Nijmegen) some of which grew rapidly in the eleventh and twelfth centuries and transformed into cities. Elsewhere – near the coast and inland – urbanization essentially started one or two centuries later (Sarfatij 1990). In the countryside hamlets generally did not develop into villages before the fourteenth and fifteenth centuries.

Norse Greenland and the extinction of the settlement there
by Jette Arneborg

Colonists from Iceland settled in Greenland in the late 980s (Fig 2.9; Arneborg 2008). The settlement was based on pastoral farming – cattle, sheep and goats – and foreign trade, primarily of high-value walrus and narwhal tusk and exotica such as furs from polar bear and white gerfalcons. Imports of commodities, especially iron for tools, were of vital importance to the settlement.

Most of Greenland is Arctic; the most southerly part of the west coast, nowadays Kujalleq Municipality, and the inner parts of the Nuuk fjord system however belong to the northern temperate (boreal) birch forest and had the potential for the pasture economy the Norse settlers brought with them from Iceland. The goods for foreign trade were obtained on hunting trips to the Arctic regions in the North and on the east coast of Greenland.

The most southerly of the settlements was the Eastern Settlement. Here about 500 groups of ruins have been recorded, most of them representing Norse farms. In the smaller Western Settlement in the Nuuk region around 100 ruin groups have been mapped. The individual farms were scattered along the fjords and in the fertile valleys that connect the coast with the Inland Ice, and subsistence depended on a combination of domestic animals and hunting especially of Greenland seal that passed the settlements in spring and autumn.

The Norse Greenlanders were Christians (Fig 2.10). Their churches were built close to the farms, and the organisation of the Church was closely connected to the elite. The churches were owned by the farmers on whose land they were raised and the users paid the owner for the services of the Church. A Greenlandic Episcopal See under the

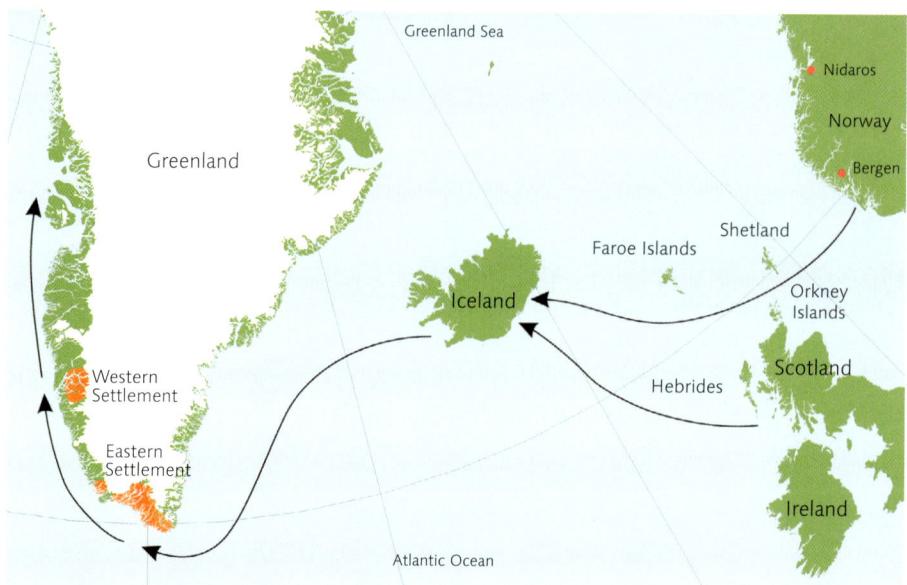

Fig 2.9   *The North Atlantic and the Norse settlements in Greenland.*

Archbishopric of Nidaros in Norway was established *c.* AD 1124 at *Gardar*, one of the largest farms in the Eastern Settlement. The last resident bishop in Greenland died in AD 1378.

Land and the ownership of land were the foundations of the social and economic structure, although local seal hunting was vital for subsistence. Zooarchaeology and an isotopic study (Arneborg & Lynnerup, in prep.) show that the dietary economy of the Norse settlers depended heavily on marine resources from the very beginning, and the dependence increased through time. This may have been caused by a combination of climate changes and non-sustainable farming.

From the middle of the fifteenth century the climate changed. Temperatures dropped, the wind intensified and sea ice increased, as did the ice cover of the fjords. It has been argued that the climate changes caused the abandonment of the settlements. The explanation for the abandonment may however not be as simple as that (Arneborg 2003). In the archaeological record we do not see a decline in the living conditions of the inhabitants (Fig 2.11). The resources of the land may have failed, but all indications are that the marine resources continued at an adequate level.

A more serious threat to the settlements was the failing of contacts with Europe. Increasing sea ice and declining markets in Europe for Greenland commodities caused a decline in navigation between Greenland and Europe (Norway) making it more difficult to maintain a north European peasant lifestyle in Greenland. In the fifteenth century, life in the Norse Greenland farms faded, coming to an end in the second half of that century.

The ruin of the Hvalsey Fjord Church in the Eastern Settlement. In front, the remains of the byre. The church is dated to after AD 1300.   **Fig 2.10**

(Inset): Liripipe hood from Herjolfsnes, Greenland (c. 1300-1450).   **Fig 2.11**

Introduction

From the thirteenth to sixteenth centuries, people lived alongside animals at a level of intimacy that is difficult for us to imagine, especially for the modern European city dweller. Medieval Europe was a predominantly rural society, and whilst this epoch sees the formation and growth of towns that would come to dominate the modern landscape, connections with the countryside and experiences of the natural world were extensive, even for the town-dweller. Animals proliferated in the symbolic systems of both Christian and Jewish communities, playing a central role in social identity, art and literature. Within the latter, the genre of the 'Beast Epic' satirising contemporary human society proliferated in a number of English, French, German and Dutch vernacular texts, producing one of the most popular medieval characters in western Europe: Reynard the Fox (e.g. Varty 1999 & 2000). This animal iconology was expressed in material culture, ranging from building decoration to jewellery, representing a vocabulary shared by peasants, clerics and the aristocracy alike. Its use could reflect the emblematised identity of an individual knight or an entire state; the lion of Venice appears from the mid-thirteenth century as one of the most distinctive material signifiers of Venetian political hegemony and commercial influence in the eastern Mediterranean, developing from a religious symbol (of St Mark) to a civic one (Rizzi 2001, 22-25).

This was also a time of ecological flux, a formative period for modern European society; the later Middle Ages in Europe can be seen as a time of massive 'niche' construction – i.e. the idea that human societies actively manipulate their environments and construct specific 'niches', reflecting their socio-economic as well as conceptual needs (see Ch 1, p 55). This can be seen in the significant environmental transformations that take place across the Continent, and is particularly evident in responses towards both domestic and wild fauna. The rapidly expanding population put pressure on natural resources, and the extent of cultivated land in many regions of Europe was at its greatest in the thirteenth century. The Black Death pandemic in the mid-fourteenth century enabled woodland to regenerate in a number of regions reaching its greatest extent in *c.* 1400, whilst the diversification of farming, largely favouring pasture in western Europe, prompted the regionalisation of natural resources (Yeloff & Van Geel 2007). The plague did not halt the growth of cities for long, and in the fifteenth century the major capitals of Europe were relying on animal products from vast and distant hinterlands. There is clearly a fundamental economic aspect to the exploitation of both wild and domestic animals in the later medieval period; trends and innovations ultimately resulted in the appearance of modern breeds and culminated in irreversible ecological transformations. Despite the regeneration of habitats in the later fourteenth century, the decline of several wild mammal species is evident in a number of European regions by the sixteenth century. Underlying these trends was a cosmology of human dominion over the natural world and a sense of separation from other species, which surfaced most vividly and explicitly in the writings of theologians from the twelfth century. The medieval period can be seen as a time where individuals and communities struggled to realise their divinely-ordained dominion. This was replicated within human society in microcosm, where animals and access to animals were frequently used as indicators of social differentiation.

Medieval animal studies

In recent decades the study of animal bones from medieval contexts has significantly contributed to furthering our understanding of the dramatic transformations across European societies from the thirteenth to the sixteenth century. The literature is growing at an exponential rate, in numerous languages and its dissemination is becoming increasingly sophisticated. Animal bones, especially in significant quantities, can yield a diverse range of information on the living communities of animals and the processes that led to their death and deposition (Fig 2.12; Choyke *et al.* 2005). Common topics include socially distinct dietary regimes, husbandry practices (such as dairying, transhumance and breeding), butchery technology, animal-related material culture (such as bone tools and ivory artefacts), the role of animals in religious and social ideology (such as elite hunting culture), as well as species biogeography, health and ecology. More recently, biomolecular techniques are revealing the provenance and long-distance movement of some species (see Ch 1, p 55). The limitations of the zooarchaeological data are evident when compared with contemporary documentary sources. For example, variable preservation and excavation techniques have meant that the consumption

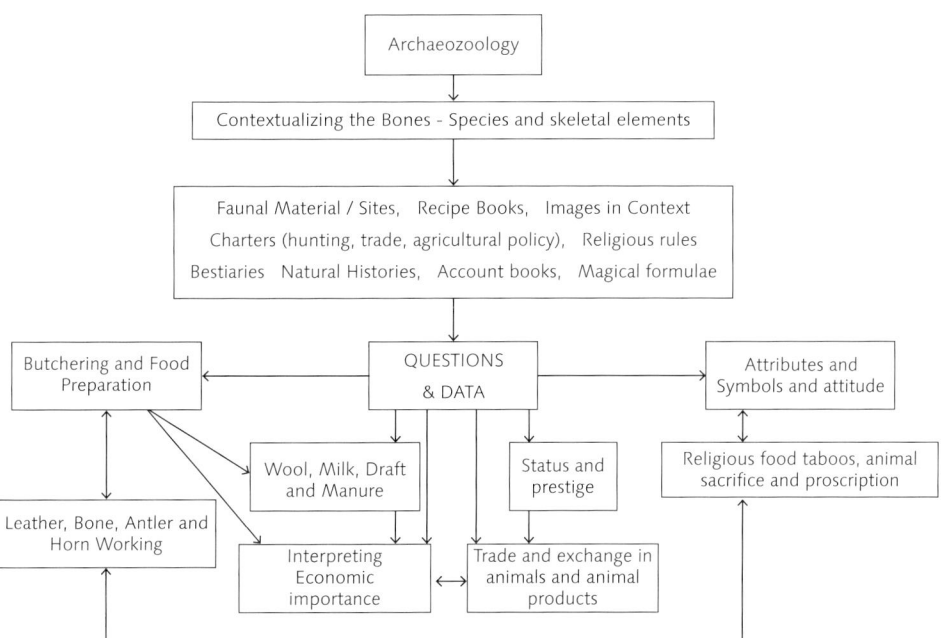

Research themes in medieval zooarchaeology, adapted from Choyke, Lyublyanovics and Bartosiewicz **Fig 2.12**
2005.

of fish is usually dramatically underrepresented in the archaeological record (Ervynck *et al.* 2003, 433). Excavations within Malbork castle in north Poland have yielded very few fish bones, in comparison to the extensive references to the organisation of fishing at the site in late fourteenth century-records (Maltby *et al.* 2009). Even in the Venetian lagoon, where high quantities of diverse species thrive in the sheltered environment today, no archaeological contexts were sieved until relatively recently. Indeed, recovering this data has shed significant new light on fish exploitation. The introduction of sieving medieval archaeological contexts at Flemish sites in the 1990s revealed that cod, previously thought common, was in fact outnumbered by many other species, and reassigned a higher-status value. A similar reappraisal has changed our perception of pike consumption in medieval Switzerland, relative to smaller, very young fresh-water fish (Ervynck *et al.* 2003, 434). In York, sieving yielded quantities of fragmented egg shell, mostly from hens, again representing a much underestimated product in medieval cuisine (O'Connor 1989, 17). Any understanding of the role of animals in alimentary culture must be combined with evidence for vegetables, fruits and other foods, but the regular synthesis of zooarchaeological and palaeobotanical data has yet to be achieved.

Limitations are being overcome with multi-disciplinary dialogue. Indeed, it is possible to speak of a sub-field of 'medieval animal' studies, exemplified by projects such as the 'Medieval Animal Database' (a collaboration between six universities; see http://www.imareal.oeaw.ac.at/animalwiki/index.php/Main_Page). This database, will enable zooarchaeological, documentary, literary and artistic sources to be cross-referenced for individual species, regions and periods, promoting both multi-disciplinary awareness and facilitating inter-disciplinary synthesis. Other databases focusing on medieval animal studies have also been launched elsewhere in Europe, and animals have been the subject of increasing numbers of conference sessions as well as conference series, such as 'Animals as Material Culture in the Middle Ages', a pan-European forum which has been running annually since 2005.

What then have environmental archaeological perspectives and the new sub-field of medieval animal studies contributed to our understanding of European society in the first half of the second millennium AD? How will these develop in the future? A useful starting point is to consider how the human niches reflected the diverse environments of medieval Europe.

The tame and wild in towns: Microcosms of civilisation

Medieval towns were quintessential human environments: bounded, built-up and regulated. The twelfth and thirteenth centuries were a period of significant urban growth in Europe and the later medieval period saw the development of certain towns into the first 'capital cities' (Spufford 2002). The process of colonisation accompanying the crusades promoted urbanisation in the Baltic and urban renewal and expansion in Palestine (Bartlett 1994). Towns, from their earliest development, required significant provisioning networks which increasingly extended to meet the demands of their markets and to complement the range of products available within their bounds; excavations of cities such as York in northern England, Novgorod in western Russia, Prague in the Czech Republic and Gdańsk in northern Poland, have yielded vast quantities of animal bone, most of which derive from livestock.

Cattle and sheep (neither of which were kept predominantly for food) were brought into towns on the hoof, slaughtered within their bounds and their carcasses processed, whilst there is evidence for keeping pigs, poultry and sometimes herds of other domesticated ruminants within the town in yards, small holdings and orchards (O'Connor 1989; Albarella 2005). Whilst cattle dominate the faunal assemblages of many medieval European towns, in some sites such as Stari Bar in Montenegro, the mountainous environment was far better suited to raising sheep and goats, reflected in recovered faunal assemblages (Pluskowski & Seetah 2006). On the other hand, the unusually high rate of mutton consumption in late medieval Basel (Switzerland) and later medieval Segesd-Pékóföld (Hungary) can be more readily linked to the local importance of wool processing (Bartosiewicz 1999, 146). The cash economy of towns also ensured that a greater diversity of wild species was available in towns than in rural areas, variation within urban sites reflecting the purchasing power of individual households (O'Connor 1989, 19). Hunted mammals and birds represent a minute fraction of urban faunal assemblages, but their presence (alongside exotic animals and their products (see below and Ch 3, p 132), reflects the specialised economies of towns in contrast to the exploitation of locally available species by rural communities (Yvinec 1993). This specialised animal exploitation is also evident in urban demand for fish.

By the thirteenth century, town populations were consuming a greater diversity of fish – particularly marine species such as cod – than in previous centuries, both reflecting and driving the expansion of commercial fishing (Barrett *et al.* 2004; see also below). By the fourteenth and fifteenth centuries, the population density in some regions of Europe outstripped its local resources and animals (as well as grain) had to be moved significant distances; for example the urban populations between Calais and Cologne relied on cattle meat raised in the Oversticht of Utrecht and in Friesland, and in the fifteenth century additional cattle were reared in Denmark for urban markets in Flanders, Brabant and Holland (Spufford 2002, 104). The late medieval international trade in fish paralleled these sprawling provisioning networks, linking the North Sea and Baltic with the Mediterranean (Salamon *et al.* 2008).

Whilst towns acquired animals from networks stretching considerable distances, they also developed their own distinct ecosystems, which urban communities sought to control. The concentrated quantities of human organic refuse resulting from food and butchery waste formed a key food source for high populations of diverse species, dominated by predators such as raptors and feral cats (O'Connor 2000b). The latter were exploited for their fur, which was the cheapest on the market and during occasional episodes of starvation for food, as in the case of seventy-nine cats recovered from a thirteenth-century well in Cambridge (Luff & Moreno-Garcia 1995). Medieval towns contained a mosaic of gardens, orchards, even fields, supporting diverse communities of plants, insects, birds and mammals (Armitage 1985). This diversity was more pronounced than in modern towns; in the later medieval/early modern period, large cities such as Paris saw the shrinkage of green spaces, as human populations grew and backyards were overbuilt (Crossley-Holland 1996, 41). The distribution of the most visible animals within a town reflected internal social stratification; higher-status complexes belonging to royalty, aristocracy, bishops, monasteries and the military orders had access to the most diverse range of animal resources, increasingly after the fourteenth century in response to emulating upwardly mobile classes such as merchants (Ervynck 2004).

This stratification is clearly represented in the diversity of dog types (zooarchaeologists hesitate to refer to them as 'breeds' as these include characteristics such as colour, coat texture and temperament). A comparison of dog remains from medieval Scottish towns demonstrated the presence of individuals used by different social groups for hunting, herding, security, and in the case of small lapdogs, kept as high-status pets (Smith 1998). Horses on the other hand, another key indicator of status, are not encountered very often in urban excavations. Although they were omnipresent in towns for transport, their disposal was usually confined to urban boundaries (Rackham 2004). The ecology of towns was distinct and largely the product of human management, corresponding to contemporary impressions of towns as enclosed centres of civilisation, their conceptual separation from the countryside often marked by walls or other boundaries. Nonetheless, urban wildlife flourished, and in some cases even large carnivores such as wolves were able to find their way into towns. There is little evidence for the difficult relationship between urban centres and rodents that characterises modern cities, but medieval towns certainly supported extensive communities of scavenging mammals and birds. The growth of towns had a significant impact on rural society, which became heavily involved in provisioning. However, whilst the town inhabitants struggled to maintain their environment as a microcosm of civilisation, there is also evidence for the imposition of the same social design on the medieval countryside, related to trends in colonisation, the spread of monasteries and aristocratic culture.

Rural society and animals: the struggle for dominion

Later medieval rural society was closely associated with seasonal rhythms, in contrast to the changing nature of urban society from the later fourteenth century increasingly dictated by more precise timing, geared to commerce and measured by mechanical clocks (Goodman 1999, 154-5). Despite the growth of towns, the majority of people in the Middle Ages still lived in the countryside, where contact with wild and domestic animals was varied and regular. The zooarchaeology of rural sites encompasses a range of social contexts: from castles and monasteries to villages and individual farmsteads, hunting shelters and shielings. This abundant data-set has been used to reconstruct trends in animal exploitation relating to the local rural economy, often comparing and contrasting individual sites. The broader context for the insights offered into local diet, pastoral farming customs and the processing of deadstock is the intention to manipulate the local environment. Whilst this has often been viewed from an economic perspective in terms of maximising subsistence strategies, it is equally important to situate this within the distinct ideological frameworks operating in later medieval society.

The impact of the Black Death on rural communities was emphatic, and had implications for animal exploitation. In the thirteenth century, the countryside was a mosaic of manorial and monastic estates, villages of varying character that had been shaped by the nature of the topography and earlier occupation, and carefully managed landscapes, particularly those in short supply such as woodland. The growth of population across Europe in the twelfth and thirteenth centuries coincided with a warm climate (see Part I above) enabling the settlement and cultivation of previously marginal areas. This saw the colonisation of the interior of densely wooded regions, such as the Scandinavian peninsula, the uplands of Swabia, Franconia and the Black Forest (Scott 2002, 79), resulting in significant deforestation in many regions of Europe and the intensification of exploitation of various terrestrial and aquatic habitats. Industries which required timber as the most important pre-requisite for their manufacturing processes developed on the fringes of woodland, such as the production of iron, leather and glass in northern central Germany (Scott 2002, 76), central Sweden and Norway (see papers in Andersson *et al.* 1998). The climatic downturn or 'Little Ice Age' at the turn of the fourteenth century prompted a series of bad harvests and the gradual abandonment of marginal areas in certain regions. The dramatic reduction in population following the Black Death pandemic enabled some woodland and their populations of wild mammals to regenerate, but this was relatively short-lived and the fifteenth century saw the resumption of pressure on the wild countryside. Socio-economic transformation following the pandemic saw a general switch from arable farming to pastoralism – tillage, stock-rearing and dairying – in many regions of Europe (Scott 2002, 73), alongside increasing access to meat at the lower levels of society, which in turn prompted the elite to diversify their exploitation of wild birds and fish in particular. This appears to have accentuated the role of animals in defining social identity in the fifteenth and sixteenth centuries.

The zooarchaeology of medieval pastoral farming

A great deal has been written on farming practices in medieval Europe, which were often aligned with local topographic conditions. All three major groups of livestock – cattle, sheep and pigs – were raised across Europe, but their relative representation varied both regionally and in terms of local exploitation. The coastal marshes of Frisia and Emsland and the lowlands of Mecklenburg between the Elbe and Oder were prime cattle-raising regions (Scott 2002, 73). Goats were better suited to warmer, rugged Mediterranean environments than temperate northern Europe, while sheep, significantly less important in medieval Germany, dominated pastoral farming in Britain in the context of wool production, especially after the fourteenth century when the 'kill-off' pattern interpreted from their remains indicates the culling of older animals (Albarella 1997, 24). Pigs were farmed exclusively for their meat and fat, and were predominantly driven into woods to feed on acorns, or raised individually in towns. They were the most unusual of the three livestock groups, partly feral, feeding off scraps or bran from milling when not roaming woods. Indeed, their presence is often used as a proxy for woodland, but it can also be a convincing indicator of social control and culinary preferences. The highest quantities of pig remains are found on aristocratic sites, and the conspicuous consumption of young animals, killed before their optimal slaughter age (acquired in part through taxation) is a hallmark of elite diet at least from the latter centuries of the first millennium (Loveluck 2005, 241). On the other hand, the steady rise of pork consumption in medieval Hungarian towns has been linked to the influx of German colonists, bringing with them a new culinary culture (Bartosiewicz 1999, 146).

Husbandry regimes also varied from one region to another; cattle-rearing in northern Germany tended to serve the market for both meat and dairy produce, whereas in the Alps there was more emphasis on dairying. As such, the growth of southern German towns outstripped local meat supplies and necessitated importing livestock on the hoof over considerable distances (Scott 2002, 83). Monasteries often maintained significant herds, a portion of which was harvested at an early age for their soft skin, which was made into parchment (see below and Fig 2.13). But the relationship between husbandry regimes and industry was not one-sided. The Upper German linen industry in Swabia required vast quantities of milk for the various stages of cloth production (it catalyzes the retting of flax), which depended on widespread dairying, thus specific pastoral regimes functionally conditioned the development of the linen industry (Scott 2002, 73). While animals were bred mainly for urban consumption, meat also played a role in the dietary regimes of rural communities. Here, older animals were typically

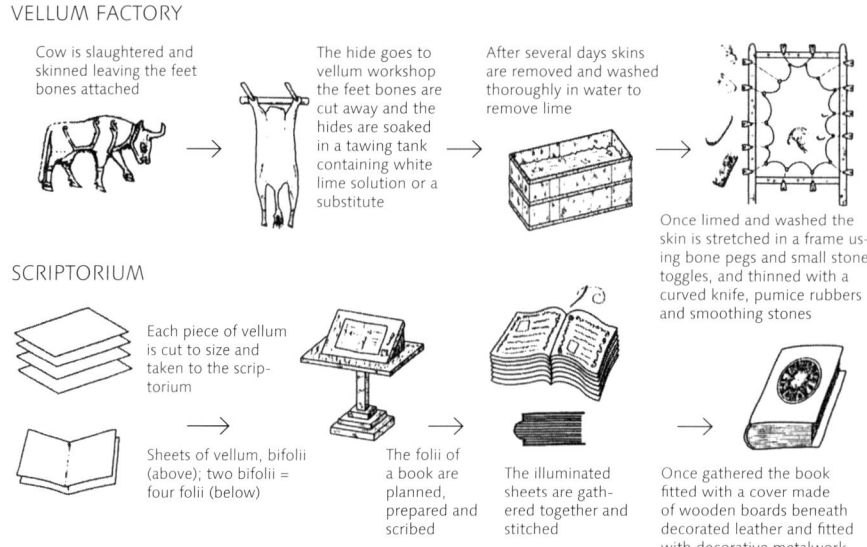

Fig 2.13   *Diagram showing the process of making parchment or vellum (from Carver 2008, Fig. 6.6; reproduced by courtesy of Martin Carver)*

consumed, a reflection of relative wealth and husbandry regimes geared to exploiting secondary produce. This trend can be seen from Ireland to Moldova; in the latter region, the majority of cattle, for example, were slaughtered between four and six years old (Bejenaru 2009, 32). Regional variations in the size of livestock are evident from the study of faunal assemblages, whilst a combination of local improvements and imported breeds resulted in generally faster growing, larger animals from the later fourteenth to the seventeenth centuries (Thomas 2006). By the fourteenth century, horses had begun to replace cattle as traction animals, resulting in the selection of larger and stronger animals, reflected in a noticeable difference in size between early medieval and later medieval animals (Albarella 1997). The success of the extensive cattle trade in central Europe prompted the selection and breeding of local stock to produce the famous Hungarian Grey (*Magyar szürke szarvasmarha*) by the sixteenth-eighteenth centuries (Bartosiewicz 1999, 148).

The complex roles of the major livestock groups in medieval European societies are difficult to extract from the fragmentary sources, although it is important to move beyond using animal remains simply as economic and environmental proxies. Claudine Fabre-Vassas' (1997) ethno-historical study of pig keeping, killing and eating, and its links with religious festivals, social networks and identities in southern France, illustrated the centrality of animal husbandry in the life of rural communities that was evidently developing within the Christian milieu of medieval society. In particular, the consumption of pork as a visual definer of Christian communities was explicitly and consistently juxtaposed with Jewish identity, and became central to the anti-Semitism of European communities that developed particularly from the fourteenth century. Jewish attitudes to animals, in turn, reflected specific religious ordinances and have been used to identify these communities on the basis of contrasting faunal assemblages (see below, and Ch 10, p 411). The fourteenth century also saw the increasing (re)appearance of animal disguise in local folk games and mumming, a trend which Michael Camille (1998) linked to apotropaic attempts at reviving depleted natural resources. Occasional archaeological examples of the ritualistic treatment of animal remains in the later medieval period (e.g. Merrifield 1987, 118-19), hint at a diversity of folk practices that have yet to be fully documented and understood. Although livestock had been hit hard by the famines of the early fourteenth century, wildlife was to be more severely affected by the development of the medieval human niche.

Predator and prey

The woods, moors and mountains of medieval Europe were home to wolves, bears and lynx (and on the Scandinavian peninsula, wolverine) that preyed on a diverse range of wild ungulates and smaller mammals. These top terrestrial predators in turn became the occasional targets of human depredation, with both groups competing for the same prey. In various regions of Europe, the aristocratic impulse to control environmental resources had developed by the twelfth century, and was conceptualised as a defining feature of lordship. The Norman Conquest had introduced *foresta* into England;

a system of controlled land-use designed to preserve populations of deer for exclusive hunting by the aristocracy; one which reached its zenith in the thirteenth century (see Ch 3, p 132). Although this system was virtually unique in Europe, the control of hunting space developed alongside the growing political power of the French and Danish kings, the Scottish kings adopted a version directly from the Anglo-Norman system while across the Empire and in Italy various laws sought to regulate hunting. Comparative analysis of faunal assemblages in England, France and central Europe (e.g. Sykes 2007a; Yvinec 1993), have indicated a close correlation between the presence of hunted animals and aristocratic sites. In north Italy, the infrequent exploitation of game at all levels of society in the early medieval period (Baker 1993) becomes associated with aristocratic sites from the ninth century, and increasingly from the eleventh century (Valenti & Salvadori 2007). In his seminal work on medieval hunting, John Cummins (1988) sub-divided quarry species into edible and non-edible categories and indeed, some species were introduced into western European landscapes – exclusively it seems at first for hunting and consumption (see below). In fact, while cervids were widely perceived as the ultimate prey item, this appears to have varied across Europe and bear meat was consumed in Flemish and Baltic regions, appearing in low quantities at high-status sites (Ervynck 1993).

The exploitation of game fits the concept of the aristocratic meat-eating class as top predators, characterised as independent wild carnivores in contemporary literature and adopting bestial emblems in the formative century of heraldry. The hunt became a theatrical aristocratic pageant in some regions, an elaborate expression of the microcosm of the court. This in fact extended to the seigneurial manipulation of the landscape, configuring local ecosystems to meet (and create) cultural ideals expressed in literature and art. Some of the most symbolically intricate examples of later medieval art centre on the aristocratic animal world, often within the context of hunting or related 'landscapes of lordship' (see Creighton 2009). Whilst there were famous aristocratic hunters, such as Gaston Phébus, the third Count of Foix, who wrote the most influential book on hunting of the fourteenth century (Fig 2.14), a significant proportion of hunting was carried out in proxy by professional retinues, who would essentially provide venison on demand. Moreover, there is zooarchaeological and written evidence for the systematic redistribution of game carcass parts 'down the line' of the hunting party hierarchy (Sykes 2007b), and a remarkable assemblage of eighty-one roe deer antlers from pits in London, dating to c. 1180-1300, represents the end of this chain, stretching from the aristocratic hunting retinue to urban leatherworkers (Armitage & Butler 2005). Alongside this controlled exclusivity, there is also documentary evidence for poaching and black markets in this restricted meat. The fundamental role of animals in expressing social relations is particularly emphasised in western European regions from the fourteenth century, when the increased diversification of wild bird consumption noted in English and French aristocratic sites represents the redefinitions of social boundaries at a time when meat had become more widely available (Clavel 2001).

In eastern Europe, as well as the Scandinavian peninsula, there was relatively less control over animal resources, perhaps reflecting a combination of topography and

Illustration from a 15th-century copy of Le Livre de La Chasse by Gaston Phébus, showing a wild boar **Fig 2.14**
hunt (Paris, Bibliothèque nationale, Ms. fr. 616, folio 95). Reproduced under non-commercial licence
http://www.bnf.fr/fr/collections_et_services/reproductions_document/a.repro_reutilisation_docu-
ments.html.

political systems. But even here there was an impulse from ruling elites to appropriate wild animals. In Norway, the mass-trapping of reindeer at sites such as Dovre in the mountainous interior during the thirteenth century, supplied royal towns like Bergen with antler, hides and meat (Barth 1983; see also 'Wild reindeer hunting as world heritage' project, http://www.villreinfangst.no/eng/). The extensive woods of eastern Prussia and Lithuania remained a militarised zone for much of the thirteenth and fourteenth centuries due to the ongoing crusades of the Teutonic Order, and supplied game for the Order and its guests. Because of their limited population and their diverse and plentiful supply of wild ungulates, including European bison, these woods became famous hunting grounds for the Polish kings and Lithuanian dukes in the fifteenth and sixteenth centuries (Samojlik 2006). At the frontiers of Christendom hunting and trapping appears to have been more widely practiced, but even here local elites exerted strong control over animal resources which represented important luxury commodities for the European market. In the Russian principalities, this control focused on the acquisition of fur; in Arctic Norway furs and also fish and whale products; in the Scandinavian Atlantic colonies, especially Greenland, virtually all exports, particularly the highly valued narwhal and walrus ivory, as well as live gyrfalcons, were monopolised by local chieftains (Pluskowski 2009). Sustained hunting and trapping inevitably resulted in ecological transformations, the regional effects of which are only beginning to be appreciated.

Ecological transformation

Hunting and trapping could result in the collapse of wild mammal populations, and there is evidence for excessive environmental exploitation throughout the Middle Ages. In the tundra frontier of the Russian principality of Rostov, a series of settlements developed around Lake Beloe from the ninth century and began to prosper as a result of exploiting local fur-bearing mammals, especially beaver. The faunal assemblages of these settlements show a marked decline in exploitation from the second half of the thirteenth century, which ultimately resulted in the abandonment of some sites, the reorganisation of others and the relocation of the regional urban centre; this trend may be explained by the collapse of local fur-bearing mammal populations (Zakharov 2002). This is not the case in all regions where furs were systematically harvested; in Livonia beaver populations survived into the seventeenth century, but faunal profiles from Latvian and Estonian sites do not indicate a similar intensity in exploitation. Overexploitation is also evident as a consequence of aristocratic hunting culture in western Europe, resulting in the dramatic decrease of wild ungulates. Wild boar had been hunted to virtual extinction in England by the thirteenth century, but by the fifteenth century the decline of red deer is documented in a number of royal *foresta* (Pluskowski 2007a); similar trends are evident elsewhere in north-western Europe (e.g. Clavel 2001) and eastern Europe (e.g. Bejenaru 2009). The mass hunting of reindeer in central Norway appears to have prompted herds to shift their migration patterns in the late thirteenth century, whilst the pressure of local hunting and/or habitat transformation on elk populations in southern Sweden prompted comb makers in Skara (Västergötland) to switch from using shed elk antler to cattle bones by the late thirteenth century (Vretemark 1990).

Aristocratic hunting culture was conceptualised in literature as an adventurous, potentially perilous chase through a wooded and partly mysterious landscape. This is most likely to have been the case in some regions of Europe; the bear hunts documented in the Pyrenees, one of which resulted in the death of Gaston Phébus, were complicated, dangerous affairs requiring the mobilisation of extensive manpower and resources, crossing through farmland, meadows, woods and mountains. However, a significant amount of hunting, and its culture, was carefully engineered and choreographed. This resulted in a high degree of ecological manipulation. Fallow deer and rabbit were imported into England, France and other parts of northern Europe as exotic quarry to be bred and contained for the aristocratic hunt. Domesticated ferrets were kept for coursing rabbits, and a rare find from the Flemish castle of Laarne indicates that their canines were filed down, enabling rabbits to be caught alive and the population selectively managed (Van Damme & Ervynck 1988). From the twelfth century these animals were confined in enclosures – parks and warrens – which represented paradise in miniature (Pluskowski 2007a). The kings of Denmark reserved whole islands as parks, attaining the ideal of heaven mirrored on earth. The number of parks rose dramatically in the thirteenth and fourteenth centuries, along with their populations of fallow deer and rabbits. This is reflected in changing representation of cervid species at high-status sites. In northern France, the decline in hare remains parallels the rapid increase in rabbit bones at aristocratic sites (Clavel 2001). Animals escaping from warrens were almost certainly the progenitors of post-medieval wild rabbit populations, which proliferated due to the reduction in predators, landscape clearance and milder winters (Van Damme & Ervynck 1988, 283). While this may have reflected dietary preference, rather than an actual collapse in the local hare population, there is certainly evidence that some species were disappearing from the unbounded landscapes of northern Europe. Systematic persecution developed alongside aristocratic hunting culture. Large carnivores, particularly wolves, became perceived as unwelcome competition for wild ungulates and in England they were hunted to extinction, with the last pathetic example of the lupine population housed in the Tower of London. Even then, there is no evidence that this particular animal was obtained in England, and the last reliable documentary reference to wolves dates from Whitby Abbey at the end of the fourteenth century (Pluskowski 2006).

The aristocracy were by no means the only group associated with ecological transformation. The process of colonisation in various regions of Europe, particularly the Baltic, had a significant impact on local environments which written sources hint at, and which are increasingly beginning to attract the attention of archaeologists. But the most explicit expression of the need to cultivate land can be found in the activities of some of the coenobitic monastic orders, particularly the Cistercians. In the twelfth and thirteenth centuries, this order of monks sought to locate their houses in areas of 'wilderness' in order to cultivate it and make it productive. On the one hand, the ecological impact of such religious communities was potentially very significant as they certainly

promoted settlement growth, but on the other, the order often took advantage of existing infrastructure and its obsession with wilderness quickly developed into a carefully
constructed mythology. Despite the significant political and territorial power many
monastic houses wielded, they distanced themselves from one of the defining features
of the secular elite, their communities avoided hunting and to a great extent the consumption of meat from quadrupeds was replaced with aquatic fauna. The monastic
quest for physical and spiritual purity resulted in the creation of a significant European
market for fish, considerably contributing to trends in commercial fishing, and laying
the foundations for one of the major ecological crises of the modern world.

Religion, commerce and the aquatic environment

Fish were ideologically central to the medieval Christian diet, and this probably had a
direct impact on the development of commercial fishing. The Church prescribed the
consumption of fish on Fridays, and during festivals such as Easter and Christmas,
accounting for nearly half the year. One of the most important consumers of fish was
represented by monastic communities (Ervynck 1996, 162). Although they constructed impressive fishponds within their precincts, there is little evidence these sustained
viable stocks, and many houses relied on the purchase of marine fish. This alimentary
ideology was exemplified by monastic communities as suggested by isotopic studies in
England (Mays 1997) and Belgium (Polet & Katzenburg 2003), but had clearly filtered
through to Christian society in general. Isotopic studies of north English medieval skeletons emphasised the role of aquatic resources in everyday subsistence for a significant
portion of the population, reflecting the influence of the Church on alimentary culture
(Müldner & Richards 2005). Freshwater fish, mostly cyprinids, could be obtained from
rivers and lakes across Europe it developments in marine fishing by the end of the first
millennium AD in turn spawned an international market for cured fish, predominantly
cod, haddock and mackerel (Barrett *et al.* 2004).

The consumption of fish as prescribed by medieval Christian ordinance could encompass any aquatic animal, following the elemental categorisation of the natural world
in contemporary intellectual thought. The hunting of pinnipeds (seals) and cetaceans
(dolphins, whales) is attested by occasional remains in high-status sites, but in the case
of whales appears to have been infrequent and largely the result of scavenging beached
carcasses; commercial whaling would not develop until the early modern period. Whale
meat was expensive – or nominated as an aristocratic privilege – and it is unsurprising
to find their remains associated with high-status sites in many parts of Europe (Ervynck
1991). This is in contrast to circumpolar Scandinavian regions, such as Arctic Norway,
Iceland and Greenland, where a range of whale species appear to have been hunted
more regularly. The Christianisation of the eastern Baltic frontier invariably brought
fish into a new ideological role, but the process of colonisation also shaped patterns
of consumption. Bones and references to carp appear in the conquests of the Teutonic
Order's state only from the fifteenth century, before they appear in other regions of the
Baltic. This has been associated with incoming German colonists importing a culinary

tradition that was otherwise unknown in Slavic regions, corresponding to the dramatic increase in cod remains from major Hanseatic towns such as Gdańsk (Danzig) and Kołobrzeg (Kolberg) (Makowiecki 2001). The human niche reached its limit at the water's edge, but with the commercialisation of marine fishing, it responds to growing demand rooted in Christian alimentary ordinance; this established the means and the impulse that would lead to the modern overexploitation of the oceans. Fish were not only a key ritual food for Christians in later medieval Europe, but featured in the alimentary cultures conceptualised as 'other'.

Animals, ethnicity and otherness

In her seminal work on animals in medieval society, Joyce Salisbury (1994) argued for a hardening of the species boundaries in the minds of north-western European Christians from the twelfth century onwards. This was the final break with the *longue durée* of the pre-Christian past where such boundaries had been fluid. Although Salisbury's work has been criticised, there is plenty of evidence for the codification of morally correct behaviour which came to govern when meat could be consumed, whether it was acceptable to have sexual relations with other species and what value could be assigned to different animals. All of these are evident in Christian countries in the latter centuries of the first millennium AD, but the twelfth century sees a proliferation of literature discussing and representing animals on an unprecedented scale. At the heart of these ruminations was the very idea of what it meant to be human. Animals themselves were rarely elevated to the status of people; occasional trials of species as diverse as rats, pigs and locusts and a couple of local cults centred on the healing power of certain animals – many of these examples from France – are exceptional and remain to be fully understood. More typical was the animalisation of undesirable groups of people: political enemies, often entire countries, could be de-humanised and peasants were perceived as partly bestial by urban commentators, although the most extensive animalistic stereotypes were employed for heretics and non-Christians. In some extreme cases sexual relations between Christians and Jews were considered legally on a par with bestiality – a capital offence (Dean 2001, 59). But these minorities also defined themselves in relation to animals, primarily, like mainstream Christians, by what could and could not be eaten.

Although there is clearly evidence for considerable dietary diversity across Europe, in some instances what was eaten or not eaten came to define attitudes towards non-Christians. In the castle district of Buda in Hungary, the location of the first Jewish settlement (1250-1360) was confirmed by contrasting faunal assemblages from a well, particularly a comparison of fish species; the upper contained scale-less catfish and sturgeon, and the lower exclusively derived from scaly fish (as well as an absence of pork bones) corresponding to Jewish dietary restrictions (Bartosiewicz 2003). Ashkenazi Jews from central Europe were noted for their strict ideological adherence, but Sephardic Jews in Iberia were also identified by their 'unusual' treatment of animals, sometimes with lethal consequences. Muslims shared Jewish avoidance of pork, and although the absence (or comparatively limited presence) of pork is a truism of the zooarchaeology of Islamic sites, there are clearly levels of complexity in animal exploitation that relate to the 'frontier' contexts of the regions where Christendom was expanding. Faunal assemblages from medieval Spain indicate that Muslims and Christians adopted varying animal exploitation strategies. For example, the Islamic period at the Castillo de Albarracín in Aragón was dominated by the consumption of sheep, whilst the succeeding Christian phases saw noticeable diversification with the additional presence of beef, pork and venison. The opening up of the frontier saw a shift from the management of sheep and goat for subsistence to a more specialised economy associated with wool, associated with the introduction of transhumance (Moreno-Garcia 1997). In the Middle East, the installation of Frankish rule corresponds to a distinctive rise in pork consumption (Boas 1999, 84) while in eastern Europe, the fourteenth-century faunal assemblage from Orheiul Vechi (modern Moldova) during its occupation by the Mongolian Golden Horde is dominated by ovicaprid remains with only a tiny amount of pig remains, reflecting the Islamic alimentary culture (Bejenaru 2009, fig. 3.6). The religious impetus behind what were effectively culinary choices, remind us of the importance of social ideology in determining material practices involving animals.

A less visible group of outcasts which subscribed to specific dietary regulations were the preaching 'good men and women' or 'perfects' of the group later popularly branded as Cathars, who were said to have rejected all animal produce as the creation of the Devil, along with the rest of the material world and in some testimonies recognised animal bodies as vessels for transmigrating souls. These dietary preferences were subsequently used by the Inquisition to identify heretics under interrogation. But faunal assemblages recovered from sites associated with heretical groups in the literature, such as the castles of Montségur and Queribus in Languedoc, represent chronologically broad aristocratic signatures of animal exploitation. Until microstratigraphic and isotopic analyses target some of these contexts, the relatively short-lived presence of heretical communities can only be known from written sources, virtually all written by their persecutors. Moreover, the revisionist idea that the designation of heresy in the Languedoc represented a contemporary misunderstanding of Occitan social complexity (Pegg 2008) can be scrutinised through the lens of integrated environmental archaeology. It is clear that in the context of alimentation – food culture and access to different species, represented not only social status but also ideological standing.

Animals as material culture

Most fragments of animal bones recovered from medieval archaeological contexts can be defined as 'material culture', in that they represent human manipulation and re-use of animal bodies, whether for cooking or manufacturing into bone objects or skin garments. The extent to which animal bone and skin was used in medieval European society is analogous to modern plastic; all of the elements of a carcass — meat, skin, bone, horn or antler and hooves – could be used and towns contained concentrations of inter-connected industries processing this range of 'deadstock'. In the case of artefacts, it is not always easy to determine which species the raw material derives from, and in the case of objects derived from the bodies of exotic (i.e. foreign) species, there is even evidence for the active transformation of their zoological identity. Exotic animal body parts represented artefacts with their own specific biographies, which more often than not involve the transformation of the part's zoological identity (see Ch 5, p 213; Ch 8, p 357). The narwhal tusk became the unicorn horn; the ibex horn a griffin claw; the crocodile skull became a dragon. Rationalist accusations of medieval naivety offer little to our understanding of why these transformations took place. Examples of exotic animals that were imported alive into medieval Europe have been occasionally found, as discarded fragments in rubbish pits. This suggests that such animals had no real value after expiring; there was no attempt to preserve the skins of the lions held in the Tower of London after the animals died, in contrast to the use of lion pelts in the regions where these animals were indigenous. Interestingly, by the thirteenth century there was a pan-European market for leopard skin products, largely driven by middle-range groups such as merchants and the Teutonic Order. Examples of leopard-lined garments can be seen on some fifteenth-century Burgundian tapestries, and two fragments of leopard have been recovered from archaeological contexts in Hungary (Fig 2.15) (Bartosiewicz *pers. comm.*), originally attached to hides which would have been used as rugs or coverlets.

Exoticism and luxury were far from the minds of the authors of compendia of Christian animal symbols or 'bestiaries' from the thirteenth century. Here the leopard or *pardus* symbolised bloodthirstiness and became an appropriate metaphor for criticisms of the violence of the knightly class (Haist 2000, 11). But there is some evidence that

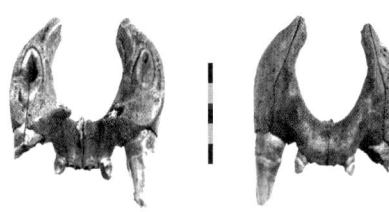

Fig 2.15

(above) Fragment of leopard crania from Hungary (reproduced with the kind permission of Laszlo Bartosiewicz).

Fig 2.16

(left) Bear claw amulets of 'Type I/variant 2' from late-14th to 15th century (predominantly female) graves in western Lithuania, from the territory procured and ruled by the Teutonic Order (Svetikas 2008 by kind permission of Eugenijus Svetikas).

the body parts of carnivores were used to express complex ideas of spirituality. In later fourteenth and fifteenth century western Lithuania, 114 bear claw amulets have been found predominantly in the graves of older women (Fig 2.16). Rather than representing expressions of a pre-Christian cult, their specific chronological context and their combination with Christian symbols may suggest a local interpretation of Christian ideas of resurrection (Svetikas 2008), perhaps drawing on the bestiary image of the bear bringing its young to life. This is likely to have differed from the use of bear pelts in early Scandinavian funerary rites, which is convincingly linked to pre-Christian cults and ideas of species permeability, and contrasts strikingly with the contemporaneous burial of whole bears by the Saami in medieval northern Scandinavia (Zachrisson & Iregren 1974). The example of the leopard in the West and the bear in the East exemplify the diversity of complex meanings attached to the same animal (and the same category of large carnivore recognised by contemporaries) in different contexts, much like in modern European society.

Conclusion

The study of animal bones, particularly on a site-by-site basis, is predominantly concerned with the types of patterns described above; dietary signatures, local ecological transformations and the diversity and extent of exploitation. At the European scale it is possible to see how this varied from one environmental context to the next, although we can also see the development of supra-regional class identities in relation to animal exploitation; an aristocratic identity associated with hunting and meat and a general Christian identity associated with the cyclical consumption of fish exemplified by monastic communities. Overall, there is a theme of people seeking to control their environments, in part by manipulating their resident fauna and by introducing new species. In some cases the very identity of a species could be re-constructed, or at least re-contextualised, and invested with new meaning within medieval Christian culture.

The field of animal studies, and the multiple application of environmental archaeology to medieval contexts, is growing at an exponential rate. As multiple strands of data from local, inter-regional and international scales are synchronised and synthesised, new light will invariably be shed on how people in the Middle Ages responded to and thought about animals. In this process we will have a better understanding of how people perceived themselves. We will also have a better sense of how different species responded to the explosion of the human niche, at different rates and in different regions. Extensive isotopic research on fishing has already demonstrated how the modern overexploitation of the marine environment was founded in the Middle Ages. But human dominion over the natural world, although divinely ordained, could be contested and its uncertainty remained a constant source of anxiety. The extent to which the Christian world-view, which united otherwise unconnected regions of Europe by the later Middle Ages, dominated attitudes towards other species, and how it related to established traditions, to experience and to imagination, awaits further investigation.

CHAPTER 3

LIVING ON THE LAND

Jan Klápště

PART 1: INVESTIGATING RURAL SETTLEMENT *by Jan Klápště*

Introduction to the sources

Archaeology opens a wide window onto medieval settlement and its principal activity, agriculture. It builds on the study of artefacts, provides ecological information ('ecofacts') drawn from the natural sciences (especially archaeobotany, palynology and archaeozoology) and studies the context of agrarian production, especially farms and fields. Archaeologists aim to integrate their evidence with that of other scholars of agrarian history – using written documents, illustrations and ethnographic observation – and may use also experiments to endorse their interpretations. Especially we aim to integrate the evidence for the environment, the land and its resources (Ch 2), with that for rural settlement and agricultural production (this chapter). Our focus is on the period 1200-1600 (for the period 800-1200, see AME I, Ch 3).

We begin by discussing aims and approaches and then review the archaeological evidence available. The most important survivals for settlement studies are the medieval villages, whether deserted or still occupied. The investigation of both kinds of sites is challenging, as their material is very vulnerable to the passage of time and the footprint they leave is elusive. The different survivals of houses and assemblages can lead to different perceptions of the medieval village – a point which I illustrate using two case studies.

In the sections that follow this, we explore four villages and then four examples of evidence for food production. Taken together, they demonstrate the significance of the medieval farmers for the later Middle Ages – and also how much we still have to learn about them.

Aims and methods in the study of rural settlement

Rural settlement archaeology of the twelfth to sixteenth centuries can be linked to two fundamental processes of European history: transformation to the feudal mode and subsequent transition to the early modern era. Across Europe, the two stages took place

Fig 3.1   *Très Riches Heures du Duc de Berry (The Very Rich Hours of the Duke of Berry) from 1412-16 illustrated March with a depiction of the beginning of agricultural work. In the foreground, ploughing; on the left, the trimming of vines; in the background, the pasturing of sheep. While illuminated books do not exactly represent medieval reality, they provide valuable context and support for archaeological reconstruction. Chantilly, Condé, ms. 65 (1284), f. 3v.*

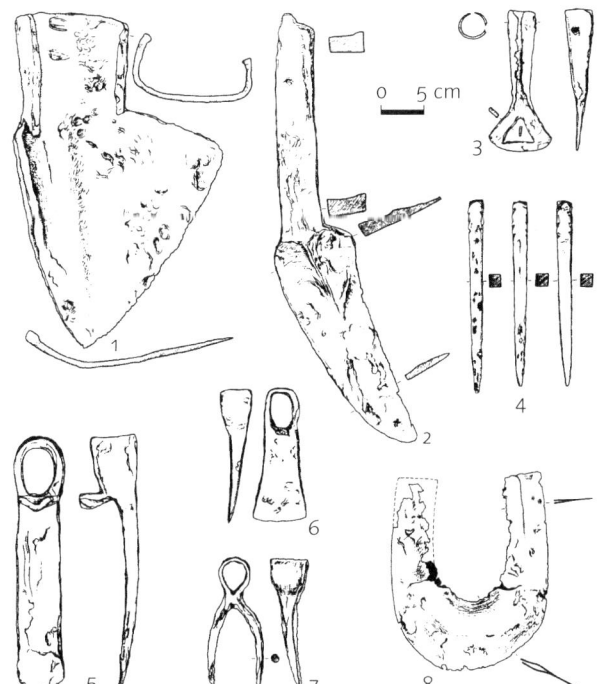

Semonice in Eastern Bohemia, early 14th century, iron parts of implements used for cultivation. 1 plough-share (2921 g), 2 coulter (2757 g), 3 plough-staff, 4 harrow, 5-7 mattocks, 8 spadeshoe (after J. Klápště 1998).

Fig 3.2

0   5 cm

at different times. For instance, while medieval transformation was completed in Western Europe by the twelfth century, in Central-Eastern Europe it only began in the thirteenth century. No less jarring are the disparities of the age in transition; the first steps of industrialization were concentrated only in certain parts of Europe. Despite many open questions, there is no doubt that the twelfth to sixteenth centuries presented the European landscape with a heritage whose impact is felt to this day.

Overall, the rural settlement landscape of the twelfth to sixteenth centuries enjoyed relative stability and order. Residential and utility buildings were conservative in function, sturdy and built to last. That is why many buildings that still stand today continue to shed light on medieval farmsteads, including living houses and economic and auxiliary buildings. Utilitarian artefacts from medieval contexts often correspond to those collected and documented by ethnographers in the nineteenth century. Contemporary illustrations captured rural life, the village appearance, its hinterlands, and the peasants' everyday life, as seen in some illuminated manuscripts (Fig 3.1) and later in the work of Albrecht Dürer (1471-1528) (see also Box 5.1). Written sources provide outstanding testimony and their number and variety grew as the Middle Ages drew to a close. Analyzing secondary sources like Early Modern cartographic documents also helps to decipher medieval situations (see e.g. Ch 3, p 110).

Current rural archaeology confronts two challenges. On the one hand, it must take its opportunities from the numerous mitigation projects that are consequent on the growing concern for archaeological heritage. On the other, the archaeological agenda must be integrated with those of the traditional students of the rural landscape, historians and geographers.

Archaeological evidence: tools

The considerable diversity of European agriculture makes it possible to emphasise trends over a wide scale from the thirteenth to the sixteenth centuries. Crucial is the increased supply of iron, which significantly contributed to the greater efficiency and availability of tools (Astill & Langdon 1997; Fig 3.2). New heavy ploughs with iron shares and coulters were utilised on the heavy soils in the European moderate climate belt (for the early medieval plough, see AME I, 98-9). Whereas the weight of ploughshares in the ninth century was often around perhaps 0.5 kg (Klápště & Nissen Jaubert 2007, 99), shares of the late Middle Ages weigh around 3 kg (Pesez 1991, 138-42). Heavy ploughs turned over soil to a depth of 30cm or more, and harrows would be required to break up the clods and cover the seeds. Both of these tools placed significant demands on the pulling power of traction animals. A great many iron parts were utilised in the hand tools of cultivation: for example, mattock blades and shoes for spades. Narrow, long sickles, suitable for cutting the upper parts of the stalks with ears, were used for the harvest throughout the Middle Ages. This practice minimised the loss of grain and left weeds in the fields with high stubble. A substantially more effective scythe did not begin to be used for harvesting grain until the sixteenth century.

Fields

For the vast majority of the population, cereals formed the basis of the diet and extensive parts of the agrarian landscape were allocated to their production. When the fields subsequently reverted to pasture, as in fifteenth and sixteenth century England, the arable fields were fossilised as earthworks, recognisable from the air and the ground (Fig 1.7 and Fig 3.11). *Ridge and furrow* can be recognised as curvilinear parallel ridges, ranging from 3 to 20 m apart and up to 0.6 m high, and *strip lynchets* take the form of step-like features on hillsides. Throughout the twentieth century, examples of both categories have been widely documented through archaeological fieldwork and aerial photography (e.g. Taylor 1975), including regions now covered by secondary forest (e.g. Černý 1994). The contribution of the evidence of the erstwhile fields is unusually revealing, because they mark out the capacity potential of the hinterlands of the contemporary agrarian settlements (Astill 1988a).

The expansion of arable open fields, typical for the later Middle Ages, reduced the area of grazing for domestic animals, which remained, however, essential for the function of the overall agricultural system. The solution lay in the stabling of animals and in the cultivation of meadows (often artificial in origin), which provided supplies of hay for fodder in the winter months. It was the cutting of this hay that made the long scythe an indispensable tool. Stabling substantially influenced the capacity of the animals as well as their relation to people. It allowed the development of dairy husbandry, and accumulated supplies of manure. The manure could then be used to fertilise the fields, and it is this process that is often responsible for the spreads of pottery sherds picked up in surveys.

In some parts of Europe, the quality of the soils was improved by the systematic transfer of soil from one place to another, as has been documented by soil science. A distinctive manifestation of this procedure, developed in the Netherlands and practised on the Atlantic coast from Norway to Portugal, was the deposition of *plaggen* soils. These soils were created, from at least the later Middle Ages until the beginning of the twentieth century, by the application of a mixture of manure and cut sods, forming layers with an average thickness of 70-80 cm (Spek 2006, Groenewoudt 2002).

Evidence from farmsteads includes bones, seeds and the form of buildings from which activities such as the threshing and storage of grain and the management of cattle may be inferred. New excavation techniques, using chemical and physical plotting can indicate where animals were stalled or manure was heaped up (see Ch 1, p 35). Strong regional differences are expected, with different emphases on cultivation, sheep or cattle. These are often reflected in animal bone or plant assemblages, as contributors to this chapter show.

Rural industry

Medieval rural territories have become synonymous with farming, but this equation was not invariable. Rural industries include activities connected to the extraction of raw materials: these included ferrous metallurgy, glass production or charcoal burning and tar production (Jeute 2007; *Ruralia* 2007; and see Ch 7, p 277 and p 113, below). Craftsmen normally associated with urban contexts and detectable by archaeology, such as metalsmiths and potters, also occur in rural areas. Some exceptional rural conurbations were created, for example the pottery production centres surrounding Köln (Cologne) on the River Rhine or near Saintonge north of Bordeaux (Janssen 1983). On the other hand, even in the later Middle Ages large sectors of European towns retained a distinctly agrarian character, which can also be identified to a significant degree by archaeology. Rural settlers practised their own version of an overall production portfolio, consisting of interlinked agrarian and industrial activities (Dyer 1997b).

The study of deserted villages

The principal source for life in the countryside is the rural settlement itself, a target of later medieval archaeologists since the subject began to develop in the 1950s. The modern project has benefitted from the formation in the mid 1990s of the *Ruralia* Association, with its Jean-Marie Pesez Conferences on Medieval Rural Archaeology regularly reflecting the current state of research (*Ruralia* proceedings, www.ruralia.cz). Rural settlement archaeology first focused on settlements that had permanently and completely disappeared below ground. Systematic research of these deserted medieval villages (DMVs) followed agendas set by economic history and geography, while adopting methods of open-area excavation that had proved successful in prehistoric archaeology (cf. Bentz 2008).

A pioneering project was the lost village of Hohenrode, Harz, Germany, which Paul Grimm (1907-1993) investigated in 1935-1937 and published in 1939. The undertaking arose from questions typical to ethnography, using programmed excavations to enhance appreciation of still-standing rural architecture and medieval illustrations, to support an image of the vanished German countryside. Following Grimm's project, it was the Danish ethnologist Axel Steensberg (1906-1999) who influenced much of European practice via British archaeology. As early as the 1940s he applied controlled excavation procedures to rural sites using open-area excavations.

The earliest research into DMVs was governed by the idea that rural settlement had passed through two different and successive stages: growth and development in the eleventh to thirteenth centuries followed by a fourteenth and fifteenth century crisis (for a classic example, Abel 1935). DMVs, presumed typical only for the later Middle Ages, were seen as symptomatic of this crisis, implying a rural depopulation (already in Grund 1901; Abel 1943; Genicot 1966 among many others). But archaeology soon showed that, for settlements, collapse and disappearance was a constant fact of life (Janssen 1968, 348). People had deserted settlements in the Early Middle Ages as well as in prehistoric times or the Post-Medieval era. In addition, the 'late' desertion wave attributed to the fourteenth-fifteenth centuries, was in reality highly varied in different parts of Europe, arriving for example between 1250 and 1300 in the Eifel region (Janssen 1975), and in the mid-fourteenth century in the Weserbergland (Stephan 1978). The discussion about the causes of disappearance became more complicated when it was realised that settlement desertion could happen without any noticeable regional depopulation or reduced production. From the 1930s, German settlement geography began to classify desertion using three criteria: (1) did the desertion affect both the settlement and the hinterland? (2) was it complete or partial? and (3) was it permanent or temporary?

The archaeological agenda first addressed basic questions of where? and when? (i.e. the location and date) and then why? – the reasons for settlement desertion. Answers that cited circumstantial causes (fires, wars, etc.) were soon modified to include drivers of lasting collapse (structural settlement changes, ecological changes for example in the water regime, see Ch 2, p 68). Human decision-making was recognized as another key factor. Archaeology fuelled this inquiry through its links to other disciplines that relied on written and cartographic documents, including place- and field names. Unique to this early era was the monograph, *The Lost Villages of England* by economic historian M.W. Beresford, first published in 1954, a book that practically invented a new subject of historical, geographical and archaeological investigation. By then, the Deserted Medieval Village Research Group (DMVRG) founded at Wharram Percy in Yorkshire, England, in 1952 was already nurturing the growing interdisciplinary interest, and during the 1950s and 1960s, the topic of DMVs was winning a place in European economic history. The state of research in 1965 was reviewed in the International Economic History Society Conference in Munich, and in 1971 in an updated report on the state of British research (Beresford & Hurst 1971). The British situation demonstrated the value of an integrated approach supported by inspecting maps, aerial photographs and fieldwork. The original Beresford list of 1954 had registered 1353 DMVs, but by 1968 that number had risen to 2263.

At first, DMVs were seen as "time capsules of medieval rural occupation, undisturbed and unpolluted by modern features" (Dyer 1997a, 55), and the original intention was to produce a generally relevant historical sequence. In 1948, British DMV archaeologists chose Wharram Percy as their flagship, and work continued there for half a century (Bell et al. 1987; Mays et al 2007) (Fig 3.3). The evolution of research methods at Wharram Percy thus offers a history of the ways that a group of archaeologists sought to understand rural settlement. After the first timid steps in 1948, programmed research took off in the early 1950s and, under the joint direction of historian Maurice Beresford and archaeologist John Hurst, operated in brief research seasons until 1992 (Beresford & Hurst 1990). This study too started out with questions on the dates and causes of collapse. Although Wharram Percy's disappearance was initially interpreted as a result of the Black Death in 1348-9, the effects of 'enclosure' and the fifteenth century's economic changes soon came into the picture. The evolution of house-types and the complexities of house construction and material extended the list of new topics. Thus the priority in the 1950s was to excavate completely a single peasant house. Later, information on the daily life of the peasants, both at home and in the fields, gained special significance. The diachronic study of the whole village was a subsequent objective. Finally, the ever-widening scrutiny was crowned by a systemic approach treating Wharram as one element of the settlement pattern in a broader landscape (Hurst 1985; Gerrard 2003a, 103-4).

It must be emphasized that despite their protracted duration and deep significance, the excavations of Wharram Percy remained modest in scope and the excavated sample only uncovered five per cent of the entire site. This should be compared with examples of large scale European DMV excavations, e.g. Königshagen (Janssen 1965), Rougiers (Demians d'Archimbaud 1980), Sarvaly (Holl & Parádi 1982), Brucato (Pesez 1985), Pfaffenschlag (Nekuda 1975) and others. Changes in the study of the medieval village, stemming from fundamental shifts in medieval archaeology, began to emerge in the 1970s. Gradually, the great era of long-term programmed excavations of selected DMVs was ending. At the same time, rescue interventions had expanded the mosaic of evidence by means of mostly small-scale excavations. The once-dominant position of rural archaeology ended and archaeological interest turned unapologetically towards historic towns, then feeling the pressure of expansion and redevelopment (see Ch 9, p 370).

Although less threatened, and thus less eligible for mitigation funding, rural archaeology had been transforming its research strategy (see Ch 1, p 28). It began to treat the landscape as a theatre with a full spectrum of settlement types including their agrarian and non agrarian hinterlands. In this new stage, fieldwalking gained special status employed at multi-disciplinary projects of which Shapwick was notable (Aston & Gerrard

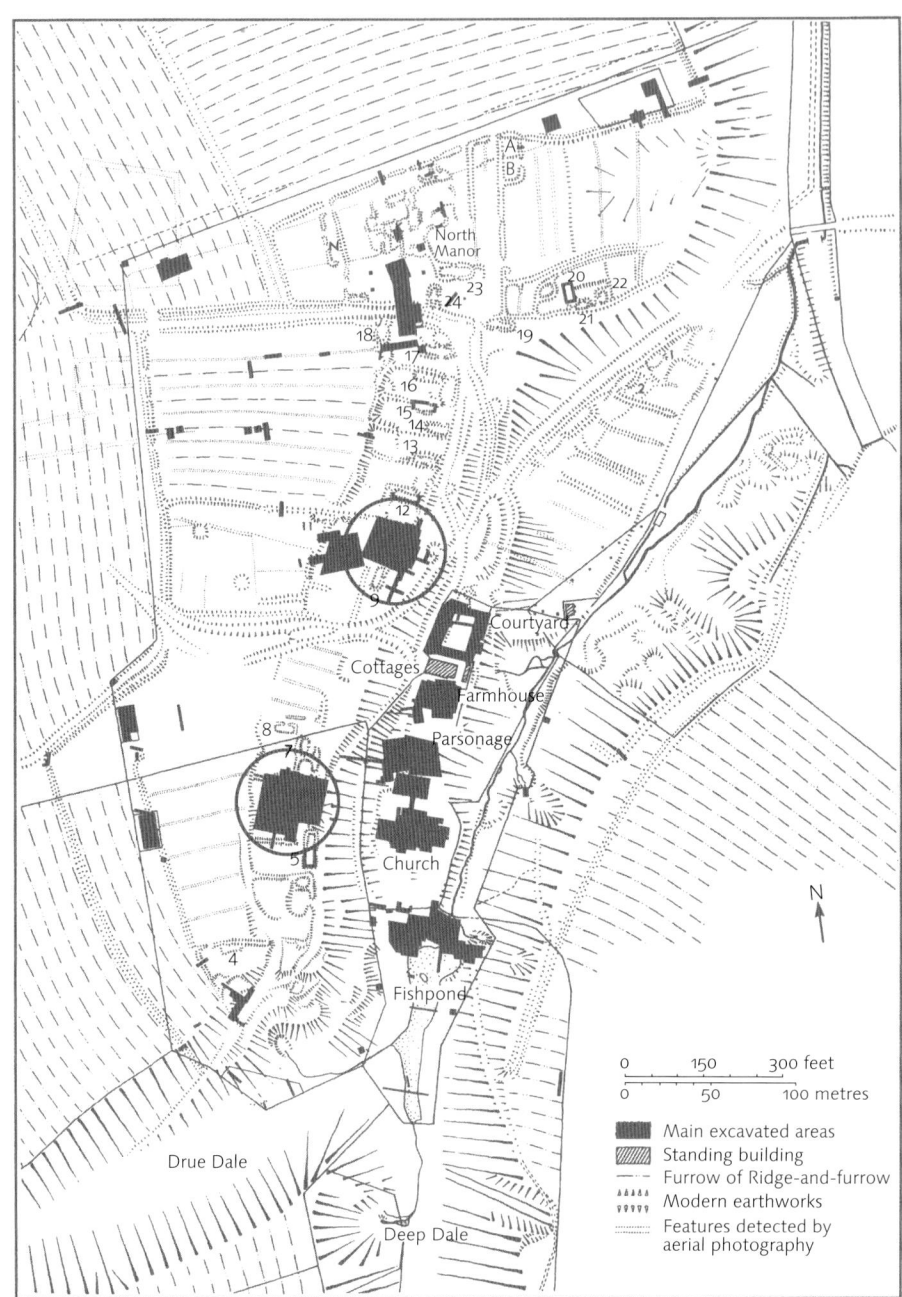

Fig 3.3 *Wharram Percy, Deserted Medieval Village in northeast England (Yorkshire). The earthwork remains indicate that the settlement contained thirty to forty farmsteads. Each farmstead included a living house, outbuildings and farmyard in its toft; the adjacent croft was an area of a small field. The research programme at Wharram Percy was a flagship not only for British medieval rural archaeology for over almost half a century (© English Heritage).*

1999 and see Box 1.1). The use of multiple archaeological techniques became routine, emphasizing the interpretive value of biological data (biota) and the full integration of historical information.

Site formation processes

Archaeology relies to a great extent on what was done and what survived at a particular place, and without taking this survival into account, comparisons between one village and another are not strictly possible (Ch 1, p 21). This is best illustrated with a number of case studies, which will both report examples of rural settlements and equip us with a critical eye in archaeological design.

Large areas of the European landscape contain dispersed potsherds that are remnants of later Medieval and early Modern manuring (e. g. Parry 2006, 132 ff.; Gerrard & Aston 2007, 156ff.; and see Ch 1, p 28). But areas only defined by a few potsherds (e.g. three or five) cannot be designated as settlements. Similarly, a continuously occupied settlement is hard to distinguish from a shifting settlement using surface indications alone. The existence of a settlement and its status as a new or developing place of occupation usually requires an endorsement by excavation.

Excavation hopes to define buildings and settlements that can be placed in time and interpreted in function by means of their shape; in practice the itinerary of the rural house had a great deal of local diversity. A two-bay two-storey stone house of fourteenth century appearance in the former cloister-vineyard village of Matting, southwest of Regensburg gives an example (Fig 3.4). This house was lifted and transferred to an open-air museum, and archaeologists profited from the occasion to examine beneath it. Excavations showed that its development had begun with a two-part construction on a 10 x 6.2 m area, probably from around 1300. The diagnostic factor was the earth-fast construction, a framework supported by posts embedded in holes 0.8 m deep. Dendrochronology showed that the house had already undergone its first reconstruction by 1411, the house now measuring 15 x 10 m (Alper *et al* 1994). Evidently, in the immediate hinterland of a large medieval town with noteworthy secular architecture, traditional civil engineering prevailed until the mid-fourteenth century (Kirchner & Kirchner 1998). The Matting example is in no way exceptional. New modes of construction may have emerged, but their systematic application was often slow to take hold over the broad span of the eleventh to fourteenth century AD (Zimmerman 1998). The causes of the lag, reflecting different rural attitudes towards innovation were numerous: a strong local building tradition, a good supply of certain building materials, the landowners' involvement, social differentiation or farming practice are among the variables.

The same considerations affect the development of a village as a whole. If all these factors were coincident, a later Medieval rural settlement would gain its distinctive shape in a relatively short time. But if those same factors surfaced at different times, it might take centuries before a rural settlement reached a characteristic late Medieval form. The excavation of a farmstead in Filborna village in Sweden (province of Skåne) showed these agencies at work. This historically-known settlement location dates back

Fig 3.4 *Matting, Bavaria, a late medieval stone house currently transferred into an open-air museum in Bad Windsheim. The stone house replaced a house with earthfast post constructions revealed by archaeological excavation.*

to about 1100, which was the time of nucleation, with dwellings gathered together and outbuilding functions segregated. It is reasonable to relate the impetus for the formation to shifts in the social context and to new strategies of rural economics. In theory technical evolution should follow the course: earth-fast posts, timber-framing and use of stone. But principles of local building and traditional technologies evolved at different rates. Timber-framing together with the stone sill was introduced between the years 1250 to 1500, but new buildings erected in the period 1500 to 1668 featured posts set in the earth and on stone sills. The general use of stone sills only began with the reconstruction that followed the fire of 1668. The Filborna village case shows the separate influence of each factor, dispelling the presumption that one change need imply the others (Söderberg 1997).

Two case studies

Villages recently examined in the Czech Republic provide good examples of varied origins and development, and of the importance of archaeological survival in interpretation. Svídna, located in Central Bohemia (30 km from Prague), lies in a landscape that was only settled in the thirteenth century, on a site favoured with high quality building stone. Svídna´s existence stretched from the late thirteenth century to the period around the year 1500. After its gradual desertion, the entire area was reclaimed by forest. Topographical survey showed that the village extended on a flat plain over

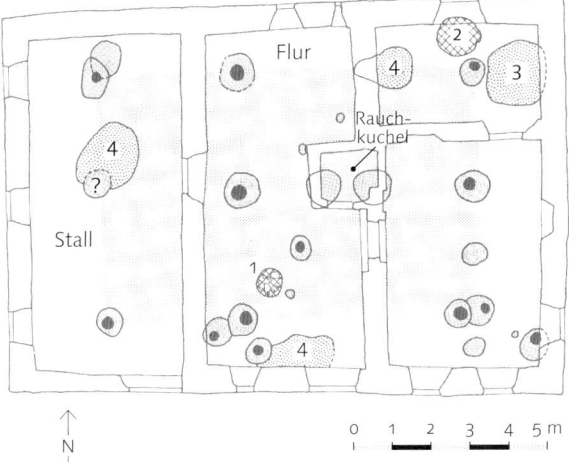

Fig 3.5

Svídna, Deserted Medieval Village in Central Bohemia, the plan of the surface features. (above) In the fourteen identified settlement units (thirteen farmsteads and one manorial farm), the width of the plots is indicated, with the basic module being approximately 21 m long. The differences reflect the social structure of the medieval village (after Smetánka 1988). (below) A multipartite residential house at Svídna, DMV in Central Bohemia was built within a single building plan. Considering the absence of any further structural relics, it could be presumed that this house as a whole was established at the time of the foundation of Svídna before around 1300 (After Smetánka 1988).

some 4.1 ha, which included the village-green and the plans of 14 settlement units, i.e. thirteen peasant farmsteads and one manorial farm (Fig 3.5a).

The archaeological appearance of Svídna inspires confidence: its surface remains have been well preserved and the conditions for studying the construction of the farmsteads have been favourable (Fig 3.5b). Among its outstanding remains are the base portions of the walls built of local hard chalk bound by clay, some surviving more than a metre high. Three area excavations have also contributed to a better understanding of the farmsteads. The excavated sequence tracks the gradual construction of farmsteads, along with fragmentary modifications of the layout, allowing the archaeologists to address key questions about the origins of the multipartite residential houses (Smetánka 1988).

But even the clearly visible components of this site are still lacking in important aspects. Two of the excavated farmsteads retained either no, or only minute, traces of the outbuildings that were crucial to any rural community. Perhaps built of timber and mud, they were not supported by earth-fast post constructions and thus left no archaeologically identifiable traces. This is a common problem of settlement archaeology: different building technologies that had served side-by-side leave a very different record. Specific problems plague the identification of non-earth-fast wood and clay buildings. The indicators of such technologies are usually padstones. When desiring a more in-depth determination, daubed wattle, recognised mainly in buildings destroyed by fire, are especially important. Stone walls bonded by clay leave noticeable positive upstanding features but in places where the wall footings lay on the ground surface they can disappear without a trace after stone robbing. In regards to Svídna, it must be emphasized that the conditions were not conducive to stratigraphic analysis: the entire two hundred years of existence of this medieval village had left behind just one layer, which was totally homogenous and only a few centimetres deep. There is a temptation to regard Svídna as type-site, reflecting a belief that farmsteads and multipartite residential houses were built at the earliest stage and that succeeding generations only made fragmentary changes and improvements. Such thinking makes the DMV of Svídna a distinctive example of a 'new village' founded before 1300, followed by a basically smooth development until its desertion around 1500. Though the archaeological evidence does not deny such an interpretation, it is impossible to judge whether its archaeological record is sufficiently representative.

The Moravian DMV of Bystřec offers a contrasting model. Located about 20 km from Brno, this village was established in the middle of the thirteenth century and deserted following a violent attack in the early fifteenth century. The settlement pattern of two rows of farmsteads and fields behind them was typical of a 'colonization' or 'new village' of Central Europe. The original name of Bystřec was probably Mehrlinschlag in German, since some settlers came to this region from the Austrian Danube river basin. A stream ran straight through the village centre, for about half a km. Most farmsteads of the DMV at Bystřec were indicated by surface finds alone and only long-term excavations could proffer a deeper insight (Belcredi 2000, 2006).

The archaeological survival at Bystřec was determined by several factors. The buildings, primarily timber and clay were affected by extreme conditions, including fire and war. The clearance of the forest above the village soon destabilized the slopes, and rainfall caused mudslides. The overall plan of the village was quickly determined, but defining the construction sequence on individual plots and in-field systems (and thus assessing the growth in population) was more difficult. But it still proved possible to discover changes in building practices over time. Construction began with earth-fast posts that were then gradually replaced by walls of timber and earth set up on stone sills.

The nature of the settlements and the changes that occurred to them should be reflected in the assemblages of both artefacts and biota. But comparisons are only possible where the survival is similar – and it rarely is. When Svídna was a living village, no situations occurred that were favourable to the stratigraphic deposition and preservation of assemblages. Furthermore, during its gradual desertion, everything usable was removed. Thus archaeological excavations at three farmsteads produced only a meagre collection of discarded items. In addition, local conditions did not permit organic material to survive. As a result, the artefactual assemblage consists of ceramic fragments, mostly from the time of the settlement's abandonment, with a few remnants of iron artefacts. The only biota here are a small group of animal bones (111 identifiable fragments). At Bystřec, on the other hand, the adversity suffered by the inhabitants, culminating in the sudden and violent annihilation of the settlement, created favourable conditions for the capture of assemblages, which included some 40,000 ceramic sherds and 116 metal objects. On the other hand, animal bones were virtually absent from this site due to the chemistry of the soil.

A comparison between the sequences at Svídna and Bystřec reveals other fundamental differences. While the first DMV looks like a fairly static example with only minor modifications, the second manifests a number of considerable changes. These differences between two examples from the Czech Republic could be multiplied elsewhere. For archaeology, which directly depends on recorded evidence on the ground, this variation in site formation is the major factor to be taken into account when attempting to describe and explain the experiences of medieval rural societies. A priority for archaeology today is the development of new methods of investigation, allowing us to define with much greater precision the nature of dwellings and their chronological context, even if much of the material has disappeared (see Ch 1, p 25).

Studying rural settlement today

Rural settlement archaeology of the twelfth to sixteenth centuries remains a major field of research. Archaeologists examine fossil landscapes, including deserted settlements, making full use of modern methods of mapping from the air (aerial photography and lidar) and on the ground (using total station surveys). In some cases, the entire plan of a village may still be visible, with the layout of individual farmsteads and houses, together with the remnants of tracks and field systems. Such settlements may lack direct evidence for dating, but can be recognised as medieval from their morphology. More often, deserted medieval villages are incorporated into arable land and are subsequently ploughed out. In these cases, the main instruments of inquiry are those of remote mapping, from the air (using cropmarks) and on the ground (by recording the surface patterns of pottery and geophysics). Here the settlement area and its extent can be inferred from the distribution of artefacts on the surface and the signals of buried features beneath it. In excavation, opportunities to examine medieval settlement on a wide scale are often offered by mitigation archaeology (e.g. Ch 3, p 119). Scientific techniques of chemical and physical mapping have been developed in periods and areas well-known for their lack of artefacts and visible buildings (see Ch 1, p 35); these will find increasing application to the medieval house and its elusive occupants. More research is also being applied to villages that are medieval in origin, but still lived in today (see Tårnby, below, and Shapwick in Ch 1, p 28). The majority of medieval settlements escaped desertion and became buried in the soil or the architectural fabric of villages that still exist. Taken together, study of these localities offers a chance to understand short-term and long-term, local and general changes in houses, farmsteads, large settlements and landscape, as as demonstrated by examples that follow in part 2.

Skramle: A Deserted Medieval Hamlet in the Scandinavian Forest
by Eva Svensson and Sofia Andersson

According to a tradition written down in the eighteenth century, the Åmot and Skramle farmsteads in the parish of Gunnarskog, western Sweden, were abandoned during the Black Death in the middle of the fourteenth century and never resettled (Anderssen & Svensson 2002). The name 'Skramle' has survived on a peninsula in the central lake system in Gunnarskog, south-east of the parish church, today built only with summer houses. Studies of maps from 1641, 1709, and 1832-33 give clear indications of a deserted settlement on the peninsula (Fig 3.6). An archaeological survey carried out at the site in 1990 located a hearth subsequently dated by radiocarbon to the mid-fifteenth century, some hundred years after the plague, suggesting the continued presence of a medieval farmstead. This first reconnaissance was followed by a major campaign of excavation and regional survey (Svensson 2008, 97-118).

Excavation determined that the site was occupied intermittently from the sixth to the early sixteenth century, with a peak in occupation from the second half of the thir-

Fig 3.6   *Historical map of the Skramle peninsula, dated to 1641 (©Lantmäteriet).*

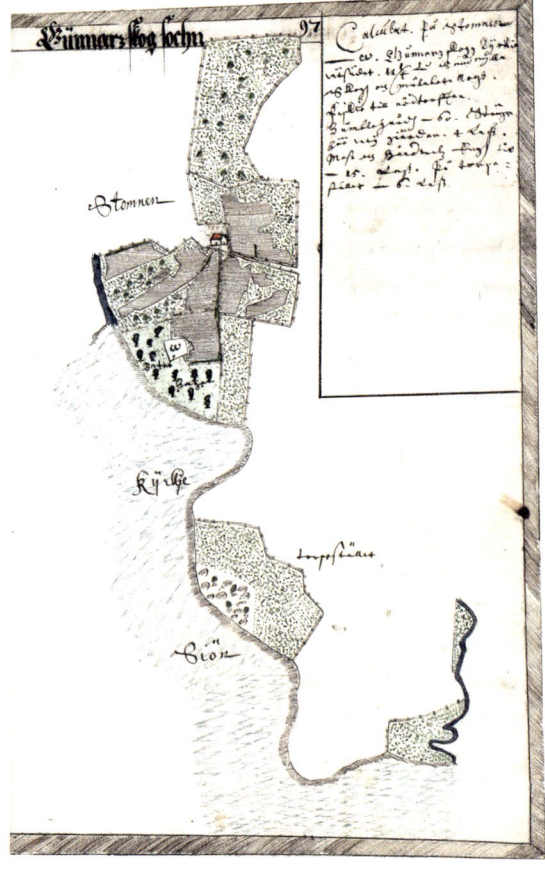

teenth to the first half of the fourteenth century. Skramle was deserted quite abruptly in the mid-fourteenth century, perhaps following the Black Death, just as tradition has it. The houses and their contents were abandoned and left to decay, something that can clearly be seen in the excavated cultural layers of the houses. The relative abundance of artefacts also suggests a sudden desertion at this time. A total of 589 artefacts was recovered from the period c. 1250-1350, while there was just one artefact from the preceding phases and 22 artefacts from the later phases. The settlement at Skramle was permanently abandoned after the early sixteenth century, although the surrounding area continued to be used for fields and meadows.

The foundations of at least twelve houses were defined, from three main periods (Table 3.1). For the sixth to eighth centuries, partial house remains (H IX and H XII), an (unexcavated) grave and a rune stone engraved with runes from the older *futhark* (Scandinavian runic alphabet) were recovered.

The main period of occupation included three dwellings (H VI, VII and X), one with a smithy attached (VIb), in use from the second half of the thirteenth century. A fourth dwelling (H VIII) was a structure of two rooms, one with a hearth, dating to the first half of the fourteenth century. Other dwellings had one room, with a fireplace away from the walls. In this period, there were also two outhouses (H V and XIII) and an outhouse-cum-cattle byre (H XIV) with an adjacent cattle path.

In a later period, mid-fifteenth to mid-sixteenth century, the settlement had two dwellings (H I, XI), two outhouses (H II and IV) and a barn (H III), with possible outhouses on the site of H XIII and XIV).

TABLE 3.1 EXCAVATED STRUCTURES AT SKRAMLE		
STRUCTURE NO.	FUNCTION	DATE
H I	Dwelling	c. 1450-1550
H II	Outhouse	c. 1450-1550
H III	Barn	c. 1450-1550
H IV	Outhouse	c. 1450-1550
H V	Outhouse	c. 1250-1350
H VI	Dwelling/smithy	c. 1250-1300
H VII	Dwelling	c. 1250-1300
H VIII	Dwelling (two-room)	c. 1300-1350
H IX	[fragments]	c. 500-600
H X	Dwelling	c. 1250-1350
H XI	Dwelling	c. 1500-1550
H XII	[fragments]	c. 700-800
H XIII	Outhouse	c. 1250-1350; reused 16th c
H XIV	Outhouse/byre	c. 1250-1350; reused 16th c

All the buildings shared a location that sloped southwards slightly, which creates the impression that the settlement faced south towards the lake. To compensate for the slope, but probably also to create a stronger impression for the visitor arriving from the lake, the southern walls of the buildings were terraced and rested on the largest sill stones. In some cases, the northern walls were resting almost on the ground. All houses were small and rectilinear, and built using the log-cabin technique. H VI was around 5.5 x 5 m (E–W), H VII around 7.5 x 4 m (E–W), H VIII around 9.5 x 4.5 m (NE–SW) and H X around 7 x 6.5 m (E–W) (Fig 3.7).

The hearths were designed slightly differently. In H VI and H VIII the hearths were almost perfectly round and made of stone and located at floor level on top of a pit filled with stones. In H VII and H X the fireplaces were smoke-ovens with brick-lined fire surfaces and arched domes of burnt clay and earth. Finding smoke-ovens and brick at such an early date was unexpected and might suggest outside influences and contacts. In all of the houses there were remains of benches attached to the walls. In H VI and H VII, large boulders had been brought inside, presumably to support timber planks. In H VIII and H X there were stone- and earth-filled benches. Otherwise nothing was found that could relate to furniture or other fittings. There were no traceable signs of doors or door openings. The find material includes a great many artefacts belonging

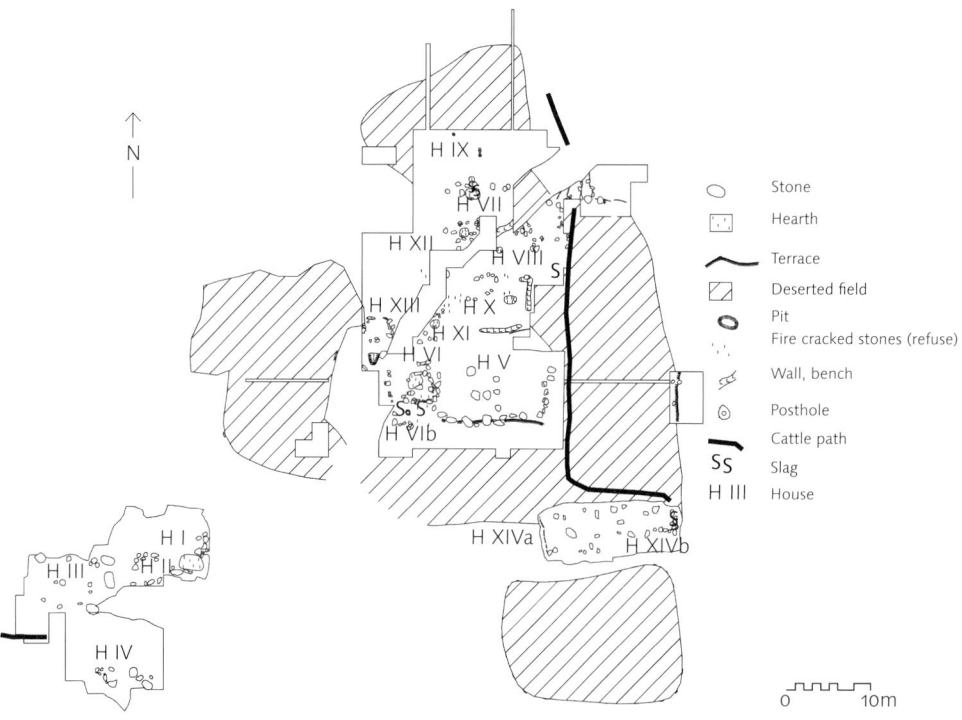

Fig 3.7   *Plan of the excavation site of Skramle (after Svensson 2008, fig. 23).*

to doors, such as hinges, but they were not found in places where one would expect to find a door. The doors were probably located on the long walls opposite, or at an angle to, the fireplaces.

The cultural material from the medieval period comprised items related to house-keeping, cooking, clothing, personal adornment, domestic animals, hunting, fishing, agriculture and craft. Some artefacts may also have had a secondary amuletic use, reflecting popular belief. Among the artefacts collected from the medieval period were knives, whetstones, sherds of soapstone vessels, arrows, sickles, strike-a-light flints, plates, nails, rivets, mountings, locks, hooks, buckles, strap-plates, eyes, needles, pig spikes, scissors, bridles, horse shoes and spindle-whorls. No pottery was recovered, a common absence in medieval settlements in the region. There were also a few more exclusive artefacts, such as ring-brooches, buckles and vessels of bronze and a heraldic mounting. Crafts detected were blacksmithing, brass casting, textile production, soapstone carving (including attempts to use ordinary rock) and fur handling. The first three were for use among the households at Skramle, whereas soapstone and fur products were produced for sale.

In addition to the building remains, there were four fossilised fields, of which three were adjacent to the toft. The pollen analysis shows that the main crop here was barley, although wheat, oats and rye were also cultivated. Several crafts imply resources from a wider environment. The forest was used both for the production of various items, e.g. iron production, hunting, tar production and stone quarrying, and as a complement to the infield, for cereal cultivation, pasture and hay-making. In the parish of Gunnarskog pitfalls for capturing elk, a few sites associated with bloomery iron production, two soapstone quarries, from which the soapstone used at Skramle was extracted, and shielings (dwellings for shepherds supervising summer grazing) that may belong to the medieval period have all been documented in the vicinity (Fig 3.8). However, the immediate area that should have formed part of Skramle's hinterland has yielded very little evidence of activity: a shieling of unknown age and a stone quarry where only small amounts of stone have been extracted. In addition to the quarry and shielings, fishing must have been important for the inhabitants of Skramle, since the hamlet was on the shore of a lake. The remains of a jetty have been found on the shore close by.

From the number of houses and fields dated to the medieval period it is clear that Skramle was a small hamlet. In the second half of the thirteenth century there were three farmsteads/households there, and just two in the first half of the fourteenth century. The fossilised fields at Skramle are small and do not appear to have been divided up, which suggests that the different farmsteads did not have shares in different fields. Co-operation in the hamlet was focused on crafts and cattle breeding. There was only one site for each craft, apart from the textile production and fur handling that was conducted within the separate households, and just one barn, one cattle-byre and one cattle path. The cattle belonging to the different households thus shared a single cattle-byre, and the animals presumably grazed together nearby.

The farmers at Skramle, although living in what appears to be a marginal area, were involved in external networks and market relations. At the local (parish) level, labour

Fig 3.8

Gunnarskog parish with medieval settlements and remains of outfields. Map by Stefan Nilsson (after Svensson 2008, fig. 21).

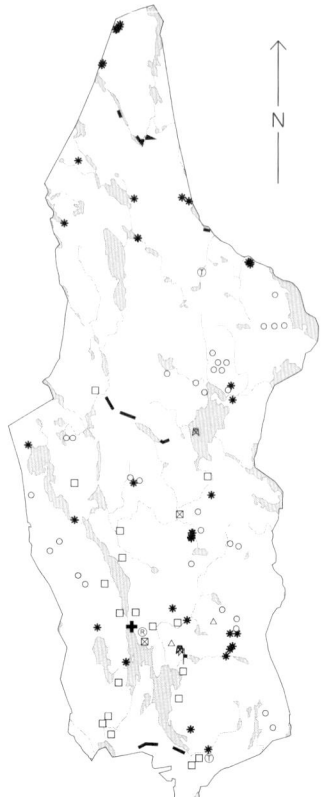

□ Medieval rural settlement, currently inhabited
⊠ Deserted medieval rural settlement
✳ Pitfall
〰 System of pitfalls
○ Shieling
△ Occurrence of slag
ɼ Iron works forge
▨ Charcoal pit
® Runestone
ⓣ Soapstone quarry
✚ Parish church
▨ Waterway

0   2.5   5   7.5   10 kilometer

division and mutual trade relations are discernable. Different hamlets, sometimes in collaboration, appear to have focused on different resources and production relating to outland use, such as pitfall hunting, iron production, soapstone quarrying or shieling management. Presumably, the farmers traded products with each other, maybe during regular meetings at the church. The soapstone industry at Skramle appears to be geared towards the local community. The Skramle farmers also operated over longer distances, probably trading furs. From the outside world they brought home novelties, such as smoke ovens and bricks.

A farm in Tårnby, Denmark *by Mette Svart Kristiansen*

The excavation of an area of 7,500m² in the village of Tårnby south of Copenhagen uncovered a farmstead with its toft and associated structures (Svart Kristiansen 2005). Well-preserved and deep cultural layers with sequences of floor-layers up to 0.7 m thick made it possible to follow its establishment from around 1050/1150 to 1858, when the area was built over by smallholders (Fig 3.9, 3.10). The medieval phases were particularly well preserved. Some of the most notable structures in the excavation were the complicated systems of ditches and the many buildings founded on sills.

The farmstead was probably laid out in connection with reorganisation in the village, and is supposedly the southern farm in a long, planned row of tofts. The toft,

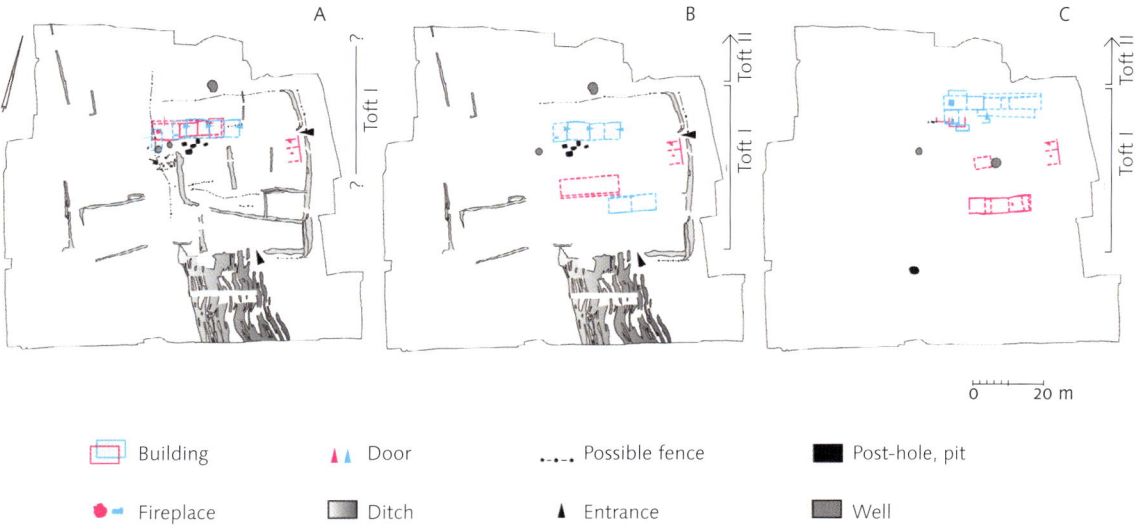

General plans of selected features showing the structural development on the farm at Tårnby. Left to right: (a) 1200-1250, (b) 1250-1300, (c) 1300-1400. Earlier and later phases are omitted (after Svart Kristiansen 2005, fig. 1.8b-c, 1,9).

Fig 3.9

clearly demarcated towards the street by a ditch, was 42-45 m wide and at least 4.5m deep deep with its buildings arranged towards the street. In the earliest phases the toft was divided into small areas of unidentified function, some probably orchards and vegetable gardens. During the twelfth-thirteenth century the farm had two, and in a later period possibly three, contemporary wings (Fig 3.9 a-b). Around 1300 the toft underwent substantial changes as it was extended to the north and an impressive 27m-long main building was erected. A physical boundary to the new toft could not be found (Fig 3.9c). Around 1400 the main building suffered a fire and was replaced by a series of small buildings in succession. Later phases of the farm structure appear very fragmented, but in the post-medieval period it is possible to distinguish four farmsteads along the road. It was only feasible to a limited extent to relate these sites to written sources and historical maps.

The excavation uncovered up to 43 buildings, and at least 16 of these are medieval. By far the greatest majority are single-aisled, with roof-bearing posts placed in the outer wall. In the twelfth century, the buildings were constructed with roof-bearing posts set in post-holes. In the later phases, building fashion changed and the posts were erected on various forms of foundation. Several buildings provided good opportunities for the reconstruction of ground-plans. However, the function of the rooms could seldom be identified as they have been thoroughly cleaned out. Sometimes the furnishing of the rooms had left traces in form of impressions in the floor by fixed constructions such as benches, bed areas and raised wooden podiums and by special flooring for furniture or barrels.

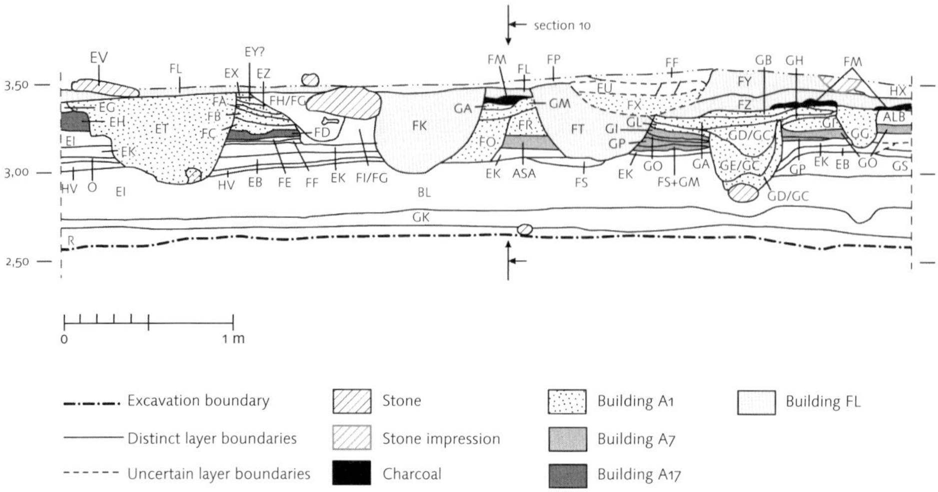
section 10
3,50
3,00
2,50
EV
FL
EY?
EX
EZ
FM
FP
FF
GB
GH
HX
FY
FZ
EG
EH
ET
FA
FB
FC
FH/FG
FD
GA
FK
GM
FR
FO
FT
FX
GI
GL
GP
GD/GC
GE/GC
ALB
GG
EI
EK
HV
O
EB
FE
FI/FG
BL
ASA
FS
GO
FS+GM
GP
GS
GK
R
0
1 m
Excavation boundary
Distinct layer boundaries
Uncertain layer boundaries
Stone
Stone impression
Charcoal
Building A1
Building A7
Building A17
Building FL

Fig 3.10 *Part of section showing sequence of floor-layers from four buildings at Tårnby dating from 13th to 16th century. Ploughing on this site would have caused much loss of data from 13th century and onwards (after Svart Kristiansen 2005, fig 3.13).*

The village was situated ideally, with abundant fish in the nearby Øresund, and access to rich clay soil for cultivating crops and extensive meadows for livestock. Some 7000 artefacts were found and, along with comprehensive archaeo- botanical and zoological material, they give a rich insight into the daily life on the farm and agricultural production for home consumption as well as for trading at the growing market in Copenhagen.

Rattray in Moray, north-east Scotland

by Martin Carver (after Yeoman 1995)

Medieval settlement in Scotland primarily took the form of dispersed *fermtouns*, each with a small number of farming families sharing resources, surrounded by the curving selions of their rig and furrow (Fig 3.11). Some small burghs (towns) had a strongly rural aspect to them, as at Rattray on the shore of the Moray Firth, where excavation (by Charlie and Hilary Murray) has shown how lairds (lords) and farmers lived adjacent lives between the thirteenth and the fifteenth centuries. The settlement was focused on a manorial castle, where clay-bonded stone buildings with simple mouldings for doors and glazed windows were constructed on top of a motte (Fig 3.12). On this site, the animal bone assemblage showed that the lairds were hunting red deer, roe deer, fallow deer, wild boar, hare, rabbit and wolf. A forested hunting reserve was located to the west. Among the finds were arrowheads, a ceramic hunting horn and a silver brooch decorated with four leopard heads.

The farmers' settlement was laid out at the foot of the castle mound in tofts marked out by ditches and arrayed on either side of a road (Fig 3.13). The two largest tofts in

The fermtoun at Wardhouse in Aberdeenshire, Scotland. The rectangular buildings are surrounded by the **Fig 3.11**
curves of the rig fields, with (top) small clearance cairns where stones removed from cultivated areas are
stacked (Yeoman 1995, fig 91, 109).

Foundations of the 14th-century **Fig 3.12**
stone hall on the earth motte at
Rattray (Yeoman 1995, colour
pl. 13).

the centre of the village contained the smithy and the potters' workshop. In the thirteenth century, the farmers' houses were constructed with turf walls with timber roof supports. But in the fourteenth, they had thick clay walls and clay-bonded stone gable ends, perhaps reflecting a change in climate or a rise in income. Rig and furrow was detected on the landward side, and excavation showed that household rubbish had been scattered there to manure the fields (Yeoman 1995, 93, 111-12, 116-17).

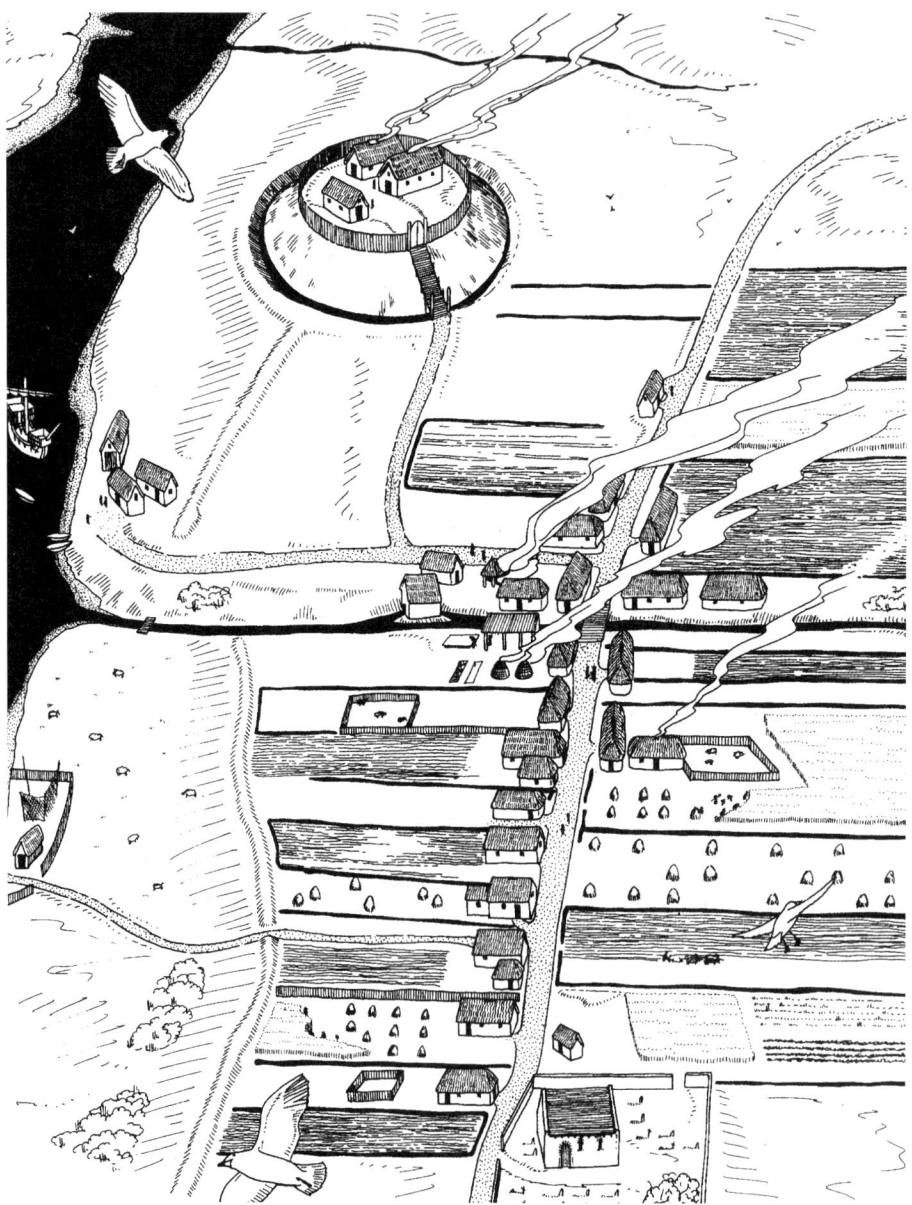

Fig 3.13 *The burgh of Rattray, showing the earth castle and planned village (J. Dunbar; Yeoman 1995, fig 96, 117).*

The diet was drawn mainly from meat, fish and oatmeal, with some barley. Corn dryers (and later kiln-barns) were used to facilitate grinding and save crops that often came in wet. Oat grain may also be burnt off its stalks, without the need for threshing (*graddanning*). The oat grains would be ground into oatmeal using a quern or flaked with a wooden mallet and mortar. Mixed with water the oatmeal is rapidly baked to make an oatcake or *bannock*. Examples of oat bannocks recorded in twentieth- century Scotland were 2-3cm thick and up to a metre in diameter and they could be baked over or next to an open fire. Oats were also eaten mixed with hot water, as *brose*, or boiled and mixed with ale, *pottage*, or the hull boiled into a paste, known as *sowens* (Fenton 1999, 98-9, 104-6, 168, 176). At Rattray, cattle was the main source of meat for the farmers, and sheep the main source of milk and dairy products (as well as wool). Kail was grown in the tofts to feed animals, which were in the main sustained through the winter. The animal bone assemblage also showed that whale, porpoise and dolphin were also eaten.

The community here was designated a *burgh*, i.e. a trading port, and it is possible that hides, wool and smoked fish were traded over and above their supply to the laird, and thus the community would have been on a trajectory towards greater autonomy. However the archaeological evidence showed that it remained essentially a rural settlement and its economy was weak, leading to its collapse and abandon in the fifteenth century.

In the path of a high speed train: Beaume, a hamlet in the Rhône Valley
by Odile Maufras, Michèle Bois and Nathalie Valour

The Rhône valley forms the principal communication route between north-west Europe and the Mediterranean Sea. The north–south corridor of the valley was served by a dense network of parallel and transverse routeways that connected towns and villages, the floodplain and its environs. A major road ran along its left bank between Lyon and Arles which formed part of Agrippa's Roman network and was still in use during the Middle Ages (Planchon *et al.* 2010). The river itself is crossed by numerous fords and ferry points that complement the bridges or stand in for those destroyed by the river when in spate. Among the most important crossing points were La Guillotière at Lyon, bridged in timber from the twelfth century (Burnouf *et al.* 1991), Saint-Bénezet in Avignon, bridged in stone in the same century and Saint-Saturnin du Port (today Pont-Saint-Esprit) bridged in 1309. The river was not crossed at Arles until the building of a pontoon in the seventeenth century, and although it had a port accessible to seagoing vessels, the market only flourished at a regional scale (Stouff 1986).

The pattern of Carolingian *villae* (which are open villages in this part of France) changed in the eleventh century, some staying open, others disappearing, others becoming fortified. The sites of towns and villages became fixed in the thirteenth century, forming a network that has largely persisted until today. However, between the thirteenth and sixteenth centuries, the settlements – and the landscape as a whole – were modified in numerous ways. For example, documents tell us of the clearing of forests, such as that of Bayanne in the Valentinois, to make way for Cistercian and Hospitaler's granges. All through the thirteenth century, occupation was intensified: more land was brought under the plough, farming and light industrial centres sprang up, and an increasing number of mills is implied by the documented demand for millstones as well as from the remains of waterworks. The century saw an increase in production, unequal from place to place, but palpable overall and with a consequent development of fairs and markets.

Production in the lower Rhône valley accelerated further in the early fourteenth century through the arrival of the papal court in Avignon, which generated a large number of artistic and architectural commissions as well as orders for furniture and food. The process was brutally halted by a wave of epidemics, starting with the Black Death in 1348, followed by social unrest, floods and famines that continued to affect the region until the fifteenth century. As elsewhere, the consequences included a fall in population, the desertion of some rural settlements, the provision of ramparts at others and a downturn in trade.

The economy rallied after the mid fifteenth century, with the areas outside the towns that were still peopled turning to food production and particularly to pasturing sheep, which, requiring few hands, could be accommodated within the modest rise of population. This was augmented by migration prompted by the acquisition by France of Provence and Dauphiné, the Italian wars and the troubles of the Reformation. Population movement and the redistribution of wealth allowed the progressive reconstruction of former settlements and buildings that had been left destroyed or abandoned in the times of unrest.

In the 1990s, the Rhône valley, lower Provence and eastern Languedoc were affected by the construction of a railway for high speed trains that was to connect Lyon, Marseille and Montpellier, and required a corridor 310 km-long across land of high archaeological potential. In contrast with the salvage operations of the 1980s, the archaeological programme was carefully planned in advance by the Archaeological Services of the three regions affected. The operation was divided into stages, beginning with an appraisal of the route using maps, photographs and documents in archive, followed by surface inspection and test-pitting along the whole route. Two hundred sites were located in this way, of which 130 were then excavated. Specialists were involved at every stage, with a view to integrating the different kinds of evidence: geological, sedimentary, stratigraphic, artefactual, floral and faunal. The objectives embraced not only the sequences at the particular settlements excavated, but changes in climate and the broader environment, and the human interaction with them. The archaeological response over this vast area was achieved in 22 months (between autumn 1994 and summer 1996), involving scientific recording of sites of all periods due to be destroyed by the railway (Bel 2006).

In the lower and mid Rhône valley, the TGV-Méditerranée corridor ran for the most part through vineyards, olive groves and orchards which for the past half-century have been cultivated by turning over the soil mechanically to a depth of about 90cm. This resulted in the destruction of the upper levels of stratification and most of the shallower features. Sites of the medieval period were hit particularly hard, and only 14 were found along the whole length of the route (Fig 3.14). In addition, in order to lessen its impact,

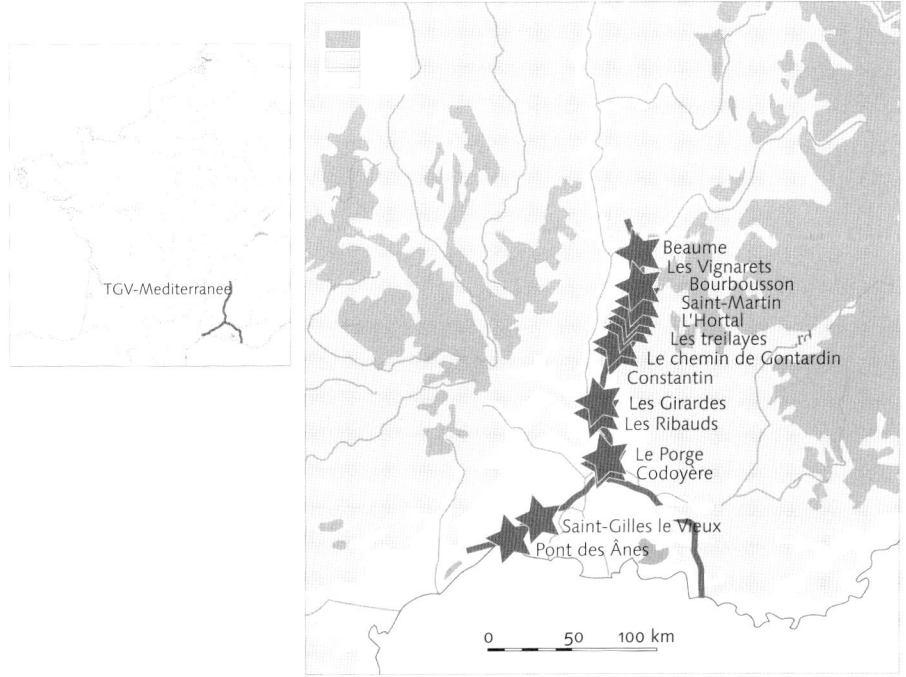

Medieval sites of the 7-15th century located on the route of the TGV-Méditerranée (drawing: O. Maufras/Inrap).

Fig 3.14

the railway line was carefully laid out so as to avoid all the present villages; in other words the sites of most of the nucleated and fortified settlements of the twelfth and thirteenth centuries. Therefore the chances of encountering a village, castle or church, or a town of the later Middle Ages were small. Of the 14 medieval settlements located on the route only one belonged wholly to the later period. This was the site of Beaume, located at the northern end of the line, and occupied between the twelfth and fifteenth centuries.

Beaume is a small rural settlement, a hamlet or farmstead, at the edge of the forest of Bayanne, on the left bank of the Isère, 10 km north of Valence and 3 km from the medieval *bourg* of Châteauneuf. It was built on the floodplain in a shallow depression about 100 m across and between 2 and 2.5m in depth. When occupation ended, the depression was rapidly filled in, allowing a good state of preservation, and preservation was further enhanced by a fire that had ravaged the hamlet at the end of the thirteenth century, allowing the earth walls to survive in a recognisable state: parts of the walls had collapsed to the ground where they were partially baked. The settlement had begun in the twelfth century and experienced three further main phases of development up to the fifteenth century, when it was abandoned (Fig 3.15).

From Phase 1, there survived two pieces of earth wall at right angles with a third adjacent, founded on a base of pebbles, with a patch of beaten earth alongside. These were

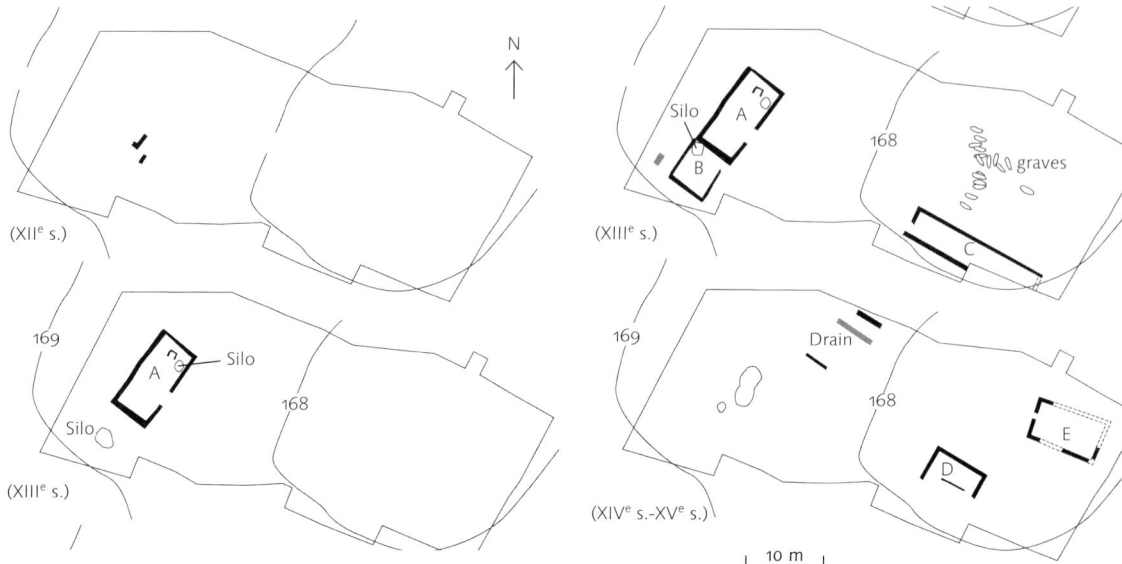

Fig 3.15 *Four phase development of Beaume from the 12th to the 15th century: G. Macabéo/Inrap (Maufras 2006, fig 7; courtesy of Documents d'Archéologie Française).*

associated with sherds of twelfth-century jugs and cooking pots, together with a coin of the Bishop of Die of the same date. The main period of occupation took place during the thirteenth century and began with a building (A) with a hearth and accompanied by a storage pit (Phase 2). Building A was extended by an annexe to the south-west (B) and joined by a long agricultural building to the south-east (C). A small cemetery developed beside and to the north of Building C. There may have been other buildings beyond the limits of the excavation.

Building A measured 73 m² or 110 m² with its extension. It had a hearth 1 m² placed up one end, but away from the walls, made of a clay base edged with tiles, and there was a structure for suspending a cauldron, as suggested by two stake-holes. Other stake-holes ran all along the west wall and in the south-east corner. These must have supported furniture or fittings of some kind. There were two large storage pits, one in Building A with a capacity of 7 m³ and the other in *Annex B* of 5.25 m³. The floor area of Annexe B was less well maintained than that of the main building, and a much larger number of artefacts was left in place there; it must have had a domestic or agricultural function (Fig 3.16 A, B).

Building C was 16.6 m long and 4.15 m wide, with no openings on the long side. Entry was via a door in the west gable, and there may have been a similar entrance in the short side at the opposite end. The interior floor had been reinforced with a layer of crushed tiles, witness to intensive trampling that had caused subsidence in the central area. The character of the floor and the long form of the building suggested its use as a stable or sheep fold.

All three buildings were constructed of mud walls placed directly on the ground without any foundations. The lower parts of the walls were made of a mixture of clay, silt, sand and gravel without any wood shuttering. The absence of timber suggests that the wall was made up with wet layers of mud, rather than daubed on a timber frame. The only framing still conserved came from the upper part of the north gable of Building A. It consisted of wickerwork made from branches of deciduous oak, elm and beech, held in place by uprights of oak and filled in with clay. The wall faces were finished with a slip of red or yellow clay and the roofs were covered by curved tiles. The structures made no use of stone. The pebbles on the thresholds had apparently been recycled from the previous phase where they had been used as sills for the walls of the twelfth century.

Agricultural production is suggested by the character of Building C and by the rare finds of animal bone: cattle, sheep/goat, pig and horse. Butchery marks show that these animals were eaten. There were also the remains of dogs large and small that may have been used to guard flocks or for hunting (Forest 2006). There were abundant remains

(right) Plan of Building A by: G. Macabéo/Inrap (Maufras 2006, fig 9; courtesy of Documents **Fig 3.16a** *d'Archéologie Française).*

(left) Building A and annex B seen from the south (Maufras 2006, fig. 135; courtesy of Documents **Fig 3.16b** *d'Archéologie Française).*

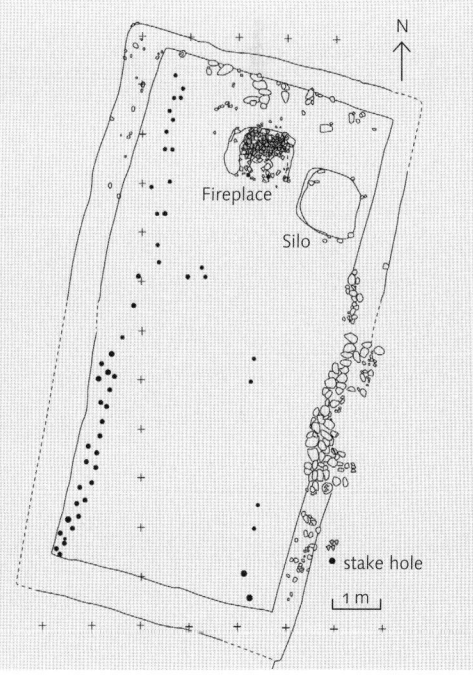

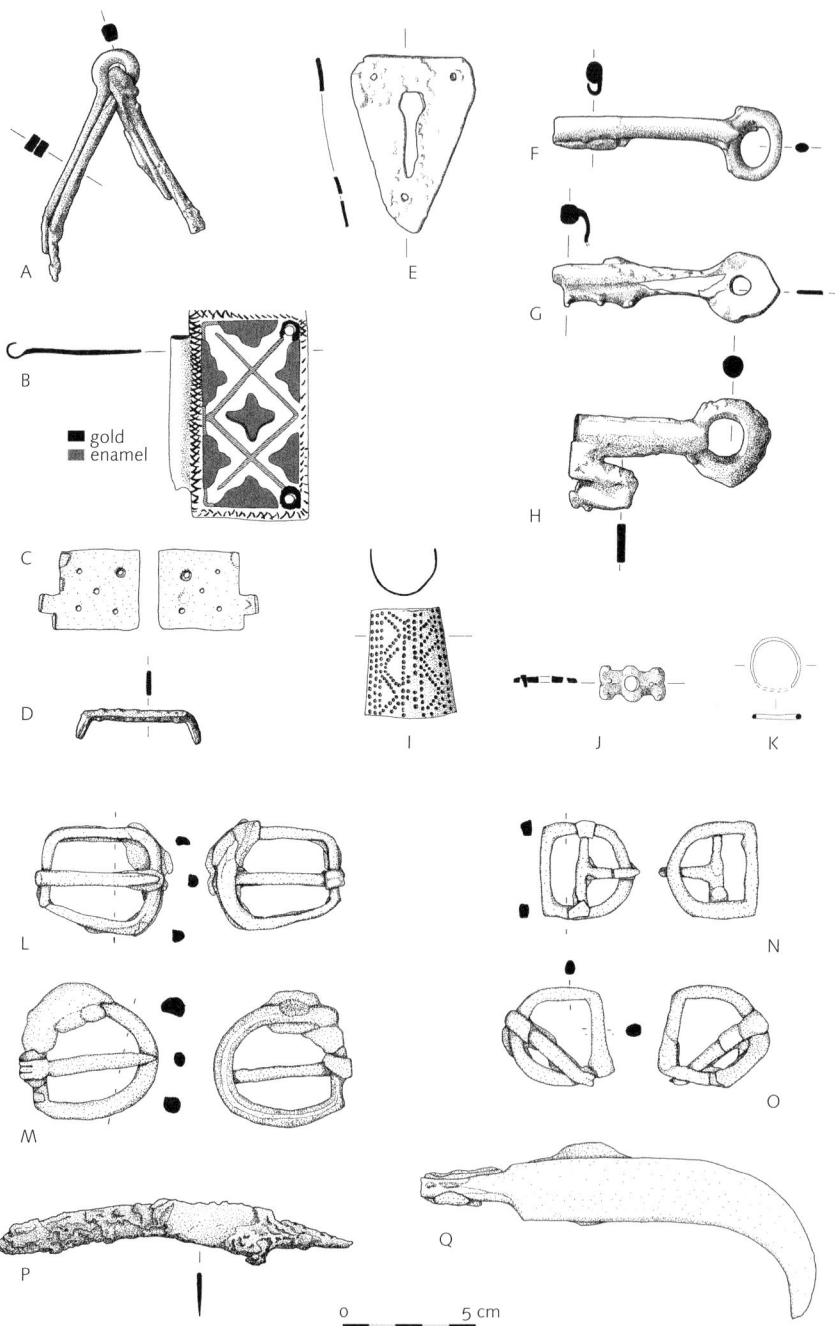

■ gold
■ enamel

0   5 cm

Fig 3.16c *Objects from the 13th-century phase at Beaume: A-C: hinges; D: hook; F-H: lock and keys; I: thimble;*
J: sequin; K: finger ring; L-O: belt buckles; P-Q: sickle blades (P. Mélony, K. Mokaddem, C. Plantevin/
Inrap).

of three plants: lentils within Building A, and rye and oats in the storage pits. As well as being stored in the pits, cereals were certainly cultivated in the region: the landscape was marked by a mosaic of fields bordering the woods in the territory. Other foodstuffs were accessed by the inhabitants, but not necessarily grown locally: apples, grapes, nuts and blackberries (Bouby 2006). Objects of everyday use were also recovered from the phase 2-3 site (Fig 3.16C), coming from the buildings (a lock plate and keys), from wooden furniture (a hook and hinges), from work (a thimble, sickle blades) or from items of clothes or personal adornment (belt buckles, a ring, a sequin).

The *cemetery* occupied an area of around 30 m², and was laid out in a T-shape, a plan no doubt constrained by factors that are no longer visible. It consisted of 24 unmarked graves of which a few overlay or cut into others; all were apparently laid down in a short space of time. There were coins accompanying the dead in three graves, one of them eleventh-twelfth century, the other two from the very end of the twelfth and the thirteenth century. Given the poor stratification, it is not excluded that some burials belong to the twelfth century.

All the bodies were buried in graves with a concave bottom with the exception of one that was placed in a pegged wooden coffin or box. The group as a whole was rather different from the type of medieval population usually encountered. There were no children. There were three adolescents – a relatively rare age group with a low mortality – and the majority were adults of advanced age (Blaizot & Martin-Dupont 2006, 45-8). The skeletons revealed an abnormal level of pathology, some examples due to old age, others to violent incidents. The injuries were varied and showed that the group had not all been exposed to the same source of trauma (*ibid.*: 48-54).

The phase 3 buildings were burnt down at the end of the thirteenth century, giving way to Phase 4. The storage pits had been emptied of the grain spared by the flames, one to down to the bottom, the other down to a protective layer of straw that carpeted the base. The unusable burnt grain was dumped in the storage pit of annex B. After the fire, the hamlet was reconstructed further east and south in the direction of the Valence road. Two buildings (Fig 3.15: D and E) were defined, which probably only constitute a part of the new development. They were badly preserved, but used a new form of construction. If the wall elevations were still fashioned from raw earth, the foundations were now of cut stone blocks bonded with clay or mortar. Contemporary with the buildings were pits containing material, principally fifteenth century pottery, which showed that the place had remained a residence within an agricultural economy.

In sum, Beaume was a rather atypical establishment, serving an agricultural venture with a settlement consisting of a few houses. At its heart was a burial ground, but there was no sign of any church, and this at a time when burial in consecrated ground was the norm. The status of the site has been clarified, both by the documentary archives and by the study of the palaeopathology of the buried persons. Neighbouring Châteauneuf and its territory constituted a lay lordship until 1157 when it was passed to the Bishop of Valence, at a time when religious possessions were multiplying in the district. The Cistercian abbey of Léoncel increased its holdings during the twelfth and thirteenth century, at first through the areas of transhumance and then through the founding of granges, acquiring properties scattered in the neighbourhood of Beaume. Other religious orders also owned land in the plain of Valence, among them the Hospitalers who from 1170 controlled territory that must have included Beaume, judging from the limits of their estate in the area of Chambaud in 1260-1 (Valour *et al.* 2006).

The earliest occupation belongs to a documented period in the twelfth century, and was one of a number of hamlets on the outskirts of Châteauneuf that grew up following a wave of forest clearance. Beaume may have developed into a hamlet with a special function. The pathology of the thirteenth-century population resembles less a community that had been born and died in the same place, more one gathered together by virtue of their physical condition. Given that Beaume was probably located on an estate of Hospitalers, one is tempted to suggest that it was a hospice for the aged and handicapped (Blaizot & Martin-Dupont 2006, 55-6).

Documents show that at the time of forest clearance, placenames were not yet finally fixed. Beaume was first known by the name of neighbouring places, such as Chirons to the north and Chambaud to the south, and subsequently as *Gros Bosc, maison blanche près Gros Bosc, terre à la Bôme* or *Do camina*. The name Beaume only appears at the end of the fifteenth century, probably the period represented by Phase 3.

PART 3: GROWING FOOD

Food in northern Europe from the thirteenth to the sixteenth century
by Reidar Bertelsen

Method

The complex and fascinating subject of food production and consumption was discussed in Volume I for the period 800-1200 (AME 1, 181-200), and many of the observations made there are valid for the later medieval period too. Food as subsistence is the aspect that dominates the archaeological perspective. But other aspects of food as material culture should not be overlooked; food links with life in many other ways from nutrition to social structure, religion and to the manner in which we alter the landscape. The study of food in the past is one sector of archaeology where our discipline meets others: history, chemistry, physics, botany, geology and zoology.

We have much to do: our data are fragmentary and our research strategies have been so diverse and incomplete that we are still far from being able to give a valid and comprehensive overview. A comparison between southern, central and northern Europe will be difficult from the very beginning because nature has given such dramatically different conditions for the survival of data in these regions. The historical records give us detailed and plentiful information about food in the late Middle Ages, but they are almost exclusively reporting the life of the aristocracy. The Renaissance has given us a number of fascinating dietary accounts, but we would be misled if we read those as representing the late medieval population at large.

Changes in diet: the example of England

As a first difference from the earlier period, we can note that there was a marked increase in the urban population. New towns were established and old towns expanded (Ch 9). This meant that a larger part of the population was not directly involved in food production. On the other hand, the growing urban middle classes and the urban contact network within and between regions and countries helped to establish a strong and influential trade in foodstuffs. Other factors such as climatic changes and technological innovation may also have contributed to change.

England is one of the best studied areas for mapping the pattern and variation of diet onto geography and social status. A large number of sites have been compared systematically on the basis of both the archaeological and the documentary evidence from the Saxon period until AD 1540. The late Middle Ages are in most respects a continuation from the early Middle Ages and the changes that can be identified came gradually in the form of socially restricted differences in the distribution of foodstuffs, rather than in access to new commodities. But the fifteenth century appears to be a period of change, especially in urban contexts. Meat of domestic animals (beef, mutton and pork) was still the main protein source, but there was a significant addition of game and birds that widened the urban diet. As for the increase in the consumption of fish, which happened in the twelfth century, it was the upper classes that were able to make such choices when it came to diet. The urban diet differed from that of the countryside mainly because out of town the contrasts between social classes became more marked (Woolgar *et al.* 2006).

Field crops, such as wheat, barley, rye and oats, legumes, peas and beans were the most important sources of calories as in earlier periods and they were grown all over the country. These crops were mainly consumed in the form of bread, ale or pottage and it is demonstrated from documentary evidence that wheaten bread and ale brewed from barley were preferred by the higher social groups (see above). Our knowledge of the consumption of plant food is rather difficult to compare with the consumption of meat based on the archaeological record. We do however know that both types of food were generally available.

Bones from cattle and sheep account for the majority of animals consumed in the late medieval as in the early medieval zooarchaeological records. Towards the end of the period, there was an increased consumption of beef among high status households. There was also a marked difference in cooking methods: stews were more common among ordinary people and roasted meat became the favourite in the higher circles (see also Ch 1, p 47).

As in the previous period, pork was a frequent element in the diet, but the number of pig bones found in the later Middle Ages diminished in comparison to cattle and sheep/goat. This must partly have been compensated by an increase in the size of the pigs. It is also likely that pigs were stalled or yarded because the area of open woodland diminished (Albarella 2005).

The consumption of dairy products is as hard to assess from archaeological evidence as that of plants. Since this part of the diet was closely linked to animal husbandry we must assume that the milk of cattle and sheep/goats was as important as it had been earlier. The conservation of fresh milk was a problem during the main production period, the summer. Butter and cheese were therefore the main products, especially for consumption in the towns (Woolgar *et al.* 2006).

Cod and other large preserved fish as well as herring provided the volume of medieval fish consumption from at least the twelfth century, possibly already from the eleventh century. It seems evident that high status households, religious houses and the growing urban population favoured stockfish and other dried variants of large saltwater fish. It is likely that this consumption was favoured both by demographic changes and by the observance of religious customs (e.g. the season of Lent). The consumption of freshwater fish diminished throughout the period (Woolgar *et al.* 2006).

Geese, duck and capons became increasingly popular among the higher social classes, as did a variety of wild birds. Chickens and their eggs remained a common part of the diet for all social groups. Like fish, birds were not subject to ritual restriction.

The northern margins

Although the investigation of diet in other parts of Europe has been less comprehensive than in England, there are several other good examples. Starting from the far north, in Arctic Norway, we find Saurbekken (at 69° N), a small one-family holding first settled towards the end of the tenth century (Bertelsen 1973). It came into the ownership of the Trondenes church, probably before AD 1250. The little settlement was placed on flat land beneath a forested hill and 500 m from the shore. Saurbekken was abandoned after the Black Death and its 'farm mound' (the mound formed by the deserted settlement) was subsequently quite well preserved. The majority of the midden material excavated was accumulated during the thirteenth and first half of fourteenth centuries. Beef, mutton and pork seem to have been the dominant foodstuff. But wild mammals such as seals, small whales and reindeer were abundant as well as a wide range of wild birds such as grouse, wood grouse and different types of seagull. From other excavated settlements in the region, we can add eider ducks, geese, cormorants, puffins and thick-billed guillemots. The midden also gave evidence that various kinds of shellfish and molluscs had been eaten occasionally.

Cod and other marine species like coalfish, haddock, ling and cusk were abundant. More rare species were halibut, herring and golden redfish. Plant remains were not analysed, but judging from pollen analyses in the region, barley was commonly cultivated as far north as 70° N from the Neolithic period. We are lacking evidence for the consumption of wild berries of different kinds that were abundant in the nearby forests. The strong marine element in the northern diet was not new in the Middle Ages, but had been a tradition that endured all the way from the Mesolithic period.

In sum, the household at Saurbekken had a complex diet which was linked to a broad subsistence strategy. A sherd of thirteenth century Yorkshire pottery indicates an indirect link to a distant world. Perhaps this should be interpreted as an indication of participation in the commercial fisheries that had gradually developed since the eleventh century as the main economic link between the capital of the early Norwegian kingdom, Bergen, and the northern coast. The winter fisheries of the Atlantic cod and the production of stockfish had been an integrated part of the subsistence for the northern coastal population since the Mesolithic period (Mook *et al.* 2008), but the 'fish-event' (Barrett 2007, 201-3) initiated a new economic system that included long distance trade in large quantities of food.

Alstahaug (66° N) was, in contrast to Saurbekken, a large settlement rooted in the Early Iron Age. It became a church centre of regional importance in the late Medieval and post Medieval periods. The excavation of four trenches of the farm mound has been published recently (Berglund 2007) and it is phases 2 and 3 that are of interest for us (AD 1200-1500). Judging from the osteological record, the diet was almost in every detail similar to that at Saurbekken. However, the assemblage included artefacts related to the preparation and serving of food. Fragments of continental stoneware and bronze cauldron showed a strong influence from urban households in the kitchen as well as in the arrangement of the table.

The centre of Norwegian medieval cod fisheries, Vágar on the easternmost of the Lofoten islands (68° N), has been partly excavated (Bertelsen *et al.* 1987; Urbańczyk 1992). Based on documentary evidence we know that most of the stockfish exported from the city of Bergen to Europe came from Vágar (Fig 3.17). The rich zooarchaeological material from households living close to the main harbour give a similar picture

Storvågan in the Lofoten islands in March 2009. This was the main harbour of the medieval Vágar urban **Fig 3.17**
community (Bertelsen et.al. 1987) where most of the dried fish that was exported from Bergen was pro-
duced. Cod fishing mainly happened during the late winter/early spring. By June the fish was dried and
ready for shipment (photo: R Bertelsen).

Fig 3.18   *Dried stockfish on a traditional rack at Å in the Lofoten islands, June 2009 (photo: R Bertelsen).*

of the late medieval diet as the material from the farm mounds of Saurbekken and Alstahaug, even if meat was rarer and cod more abundant (Perdikaris 1999) (Fig 3.18).

These sites by no means represent the majority of the medieval European population. They must be considered marginal when it comes to agricultural resources and the distance from urban centres, but optimal when it comes to access to wildlife resources, both maritime and terrestrial. Did they have anything in common with the people in more central parts of Europe?

Scandinavia and the Continent

This question can be addressed by comparison with households in farmsteads and castles further south, drawing information from a wide range of investigations in Sweden, Germany, the Czech Republic, Switzerland, England and Wales (Svensson 2008, listed in Table 3.2). Even if the material at hand represents contrasts in geographical and social context, quantity and quality of the investigations, the dominant pattern of the diet is the same. Beef, mutton and pork (in order of quantity) were the dominant source of animal protein all over the northern continent and in Great Britain and this pattern is the same all over the rural landscape. The main diet of the aristocracy was similar to that of the peasants. Some indications of wild game, fruits, hazelnuts and walnuts were found at the farmsteads, but there is more abundant evidence for game, wild birds and, most of all, fish like carp, trout, salmon, bream and cod, represented in images. An example is provided by Christ at supper with Simon the Pharisee by Dierec Bouts the elder *c.* 1440 (oil on wood) which may be seen in the Gemäldegalerieat the Staatliche Museen zu Berlin. The table is laid with bread, wine and fish and we recognize the main types of German stoneware and glass.

TABLE 3.2	RECENT INVESTIGATIONS OF DIET AT DIVERSE SITES			
PLACE	COUNTRY	TYPE OF SITE	DATE	REFERENCE
Skinnerud	Sweden	Farmstead	900-1250	Svensson 2008
Skramle	Sweden	Hamlet	1250-1350	Svensson 2008
Saxholmen	Sweden	Island castle	1250-1300	Svensson 2008
Edsholm	Sweden	Island castle	1370-1434	Svensson 2008
Huis Malburg	The Netherlands	Farmstead	1050-1225	Oudhof et al. 2000
Cefn Graeanog	Wales	Farmstead	abandoned late 13th century	Kelly 1982
The Hill Top Farm	England	Farmstead	12-14th century	Makepeace 2001
Bystrec	Czech Republic	Village	13-15th century	Belcredi 2000; 2006
Konůvky	Czech Republic	Village	13-15th century	Měchurová 1997
Dalem	Germany	Village	600-1340	Zimmermann 1991
Ulm-Eggingen	Germany	Village	600-1300	Gross 1989
Oude Huys	The Netherlands	Castle	1175-1375	Arts 2001
Alt Wartburg	Switzerland	Castle	*c.* 1100-1415	Meyer 1974
Lewes, phase 2	England	Castle	13th century	Drewett 1997
Koválov	Czech Republic	Castle	13th century	Unger 1994
Lelekovice	Czech Republic	Castle	14th century	Unger 1999
Schnellerts	Germany	Castle	13-14th century	Unger 1999

Urban contexts

The extensive excavations of habitation areas in medieval Oslo (1025-1624) were rich in zoological and botanical remains. According to Griffin (1988) these included cereals, mainly oats and barley, in addition to peas and beans, onion and turnip, cherries, apples, crowberries, strawberries, rosehips, cloudberries, raspberries, blackberries, buckthorn berries, cranberries and hops. These give a picture of a multifaceted late medieval diet of fruit, bread and beer. Lie (1988) noted an increased consumption of beef in addition to mutton and pork and increased presence of horse, dogs and cats. Hare, reindeer and seals were the most commonly eaten wild game. Many of the wild animals of the early medieval period such as elk, red deer and small whales were lacking. But a series of animals mostly hunted for their fur (beaver, otter, pine marten, brown bear, squirrel, fox and wolf) was also present in the early medieval middens. Wild and domestic birds decreased towards the late medieval period, but chicken, geese, capercaillie, black grouse, grouse, fulmar, black-throated diver, guillemot, swan, seagulls, hawk, eagle and raven were represented. The sea fish cod, ling and pollock were found in quantities. Occasional bones of haddock and bluefin tuna completed the marine diet. There were fewer species than in the early Middle Ages, but the relative numbers of fish (mainly ling) had increased. Stockfish probably accounted for most of the cod bones.

Bone assemblages have also been published from Århus (Møhl 1971) and Viborg (Hatting 1998) among other towns. The Viborg material is not divided between the early and the late medieval period, but it is fair to say that the Oslo pattern is repeated when it comes to the list of species represented. In the Danish towns, beef was more abundant. The Århus material also shows an increase in beef consumption towards the late medieval period. In both towns, cod dominated the consumption of fish, but the Århus material shows a decrease towards the fourteenth century.

A general northern diet?

Continuity throughout the Middle Ages as well as a common northern European diet seems to be distinctive features of the late Middle Ages. But there were variations due to regional ecological differences as well as a more distinct tendency for the high-status groups to adopt a more luxurious diet. This would be greatly enhanced in the sixteenth century, consequent on the discoveries of the richness of foodstuff in the rest of the world.

Hunting and venison in medieval England
Naomi Sykes

On many medieval excavations, animal bones and teeth are some of the most common archaeological finds, usually representing the remains of human meals or industrial processes such as butchery, bone-working and tanning. Traditionally, analyses of these remains have focused on domestic animals, with zooarchaeologists studying their relative proportions and age structures (amongst other things) to reconstruct dietary regimes, economies and local environments (Ch 1, part 2). Less attention has been given to wild animals – an oversight given that in farming societies, where hunting is unnecessary for survival, the exploitation of wild animals usually involves a social and political performance bound up with expressions of identity (but see Ch 2, part 3). This brief case-study presents evidence for hunting and, more specifically, the distribution and consumption of deer in later medieval England. It sets out to demonstrate how zooarchaeology and historical studies can be integrated profitably to provide new perspectives on the structure, behaviour and ideology of medieval society.

In 1159 John of Salisbury complained that "In our days, the scholarship of the aristocracy consists in hunting jargon" (*Policraticus* 1.4, I.23). He was referring to the complex rituals that, following the Norman Conquest, came increasingly to surround elite hunting (Sykes 2007a & b). Knowledge of these rituals was deemed a mark of nobility and, by the thirteenth century, a common aristocratic hunting culture was established across Europe (Ch 2, p 80). Its cultural importance is demonstrated by the many later medieval hunting manuals that were written to provide tuition in the methods of capturing, killing and butchering different quarry. Following medieval humoural theory, it makes sense that the aristocracy hunted and consumed wild boar, the violent *bête noire*, in order to embolden themselves and increase their military prowess. Ecclesiastics on the other hand, keen to avoid animals whose capture and consumption might induce aggression, opted for species deemed meek in temperament and chaste in character (Larioux 1988; Yvinec 1993).

But the perception of medieval England as the home of deep woodland where wild boar abounded is an illusion created by the fact that most of the English hunting manuals were copied from continental originals – for example the *Master of the Game*, by Edward Duke of York, is a translation of Gaston Phébus' *Livre de Chasse* (Fig 2.14). In France, wild boar were indeed the focus of hunting, their remains often found in high frequencies on settlements belonging to the secular aristocracy. But even in France wild boar were not hunted by all sections of society; the species is seldom found in assemblages from religious houses, where roe deer and hare are usually the best represented wild animals (Yvinec 1993).

In England, wild boar was very rare, if not extinct, by the thirteenth century (Albarella, 2010). The remains of other game animals are found unevenly distributed in different kinds of medieval site (Fig 3.19a). That roe deer are fairly well represented in assemblages from religious settlements is all the more interesting given that they are very poorly represented on other site types; indeed, it would seem that by the end of the fourteenth century this species too was largely extinct in England. Red deer numbers also appear to have been in decline at this point. This is particularly apparent for elite sites, brought into relief by the overwhelming abundance of fallow deer which presumably reflects the later medieval fashion for deer parks, of which this species was the principal inmate. Assemblages from the residences of parkers and foresters indicate that these individuals ate large amounts of the available venison. Indeed the assemblages from Lodge Farm in Dorset (Locker 1994), Donington Park Lodge in Leicestershire

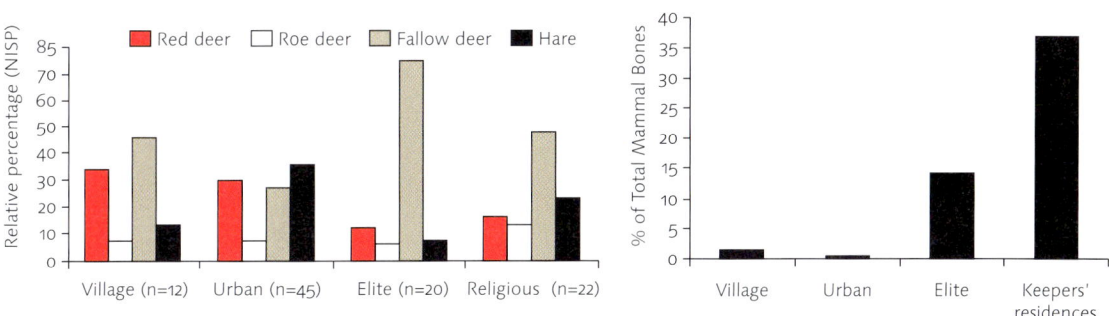

(a) (left) Relative frequencies of the main game mammals found on types of late medieval site in England. **Fig 3.19**
The data are presented in terms of fragment counts (NISP) and shown by site type, n = the number of sites included in each category. (b) (right) Overall proportions of game mammals at different site types.

(Bent 1977-8) and Stanstead Lodge in Essex (Framework 2008) contain deer remains in far higher frequencies than is seen on elite sites, suggesting that, for parkers and foresters, venison was less a luxury and more a tedious dietary staple (Fig 3.19b).

It is tempting to interpret these inter-site variations in species representation as reflecting differences in resource availability; but this would be too simplistic. No human society, either now or in the past, eats all of the edible animals available to them – some limbs become dietary staples, others are avoided. All decisions are governed by personal attitudes and wider cultural views. According to the manuals, the crescendo of a day's hunt was the 'unmaking', a highly ritualised event where the quarry was dispatched, skinned, butchered and certain body parts given away. Instructions on this procedure vary between the different manuals but, generally, they agree that the hunting dogs received much of the offal, the 'corbyn bone' (the pelvis) was cast away as an offering to the 'corbyn' (crown or raven), lower quality cuts (e.g. the head) were given to the poor, and the meat-bearing parts of the carcass were gifted to different people: the left shoulder going to the forester or parker as his fee, the right going to the best hunter or breaker of the deer, with the haunches being taken back to the lord's residence (Cummins 1988).

The zooarchaeological evidence indicates that where deer were hunted, not only were the unmaking rituals followed, they were adhered to quite rigidly. Fig 3.20a shows the combined skeletal representation patterns for red and fallow deer from three late medieval English sites of high status: Guildford Castle (Surrey), Stafford Castle (Staffordshire) and the manorial site of Faccombe Netherton (Hampshire). As would be expected from the historical evidence, they show a clear over-representation of the hind-

Fig 3.20 *Anatomical representation of red and fallow deer in archaeological assemblages, shown as a percentage of the total count of mammal bone fragments (a) from elite sites (b) from foresters' sites (c) from villages and (d) from urban sites (source: Sykes 2007).*

Fig 3.20a

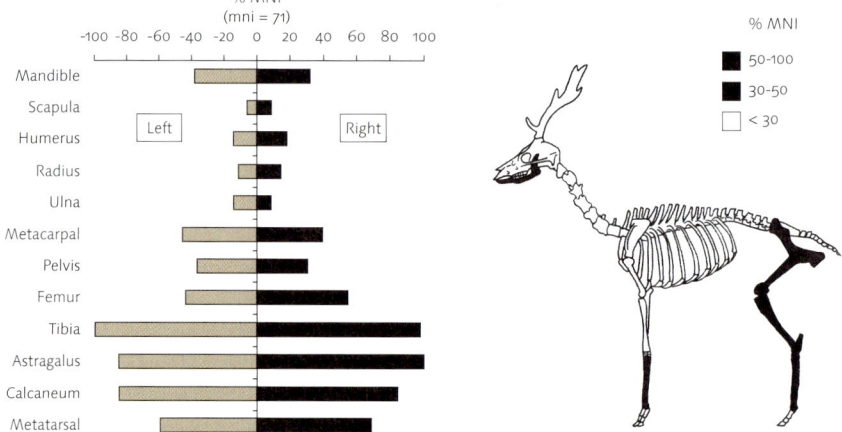

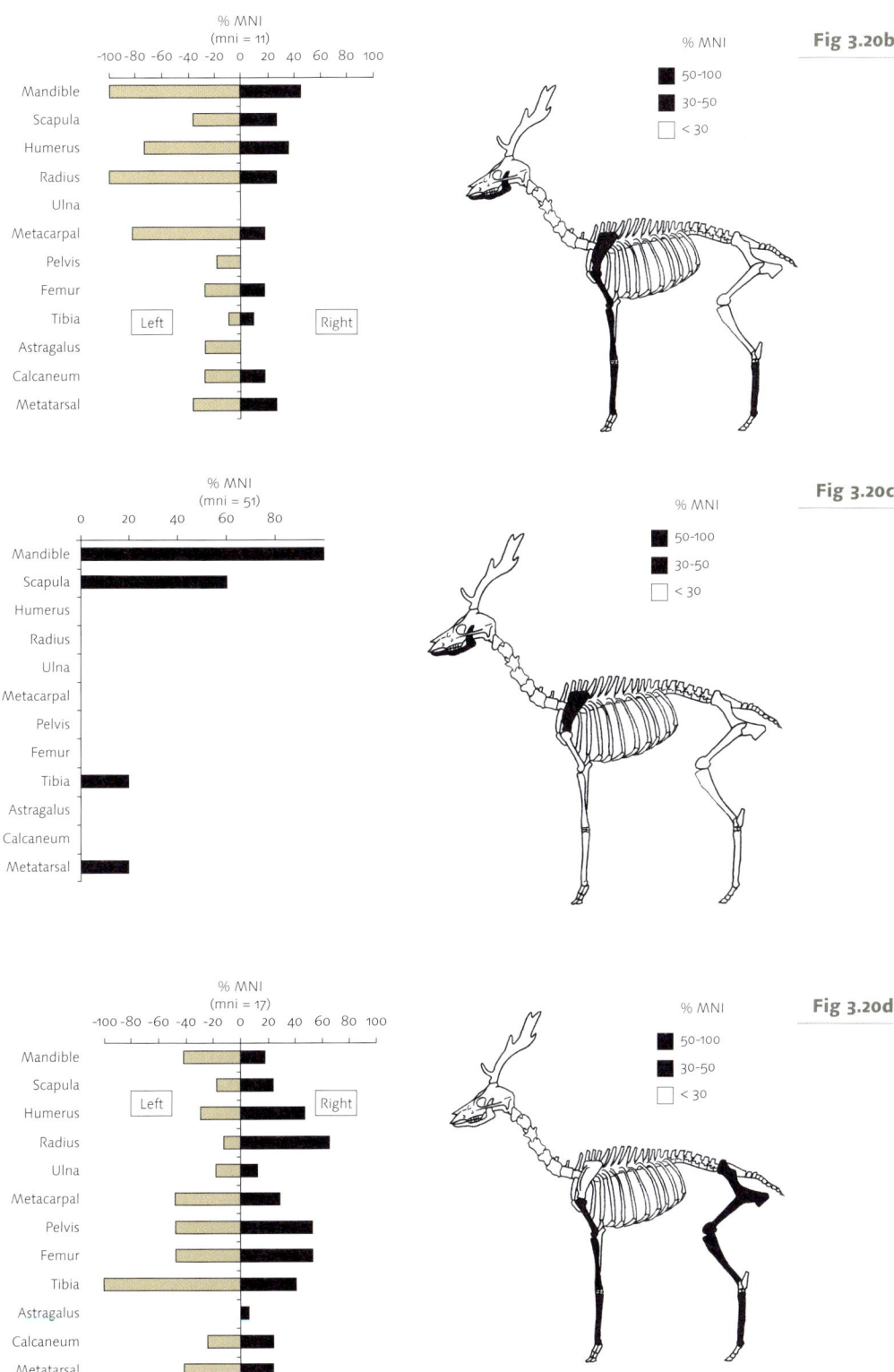

% MNI
(mni = 11)

-100 -80 -60 -40 -20 0 20 40 60 80 100

Mandible
Scapula
Humerus
Radius
Ulna
Metacarpal
Pelvis
Femur
Tibia
Astragalus
Calcaneum
Metatarsal

Left   Right

% MNI
50-100
30-50
< 30

Fig 3.20b

% MNI
(mni = 51)

0 20 40 60 80

Mandible
Scapula
Humerus
Radius
Ulna
Metacarpal
Pelvis
Femur
Tibia
Astragalus
Calcaneum
Metatarsal

% MNI
50-100
30-50
< 30

Fig 3.20c

% MNI
(mni = 17)

-100 -80 -60 -40 -20 0 20 40 60 80 100

Mandible
Scapula
Humerus
Radius
Ulna
Metacarpal
Pelvis
Femur
Tibia
Astragalus
Calcaneum
Metatarsal

Left   Right

% MNI
50-100
30-50
< 30

Fig 3.20d

Living on the Land   **135**

limbs, with elements from the left and right hand side of the body represented in equal frequencies. Less abundant are those parts of the body that the texts suggest would have been gifted: the pelvis is poorly represented as are skeletal elements from the upper fore-limb. Add to this the fact that household accounts and recipe books frequently mention haunches but seldom mention shoulders (see Birrell 2006) and it would seem that the forelimbs are genuinely absent from elite sites. If it is accepted that only two thirds of each deer was regularly transported to lordly residences then, by concentrating exclusively on elite sites, we are overlooking at least one third of all venison consumption that took place in later medieval England – there must have been plenty to go around. The skeletal representation patterns for foresters' and parkers' residences are in complete opposition to the assemblages from elite sites: Fig 3.20b demonstrates that few elements from the hind limb are present but there is an over-representation of shoulder bones, particularly those from the left hand side, as indicated by the hunting manuals.

What then of the hunters' portion, and the right shoulder in particular? Unlike foresters and parkers, hunters did not receive accommodation as a perquisite of office; most were yeoman and lived within the rural community. Unfortunately, animal bone assemblages from medieval rural settlements are notoriously scarce and even where bones are preserved, deer remains are present only in low frequencies (Fig 3.19b). Fig 3.20c shows the available skeletal data for deer assemblages from village sites. Jaw bones are the best represented body part and, although this may reflect preferential preservation of this robust element, it could feasibly confirm that heads were occasionally given to the poor. The only other skeletal element present in any frequency is the shoulder blade. At Seacourt in Oxfordshire (Jope 1961-2), for instance, three of the four deer bones recovered were shoulder blades and, interestingly, all were from the right-hand side of the carcass. Whilst this sample size is exceptionally small, its significance becomes apparent when compared to the evidence from Faccombe Netherton where, out of 784 deer bones, just two shoulder blade fragments were identified. Thus even the limited dataset for rural settlements would appear to confirm that venison redistribution was carried out in the fashion suggested by the texts.

For those not permitted to hunt, poaching provided an exciting alternative, with the distribution and consumption of ill-gotten venison carrying its own cachet, either as a statement of defiance or in terms of social emulation (Manning 1993, 20; Birrell 1996, 84). A classic example of peasant poaching comes from the village of Lyveden in Buckinghamshire, a settlement where poaching is attested by both the historical record (Birrell 1982, 21) and the zooarchaeological evidence: the animal bone assemblage contained a heavily-butchered red deer skeleton that was 'hidden' down a well but also a range of other deer bones from all parts and sides of the body, a pattern in no way suggestive of the unmaking procedure.

That poached venison was percolating into towns via the urban black market is also indicated by the zooarchaeological evidence. Fig 3.20d shows the deer skeletal representation data for urban assemblages and the overriding impression is that it does not conform to the structured anatomical patterning seen on other site types. We may envisage that individuals brought a haunch here or a shoulder there, but the presence of mandibles and foot bones suggests that a few complete carcasses were also arriving. The acquisition, man-handling and distribution of a whole carcass would have been beyond a single individual, requiring a great degree of collusion and cooperation. Indeed the difficulties of smuggling and fencing a large deer carcass may explain why urban assemblages contain the highest frequencies of hares (Fig 3.19a). The zooarchaeological evidence must surely be recording the organised poaching gangs that operated out of urban taverns and alehouses, where they also consumed and sold their bag (Manning 1993; Birrell 1982, 14).

It is reassuring when historical and archaeological evidence concur, but it is not enough to identify past patterns of behaviour: we need to understand their meaning. This is where both historians and archaeologists can benefit from insights offered by the disciplines of anthropology and sociology. In most traditional societies today, animal carcasses represent more than just 'protein'; the cutting up and redistribution of meat is laden with rhetoric tied into expressions of land-ownership, social position and group identity (Lokuruka 2006; Symons 2002). Medieval hunting and venison redistribution can certainly be interpreted in these terms: social hierarchy was reinforced by gifting different cuts of venison as meaty symbols of social position, but those who received portions of meat could be sure that they *had* a position *within* a group. In this way, rather than being socially exclusive, hunting and venison consumption could actually create community and narrow the gap between lord and peasant.

Stories from seeds: the late thirteenth century granary at Durfort (Tarn)
(paraphrased by M. Carver, from Ruas 2002 with the author's assistance)

The castle of Castlar is located at the west end of the Montagne Noire (Massif Central) above Durfort in the region of Midi-Pyrénées, France. Among the spaces excavated in the castle was a rectangular granary measuring 5 x 6 m, cut into the rock on one side and overlooking the ravine at the other. The room had burnt down at the end of the thirteenth century, leaving pots and a brazier smashed and burnt where they had stood (Fig 3.21). The sediments that remained (up to 5 cm thick) were carefully mapped and sieved, producing a total of 392,563 identified seeds, an average density of 5537

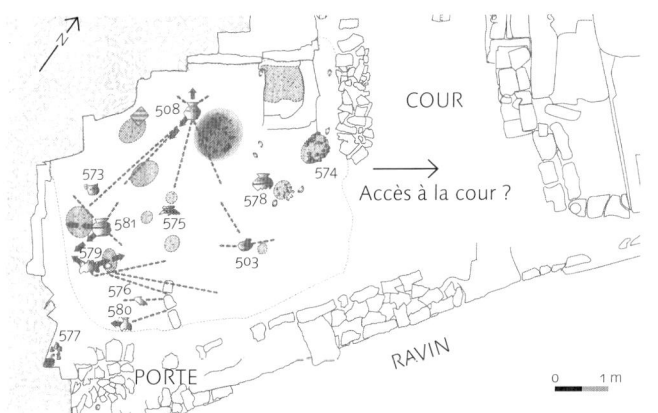

Plan of the granary at Durfort Castle (Tarn, France), showing position of pots, conjoining sherds (dashed lines) and brazier (circle of black wood pieces) (Ruas 2002, 31). **Fig 3.21**

seeds per litre of processed soil. By means of this exceptional preservation and high precision recording, the species were not only identified, but they could be assigned to particular places in the store, where they had been kept in pots, bins or sacks, mainly round the edge of the granary (Fig 3.22).

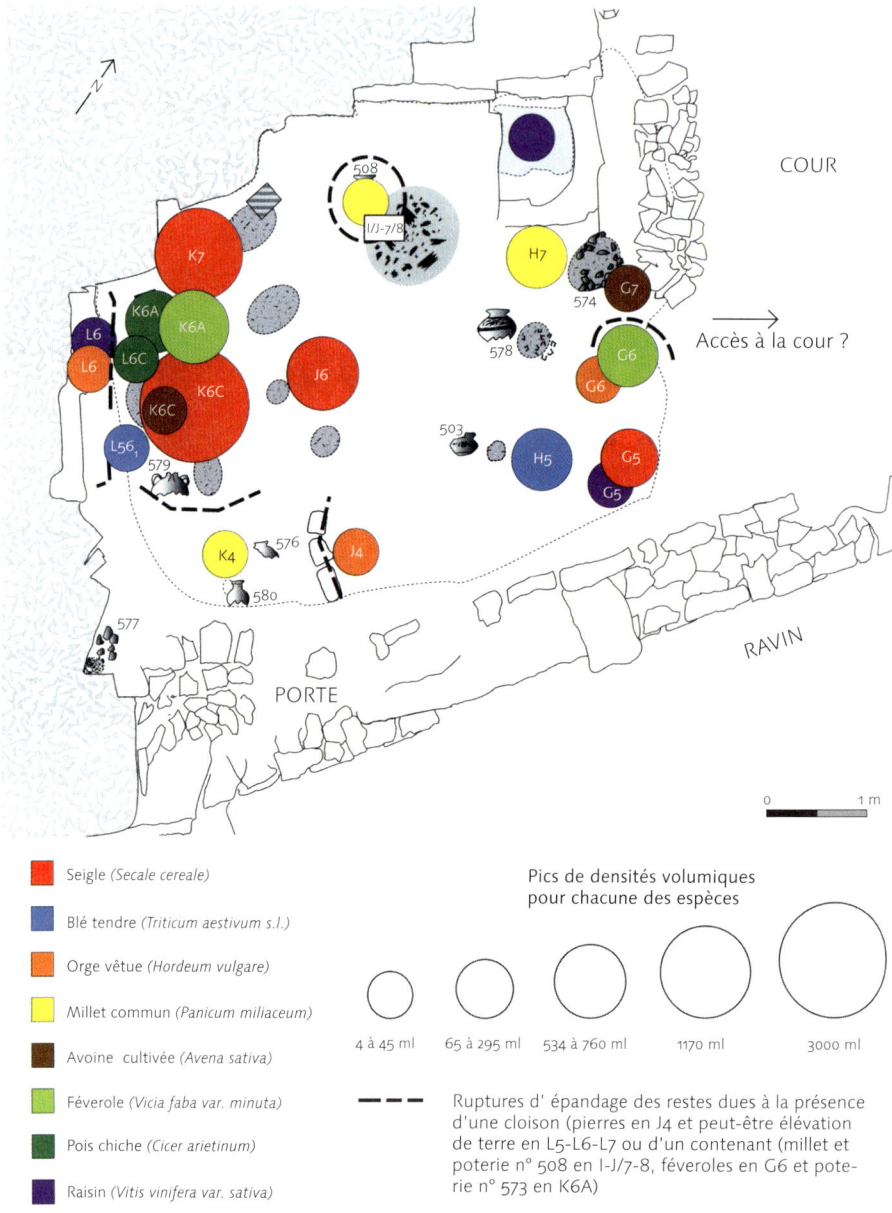

Seigle (*Secale cereale*)

Blé tendre (*Triticum aestivum s.l.*)

Orge vêtue (*Hordeum vulgare*)

Millet commun (*Panicum miliaceum*)

Avoine cultivée (*Avena sativa*)

Féverole (*Vicia faba var. minuta*)

Pois chiche (*Cicer arietinum*)

Raisin (*Vitis vinifera var. sativa*)

Pics de densités volumiques pour chacune des espèces

4 à 45 ml   65 à 295 ml   534 à 760 ml   1170 ml   3000 ml

– – – Ruptures d' épandage des restes dues à la présence d'une cloison (pierres en J4 et peut-être élévation de terre en L5-L6-L7 ou d'un contenant (millet et poterie n° 508 en I-J/7-8, féveroles en G6 et poterie n° 573 en K6A)

Fig 3.22 *Plan of the stored species. Red - rye; blue - wheat; orange - barley; yellow - millet; brown - oats; green - broad beans; dark green - chick peas; purple - grapes. (Ruas 2002, 52).*

The assemblage included crops, dominated by rye and broad beans, with some bread wheat, millet, barley, oats and chickpeas. There were cultivated fruits: grapes, figs, cherries, plums, peaches and medlar; and fruits of the wild: strawberries, blackberries, elderberries, sloes, hazel nuts and walnuts. Other seeds, mainly found with cereals, belonged to 131 different taxa, of which some were weeds, some were potentially dyes, some were toxic and others had medicinal properties.

Drawing on her detailed analysis, archaeobotanist Marie-Pierre Ruas deduced that the produce was mainly local. The cereals had been stored as grain rather than flour, and milled for the kitchen as required. The variety and quality of foodstuffs allowed her to conclude that they were grown, gathered and prepared at the instigation of the castle's governing lords (source: Ruas 2002).

Inferring diet by stable isotope analysis: case studies from the French Alps *by Estelle Herrscher*

Advances in chemical techniques now permit the reconstruction of the diet of an individual through the direct analysis of the human skeleton (Herrscher *et al.* 2002; Privat *et al.* 2002; Prowse *et al.* 2005; Müldner & Richards 2007). Here we present a brief description of the method, and its application to a population living in the later Middle Ages in the foothills of the French Alps.

Elements such as nitrogen (N) and carbon (C) occur in nature in atoms of different weight, with different numbers of neutrons in their nucleus. These different *isotopes* of each element are taken up in different quantities by plants and animals in the food chain and end up in the protein (collagen) in human bone. Thus bone collagen contains within itself information about the proteic part of the diet followed by a deceased person during their last years of life (Ambrose & Norr 1993; Hedges *et al.* 2007). The relative amount of the rarer isotope is expressed as a ratio (δ); thus $\delta^{15}N$ indicates the amount of ^{15}N relative to ^{14}N, and $\delta^{13}C$ indicates the amount of ^{13}C relative to ^{12}C of each sample compared with the same ratio of international standards. These are the *isotope signatures* that imply access to certain foodstuffs. The interpretation in isotopic data and the reconstruction of past diets has been validated by ecological studies of mammals (Ambrose & Norr 1993, Ambrose 2000, Sponheimer *et al.* 2003) and human populations (Minagawa 1992; Froment & Ambrose 1995; O'Connell & Hedges 1999, 2001) whose dietary regimes are known.

It has been found that the collagen of predators contains $\delta^{15}N$ values that are higher, by 3 to 5‰ (parts per thousand), than those found in their preys (Minagawa & Wada 1984; Bocherens & Drucker 2003). Therefore, the higher the position of individuals along the food chain (higher trophic level), the higher the $\delta^{15}N$ value in bony tissue is, and this enables us to distinguish the dietary trends of individuals, i.e. plant eating, meat eating, fish eating or omnivorous (DeNiro & Epstein 1978, 1981; Schoeninger & DeNiro 1984).

The collagen of predators shows $\delta^{13}C$ values that are slightly higher, between 0 and 1‰, than those of their preys (Minagawa & Wada 1984; Bocherens & Drucker 2003).

Plants have carbon isotope signatures that differ depending on photosynthesis: plants and tissues of plant eaters who lived in temperate, closed environments show isotopic $\delta^{13}C$ values that are lower than those which lived in warm, open environments (van Klinken *et al.* 2000). The isotopic signatures of carbon therefore allow us to trace the type of environment in which the original foodstuff grew (Park & Epstein 1960). There is a notable variation in $\delta^{13}C$ in the case of fish and fish eating, since the plants on which they fed grew under water (Schoeninger & DeNiro 1984).

Collagen is extracted from bone according to a chemical protocol that follows Longin's method (1971) as adapted by Bocherens (Bocherens *et al.* 1991a). Samples are ground to bone powder, the collagen extracted and the relative proportions of isotope measured by mass spectrometer (DeNiro 1985; Ambrose 1990; van Klinken 1999). Before reconstructing the diet of human individuals, it is important to identify isotopically the different sources of food potentially available in the local environment as a control (Herrscher & Le Bras-Goude 2010). Animal remains recovered in association with the human skeletons are ideal (Hedges & Reynard 2007). If the skeletal remains are not directly associated to animal and plant remains, it is possible, with care, to use data available in the literature, if possible from contexts related as closely as possible in time and geographical area. These animal/human comparisons constitute an important step in modelling the resources that were consumed (Bocherens *et al.* 2006; Drucker & Henry-Gambier 2005). Given that quantities of isotopic data are now available on a Europe-wide scale for the historic periods, it is possible to build a general isotopic framework for several types of food resources potentially available in locations in England, France, Belgium and Italy dated between the second and nineteenth centuries AD (Table 3.3). Two case studies follow, demonstrating how stable isotope analysis may contribute directly to an understanding of diet and its social and economic implications.

The medieval population at Saint-Laurent in Grenoble (Isère)

The church of Saint-Laurent-de-Grenoble is located beside the valleys of the rivers Drac and Isère on the outskirts of the city of Grenoble in the department of Isère in France (Colardelle 2008, here Fig 3.23). The excavation of its cemetery produced a human bone assemblage of the late medieval period that contained 252 adults and 84 immature individuals (Herrscher & Valentin 2005) spread over three successive phases: Phase 13 (thirteenth-early fourteenth century), Phase 14 (1320-1430) and Phase 15 (1430-early sixteenth century). This key historic period is characterised by the growth of a market economy in the region (Flandrin & Montanari 1996; Laurioux 2002), as well as by climatic and epidemic crises, famines and political unrest (Chomel 1976; Le Roy-Ladurie 1983). The isotopic analysis of the diet of the inhabitants of the quarter of Saint-Laurent pursued two objectives: the reconstruction of the diet of the adults and the diet of infants (Herrscher 2003).

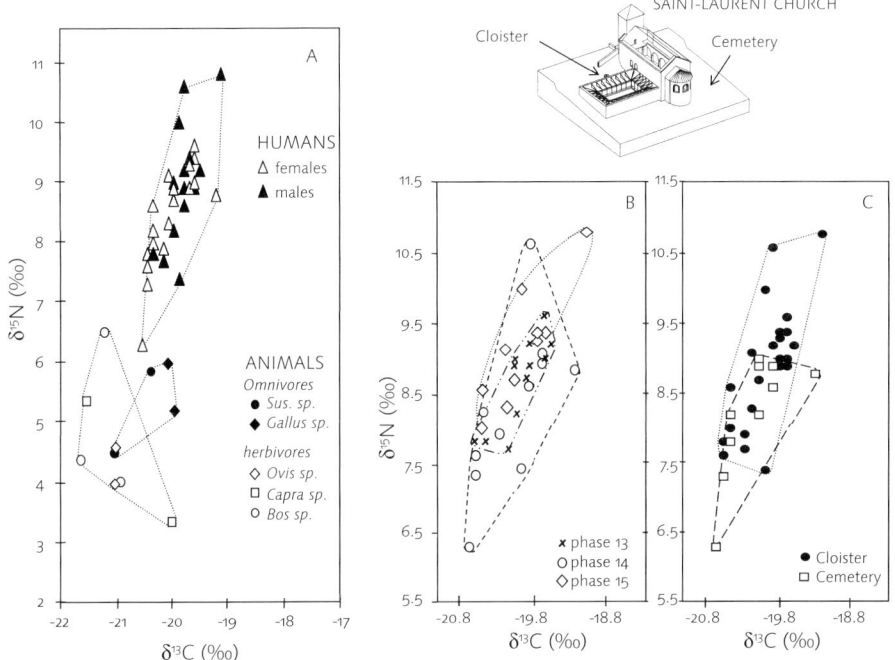

$\delta^{13}C$ and $\delta^{15}N$ ratios for human population and animals from Saint-Laurent site. *(left) by sex and species* **Fig 3.23** *(centre) by phase and (right) by location.*

The diet of the Grenoble adults

The sample comprised 34 adults (20 females, 14 males). Samples were taken for each individual from the cortical bone of the hand phalanges. The local isotopic control group was an animal bone assemblage consisting of 13 specimens (cattle, pig, goat, chicken) recovered in the backfill of the graves. Isotopic variations ($\delta^{15}N$ and $\delta^{13}C$) were assessed according to archaeological criteria (date, position of burial within the cemetery) as well as biological ones (age at death, sex, state of health).

The $\delta^{13}C$ values conformed to the geographical location of the site and are commensurate with a temperate environment. The relative animal and human isotopic signatures show that the animal species considered (chicken, pig, cattle and goat) had probably been consumed. The mean $\delta^{15}N$ values of the adult humans show that they did not regularly consume aquatic resources, either freshwater or marine. Interestingly, an increase in the $\delta^{15}N$ values is noticeable from the thirteenth to the fifteenth century, suggesting that there was an increased intake in animal proteins as time went on. This change in the diet was related to an increase in stature and a decrease in tooth wear, but an increase in dental pathology among the population of the period (Herrscher *et al.* 2007).

An increase in the degree of sexual differentiation (dimorphism) would indicate that living conditions were better, both socially and nutritionally, during the fifteenth century. This improvement may have been be due to an increase in the amount of food containing glucose and animal proteins as well as to the consumption of bread of better quality (Herrscher *et al.* 2006). These results are in keeping with the historical documentation. While the nutritional health of the inhabitants of the quarter of Saint-Laurent deteriorated during the fourteenth century, due to economic difficulties and harsh climatic conditions that triggered famines, the fifteenth century saw a return to political and economic stability in the region (Chomel 1976).

However, this generalisation needs refining. The analysis of the distribution of $\delta^{15}N$ values according to the position of the graves in the cemetery (cloister/Place Saint-Laurent) shows that those individuals buried in the cloister – which are presumed to be of higher status – consumed more meat than the rest. Therefore, improvements in health and diet observed amongst the inhabitants of Saint-Laurent may actually be due to the higher social status of individuals buried in the cloister during the fifteenth century, compared to those buried in the parish cemetery.

Infants at Saint-Laurent: breastfeeding and weaning

Food historians are not all of the same opinion concerning the age of weaning in the later Middle Ages. Some propose weaning at one year old (Loux 1978; Alexandre-Bidon & Closson 1985), others between the ages of 3 and 4 (Flandrin 1984). At Saint-Laurent, analysis of the diet of infants was based on a sample of 12 infants who died between birth and 5 years of age, spread over the three phases (Phases 13, 14 and 15, thirteenth-fifteenth century) (Herrscher 2003). Infant tissues are gradually enriched with ^{15}N during the time they are breastfed and the quantity decreases during weaning. This effect is similar to the isotopic fractioning that happens between 'predator' and 'prey' (in this case the child and its mother): it leads to a systematic increase in ^{15}N of the order of $+3‰$ in the tissues of infants compared to those of the mother. This effect has been tested on infants alive today whose diet is known (Fogel *et al.* 1989).

Two samples were taken from each individual, one from a bone fragment, indicating diet some time before death, and the other from the root of a growing tooth, indicating diet at the time of death (Balasse *et al.* 1997, 1999, ; here Fig 3.24). An increase of the $\delta^{15}N$ values between the two tissues (bone and tooth root) means that the infant was still breastfeeding; a decrease that weaning had begun. If the values were the same, the result was less conclusive: the infant had not undergone a change in diet, either because she had been fed animal milk, or had just stopped breastfeeding and begun the weaning process. Though the small number of samples does not permit a comparison of weaning practice through time (phases 13, 14 and 15), some remarks can nevertheless be made (Fig 3.25). In the fifteenth century (Phase 15), two infants show negative results indicative of a weaning earlier than for the third infant with a positive result suggesting prolonged breastfeeding. Caution is needed since those infants suffered from non-specific infectious lesions that could imply a rejection of their mother's breast. Nevertheless given the age at death, the overall results suggest that infants were breastfed up to the ages of 2.2-2.6 years old, and weaning took place between the ages of 2.6 and 3.3 years old.

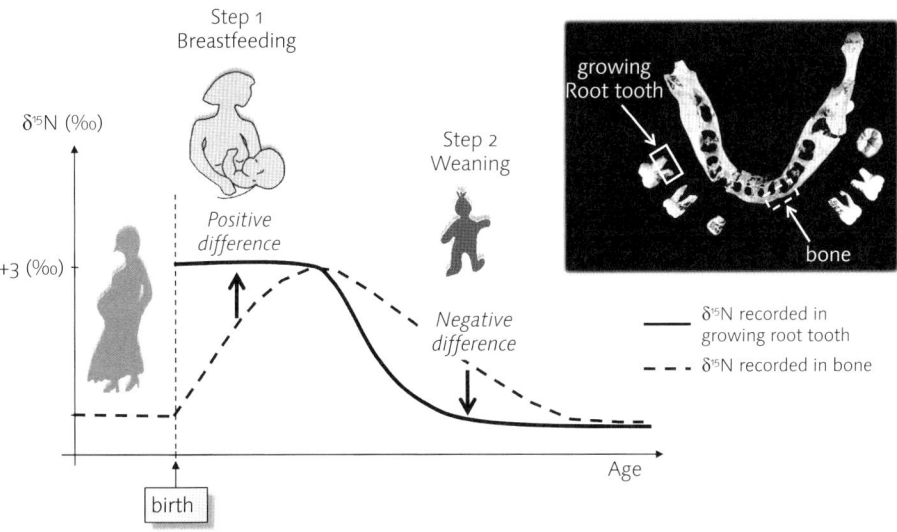

Changes in δ¹⁵N ratios recorded in the growing tooth and bone tissue of babies during the breastfeeding **Fig 3.24**
and weaning process.

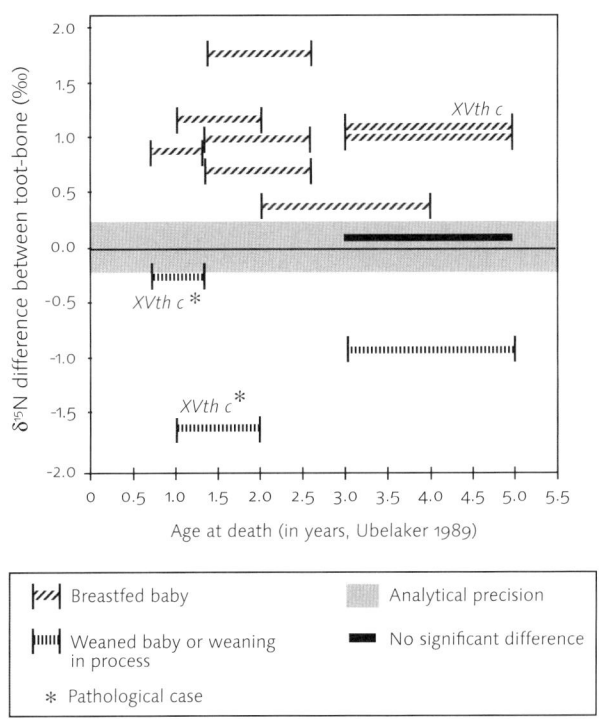

Changes in δ¹⁵N ratios recorded in the growing tooth and bone tissue of babies during the breastfeeding **Fig 3.25**
and weaning process.

The excavation of the archaeological site of Brandes, located on a high plateau in the massif of the Oisans (1800m asl.) revealed an abandoned mining settlement, complete with workshops connected with the extraction of silver, and a cemetery in front of the village chapel (Bailly-Maitre 1998; Bailly-Maitre & Bruno Dupraz 1994; Bailly-Maitre & Simonel 1996; also p 326 below). According to the archaeological data, the site was occupied for two centuries, from the mid-twelfth to the mid-fourteenth century. The population buried at Brandes, estimated to be 100 adults and 42 immature individuals, is reported as showing a normal mortality profile (Bailly-Maitre *et al.* 2008). Stable isotope analysis of nitrogen and carbon was carried out on 24 adults (7 women, 13 men and 4 undifferentiated individuals). The local isotopic control was established from 21 fragments of animal bone (cattle, goat and pig).

The distribution of the $\delta^{13}C$ values, comprised between -22 and -20‰ for the animals and between -20 and -19‰ for the humans, reflects the geographical location of the site in a temperate environment (Fig 3.26a). The distribution of the $\delta^{15}N$ values, within a range of 4 and 7‰ for the animals and 7 and 10‰ for the humans, is typical of a consumer-consumed relationship: animal proteins procured directly through husbandry practiced by the inhabitants of the plateau of Brandes. The distribution for the humans shows a discontinuity in nitrogen isotopes, with two individuals possessing significantly lower $\delta^{15}N$ values (6.9‰). Two scenarios are possible: either the majority consumed food enriched in ^{15}N, probably animal proteins, or the two individuals with

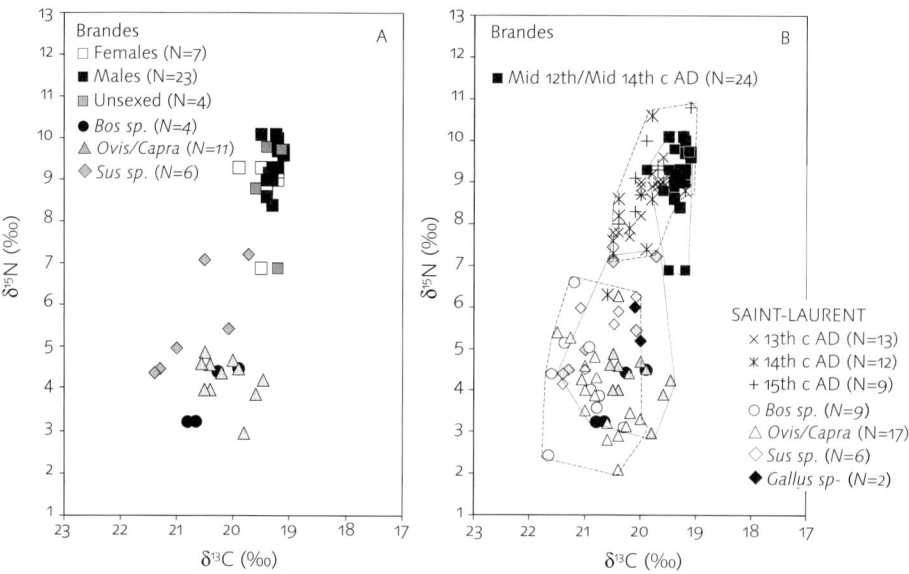

Fig 3.26   *(a): $\delta^{13}C$ and $\delta^{15}N$ ratios for human population and animals from Brandes-en-Oisans site and (b): comparison with $\delta^{13}C$ and $\delta^{15}N$ ratios for human and animals from Saint-Laurent site by chronological period.*

low ^{15}N compared to the rest of the group had consumed leguminous plants. Leguminous plants have low nitrogen isotope values because they fix atmospheric nitrogen directly at root level (Virginia & Delwiche 1982). The latter hypothesis is possible since fossilised remains of such plants were identified during palaeobotanical analysis.

Comparison between the isotopic data obtained for the inhabitants of Brandes and of the quarter of Saint-Laurent in Grenoble throws up notable differences (Fig 3.26b). Indeed, the herbivores (goats) as well as the humans of Brandes exhibit significantly higher δ^{13}C values than those of the individuals at Saint-Laurent. Such a result could be due to the more open environment at Brandes, located at 1800m asl., as opposed to the local environment near the city of Grenoble in the valley bottom. The δ^{15}N values from Brandes are significantly higher than those obtained for the thirteenth and fourteenth centuries but similar to those of the fifteenth-century individuals at Saint-Laurent. Such a result indicates that, during the mid-twelfth to mid-fourteenth century, the inhabitants of Brandes consumed more animal protein than the inhabitants of Saint-Laurent. As at Saint-Laurent, it seems that the men had privileged access to animal protein and that consumption of sweetening agents was not important. Although the individuals lived under harsh conditions of isolation and climate, the analysis of the skeletons did not show any major dietary or health disadvantages among the miners of Brandes-en-Oisans as compared to their contemporaries in the valley of the Isère at Grenoble (Bailly-Maitre *et al.* 2008). It seems that the mining community at Brandes was able to live well in its geographical isolation, no doubt thanks to regular deliveries of silver to the valley (Bailly-Maitre 1998).

Conclusion

Stable isotope analysis has the potential to reveal dietary practices that in turn reflect the environment, health, economy and social structure of a community through time. The urban population of Saint-Laurent in Grenoble saw an increase in the amount of animal protein consumed between the thirteenth and fifteenth century AD, reflecting a rise of prosperity towards the end of the Middle Ages. Their neighbours at Brandes, mining at high altitude between the twelfth and fourteenth centuries, already had a higher meat intake from local stock than their contemporaries in the valley at Grenoble. The intra-individual isotopic analysis of a group of urban infants allowed us to propose that prolonged breastfeeding was practiced, beyond the age of 2.5 years, probably associated with a complementary diet.

The biochemical study of skeletal remains is providing a new source of information about medieval life, one that complements the study of sites and artefacts and goes beyond written and illustrated evidence. It enables us not only to identify biological lifestyles, but to infer matters relating to the economic, cultural and political management of food.

TABLE 3.3 ISOTOPIC DATA OF TERRESTRIAL AND AQUATIC FOOD RESOURCES

TABLE 3.3 ISOTOPIC DATA OF TERRESTRIAL AND AQUATIC FOOD RESOURCES from European archeological animal remains (2nd-19th century AD).							
	$\delta^{13}C$			$\delta^{15}N$			References
Types of food*	mean	SD	N	mean	SD	N	
Terrestrial resources							
Herbivores	-21.4	0.8	128	5.2	1.4	128	1, 2, 3, 4, 5, 6, 7
Omnivores	-21.4	0.6	64	6.9	1.5	64	1, 2, 3, 4, 5, 6, 7
Carnivores	-20.3	1.0	26	9.0	1.7	26	1, 3, 4, 5, 6, 7
Domestic fowl	-20.5	1.1	21	9.4	2.1	21	2, 5, 6
Wild fowl	-21.5	0.8	9	9.3	3.7	9	6
Aquatic resources							
Freshwater	22.0	2.3	8	14.2	4.3	11	5, 6
Anadromous species	-15.0	0.6	6	11.2	2.5	6	6
Catadromous species	-23.2	2.4	11	11.2	1.3	11	5, 6
Marine fish	-13.8	1.7	35	13.1	1.8	35	1, 5, 6

*Herbivores = *Bos* sp., *Ovis/Capra*; Omnivores = *Sus* sp.; Carnivores = *Canis* sp., *Felix* sp., *Vulpes vulpes*; Domestic fowl = *Gallus* sp., Wild fowl = Duck, Goose; Freshwater = Cyprinid, Pike; Anadromous = Salmonid; Catadromous = *Anguilla* sp.; Marine fish = Haddock, Cod, Herring.
(1) Bocherens *et al.* 1991b; (2) Herrscher *et al.* 2001; (3) Privat & O'Connell 2002; (4) Polet & Katzenberg 2003; (5) Müldner & Richards 2005; (6) Müldner & Richards 2007; (7) Herrscher, unpublished.

CHAPTER 4

HOUSING

PART 1: PALACES AND PALACE LIFE IN THE NORTH *by David A. Hinton*

Although the appropriateness of attaching the label 'Feudal' to the hierarchical society of later medieval Western Europe has been called in question (eg Reynolds 1994), only in Italy was the balance of power in favour of an urban aristocracy rather than a landed one, however much a ruler's wealth came from the profits of tax on trade, rather than the products of rural estates. Further north, kings, dukes, counts and barons mostly had a level of wealth far above that of even the richest merchants, although it was less disposable and they therefore frequently needed loans, for which their jewels and plate served as pledges. The aristocratic home was more than a residence; it also served to display secular power, which in our period frequently involved a fortified building, a castle. However questionable the defensive need for castles may have been, except in frontier zones, they remained symbols of military capacity; a ruler had strong-points to show his rule, his subjects to show that they could give him their support. Castles are discussed in Ch 6, and see AME 1, Ch 12 for a discussion of the display of secular power in the preceding centuries.

Buildings and Physical Settings

The distinction between a castle and a palace was often a narrow one, but the thirteenth century saw increasing use of what might be quite sprawling complexes, enclosed, but with no serious fortification (Fig 4.1; and see Fig 1.14). A ruler who was internally strong dominated through control of the law courts. In the great kingdoms, power became more centralised, represented by a permanent presence of the king's officers even when the king himself was absent. Royal houses also grouped around favoured centres, as kings became less dependent on itinerancy to exercise control, let alone to consume the payments in kind that had once sustained them.

The growing power of the thirteenth-century kings of France is reflected in the growing importance of Paris. The kings had long had a great residence there, but the *Palais de la Cité* became a display centre in which justice and hospitality were dispensed, a magnificent hall dominating a public open space to emphasize that only a select few were entertained inside. Linked to the hall was a processional way into the triumph of European Gothic architecture, the Sainte Chapelle. The Capetian dynasty established

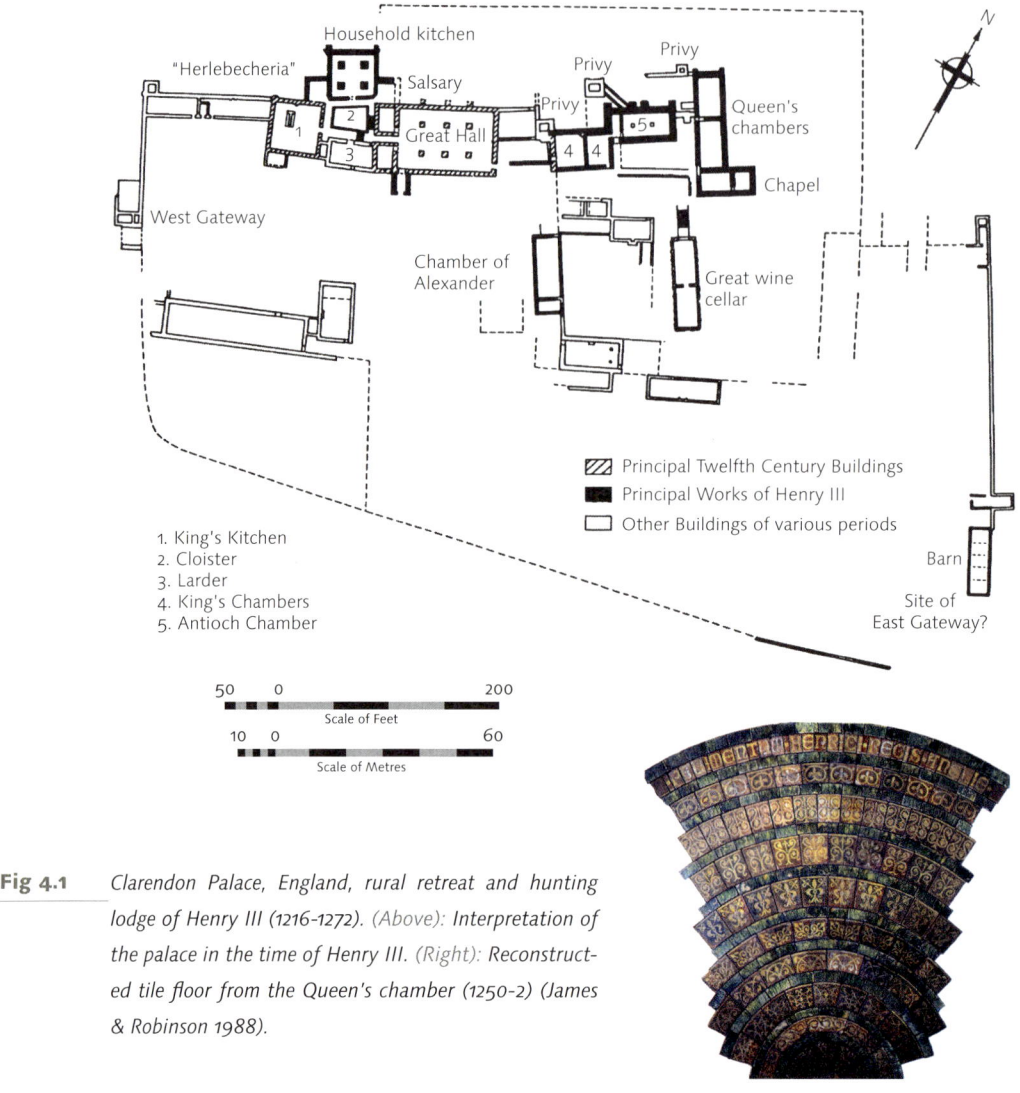

Household kitchen

"Herlebecheria"

Salsary

Privy

Privy

Privy

Queen's chambers

Great Hall

West Gateway

Chapel

Chamber of Alexander

Great wine cellar

Principal Twelfth Century Buildings

Principal Works of Henry III

Other Buildings of various periods

1. King's Kitchen
2. Cloister
3. Larder
4. King's Chambers
5. Antioch Chamber

Barn

Site of East Gateway?

50   0   200
        Scale of Feet
10   0   60
        Scale of Metres

Fig 4.1   *Clarendon Palace, England, rural retreat and hunting lodge of Henry III (1216-1272). (Above): Interpretation of the palace in the time of Henry III. (Right): Reconstructed tile floor from the Queen's chamber (1250-2) (James & Robinson 1988).*

itself as pre-eminent in the minds of Europe's élite, the Ottomans having already been eclipsed long before the Sack of Constantinople in 1204, an event that brought a final load of Byzantine treasures to the west.

A hall was where its owner dined in state – on a dais to raise him and his family above those at the lower end. Elaborate service was involved; even when, as often happened, a lord dined in the less formal surroundings of chambers, the food might still be processed through the great hall on its way to him. The great hall was also usually where business was conducted; the hall served as a law court. As a building, the hall was not necessarily very convenient for such purposes, particularly when several different cases were being heard at the same time, but a large space remained an essential element for most magnates in which to entertain and to receive their dependents. Practice varied

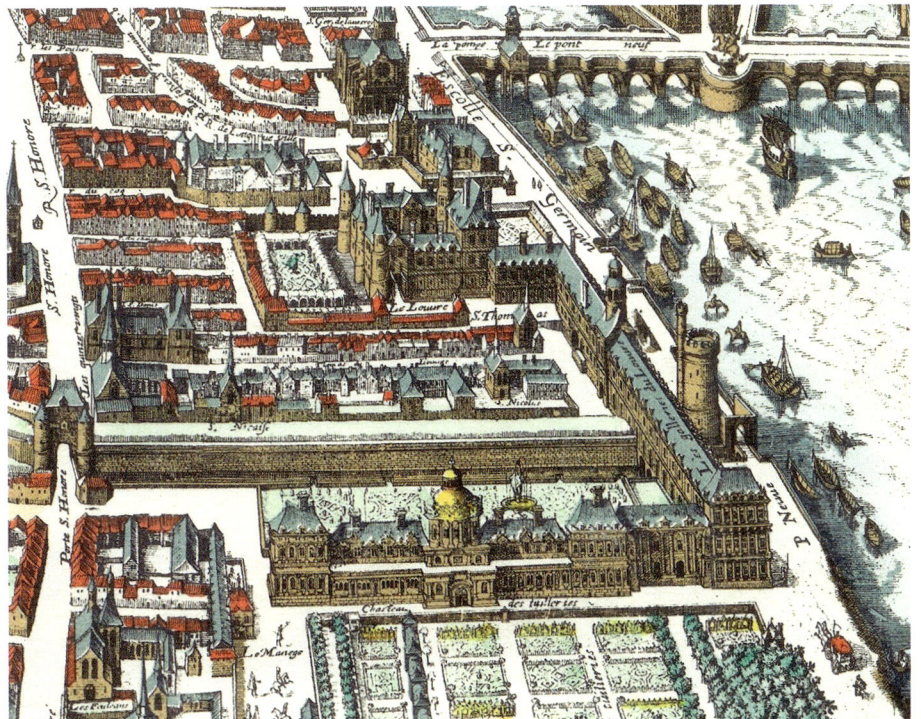

The medieval Tuileries Palace and the Great Gallery at the Louvre, as depicted by Merian in 1615 (Wikimedia Commons).

Fig 4.2

over whether it was at ground- or first-floor level, and in the latter case whether the undercroft space was used for kitchens and storage, or as a second hall, where inferiors were fed.

For all its grandeur, the *Palais de la Cité* was hemmed in; increasingly France's rulers preferred to stay at the Louvre, which had immediate access to the great forest of Vincennes (Fig 4.2). A previous impressive stone manor-house and some suburban sprawl were removed, and a riverside complex – access by water was often as important as access by land for grand houses – was enclosed and moated (Van Ossel 1998).

Similarly, further north, the counts of Brabant deliberately built for themselves the most imposing stone residence within their newly founded town of s'Hertogenbosch at the end of the twelfth century, but in the 1230s moved out, granting the *domus ducis* to Italian bankers (Janssen 2002). For the counts of the Low Countries, French and German kings were far enough away for royal vassalage not to be a major issue for most of the Middle Ages, though it was a deliberately symbolic act for the king of France to raze the palace of the counts of Flanders in 1553. In the south, the growing ambitions of the counts of Provence led them to extend their existing stronghold at Drôme with a great hall and chapel, effectively at the same time as they were drawn through marriage into the French and out of the Spanish ambit, which was to lead to their title's incorporation with that of the kings of France at the end of the fifteenth century, without a power struggle (De Meulemeester & Poisson 2002).

Status of place

By the time that the Provence title merged with that of the crown, the kings of France had shifted their court southwards to Amboise and other centres. A grand façade could be achieved at such places, leading into a series of courtyards, graded in importance according to the uses of the buildings – stables in the outer yard, then lodgings in ranges and towers for the grandest visitors, and finally for the owner's family, which might involve separate households and spaces for wives and sons. At Amboise, the local hunting was good. It was not infrequent for new sites to be used despite their not having long traditions of royal association. Dynasties in general no longer felt the need to associate themselves with origin myths and supposed ancestors when conquest by force was seen as providing sufficient rights. Inauguration by placing a foot into a rock imprint was ousted by unction with papally blessed oil; a sufficient vestige of antiquity hung around Scotland's Stone of Scone, a place where abbey and palace co-existed, for England's Edward I to symbolise his conquest of the Scots by removing it to put under the coronation chair in Westminster Abbey; but the Scottish kings themselves had already lost contact with most of the rest of their Pictish and Gaelic past. It was Perth, a few miles to the south on a navigable river, which provided them with a headquarters in the castle, although even that was dispensed with during the thirteenth century, the king staying in one of the town's religious institutions instead. Scone Abbey was the setting for some early meetings of the Scottish Parliament, but Perth came to be preferred, and Scone even ceased to host coronations. In England, a crowning at Westminster rather than Kingston became essential for validating the claims of competing families, although the French monarchs remained loyal to Reims, where a huge new thirteenth-century nave could accommodate an enormous audience for such events.

New tradition did not become strong enough to make Perth a permanent base for the parliament meetings, unlike England's Westminster, where Henry III's lavish patronage created a centre not only for coronations, but for royal burials and for the highest courts in the land, a centre that was to endure all the changes of dynasty that were to follow the thirteenth century (Fig 4.3). In the sixteenth century, Henry VIII developed Whitehall for executive purposes where his Privy Council met, leaving Westminster for the law courts and parliaments (Thurley 1999). Westminster Abbey was used for public events, but Henry III also sought to build a more private chapel to rival Sainte Chapelle (Binski 1999); other kings followed different trajectories, the Hungarian dynasty preferring to enhance what was already on the site at Prag (Boháčová *et al.* 1992, 86-7). Association with the Church varied: the presence of a cathedral alongside a royal house was not unusual, but kings and bishops did not always make good neighbours.

Processions were important modes of display, for a variety of ceremonies. Kings and great nobles expected to be received with due deference; mayors and corporations assembled outside town gates to greet them and to usher them inside, where they would be

The interior of Westminster Hall, London, founded by William Rufus in 1097, and developed by subse- **Fig 4.3** *quent kings of England. The hammerbeam roof was commissioned by Richard II in 1393 and completed 1401. Pictured in 2010, the hall now forms the public entrance to the Houses of Parliament (M. Carver).*

fêted in the hope of favour. Towns might have origins so ancient that they could claim mythical, often royal, founders, but even the oldest needed support, and many were either royal foundations, or had royal licences for their walls, urban privileges and markets. Kings knew too that, in general, towns paid fees, even if at times maintenance costs meant that these had to be temporarily reduced or rescinded. Magnates could not fail to observe the private wealth that merchants showed in their stone houses as well as in what towns spent publicly on their town halls, market halls, and walls. In northern Italy, rival patrician families built needle-like towers as high as cathedrals, which were forcibly lowered when their ambitions were brought down to earth. This was a factor of constrained ground space; most northern European cities had neither the wealth nor the same degree of constriction, though late medieval towers of several stories were certainly built.

Status in death

The English king Henry III was associating himself with a saintly predecessor, Edward the Confessor, by developing that king's foundation at Westminster. Burial at places with family associations remained important for many. For the Capetians, it was Saint Denis with its Merovingian ancestry. The Scottish kings associated themselves with the cult of their own family member St Margaret by their use of Dunfermline as a mausoleum, but just as the use of Scone for coronation was not regarded as an essential part of the acceptance of a new incumbent's claims to the throne, so burial with St Margaret fell into disuse in the fourteenth and fifteenth centuries (Oram 2008; Fawcett 2005).

Kings and queens expected to be buried inside churches, not in outside cemeteries like most of their secular subjects. The east end of the nave, and at the crossing, as close as possible to the high altar, were the preferred locations. The German emperors used Speyer cathedral, where the town's main street was axially aligned with the great west entrance, so that it became a processional route for a succession of dynasties from the Salians to the Hapsburgs (Meier 2002, 180-1). Prague was also replanned, creating a grand processional route across a towered bridge and up into the palace complex. Other magnates made a range of choices; even if they could not claim to have had a saint in the family, many had ancestors who had founded monasteries where family burial was appropriate. A few selected churches on their estates, adding chantry chapels that outgrew in proportion the buildings to which they were attached – but where no priest would dare to challenge the family's right to choose where and with what monument they should be remembered.

Military emphasis inevitably made for a gendered society, although some wives and widows were effective household controllers. Analysis of palace sites has shown that gender difference was incorporated into their design, and this gradually changed throughout the period: in the thirteenth century, the king fronted the political access while the queen was contained in more private space, more difficult of access. By the early sixteenth century, the layout had become more complex, with the king's and the queen's households operating with a certain independence (Richardson 2003b; here Fig 4.4). Some brides brought family connections that enhanced their husbands' status; complex heraldry identified those who claimed ancient rights. Again with Italy as an

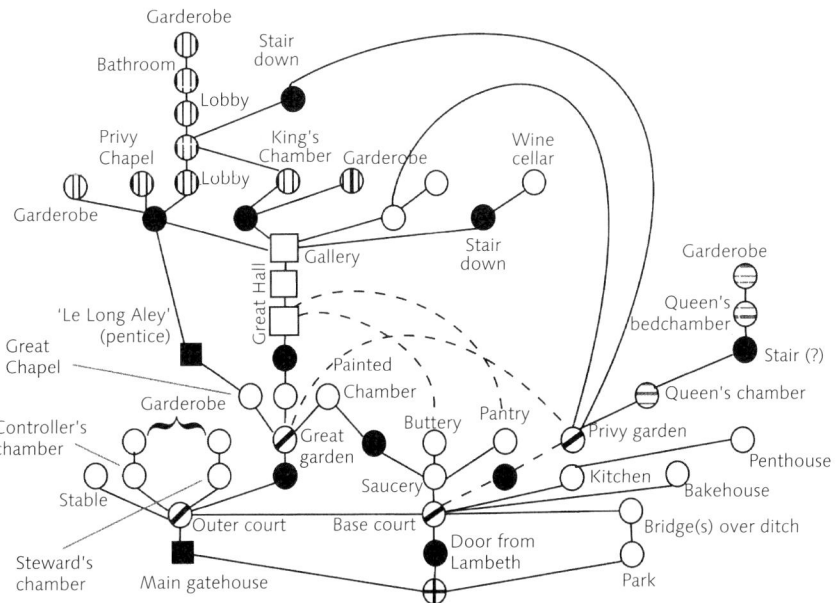

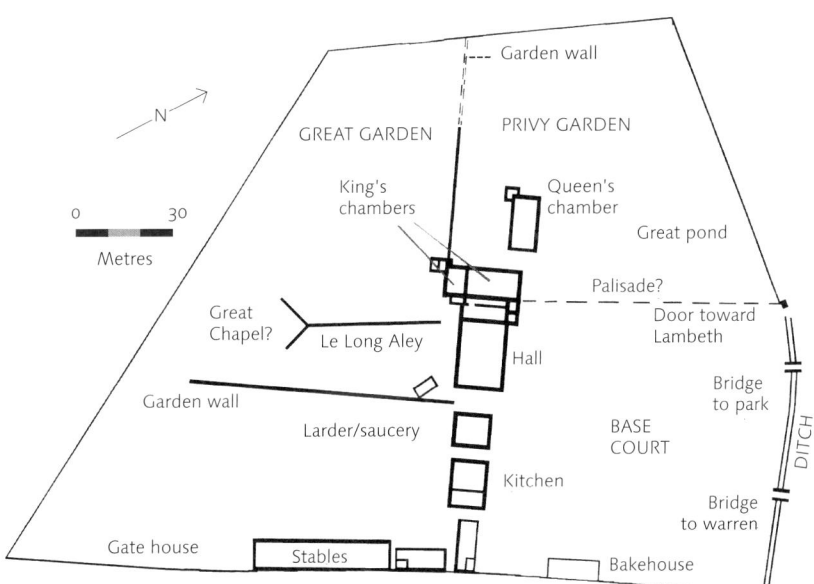

(above) An example of access analysis by Amanda Richardson, used to map ease of movement in Ken- **Fig 4.4**
nington Palace, England, during the 1380s. The rooms are marked by open circles, the passages by black
spots. The hatched circles distinguish the king's and the queen's apartments. A schematic plan of the
palace is shown below. (Richardson 2003b, fig 14).

exception, most countries increased the number of noble titles, creating extra tiers in the stratification of society, which sumptuary laws enhanced, setting out codes of what was appropriate for all ranks to wear and eat.

Conspicuous consumption

The association of the Louvre with the forest of Vincennes was a medieval common-place. Forests and parks were one of the most potent symbols of power – not only for secular society, of course, since prelates and abbots also hawked and hunted, and want-ed to dine on venison and wildfowl. Laws protecting game varied in detail, but were widely instituted (Ch 3, p 132). Houses increasingly had fenced parks attached directly to them, or indeed all around them, with windows or galleries placed to give views over parks and gardens, implying ownership as far as the eye could see. Although parks might be grazed by domestic stock, and even on occasions ploughed, access to them was exclusive, and the space that they took up was largely removed from normal exploita-tion. This applied with perhaps greater force to fish-ponds, as those had to occupy low-er ground which would otherwise have provided farmers with the best hay meadows, essential for keeping stock through the winter in most of western Europe. To the élite, however, it was more important to have a supply of freshwater fish such as pike, bream and carp for their own tables; swan and duck shared the water; peacocks were kept, as were hawks to provide game birds and wildfowl. Doves, raised usually in separate build-ings but also in nesting-boxes built into castle walls, were another delicacy and another form of lordly exploitation of tenants, who were not permitted to chase the birds away from their crops. Netted song-birds were also cooked. Faunal remains show the residues of the feasts at which these, and the flesh of young animals killed before they had bred, were principal components. Elaborate cooking methods and profligate use of imported spices further emphasized the distance between the exceptionally powerful and the rest of society (Woolgar 1999; Woolgar *et al.* 2006). Etiquette books set out the courtesies of service, though they may have been aimed at aspiring gentry, expressing ideals rather than showing what actually happened in noble households.

Wine was the expected drink at royal or noble tables, although it could also be bought in urban taverns. In England, to which it had to be imported at considerable expense, a barrel made a good gift, one reason why kings exercised purveyance rights and maintained their own cellars in Southampton, one of the principal entry points. Several royal palaces, and even some lesser royal houses, had below-ground cellars, though storage in the basement of a tower usually sufficed, and few magnate houses had other provision for it. A few examples of the gold, silver-gilt, and enamelled goblets in which it was served, at least on the greatest occasions to the host and greatest guests, have survived (Fig 4.5). Glass was rarely used, and wood (*treen*) let alone pottery, was considered too base for such a superior liquid, at least until the very end of the Mid-dle Ages. The plate had to be carefully stored and accounted for, requiring iron-bound chests and strong-rooms, often in towers with tiled floors which were fireproof, where the owner's charters and deeds could also be kept – a source of resentment and a target

Fig 4.5

Luxury silver gilt bowl or porringer on foot ring, engraved with the alphabet on lid and body (The Studley bowl, c. 1400). Possibly made for a noble child to eat from and learn the ABC at the same time (Victoria and Albert Museum; Alexander & Binski 1987, pl. 728).

for revolt by tenants. Designs, of plate, jewellery, architecture and tombs, tended to be conservative, and usually took their lead from Gothic France and the workshops of Paris, but Henry III looked to Rome for Westminster's internal fittings, and increasingly 'Renaissance' classical imagery and use of materials such as terracotta and maiolica tiles percolated into fifteenth-century western Europe from Italy (see Ch 8).

Access to luxuries and the ability to entertain were essential for anyone seeking to build up a network of retainers; 'feudal' ties of army service proved unreliable for foreign campaigns, and professional soldiers had to be paid. The nobility was still generally expected to fight alongside its rulers, gaining family honour and showing the right to bear arms, as well as the hope of winning financial reward through ransoms; a difference between England and much of the rest of Europe was created after the middle of the fifteenth century, as such opportunities disappeared alongside the development of more realistic royal ambition. Being successful in war, skill and courage in horsemanship and in wielding arms, and learning to take hard knocks and falls, were necessary. Hunting provided training, but jousts and tournaments gave the extra lure of prizes and of fame in competition with social equals, where flaunted wealth would be admired by the wider audience of spectators. Rulers who provided a round table or other ceremony associated with feasting and fighting could expect to add lustre to their own names.

Tailored clothes in the finest woollens and linens gave new awareness of the body's shape; dyes gave colour, but not always for brightness – some of the most expensive were deep, dark reds, purples and blues. Silk was even more costly, but above all, furs were noticed; fourteenth-century sumptuary laws in England at first tried to restrict them all to the highest ranks, then created grades by which ermine and *budge* (actually imported lambswool, but who knew that?) were for the highest, the richer knights could wear *minever* – but the less prosperous could only have fur facings, not whole robes. Even in 1532, sable was only for royalty, reflecting the lure of the darkest shades (see Ch 8, p 359). As for jewellery, sumptuary legislation in most Italian cities again had different intentions from elsewhere in Europe, as great expenditure could have led to the creation of a nobility, especially if head-gear such as coronals were permitted, as those could have seigneurial implications; elsewhere, even in Milan where a dukedom existed, the purpose was to preserve its privileges (Lightbown 1992, 79-89).

In the archaeological record, such organics as furs rarely survive. Expensive gold and silver plate has mostly been melted down – ironically, survivals of metal-mounted co-coa-nut and nautilus shells, ostrich eggs and burr maple cups survive as they were more valuable in the late Middle Ages than they were to be later. Ostrich eggs in particular were exotica, as were the strange creatures acquired by a few western rulers for their zoos; animal qualities of fearlessness and fighting skill led some kings to associate them-selves with lions and leopards, which became heraldic devices (see above, p 116 and Ch 8, p 358). Heraldry is displayed on small metal harness pendants, on buildings, and on tombs and effigies; some badges associated with particular families have also been found, such as the gold and enamel Dunstable swan in England, a Lancastrian symbol. Base-metal badges for family retainers are more commonly found. Chains showing devices in their links and on pendants suspended from them became statements of family allegiance, and collars expressed office, in the fourteenth century; again, a few have survived in treasuries.

Lavishly illustrated books have had a better survival rate, most notably the *Très Riches Heures* painted for the zoo-owning Duc de Berry, lord of most of the south of France at the end of the fourteenth century, which shows not only his fantasy castle at Mehun-sur-Yèvres, but also the orderly world of people working in his fields to sustain him in his great wealth (Fig 3.1). The Duc was a famous collector of treasures, especially jewels (Camille 2001). Such unabashed acquisition and delight in ownership is seen in others: King Richard II 'secretly' visited his treasury in London's Tower; Henry III's frustration at not being able to buy a cameo from a German merchant rings out from the austere pages of royal accounting records.

Objects of display were not just expressions of status, but a reassurance of their owners' ability to maintain their social position. Sales were rarely necessary, and it was even rare for a merchant's child to be married into an aristocratic creditor's family; in any case some of the wealthiest lenders were Jews, who as non-Christians were unable to join any Christian kin network. Their precarious position meant that Jews' houses and cemeteries were often placed where a royal or lordly power-base protected them – until they became superfluous and persecuted. For Christians, however, the difference for most purposes between aristocrat and merchant was that the former acted within a military theatre, whether real warfare or regulated tournament, for which the base-born were not trained. The bearing of arms on horseback was still the symbol of knighthood, even as more lethal projectiles made cavalry charges with lances and swords less effec-tive; gun-powder was not handled by medieval gentlemen.

The symbolic character of objects at every social level is discussed in the next chapter, and the effects of war and the knightly ethos on residential buildings are further ex-plored in Chapter 6.

BOX 4.1   HUNGARIAN TILED STOVES

Northern houses require heating, achieved by burning logs or peat in open hearths and ovens and occasionally by underfloor systems using hot stones (AME 1, 175). In the south, sub-floor and hot flue systems were used to make heated bath-houses in the Roman tradition. The tiled stove represents a late medieval innovation of great significance for northerners, providing a high level of heat by means of a safe device for retaining and diffusing warmth. The oven was clad in decorated tiles that in turn provided a medium for the exchange and distribution of culture (Fig 1). Here we briefly consider the achievement of Hungarian designers (Sabján 2007; for production and trade in northern Europe, see Ch 9, p 340).

Fig 1

The late medieval tiled stove. An example dating from the end of the 14th century from a house in Cressier, Switzerland, reassembled in the Laténium Museum, Neuchâtel. The spectator is age 6 (M. Carver).

Tiled stoves began to spread in the Hungary of the Anjou-period (1301-1386). By the late-fourteenth century all types of tiles can be found among the remnants of Hungarian stoves. Tiles with closed front and relief-decoration or with barrel-back and jagged-pierced front became popular. The stoves built from these tiles are rich Gothic constructions, designed and decorated under the influence of architecture (Fig 2). Their lower part was built from flat tiles with patterns in relief. At the top, triangular tiles, decorated with small towers at the tips formed a gable. Behind them, a pointed dome rises with a ceramic pinnacle at the top.

In the Sigismund-period (1387-1437) stoves were made to royal and aristocratic order in great variety: virtually all sizes and decorations can be found this time, using tiles varying greatly in size. The influence of architecture can be seen in tracery, and heraldic devices provide the subject of images. After 1408, the arms of Sigismund were featured, encircled by the badges of the 'dragon order'. Tiles of many different colours are employed.

The stoves of the Matthias-period (1457-1490) dazzle with delicate sculptural work. The stove with the knight-figure, constructed in several varieties, originates from the best-known workshop of the age, and had a great impact on the formation and development of Hungarian stove-building. The front of the older type was made with delicate tracery and smaller sculptures; the back is a semi-cylindrical niche. The first examples of these stoves were made in the pre-fifteenth century, later pieces date from the end of the Matthias-period. The tile mantelpiece, differentiated by its brown glaze, appears first on late Gothic refined stoves of the Matthias-period. It is characterised by corner pieces decorated with coats of arms and gables with finials, and huge tiles decorated with blind tracery.

The use of stoves became widespread in the second half of the fifteenth century. Aristocratic mansions, priests' houses, guestrooms of monasteries, rural castles and even country peasant dwellings were heated by stoves. In the sixteenth century, most of the ceramics now had a curved pot-like shape and were made on a potter's wheel. All were unglazed, although sometimes decorated with red or white colour (Fig 3). These stoves followed aristocratic prototypes; their construction could include between 6 and 10 types of tiles. The production of new types in the centre of Hungary was stopped by the Turkish occupation, but tradition lived on in the Uplands and Transylvania.

The late Tibor Sabján

Fig 2

Reconstruction of a late 14th-century stove from the Anjou-period in the castle of Diósgyőr (after Boldizsár et al. 2007).

Fig 3

Stove of unglazed tiles from the 16th century or earlier in an outbuilding of the mansion of Baj (after Sabján 2007).

History of research

Archaeologists have long been interested in the study of houses as the focus of medieval domestic life. In the nineteenth and early twentieth centuries, English architectural historians concerned themselves primarily with studies of elite domestic buildings such as castles, palaces and manor houses (Turner and Parker 1851, 1853, 1859; Gerrard 2003). Gradually, however, the study of English 'house history' more generally attracted the attention of pioneering scholars such as Addy (1898) and Innocent (1916) and was exemplified in the regional study of Monmouthshire houses by Fox and Raglan (1951). Early attempts to develop a systematic understanding of the medieval house were aided by the work of both the *Victoria County History*, with its parish-by-parish surveys, and the regional and town-based inventories of the Royal Commission on Historic Monuments. Interest in this vernacular housing – the term essentially refers to houses of indigenous type serving the population at large – was further reflected in the foundation of the Vernacular Architecture Society in 1952 and the Society for Medieval Archaeology in 1956-7. The study of houses also became an important aspect of rural settlement studies, for example at Wharram Percy by Maurice Beresford (1954), and the analysis of towns, such as W.A. Pantin (1962-3; Gerrard 2003: 95-99). These studies focused on the construction traditions apparent in the wall frames and roof trusses of buildings, or in the geology of stone or use of early brickwork. Such patterns were linked with established regional and agricultural 'zones' (Clifton Taylor 1965; Smith 1965 and see synthesis in Le Patourel 1991). They also focused on the plan form of buildings, stripping away later accretions to reveal simplified or schematic plan forms, to which labels such as 'hall', 'services', 'solar', 'chamber' or 'parlour' were variously applied.

Many early studies were concerned to establish the basic typologies of medieval housing and those of Faulkner (1958), Wood (1965) and Mercer (1975) had an enduring influence on the study of high status buildings, whilst those established by Eden in the 1968 Cambridgeshire RCHM(E) volume became the basis for subsequent lower status housing typologies (RCHM(E) 1968; Longcroft 2002). Since then, an important group of regional studies has been published, such as that for Hampshire (Roberts 2003), North Avon and South Gloucestershire (Hall 1983), Hertfordshire (Smith 1992) Lancashire (RCHM(E) 1985), Kent (Pearson 1994), Shropshire (Moran 2003), Suffolk (Johnson 1993a), North Yorkshire (Harrison and Hutton 1984) and West Yorkshire (Giles 1986). These have been greatly enhanced by the systematic use of dendrochronological dating, and useful syntheses of this dating evidence have recently been published (Pearson 1997, 2001; see also Ch 1, 00). Numerous local studies, published by vernacular architecture groups and scholars, have added important colour and detail to the picture (Pattison *et al.* 1992, 1999).

Some of these studies have been quite traditional in nature. However, increasingly, vernacular architecture has adopted a social and cultural perspective. The development of houses has been linked to changes in the specific economic circumstances and social status of groups of wealthy peasants or yeomen (Pearson 1994; Dyer 1997c; Roberts 2003). The organisation and cultural meaning of space within houses, access routes around them, and relationships within and between rooms, has also received much attention (Alcock and Currie 1989; Barley 1991; Johnson 1993b; Martin 2003; Gardiner 2000, 2008). The ways in which vernacular houses were transformed during the early modern period, has also been the focus of much debate (Hoskins 1953; Machin 1977a, 1977b; Alcock 1983; Johnson 1993b). Many of these studies have been enhanced by a critical awareness of the intellectual discourses and disciplinary methods through which buildings have been studied, in the past and present (Johnson 1994, 1997; Dyer 1997c; Grenville 1997; Mercer 1997; Currie 2004;). The drive towards interdisciplinary study has also encouraged medieval archaeologists and historians to think more critically about the material context of the household and the archaeology of domesticity (Beattie, Maslakovic and Rees Jones 2003; Kowaleski and Goldberg 2008; see also Box 1.2).

High status medieval houses

The study of high status medieval houses has always been closely linked to other forms of elite domestic architecture, particularly castles and palaces (see above for palaces, and Ch 6 for castles and moated houses). Early attempts to understand the different forms of post-Conquest manor houses suggested the existence of two very different structural forms (Wood 1950, 1965; Faulkner 1958). The earliest form of surviving medieval domestic building dated to the twelfth and thirteenth centuries is the stone-built, two storeyed 'first-floor hall', with a high status first-floor or 'upper hall' located over a vaulted, ground floor undercroft. One of the most frequently cited examples of the type is Boothby Pagnall (Lincs) and importantly, the type was also found in urban locations, such as the late twelfth century 'Norman' house in Lincoln (Faulkner 1966) (Fig 4.6). Access within the building was usually provided by an external stair to first floor level, although the undercroft was also accessed internally by a newel stair from the hall. The second type of early domestic building was the ground floor aisled/non-aisled or 'end hall', where the hall was attached to other rooms used for services or accommodation, such as the Bishop's Palace at Hereford (Blair 1987).

Traditionally, debate has centred on questions concerning the origins of these types, whether in Norman France or England, and whether the two types were contemporary, or if aisled halls were a slightly later development. However, more recently the debate has been advanced by Blair's (1993) suggestion that many so-called 'first floor halls' may in fact be detached 'chamber blocks', once associated with (now lost) free-standing open halls. Blair's argument drew carefully on linguistic, literary and historical evidence, but although it sparked lively debate during the 1990s, the archaeological evidence to support Blair's hypothesis has yet to emerge consistently. Whatever the conclusion, it is clear that the 'first-floor hall' did exist, in buildings such as castles, and endured as a late medieval type in public buildings (see Ch 9 below, on guildhalls). But the difficulty in proving whether a building was indeed a hall or chamber may itself be telling. The ambiguity of the archaeological evidence may, as Quiney (1999) has sug-

The stone house at 47, Steep Hill, Lincoln, dating between 1170 and 1190 and known as the Norman **Fig 4.6**
house (formerly 'Aaron's House'). Not to be confused with 'The Jew's House' a similar building on the
same street at no 42.

gested, indicate that such buildings were far more flexible, multi-functioning spaces that we have previously assumed.

The evolution of high status houses in the late medieval period has often been presented as one of gradual accretion, through which a characteristic 'tripartite' layout developed. The tripartite plan consisted of a central open hall, with a 'low' end containing services (usually a buttery and pantry, with detached kitchens elsewhere) and a 'high' end leading to high status chambers or solar wings (Fig 4.7). Within this there was enormous variety, as has been revealed by the regional surveys cited above and the important gazetteers of Emery (1996, 2000, 2006). The late twelfth century appears to have been a pivotal moment in the coalescing of the tripartite plan (Grenville 1997: 93-95; Gardiner 2000, 2008).

Gardiner's work raises important questions about the social functions of the open hall throughout the medieval period. It has long been acknowledged that the tripartite plan had symbolic meaning as well as functional advantages in late medieval society. The spatial hierarchies apparent in its 'high' and 'low' ends could – and were – used to reinforce and reproduce feudal and patriarchal power over the family and the wider household (Johnson 1993a; Grenville 1997: 89). But Gardiner (2008: 61) suggests that the increasing formalisation of such arrangements must be viewed in the context of the

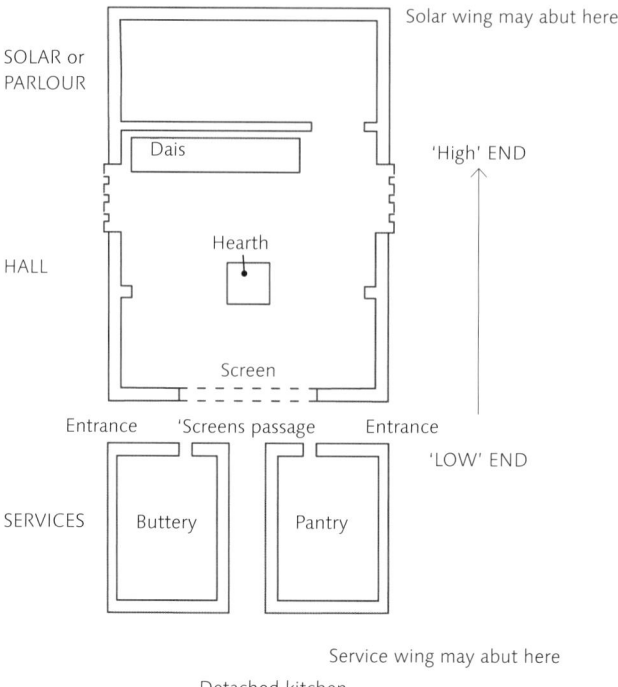

Solar wing may abut here

SOLAR or
PARLOUR

Dais

'High' END

Hearth

HALL

Screen

Entrance   'Screens passage   Entrance

'LOW' END

SERVICES   Buttery   Pantry

Service wing may abut here

Detached kitchen

Fig 4.7   *The late medieval tripartite plan, showing the hall, solar and services, separated from the hall by the screens passage (after Grenville 1997).*

codes of behaviour prescribed in the contemporary courtesy books and the increasing formalisation of rituals of domestic ceremony in elite households. At the other end of the chronological scale, Phillips (2005) has demonstrated how late medieval household ordinances codified particular forms of ritual behaviour which evoked powerful para-liturgical symbolisms in the treatment of the person of the late medieval lord.

Some scholars have argued that the importance of the open hall in elite houses was waning by the end of the Middle Ages, as the desire for 'privacy' encouraged lords to withdraw from the hall and use rooms such as chambers and solars for the hitherto public rituals such as eating (Girouard 1979; Thompson 1995). Grenville (1997: 108-9) has challenged this hypothesis. The evidence of the size and investment in buildings such as the courtyard arrangement at Gainsborough Old Hall (Lincs) suggests not only that the open hall endured throughout the late medieval period, but actually got larger during the fifteenth centuries. Understanding how – and why – the elite held onto the tripartite arrangement alongside the use of subsidiary buildings such as private accommodation ranges, parlours and lodgings, is an important question for future research. It might be suggested, for example, that late medieval lords were desperately holding onto the symbols of feudal power in a period of economic and political uncertainty and rapid social change.

Lower status 'peasant' houses

The study and interpretation of lower status English medieval housing must be understood in the context of the work of the RCHM(E) and the Vernacular Architecture Group mentioned above. But it was also influenced by the development of landscape and local history, particularly the work of the Department of Local History at Leicester University and scholars such as Beresford (1971) and Hoskins (1953, 1967), and the discovery and excavation of 'deserted medieval villages' such as Wharram Percy (N Yorks), Hangleton (Sussex), Upton (Gloucs.), Gomeldon (Wilts), West Whelpington (Northumberland), Dartmoor (Devon), Grenstein (Norfolk) during the 1950s-1980s (Astill 1988b; Austin 1990; Le Patourel 1991). These studies revealed important information not just about houses, but also their associated landscapes of tofts and crofts, and the subsidiary buildings such as barns, stables, kilns and bakehouses, found on rural sites (see Ch 3, p 97). Such studies were important in demonstrating that houses could contribute to academic debates in rural history, particularly Beresford's (1954) hypotheses about desertion. From these studies, a picture emerged of peasant houses as rather flimsy and impermanent structures, which had to be rebuilt every 20-30 years. It led Mercer (1975: 8) to conclude that 'rural vernacular houses prior to the late middle ages appear from the evidence of excavation, to have been of uniformly poor quality throughout the whole of England'.

However, during the 1980s, several important challenges to this hypothesis emerged, and are summarised in detail by Grenville (1997: 123-128). Initial challenges came from historians such as Dyer (1986), highlighting a range of documentary evidence to suggest a reasonably high standard of living amongst the peasantry in the post-Black Death period. Evidence from the study of surviving buildings in North Yorkshire (Harrison and Hutton 1984) and sites deserted only in the eighteenth century, such as West Whelpington (Northumberland) encouraged the re-examination of the excavated evidence to suggest that such buildings were originally cruck-framed – a much more permanent form of construction than previously thought (Wrathmell 1989). Interdisciplinary research by Dyer (1986), provided documentary evidence for peasants not only using crucks but also employing professional carpenters. From this work emerged the idea of medieval peasant buildings as 'semi-permanent', requiring little initial financial outlay but regular maintenance over time (Fig 4.8).

Although the earliest surviving examples of lower status housing in England date to the mid-fourteenth century, the majority of standing examples date to the end of the fourteenth or fifteenth century. The systematic application of dendrochronological dating to vernacular houses means that it is now possible to identify particular patterns in the construction dates of surviving houses. It is important to remember that this data may tell us as much about patterns of survival as construction, and about the ability of certain types of building to be adapted or modernised in subsequent centuries (Currie 1988). Nevertheless, the evidence suggests that there were periods of large-scale investment in the construction of rural houses in the late fourteenth and early fifteenth centuries. It does not seem unreasonable to suggest that such investment represents the

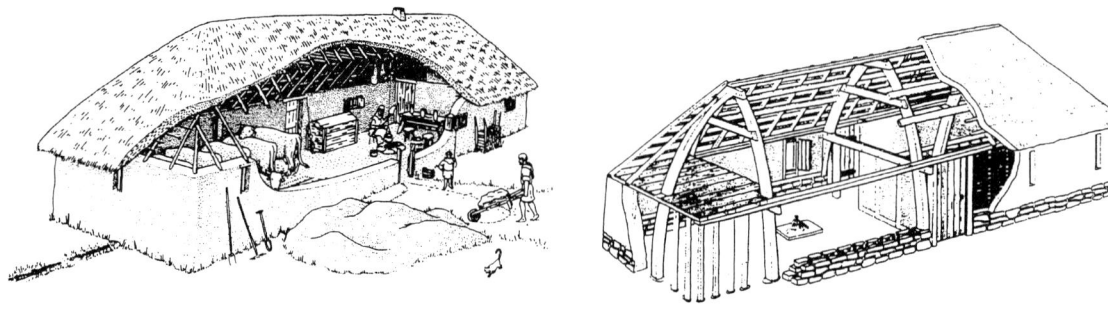

Fig 4.8 *Peasant Houses. Cob wall (left) and cruck with studding (right) (Grenville 1997).*

growing confidence and economic wealth of the upper levels of the peasantry – what we might think of as a proto-'middling sort'.

What of the structure and form of lower status medieval housing? Over the past fifty years, landscape history has shed light on the underlying frameworks of topography, geology, settlement patterns and agricultural specialisms of late medieval England (Miller 1991). Vernacular architecture studies, too, have appeared to reveal clear regional patterns in the distribution of construction traditions, such as crucks, or the timber-framing of wall and cross frames (Smith 1965; Harris 1978) and cruck construction (Alcock 1981). However, although as Roberts and Wrathmell (2000: 27) note, it might be expected that such provincial frameworks would have impacted on the functional arrangement and plans of medieval houses, in reality they, like their high status counterparts, show 'a remarkable consensus about the organization of social space' (Gardiner 2000: 179; Le Patourel 1981).

A basic typology of lower status medieval houses emerged from early regional studies such as those of Fox and Raglan (1951) and the RCHM(E) (1968; Longcroft 2002). Early scholars may have presumed that the adoption of the open hall was a result of the diffusion of ideas from elite housing, or the deliberate emulation of these forms by the late medieval peasantry. However, Gardiner's (2000) important article raises questions about this hypothesis, demonstrating the early origins and presence of the form, *across* the social scale.

The longhouse has traditionally been considered a distinctive type of lower status peasant house, associated particularly with areas of marginal, pastoral farming. Its distinctive function was to provide accommodation for both people and their animals, usually presumed to have been cattle, oxen or horses. Much debate has surrounded its identification through distinctive features such as the presence of a cross passage indicated by opposed doorways; the separation of a 'low' end containing a byre or *shippon* (cattle shed), evidenced by a drain and/or tethering device; a central hearth and cooking pits in the body of the house; and separate spaces beyond this for sleeping, often provided in an annexe (Alcock and Smith 1972; Mercer 1972; Meirion-Jones

1973; Austin 1985: 76; Harrison 1991; Grenville 1997: 134-141). The 'story' of long-house development was traditionally presented as that of conversion and rebuilding into 'farms', as animals were gradually removed from the house and accommodated in separate buildings, freeing up the low end for conversion and adaptation to domestic use (Beresford and Hurst 1971). This in turn has provoked debate about the equivocal nature of the evidence, of rebuilding and of the original functions of such buildings. These problems are raised in Meeson's (2001) study of Hill Top, Longdon (Staffs). Previously interpreted as a rare example of a surviving hall-house within the region, a disastrous fire and subsequent stratigraphic analysis revealed important evidence to suggest that the 'low end' had previously been used as a form of byre and platform for the (seasonal) storage of agricultural produce. Indeed, Harrison and Hutton's (1991) study of inventories from longhouses in the Vale of York suggests not only that longhouses could be associated with areas of arable, as well as pastoral farming, but also that the presence and therefore the 'visibility' of animals and/or crops in such buildings was a seasonal phenomenon.

Our insistence in drawing a distinction between the longhouse and other medieval house forms may tell us much more about modern cultural assumptions about living with animals than it does about medieval practice. Green (2007) has recently demonstrated how the idea of the 'vernacular' emerged from particular discourses of the early modern period. More recently, Gardiner (2000:168) has therefore suggested that the longhouse should simply be seen as a regional adaptation or variation of the tripartite plan.

Traditionally, regional surveys of lower status housing have sought to understand the number and distribution of variants of the open hall in particular areas. These include the use of cruck or box-framing, associated roof types and other features such as jettying, the presence or absence of aisled and non-aisled halls, and the gradual accretion of storeyed wings, in line with or at right angles to the hall, containing services and/or more private accommodation. Some of the most interesting patterns to emerge from these studies shed light, not on regional, but rather on social differences in the choice of house type. In Kent, for example, Pearson (1994: 134-5) has shown how the lower levels of the gentry preferred halls with wings set at right angles, whereas the upper levels of the peasantry often occupied two-storeyed buildings with their ends in line with the hall, such as Wealdens, jettied and unjettied houses (Fig 4.9). In late fifteenth century Hampshire, Roberts (1995) has shown how new demesne lessees did not simply adapt or rebuild previous houses on manorial sites, but often relegated these to service functions, preferring to build new fully-floored houses with internal chimney stacks and chambers for public use.

These variations of the open hall type remind us that our focus on the universality of the open hall and tripartite plan can cause us to overlook important evidence of the ways in which late medieval houses were constantly adapted and altered throughout the fifteenth and early sixteenth centuries. Many buildings provide evidence of what is often termed 'piecemeal' rebuilding. In Sussex, the Rape of Hastings survey revealed that 40% of houses had experienced partial or piecemeal rebuilding from the late fifteenth century onwards (Martin and Martin 1987, 1999; Martin 2000). More detailed studies

Fig 4.9   *Chart Hall Farmhouse, Chart Sutton (Kent). An early Wealden house (1379/80) (©RCHME).*

of individual buildings within the area show how such rebuilding was often designed to meet the changing needs of the late medieval household, by creating 'suites' of rooms, which in turn required new access arrangements (Martin 2003). In Devon, the study of a series of peasant houses revealed important evidence for their 'modernisation', and for the partial flooring of open halls through the use of internal jetties which extended the space of first floor chambers, possibly for semi-industrial activities such as spinning and weaving (Alcock and Laithwaite 1973). The tripartite plan itself could also be adapted for storage or industrial use, as in the aisled houses of West Yorkshire, where the aisles of the halls then appear to have been used as services (RCHME 1984).

One of the problems with making sense of these processes of adaptation and altera-tion is the tendency to interpret them as evidence for an inevitable process of transition from the medieval to the early modern house type. Early discussions of this transfor-mation of medieval houses as part of a process known as the 'great rebuilding' were outlined by Hoskins (1953; see subsequent debate in Machin 1977a; Alcock 1983; Johnson 1993). The typological model of this shift from 'medieval' to 'early modern' house type was laid out by the RCHM(E) (1968) and discussed in syntheses such as Mercer (1975: 23-33). Most recently, it has found its way into the theoretically-informed account of the transformation of medieval housing through a process of 'closure' associated with large-scale social, economic and ideological shifts of capitalism, Renaissance and Reformation, which occurred during the sixteenth and seventeenth centuries (Johnson 1993a).

The retention and/or abandonment of the open hall to facilitate fully-floored, multiple-storeyed accommodation throughout the house, and the introduction of new forms of heating is often seen as one of the defining characteristics of this shift, particularly when associated with the transformation of traditional access routes into the house through the creation of the lobby entry (Grenville 1997: 153-156). The evidence emerging from dendrochronologically-dated buildings in Kent and Hampshire is particularly important here. It indicates both that although the open hall persisted in both areas well into the sixteenth century, some halls had begun to be floored over as early as the 1470s, and that new fully-floored buildings were also being built at this early date. Clearly, in many regions from the late fifteenth century onwards, inhabitants and craftsmen were able to choose from a wide range of options, depending on the changing needs of their households. Indeed, Dymond's (1998) study of five building contracts from Suffolk, dating to the early 1460s, demonstrates that contemporaries deliberately identified 'advanced' features such as parlours, continuous jetties and oriel windows, in neighbouring properties, that they wished to emulate in the design of new houses.

Urban housing

The earliest surviving examples of medieval townhouses are the stone-built, two-storeyed, 'first floor halls', such as the Jew's House, Lincoln (Faulkner 1966). At first glance, these would seem to reinforce the idea of a universal adoption of the tripartite plan. However, as yet unpublished work by Harris (1994) has argued that such buildings must be understood on their own terms, operating commercially on two storeys. Faulkner's (1966) study of medieval undercrofts in Southampton and Winchelsea, and in-depth studies such as those of the rows of Chester (Brown et al 1999) provide further evidence for this. Undercrofts could be let separately from the houses above them as warehouses, shops or taverns, and contain impressive architectural features to suggest they were spaces of display as well as function. It might be suggested that the urban first floor hall needs to be reinterpreted in the light of Blair's 'chamber block' hypothesis. However, what seems more likely is that these early forms of urban house reveal evidence both of a commercially distinctive function, and the ability of urban (as well as rural) buildings to host spaces with multiple functions (Quiney 2003).

The houses of the urban elite have received far less attention than their rural counterparts. In part, this reflects problems of survival. Many of the largest houses in London and other provincial cities were associated with episcopal and monastic dignitaries, and were confiscated or sold during the Reformation. The changing fortunes of England's aristocracy also impacted on the maintenance of expensive urban mansions and palaces. Schofield (1994) and Quiney (2003: 187-216) have shed important light on these buildings. As London and Westminster in particular became established as the permanent seat of government, both spiritual and secular lords sought to establish urban bases in the capital. By the end of the Middle Ages, the archbishops of York and Canterbury, and all bishoprics except St. Asaphs, as well as twenty-two abbots and six priors, had established such residences in the city, such as Winchester House, built on the Southwark bank of the Thames. These complexes might be accessed through gatehouses and were arranged around courtyards. They contained great halls, often raised over undercrofts, accommodation and service ranges and subsidiary buildings such as kitchens and chapels. Their close relationship to rural building forms was also emphasised through the addition of towers, such as that at Sir John de Pulteney's inn, which was granted a licence to crenellate in 1343 (Quiney 2003: 194-6).

At present, there has been little comparative analysis of the rural and urban houses of individual aristocratic patrons, which might shed light on differences between both urban and rural 'ways of living' and respective household structures (for rural palaces see above). Nevertheless, the apparent retention of 'traditional' building forms in these elite residences may tell us something important about the conservative ways of living amongst the spiritual and the secular elite. However, another important and as yet under-studied aspect of these buildings was the way in which these buildings were subsequently converted into inns for pilgrims and travellers; a type of building that has received comparatively little attention from archaeologists, but warrants further study (Quiney 2003: 201-212).

The majority of surviving middle-lower status urban houses in England date to the later medieval period. However, from an analysis of the dendrochronological data it is possible to identify patterns in their investment and construction. Pearson (1997, 2001) notes the survival of a significant group from the period c. 1275-1375, a slowing down during the late fourteenth century, a further increase during the early fifteenth century and subsequent decline in the later fifteenth century (but see Roberts 2003: 193 for some regional differences within this pattern). The sheer diversity of late medieval urban communities has meant that traditionally, it has seemed difficult to differentiate the houses of the lower gentry from those of the upper levels of the merchant classes. However, recent research has begun to reveal important information about the distinctiveness of late medieval urban English houses.

Traditionally, the open hall yet again formed the focus for the typological analysis of urban houses. The key scholar in this field, Pantin (1962-3), started from the presumption that medieval urban houses were 'rus in urbe': urban adaptations of the tripartite form, developed first in the countryside and then adapted to the constraints of the urban burgage plot. The simplest adaptation of the rural model was the parallel plan, where the hall was placed parallel to the street, with services and solar in a linear form. Variations of this plan included the creation of a row of often separately-let storeyed shop-and-chamber units in front of the hall, or a full courtyard arrangement, as at Tackley's Inn, Oxford (Fig 4.10). The alternative type was the right-angled plan, where the house was set with its gable at right angles to the street, facilitating the creation of an individual shop with undercroft below and chambers above it, as at 58 French Street, Southampton (Fig 4.11). Pantin's typology has proved enduringly successful, partly because it seemed to fit the evidence of the buildings themselves, but also because it supported the idea of a common use of the tripartite form across all medieval houses. Indeed, Grenville (2008: 117-119) has argued that its use was an important mechanism

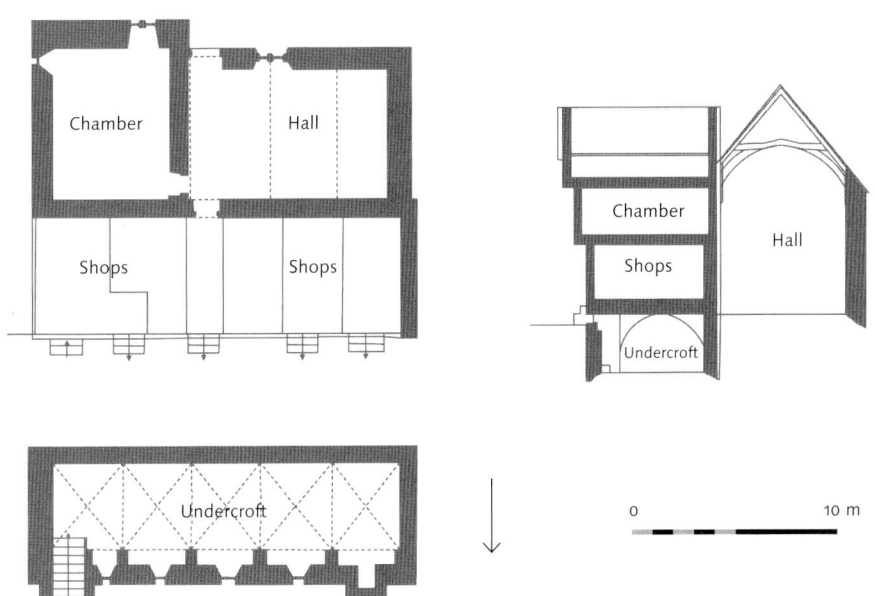

Town house parallel to the street: Tackley's Inn, Oxford, plan and elevation, showing a row of separately- **Fig 4.10**
let shops in front of the hall (after Grenville 1997; Faulkner 1966 and Harris 1994).

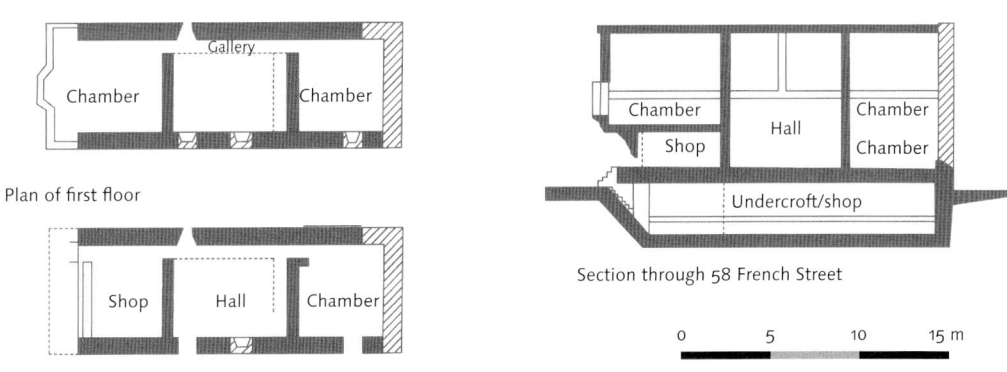

Town house gable-end-on to the street: 58 French Street, Southampton, showing the central hall with **Fig 4.11**
shop in front, chambers above and undercroft below (after Grenville 1997 and Faulkner 1966).

through which immigrants into towns, particularly young men and women entering service in urban households, gained a form of security and learned how to behave, in the otherwise unfamiliar surroundings of the city.

The power of Pantin's thesis has meant that alternative typologies of urban houses, such as those of Schofield, which sought to categorise buildings according to their size and scale, have largely been overlooked (Schofield 2003: 89). However, Pearson (2005, 2009) has now provided a fundamental challenge both to Pantin's typologies and to the assumptions on which they are based. Pearson criticises Pantin's relatively small and selective sample of forty houses and argues for much greater diversity in the size and scale of medieval houses. But most importantly, she suggests (like Harris) that urban houses were distinct from their rural counterparts because of their commercial functions. She argues that the hall was far less significant in such contexts. Many urban houses at the lower end of the scale, such as Lady Row, York cannot be said to have had halls at all, whilst others such as the Wealden terraces of Spon Street, Coventry, had halls of only a bay, or one-and-a-half bays. In many urban buildings, commercial and storage space, in undercrofts, shops, chambers and outbuildings, seems to have been much more important. Moreover, far from being '*rus in urbe*', Pearson suggests that the constraints and opportunities of towns may have led to different priorities, such as the provision of commercial and storage space at ground floor level, or the development and prominent display of multi-storey timber-framing. Indeed, Pearson suggests that rural buildings may subsequently have sought to emulate their urban counterparts through the adoption of features such as multiple storeys within the rural context.

Pearson's work raises broader questions about the identification of different kinds of spaces in all types of lower status medieval housing. In towns, it is clear that some halls, such as Dragon Hall in Norwich or Hampton court, King's Lynn (Norfolk) were always more than domestic spaces. Halls could be used to store and display goods, and to negotiate commercial transactions as well as accommodating the domestic life of families and households. But halls could also be reduced in size, to provide more space for shops. Shops often adopted characteristic pairs of windows with internal rebates for shutters, under which there were stalls or sills, and a door to one side (Stenning 1985; Clark 2000; Quiney 2003). In contrast, workshops have always been much more difficult to identify (Grenville 1997: 172, 2004). Such structures are often assumed to have been located to the rear of properties, and therefore to be particularly vulnerable to subsequent alteration. However, the ephemeral nature of their fixtures and fittings has meant that it is often impossible to identify clear archaeological evidence for their location. This apparent absence of evidence may be more significant than we realise. Evidence from several studies, and from surviving documentary sources such as inventories suggest that the divisions between shops and workshops may not have been so clear cut (Alston 2004a). Indeed, given that the household was often heavily involved in production and retail, it seems likely that halls, chambers and solars were used as alternative working, as well as domestic spaces.

The material household

The sections above have sought to synthesise recent research on the archaeology of medieval rural and urban houses. Such studies tend to focus on the plan form and structural framework of such buildings. Whilst they reveal a certain amount about the appearance, location and access of spaces within houses, they tell us far less about the materiality of houses: their decoration, furnishings, fittings and fixtures and the ways in which they were used by the households who inhabited them. Traditionally, medieval historic interiors have been poorly understood in England, with attention focusing on the architecture, decoration and subdivision of houses, rather than on the objects and assemblages used within them (but see Alcock 1993; Barnwell and Adams 1994; Ayres 2006; Gore & Gore 1991). However, the flourishing of interdisciplinary approaches has recently begun to demonstrate the potential of more integrated studies of houses, people and objects. Collaborative research projects, such as the work of the Centre for the Study of the Domestic Interior have demonstrated the potential of historic interiors in Renaissance Italy to be approached more holistically (Ajmar-Wollheim & Dennis 2006; Ajmar-Wollheim et. al 2007; Aynsley & Grant 2006; Olson et. al 2006; see also Ch 5, p 190).

English scholars are now beginning to realise the potential of sources such as probate records for revealing the material culture used in medieval houses. Goldberg (2008), for example, uses a wide sample of rural and urban inventories to shed light on the different value systems of rural peasant and urban bourgeois households. Importantly, Goldberg suggests that the multiple functions of urban houses may have made them more 'permeable' than their rural counterparts, resulting in the increasingly sophisticated use of textiles and objects in urban houses to delineate private and intimate spaces, such as the marriage bed, or chamber. Similar support for the idea of late medieval houses as multiple-functioning spaces emerges from Richardson's (Richardson C 2003) study of probate inventories of the fifteenth century from Sandwich (Kent). Richardson suggests that the lack of firm associations between the objects and the spaces listed reflected the use of rooms for a variety of household functions. The emergence of much more fixed relationships between objects and the spaces in the sixteenth century is therefore interpreted as evidence of the emergence of single-function rooms in the early modern house.

These more recent interdisciplinary studies seek to engage with a rich vein of material culture studies, particularly so-called 'geneaological' or 'biographical' approaches to the analysis of people, places and artefacts (Lucas 2006: 39-42). Genealogical approaches seek to study the biographies of individuals or households and their material remains. In contrast, biographical approaches to objects seek to understand the changing cultural meanings of sites and objects (Appadurai 1986; Hoskins 1998; Gosden & Marshall 1999; Caple 2006; Olson et. al 2006). Both of these approaches have considerable potential to be applied to the rich palimpsests of surviving buildings, and the documentary and artefactual remains of medieval domestic material culture (Egan 1998; Ottaway 2002; and see Ch 5, p 213).

BOX 4.2   ENGLISH HYGIENE

There is a prevailing belief that medieval and early modern towns and villages were unremittingly squalid, and their occupants slovenly. This idea has been widely endorsed in art, historiography and literature from the nineteenth century to the present. Some scholars have challenged the notion, arguing that conditions were generally better than commonly supposed and warning against 'regarding as a lineal heritage from the Middle Ages bad new conditions which actually resulted from the industrial revolution of the eighteenth and nineteenth centuries' (Thorndike 1928: 193; see also Sabine 1933, 1934, 1937; Palliser 1990).

Palaeopathologists studying morbidity in excavated human skeletal remains

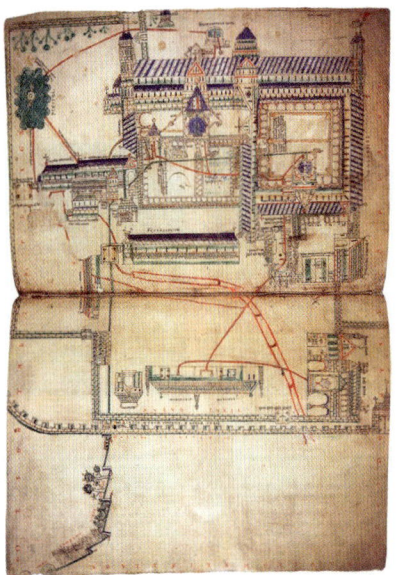

Fig 1

Waterworks of the Priory and Christ Church Cathedral in Canterbury, illustrated c. 1165, showing the latrine block with fifty-five cubicles (Cambridge, Trinity College Library, MS R.17.1, fols. 284v-285r).

have lent support to this suggestion. One study indicates that children from medieval York (c. 950-1550) showed less evidence of physiological stress than their counterparts in eighteenth- and nineteenth-century London, indicating that (in addition to any genetic advantages) they were exposed to fewer environmental pathogens (Lewis 2002; see also Ch 12). Recent surveys on the subjects of personal care and sanitation further revise the preconception that people were universally lousy, dirty and unhygienic (Gläser 2004; Smith 2007; Vigarello 1988 cf. Crawford 2007: 82). Attitudes to dirt and disease are relative, circumstantial and socially constructed (Douglas 1966). In other words, the criteria used to judge good hygiene in our period were different to those advanced by modern germ theory. Because of this, it is increasingly considered anachronistic to transpose biomedical paradigms of bacterial sanitation onto the evidential record (Horden, 2000; cf. Cooper, 1913). Now scholars are asking: by what standards did men and women of the period identify hygiene, and what steps did they take to foster it?

The answer lies in a set of beliefs inherited in our period from the ancient Greek world. In its original sense, the word *hygiene* signified an 'art' (or set of practical techniques) for maintaining health, and it referred to a wide range of behaviours in addition to physical cleanliness and grooming, such as diet, exercise, and even the cultivation of a balanced emotional state. The management and regulation of a person's immediate environment was also of principal importance, according to the Hippocratic tract *Airs, Waters, Places*, written at some point between 430 and 330 BC (Smith 2007: 95). Encyclopedists like

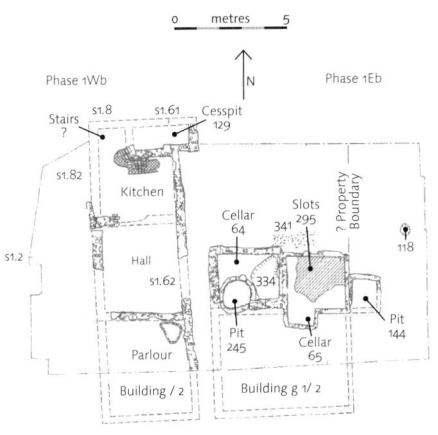

Fig 2

Plan of late medieval tenements excavated at Pottergate, Norwich, showing cesspits 245 and 129 (©Norfolk Museums and Archaeology Service).

Bartholomaeus Anglicus (fl. 1230-40), codified these ideas, and from about the mid-thirteenth century, they were disseminated in Europe via the *regimen sanitatis*, or 'guide to healthy living'. According to this developing genre of medical literature, anything that putrefied and compromised the quality of air and water was a serious health hazard. Carrion or butchers' waste, blood, stagnant water, 'foul things' cast into streets, privies situated too close to living spaces, manure and dunghills, corrupt gutters, compost heaps, smoke and industrial waste were all judged especially injurious (Horrox 1994, 174). The 'information revolution' of the later fourteenth century gave men and women direct access to these ideas, which were formerly the preserve of the academic and medical elites (Murray Jones 1994; 1998). The advent of printing and the repeated onslaught of virulent epidemics further stimulated the

production of neatly packaged manuals for literate, middle-class town-dwellers (Wear 2000: 158, 184-209). These manuals recommended prophylactics including fumigants, the cultivation of sweet smelling gardens, and gentle exercise in clean air (Fay 2007).

Armed with this knowledge, we can identify circumstances in the archaeological record that men and women of our period would have judged unhygienic. The state of two of London's minor watercourses – the Fleet and Walbrook – clearly failed to meet the standards. Blood and muck from nearby slaughterhouses were dumped into the Fleet (Sabine 1933: 343). Excavations have demonstrated that other kinds of noxious waste were also deposited in and around ditches, dating to between the mid-eleventh and late thirteenth centuries, which drained into the two streams. The material included inedible by-products from butchery (predominantly, head and feet-parts of oxen), and the skinned remains of animals, including cats and dogs, killed for fur, as well as domestic and industrial refuse, leather working scraps and quantities of old, worn-out shoes (Telfer 2003; Drummond-Murray & Liddle 2003). Sedimentary analysis shows that the Fleet became increasingly contaminated during the fourteenth century, after its stagnant drainage ditch, mentioned above, was back-filled and the area surrounding it was developed (Schofield and Vince 2003: 179; Telfer 2003). Possibly, the pollution occurred precisely because such former dumping grounds were no longer available, forcing people to deposit waste directly into the stream. At any rate, the deteriorating situation caused alarm. In 1357 a royal writ forbade men and women from throwing waste into London's watercourses, and directed them to make use of the city's waste collection facilities (Sabine 1937: 37).

For sewage and drainage, the most desirable sanitary arrangements were located within wealthy institutions such as monasteries, friaries and the larger hospitals (Bond 2001). At Norwich Benedictine Cathedral Priory, for example, numerous wells and a flint-lined culvert provided water for cooking, housekeeping and the laundry, as well as the monks' personal and religious ablutions. The wells' supply was remarkably clean; it was filtered by the chalk and gravel on which the priory precincts were built. Running water, channelled by the culvert, flushed out sewage from the latrines of the infirmary as well as the commodious facilities at the monks' dormitory. This arrangement prevented the water table from becoming contaminated. An excavation of one portion of the culvert revealed an enormous barrel vaulted drain, supported by Caen stone arches, that spanned 3 metres in width and 2.5 metres in height. The monks' latrines were scoured regularly; access to the culvert for this purpose was provided via special cleaning hatches. Similar systems were found at the hospital of St Mary Ospringe and St Mary's Abbey, York (Gilchrist 1992: 108; Gilchrist 2005: 36-8, 120, 138, 140, 177; Addyman 1989: plate 2) and the Priory and Cathedral at Canterbury (Fig 1).

Access to high quality facilities was not limited to the residents of large institutions. At the late fifteenth-century tenements at Pottergate, Norwich, rented by the affluent, aspiring middle-class, cesspits constructed in flint rubble and mortar were situated in cellars which probably communicated with,

and thus serviced, first floor, timber-framed en-suite accommodation in the adjacent domestic blocks, by means of a connecting chute (Fig 2, cesspits 245 and 129: Atkin, Carter & Evans 1985, 12-15, 21). The large cleanable cess pit at Cuckoo Lane, Southampton had a wooden floor supported by wooden struts. On its excavation the pit was discovered to have preserved small bits of cloth, probably used for wiping or feminine hygiene, together with a huge secondary assemblage of pottery, glass, wood and leather, dumped in the disused toilet around 1300 (Platt & Coleman-Smith 1975, 293). A different arrangement was found at an impressive stone-built merchant's house at Winkle Street, Southampton. Here, a well-constructed stone drain, probably dating to the fourteenth century, sluiced the contents of a garderobe pit out to sea (Platt & Coleman-Smith 1975: 273-5). In both cases, excreta were kept well away from the main accommodation. These examples can be compared with the malodorous situation at one fly- and maggot-infested latrine situated in a fifteenth-century tenement in Sidbury, Worcester. Its cesspit was contrived out of old barrels, which fostered anaerobic conditions. When excavated, the material preserved in the barrels contained large quantities of human parasite remains (an indication of poor manual hygiene routines following defecation), as well as partially decayed domestic refuse, including food waste, feather and bone. In order to diminish the bad smells, small bundles of straw, hay and sedge were periodically thrown in the latrine to seal it (Greig 1981: 279; see Fig 9.8 for an example of a latrine pit of 1290 from Germany).

The belief in the importance of clean air for health had implications for the ways in which people in our period treated their living spaces. Excavated evidence gives the lie to Desiderius Erasmus' oft-quoted statement that the rush-strewn floors in English houses were left "sometimes for twenty years", festering with "spittle, vomit, dogs' urine and men's too, dregs of beer and cast off-bits of fish, and other unspeakable kinds of filth" (Mynors and Dalzell 1992: 471). The floors of fourteenth and fifteenth-century peasant houses excavated at Wharram Percy were swept so often that they were worn concavely, whilst floors in the urban tenements at Winchester were also kept scrupulously clean (Keene 1982, 28-9; Hurst 1984, 99). Medieval men and women were expected to keep the streets outside their front doors equally tidy. A recent reassessment of archaeological evidence suggests that people lived up to their obligations for much of the time, and argues that layers of rubbish excavated from medieval streets are unlikely to represent jettisoned waste, but were deliberate deposits for making-up and stabilising the subsoil (Jørgensen 2008: 560).

In fact, the problem of disposing of waste varied in severity at different points during our period. When settlement density was low, following the crash in population suffered during the Black Death of 1348/9 and subsequent epidemics, or in spacious rural or suburban plots, it was possible to bury sewage and refuse on a property without overburdening it. Land pressure intensified as urban populations recovered (or were augmented by immigration) during the early fifteenth to sixteenth centuries. Whenever the quantity of waste material threatened to exceed a level that could be safely and easily disposed of, new measures had to be employed. One solution was to line rubbish or cesspits with timber or stone; these linings made it possible to clear out the pit's contents. The removed waste might be put to a useful purpose, either as agricultural fertiliser, or to shore up riversides and consolidate ground (great quantities were disposed of in these ways, particularly up to the early part of the fourteenth century, when agriculture was intensive and towns were rapidly expanding into hitherto uncolonised land: Rawcliffe 2004; Gläser 2004: 18, 34, 80-1, 101). Other materials (including bone, ash, metals and wood) might be recycled in a manufacturing process or used in a new product, thus avoiding disposal in the first place (Carver 1987, 82). Finally, if no further use could be found for it, refuse might be carted to a civic dump (Carver 1987, 98; Harbottle and Ellison 1981). From the late fourteenth century and throughout the fifteenth and sixteenth, several larger towns devised schemes to fund waste collections, which regularised the process (Jørgensen 2008). Archaeologically, we see a discernable decrease in the amount of human waste and rubbish that was permanently deposited within tenements at this time (see Ch 9, p 392; Atkin and Evans 2002: 31; Gläser 2004: 63, 101, 121; Platt and Coleman-Smith 1975: 34; see also AME 1, 177).

by Isla Fay

Conclusion

It is clear that the historiography of medieval houses creates an important legacy for modern scholars. But modern studies are beginning to question many of the assumptions that have hitherto dominated our understanding. It can no longer be presumed that innovation occurred amongst the elite and filtered down the social scale to rural peasants or the urban bourgeoisie. Rather, a gradual emergence of common ways of organising and using space can be traced through the medieval period, particularly in the use of the tripartite plan. But this common template should not be seen as a rigid model, imposed on the rural and urban landscapes. It was a form that could be adapted and altered to meet the very different social, domestic and economic needs of medieval households, in rural and urban areas. Indeed, what seems to characterise middling-status houses in late medieval England is the flexibility and the multiple uses of domestic space. The significance of these new ways of thinking about medieval houses is considerable. It begins to shed light on the distinctive 'ways of living' of the inhabitants; ways of living which were carried forward into other sites and spaces, such as the public buildings and churches of late medieval England, which form the focus of other chapters in this volume.

PART 3: SOUTHERNERS: HOUSE AND GARDEN IN AL-ANDALUS
by Julio Navarro Palazón & Pedro Jiménez Castillo

For a map and historical framework of al-Andalus, please see Ch 1, p 19.

Houses: History of Research

While some written records do mention the medieval Andalusian house, they are not very informative. Chronicles and poetry refer mainly to princely dwellings and legal documents tend to be ambiguous. Other texts, such as the inventory of properties belonging to the churches of Granada in the beginning of the sixteenth century, contain relevant information, but must be used with caution as they reflect the situation after the Castilian reconquest. However, the form and function of the Islamic house is becoming better known through archaeology. Archaeology can establish the plan of a house, the use of the rooms and the way the house interacts with the rest of its settlement area, in both town and country. These studies should lead to a greater understanding, not just of practical and technical matters relating to construction, but of the social organization that reflect the way space was structured.

We still know very little about the houses of the Emirate period (eighth-ninth century). In recent years archaeologists have made contact with remains in the countryside at Majada de las Vacas (Granada) and Peñaflor (Jaén) and in modern cities such as Valencia, Mérida and, especially, Córdoba, where a large area of the Segunda district has been uncovered, abandoned in the early ninth after the notorious "revolt of the suburbs" (*revuelta del arrabal*). The information available from the Caliphate (tenth century) is significantly fuller, provided especially by the splendid courtly city of Madinat al-Zahra, the site of Pechina (Almería) and, more recently, traces of houses that have appeared in urban excavations in Córdoba and Murcia. The Taifa period (eleventh century) includes houses in Vascos (Toledo) and the interesting urban complexes recently unearthed in Zaragoza.

Archaeological knowledge of architecture in the twelfth and thirteenth centuries, including that of citadels and palaces, has experienced a quantum leap (Navarro 1995), and the domestic residence in particular has been illuminated by the study of dwellings in the abandoned town of Siyâsa (Navarro 2002; Navarro & Jiménez 2007b) (Fig 4.12). There are other sites known in the countryside, such as Yecla (Ruiz 2000) and Calasparra (Pozo 2000) – while in towns most contact has been via rescue archaeology, for example in Valencia, Denia, Orihuela, Elche, Lorca and Murcia. In Gharb al-Andalus (the West) the most important archaeological sites for domestic architecture are Saltés (Bazzana & Bedia 2005; see AME 1, 157), Mértola (Macías 1996) and Silves (Varela & Varela 2001), the last two in Portugal.

In the later phase, corresponding to the Nasrid kingdom of Granada and the Marinid kingdom of the western Maghreb (thirteenth to fifteenth centuries), there are more

Plan of the excavated area at Siyâsa (Cieza, Murcia).

Fig 4.12

examples of domestic buildings still standing on either side of the Straits of Gibraltar. To these may be added the information provided by archaeological excavations, some classic such as the Alhambra itself (Orihuela 1996), others more recent, such as the annexe to the Cuarto Real at Santo Domingo and the housing complexes at Ceuta (Hita and Villada 1996 and 2000), Qasr as-Saghir (Redman 1986) and Belyounech (Cressier, Hassan Benslimane and Touri 1986), the latter two in Morocco.

The territory of Al-Andalus, as all medieval Islam, inherited the Mediterranean courtyard house, the origins of which can be traced back to Mesopotamia. By 2000 BC courtyard houses in the city of Ur already featured rooms on two storeys opening onto a central courtyard with an elaborate water collection system. We see the same arrangement twenty-five centuries later in Sassanian examples. In the Aegean world we know of courtyard houses at Gurnia (Crete) abandoned around 1200 BC, and from the fourth century BC courtyards are found flanked by lobbies *(prostas)* or perimeter porticos *(peristylon)*. By the third century BC, paved patios surrounding houses are featured in Phoenician Kerkuan and Carthage, on the coast of Tunisia.

Layout

While Islam adopted the courtyard house, it took it to fresh levels of development, largely aimed at improving privacy, especially in towns. Modifications included the reduction of openings to the street and measures to prevent a direct view of the interior, either through an open door or from the roof-tops or terraces of adjacent houses. However, the courtyard house was not universal under Islam: courtyards could become redundant or inconvenient in cold wet climates. Muslims living in the Balkans, on the shores of the Caspian Sea, northern Iran, Afghanistan, Yemen or some mountainous areas of the Maghreb preferred houses without doors leading onto patios, and employed openings that were high up, narrow slits or arched windows with stained glass or shutters to achieve ventilation and maintain privacy.

In al-Andalus, the courtyard house was the main type, but simpler forms can be encountered in the countryside, the direct heirs of pre-Islamic traditions, in which the structural units grew (with the family) as contiguous cells. Rooms with a number of different functions might be added and eventually surround an open central space, thus in effect creating a courtyard plan. It is sometimes difficult to draw a clear line between these examples and houses with an original courtyard design, just as written sources fail to distinguish between occupancy by single or multiple family groups.

A surviving house-plan that has a central courtyard surrounded by four wings often means that it was built at a time when there was plenty of space available – as in large farms or early houses in towns. Small plots and the absence of one or more wings may imply a more recent construction adjusted to fit the land available (Fig 4.13). A plot may subsequently be transformed by inheritance. The medieval Islamic house developed on the ground floor, and an upper floor, by no means universal, was the result of the search for more space on a cramped plot, or in consequence of partition of the property.

Andalusian house excavated on a plot on Alfaro Street, Murcia.

Fig 4.13

Interiors

To appreciate the interior of the Medieval Islamic house, we might pay it an imaginary visit, beginning by handing over one's horse to an ostler at the entrance. Houses were equipped with stables (as determined at Siyâsa by the presence of mangers), situated away from the main living area of the house, to keep the noise and odour at a distance. In some cases, the stables formed an annex to the house and had their own door opening directly onto the street. In towns, it was never necessary to go through the living space to get to the stables.

An L-shaped entrance hall, the *ustuwan,* leading from the street into the courtyard, was the feature that did most to transform the Mediterranean house for Muslim use. The door leading in from the street, and the door leading out into the courtyard were offset, so that it was not possible for passers-by to see into the courtyard or beyond into the house, even when both doors were open. The entrance hall served as a holding bay for visitors before they were admitted to the main house and often had a stone bench for them to sit on while waiting.

Regardless of the size of the Andalusian house, the central courtyard *(sahn)* was its essential feature (Fig 4.14). It let light and air into the rooms and was the focus of most

Fig 4.14　*Digital Reconstruction of House 8 at Siyâsa (Cieza, Murcia).*

of the daily activity – a role that led to its being the chief subject for architectural ornament. Where the house was laid out on a spacious plot, the courtyard had a generous
size and was symmetrical in form; but on small plots it might amount to less than 4 or 5
square metres. In the palaces and richest households, the shape is generally rectangular,
running north-south, but in more modest homes it may be square. On at least one side,
usually the north, it was usual to have a portico, intended to dignify the range containing the principal reception room and to link the upper floors by the gallery that the
portico supports. Where a water supply was available, the courtyard provided the site
for a sunken garden, sometimes occupying almost the whole space (see below).

The Andalusian house was characterized by the presence of a long and narrow salon
that acted as a reception or living room (*majlis*). Its location was typically in the north
wing, looking south to catch the early sun. It was intended for family gatherings and
the reception of guests, and at night it could be used for sleeping. Larger houses might
acquire a second salon in another wing, and the two rooms might be used alternately,
depending upon the seasons (as in Houses 4 and 6 at Siyâsa), although they might also
be intended to serve separate branches of the family.

The living room occupied the central part of a wing, and their ends were often
stopped by partition walls, leaving small enclosed areas beyond known as *alhanías* or
alcobas. This word is glossed as 'bedroom' in the Diwan of Ibn Quzman (d.1160 AD),
in the Leiden Glossary of the late twelfth century and in the *Arabic Vocabulary* attributed to Friar Raimon Martí of the thirteenth century. Sebastian de Covarrubias, in his

dictionary of 1611, states that the alhanía is a *"chamber, place of rest and sleep, where you sleep and the bed is located, because the alhania, says Father Guadix, is as good as the bed."* There is evidence that the floor was higher than in the living room and in some cases, there was a platform on which was installed a wooden structure or *tarima* (a term of Arab origin) that served as a bed.

The kitchen was an essential element, and occurred regularly in the twelfth and thirteenth century houses of Siyâsa. There the kitchens have three main characteristic features: the hearth, the cupboard and the work surface. The main hearth, rectangular with an apsidal end, was usually paved with slabs of stone and sunk about 10 cm into the floor in order to contain the ash and cinders. The cupboard, containing the cooking pots and other utensils, was constructed of stone or wattle-and-clay, and plastered, and it was located adjacent to the hearth. The bays of the cupboard (or dresser) were formed by ornamental arches, consisting of at least two shelves and a variable number of compartments. The work surfaces took the form of L-shaped benches built around the hearth, with a height ranging between 10 and 30 cm, and were designed to function as tables for processing food.

According to Fray Pedro de Alcalá's *Arab Dictionary,* the name given to a latrine was the euphemistic *bayt al-ma,* or water-closet (as it is still called in Morocco). At least since the Caliphate period it had the same characteristics: a small building usually located in a corner of the courtyard, and entered through an L-shaped passage. The better-preserved examples have a high narrow window to admit air and light.

Conclusion

The design of the house was practical, drawn from centuries of experience in living in Mediterranean climates. But it was also influenced by a concern for privacy common to all Islamic societies irrespective of their geographical location. Controlled breeding (endogamy) and the concept of family honour *('ird)* characteristic of Arab society, confined women to private quarters *(haram,* literally 'forbidden'), which must be carefully preserved from strangers. These precautions were particularly needed in the city, where promiscuity among individuals, families and clans was much higher than in rural areas. Therefore, the house, where women spent most of the day, was a building that had to be well guarded against any uncontrolled physical or visual relationship with the outside world.

This architectural scheme was applied to simple houses and to palaces alike. In the palaces, it characterized the domestic areas of courtly buildings, where the king and his family lived, together perhaps with noble associates. The same model was also adopted for ceremonial areas, those that genuinely represent the power and the government, but on a larger scale and adding specific elements such as the throne hall and a developed courtyard, featuring gardens, *qubba,* pavilions and large ornamental pools (see below).

The Gardens of Al-Andalus, History of Research

The conquest of the Kingdom of Granada in 1492 introduced Europeans to the orchards and gardens located on Andalusian soil, in particular at the palaces of the Alhambra and the Generalife. The unanimous appreciation of their striking beauty and amenity was celebrated in many chronicles at the time, an admiration maintained throughout the seventeenth and eighteenth centuries. James Cavannah Murphy (1815) carefully described and drew attention to those "Moorish" elements that seemed typical of the gardens, all very different from those known in the rest of Europe. Of the authors of the first half of the twentieth century, Valladar and Forestier exposed for the first time the elusive nature of the Andalusian garden, and the need to draw on new sources to discover its medieval origins. Forestier (1915) recognized the difficulty of extracting the essence of the medieval garden from those preserved in the Alhambra and the Generalife, which had been modified over five centuries. Forestier's insights were influential; for example, he claimed that medieval gardens had raised walkways or promenades, a design only seen in traditional Moroccan courtyards; these features have been subsequently confirmed by many archaeological excavations. Intuitively he suggested that medieval gardens featured architectural topiary, an attractive hypothesis not yet endorsed. However, he also promoted the idea that edible and ornamental plants would grow on the same parterre, which seems unlikely, especially in the palaces.

The second half of the twentieth century saw the continuation of interdisciplinary attempts to recover and to analyze the early Islamic garden. Researchers such as the eminent architect L. Torres Balbás refrained from making speculative reconstructions, but not so Prieto Moreno (1952), who based his image on tenuous conjecture and personal impressions. G. Marçais's 1941 lecture (published 1957) entitled "Les jardins de l'Islam," introduced a strategy that was to be followed in future investigations on the subject; it would be necessary to use sources as diverse as literature, iconography and archaeology, all embedded in the broader context of the history of gardening. James Dickie (1965-1966, 1992) took a traditional line, exploiting the limited information contained in the written sources combined with the testimony of the standing architecture. In 1973 an international congress on Islamic gardens was held in Granada, at which were presented several studies relating to gardens in al-Andalus. Some were general and some more specific topics, such as the use of water in Nazari gardens, references in the poetry of the time, the Geoponica texts and even the contribution of palaeontology (AAVV. 1976).

At the end of the twentieth century, the character of the Islamic garden was encapsulated in a suite of ideas originally owed to Forestier, namely that it had a spiritual purpose, evoking paradise; it instilled tranquillity through standing water (with occasional fountains); it combined ornamental and vegetable plants in the same garden; and, in general, that the form and character of the inherited Medieval Islamic garden can be read from the gardens of the al-Andalus area.

These diagnostics were challenged and critiqued by modern scholars, especially Tito Rojo (2001, 2007). Although the early authors, and later romantic travellers, had regarded the surviving gardens as 'Islamic' this was not strictly true, since they had been developing in a local milieu for two or three hundred years before the lands were conquered by the northern Christian Kingdoms. Much of the later literature on the medieval Islamic garden in general, and al-Andalus in particular, has simply repeated the list of defining attributes without demonstrating their validity. Most are simplistic, or even in contradiction with the reality that we now know better, thanks to a small group of specialists who, following Tito Rojo's lead, have been extensively studying the writing, illustrations and materiality of the garden.

The archaeology of gardens

In addition to the interdisciplinary harnessing of Arabic studies, history, ethnobotany and literature, much of the new reality of the medieval garden is owed to archaeology. Recent syntheses which reflect these developments are Tjion Sie Fat and de Jong (1991), Petruccioli (1994), the doctoral thesis of Rafael Fernández García (1995), Ruggles (2000), Navarro (2005) (on the archaeology of garden architecture in al-Andalus), Antonio Almagro (2007) (on the visual analysis of such spaces), Zangheri, Lorenzi & Rahmati (2006), Conan (2007), and García & Hernández (2007).

Unlike architecture, a garden is a living organism composed of things which flourish and die, sensitive to changes in fashion, neglect and abandonment. Archaeology, therefore, reports principally on architectural elements such as the provision of flower beds and promenades, porticos and pavilions, pools, fountains, wells and ditches supplying water for irrigation, all of which were part of the garden landscape. The enormous volume of new information provided by medieval archaeology includes not only the gardens of palaces, but also details of the little-known domestic garden. New techniques applied to archaeological research, especially palynology and paleobotany, are yielding valuable first-hand information on the species planted through the analysis of pollen and seeds, as demonstrated by the work at the Generalife (Casares, Tito & Socorro 2003).

The garden has been linked to power in a special and intimate manner: it provides pleasure to its owners, and becomes a sign of distinction and authority. In al-Andalus, there was virtually no palace without a garden. In most cases, the garden was built inside the palace, within available courtyards of sufficient size to allow the planting of trees, shrubs and ornamental plants. Water was provided for irrigation as well as being itself a garden feature. In many cases, gardens and surrounding orchards also lay outside the buildings, enhancing the glories of the royal house and adding the production of fruit to the simple pleasures of ambience.

Thanks to archaeology, we now know that, in addition to palaces, domestic dwellings from the humblest houses to the richest exhibited the Andalusian taste for gardens in their residential courtyards. They were almost always square or rectangular, equipped with perimeter gutters to collect rain-water and sunken to prevent flooding. Larger houses might also feature ornamental ponds and fountains. In more humble domestic properties, conditioned by the small size of the courtyards, the garden shrank to a square in which only one tree could be planted.

It will be convenient to present now a summary historical synthesis, intended both to offer an assessment of current knowledge and pointers for future work.

A History of the Andalusian garden

The oldest known Andalusian gardens in a town, now in ruins, is at Madînat al-Zahrâ' built by the Umayyad caliphs of Al-Andalus in the tenth century. It featured both large landscaped open spaces and smaller, more formal parterres with pools, fountains, promenades and water-channels. The gardens of al-Zahra were seen as part of its geography of reception. In the garden fronting the reception hall of 'Abd al-Rahmân III stood a central pavilion on a raised platform with promenades and pools. At the end of one of the promenades of this enormous garden was another pavilion, which looked out over another stretch of pasture and a garden lying at a lower level divided in the shape of an axial cross. The presence of water, both moving and still, in the gardens of the palace of Madînat al-Zahrâ' was important. Large pools, still and silent, formed mirrors that varied in tone depending on the depth of the pool. They reflected the architecture and threw light back into the interior of the rooms. By contrast, the streams were incorporated into the architecture by means of systems of channels, watering the flower-beds while their murmuring sound filled the garden space. On a terrace at a higher level still was a residential area known as Casa de la Alberquilla, structured around a square courtyard faced with two porticos and a central garden, with a cruciform layout of promenades, interrupted on one axis by a pool. This first example provided a model of the design to be adopted later in family houses and palaces.

From the late eleventh century, after the brilliant but unstable period of the first Taifa (tenth-eleventh century AD), the African dynasties began to develop the courtyard gardens first known from the Umayyad period. The Taifa Palace of Aljafería (eleventh century), built by King Abu Jafar Ahmad Ibn al-Hûd Muqtadir Billah, near the city of Zaragoza, provides an important link in the evolutionary process of the Andalusian patio garden. This now has two pools, one appearing before each portico, but each of different sizes. Scarcely any remains of Almoravid (eleventh century) residences exist, and we know only the walls of the palace that Ali Ibn Yusuf ordered to be built in Marrakesh, exhumed when the site of the first Kutubiyya was excavated. This is a small cross-shaped courtyard which possibly formed part of his private premises and that was possibly preceded by two pools, similar to what was to be constructed few years later in Castillejo de Monteagudo.

The Castillejo de Monteagudo, known in Arabic sources as Qasr Ibn Sa'd, palace of Ibn Mardanish, or King Lobo, is the best surviving example of Andalusian residential architecture from the mid-twelfth century. Although dated to the second Taifa period, we can consider it, from its architectural decoration, as a late example of an Almoravid building. Situated a few kilometres from Murcia, this recreational residence was laid out around a cross-shaped rectangular courtyard, fronted by small pools on the shorter sides. The remains of another Mardanisí palace, the Dar al-Sugrà, discovered beneath the monastery of Santa Clara at Murcia, comprised part of a garden of two broad platforms with small longitudinal water channels at whose intersection stood a pavilion or *qubba*. This courtyard was three times bigger than that of Castillejo de Monteagudo.

The Almohad caliphs (*c.* 1147 - *c.* 1269) came to exercise control over a vast territory extending between Africa and the Iberian Peninsula, and inaugurated an era of demonstrative building. They had their capital at Seville, notable for its magnificent homes, especially those built within the palace complex of the Alcázar of Seville. Their gardens all adopted the courtyard cross formation, now combined with pools arranged at each end of the long axis. The first and best known is called the *Crucero*, a large courtyard divided into four gardens, each subdivided in turn into four. The gardens lay 4.70m below the level of the house, the deepest we know. Another courtyard garden in Seville, completely destroyed in 1356 to build the residence of King Don Pedro, has been rediscovered under the *Patio de la Monteria* (Fig 4.15). Exceptionally, the garden here was square and appears to have featured a high platform surrounding its perimeter. On each side of the garden, steps descended from the platform to the paths of the cross-formation, located one metre down, while the surfaces of the four garden areas were 0.50 m below that. A channel at the base of the platform collected rain-water from the roofs and prevented it flooding the cultivated areas.

Between the period of the Alcazar palace complex of Almohad Seville and the first buildings of the Alhambra, there is a gap of a century in which we have only one single example, – the residence erected in Murcia for Ibn Hûd al-Mutawakkil (1228 – 1238). This building, known in the thirteenth-century Christian sources as "Alcacer Ceguir" (al-Qasr al-Sagîr), is still partially standing in land that now belongs to the Monastery of Santa Clara. Its architectural organization and decoration are essential for under-

Cruciform garden discovered beneath the Patio de la Monteria at the royal palace of Seville, 12th century **Fig 4.15**
(digital reconstruction by A. Almagro).

standing the birth of Nasrid art in Granada. The new plan was laid over the ruins of the Dâr al-Sugrà (above). One of the most innovative aspects of this garden is a central large rectangular pool running north-south, with garden spaces placed on each long side, a design that was to be adopted in the Nasrid palaces of the Abencerrajes, and Comares, both of them located in the Alhambra.

The Nasrid emirs established their capital in Granada in 1238 and maintained a kingdom in its name for more than two and a half centuries – until 1492. Most of the gardens and orchards preserved from this period are in the palace-city of the Alhambra and the Generalife. El Patio de la Acequia in the Generalife, whose construction may have started in the last quarter of the thirteenth century, is noted for its exceptional state of preservation (Fig 4.16). The rectangular shape is more elongated than usual and the four gardens in the cross arms, each 48.60 x 12.70 metres, contained plants typical of the genre. Recent palynological studies have indicated that the beds were occupied by meadow grass with colourful flowers enclosed with myrtle hedges. Also indicated is the presence of citrus fruits (bitter orange, lemon, citron), pomegranate, jujube, grape vines, and other ornamental types of trees such as the cypress, laurel, jasmine and roses (Casares, Tito & Socorro 2003).

The most common type of garden now being adopted for palaces and houses of this period had a tripartite organization, in which two rectangular parterres flank a large central pool that occupies the entire elongated length of the courtyard, with porticos standing on the shorter sides. The most famous example of this type of garden is in the Comares Palace, the ruling sultan's private residence built by Yusuf I (1333-1354). Currently, the parterres are occupied exclusively by myrtles on raised platforms, but a wealth of iconographical evidence shows that they had once contained fruit trees. Drawings and antique prints also show fountains in the centre of the pool, now disappeared, and on the short sides, now levelled.

Of the Nasrid dynasty of Granada, Sultan Muhammad V (1354-1359 and 1362-1391), had a great interest in architecture, and in the Palacio de los Leones he set out to do something new, influenced by the architecture of his ally Peter I (1350-1369), king of Castile. But even today there is no consensus that there was a garden there during the Middle Ages. However, archaeological excavations since 1995 at Cuarto Real de Santo Domingo, located in the historic centre of Granada, have discovered a new garden of the greatest interest, with elements indicating a date in the Nasrid period, and probably the reign of Muhammad II (1273-1302). It was rectangular, measured 42.30 x 34.40 metres and was bordered on three sides by a high wall. The lower south side was flanked by a portico with five arches in front of a *qubba,* perfectly preserved, with two small outbuildings on either side. The garden was divided into two large parterres by a central promenade running from the portico, opening into a square platform containing an octagonal pool of 1.43 metres a side. The pool was fed by water led via a channel from a fountain of white marble located in the portico. The edge of the pool was surrounded on all sides by a raised promenade, which, like the base of the pool, was composed of bricks laid in a pattern (Fig 4.17).

Patio with central channel at the 14th-century Generalife in Granada.

Fig 4.17

The palaces and gardens of Al-Andalus transcended the boundaries of Islamic territory and were adopted as a sign of prestige by Christian Castile. As Castile became the strongest kingdom of Spain it employed its growing wealth to develop with renewed vigour this architecture of Islamic tradition. Models of Andalusian origin were selected, modified, reworked and recreated, so renewing the influence and development of Islamic art, especially in the city of Toledo. A typical example is the palace of Don Fadrique, a building closely linked to the Toledo plaster artisans, which was built in Seville a few years after the Christian conquest in the middle of the thirteenth century.

Paradoxically, while typical Islamic elements such as cross-shaped courtyards fell into disuse in later thirteenth century al-Andalus, they were maintained and developed in designs owed to the Mudéjar (Islamic residents of Christian Spain). The recently excavated Alcázar of Guadalajara, which is providing valuable information about the interactions between Christian and Muslim in the architecture of the thirteenth and fourteenth centuries, featured a courtyard with a great cross-shaped area. Instead of a pavilion, it had at its centre a large rectangular pool lined with concrete in which were embedded ceramic pots to encourage the breeding of fish (Fig 4.18). This is a valuable example of the Castilian Mudéjar contribution to Andalusian architecture, since this model of cross-shaped court with great central pool, appears later in the Nasrid palace of Alijares.

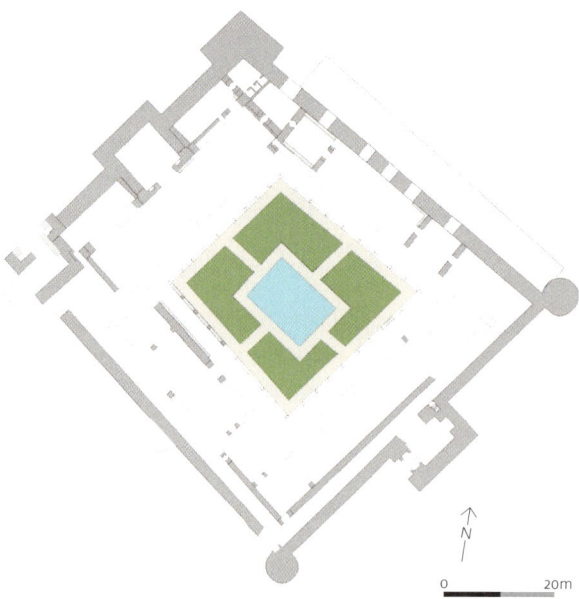

Fig 4.17 *The garden and pavilion of the Cuarto Real of Santo Domingo, Granada, end of the 13th century (digital reconstruction by A. Almagro).*

Fig 4.18 *Plan of the fortress at Guadalajara (13th–14th century), which featured a courtyard with a great cross-shaped area. Instead of a pavilion, it had at its centre a large rectangular pool lined with concrete.*

CHAPTER 5

MATERIAL CULTURE
– ARTEFACTS AND DAILY LIFE

Else Roesdahl and Frans Verhaeghe

Introduction

The material world of communities and individuals in medieval Europe (and else-where) included their physical environment, man-made landscapes, settlements, major buildings and housing, all of which relate in one way or another to power, economy or religion. This material world also comprised a wide range of portable objects and com-modities, which shaped the daily lives and behaviour of medieval people, and form the subject of this chapter.

All objects are vehicles carrying many kinds of information – about raw materials, production and technology, consumption and consumption patterns, functions and disposal, trade and exchange, processes of change (including fashion, innovation and transfer of technology), and more abstract properties, including religious and ethnic identities. Objects could have many different meanings depending not only on their function but also on their social, cultural and economic contexts. They also help with chronological queries, but we should keep in mind that an artefact may have had a long life-span and a complex biography.

Nor should we forget that artefacts never emerged or functioned in isolation: each was an integral part of a much larger assemblage. Although important in basic practi-cal terms, they were also set in specific technical, cultural and even 'artistic' traditions and were used – consciously or otherwise – in complex social relations. They were, of course, also linked to other components of material culture and just like these, they were agents, playing an 'active' – not a passive – role in people's behaviour and in the evolution of material culture and society through time.

Archaeology documents the intricacy of such links with numerous examples. Among them are the changes in housing and housing culture and its relationship with heating arrangements, fittings and other material equipment; the development of paper and printing; the invention of guns; or – on a more modest level – the copying, adapt-ing and adopting of new fashions and their attendant objects. Such complexities and interactions between artefacts and the many spheres of (domestic) life deserve more attention in future research.

Given the broad and fast-growing repertoire of portable goods over the period – up to and including toys and miniature objects (Forsyth with Egan 2005) – it is not possible here to list and discuss in great detail every kind of medieval object that has been archaeologically documented. We offer first a broad descriptive overview of the principal categories of medieval artefact (Part 1), and then a discussion of methods of study and approaches to interpretation (Part 2, pp. 213-227). Readers will also be referred to other chapters as we proceed, since in many ways artefacts constitute the basic vocabulary of medieval archaeology.

PART 1:   MEDIEVAL PORTABLE ARTEFACTS – A SURVEY

Because of the enormous range and complexity of the portable artefacts in use in Europe from *c.* 1200 to *c.* 1500, this section will only provide a brief user-guide to some of the main categories of objects concerned with everyday life in the household (see Ch 3, p 99 for agricultural tools, and Ch 6, p 272 for weapons). We adopt a broad functionalist approach in selecting these categories: cooking and dining, furnishing, dress, leisure, body care, reading and writing, and religion, further subdivided by material: ceramics, wood, metal, textile. This approach is purely for the convenience of the reader and is not intended to imply that this was the way medieval people saw or categorized the objects that surrounded them – or even that some categories of objects were more important to them than others. For practical reasons, the chapter will focus on North-Western Europe.

Cooking and dining: eating, drinking and attendant ritual

A wide range of objects and materials was intimately linked with this hugely important sphere of daily and social life, notably for storing, preparing, cooking, trading, transporting and consuming foodstuffs, and with the attendant social and behavioural aspects related to eating, drinking and feasting (Fig 5.1).

Pottery survives from the Middle Ages in large quantities and is found almost everywhere (Ch 7, p 287; Ch 8, p 340). This ubiquity biases the overall picture as it obscures the fact that in many places wooden vessels were at least as important as pottery, while in some areas stone vessels were used instead (see below). Still, by the twelfth-thirteenth century, pottery production had become a fairly important specialized economic activity, impacting strongly on the daily material scene and behaviour. The weight of local or regional traditions (on the part of both the consumers and the producers) and the emergence of larger workshops explain aspects of the rather strong regional diversity. Recent work shows that detailed regional analysis has much to offer in terms of understanding the dynamics of production, exchange, change, innovation, and consumption (e.g. De Groote 2008; Endres & Lichtwark 1995).

Regional diversity was intertwined with major supra-regional developments that co-determined pottery usage. Apart from the generally increasing range and diversity of

Table-ware of pottery, glass and wood, with some cutlery from southern Germany and northern Swit-   **Fig 5.1**
zerland. Around 1300 (photo: Schweizerisches Landesmuseum Zürich).

objects, many regions clearly also show tendencies towards more uniformity in terms of fabrics, range of pottery types and of decoration, and cooking wares. More over-arching developments are seen in the tableware, which included most of the quality pottery. Jugs emerged as a major new type, their success probably linked to changing drinking habits and table manners. The development of three major types of ceramics was crucial: the maiolicas (tin-glazed wares with painted decoration) in the Mediterranean world, and the highly decorated wares and the stonewares in the North. The first two also exemplify the 'colouring' of daily life in this period.

Rooted in Islamic culture, the maiolicas were developed by potters in Spain, where some production regions (e.g. Malaga, Paterna, Valencia) were of major importance (Fig 5.2; see also Ch 7, p 296, 302). Through Mallorca and/or Malaga (whence the name maiolica according to some), the objects and techniques reached Italy where maiolica production rapidly gained foothold. Bowls, plates and *albarelli* were the main types, and Spanish examples reached the North Sea and Baltic regions by the late four-

Fig 5.2   *Fragments of bowls of Valencian (Spanish) maiolica with Gothic lettering (c. 1425-1450) found at the fishing village Raversijde near Ostend, Belgium (photo: Hans Denis, Marnix Pieters ©VIOE).*

teenth century, becoming more widespread there in the fifteenth century (Norway, see Reid 1982; the British Isles, see Gerrard *et al* 1995; Ch 8, p 328). Regularly, bowls were traded as containers for expensive exotic fruits, such as dates. Around 1500, the northern urban markets became sufficiently interested and interesting for Italian maiolica potters to establish themselves in Antwerp. With this transfer of technology, production gradually spread throughout north-western Europe. Another way north, particularly for Italian wares, was via southern France, but only limited numbers of Italian maiolicas reached the North Sea regions (e.g. Veeckman *et al* 2002).

Basically a North Sea region phenomenon, highly decorated glazed wares started to appear around 1150-1200, possibly in France (Île-de-France?). The fashion spread rapidly to Normandy, the Low Countries, England and Denmark (Fig 5.3). The potters revitalized older decoration techniques with lead-glazing and oxidizing firing, introducing new colours and colour contrasts. Often designed locally (e.g. in Flanders), potters from different towns competed extensively, copying and adapting products to local circumstances and tastes. In England, for example, some potteries developed jugs with highly sculptural decoration. Some forms of decoration, however, were internationally popular: applied human faces, mostly bearded, appear for instance in many places on so-called face-jugs; the feature doubtless had a particular meaning that remains to be explained.

Jugs were by far the most common highly decorated product, but already in the thirteenth century other objects occasionally turn up: roof-finials, salt-pans, covers. In the fourteenth century, these jugs go out of fashion, probably forced out by the German

(above) Highly decorated jugs and cover (for plate) with green (copper) lead-glaze. Decorations include rouletting, ribbing, stamping and a face-mask. The glaze is applied on a white pipe-clay which masks the reddish fabric and was used to compete with the whitish French highly decorated imports. The green glaze is characteristic for parts of the Bruges production (13th century). From Bruges, Belgium (photo: B. Hillewaert. ©Raakvlak). (left) Highly decorated face-jug with applied yellow slip. The colour contrasts are fairly characteristic for the production in Brabant, Belgium. Found in Mechelen (Malines), Belgium (photo: F. Verhaeghe).

Fig 5.3

stonewares (see below). But the decoration techniques survived. In the fourteenth- and fifteenth-century Low Countries, they were used on dishes, candle maker's boxes, ewers, lamps, lanterns, chafing-dishes, aquamaniles, basins and wine coolers, whistles, many of them skeuomorphs (see p 223 below). Decorations were continuously adapted, offering alternatives for maiolicas and metal objects and living on in post-medieval times as shown by the slip wares (Verhaeghe 1989; 1996). Similarly, lead-glaze, which was still a quality marker in twelfth-century north-western Europe, became a common feature by the end of the fifteenth century; most common wares, including cooking wares, would eventually be glazed.

The German stonewares represent the third major development. Mass-produced at high temperatures in stone-hard fabric by specialized potters, they featured mainly jugs and beakers and dominated drinking for centuries, forcing potters elsewhere to specialize in other products. Traded throughout the North Sea and Baltic regions (cf. Gaimster 1997), they did not penetrate France. Here, production emerged in the Beauvaisis (fifteenth century) and the products (including copies of German Siegburg items) found their way to Central France and England but not further north, probably because of the German stonewares (Ch 7, p 291; Ch 8, p 340).

Long-distance trade in pottery intensified and was essentially by shipping – though often as collateral items in mixed cargoes. It concerned mainly quality products and notably tableware; but some items travelled in other ways, and some types of pottery were used as containers. The general picture is one of redistribution combined with overlapping and interlinked networks for the regional goods, and with competition between workshops, production centres and products.

In most of Europe, *wooden household utensils* were very important (Fig 5.4), more so than pottery, and particularly in regions with easy access to the right wood species (see also AME I, Box 8.2). They are very common finds if preservation conditions are favourable, which means that most come from waterlogged strata in town and castle sites, for example Freiburg and Konstanz in Central Europe and Boringholm castle in Denmark (Müller 1992; 1996; 2006; Andersen 2005). But rural sites have also yielded many examples, e.g. from wells, or preserved by permafrost as in arctic Greenland (Roussell 1936, 135ff). In places like Norway, which did not produce pottery in the Middle Ages, such goods were extremely common, while the Sami population also used containers of birch bark, which can be made water-proof. Linked to these materials, basketry was probably widely used but rarely survives.

The types of household goods used during this period were much the same as before: most important were stave-built barrels (both for storage and transport), buckets, jugs and drinking-vessels; turned bowls, plates and beakers; carved troughs, bowls, ladles, spoons, hooks. Carved ornament is sometimes found on tableware, as are incised or burnt 'owners' marks, graffiti, or (on barrels) boards for games. Pigment traces demonstrate that some tableware was painted (jugs), and some fine bowls and beakers were turned from maple and mounted with brass or silver.

Wooden artefacts had an advantage over pottery: they were more break-resistant, although repairs are sometimes seen. They were therefore also used for travel. Depend-

Heaps of wooden vessels, turned and coopered, including a decorated bowl and some spoons. From Lübeck, 14th-16th centuries (after Meckseper 1985). **Fig 5.4a**

Selection of household goods from Greenland farms including a knife, spoons of various materials, a spoon case of wood, and three vessels of soapstone. The other objects are of wood. 14th century (©National Museum of Denmark). **Fig 5.4b**

ing on the wood species and the technique used they were also cheap, and some carved and hollowed-out items like simple bowls and ladles were surely home-made. But many objects, notably coopered and turned ones, were produced by craftsmen, requiring professional skills as well as specialized tools and sometimes imported wood materials (e.g. pine-wood for stave-built drinking-vessels produced in Denmark). Conversely, dendro-provenancing using regional tree-ring patterns (Ch. 1, p 28), has also demonstrated that artefacts made from wood species which were available locally were in fact sometimes imported from elsewhere, like some fourteenth- and fifteenth-century oak barrels in Denmark and Flanders which came from south Germany and Poland (Malmros & Daly 2005; Pieters 2002, 294-9).

A wide variety of wood species was used and the qualities of each were well known. Particular species appear to have been very often used for specific types of objects and techniques – species identification can therefore sometimes help to identify a very fragmented wooden object. Use patterns could, however, change with time. At the fourteenth-century Danish castle-site of Boringholm, for example, only oak was used for coopered barrels, buckets and jugs while ash was preferred for turned bowls and dishes; it also emerged that materials for knife handles here and elsewhere were different from those of the Viking Age, when ash was normally used (Malmros & Daly 2005).

As in earlier times, *metal vessels* included copper-alloy and iron cauldrons of various sizes made of sheet-metal. But from the late twelfth century onwards, cast copper-alloy vessels for kitchen and table were increasingly used, and by broader levels of society. In the later Middle Ages the same goes for pewter tableware, particularly jugs and plates. In short, metal artefacts became much more common (e.g. Blair & Ramsey 1991). But as metal was likely to be re-used, the finds do not reflect the frequency of use. Metal pots had advantages over pottery, wood and stone vessels: they could be more efficiently cleaned, and heat spread more evenly when used for cooking. They were also more expensive and probably reflect a measure of status.

Solid cast copper-alloy tripod cauldrons with two handles and horizontal ribs (German 'Grapen') may have originated in North German towns and gradually spread to Scandinavia, the Baltic countries, the Low Countries and south along the Rhine, as well as to Britain and (at least parts of) France (Fig 5.5). They could be hung over the fire or set in the fireplace or on the table and were both cooking and serving vessels. Fragments occasionally appear in excavations. But many complete cauldrons have been found as containers for hoards, deliberately hidden in times of unrest and not recovered. These provide good chronological and typological sequences. A few workshops have also been excavated, and from the fourteenth century onwards some of the products have marks linked to both the individual craftsman or workshop, and the town – the mark of the town of Stralsund, on the German Baltic coast, was, for example, an arrow. This, together with marks on other cast copper-alloy artefacts such as church-bells, helps to document production and consumption patterns. As they had some value, they are sometimes mentioned in written sources and occasionally shown in pictures (Drescher 1968; 1969; 1982; Vellev 1998; Krabath 2001, 32-40). Cast copper-alloy pans are known but rare.

Two cast copper-alloy tripod cauldrons full of coins. Made in Stralsund, north Germany; found in Kirial, **Fig 5.5**
Denmark, where they were buried c. 1370 (©National Museum of Denmark).

There were also cast copper-alloy jugs, sometimes with ornaments. A particularly interesting example is the large jug found in 1896 in the royal palace of the Ashanti at Kumasi, Ghana; it bears the arms of the kings of England together with the badge of Richard II (1377-99) and a decorative inscription (Fig 5.6). How it ended up in West Africa is a mystery. A very similar jug – preserved in an English manor and possibly from the same workshop – shows that the Ashanti jug was not unique (Alexander & Binski 1987, cat. nos. 726-27; Cherry 1991a, 50-4). Aquamaniles (Fig 5.7) served in both liturgical and secular rituals and their iconography – particularly knights on horseback and animals – has strong status implications (Hütt 1993). The repertoire further comprised double-spouted hanging-vessels or lavabos designed for hand-washing and sometimes seen in paintings. Another type of vessel in the North Sea region is the copper-alloy tripod ewer, used in liturgical contexts but also in formal vernacular hand-

Fig 5.6   (left) English copper alloy jug found in Ghana. Height 40.2 cm. Late 14th century (©The Trustees of the British Museum).

Fig 5.7   (right) Two 14th-century figural aquamaniles from excavation of a ship-wreck at Vigsø, Denmark. Probably of German manufacture (©National Museum of Denmark).

washing. These objects could be used together with copper-alloy hand-basins – known also in earlier times (AME 1, 244, 355 and Fig 12.7) but now often undecorated (see also Müller 2006).

Throughout the Middle Ages, *soapstone* was also used for household vessels (including cooking pots), notably where the raw material was readily accessible and pottery production limited or non-existent, as in Greenland (an example in Fig 5.4b), Norway and Alpine parts of Switzerland and Italy (Roussell 1936, 143f and passim; Lossius 1977; Boscardin 2005). During our period such vessels were, however, no longer traded over large distances in the Scandinavian world as they had been in the earlier Middle Ages (AME 1, Box 10.2). Slate plates could be used for baking, as in Norway.

Sturdy *mortars and pestles* were necessary items for medieval cooks who had a liking for mashed food (Fig 5.8). Many were probably made of wood and fragments would be difficult to identify. Fine complete mortars survive in cast copper-alloy, and some pestles are known from excavations (e.g. Drescher 1968; 1982; Andersen 2005, 123-4). Excavations have also yielded thirteenth-, fourteenth- and fifteenth-century mortars made of various stones. Geology often allows the stone to be identified, as with the Caen limestone from Normandy, the Purbeck marble and Quarr stone from southern England or the soapstone from Norway, and details of form are specific to the stone type and the production centre. Such mortars were traded within the North Sea and Baltic regions, but mortars were of course also used elsewhere. They are often found on high-status sites like castles and in international trading centres (Bencard 1971; Dunning 1977).

Cutlery was normally fairly simple (examples in Figs 5.1 and 5.4). Hands and knives were used for eating solid food, even at formal dinners of the aristocracy – forks in the modern sense were not used before the sixteenth century (Felgenhauer-Schmiedt 1993, 143-45; Cherry 1991a, passim). Hand-washing was therefore a preferable ritual before and after meals, and types of metal jugs and hand-basins are mentioned above. Less affluent levels of society probably used wooden or ceramic equivalents. As in earlier times, knives constituted by far the most important form of cutlery. They were personal items and used by everybody. In addition, there were big carving knives. Knives varied widely in terms of materials, workmanship of the handle (visible and therefore a potential status marker) and also blade quality. Finds show that blades were often worn down before being discarded. Handles were made of various woods, bone or ivory (sometimes finely carved), and some had metal mounts. They were kept in leather sheaths, sometimes with ornamental stampings and metal mounts (e.g. Cowgill *et al* 1987; Harjula 2005). Spoons for liquid food were rare until the fourteenth century, when they gradually got more popular. They occur in many materials – woods, tin/lead, silver – and were of widely varying qualities, the finest being masterpieces in gold. They were probably personal items, as in later times, brought along when needed outside the home. Spoon-cases are also known.

Apart from the enamelled beakers (see below), *drinking-glasses* became more widespread from the thirteenth century onwards – particularly among the aristocracy and the better-off classes. In north-western Europe, where greenish fern-glass (*Waldglas*) long dominated, tall-stemmed glasses with a shallow or tulip-shaped bowl became relatively prominent in the late thirteenth and the fourteenth century and were soon joined by a whole range of beakers and goblets of different sizes and shapes and with varying decoration (examples in Fig 5.1). Simultaneously, Mediterranean and particularly Venetian production flourished and exported items to the north, often influencing local production (e.g. Baumgartner & Krueger 1988; Foy & Sennequier 1989; Henkes 1994, 21-118 for the Low Countries; Tyson 2000; Stiaffini 1999).

Other objects, generally of high quality and destined for aristocratic tables and other formal meals, include fine beakers and plates in gold or silver, *nefs* (see below) and even drinking horns (particularly in Scandinavia but also known in England and other places) with copper-alloy or silver mounts. The latter, normally of fourteenth-fifteenth-century date, were probably based on old (perhaps revived) traditions and had ceremonial purposes (Olrik 1909; Cherry 1989; 1991a; Grinder-Hansen 1997, cat.nos. 7, 247). Obvious status markers and expensive, most of these objects survived as collection items and are discussed in various exhibition catalogues.

Furniture and furnishing

Nowhere in Europe has a furnished medieval room been preserved. Most surviving medieval buildings have undergone extensive rebuilding and/or heavy restoration. However, it is still possible to deduce in general terms how houses were furnished and to gain some understanding of how people actually lived in their houses, and how and why the styles of living changed through time. The rapidly growing interest in 'housing cultures' (Ch 3, Ch 4; AME I, Ch 5; Roesdahl 2009) means that many new questions can now be addressed, such as the development of heating technologies and its consequences, the search for increased comfort, the use of furniture and fittings to express identities, social standing and political preferences, diversification in room function and private versus public life.

So far, we know more about the furniture and furnishing of town-houses than of farm-houses, but information on the latter is accumulating. There was little difference between town and countryside regarding furniture and fittings in equivalent social circles; but patterns could vary depending on room-sizes and heating systems: open fireplace, wall-fireplace, stove or sub-floor heating (AME 1, Box 5.2), which was decisive for the use of floor space and hence for the use and arrangement of furniture (Fig 5.9).

A variety of sources are available for the study of furniture and furnishings. Much furniture of all types survives in all parts of Europe, mostly from churches and grander houses and farms. Although usually out of context they demonstrate the variety and main types, and excavations may yield fragments. The archaeological study of medieval furniture must therefore maintain a balance between strongly fragmented or indirect evidence – parts of metal mounts, hinges, etc. – and complete or near-complete items. The published information on excavation finds is scattered over numerous find catalogues in excavation reports (e.g. Egan 1998, 42-64, 88-120; Brenan 1998), while synthetic work is still limited (e.g. Roesdahl 1999a; 2003a for Denmark). Most exhibition catalogues related to the Middle Ages offer examples of furniture, while most studies of the (art) history of furniture tend to link the Middle Ages with later periods and to pay only limited attention to the medieval items and the artistically less striking objects. There are, however, useful surveys (e.g. Mercer 1969; Kreisel 1981; Thirion 1998; Boc-

Arrangement of furniture and fit- **Fig 5.9**
tings in a sitting-room with a wall-
fireplace (right) *and a stove* (left),
as shown in a wood-cut printed in
England in 1506 (right), *and in Mu-*
nich, south Germany in 1488 (after
Roesdahl 2003a and Franz 1981).

cador 1988; Windisch-Graetz 1982; 1983; Albrecht 1997), some of them focussing on the Middle Ages (e.g. Karlson 1928; Eames 1977) or studying medieval collections (e.g. Tracy 1988).

Pictorial and written sources provide additional information (see Box 5.1). Pictures show furniture in use, e.g. dining scenes in various social groups. They also show important furnishing components which rarely survive, e.g. textiles for bedding, cushions, room divisions, wall-hangings, towels, table-cloths, etc. And from the fifteenth century onwards whole room interiors are shown by paintings and wood-cuts (Fig 5.9). It would appear that, at any given time, room furnishing was fairly standardised but that there were general regional variations between central and western Europe depending on the heating system used: the stove was normal in Central and parts of Northern Europe while wall fireplaces or even central fireplaces were normal in Western Europe and the western parts of Northern Europe. The individual pieces of furniture and fittings were, however, much the same during this period – as also shown by archaeology.

Important written sources from this period comprise testaments, accounts, and particularly late medieval inventories. These mention the movable furniture and other items in each room in the house in question and sometimes also the contents of chests and cupboards. To understand furnishing in its totality it is, however, crucial to realise that throughout the Middle Ages and throughout society much furnishing was built-in: there were wall niches for cupboards, built-in benches and beds and even built-in

BOX 5.1   LATE MEDIEVAL PICTORIAL SOURCES

In the later Middle Ages in particular, archaeological finds are supplemented by many pictorial sources that include illuminated books, murals, paintings, sculptures and monumental brasses on elite tombs. Archaeological and historical interest in these sources is growing, as they offer much information about material culture and behaviour. Illustrations in manuscripts and murals are particularly interesting (e.g. Haastrup & Egevang 1986-92; Mane 2001; 2006; Alexandre-Bidon & Lorcin 2003; Brown M 2006). Religious subjects clearly dominate, but the vernacular world is very much present (Fig 1). In our period, images offer varied factual information on components of the material world (e.g. dress, textiles, furniture, interior decorations, tools, weapons, dress accessories and even pottery). Fairly often it offers information not readily available through archaeology, for example the hammock shown in the Luttrell Psalter from *c.* 1320-40 (e.g. Backhouse 1989, 48, 56) or many of the toys and games seen in Pieter Bruegel the Elder's Childrens' Games (1560) (http://www.wga.hu/index1.html). More importantly, images also show the objects in context, revealing at least of some of their functions and associations with events and other objects – a distaff meant for spinning also comes in useful for man-beating (Backhouse 1989, 49). Good examples are representations of meals and set tables (e.g. Alexandre-Bidon 2009). They also add other information, such as the colours used. In short, they can complete the fragmented and partial archaeological picture. Some of them even include the word for objects shown, thus providing crucial information and links to written sources (see also Felgenhauer-Schmidt 1993, 99-110).

Visual representations are not, however, real-life photographs but manipulated interpretations of reality: they require a critical approach, preferably in collaboration with art historians. An artist may have copied a scene of foreign origin or used a foreign or older object. Some objects are depicted correctly, while others are not. Sometimes, the presence of an object has symbolic meanings changing its normal functions and setting. Thus, the realistically depicted Valencian albarello (unguent vase) and glass in Hugo van der Goes' Portinari Tryptich (*c.* 1475) (http://www.virtualuffizi.com/uffizi1/Uffizi_Pictures.asp?Contatore=14) are objects well-known archaeologically. But in the painting they are used as flower-vases (the flowers themselves having symbolic connotations), not as containers or tableware. They may well have been used as such in fifteenth-century Northern Europe, but they were hardly made with this function in mind (see also the bote in Fig 7.14).

None of this diminishes the value of visual representations for the archaeological study of medieval material culture. Rather, it emphasizes the complex and multi-faceted nature of objects and the way they were perceived. It also shows that such sources should not be used anecdotally or superficially. Conversely, as with written sources, archaeology has much to offer in return, because it documents objects differently and helps to understand their technical, functional and social complexities.

by Else Roesdahl and Frans Verhaeghe

Fig 1

Mural c. 1480 in Keldby Church, Denmark, showing a rich and a poor man kneeling at prayer either side of the cross. Each is dressed according to their means, and holds a rosary of appropriate quality. The thin lines show the secret thoughts of each: the poor man fixed on the wounds of Christ; the rich man with his dagger and purse thinks about clothes, money, drink, a fine horse, and food prepared by a woman (photo: Ebbe Nyborg).

tables. Written sources also remind us that folding furniture was fairly common: chairs, benches, tables. This made storage easy and was useful when travelling.

Furniture used to be studied only by art historians but the potential of archaeological study is increasingly recognised. Most furniture was simple carpenters' work, but it could be decorated with iron mounts which at the same time strengthened the construction. During the thirteenth to sixteenth centuries, carved decorations grew more common and constructions became lighter and more sophisticated, undoubtedly through the influence of cabinet-makers and designers of altar-pieces. Towards the end of the Middle Ages, panels were commonly used in the construction of chests, cupboards and doors. Colour is mentioned in written sources, and occasionally traces are found on existing furniture. Furniture can often be dated only within a fairly wide time-frame using decorative elements including mountings and construction features; some series of dendrochronological dates are sorely needed.

Furniture items can be grouped conveniently according to function: storage and safety, sitting, eating, sleeping (e.g. Roesdahl 2003a). Furniture for storage comprised chests and cupboards. Chests were the most common type of furniture, and some are still in use. Used for storing all sorts of things, some were also meant for travel. There were several types of construction, and they were decorated according to use. Further work will probably reveal workshops and certain regional groups (Fig 5.10).

Cupboards became increasingly popular and appeared in all sizes, often with iron mounts. Finer examples also allowed for the display of luxury items at feasts (as with the dressers). Chests, but also cupboards might have one or more solid locks for safety purposes; so far, these have hardly been studied.

Fig 5.10   *Carved chests, probably around 1400: (above) From Vadstena, Sweden (after Karlson 1928). (below) From Lyngby, Denmark (©National Museum of Denmark). This type of architectural decoration is found in north Germany, Denmark, Sweden and the east Baltic lands.*

Furniture for sitting comprised small stools, chairs and benches, the latter two furnished with cushions. Chairs and benches could be quite elaborate, with tall posts, carvings or lathe-turned posts and other details, some of which occasionally appear in excavations. Tables might consist of just a loose table-top on some support; decorative table-cloths were popular. Fine beds, with rich bed-clothes, were status symbols, and throughout the Middle Ages their place was in the 'sitting-room'. They probably also symbolised marriage, and there appears to be a specific Scandinavian type with prominent head-posts, following a tradition going back to the Viking Age (Roesdahl 2009, 274-5).

In the late Middle Ages 'sitting-rooms' became increasingly crowded with objects, as shown by written and pictorial as well as by archaeological sources. There might be a wash-basin and a towel on a holder, candle-sticks, an iron or brass chandelier, a flower-vase, etc. Where used, stoves constituted a dominant piece of furnishing with brightly glazed tiles with chosen motives (Fig 5.9; Ch 4, p 157).

All this reflects a changing way of life, with new levels of comfort, growing specialisation of room functions, probably a growing focus on private life, a certain concept of what was 'the right way of living' shared across fairly wide regions. It was the start of modern 'living' in a house – very different from what it was like in earlier times.

Dress, dress accessories and jewellery

Vernacular dress functioned as protection against the weather, but it also had (and has) a crucial role as a marker of gender, sometimes age, social status and wealth (cf. Fentz 1999; Piponnier & Mane 2000). This could be achieved through types and colours of cloth, fashionable (and sometimes highly impractical) cuts and fashions, and accessories and jewellery. Probably the best of all potential status markers, it consisted of an array of individual items, each changing according to fashion but forming characteristic ensembles together. The evidence also indicates that some of the elements of high fashion, which of course developed among and for the aristocracy, spread to all levels of society – e.g. male hoods with *liripipes* (tails) (see Fig 2.11). Clothes for physical work of course retained features such as a practical length. Given certain circumstances, some dress elements might fossilize in some societies or at some social levels, or local features could develop.

Both the archaeological evidence and the relevant literature are fragmented. Dress items are often studied separately from accessories and the textiles themselves are often looked at from a mainly technical perspective (Ch 7). But all in all, there is now a considerable and comprehensive corpus of material, and a modern synthesis, looking also at regional and social variations and at the origin and spread of fashions, is much needed.

Conditions for the survival of dress are variable. Wool, by far the most common material and sometimes mixed in with goat's or cattle hair, may survive in waterlogged or frozen conditions, but linen, much used for underwear, does not. Important finds include the fourteenth-century full dress of a man who disappeared in the Bocksten bog, south-western Sweden (tunic with belt, cloak, liripipe hood, suspension hoses with feet, shoes) and the many late thirteenth-early fifteenth-century dress items used as body wrappings for men, women and children at the Herjolfsnes cemetery, southern Greenland: tunics, coats, dresses, stockings/hoses, liripipe and other hoods, caps, a hat (Fig 5.11). These show that European fashions reached and were adopted even by the distant farming society of Norse Greenland (Nockert 1997a; 1997b; Østergård 2004).

There is also a rapidly growing corpus of items from town and castle excavations, though usually consisting of small fragments, as textiles were normally re-used intensively (e.g. Crowfoot *et al* 1992). Some aristocratic dress, made of rich materials, survived in graves with clothed deceased (although such dress may have been modified), as in the monastery of Santa María la Real de Huelgas in Burgos, Spain (e.g. Carretero, nd). Other aristocratic items are preserved as 'treasures' in churches, e.g. the 'pourpoint' (a tight jacket) of Charles de Blois (killed in battle in 1364), or the so-called Queen Margrete's golden dress from around 1400 (Nockert 1997a).

Fig 5.11   *Dress for man, woman and child, from the cemetery at Herjolfsnes, Greenland (c. 1300-1450). See also fig. 2.11. (©National Museum of Denmark).*

Such finds provide crucial information on materials, textile techniques, cuts, details, dyes and colours, and dating (Crowfoot *et al* 1992; Østergård 2004). However, the mass of coloured and often quite detailed pictures of fully dressed men, women and children from all levels of society, set in all kinds of situations, provide invaluable additional information for understanding dress and its contexts and developments (Box 5.1); some pictures with sick people even show underwear. Written sources also have much to offer: names of dress parts, lists of dresses in inventories, dress donations in testaments, costs of and trade in fine textiles, reactions to extreme fashions such as liripipe hoods or royal decrees against the nobility's extravagant dress displays.

All this clearly was of huge economic, social and practical importance and there was staggering variation – from clothes made of coarse wool in natural colours to pattern-woven silk ones in strongly contrasting colours and items made of finely processed wool. Padding and fur linings, which very rarely survive, was also used, while ermine symbolised and was the prerogative of royalty.

The period probably experienced the most extravagant fashions ever seen in Europe and shows developments in which many factors were at play. Male tunics, for instance, normally reached the knees in the twelfth century, became long in the thirteenth, then shortened again and became tighter in the fourteenth century, when they combined with liripipe hoods (as with the Bocksten dress). From around the mid-fourteenth century young fashionable men wore tight jackets with broad padded shoulders which barely covered the buttocks, together with tight stockings and pointed shoes – leaving little to the imagination (old men wore long dresses). Women's clothes had an equally tight top but a full long skirt. From the thirteenth-fourteenth century onwards, it became fashionable for both men and women to wear layers of clothing of different colours, allowing one item to be seen through openings in the other. Both sexes also wore all sorts of fashionable head-gear. Married women's hair was expected to be covered, and archaeological evidence of female headdress mainly consists of masses of small metal pins, used to keep this in place.

The fourteenth century also witnessed the introduction of buttons, which became high fashion, with very many of them at the front opening and on narrow sleeves. Alternatively, metal hooks and clasps were used to fasten tight dresses, and, following the general trend, small metal mounts and even bells became popular as pure dress decoration; these often appear in excavations. Gussets continued to be used in order to provide width in skirts and sleeves of male and female dress, but new patterns were also introduced, such as sleeves '*aux grandes assiettes*' allowing for better arm movement in tight jackets and dresses.

Dress accessories and jewellery appear regularly in excavations, and very fine examples survived in old collections (Lightbown 1992; see also Exhibition Catalogues and sources summarised in Box 5.3). Additional information is gained from inventories and other written sources, while function is seen in pictures and sculpture. Accessories were linked to dress fashions, types, forms, materials and qualities, and to dress context. They show wide variation and include leather belts with buckles, often embellished with metal mounts; belts could also be made of other materials, for example textile with metal, bone or ivory mounts, or be entirely of metal. Practical objects might hang from male and female belts (particularly useful in the period before pockets). In the four-teenth-fifteenth centuries, when male belt fashions flourished, it was also fashionable to wear kidney (or bullock) daggers for display, prominently placed at the front middle, above the crotch (see Box 5.1). Swords were worn with formal aristocratic dress. Purses of leather or textile, sometimes with metal frames, were also used by men. Lead or tin badges with political, religious (pilgrim badges) or other significance were worn on hats or elsewhere and signalled loyalty or devotion (Fingerlin 1971; Egan & Pritchard 1991; Goubitz 2007; Ch. 10, p 420).

Jewellery was, likewise, closely associated with dress – particularly brooches, many of which had practical functions (Egan & Pritchard 1991; Lightbown 1992; Tegnér 1996; concise survey in Hinton 1982). With the growing attention to fashions from the mid-fourteenth century onwards, jewellery also became increasingly decorative and colour-ful. There were many types, forms and materials that naturally signal status and wealth – some of it was magnificent and extravagant art for display. But excavations provide increasing amounts of cheap jewellery, which often imitate expensive materials, such as brass rings with inset 'stone' of glass paste. In some places, as in England, wearing some kinds of jewellery (gold, silver, precious stones) became a formal sign of rank and was regulated by law. Precious metal jewellery was also moveable wealth, and collections of this are known from hoards (e.g. Jensen *et al.* 1992) – which of course provide good chronologies. The metal dress-mounts, hooks and clasps mentioned above should also be seen as jewellery and might take decorative forms like rosettes, heraldic weapons or animals.

Much jewellery implied symbolic meanings through materials (types of inset stones for example), shape, inscriptions or images. This was particularly so with finger-rings and ring-brooches, and symbols mainly referred to fidelity and love (e.g. a heart shape or two clasping hands), or to beliefs (religious motives) (Fig 5.12; Ch 10, p 432). En-gagement rings were introduced during this period, and certain religious images prob-ably symbolised the formal entry of a nun into an order – as the bride of Christ.

The main types of jewellery were brooches, finger-rings and, particularly in the fif-teenth century, also necklaces with decorative pendants. Fashions spread all over Eu-rope, often following cultural and political affiliations (Box 5.2). Brooches were pre-dominantly ring-brooches. These appear from around 1200 and continued throughout the Middle Ages and sometimes beyond. They consist of a full 'ring' (of many forms and often flat) with a constriction for attaching the movable pin. There was no catch: the brooch was held in place by the pull of the material through which it was pushed. Many were of simple materials and undecorated, but the form allowed for much deco-ration, such as inscriptions, inset stones, clasped hands, filigree. They were used by both sexes, and numerous pictures demonstrate how they were used on dress. Huge display brooches and clasps moulded in relief were used for formal secular and ecclesiastic dress.

Finger-rings were used by both sexes and some had ecclesiastic functions. They var-ied widely and allowed imaginative craftsmen much leeway. Some had one or more in-set coloured stones, others a small sculpture or an engraved bezel; the whole ring might

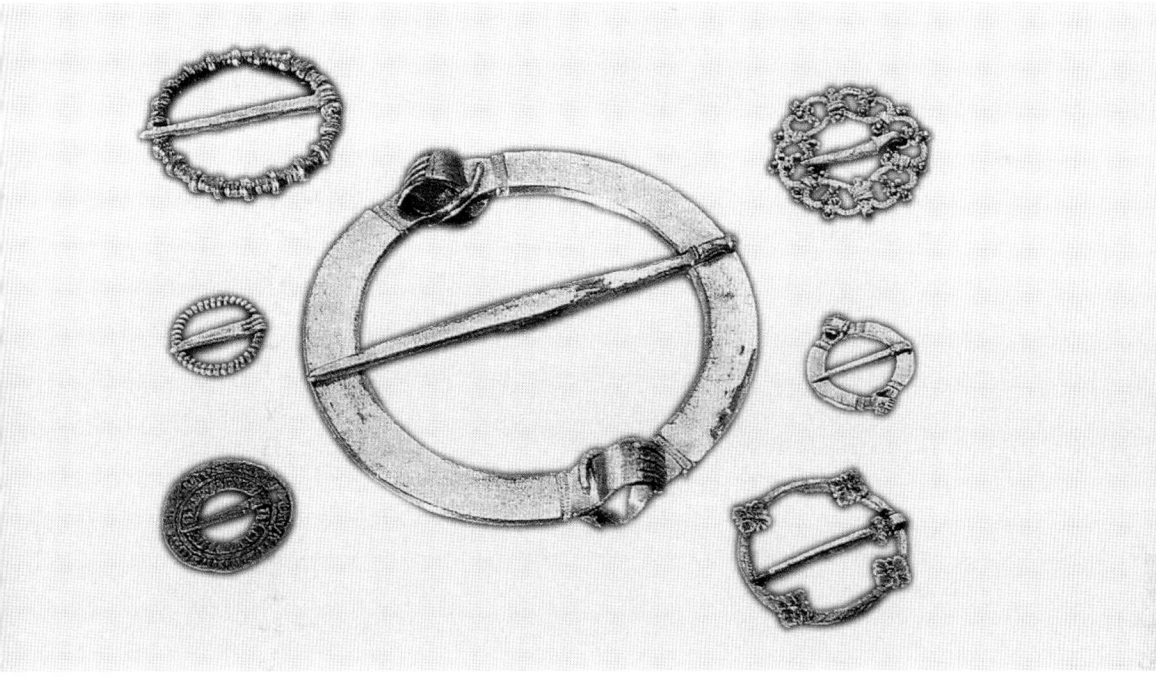

Ring-brooches of various materials and forms, including a symbolic one with clasping hands. From sites **Fig 5.12**
in Sweden. 13th-14th centuries (©State Historical Museum Stockholm).

be engraved and inscriptions also occur. Pictures show that a number of rings might be worn at the same time (Oman 1974; Lindahl 2003). Necklaces looked particularly good on bare throats and necks, as was the fashion for women in the fifteenth century, or, when these parts were covered, on plain cloth. They gave rise to pendants in many forms and of many meanings, sometimes an intricate and enamelled miniature sculpture; pendant crosses occurred quite often, which is linked with the growing popularity of devotional artefacts at the time (see below).

Waterlogged contexts in towns and castles have yielded large numbers of *leather shoes and boots* and pictures show that all levels of society used footwear (Fig 5.13). The finds are often discarded soles and uppers or fragments thereof, but much complete foot-wear is also known and some typologies have been presented. Footwear followed general fashions and some particular forms developed, like the late fourteenth-fifteenth century shoes with long pointed toes ('poulaines' or crackowes), followed around 1500 by the opposite, square-toed and low-cut shoes. The extreme forms were highly unpractical and would have been used on formal occasions. The same would be true with embroidered or otherwise decorated footwear. Shoes might be protected from contact with muddy roads by wooden pattens (e.g. Grew & de Neergaard 1988; Goubitz *et al* 2001, passim; Schnack 1992; Harjula 2008).

Fig 5.13   *Reconstruction of three late medieval shoes of different types from Konstanz, South Germany (after Scholkmann 2009).*

Leisure, entertainment and sports

Entertainment was an integral part of daily life, and manuscript and painted pictures of many kinds, offer interesting and sometimes surprising examples, such as performing dogs, horses, monkeys and bears, stilt walkers and acrobatic dancing, peculiar drinking situations and much more (for example images in the Luttrell Psalter, Backhouse 1989; Brown M. 2006). *Hunting* was a favourite sport of the aristocracy (Ch 3, p 132); arte-factual evidence consists largely of symbolic carvings (e.g. on knife handles, see above), rare hunting horns or ecofacts (like wild animal bones). Grand entertainment, like tournaments had high symbolic and political content; many armour items are related to jousting (see also Mehl 1990; Wilkins 2002).

A wide variety of *musical instruments* are known, partly from pictures and partly through archaeological finds of components of such instruments. Clearly, all levels of so-ciety had some form of music apart from what was heard in church. Artefacts range from simple home-made flutes and other wind instruments to mass-produced iron or copper-alloy jew's harps to string instruments and composite items like organs. A particularly fine gittern from the early fourteenth century, now in the British Museum, demonstrates the social importance of music (e.g. Cherry 1991a, 2-3, 7-8; Homo-Lechner 1996).

Board games were also widely spread throughout society. The materials and craftsman-ship of the related artefacts ranged from artistic gold and ivory pieces to simple wooden, bone or even natural stone ones. Some boards were incised on barrel lids or bottoms or on ship planks, suggesting their use as popular pass-times; others were elaborate artefacts. Pictorial and written sources inform us about the symbolic meanings of games and their functions in relation to feasting and other social meetings. Chess was the queen of games: it came to be played all over Europe – from imperial courts in Sicily to isolated farms in distant Greenland. Dice and discoid gaming counters (for the equally widespread but more aristocratic backgammon game), mostly made of bone but sometimes of more expensive materials, also turn up regularly in excavations (e.g. Murray 1913 [2002]; 1952 [2002]; Wichmann & Wichmann 1964; Zangs & Holländer 1994; Seipel 1998).

Body care

Health, hygiene and toiletry were part and parcel of daily life, and a series of artefact types in a variety of materials relate to these spheres of behaviour. Some like the many types of flask-like glass urinals (Fig 5.14), used to examine urine for medical diagnosis, or the unguent vases are fairly well documented. This also goes for combs in bone, antler, wood or more expensive materials (Fig 5.15). Other medicinal instruments and many smaller objects used for toiletry purposes – small pairs of tweezers, ear-picks, tooth-picks, small spoons for applying unguents, and others in bone, copper-alloy or even ivory – are also found occasionally and still require detailed study. They remain difficult to identify correctly, the evidence being scattered in many catalogues and notes. The unique find of a wooden leg from the fourteenth-century Boringholm castle in Denmark demonstrates the harsh realities of life (Fig 5.18; Andersen 2005, 137f).

Next to *mirrors* in metal, glass mirrors with a backing of lead or other metals became much more widespread from 1300 onwards. Fragments are excavated occasionally as are parts of the mirror frames or cases (varying from simple to costly) (Krueger 1993; Kock & Sode 2002).

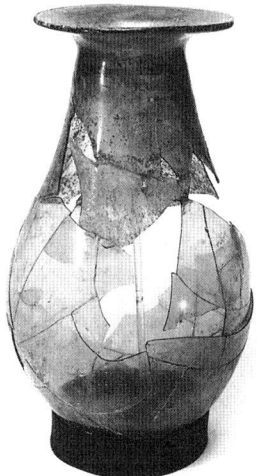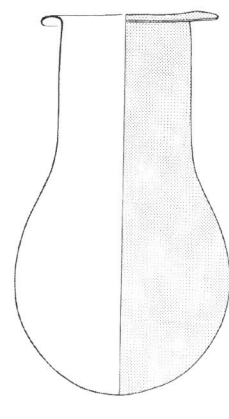

Glass urinals. Around 1500. Left: from London; height 22.5 cm. Right: from Strasbourg; height 16.6 cm **Fig 5.14**
(after Baumgartner & Krueger 1988, cat. no. 542; Foy & Sennequier 1989, cat. no. 371).

Combs from Bryggen in Bergen, Norway, dating from c. 1200 (centre) to the late 15th century (lower right side). Most are of antler, but one big double-sided comb (top centre, c. 1400) is of wood, and a small one (top left, c. 1250) is probably of whale bone (©University Museum of Bergen).

Reading and writing

The introduction of paper (thirteenth-fourteenth centuries) and printing (fifteenth century) gave occasion for the rapid application of reading and writing to much broader purposes and levels of society. Writing tools therefore become much more frequent in the archaeological record, and archives and libraries hold many examples of their products. Finds include styli of different materials, wax-tablets of wood or ivory, parchment-prickers, leaden line-markers (many were used for writing on vellum), pens, pen-cases, pen-knives, inkwells and seal-matrixes. Reading-glasses were also introduced. Excavations yield book-cover clasps, mounts and ornamented leather, to be compared with the material in libraries, and sometimes inscribed objects – in Scandinavia and Greenland runic inscriptions still appear. Reading, and the process of writing is seen in many pictures (e.g. Fig 5.9), and there was special furniture for reading, writing and book-keeping (surveys in e.g. de Hamel 1992; Grinder-Hansen 1997, 148-153, cat. nos. 85-102, 176-77 and passim; Roesdahl 1999b, 238-56), but note that identification of some writing tools is disputed).

Religious artefacts

The variety and mass of religious artefacts owned by laymen in the later Middle Ages corresponds to the mass of religious pictures, sculptures and other fittings now seen in churches and to the popularity of religious plays; they reflect new religious concepts and devotional patterns (cf Box 5.1). Artefacts include pilgrims' badges (AME 1, Box 13.2; here Ch 10, p 420), pendant crosses, burial crosses, devotional crosses, small portable alters, rosaries (Ch 10, p 428); figurines of holy persons, amulets (some Scandinavian lead ones had 'secret' runic inscriptions), printed religious images, books.

To gain some understanding of all this diverse material, different approaches and techniques are required – most of which are part and parcel of good archaeological practice. Together they offer the basic data needed for further understanding: object characterization and identification, the identification of materials (organic and inorganic), production technology, possible origins, chronology and evidence of use (for a general survey, see e.g. Caple 2006). In passing we may note that while scholarly interest in typological work has been declining, it remains essential for our period in order to manage the masses of material, for example the huge amounts of pottery recovered from excavations every year.

The main difference between the study of artefacts from earlier times and those from our period is that from around 1200 onwards the factual and contextual information provided by other sources, notably written and iconographical (or pictorial) material increases significantly. New types of texts emerge (e.g. inventories), more segments of society are documented and so are conditions of production, sources of raw materials, and information about guilds and particular commodities. Pottery studies provide a good example of what a combination of texts and archaeology can offer, for instance concerning medieval and later production centres (e.g. Flambard-Héricher 2002).

Texts offer insights of a contextual nature, allowing us to put objects in a social setting. This may be of a more general nature (e.g. production organization and economics) or more particular (e.g. an inventory of furniture or imports). In the latter case, we also gain insights into social meanings, values and prices. There remains much to do in this area and closer collaboration with historians is advocated. In our period, pictorial sources also offer direct evidence for the appearance, use and context of artefacts, as well as for the love of colour (Fig 5.16 and Box 5.1).

Unlike archaeology, texts and pictures rarely document the objects themselves in any detail. But archaeology has limitations of its own. Not all medieval artefacts are now available for study: some deteriorate fast underground, and only survive when conditions are favourable, as for example textiles in waterlogged deposits. Others have disappeared due to recycling, for example metals melted down to make new objects or wooden artefacts used as fuel. Thus, the best surviving material does not represent the highest social value. Pottery, for instance, was much less important than its archaeological occurrence suggests: sherds offer few possibilities for re-use and survive very well in the soil, but the average household probably had only a few items at any given time. Textiles on the other hand were ubiquitous, but they were extensively re-cycled and rarely survive underground. A long stay in the soil may also entail loss of information in metal and glass through corrosion, loss of colour, or abrasion of the original surface treatments.

Some high quality items, such as textiles, jewellery or liturgical objects were never buried and various exchanges and acquisitions have subsequently led them to modern collections and museums (see Box 5.3). The contextual information is often limited, but such items were an integral part of the material world. If they bias the evidence towards the higher and richer social groups, they do offer information on technologies,

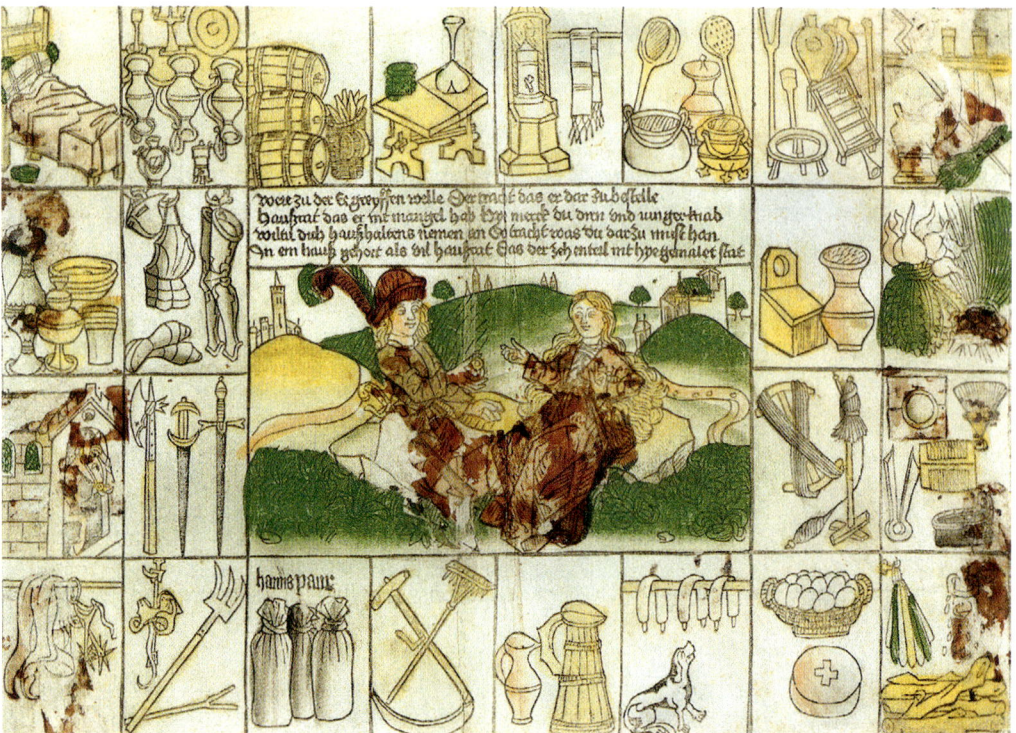

Fig 5.16   *Block print c. 1475 by Hans Paur, Nuremberg. 24 pictures of household equipment surround a young couple about to be married. The text above them explains the importance of the objects depicted and reminds them that they constitute only a tenth of what is necessary. The print is a visual variant of the detailed household poems of the time and may have been meant as a didactic house ornament. The same types of objects would have been used in large parts of Europe (©Staatliche Graphische Sammlung, München).*

materials, exchange, trade, production, culture and other aspects of material life, not forgetting their role in terms of identity and status. Contextualizing them with historical and art historical information can be illuminating (see for instance Cherry 1991a). And they regularly influenced the production of more lowly imitations, for instance as skeuomorphs (see below).

The study of objects today generally takes one of three forms: the basic presentation and discussion of finds in excavation reports, the study of specific assemblages and the more thematic and systematic study of specific categories or sub-groups of objects. In all cases, the approaches, criteria and questions should take into account the specific nature of the type of object involved – pots are not dress accessories: their life-trajectories and dynamics are different.

Syntheses concerning select categories generally have a regional or supra-regional scope and tend to pay systematic attention to origins, production, technologies, distribution and exchange, functionalities, social distribution and (possible) meanings, intra-site and inter-site comparisons and analyses. They constitute essential stepping-stones in the continuous study of these commodities, to be re-evaluated regularly as new finds turn up. For large numbers of finds, specific methodologies are required, including the building of databases (with relevant and discrete criteria) and quantification. The inter-site comparisons enhance the study of spatial and social distribution and meanings. More recent approaches also look at the movable finds from specific elites in a regional setting (e.g. Krauskopf 2005). Again, the quantification techniques depend on the kind of find under scrutiny (for pottery, see e.g. Orton *et al.* 1993, 166-81).

Some topics, such as function, social distribution, identity and status, economic significance and technologies, are fairly well rehearsed today. Each poses complex problems that in fact require a multidisciplinary approach and a good measure of critical reflection. The many interpretative issues in the study of medieval artefacts cannot all be discussed here. Suffice it to say that history, anthropology, ethnology and sociology may all provide interesting analogies and other clues, although their limitations in relation to archaeology should be kept in mind. The main point is that all objects have multiple meanings depending on their contexts, which change through space and time (e.g. Hundsbichler *et al* 1998).

Spatial analysis, and notably distribution maps, help to assess distribution, exchange and trade. But they are biased, as they also reflect the density and intensity of archaeological fieldwork. Furthermore, a foreign item in a particular agglomeration does not necessarily reflect direct trade: objects may travel in many ways (e.g. as gifts, souvenirs, taxes or group affiliation). Quantification can help, but even then issues such as the kind of trade involved, its relative importance, the routes followed and the way(s) the goods travelled are not necessarily resolved: these require additional information (e.g. through other sources) and critical assessments (for examples of interpreting finds in terms of trade and exchange, see Gläser 1999 on finds in Hansa towns; for medieval pottery, see for instance Verhaeghe 1999). The fifteenth-century Iberian maiolicas found in fishing settlements along the Belgian coast (Fig 5.2) illustrate this: neither rich nor poor, all sites yielded small numbers of such goods, and indirect evidence suggests that relatively easy access to these – not necessarily trade – explains their recurrent presence. In contrast, such goods were normally traded through nearby Bruges and included richer items destined for better-off societies in inland Flanders. The evidence also suggests that in the fishing communities these objects had other functions and probably other meanings (Pieters & Verhaeghe 2009).

Artefacts and identities

Related to issues in politics, culture past and present, globalization versus isolation, and many more topics, identity studies have become particularly important in recent years (Ch 1, p 21). Archaeology has embraced the subject, mostly drawing on anthropological theory (e.g. Driessen & Otto 2000). Identity may be defined as a set of common ideals and features specific for a smaller or bigger group and distinguishing it from others. This may take many forms and be expressed in literature, history, family patterns, cooking techniques, buildings, housing culture or personal ornaments, etc. The purpose is basically to help an individual to identify with a certain group and thus set her or him – for whatever reason – apart from others.

Objects provide an efficient means to express identities deliberately through clearly visible variations of form, decoration, material or technique, or through specific functions, for example in relation to a religion – Christian, Jewish, Islamic or other (Ch 10). Sometimes an earlier tradition is continued or re-invented as an identity marker, as with medieval beds in Scandinavia or late medieval and renaissance Icelandic and North Scandinavian furniture drawing heavily on Romanesque features (Roesdahl 2009 with refs). The systematic rejection of a cultural practice – for example the eating of pork by Muslims and Jews – is another means (on theory, see e.g. Otto & Pedersen 2005).

Identities as expressed through artefacts may relate to many kinds of groups, for instance religious ones. Others may be of a political nature, as reflected in badges, or ornament on late medieval-renaissance stove tiles in central and northern Europe (see below and Ch. 4, p 157; Cherry 1991a). Social or socio-economic groups may have used specific tableware, while monastic orders had their specific clothing. Opposing ethnic identities were sometimes expressed through types of personal ornaments, as in Baltic lands (see Box 5.2), while gender identities were almost always linked to dress. In geographically wide-spread societies, the urge to emphasize a common identity may be particularly strong, as was probably the case with Norse Greenlanders who tried hard to follow the culture of the Scandinavian homelands (Høegsberg 2009). A single individual could also signal multiple identities through a number of different artefacts.

But there are many questions. Was there, for example, a distinct burghers' identity as opposed to a farmers' one? (e.g. Roesdahl 2009). Did late medieval and renaissance stoves with glazed and highly ornamental figural tiles express a 'Hanse-identity', specifically related to the Hanseatic trading league, as has been suggested? (Ch 8, p 340). Or were they rather an efficient and decorative Central European form of heating system, which spread north and in some places perhaps signalled a burghers' identity?

Closely linked with factors such as tradition, socio-economic conditions or even status (see below), many artefactual expressions of identity had a local or regional distribution (as with many local pottery types), while others had a largely European coverage (as with the aristocracy's swords or certain pilgrims' badges; see AME 1, Box 13.2; here Ch 10, p 420). However, during the later medieval period, many artefact types and figurative motives were taken increasingly into common use over larger areas of Europe. Examples include fourteenth-century knives with a bone or ivory handle carved as a person holding a falcon, an aristocratic symbol, fourteenth-fifteenth-century stoneware jugs and goblets (see Ch 7, p 291), stove-tiles and their decoration motives (Ch 4, p 157, and Ch 8, p 347), mass-produced fifteenth-century brass candlesticks with a human figure (originating from Nuremberg in southern Germany, but copied in many places), the decoration of fine boxes, mirrors, chests or floor tiles with figural scenes from European literature, such as the story of Tristam and Isolde (e.g. Cherry 1991a) and particular fashions in dress and shoes (see above). The vastly expanding trade and other kinds of communication helped in this dissemination (see below and Ch 8).

Such objects were instrumental in creating new frameworks for daily life and a growing sense of being European, or for example North European. They also helped to create identities across natural and political borders. And some societies developed distinct cross-border cultures as in Sicily and Spain, even after the Christian Reconquista (see Ch 1, 4, 7, 8 and 11).

Influences from beyond Europe

Artefacts from distant lands were always an important part of aristocratic material culture, reflecting status and bringing pleasure, wonder and excitement. But the expanding long-distance connections of the period gradually also allowed other segments of society to gain access to items of distant origin, which then became part of their own material culture. Furthermore, exotic objects could be seen in public (e.g. in churches, processions and ceremonies) and would thus have some influence at all levels of society.

Many such foreign and often (near) complete artefacts have ended up in museums via old collections. More recently, however, more examples – mainly small fragments – have been identified among excavation finds, and gradually a better understanding of the meanings and functions of 'exotic' artefacts (and ecofacts) in the material culture of the time and of the influences of foreign cultures on European artefacts is developing. At any given time, different parts of Europe also had very different perceptions of what was foreign, exotic and valuable. In Trondheim, Norway, for instance, glass and silk was much coveted, while in Venice, Italy, fine furs were clearly status symbols.

From *c.* 1500 onwards, the Far East, Central and West Africa, and the Americas became more accessible, and their influence on Europe expanded, when new intercontinental sea-routes allowed for the transport of much larger quantities of exotic goods at much lower prices than before. Up till then, Mediterranean trade and other communication with the Far East followed the long caravan routes across Asia (the Silk Roads). Artefacts and materials from Afghanistan, India and China were therefore rare, exotic and very expensive; goods included spices, porcelain, semi-precious and precious stones and silk (although silk was now also produced in Mediterranean lands). New ideas and skills also travelled. From China, paper-making reached Europe in the thirteenth century. By 1300, this new writing material – so much cheaper than parchment and vellum – was produced in northern Italy. Already in the fourteenth century, paper became cheap enough to be used for mundane purposes such as accountancy, inventories, letters, pictures and announcements (see above). Similarly, gunpowder reached Europe from India in the mid-thirteenth century. Soon adapted for military purposes and combined with newly invented and continuously developed types of firearms, it had a dramatic impact on warfare, fortification, naval battles and ship constructions, as well as on society, politics and European expansion (see Ch 6, p 260).

Europe always had some contact with the Mediterranean Muslim world and its many cultures. Expensive incense from Arabia was used in the censers of rich churches and also enjoyed by many there; the material itself is (so far) difficult to identify, but written sources provide some information. Many links were with or through southern

BOX 5.2   OBJECTS AND IDENTITY IN MEDIEVAL ESTONIA

Fig 1

Images of people with penannular brooches carved on the arches in the churches of Saaremaa. (Left) male figures in Pöide Church (damaged by the Soviet army after World War II); (Right) female figures in Karja Church (photos: Kaur Alttoa).

The area of Medieval Livonia, i.e. present-day Estonia and Latvia, offers an interesting insight into the way that portable material culture was used to signal identity at the lowest as well as the highest levels. The region was conquered and Christianized during the thirteenth century, and as a result of the conquest, the population was split into two major ethno-social groups: the new nobility, mostly of German origin, and the lower classes, mainly indigenous peasants. Medieval written sources repeatedly reflect the presence of two communities: *Deutsch* and *Undeutsch*, i.e. the Germans and the natives, and these terms also occur in relation to ornaments and dress (Johansen & von zur Mühlen 1973).

The polarization of society is reflected very clearly in ornament. In Fennoscandia, transition to medieval Christianity caused a big change in fashion, and ornaments characteristic of pagan times were abandoned. In the Baltic countries, however, several ornamental forms of the Late Iron Age – penan-

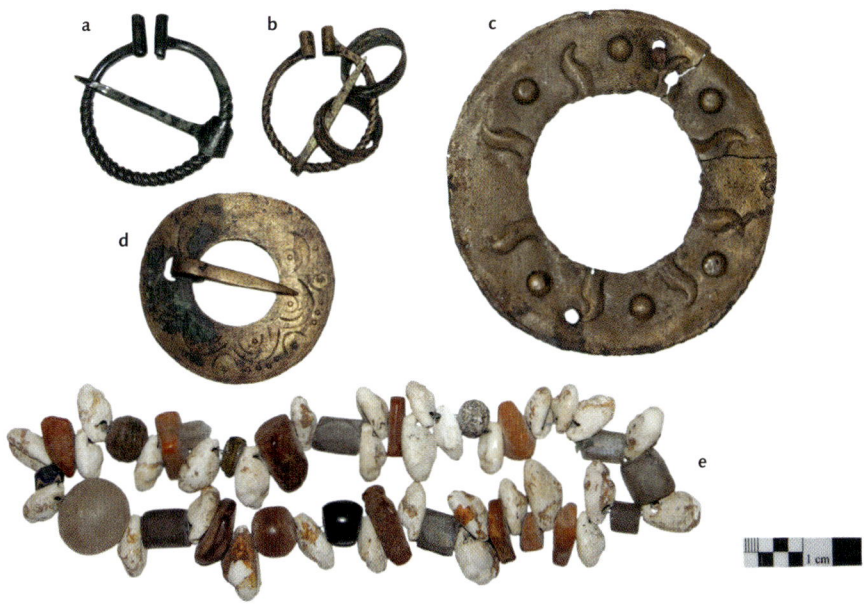

Fig 2

Late Medieval ornaments from Vana-Kuuste village cemetery, southern Estonia. Left to right, from top: a-b: penannular brooches and spiral rings – ornaments based on Late Iron Age traditions. c-d: local derivate forms of the "Hanseatic brooches". e: necklace of cowry shells, amber, glass and quartz beads, a sign of south Estonian identity.

nular brooches, spiral rings and traditional festive necklaces with big sheet pendants – remained in use in medieval times and even later, for both everyday and special occasions.

In the thirteenth century, after the conquest, the old fashions and ornamental traditions persisted among the native elite of Estonia, including those who became involved in new power structures. Traditional Iron Age identity is expressed, for example, in sculptures at the churches of Pöide and Karja on Saaremaa, island of the Baltic Sea, where figures on the arch of the crossing are shown wearing coats fastened with penan-

nular brooches, in the case of Karja as late as the fourteenth century (Fig 1). The figures are located in the position where images of donors are normally positioned in church architecture. Evidently, the depicted persons are not ordinary peasants but representative of the local social nobility, which had preserved its social position within the post-conquest social system. Written and other archaeological data also indicate that the Iron Age nobility preserved its status on Saaremaa (Mägi 2002, 148-150, 154-156).

Another example of such cultural conservation is Pada Cemetery (Tamla 1998) in Virumaa, north-eastern Estonia, an area that was conquered and Christianized by the Danes in 1219-20. The excavations of this late twelfth – mid-thirteenth century cemetery showed continuity of pre-Christian ornaments and fashion into post-conquest times: there was evidence of traditional Late Iron Age costume in graves with coins from the 1220s-1230s, and the dead were furnished with penannular brooches, wire bracelets, necklaces with pendants, and in one case with a breast chain with cross-headed pins. The cemetery is located beside a Late Iron Age hillfort which probably functioned also in the thirteenth century, and which was evidently inhabited by the people buried in the cemetery. Similar ornaments are known from the earliest graves in the churchyard of Viru-Nigula, located 3 km from Pada.

The two main places where European and the native culture met at the level of everyday life were towns and manors. It was in this way that the round 'Hanseatic' brooches spread widely in the thirteenth and fourteenth centuries. In the fifteenth century, when the round brooches went out of fashion in Medieval Europe, local forms emerged in Livonia. These derivatives developed continuously into the large ethnographic silver brooches of the eighteenth and early nineteenth centuries. Among the ornaments, there exist, however, also such specific 'European' forms which occur neither in the numerous peasant hoards from the time of the sixteenth-seventeenth centuries wars (1558-1625), nor in the peasant graves – both village cemeteries and churchyards. A good example is here the signet rings, where 'native' types can clearly be distinguished from the large rings of the nobility, made of precious metal.

In the south-easternmost corner of Estonia, on the basis of specific ornaments and costume, an identity characteristic of north-eastern Latvian Adsele County was expressed until the mid-fifteenth century (Laul & Valk 2007). In this area, women wore shawls decorated with bronze clips, headbands ornamented with beads, bronze and tin, and wide shield-shaped bracelets. Within Estonia the southern part can be distinguished by a large number of different kinds of traditional ornaments (Valk 2001) while the northern part is poor in ornament finds. These two macro-areas coincide well with the two major dialect areas of Estonia and are clearly reflected also in the ethnographic data (Valk 2006a).

The stressing of ethnic identity, however, only lasted among the native elite for a few generations. It was probably the 'Europeanization' of the native nobility involved in the feudal system that caused a break in the ornamental traditions of northern and western Estonia in the second half, or towards the end of the thirteenth century. In southern Estonia, where the elite was not involved in the new power structures and where the ethno-social polarization of society was strongest after the time of conquest, the old 'non-German' ornament forms (Fig 2) continued more broadly throughout the Middle Ages and until the seventeenth century (Valk 2001, 42-53; Laul & Valk 2007, 68-68). In this area local 'non-German' derivative forms of 'European' ornaments also emerged; they were produced both in urban and rural environment (see also Ch 10, p 430).

by Heiki Valk

Italy and the Iberian Peninsula, and the western Mediterranean developed its own versions of Islamic goods and technologies. High-quality sword blades from Toledo were famous throughout Europe. In the fifteenth century, Spanish and other Mediterranean maiolica luxury tableware (see above), wine and olive oil in amphorae, and other commodities like exotic fruits reached the North Sea and Baltic regions more or less regularly.

Contacts with Byzantium also continued and Byzantine luxuries were owned, or seen, by many in Roman Catholic Europe – some of it looted from the town of Byzantium itself (1204, Fourth Crusade). The Crusades and the new Christian principalities in the East Mediterranean strengthened ancient connections with both the Byzantine and Muslim worlds and helped to introduce new artefact types and technical skills into Europe. Aquamaniles (Fig 5.7 and AME 1, Figs 8.3 and 12.6) provide an example: based on Muslim tableware, they became popular with the wealthy for centuries and were soon produced in metal-working centres. Many survived in churches, but secular use is documented by the occasional example of a metal aquamanile excavated on a castle site, and by the cheaper pottery copies.

Surprisingly often, fine glass beakers, with coloured enamelled ornaments and sometimes inscriptions, are found on castle and town sites all over Europe. Generally of thirteenth-fourteenth-century date, they were based on Near Eastern Islamic glass traditions (Syria/Egypt), but many were produced in Venice. Rosaries (Box 5.1) are also inspired by the Muslim world and came to be used for prayer throughout society (see Ch 10, p 428). By the fourteenth and fifteenth centuries, many towns had workshops producing them (Fig 1.15).

Imports from Africa included gold, mainly used for jewellery, gilding and coins, and elephant ivory (see also Ch 8, p 357, p 363). From the mid-thirteenth century onwards these materials were available in increasing quantities, and until *c.* 1400, ivory was used frequently for religious as well as vernacular items, such as mirror cases and mall boxes with pretty mounts, which were sometimes also finely carved and painted. In the fourteenth century, huge numbers of small portable altars were produced in Paris and elsewhere, spreading all over Europe (Gaborit-Chopin 1978, passim).

Northern Russia, Scandinavia and Greenland provided walrus ivory, used mainly for gaming-pieces, but also for all sorts of carving, until elephant ivory became more readily accessible (Roesdahl 2003b, 2005). Another commodity from these regions consisted of quantities of quality furs used to line and decorate the clothes of the wealthy; it provided protection against cold weather and also signalled status, particularly in places with no natural access to such materials. The fur trade and functions of fur are well documented in written sources (e.g. Delort 1978; Ch 8, p 360); pictorial evidence shows how it was used, and natural sciences are starting to complement the information, including evidence for cheaper furs (e.g. cat and rabbit furs).

Diversification, increasing comfort and standardization

The period *c.* 1150/1200-1550 shows a number of interesting and complex general trends related to practical and functional aspects of objects. First, it seems that individual sites on average yield a larger number of items than they did before, probably due to a growing range of available artefact types. In pottery, for example, in the twelfth century new vessel types emerged, particularly among table-wares, starting with a variety of jugs and – from the thirteenth century onwards – the occasional dish, new types of drinking vessels, tripod cooking-pots. By the fourteenth and fifteenth centuries, chafing dishes, salts, beakers and mugs, dripping dishes, colanders, a variety of plates, curfews, money boxes, candlesticks, watering pots, flower pots, whistles, and quite a few others were part of the normal picture. This development was linked to the phenomenon of functional specialization (e.g. Verhaeghe 1987). In addition, new groups such as highly decorated wares, stonewares and maiolicas gradually conquered the tables of the wealthier and later also of other classes. Glass drinking vessels provide a comparable picture as do other object categories, e.g. jewellery, dress accessories and furniture, though the documentation is somewhat less explicit. All this suggests a recurrent pattern of diversification and at the same time – from the consumers' point of view – a gradually increasing measure of material comfort. The latter is consistent with what buildings and other components of material culture (e.g. food) tell us.

At the same time, the finds reveal phenomena of what may be called standardization or a trend towards more uniformity. This is manifested at different levels – firstly in the commodities themselves; and again pottery provides an example. Although the variety of types and groups increased, objects became more uniform within specific regions. Sometimes – as with Rhenish stonewares (cf. Gaimster 1997) – the concentration of a specialized product in associated workshops played a part. So did other factors, particularly the supremacy of specialized producers, transfers of technology and craftsmen, and mass production. However, regional differences did not disappear. On the contrary: idiosyncratic characteristics in terms of form and/or decoration occur in most regions (see below). This can probably be explained through particular economic, social and cultural circumstances combined with local or regional traditions.

There was probably also another form of standardization linked to particular social groups. This comes close to, but is somewhat different from, identity (see above), having more to do with Bourdieu's *habitus* concept combined with local or regional socio-economic, environmental and cultural conditions – it results from behaviour and consumption patterns rather than from conscious choices. The religious communities in the Dutch town of 's-Hertogenbosch seem to reflect such patterns by using, in part, a common range of goods and equipment. Other groups may well have done the same, and this research avenue deserves further exploration (Janssen H 1985; 1990: 408-9).

Social communication, status markers and changing worlds

Artefacts were (and are) an effective if mute means of social communication. Some were used to affirm one or more identities of the owners (see above), and some, such as secular or religious badges fixed on dress or hat, also allowed the wearer to project a particular message or commemorate an event (e.g. a pilgrimage; Ch 10, p 420). The significance of these signals is not always clear to us, but their range may have been extensive; the symbolic content often referred to religion but other beliefs, customs, politics, literary allusions and erotic signals were also on the agenda. Some were even mass-produced (Koldeweij A 1997; Koldeweij J 1999; Spencer 1998).

Objects are often both utilitarian goods and status markers – just like castles and palaces with practical military and/or residential functions and a deliberate message of power (cf Ch 6, p 230). With common tools, cooking pots or agrarian equipment, practical considerations took precedence over social ones. Things were different with goods that could literally be put on display, such as jewellery, dress and dress accessories, tableware (including cutlery), riding and other travelling equipment, furniture and fittings. These allowed users to signal status and/or wealth through the quality of the craftsmanship, the use of costly or exotic materials and/or objects that were not a real necessity. The expensive large mirror, elaborate chandelier and high quality dresses in van Eyck's painting of the Arnolfinis (1434) illustrate this.

If we include the objects transmitted through collections and museums, the record boasts a wide array of high quality goods. The interpretation in terms of status is sometimes easy, as with costly jewellery (Lightbown 1992). Other examples include expensive textiles and dresses or the often intricately ornamented armour suits of the high nobility, or the late medieval *nefs* – high quality table-ornaments in the shape of a ship and used for presenting salt or spices or even for keeping eating utensils (e.g. Oman 1963; Kovacs 2004, 193-6; Lightbown 1978 passim). High quality reliquaries and liturgical dress, sometimes preserved in church treasuries, project similar messages, mixed in with religious symbolism.

Metal objects such as copper-alloy ewers, chafing dishes, aquamaniles, lavabos and others were regularly copied in ceramics, the latter being *skeuomorphs*, cheaper imitations with some embellishment such as coloured decoration (Fig 5.17). Several factors may have been at work here: potters trying to gain a foothold in the market for quality goods, and consumers looking for cheaper versions of high status possessions. Such products could be profitable, as suggested by pottery copies of tripod metal cauldrons (see above) circulating in the North Sea region from around 1200 onwards.

High quality display artefacts (including exotic items from abroad), in combination with technical innovations, also contributed to other changes in daily material life. More objects were decorated – often intricately, and from the twelfth century onwards, daily life as a whole became more colourful. Blues, reds and other colours flourished in stained glass windows, a hallmark of Gothic religious architecture. Coloured enamels on quality goods from reliquaries to tableware enjoyed a renewed success; the French town of Limoges is iconic among production centres (e.g. Gauthier 1972; Taburet-Delahaye & Drake Boehm 1995). Walls sometimes carried painted scenes in vivid colours (Box 5.1). Woven tapestries with figural scenes adorned the walls of the wealthy in the late Middle Ages. Colours also adorned less expensive goods – dress and table-cloths for example. In Mediterranean regions the green and brown painted pottery was flanked

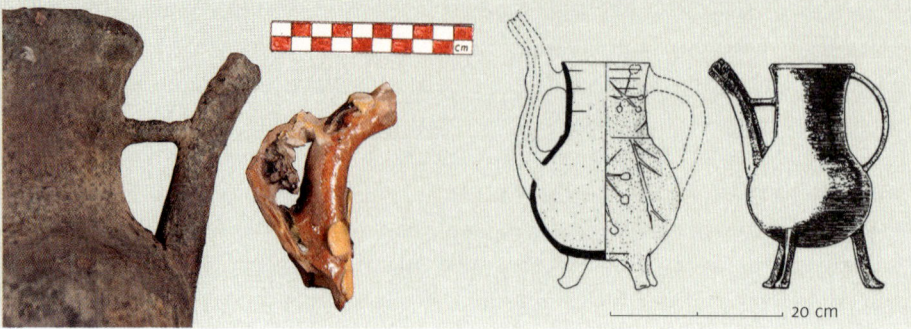

Fig 5.17   *Metal ewers and skeuomorphs. Flanders, Belgium, c. 1350-1450. (right) Highly decorated ceramic ewer with applied pipe-clay stripes and a typical copper-alloy ewer. (left) Copper-alloy ewer and fragment of a highly decorated ceramic copy with characteristic applied decoration and colour contrasts. The decoration includes a face-mask (lips, beard and nose), a copper green strip around the spout, an applied flower (petals) and animal ears and eye on the spout. From Raversijde, near Ostend, Belgium (photo: E & A Cools-Mortier).*

with white maiolicas decorated with blue, reddish, green and brown; in the North, highly decorated wares expanded the range of mainly grey and buff wares with reddish fabrics and green and yellow glazes, often using colour contrasts to enhance the decoration.

The development of heraldry was another element (see Ch 3, p 88). Colourful coats of arms – the colours gradually gaining definite symbolic values – were now used to adorn not only weaponry, buildings and monuments but also other artefacts, conveying an explicit status signal. By the fourteenth and fifteenth centuries, coats of arms were also used on some glass vessels and expensive ceramics like larger maiolica plates. A few highly decorated jugs and finials with heraldic ornament suggest that the practice became more widespread, and that some of these objects were made to order.

Finally, a developing archaeological research theme concerns the relations between town and countryside. The prevailing idea is largely that the urban context was more conducive to innovation and the development and adoption of new and more varied goods. In contrast, the rural world is – often unconsciously – perceived as more tradition-bound and also 'cruder'. The latter is not, however, really borne out by the record. Recent work on English finds (Egan 2005b) suggests that there were some artefactual differences between town and countryside and that these were mainly related to specific activities and easier access to some commodities in towns. But the differences were far more limited than surmised: the finds (and other indications) suggest that the two material worlds were closely intertwined. The coastal fishing settlements in Flanders (Pieters & Verhaeghe 2009) and many of the commodities seen on rural sites bear this out. Socio-cultural and economic networks between town and countryside may go a long way to explain this situation.

Conclusions

Our brief survey offers an indication of the wide range, large numbers and general complexity of portable artefacts of the period (Fig 5.18). It also reveals a few general developments, notably growing diversification and specialization and hence also growing numbers of artefacts and artefact types. In terms of purely material well-being, the conditions of daily life improved, and cheaper versions of high quality items also ensured a wider social distribution of many commodities. At the same time, most of these artefacts had complex social meanings and were used – deliberately or unconsciously – to convey all kinds of messages.

As in earlier periods, artefacts were markers of social and economic diversities. This appears not only from variations within individual object groups but also from inter-site comparisons – locally, regionally and supra-regionally – of find assemblages. Finds from different parts of a town often reflect differences in terms of economic and social strata; finds from different towns or regions often reflect variations in economic prosperity and/or access to goods. The differences in numbers, range and/or quality of finds between some of the richer southern towns and some of the northern regions illustrate the point. Finds from a specific site should, therefore, also be set within their specific local and regional contexts. The artefacts from the bishop's seat Gardar in Greenland, for instance, should first and foremost be interpreted within their own regional context, i.e. in comparison with those from other Norse farms in Greenland, in order to assess their meanings. These may well be very different from those of similar finds from a major harbour in France or from a bishop's seat in Central Europe. It would be risky indeed to use only the finds, as opposed to the assemblage in its context, to assess social similarities or variations between sites in northern Europe and Sicily, for example. Things also remain very difficult when it comes to an assessment of the material culture of the lowest classes and the very poor, as they left little diagnostic material evidence.

The evidence demonstrates that regional diversity was wide and studying it can offer very interesting clues as to the dynamics of production and consumption, the transfer of technologies and the mechanisms of adoption and adaptation of new fashions and behavioural patterns. But the artefacts also show this regional diversity to be intimately intertwined with more over-arching socio-cultural developments pointing to both a common European culture in some respects and supra-regional cultures in others.

Medieval artefact studies have progressed very significantly since the inception of modern medieval archaeology in the 1950s and numerous excavations have turned up a truly immense amount of material and data. But much of it remains to be exploited to the full, preferably in collaboration with historians, art historians and others. There is a continued need for both detailed study of the finds (including regional chrono-typologies) and new synthetic work – as the literature clearly shows. The evidence demonstrates that portable artefacts have much to tell us when we take their study beyond simple description and dating.

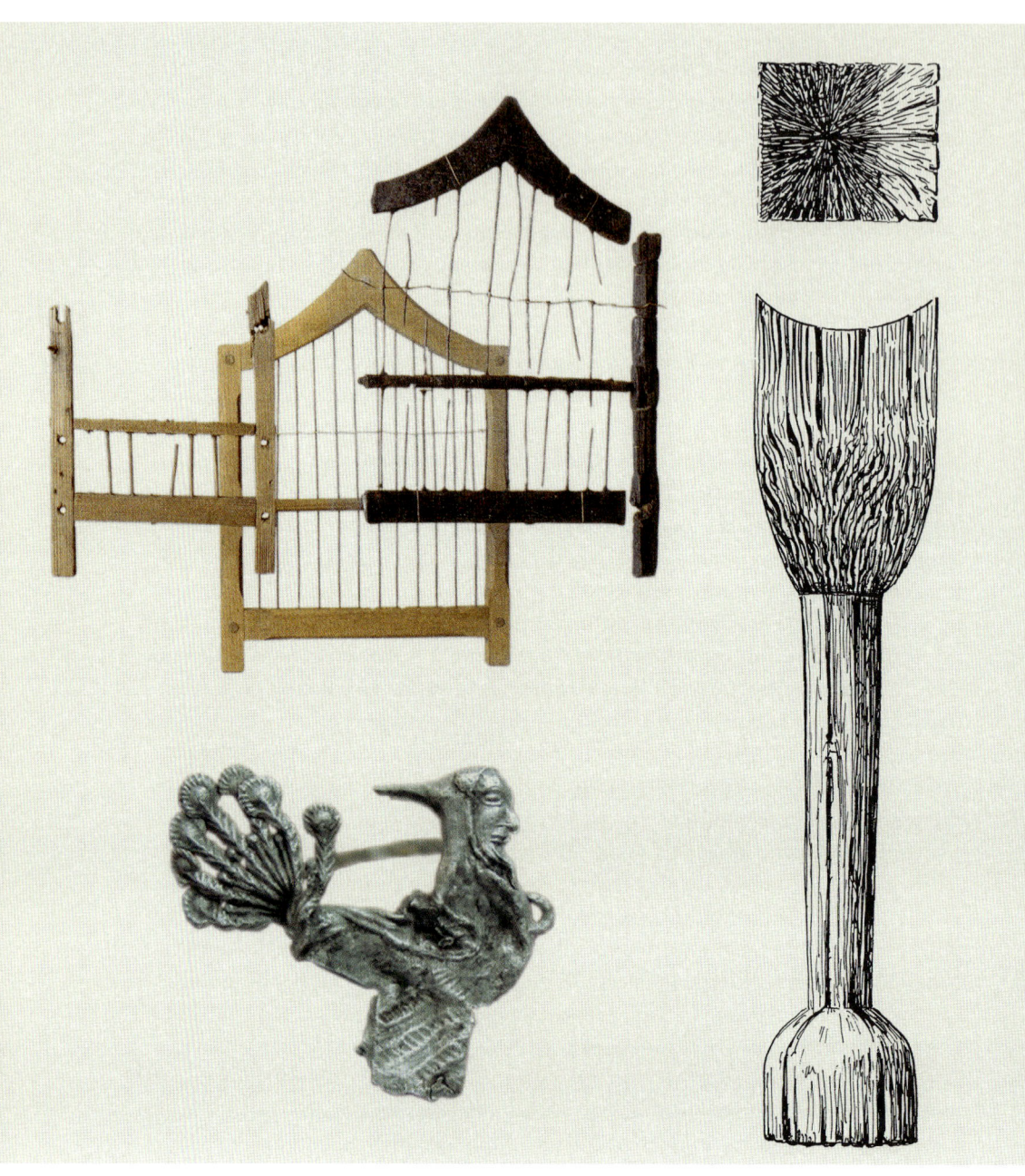

Fig 5.18   *Three unusual finds. (top left): birds cage from a monastic latrine in Freiburg, south Germany; 13th-14th century. (right): wooden leg from Boringholm castle, Denmark; late 14th century. (below left): pewter trinket found in Ribe, Denmark, probably of English origin (photo: Archäologisches Landesmuseum Baden-Württemberg (top left); Sydvestjyske Museer Ribe (below left); (right): after Andersen 2005).*

BOX 5.3 BIBLIOGRAPHICAL SOURCES

The literature related to the extensive domain of medieval cultural material has grown exponentially: it is vast, widespread and scattered over numerous types of publications. Conversely, syntheses – which at any rate rarely cover Europe – have become far and few between, particularly in recent years. In the case of pottery, for instance, only few comprehensive surveys are available (e.g. Lüdtke & Schietzel 2001; McCarthy & Brooks 1988; Gaimster 1997). But bibliographies are provided by the British Medieval Pottery Research Group (http://www.medievalpottery.org.uk/ click bibliography) and by the French Réseau d'Information sur la Céramique médiévale et moderne (ICERAMM) (http://iceramm.univ-tours.fr/ click bibliographie).

The situation is comparable but more difficult for other artefact categories: different specialist associations may offer some help (e.g. the Finds Research Group – http://www.frg700-1700.org.uk/). But by and large, bibliographies remain a problem. Useful (often regional) surveys may be starting points (e.g. Blair & Ramsay 1991; Clark 1995; Cowgill *et al* 1987; Crowfoot et al 1992; Egan 1998; 2005a; Egan & Pritchard 1991; Felgenhauer-Schmidt 1993; Gläser 2006; 2008; Grew & de Neergaard 1988; Hinton 2005; Roesdahl 1999b).

Exhibition Catalogues

Perhaps the most useful guide for modern students of medieval artefacts is provided by the Catalogues prepared for various thematic exhibitions: Ward-Perkins 1967; Wittstock 1983; Meckseper 1985; Alexander & Binski 1987; Baumgartner & Krueger 1988; Foy & Sennequier 1989; Schnitzler 1990; Flüeler, M & N 1992; Luckhart & Niehoff 1995; Grinder-Hansen 1997; Seipel 1998; Krüger *et al.* 2001; Berthelot *et al.* 2002; Marks & Williamson 2003; Jöns *et al* 2005.

by Else Roesdahl and Frans Verhaeghe

POWER

Introduction *by Martin Carver*

Chapel, castle and vineyard at Tourbillon, Sion, Switzerland.

The exercise of power operated at every level of medieval society; in our previous group of chapters its influence was noted at the level of the house, the household and the settlement, in the fields, in the forests, in the reclamation of land. In this section we focus on its overt expression, and as a theme, examine the increasing transfer of power from the military aristocracy (Ch 6) to the manufacturer (Ch 7), the merchant (Ch 8) and the town (Ch 9).

Of all the buildings that were put to the service of social control, the castle and fortified house are the most extrovert. Today's research agenda emphasises the role of the castle as a settlement, but we do not shrink from considering the escalating demands of military defence and attack, their role in the administration of force, and the effects of the growing availability of gunpowder (Ch 6). The account of the wounds sustained at the Battle of Towton, as revealed by the bodies of those that were there (p 272), is a reminder that the fourteenth century addiction to violence was not symbolic. We visit fortified sites in France, Switzerland, Latvia and Ireland, noting the architecture, the use of space and the message of the assemblages, including diet, pretension, display and the relations between native and invader, commander, garrison and builder.

While violence does not recede between the thirteenth and sixteenth century, the rise of production, marketing and trade offered opportunities for power of another kind. According to our contributors, the initiative is increasingly gained by those doing the work, who find ways of keeping and reinvesting their profits out of reach of the landed gentry. To talk of a medieval 'industrial revolution' is not an exaggeration, at least in certain parts of the continent. In our period, Europe clearly moves into a sophisticated and interlinked system of extraction, manufacture and supply (Chapters 7 and 8) representing a major change from the world of AME 1 (there, Chapters 7 and 10). The emergence of industry from craft is explored in Chapter 7 for pottery, glass, leather, and oil, with special studies of stoneware, Andalusian pottery and glass, textiles and iron extraction.

Chapter 7 also offers a pen-picture of the extraordinary success of the Moravian Anabaptists in confronting their enforced marginality by winning a market niche and growing rich on it. This is an indication not only of the new rewards for ingenuity permitted by later medieval society, but of the development of ever wider arteries of trade, enabling the creation of wealth at a distance (Ch 8). While travel over the sea and across the ice have already been long possible, we are now in the era of the routine carriage of heavy freight. Some confederacies, such as the Hansa, attempted to control the network-forcing others to seek more and more exotic markets and use coinage as the gilt-edged underpinning of commerce. Islam inspired an important exchange system within the Mediterranean, and European merchants began reaching out towards sub-Saharan Africa and China in pursuit of spices, silks, gold and beasts of special potency.

The facilitating machine of this new industrial and mobile world was the town (Ch 9); not just a big place to live, but the central stage for social interaction, the place where the rising power of the merchant met the monumentality of the aristocracy and the church. The archaeological investigation of towns, town life and town histories has been a major part of the archaeological project over the last fifty years, not least because modern urban centres are amongst the most vulnerable to new development, provoking major campaigns of archaeological excavation. With their concentrations of human energy, towns also generate a rich material culture and present unparalleled opportunities to get under the skin of medieval ways of thinking. Here residence, craft, trade and religious worship can be seen in their social context, often, as with guildhalls, in the same building. Archaeology above and below ground has also overturned the twentieth century view of the Islamic town as something unstructured, in comparison to the west. In our era of widespread redevelopment, urban archaeology has brought many late medieval communities to life and helped to write town histories, as we show in examples from Poland, France, Italy and the Czech Republic.

CHAPTER 6

ARCHAEOLOGIES OF COERCION

PART 1: CASTLE ARCHAEOLOGY – AN INTRODUCTION *by Werner Meyer*

The archaeology of fortification naturally includes more than castles: urban and landscape fortifications of different construction and length (Fig 6.1), coastal and shoreline defences, short-term fortified points for mobile troops, town walls, fortified bridges and – towards the end of the Middle Ages - fortifications built for artillery warfare and conceived as places of garrison (see Part 2 below). The first part of this chapter, however, is concerned with the archaeology of castles, how they were constructed, how they were used and how we know – their investigation.

Castles of the tenth and eleventh centuries were presented in volume 1 (AME 1, Ch 11). From *c.* 1100 there is a marked increase in castle-building and the sites have a multiplicity of function. Documentary evidence for the period 1100-1500 remains relatively sparse, or incomplete, one-sided and sometimes altogether misleading. There are many undocumented castles, whose original name is unknown. Furthermore, there are – at least in the twelfth and thirteenth centuries – other castles that, while mentioned in documentary sources, are difficult to identify on the ground. The origins of European castles are particularly elusive. The earliest mentions in documentary sources are entirely haphazard and often appear only centuries after the foundation date. Even direct references to construction do not necessarily relate to their foundation, since such information can refer to additions or transformations to already existing castles.

Records concerning the building history of castles in the possession of the landed nobility or in towns begin to emerge in the form of accounts, contracts or reports of damage during the thirteenth century and then frequently up to the end of the Middle Ages. But such records are rare for the much more numerous castles of the minor gentry. As a rule of thumb, it is only a comprehensive archaeological investigation that can confer some certainty on the origin of a castle and its abandonment; while for sites occupied over longer periods attention must be paid to breaks in occupation, a problem that has hitherto received little recognition. Archaeological investigation, with its ability to analyse structures and assemblages, is also essential for determining the function of a fortified site. While castles emerge only dimly in the written sources as focal points in an economic system, the archaeological record exposes multiple facets, including agriculture, craft production and the environment. Archaeology also reports on a castle's prestige, its significance as a symbol of power and domination. This multiplicity

The town walls of Visby, Gotland, constructed through the 13th century, eventually rising to 11m high on a perimeter of 3.4 km (M. Carver). **Fig 6.1**

of functions, revealed by the assemblages and the structural sequences, helps put into perspective their defensive function – often overestimated by older research – which, apart from protection from raids, appears to have had, especially in smaller fortified sites, a more symbolic than tactical value. It would indeed be an error to understand the medieval castle purely in military terms (se below).

Investigation methods and techniques

It is a basic principle that no archaeological investigation proceeds in the same way as another, and therefore that the procedures and methods of investigation have to be re-designed in each case. This applies of course also to the archaeological investigation of castles and castle sites. But in countries with a long-standing and rich experience of castle archaeology (for example Britain and Ireland, Denmark, the Netherlands, Belgium, France, Germany, Switzerland), an extensive methodology has developed that can serve as a solid basis for future investigations of castles and ruins. It goes without saying that archaeological investigation does not consist solely of excavation. A major role is played by survey and the recording of wall fabric, including the study of building material, the composition of mortars, and the techniques of construction used in walls, joints and quoins. This applies equally to castles now in ruins as to those that are still standing, roofed and in use.

When designing the excavation, particularly on an abandoned site, it is important to take into account the often massive deposits of rubble, which can be several metres deep and bury numerous stretches of wall as well as the archaeologically significant occupation deposits. These masses of rubble oblige us not only to uncover large areas but also to implement adequate measures for its removal and storage. If original stonework from the rubble is to be used for conserving or repairing uncovered stretches of wall, it is important to record and monitor the condition of the stones. Indeed – depending on the material – stones can deteriorate, for example because they were buried for long periods in the ground or because they were subjected to heat in a burning episode, so badly that they cannot be re-used in the restoration of walls.

In contrast to towns and religious buildings that are part of a settlement complex, most castles stand freely in open country and their assemblages relate directly to the occupation of their site and its vicinity (Fig 6.2). Objects recovered from castles include tools, weapons, occupation and cooking material, horse gear, remains from butchery, food consumption and craft residues, and stem from the occupation of the castle and bear witness to the life that once took place there (see the example of Castlar in Ch 3).

It follows that the area of investigation – particularly on hilltop defended sites – should not be restricted to the built area enclosed within the defensive walls, but should include the immediate surroundings, especially the slopes of the castle hill where the richest deposits, formed from the ejection of occupation refuse, are to be expected. By contrast, the excavation of moats on lowland castle sites tends to reveal little, as the moats were repeatedly cleaned out and re-cut, and it is only exceptionally that actual occupation layers form in these contexts. The inclusion of surrounding areas in archaeological investigations is necessary for another reason. When building or re-building took place on hill-top sites, previous occupation deposits and building remains were frequently levelled to the bedrock and dumped outside the castle precinct. In some cases the evidence for earlier buildings and occupation survive only as redeposited contexts beyond the walls.

Apart from a few exceptions (for example castles of fort-type), the ground plans of most castles are not symmetrical – in contrast to religious buildings – and therefore, if we are to understand the whole castle and its functions, an investigation should ideally target the entire area of the castle and not just selected areas that appear architecturally interesting.

Castle construction and repair

Excavations and buildings analysis demonstrate again and again how much the establishment of a castle was conditioned by its local environment. This applies first of all to the choice of site. Decisive factors include topographic features related to defensibility, space requirements, access, solidity of the subsoil or bedrock; further considerations include the transport of stone, wood, lime, sand and water. Excavations have however often shown that site defects – for example an unstable substrate – were not always recognised or were ignored because of other advantages. The abandonment of a castle, forced by a deterioration in the natural environment, for example the heightening of the water table or the collapse or erosion of the bedrock, is by no means an exceptional event.

The analysis of building materials show that stone and wood were preferably obtained in the near vicinity of a castle site, not least because this avoided expensive

The Castle of Chillon on Lake Léman, developed by the Counts of Savoy from 1150, and containing rooms of 13th and 14th century date, with exterior accretions of the 16th century and later (M. Carver).

Fig 6.2

transport. There are clear regional differences: depending on its suitability, stones could obtained by excavating the defensive ditches, or as cobbles - stones transported by the last glaciation. In regions poor in natural sources of stone but rich in clay, brick building increased from the twelfth century onwards – in Italy it is based on a tradition going back to antiquity, in northern Europe it was initiated by the Cistercians. Mineralogical analyses of lime mortar, however, rarely give convincing results. Caution must be exercised in radiocarbon determinations of wood particles contained in mortar. Their dating can – for example when older mortar was re-used – differ considerably from the date of construction of a given wall.

Added to the building techniques and building forms determined by the conditions of the natural environment are stylistic developments and architectural templates which evolved in the landed, courtly and imperial prestige architecture and which extended over the whole of Europe in the wake of the culture of chivalry. The reception of such structures, in certain cases perceived as foreign, can, as some excavated examples show, lead to unexpected difficulties and prompt a return to time-honoured building traditions.

Extensive excavations have shown that on long-occupied sites which have been repeatedly transformed, the ground plan, the functional organisation, the arrangement of the building ranges, the dimensions of the whole establishment as well as the defensive apparatus were constantly subjected to intercutting modifications. Whether such transformations, which could completely change the appearance of a castle, were due to conditions in the natural environment, to a change in the requirements for living quarters and prestige, to new siege techniques, to the influence of foreign examples or the whim of the lord, must in each case be ascertained anew.

Results obtained from excavation and recording of upstanding stonework show that a castle, while it is inhabited, is a permanent building site. It is constantly being transformed, improved, pulled down, added to, reinforced or reorganised. Direct evidence for the building work is frequently found, for example in the form of lime kilns, tools, traces of scaffolding, holes in the stonework for lifting gear and abandoned piles of building material. We regularly encounter the results of building activity, for example vertical and horizontal joints, repairs, modified doors and windows, additional wall reinforcements and partitioning of rooms, not to mention the measures taken when rebuilding was required after as fire or other destructive events.

For all the building modifications that occurred during the years 1100-1500, the craftsmen used, bar a few exceptions, the same local or regional building materials. Of course, since in many regions the forests could no longer supply sufficient amounts of long trunks, wood had to be transported from further afield; some architectural elements such as window and door frames or sculpted elements used imported well-worked stone; in the later Middle Ages, to cite another exception, brick was increasingly used in repair or small transformations and in many parts of Europe traditional roofing materials – straw, reeds, shingles, stone (in the Alpine area) – were replaced by tiles.

Analyses of the stonework show that, despite using the same stone as raw material, the structure of the walls is constantly modified. The stones, if their material allows it, are worked and assembled in ways that change through time. Though this development appears strongly marked by regional characteristics, there are nevertheless indications that all over Europe in the early twelfth century quite small square cut stones were arranged in horizontal layers, whereas in the later twelfth century and particularly in the thirteenth century there was a predilection for large ashlar, whose monumental appearance was often reinforced by bumps or bosses on the visible face. Increasingly, special care was given to the quoins (corner joints). In the wake of measures for speeding up the building process which occurred during the building boom of the thirteenth century, walls built of irregular small stones whose visible face is covered by a thick mortar appear more frequently after 1250, whereas earlier it was only the joints between stones that were pointed with mortar.

To divide buildings vertically, the principle most often used was to introduce internal floors resting on load-bearing joists, which, in the case of wide spans require cross-beams, perhaps supported by posts. Wooden constructions in the form of oriels, alcoves and balconies or galleries, internal and external stairs, rarely survive from the later Middle Ages. The remains of original load-bearing joists often provide sufficient wood to undertake dendrochronological dating. Vaults of different kinds (barrel, dome, rib and herring-bone) are differently distributed and tend to be applied to specific functions, such as cellars, chapels, ceremonial spaces, tank cisterns, shooting niches.

Reconstructing the above-ground structure of a castle from excavated stretches of walls that only survive as foundations is often a matter of pure speculation. Of course comparison with extant buildings of similar ground plan or using reliable illustrative documentation can allow some conclusions to be drawn, using analogy, as to the possible appearance of a former tower, living quarters or curtain wall. Yet, even in the best of cases, there are still many unanswered questions concerning, for example, later modifications, the fitting out of upper floors with doors, windows, partitions, and in particular the form and construction of the roof. One has to remember that the structural development of a castle did not only happen horizontally through modification of the ground plan but also vertically through stacking and demolishing, through re-modelling of the upper tracts with roofs, battlements or defensive platforms. It is only rarely that the original twelfth- and thirteenth-century widely distributed clerestories, which were attached to the main towers and made of timber or half-timbered work and which could jut out by up to 2m., survive. Their former existence can be documented by carefully recording the cavities left by the beams in the stonework.

A clear tendency towards monumentality has correctly been identified in European castle building after the emergence of stone building in the eleventh-twelfth century. This trend affects only constructions with defensive or prestigious character, such as curtain walls with gates and flanking towers, halls and living quarters, and the mains towers. Less conspicuous, perhaps timbered or half-timbered are the working buildings whose remains are most often revealed by excavation only but which are of paramount importance for the understanding of castles.

Questions of typology and terminology

It is extremely difficult to classify the multiplicity of outward appearances of castles from the twelfth to the fifteenth century. The debate over what criteria to adopt is far from over. Topographical characteristics (hilltop castles, lowland castles, promontory castles) are unproblematic but of little value. An idiosyncratic type is formed by the cave castles which occur in mountainous regions (Alps, Pyrenees). Other typological distinctions are made on the basis of ground plans (fort castles, tower castles) or on the basis of size (major castles minor castles). The rock castles are a technical particularity: their architecture consists not of stonework but largely of rooms and passages hewn out of the rock. The literature also refers to types based on legal or constitutional definitions or to types which describe function (dynastic castles, earls' castles, ministerial castles, administrative castles, blocking castles) which are however of little use for characterising their built appearance and which in many cases are not applicable.

For a typology based on fieldwork and buildings archaeology, the only useful criteria are those derived from excavated data and observation of upstanding structures. It is pure fantasy to claim, on the basis of the structural observation of a small castle, that its owner was a noble lord or a dependent knight or a ministerial. It is also an error to want to assign to a particular type a castle whose appearance is owed to numerous and varied building phases. Typological assignations are only meaningful for a building in a specific phase, and even then it is just the individual components – towers, living quarters, chapels, defences – that lend themselves to typological classification. A scientifically responsible typology of castles has to base itself on the principle of a building sets, where each building element, sequenced by period of use, contributes in variable configurations to a whole which, collectively, eschews typology.

As can be shown by the example of the supposedly simple typological concept of the 'tower castle', it is essential to carry out a structural analysis and an archaeological investigation before assigning a type to such structures. Indeed, as archaeological evidence makes amply clear, the dominant tower of small castles may have been added to the precinct area of an earlier castle. The designation 'tower castle' therefore applies in such cases only to the later phase. Moreover, if only foundations survive, on what basis can we even speak of a tower? Could a square ground plan not also indicate a 'stone house', i.e. a type of building that is also known from documentary sources (*domus lapidea*)? The possibility that the building was modified in the vertical plane must also be considered, in so far as a one- or two-storey house was added to – a fact that need not necessarily be attested by the widening of walls at the level of the foundations – and acquired the aspect of a tower at a later stage.

Although special forms and principles of construction were and remained effective and imperative, certain general trends spread at a European scale at certain times. Though castles in their full appearance eschew typological classification, some buildings and building elements that characterise certain periods and certain greater or smaller regions can be defined and therefore described as types. No-one will deny that some specific leading forms of building, for example residential towers, the ground plan of forts, semicircular bastions are repeatedly found on a supra-regional scale, even though the question of their origin is not always resolved. Also attributable to a wider trend are some types of wall, for example rusticated ashlar, megalithic blocks or rubble-infill, some building techniques for example brick building, dry stone building and distinctive types of structures such as main towers, reinforced defensive walls, round chapels, semicircular and square bastions or swallow-tail battlements.

Stages in typological development can be related to the evolution of siege techniques (eg from trebuchets to cannon), to the demand for increased comfort (glazed windows) or in new models of prestige architecture (arrangement of the façade). It is however debatable whether the art historical stylistic designations Romanesque, Gothic and Renaissance are of much use when discussing castles. Of course it is possible to find Romanesque or Gothic window types, or – in later phases – a Renaissance entrance, but when we consider a castle as a whole it is difficult to use criteria derived from religious architecture to distinguish between a 'Romanesque' and a 'Gothic' castle.

It is well known that the same meaning is not conveyed by the translation of the Latin word *castrum* (Burg, castle, château, castello, castillo, borg etc.) into the various European languages, as is the fact that there are special forms which cannot be rendered easily in different languages (for example *Ansitz, Schloss, maison forte*, tower house or manor house) and which do not have an exact equivalent in other regions. However, this is more a problem for linguists than for castle research. More important for us are the questions of definition that arise out of archaeological investigations and buildings archaeology and which have their origins in the language found in medieval documents. How does one distinguish on archaeological grounds between a *castrum* and a *palatium* in the sense of a 'palace' in the absence of written documents? While for the pre-1100 period there are clear differences between castles and palaces, these distinctions fade in the twelfth and thirteenth centuries because of the emergence of defensive-residential-ceremonial forms of building, which has on occasion led to the coining of the unfortunate hybrid term 'palace-castle'. The debate continues, but it is generally accepted that a defensive-prestigious building complex in the twelfth and thirteenth centuries can only be identified as a 'palace' if documentary evidence is present and cannot be based on archaeological evidence alone.

Even more problematic is the distinction between castle and court (*curtis, curia*). The *curtes,* or territorial administrative centres of early medieval origin which were often undefended or barely defended, acquire during the course of the twelfth and thirteenth centuries – sometimes later – towers and massive enclosure walls with bastions capable of repelling attacks and these would, on their appearance, undoubtedly be described as castles. Legal documents, however, continue to refer to such establishments as *curtes* long after their transformation. When excavations on a small lowland castle site close to a settlement uncover earlier simple buildings of timber and light masonry, it is often suspected that the castle evolved out of a *curtis*. On smaller establishments that consist only of a tower with wooden ancillary buildings we might ask whether we are even dealing with a castle at all – in the sense of a *castrum* – or whether this is a monumental *curtis*. Tower castles that are designated *curtes* in documentary sources confirm this hypothesis. Secure typological criteria have however not yet been set down.

Use of Space

The multifunctionality of medieval castles implies that individual buildings and rooms were intended to meet different requirements. Using archaeology and buildings analysis can often, but by no means always, ascertain what these requirements were. Functions often change over the course of time: rooms originally used as living quarters within a tower are transformed into prison cells, gardrobes become firing stations with a defensive purpose, prestigious halls are turned into storage or dormitory areas. Upper floors have storeys inserted to maximise the use of space. In many buildings, especially in small castles with little space at their disposal, several functions can be combined either in vertical or horizontal arrangements, as shown by the archaeological evidence. So for example a solid ground-floor building may contain the stables, the upper floors heated living quarters, and the uppermost level a defensive platform with battlements. Religious buildings (castle chapels) are quite often incorporated into the defensive arrangements.

If space allows, the castle precinct is divided topographically and architecturally into a main castle area and a bailey. The latter is often less heavily defended and contains the less massively built, but nevertheless highly important ancillary buildings (workshops, granaries, stables, servants' quarters). In the large establishments of powerful landed lords, the well-appointed quarters of dependents of the lower nobility entrusted with defence – the so-called 'castlemen' *Burgmannen* – are also found in the bailey. In the thirteenth and fourteenth centuries large, densely built baileys can develop through the granting of privileges, and become small towns; this has, however, hardly been documented archaeologically. Archaeological investigations have hitherto concentrated more on the main or core castle areas with their spectacular building ranges, and rather neglected the less appetising remains of the baileys.

The assemblages recovered allow craft activities to be identified more precisely than the buildings, though specific indicators (hearths for smelting and working metals, weaving cellars) are not always easy to come by. Despite clear indications that spinners (spindle whorls) and specialist craftsmen (bone and horn workers) worked on castle sites; but who of the castles' inhabitants worked in these trades, whether men or women, whether the production was for home consumption or for trade, and – in the case of wood- and metal-working – whether it was only repair rather than production that was undertaken, all remain open questions.

Agricultural activities have left behind clear traces, not only in the form of implements (sickles, scythes, pruning knives, hatchets, cattle bells and tools used in forestry) but also in the form of numerous animal bones which are mainly the residue not of cooking and consumption but of butchery of domestic animals which were kept at the castle sites themselves when space was at a premium, often in the castles' ditches (and see Ch 3, p 137 for an excavated castle granary). While cattle, sheep and goats were generally kept in the peripheral areas, horses were often stabled in the centre of the castle. That dogs were present is attested by gnawing marks on bone food residue rather than by the few dog skeletons recovered.

As a dwelling place, the castle – as an indicator of a prestigious manorial lifestyle – can be approached from the study of its assemblage and the analysis of its built fabric. When it is claimed that living conditions in a castle were primitive, hard, unhygienic and miserable, modern conditions and expectations should not be invoked; instead they should be set alongside the now well-researched archaeological data pertaining to living conditions in medieval towns and rural settlements. This comparison reveals that a relatively affluent lifestyle characterised the castles, where all sorts of luxury items and elaborate equipment and furnishings existed, and where recreation was expected, as indicated by games and musical instruments.

On large castles which consist of several building ranges it is possible to distinguish between living quarters which would have belonged to the private arena (*camera*) and prestige rooms, i.e. halls and audience rooms used for various assemblies (*aula*). The castle's chapel (which is however not found on all castle sites) served both sacred and prestige purposes.

In the dwelling areas the built fabric and the assemblages give, for daily life, particular insights into the use of fire, attested by hearths, ovens, fireplaces, chimneys, flues, wall niches for tallow torches and especially the remains of stove heating systems which spread over wide parts of Europe and whose presence is demonstrated by stove tiles, at first plain and then glazed from *c.* 1300 onwards. Traces of hypocaust systems are only very rarely found.

On ruined castles, evidence of structures for water provision comes mostly from excavations, as these structures are buried under rubble. Shafts to reach the water table, sometimes of considerable depth, are found on hilltop castle sites. More frequent are cisterns that collect rainwater. In certain regions north of the Alps a new type of filter cistern, where the water is filtered through sand and gravel, appears alongside tank cisterns of Mediterranean origin.

Living conditions improve sharply in castles from the fourteenth century onwards, probably as a result of a flourishing long-distance trade and the increase in the production of urban industries. Glazed windows, panelling, walls and ceilings of dwelling areas and prestige rooms decorated with paintings, richer household equipment and more luxury goods have clearly left their traces, both in the archaeological record and in the built fabric. How much this steady increase in the cost of keeping up such as high status lifestyle contributed to the economic problems of the later medieval nobility remains to be elucidated.

Defence

Even if the basis of a medieval castle is a fortified site, the defensive installations are not always easily identifiable. But it must be emphasised that all the defensive elements present on a castle site are not just the architectural realisation of a defensive purpose, but also the visible symbols of power, domination and nobility. Castles can be compared to medieval swords, which are well known to have served both as weapons and as symbols.

The countless small castles of the twelfth and thirteenth centuries defence relied mostly on the principle of passive defence. The massive main tower, the solid enclosure wall with a gate that is difficult to access, as well as the obstacles put in the way (banks, ditches and moats) are designed to repel an attack and offer good protection against attacks with bows and arrows and crossbows. On the other hand, there are few establishments with evidence for active defence. Such evidence includes arrow slits, jetties for pelting besiegers, defended gangways and platforms with battlements, hornworks with staggered gates or flanking towers on the periphery. The lack of such arrangements may also be due to the limited means of the lord, the small number of defenders and the meagre amount of military equipment available. Most castles offered no serious obstacle for a determined and well-equipped attacker, even if they stood on an island or on a rocky outcrop, and this well before the advent of firearms.

The owners of large castles of political or manorial importance – mostly kings and princes – took care to enhance their defences through measures that could withstand longer sieges. Such works concerned mainly the periphery and the gates and were influenced by the highly-developed Byzantine-Mediterranean defensive architecture which had become familiar in the West since the Crusades of the twelfth century.

The enclosure walls of wealthy lords were reinforced by corner towers and flanking towers as well as by covered gangways with battlements. Added to these curtain walls were further outer defensive walls, which created extensive hornworks. The gates were protected by towers and barbicans, and access was through a passage flanked by several connected staggered gates. In order to minimise the effects of stone projectiles, which could weigh up to 150kg and which were propelled from trébuchets known in the west since the late twelfth century, circular and semicircular bastions were built and in the ditches below the walls one encounters stone cladding to reinforce the foundations (see below). The shape of the arrow slits were adapted to the weapons used, longbows or crossbows. Projectile-throwing equipment to counter a siege or an attack was positioned on the defensive platforms of the towers and other high buildings. As always, great care was taken with defence from above, since stones falling from a height are effective against storming troops in the vicinity of the walls. Burning arrows and other incendiary devices were used against wooden siege equipment. The principle of machicolation, which was well known in the Mediterranean area, is only rarely found north of the Alps.

Up to the emergence of firearms, defensive architecture follows the basic principle of repelling attacks from a heightened position, which led in the late thirteenth century to the erection of reinforced walls and slender towers with little useful internal space but offering a high defensive platform. Arrows from bows and crossbows, and later musket balls, had better chances of success in horizontal flight against storming opponents. The introduction of firearms was at first only reflected in castle architecture by new forms of slit, which were equipped with a cross beam to absorb the recoil from arquebuses. For lighter artillery, walls had to be perforated with openings near ground level.

Fundamentally new forms of construction adapted to artillery warfare developed only in the late fifteenth century. Characterising the fortifications of the fifteenth and sixteenth centuries is the increasing rejection of high buildings, walling several metres thick and earthworks designed to withstand artillery attacks as well as undermining. Distinctive buildings include rather low buildings, round towers and bastions with platforms and casemates for artillery of different calibre, while higher towers become rare, or are destroyed. The actual military worth of a fortification, however, depended less on the building than on the number, equipment and reliability of its garrison.

In many cases the defences of castles, which were built at great expense, never saw action, and often they were unable to withstand an attack. However impressive the medieval defensive architecture appears to us today, from a purely military viewpoint it was often a false investment of little practical use but of high symbolic value.

Catastrophe and war

On the whole, daily life in a castle was peacefully mundane and marked by the seasons, as shown by the archaeological evidence. Exceptional events such as devastation by natural forces, attacks and sieges or even destruction in war were rare and counted as special events mostly recorded in written sources. These refer more often to warfare than to banal destruction by natural causes such as fires, floods, landslides or rock falls.

Traces of destruction are frequently found on castle sites but are often difficult to interpret and can by no means always be related to events recorded in written sources, particularly as the events in documentary sources are frequently inaccurately reported, embellished or even pure invention. Written sources often refer to conquest and destruction, sometimes to earthquakes, but they are mostly silent about the extent of damage and about possible reconstruction measures.

When credible reports on the demise of a castle in war are found, it is no doubt tempting to try and find the traces of such events through archaeological excavation. Such investigations have repeatedly taken place in Switzerland and produced the same results: the excavated burning and destruction levels proved practically devoid of finds, which suggests convincingly that systematic pillage took place before destruction. As the documentary evidence indicates, looting was not only for material enrichment but it was also to acquire – independently of their actual worth – siege trophies to be shown off and sometimes deposited as votive offerings in churches. It follows that sterile burning and destruction levels are most likely to represent bellicose events (even if not supported by written sources), whereas burning layers rich in finds, in particular weapons and other metal objects of high value, probably originated in fires caused by lightning, defective fireplaces or careless use of naked flames.

The destruction by fire of a castle after pillage was often systematic and this has also left traces in the archaeological record: from a scaffolding 2-3m high the walls were undermined, the excavated parts were supported by wooden posts and then the building was set alight and destroyed. Fire-reddened remains of surviving wall crowns suggest that this technique was used. The collapsed stonework did not always crumble into a dump of rubble but broke up in massive blocks spread higgledy-piggledy, making it inconvenient to excavate. The wall rubble, though containing few finds, can with careful examination yield important information about the destruction and decay processes after abandonment.

While traces of deliberate razing are clearly found in the archaeological record, it is much harder to find conclusive evidence for sieges. A few dozen arrows or crossbow bolts, as frequently found spread over entire the castle area in excavations, do not prove warfare. It is different if the number of projectile points reaches hundreds, concentrates on the destruction horizon and if many points are bent or blunted. If stone balls from mobile catapults or balls from firearms are also present, it is possible to conclude that a siege took place, even if it is not mentioned in written sources that could confirm the event. Further testimonies for a siege are tunnels that were dug from the outside over stretches of varying lengths through soft subsoil under the foundations of a castle to reach its interior.

Within a few hundred metres of the castle, there may also be occasional traces of those laying siege, for example terracing for tents and artillery, encircling banks or dumps in the castle ditches which enabled siege equipment to be moved to the foot of the castle's wall or gate. On the whole the conditions for archaeological investigations of siege places are difficult. Moreover, we must bear in mind that brief actions such as night raids or diversionary strikes that are recorded in written sources, generally do not leave archaeological traces.

Considering that in the Middle Ages the number of castles on the European continent reached the tens of thousands, the few hundred written or archaeologically documented instances of sieges and other combat are statistically unimportant. Daily life for the inhabitants of the castles was not devoted to defence but to peaceful occupations which excavations have revealed and to the protection of the castle from natural elements, neglect and fires, whose effects can be seen repeatedly in excavations in the form of burning layers and fire-reddened stonework.

Abandonment and transformation

Of the countless castles that were built in the High Middle Ages, the majority, about 70 to 80 per cent, were abandoned at a time dated to between the fourteenth and sixteenth centuries and left to decay. Destruction might stem from natural catastrophes, or war, whether localised feuds or supra-regional conflict. Such documented events as the blood feud of the Habsburgs against the murderers of king Albrecht I, the sacking of castles after breaches of peace treaties, or the devastation in the Hundred Years' War and in the German Peasants' War – or natural catastrophes such as the Basel earthquake of 1356 speed up the process of the 'death of the castle' but do not provoke it. As many excavations show, most castles, particularly the many modest establishments of the lower nobility were vacated and abandoned without a fanfare. Their owners move to nearby towns or manors, seeking a career as royal or princely functionaries or taking up a commission in the increasingly important regular armies. The oft-repeated statement that the 'death of the castle' in the late Middle Ages was due to the emergence of firearms which brought into question the military value of castles is, on closer inspection, erroneous. Quite apart from the fact that the process of abandonment had already begun well before the advent of an effective siege artillery, the many small castles facing abandonment in the later Middle Ages had no military importance to lose. Only larger castles, which depended on the will, and the very considerable means, of their owners, were refurbished to face the challenge of fighting with firearms.

Frequently the castles that survived the abandonment of the late Middle Ages were stripped of their military character in later transformations. As private seats of urban patricians, as centres of landed administrative power, in many regions also as status dwellings of an ancient but politically impotent nobility, there emerged in the late Middle Ages and in the early modern period prestigious castle building of differing sizes which reflect the living standards of their time and whose legacy from medieval defensive architecture is only betrayed by some decorative features. Such establishments are either transformed from medieval castles or represent completely new builds within former castle areas. It is not rare that the old main castle building, now perceived as uncomfortable, is abandoned and new prestigious living quarters are constructed within the more easily accessible bailey. Alternatively, new more pleasant locations are sought. Undefended castles are frequently surrounded by extensive gardens following Italian influence.

PART 2: FORTIFICATION IN THE NORTH (1200-1600) *by Kieran O'Conor*

The period from *c* 1200 until *c* 1600 is prominent for the development of fortification in Europe (for the period before 1200, see AME 1, Ch 11). Castle building reached its apogee in the late thirteenth century, with the building of a number of classic castles in north Wales by Edward I of England. In the later fourteenth, fifteenth and sixteenth centuries, large numbers of tower-house castles were built in Europe. During the course of the sixteenth century castles began to fall into disuse (or were substantially rebuilt as undefended country houses) across many (but not all) parts of Europe, an event coincident with the growth of strong government by kings. Homes no longer needed to be fortified against small-scale raiding and localised warfare between individual lords due to the relatively peaceful conditions imposed across their territories by these monarchs. Many of the early functions of castles – local defence, local administration, the application of law and punishment – began to be taken over by the state from the traditional lordly class, in a way not seen in many parts of Europe since Roman times. The decline of the power of the great medieval landed dynasties and the rise in the power of central government led by a strong monarch can be seen in this shift in the importance of different types of fortification. Now that there was less need for them in many parts of Europe, fortified homesteads were replaced with comfortable houses built in the new Renaissance style with their well-lit, warm and spacious rooms (Anderson W 1970, 285), though some of these might still affect 'castellation' for purposes of proclaiming status and prestige.

On the other hand, national identities began to emerge during the later middle ages, and fortifications, such as bastioned artillery forts, were part of national schemes of defence. In this respect, it could be argued that the sixteenth century saw a shift in emphasis, in terms of fortification of the top rank, from privately-owned castles of the elite to state-built fortresses, such as artillery forts protecting territorial boundaries and strategic locations. The most modern fortresses of the day were now being built by kings and their governments to protect their subjects and their territories against attack by external forces.

The principal aim of this section is to give an overview of the main types of fortification in use in the northern regions of Latin Christendom from the very early thirteenth century up until the late sixteenth century. They will include different types of castle, linear fortifications, town walls, artillery forts, strongholds and defended farmsteads. There will also be a brief mention of the continued building of essentially medieval fortifications beyond 1600 in certain places. In this respect, it must be remembered that the end of the medieval period and the beginning of the Early Modern Age did not happen overnight. Medieval settlement forms and ways of organising society continued somewhat longer in certain places than in others (see, for example, O'Conor 1998, xi).

Communal fortifications: Urban defences

There was a huge growth in urbanism across Europe between *c.* 1000 and *c.* 1600 (Ch 9, p 370), and many of these towns and cities possessed defences (Fig 6.1). There has been a tendency amongst scholars over the last few decades to see medieval urban fortifications as being nothing more than a poor derivative of castle architecture (see Creighton & Higham 2005, 15, 37). This perception is at least partly due to the fact that the upstanding remains of medieval urban defences are now often fragmentary. Many town walls and gateways were levelled or incorporated into new buildings during the eighteenth and nineteenth centuries, when they were seen to stand in the way of economic progress and urban expansion (Kenyon 1990, 183, 191). Perhaps as a consequence, medieval town defences lack the appeal of castles and their study has suffered as a result, at least in Britain and Ireland (Creighton & Higham 2005, 15). Furthermore, there has been a tendency amongst some scholars to downplay the defensive role of urban fortifications. Instead, in an argument that mirrors a parallel debate in castle studies, it has been suggested that town walls and gatehouses were erected by medieval urban communities primarily for social and economic reasons, such as the desire to display wealth and status, to define legal boundaries and to control access so as to allow the effective collection of tolls and taxes on all commodities brought into these places (e.g. Coulson 1995).

It is clear, nevertheless, that many towns across medieval Europe were often besieged or, at the very least, experienced some sort of military threat, even if it was only endemic raiding and banditry in their neighbourhoods. For example, while status was important, one of the principal reasons, if not the primary one, for the building of quite complex defences around Edward I's new towns in north Wales in the late thirteenth century must have been a desire on his part to protect the immigrant English burgesses from the local Welsh. One of these towns was Conwy, completed by at least 1292; its 1,300m stretch of crenellated town wall had twenty-one open-backed D-shaped towers and three twin-towered gatehouses along its length (Fig 6.3). The whole circuit of Conwy's town wall and towers were pierced by a full 480 arrowloops, and a ditch ran along the outside of the wall. At least one of the twin-towered gatehouses, the High Gate, had a drawbridge and a barbican in front of it. Two heavy double-leaved wooden doors and a portcullis stood in the passageway of this gatehouse. Furthermore, a top rank castle defended the southern side of the town (Taylor 1998, 42-44). There can be no doubt that Conwy's urban defences, if stoutly manned by its townsfolk, could see off a sustained attack by the Welsh. It seems logical to presume that the lavish military nature of the defences of this new town, which in plan is not unlike a bastide, was linked to a fear of Welsh rebellion. In this respect, the thirteenth-century fortified towns or bastides of

The town walls of Conwy, Gwynedd, Wales (photo: Jeffrey L. Thomas). These strong, late 13th-century town walls were built by Edward I.

Fig 6.3

southern France, with their high, crenellated curtain walls, numerous D-shaped flanking towers, ditches and twin-towered gatehouses were built in an area fought over for decades by the kings of France and England. For example, the town of Bastide Mirande in Gers was founded in 1281 by order of Philippe III. Its high-walled defences include four twin-towered gatehouses, nine mural towers offering flanking defence and a wet moat (Lepage 2002, 250-4). When stratigraphic, cartographic, pictorial and historical evidence is put together, along with the architectural analysis of supposedly later buildings, it would appear that the defences of many medieval towns across Europe were far stronger and more extensive than their fragmentary remains would suggest today (Kenyon 1990, 191).

Far from copying the defences seen on contemporary castles, town defences could be innovative at times. For example, the closely-spaced double line of walls or concentric defence built in the mid-thirteenth century at Carcassonne, France, pre-date the great concentric castles built by Edward I and others in Wales and elsewhere by two to three decades (see below). Again, provision for firearms can be seen in town walls and gatehouses before they appear in castles. In Britain, gunloops of the 'keyhole' type (which can also be used by archers and crossbowmen) start to appear in town walls and gatehouses during the 1360s and 1370s – a decade or two before they start to be seen in castles such as Bodiam, which was begun in 1385 (see below; Creighton & Higham 2005, 37, 110-1). Nevertheless, it is fair to say that most innovations in town defences ran parallel to (rather than copied) developments in the military architecture of castles (Lepage 2002, 257). Given all of this evidence, it is probably best to take a middle line between the opposed views outlined above and state that defence against attack and local insecurity was always one of the main reasons behind many, if not most, urban communities throughout

Europe deciding to fortify their towns. It was possibly the principal one in areas of conflict and colonial expansion (see Creighton & Higham 2005, 205-7).

Mural towers and twin-towered gatehouses of semi-circular and D-shaped form, looped for archery, became a common feature along town walls from *c.* 1200 onwards, as in castles. These walls have wall-walks and crenellations, which were often pierced by arrowloops. Heavy gates and portcullises can be seen in the passageways of these new gatehouses, which also possess drawbridges and barbicans (Kenyon 1990, 195; Lepage 2002, 257; Creighton & Higham 2005, 40). It has been argued that the average medieval town wall in Europe was about 2m in thickness and between 7m and 10m in height (Lepage 2002, 257). Rectangular-shaped mural towers are relatively rare and tend to be fourteenth or fifteenth century in date, although thirteenth-century examples do occur, as can be seen along the town wall at Rindown, Ireland (Kenyon 1990, 197). Provision for timber hoarding can also be seen on some town walls from the early thirteenth century onwards and, later in the period under review, stone machicolations also appear (Creighton & Higham 2005, 40). Ditches around medieval towns could also be very formidable. For example, the ditches around the towns of Perth, Scotland, and Bristol, England, were between 4m and 5m in depth (Kenyon 1990, 190, 197-99).

The main period for the construction of urban defences in Europe was during the thirteenth and fourteenth centuries, although new towns were built with defences right down to the late seventeenth century in certain places (Kenyon 1990, 194). It should also be understood that many towns throughout Europe in the thirteenth and fourteenth centuries, and even later, including a great city like Kiev, were defended by earth and timber defences (Kenyon 1990, 183; Lepage 2002, 256; Creighton & Higham 2005, 18, 26, 28, 37-39, 89-90, 102). On analogy with timber castles, it is possible that the timber defences of these towns included palisades looped for archery, wooden gatehouses and wooden mural towers. Alternatively, some towns possessed stone gatehouses but with rest of their defences being built of earth and timber (Kenyon 1990, 185). There were also examples of fortified agricultural villages throughout medieval Europe, particularly in southern France (Creighton & Higham 2005, 79; Lepage 2002, 251).

Cannons first started to replace the trebuchet as a siege weapon during the first half of the fourteenth century (Fig 6.4). The earliest known representation of cannon comes from a manuscript dating to *c.* 1325. As cannons cost a large amount of money to buy and needed great technical skill to make, they tended to be owned and used by wealthy territorial princes and great trading cities right throughout the period under review. Cannon were beyond the purchasing power of even quite wealthy nobles (Anderson 1970, 280; Schmidtchen 1990, 3; Kerrigan 1995, 1). It is noteworthy, in this respect, that the Italian city of Florence had artillery by 1326. Other towns and rulers across Italy, England, France and Flanders quickly followed this example and there are references to cannon being used in battlefields and sieges in the latter parts of Europe during the second quarter of the fourteenth century. For example, cannon were used at the siege of Calais in 1346 (Anderson 1970, 280).

The earliest cannon in use throughout the fourteenth and for much of the fifteenth centuries tended to be great wrought iron stone-bombards capable of firing stone balls

(left) Trebuchets at Castelnaud, France (photo: Luc Viatour GFDL/CC); (right) Mons Meg, Edinburgh, **Fig 6.4**
Scotland: a mid 15th-century bombard.

of up to 700lbs in weight. These bombards were difficult to transport because of their bulk and, due to this and other reasons, while cannon were important to the outcome of specific sieges, campaigns and battles, artillery did not reach its full potential until the late fifteenth century (Schmidtchen 1990, 5). The design of cannon improved dramatically in the late fifteenth and early sixteenth centuries. This led to the development of more reliable, far smaller and, therefore, easily-transportable cannon of iron or bronze, placed on gun carriages, that fired iron balls. These iron balls had the same and, at best, more destructive force than the far larger stone balls fired from the earlier enormous and unwieldy bombards (Schmidtchen 1990, 6). Artillery became a truly formidable weapon in the hands of rulers at this time and greatly helped these men consolidate state power in the sixteenth century (Kerrigan 1995, 1).

Cannonballs, be they made of stone or, later, iron, fired from cannon had a range of 300-500m and struck their targets, usually the walls and towers of castles and towns, on an almost flat trajectory (Schmidtchen 1990, 3). This meant that these balls had far more destructive and penetrative power, causing far more damage, than the stones thrown from earlier and contemporary engines-of- war, even trebuchets (which were still in use up to the late fifteenth century – e.g. at the Siege of Rhodes in 1480; Anderson 1970, 280). The medieval defences of towns across Europe were remodelled in places to meet this new threat. Town walls were made thicker and broader by constructing earthen ramparts against their inner faces initially and then their outer ones. This act strengthened walls against the increased striking power of cannon. Earth was able to absorb the shock of cannonballs better than stone and reduced their penetrative capacity. Earthworks and breastworks were also placed as a line of defence outside town walls for further protection. Yet towns, with their high walls and towers, were still too much

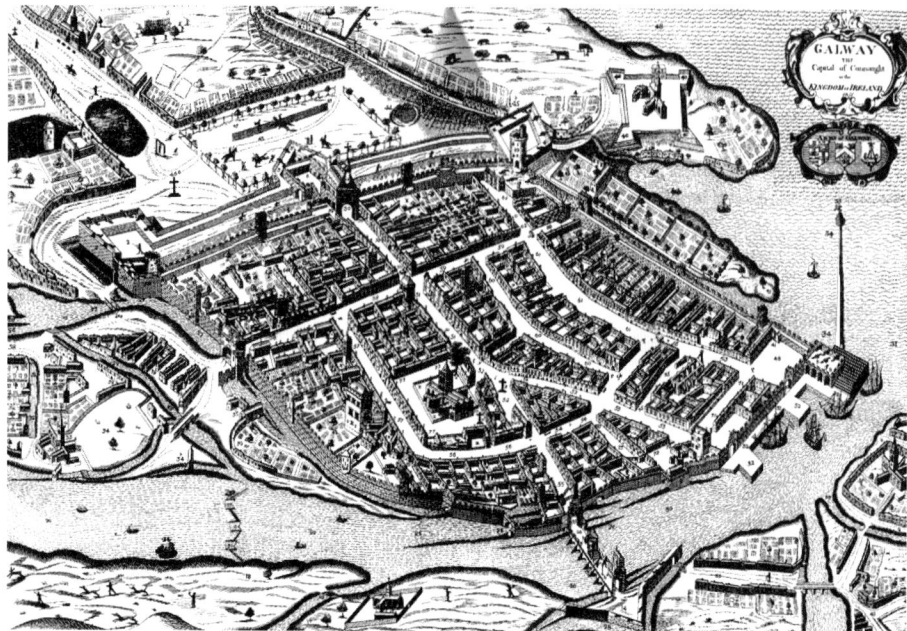

Fig 6.5   *A mid 17th-century map of Galway, Ireland, showing bastions carrying cannon on the eastern approaches to the city (Trinity College Dublin MS 1209.73).*

of an easy target for besieging artillery and, even in the late fifteenth century, remained vulnerable to cannonfire (Schmidtchen 1990, 3-9).

Another offensive method of countering fire from a besieger's battery was to place artillery on or within the towers and walls of towns but this was to prove a relatively unsatisfactory method (Anderson 1970, 283; Kerrigan 1995, 1). There was a growing realisation amongst military engineers in the second half of the fifteenth century that the high towers and walls seen on town defences and other fortifications needed to be reduced in height. The subsequent lower profile of these defences made them less of a target for besieging artillery. Also, this reduced height meant that defending artillery could fire out at attacking forces more efficiently, instead of firing over their heads as before (Schmidtchen 1990, 9). A new scientific way of fortifying towns and fortresses developed in northern Italy in the very late fifteenth century and, then, helped by the recent invention of the printing press, the ideas spread relatively rapidly across Europe and even beyond in the early sixteenth century. The new method of fortification made use of the angle bastion, first seen in Italy in the late 1480s and 1490s. This type of fortification was designed to withstand fire from besieging artillery and was also able to mount guns for efficient defence. These fortifications had diamond-shaped angled bastions at their corners and along their ramparts to provide defensive flanking fire from their sides and counter battery fire from their fronts (Fig 6.5). Cannon were also mounted on the intervening ramparts / curtains between the bastions of these defensive works. The first large-scale use of the angle bastion for town fortification was at Verona, northern Italy, where angle bastions were added to the city defences between 1525 and 1530. Other towns in Italy and Europe quickly copied this new idea. For example, Portsmouth, England, was fortified with defences that included angle bastions in the late 1540s (Saunders 1989; Kerrigan 1995, 1-2).

Linear fortifications and territorial defences

There is a belief amongst many archaeologists that great linear fortifications protecting the boundaries of territories are either prehistoric, Roman or early medieval in date. This view is only partly correct as there is evidence from different parts of Europe for the construction and use of such linear fortifications right up to the sixteenth century. It must be remembered that the last phase of the Danevirke in Schleswig-Holstein in northern Germany (which marked the frontier of the old Danish kingdom) was rebuilt in the late twelfth century by Waldemar the Great. This rebuilding included constructing a 7m-high brick wall, a ditch and forewall along much of its length. The Danevirke continued in use into the thirteenth century before becoming obsolete (Hellmuth Andersen 2001, 74). Many entrances to Alpine valleys in Switzerland were fortified by the Swiss confederacies in the fourteenth century. This was achieved by placing 1.2m-1.5m wide stone walls across them from steep slope to steep slope. These blocking walls or *Landwehren* often had ditches in front of them. Towers can be found along these walls at the point where roads cut through them. These walls were a tribute to the power and organisational ability of the Swiss confederacies at this time (Fehring 1991, 142). Linear defences were also constructed in parts of Germany during the fourteenth and fifteenth centuries to protect territories and towns' hinterlands against raiding. These lines of defence can consist of stone walls, palisaded banks and ditches or even banks surmounted by thick and impenetrable hedges. Natural obstructions in the landscape, such as rivers, lakes and marshes, seem to have been cunningly incorporated into them. Again, like Switzerland, watch-towers, often surrounded by outworks, were built at the places along these linear fortifications where roads run through them (Fehring 1991, 142-3).

Linear defences around the English-controlled city of Calais in France were built in the fifteenth century and here, again, natural defences were used to maximum effect. The control of the English government in Ireland was reduced to a relatively small area around Dublin by the fifteenth century. This area, which became known as the English Pale, constantly suffered from Irish raids. In 1495 Sir Edward Poynings, the English Crown's chief governor in Ireland, pushed through legislation in the Dublin parliament that called for ditches and 1.8m-high ramparts to enclose the 'Inglishe Pale'. This concept of territorial defence clearly originated in Calais as Sir Edward had served there prior to 1494 (Lyons 2003). No intensive study has ever been carried out on the defences of the Pale. It is uncertain at present as to whether it was ever fully constructed or what natural defences, such as rivers and bogs, were incorporated into its length. It is clear, however, that in places, including certain parts of Co. Kildare, ramparts and ditches were built and survive to the present day (Barry 1987, 181).

It would seem that these long lines of defence in France, Germany, Switzerland and Ireland were not primarily built to be held against sustained military attack, as the manpower and resources were not really available for this. Instead, these fortifications were really designed to prevent raiding and to make the theft of cattle and other livestock from the protected areas difficult. The existence of these fortifications was a physical obstacle that hindered raiders taking stolen livestock back to their home territories (Fehring 1991, 142).

State fortifications and early artillery forts

Artillery forts constructed by rulers and their governments start to be built across Europe from the late fifteenth century onwards. These forts were often used to consolidate state power, protect territorial boundaries and control newly-conquered lands. One example of this comes from Ireland where the English government regularly built artillery fortifications in its sixteenth- and early seventeenth century re-conquest of that country. For example, Fort Protector in modern Co. Laois was erected in 1548. It had a circular-shaped artillery bastion at one of its corners and it appears that its masonry walls were backed by an earthen rampart. This government fort, along with other fortresses in the area, was built to protect loyal English settlers from local Irish clans. Again, the English Crown, through their administration in Ireland, erected numerous artillery forts at strategic locations throughout the country during the bloody Nine Years War of 1595-1603 and also in its aftermath to consolidate its power (Kerrigan 1995, 2-3).

Technological developments, such as the emergence of lighter and yet very powerful artillery, meant that square-rigged ships were able by the first years of the sixteenth century to carry broadside armaments of heavy cannon. Rulers along the coasts of Europe increasingly realised that they needed artillery forts to protect their ports and anchorages from raids by rival navies and pirates. For example, the series of forts built by Henry VIII between 1540 and 1545 along the southern coast of England were designed to protect safe anchorages in estuaries and ports from attack from France and Spain (Saunders 1989; Linzey 1999, 24-25). These low-lying forts made use of round towers with attached semi-circular bastions (which often gave these fortresses a clover-leaf shape) designed to mount cannon and resist bombardment (Anderson 1970, 284). Their squat profiles made them difficult to hit from the cannon of rolling ships (Linzey 1999, 20). St Mawes Castle and Pendennis Castle in Cornwall are two of these Henrician artillery forts, built on opposite sides of the entrance to the Fal Estuary to protect the safe anchorage in it (known as the Carrick Roads) from naval attack. The fort of St Mawes consists of a central circular tower, which has three semi-circular bastions attached on to it (Fig 6.6). This tower and its bastions were all mounted with cannon firing through embrasures placed at different levels. The fort at Pendennis lies on a headland directly opposite from St Mawes, across the estuary. Its first phase, started in 1540, consisted of a three-storey circular tower, which had cannon mounted on its ground and first floors, along with its roof. Very shortly afterwards, a gatehouse was attached onto its landward side and, also, a circular gun platform was built around the tower to give it stronger

St Mawes Castle, Cornwall, England (photo: Charles Winpenny). This was one of the artillery forts built   **Fig 6.6**
by Henry VIII along the southern coast of England during the early 1540s to protect anchorages from
French and Spanish attack.

artillery fortifications (Linzey 1999). Any enemy vessels attempting to enter the Carrick Roads would have been met with a barrage of fire from the numerous cannon mounted on these two forts.

The design of these Henrician forts along the southern coast of England was already out of date by the time they started to be constructed in 1540. The sixteenth century saw the gradual introduction of the Italian-style angle-bastioned artillery fortification throughout Europe and, indeed, to European colonies in the New World and elsewhere. For example, English forces in Scotland were building forts with angle bastions by the late 1540s. This was part of an attempt by the English Crown to take control of southern Scotland and break the alliance between the latter country and France. Eyemouth Fort in Berwickshire is one of these forts and it was erected by the English in 1547. It lies on a coastal promontory jutting out into the North Sea. A massive 4m-high earthen bank, with a great ditch and counterscarp bank, was built and this cut off the promontory from the mainland. An angle bastion was erected projecting outwards from the main rampart. Accommodation for the garrison was also built within the interior of the fort (Yeoman 1995, 106-7). Again, the first evidence for an angle-bastioned artillery fort in Ireland comes from the 1550s. Its construction was linked to a decision by the English administration to defend Cork Harbour and its anchorage from naval attack (Kerrigan 1995, 35).

Further elaborations in the design of the angle-bastioned fort would occur in the second half of the sixteenth century. These developments can first be observed in Italy, as before, but can also be seen in the Low Countries at this time, as Dutch military engineers began to experiment in the design of artillery fortifications. These elaborations included the *ravelin* (a detached embanked outwork), the covered way or *chemin couvert*, the glacis and the demi-lune. In all, these new features made the angle-bastioned artillery fort, often of pentagonal plan, far more difficult to take. This form of fortification continued to be built right up to the end of the eighteenth century (Kerrigan 1995, 4-6). This was an indication of the efficiency of these forts in being able to withstand attack by trained troops.

Private fortifications: castles

The vast majority of castles were private residences, owned by and occupied for at least part of the time by a person of lordly rank. The fact that castles were residences meant that they had a number of functions. They were, for example, the centres of their owners' estates and much of the countryside of Europe was controlled from these places. While lords and gentlemen of varying ranks rented out much of their estates to tenants, some land was kept in hand and was cultivated directly from these castles. This meant that agricultural and administrative buildings (often built of wood and cob) lay within and around castles.

However, these were not the things that made them special: many moated sites (and crannogs in Ireland and Scotland) were also lordly residences and estate centres but were not regarded by contemporary observers as castles (see below). A key factor was that castles (even timber ones) held structurally-imposing buildings that dominated their surroundings. It is also becoming clear that deliberately-created landscapes (that included deer-parks) lay around castles (Liddiard 2000; Creighton 2002, 65-8). The combined effect of these great castles set within these landscapes was designed to impress all with their owners' lordly status, importance and control of economic resources. This was a propaganda exercise designed to send out the message that it would be unwise to try to undermine the power of the castles' owners, as all the resources that were needed to build such structures and landscapes could also be used to crush opposition. It was a form of 'symbolic violence' (O'Conor 2008, 334-5). It could be argued, however, that great, structurally-impressive undefended manor houses and villas set within their own parkland, built increasingly towards the end of the period, achieved this goal without being seen as castles (see Ch 4, p 147; cf Orser 2006).

This suggests, therefore, that the one thing that makes castles different from other elite residences was the scale of their defences. Castles were designed to a greater or lesser extent to see off sustained attacks in a way that other elite residences were not, although many castles were never attacked or were even threatened during the long centuries that they were occupied (AME 1, 324-5). What is meant by 'sustained attack'? Obviously great castles, such as Edward I's Caernarvon in North Wales, were able to withstand long sieges by professional armies, if stoutly manned. However, semi-defended residences, not regarded as castles, such as certain moated sites or crannogs, were capable of providing a level of defence for their occupants against outlaws and even small raiding parties. This suggests in turn that small masonry castles and most timber castles offered a level of defence that was higher than that of an elite residence. Thanks to the complexity of their fortifications they were capable of withstanding an attack by large parties of determined men, including trained troops. Let us now examine the various types of castle built and occupied during the period under review.

Earthwork / Timber castles

There are two types of earthwork castle – the motte and the ringwork. Mottes can be described as flat-topped, mostly artificial mounds of earth, on average about 5m in height above ground level, surrounded by a deep ditch (AME 1, 325-331). Such mounds often have a banked and ditched enclosure, known as a bailey, attached onto them. Ringworks usually appear in the landscape as circular, banked and ditched enclosures (Higham and Barker 1992). The original defences and internal buildings associated with these earthwork castles were made of timber and, sometimes, cob (e.g. Higham and Barker 1992, 244-325). Increasing evidence from excavations across north-west Europe indicates that these castles often carried similar defences to masonry castles but that these were built of wood and cob. Evidence for such things as substantial towers and looped palisades are coming to light in excavations of earthwork or - as some scholars now prefer to call them - timber castles (Higham and Barker 2000; Higham 2004; Mittelstraß 2004; O'Conor 2002, 175-80).

It is popularly believed that the heyday of earthwork castles was in the eleventh and twelfth centuries. But many of these castles, built as fortified lordly residences and manorial centres in the latter centuries, continued to be occupied into the late thirteenth and fourteenth centuries (e.g. Kenyon 1990, 8; O'Conor 2002, 174-5). For example, excavated evidence from the motte at Sycharth in north Wales suggests that it was occupied as a timber castle as late as *c* 1400 and this date is corroborated by contemporary literary evidence (Hague and Warhurst 1966). Also in Wales, the long-term excavation of the motte at Hen Domen, which lay on the border with England, indicated that this late eleventh-century castle was inhabited until *c* 1300. It seems to have been abandoned more for local political reasons rather than because this form of castle was then seen as being useless from a defensive point of view (Higham and Barker 2000, 159-63). Available evidence from all over northern Europe suggests that, in particular, motte castles continued to be built throughout the thirteenth and even fourteenth centuries but not in the numbers seen before 1200. For example, the twelfth-century ringwork at Aldingham in northern England was heightened and turned into a motte in the early thirteenth century (Davison 1969-70; Higham and Barker 1992, 61). There is good documentary evidence from Ireland for the construction of a motte at Clones in 1211-1212 and a couple of years later at Roscrea (McNeill 1997, 57-58, 72). Excavated evidence from the mottes of Drumadoon, Ireland, and Roberton, Scotland, suggest that these mottes were built in the late thirteenth century (Haggerty and Tabraham 1982; McSparron and Williams 2009). Mottes continued to be built in the Netherlands, Denmark and Poland throughout the late thirteenth and fourteenth centuries (Higham and Barker 1992, 83-88). For example, the excavation of the motte at Plemieta, Poland, revealed that this earthwork castle was built in the fourteenth century (Higham and Barker 1992, 86-88). It might be added that it is likely that the original wooden tower on this motte summit was up to four storeys in height (ibid.). It is noticeable that many of these late mottes in Denmark and elsewhere are square in shape. In Ireland it has been argued on distributional, morphological and historical grounds that a series of mottes, some of them square or rectangular in plan, in the Leinster region were built in the late thirteenth or very early fourteenth centuries (O'Conor 1998, 35-38). This discussion shows that earthwork castles, with timber defences, remained important places in the landscape of north-west Europe well into the fourteenth century. Due to the fact that these places are often overgrown earthworks today, it is sometimes forgotten that many of these castles originally had complex wooden defences and buildings within them. Even quite small mottes seem to have been capable of protecting their owners and their retainers against raids and minor attacks.

Timber defences, however, were not just associated with the late usage of motte and ringwork castles. A large number of important and imposing thirteenth- or early fourteenth-masonry castles across Europe had outer wards and barbicans defended in wood (e.g. Dunamase, Ireland, O'Conor 1996). Masonry tower houses of fourteenth-, fifteenth- or sixteenth-century date sometimes lay within enclosures that were defended by stout palisades. In Poland, also, many fifteenth-century manor houses were enclosed by earthen ramparts surmounted by palisades (Higham and Barker 1992, 86-88). There are also intriguing references from late sixteenth-century Ireland to some Irish chiefs living in 'wooden' castles. It has recently been argued that these were timber versions of the ubiquitous stone tower houses that were so common a feature of the late medieval period in the latter country (Donnelly et al. 2007). Wooden castles and timber defences continued to be used in places for far longer than is popularly thought.

Masonry castles

Methods of besieging castles became more effective over the course of the twelfth and early thirteenth centuries. Crossbows become more widely used at this time and the development of siege engines, such as the trebuchet, gathered pace during this whole period (above). The builders of castles began to respond to this increasing military professionalism by experimenting with the design of these fortresses. This experimentation really starts in the second half of the former century but these new ideas really became widespread after *c.* 1200 (AME 1, 333-4). Effectively, the defences of major castles became stronger to meet these new challenges (Anderson 1970, 95-104; King 1988, 78-102; McNeill 2001, 44-45). Late twelfth-century examples of castles with this greater level of defence include Framlingham and the Inner Ward at Dover Castle, England, parts of Chepstow Castle, Wales, and Château Gaillard, France, but these were really the exception, being the vanguard of this new defensive style.

Most newly-built masonry castles of rulers and magnates, however, were equipped with this stronger level of defence from *c.* 1200 onwards. Furthermore, earlier castles, including some earthwork ones, were rebuilt and re-fitted, to include the new defensive elements. These included: twin-towered gatehouses, well-equipped with arrowloops, having heavy wooden gates, portcullises and murderholes in their passageways; protective barbicans in front of these gatehouses; thicker, higher and straighter curtain walls, whose battlements included merlons pierced with arrowloops; projecting round towers, looped for archery and usually three storeys in height and, thus, rising one floor above the adjacent walls and, therefore, dominating them, occurring on the angles of the curtain; projecting half-round towers found on straight stretches of curtain walls (King 1988, 77-78, 107-25). It is true to say that keeps ceased to function as the most important defensive feature in major castles from this time onwards, although they continued to be built in many castles right down to the end of the medieval period. This discussion all shows that the defences of curtain walls and the entranceways to major castles were enhanced from the last years of the twelfth century onwards. These defensive themes were to be repeated in great castles constructed throughout the next three centuries (McNeill 2001, 45). The arrowloops set in the sides of these new projecting towers and twin-towered gatehouses allowed bowmen to fire along the bases of adjacent stretches of curtain walls and, therefore, control them. This new model of fortification, termed *scientific defence* or *scientific fortification* by certain scholars because of its carefully thought-out and logical nature, was full of arrowloops at battlement level or set in flanking towers at various levels. Sometimes, also, arrowloops can be seen at the bases of curtain walls or in fighting galleries built into the thickness of these walls well below battlement level. The arrowloops themselves were now placed in large embrasures that gave the bowmen within them a wider arc of fire. These loops also developed in form to become more efficient. Plunging loops, allowing bowmen to fire not just outwards but downwards, also make their appearance *c.* 1200. Cross-shaped arrowloops, which improved observation, start to make their appearance around the latter date too, although narrow rectangular loops always remained popular (King 1988, 116).

Experimentation in castle defences evolved steadily throughout the thirteenth century. For example, concentric defence can be seen on the town walls of Carcassone, France, by the mid thirteenth century and at Caerphilly Castle, Wales, which was begun in the late 1260s, although far earlier examples of this form of fortification can be found in the Latin East, with the idea itself seen in Late Roman times. A fully concentric castle is one built with two closely-linked lines of defence. In such a castle, the higher inner wall dominated the outer, lower one. No ditch or buildings lay in between these two walls – only flat, featureless ground. This system allowed bowmen on the inner curtain wall to fire over the heads of their comrades, who themselves were firing from points on the outer wall. In this respect, a heavy, concentrated fire came from both walls simultaneously (King 1988, 107).

English-speaking scholars have always maintained that Edward I's late thirteenth-century castle-building programme in north Wales was the high point of scientific defence in the west. These castles, built to consolidate Edward's conquest of the Welsh, are certainly very impressive and continue to inspire awe in the visitor. The erection of these fortresses, which include Caernarvon, Conwy and the concentric castles of

Harlech and Beaumaris, are a testimony to the latter king's military expertise, great organisational abilities and employment of skilled architects – in particular, a Savoyard named Master James of St George (Gravett 2007). The principle of aggressive defence is clearly seen in their plans and this made them virtually impregnable. Defensive features in these castles include: numerous arrowloops at battlement level and at different levels in the many flanking towers and twin-towered gatehouses; fighting galleries, replete with arrowloops, in the thickness of curtain walls; so-called 'keep-gatehouses', capable of independent defence if the rest of the castle had fallen; numerous portcullises, thick wooden gates, murder holes and arrowloops in the passages through the latter gatehouses (King 1988, 103-27; Gravett 2007). Early stone machicolation can be seen at Conwy Castle but this is really a defensive feature associated with castles built across Europe from the fourteenth century onwards (King 1988, 84). A heavily-defended outer wall was also added to the Tower of London by Edward I sometime in the decade after 1275, turning it into a fully concentric castle (King 1988, 112). Recent work in Ireland has shown that concentric defence was part of the original late thirteenth-century design of Roscommon Castle. This was a royal castle and, hence, this made Edward the ultimate owner, as he was lord of Ireland, although he never visited the island (Murphy & O'Conor 2008). In particular, the latter's castles in north Wales are magnificent even today and attract thousands of tourists each year, providing a sizeable income for the region. The scale of this castle building by Edward I was never seen again in Britain and Ireland.

The fourteenth century can be seen as a period of instability across much of Europe with famine, wars, peasant unrest, plagues and economic decline with a background of climatic deterioration (Ch 2, p 60). Some of these troubles continued in places well into the fifteenth and sixteenth centuries. The Hundred Years War (1337-1453) between England and France, the constant strife between nobles and princelings in Germany, inter-clan raiding and feuding in Ireland and Scotland and the threat of the Turks in Central Europe meant that castles continued to be needed, built and repaired. Great castles were still required to protect territory against invasion or to consolidate newly-conquered land.

At one level, the next generation of fortresses continued to use methods of defence perfected during the thirteenth century. Strong twin-towered gatehouses and round mural and angle towers, looped for archery and offering flanking defence, continued to be part of the design of top rank castles during these centuries. Nevertheless, there were changes and developments. For example, there was a far greater use than before of projecting stone machicolations, built on corbels, along the battlements of castles' towers and curtain walls (Anderson 1970, 183, 205; McNeill 2001, 45). The battlements at Raglan Castle, Wales, for example, which were started in the second quarter of the fifteenth century, are well supplied with machicolations. Also, the height of the curtain walls and towers of great castles, such as at the latter castle, was increased during this whole period (McNeill 2001, 45). Furthermore, gun ports start to appear in castles from the late fourteenth century onwards (ibid.). They can be seen in the gatehouse at Bodiam Castle, England, a typical quadrangular or quadrilateral castle of

Bodiam Castle, Sussex, England (photo: Kieran O'Conor). This castle dates to the late 14th century and its gatehouse is defended by early gun ports.

Fig 6.7

the time, which was started in 1385 (Fig 6.7). This gatehouse also has stone machicolations at battlement level (Thackray 1991). In this respect, with this greater use of stone machicolations and the addition of gun ports, it could be said the thirteenth-century tendency to strengthen the gatehouse was continued and improved upon during late medieval times right across Europe, especially in countries like France (Anderson 1970, 205; and see Cēsis in Latvia, below).

Minor strongholds: Tower houses, fortified houses, moated sites and crannogs

A far smaller type of castle, known as the *tower house*, was the ubiquitous form of castle built across large parts of Europe during late medieval times (Fig 6.8). Tower houses occur in areas that saw endemic low-intensity warfare associated with raiding, feuding and the breakdown of central authority, such as large parts of France, northern England, Scotland and Ireland (McNeill 2001, 44). In physical terms, the principal element of this form of castle consisted of a tall, usually rectangular tower of between three and five storeys in height. Defences seen on these towers include machicolations at battlement level, angle loops, yetts, murder holes, narrow windows and, in later examples, gun loops. In terms of dating, tower houses first start to be built in the fourteenth century but the majority of them date to the fifteenth and sixteenth centuries in places like Ireland, Scotland and northern England (see Claregalway, below).

Fortified houses, built for example in Ireland by English settlers in the late sixteenth and early seventeenth centuries, featured machicolations, gunloops, very narrow, barred ground-floor windows and provisions for yetts, and stood within walled enclosures (*bawns*) (Sweetman 1999, 175-93). Also seen in Ireland is the *stronghouse*, normally a two-storey, rectangular building with a ground-floor entrance set within a defended

Fig 6.8   *Threave tower house, Scotland (photo: Rory Sherlock). Tower houses were built in their thousands across large parts of Europe from the second half of the 14th century onwards.*

bawn. The ground floor of the central block was defended by narrow windows and gunloops, with the main living area occurring at first-floor and attic levels (Sweetman 1999, 193-98). The *bastle* house was a form of defended farmstead usually built of large stones, often bonded with clay. They are generally two storeys in height, rectangular in shape and rely on passive defence, such as thick walls, vaulted basements, first-floor entrances, stout wooden doorways, small, barred windows and stone slates, for protection. They were built by well-to-do tenant farmers as a protection against raiding (Durham 2008, 29-33). Their distribution is confined to the troubled border region between Scotland and England and they first appear in the second half of the sixteenth century. *Fortified churches* can also be found in certain parts of Europe, such as Ireland, France and Scotland, during the whole period under review and were used for both communal and personal defence (see Ch 11, p 465; Anderson 1970, 130; Bonde 1994; Creighton & Higham 2005, 103).

The majority of *moated sites* appear in the landscape today as rectangular, banked and ditched enclosures (Fig 6.9). They are often sited in low-lying ground close to a natural water source and this, in turn, means that their ditches are often wet or, at least, were water-filled when these enclosures were in use. Wedge-, square- or, occasionally, circular-shaped moated sites occur as well. Moated sites are common in Ireland, England, France, Belgium, Holland, northern Germany, Denmark and Poland, and the majority seem to have been built during the second half of the thirteenth and early fourteenth centuries (Wilson 1985, 28). About 5,500 moated sites were built in England between the late twelfth and fifteenth centuries, with the majority being erected between 1250

Moated site at Brockhampton, Herefordshire, England, with manor house (left), gatehouse (right) and **Fig 6.9**
moat in the foreground. The timber-framed buildings date from c. 1300 (M. Carver).

and 1350 (Wilson 1985, 8), and up to 1,000 moated sites can be recognised in the Irish countryside today, mostly in an Anglo-Norman / English context. These seem to have been mainly built throughout the thirteenth and early fourteenth centuries (O'Conor 1998, 58-68). However, moated sites in Jutland, Denmark, mostly date to the fifteenth and early sixteenth centuries (Wilson 1985, 28).

Moated sites appear to have been erected by men of different social classes for a variety of reasons. Across Europe, many were built by minor members of the knightly class and, therefore, functioned as their residences and manorial centres. Other moated sites were built as granges located on the outlying lands of different monastic orders, while some functioned as the hunting lodges of the elite (Wilson 1985, 7, 21, 28). Alternatively, many moated sites were the homes of prosperous, often assarting, peasants who were either freeholders or tenants of manorial lords (Wilson 1985, 28; O'Conor 1998, 58-69). Interestingly and in contrast to elsewhere, some moated sites in western Ireland were the principal residences of powerful Irish princes and lords. For example, the wedge-shaped bi-vallate moated site at Cloonfree, Co. Roscommon, was the abode of Hugh O'Conor, king of Connacht, in the early fourteenth century (Fig 6.10; Finan & O'Conor 2002). It seems to have had a defended timber gatehouse, which had a portcullis, and its banks were surmounted by substantial oaken palisades. A deep wet moat lay between the two banks (Finan & O'Conor 2002, 79-81). Nevertheless, the available evidence suggests that none of the moated sites had the complex defences of contemporary earthwork castles (Barry 2002). In this respect, Cloonfree is never

Fig 6.10 *Digital terrain model of Cloonfree moated site, Co. Roscommon (plan: The Discovery Programme, Dublin). This well-preserved but average-sized moated site was the principal residence of Aedh O'Conor, king of Connacht, in the first years of the 14th century.*

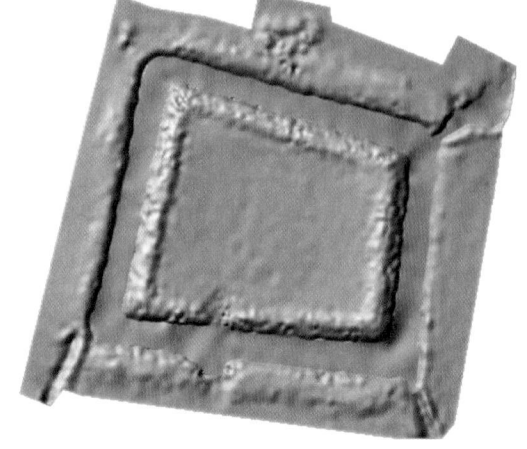

referred to as a castle in the sources, but as a *longphort* which translates as 'stronghold' (Finan & O'Conor 2002, 72).

Another defended residence in use during the later medieval period in parts of Ireland and Scotland was the *crannog*. Crannogs are best described as artificial islands located on lakes, which had a living platform that was on average about 20m in diameter. A dwelling house or houses were located on these platforms. The edges of the islands were defended by either simple oaken, or post-and-wattle, palisades. It is also clear that some small natural islands were also fortified during the period under review and, effectively, were used in the same way as crannogs. Crannogs have been traditionally viewed as being the fortified homes of kings and nobles during the early medieval period. However, more recent work has shown that many crannogs continued to be occupied, and possibly built, by members of the Highland and Irish elite right down to *c* 1600 (Morrison 1985, 23; O'Conor 1998, 79-84; Brady & O'Conor 2005). For example, the crannog of Island MacHugh, located on Lough Catherine in Co. Tyrone, Ireland, was the principal residence of the O'Neill kings of Ulster in the later medieval period (Brady & O'Conor 2005, 129-30). The crannog of Neish's Island on Lough Earn, Scotland, one of the chief seats of the earls of Strathearn in the thirteenth century, was occupied as a fortified residence up to the fifteenth century (Oram 2008, 179-80). Maps drawn up by the English military cartographer, Richard Bartlett, in 1602 show crannogs in widespread use amongst the Irish in the lakeland districts of Ulster and north Connacht at this late date (Hayes-McCoy 1964) (Fig 6.11).

The popular view that the advent of gunpowder and artillery in the fourteenth and early fifteenth centuries spelt the end of fortified sites in Europe is incorrect. Castles and fortified dwellings were built and occupied well into the seventeenth century, where they continued to function as defence against raiding and attack by small groups of men into the century's end (McNeill 1997, 228). This shows that castles were an important feature of the European landscape for almost eight hundred years and, as the homes of the elite, their study throws light on the way society was organised and developed.

Richard Bartlett's depiction of an Irish cran- **Fig 6.11**
nog being attacked by government forces
c. 1600 (reproduced by kind permission of the
National Library of Ireland).

PART 3: FOUR FORTRESSES AND A BATTLE

Town walls at Carcassonne *by Oliver Creighton*

Looming over the Aude valley in southern France, the site of Carcassonne outwardly presents an image of the 'perfect' medieval walled city, with its picture-book castle rising above crenellated town walls (Fig 6.12). But this appearance is deceptive: Carcassonne is as much a monument to the heritage industry as a monument of the middle ages, having been extensively restored in the nineteenth and early twentieth centuries (Creighton 2007).

The image of the fortified *Cité Médiéval* is also deceptive given that in places the defences were built on walls dating to Late Antiquity. Overlooking a key communications route between the Mediterranean and Atlantic coasts, there was also a proto-historic hillfort here in the sixth century BC. Following absorption into the Roman Empire the settlement became *Colonia Julia Carcaso*, and by the early fourth century AD the town was surrounded by a masonry wall studded with towers. Under Visigothic rule Carcassonne was a frontier town that was the seat of a count and the centre of a bishopric, and it is probably to this period that the first cathedral on the site dates. The castle was built from the twelfth century, and the medieval town defences date largely to the thirteenth century, including a second, lower outer wall that gave the town two concentric lines of fortification. In the valley below Carcassonne, a planned 'bastide' town was established

Fig 6.12   *Carcassone today (author).*

in the middle of the thirteenth century, its gridded street pattern symptomatic of the boom in new town foundation taking place across Europe during the period.

Carcassonne's town defences comprise two rings of walls: an inner enceinte, some 1250 metres in length and studded with 26 rounded towers (some re-using Roman fabric); and an outer wall, 1650 metres in length with 19 towers (Fig 6.13). Elements additional to the town defences included an external moat, barbicans and gates, notably the imposing double-towered Porte Narbonnaise. As well as physically enclosing and fortifying urban settlements, town walls such as these proclaiming the wealth and self-confidence of their citizens and rulers, were constructed around many thousands of settlements across Europe. Far more than features of 'military architecture', city walls were also prominent symbols of the vitality of urban life in the middle ages.

The restoration of Carcassonne from the middle of the nineteenth century was led by the architect Eugène-Emmanuel Viollet-le-Duc, whose other works included the cathedral of Notre Dame in Paris. Completed by 1910, these restorations gave the city its present appearance which, while informed by rigorous architectural analysis has attracted international criticism on the grounds of scale and authenticity. Restoration work included re-facing walls, underpinning masonry and re-creating walls to their full height, including parapet tops, while towers were capped with striking pointed roofs of slate whose authenticity has also been questioned. The restorations also included the clearance of the 'Quartier des Lices' (the flattened zone between the inner and outer walls), which removed a settlement of textile workers' houses and other buildings that were seen to encumber the medieval remains.

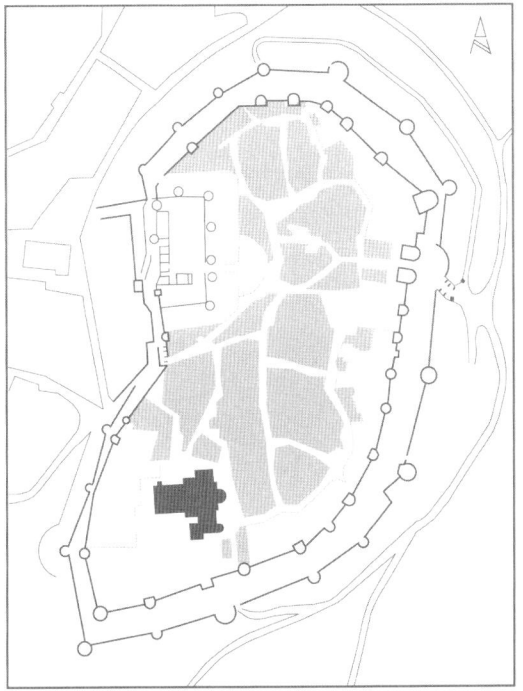

0   250m

In 1997 Carcassonne joined the list of UNESCO World Heritage Sites, its inscription recognising the qualities of the physical remains of the fortified medieval city but also the importance of Viollet-le-Duc's restorations in the history of heritage conservation (Viollet-le-Duc 1888). For some Carcassonne represents a 'Disneyfication' of the medieval past – a theme park to the middle ages; from another perspective, the restorations represent a further distinctive layer in the site's rich cultural stratigraphy (Creighton 2007).

The castle at Alt Wartburg in Aargau (AG, Switzerland)
by Maria-Letizia Boscardin

Alt Wartburg is a typical small castle of the lower nobility in the cleared woodland south-east of Olten. It was constructed around 1200, and its builders were, according to documentary sources, the lords of Ifenthal. After it was destroyed by Bernese forces in 1415, it was left as ruin. Archaeological investigations in 1966-1967 followed a comprehensive agenda, including research, conservation and some restoration of the surviving stonework (Meyer 1974; Boscardin 1982).

The fortified area (Fig 6.14) is closed on the south side by a curtain wall with a gate, which encloses a courtyard, timber buildings and a filtered cistern. A massive wall encloses the north side with small windows, which indicate defensive purpose and prestige and signal the bellicose spirit of its owner. The main feature is the impressive ruins of the residential tower, entered by means of an exterior flight of steps. An older cistern was located inside the tower.

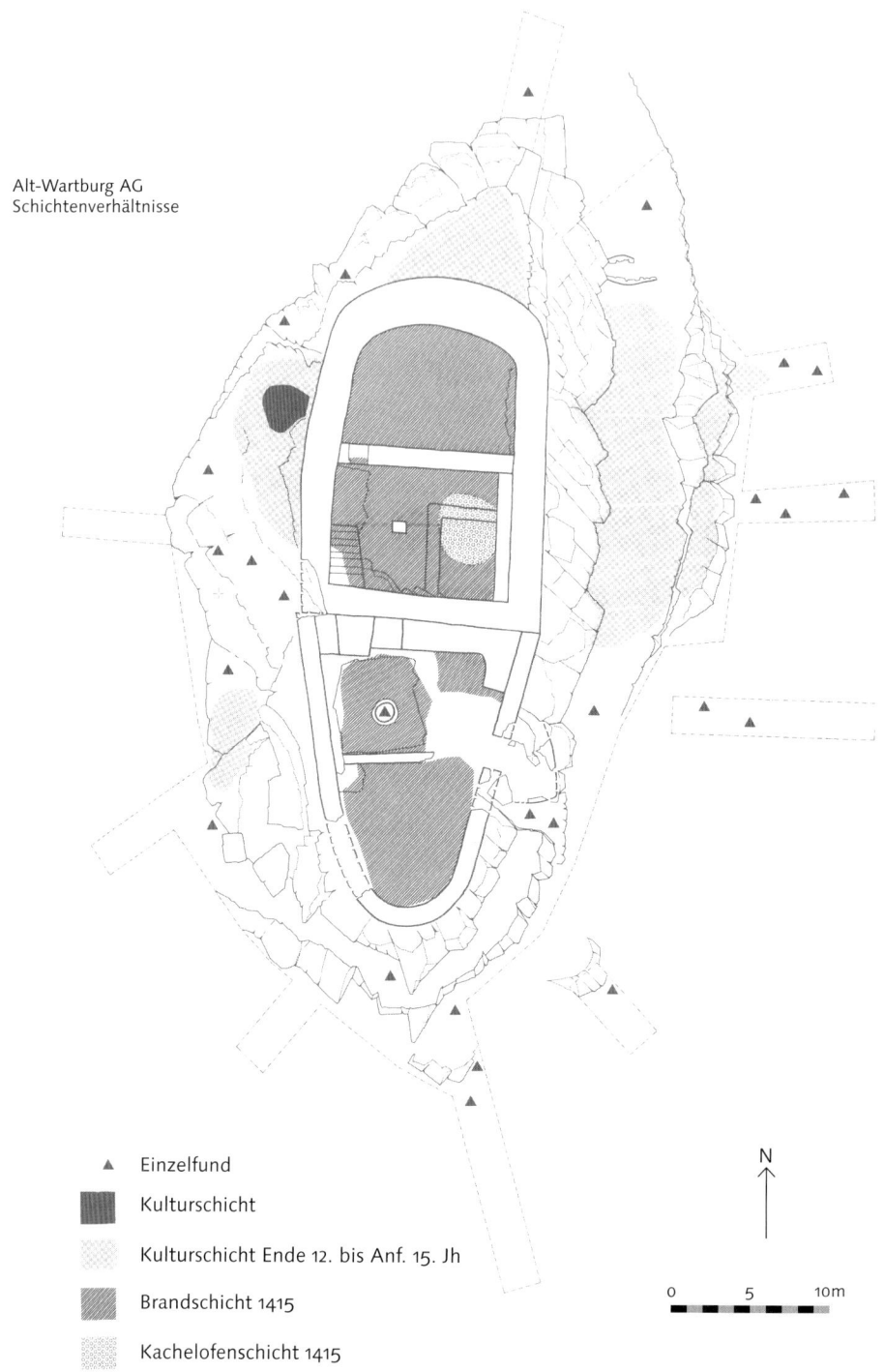

Alt-Wartburg AG
Schichtenverhältnisse

▲ Einzelfund

█ Kulturschicht

░ Kulturschicht Ende 12. bis Anf. 15. Jh

▨ Brandschicht 1415

░ Kachelofenschicht 1415

N

0   5   10m

Fig 6.14 *Alt-Wartburg AG: plan showing locations of isolated finds (triangles), stratified layers, burnt layer and debris from tiled-stoves. (Meyer 1974, fig. 3; ©Archiv Schweizerischer Burgenverein, Basel).*

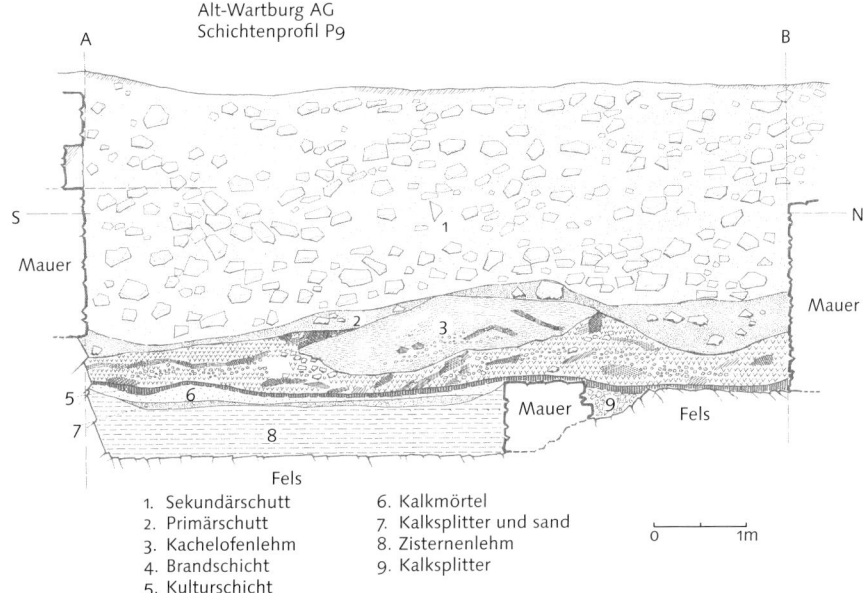

Alt-Wartburg AG
Schichtenprofil P9

A

B

S

N

Mauer

Mauer

1

2

3

5

6

Mauer

9

Fels

7

8

Fels

1. Sekundärschutt
2. Primärschutt
3. Kachelofenlehm
4. Brandschicht
5. Kulturschicht

6. Kalkmörtel
7. Kalksplitter und sand
8. Zisternenlehm
9. Kalksplitter

0   1m

Alt-Wartburg AG: section 9. 1, 2 debris; 3 ash from ovens; 4 (between 3 and 6) burnt layer; 5 occupation;   **Fig 6.15**
8 clay in cistern; 6, 7, 9 mortar. (Meyer 1974, fig. 14; ©Archiv Schweizerischer Burgenverein, Basel).

The archaeological investigations of the whole castle area and of the surroundings have clarified the sequence (Fig 6.15). The undisturbed stratification consists of occupation dumps, destruction and burning layers dated to 1415, primary rubble (plasterwork, roof tiles) and secondary rubble. The assemblage is bracketed between 1200 and 1415. The finds came in large quantities from the refuse deposits outside the castle, and in the interior of the castle traces of the destruction of 1415 were found: a massive burning layer, a collapsed and smashed tiled stove, and beneath it glazed floor tiles. Since there were no other finds in the interior, it is suggested that the castle was systematically plundered before its demolition.

The finds from the refuse deposits contained weapons, including daggers, arrowheads, stirrup from a crossbow, fragments of a gauntlet, riding gear, tools and implements, elements of dress, domestic equipment, pottery for cooking and serving, stove tiles, bone rings from rosaries, and drinking glasses. These all illustrate daily life on this simple castle. The investigations were completed by a comprehensive publication (Meyer 1974).

The Castle of Cēsis, Latvia *by Gundars Kalniņš and Kaspars Kļaviņš*

The Castle of Cēsis is not only the best preserved medieval castle site in present-day Latvia, but also, from the point of view of regional politics, culture, history and archaeology, it is one of the most important fortifications in northeast Europe (Fig 6.16). It was the key administrative centre for the Livonian branch of the Teutonic Order from the second half of the fifteenth century onwards. It has been systematically investigated in thirty-four annual seasons of work and presently it is the most extensively excavated medieval castle in Latvia (Apala 2007) (Fig 6.17).

The first castle in Cēsis, referred to in the Chronicle of Henry of Livonia as the smallest in the land (CHL: XXII, 5), was built by the Order of Sword Brethren around 1209. A series of excavations have shown that it was erected on the site of a pre-crusade hillfort inhabited by the local ethnic group of ancient Latvia – the Wends (Apala 2007). Documentary and archaeological evidence suggest that the Sword brothers lived in this castle together with the Wends up to 1214 when new stone castle was built by the Sword Brethren on the edge of the nearby plateau (Benninghoven 1965; Lapins & Dirveiks 2009). Traditional discussions of the thirteenth-century conquest of the eastern Baltic regions often ignore regional factors, forgetting that Livs, Letts and Wends mostly allied with the German immigrants from the start, fighting on their side and thus participating in the genesis of Livonia. Throughout the medieval period a synthesis occurred between the Western and the local societies, which was often determined by their living together in castles (Kļaviņš 2009). The local people not only stayed there in times of danger, but also lived there permanently – as artisans, and they also entered the ranks of the Teutonic Knights as brother-sergeants. It resulted in interaction in ways of life and technologies. This is clearly represented by the artefactual assemblages from

Fig 6.16   *Aerial photograph of Cēsis Castle (photo R. Jelevics).*

Cēsis castle where a considerable number of recovered artefacts were made and used by local population. Fig 6.18 gives an example: a horseshoe-shaped brooch, exclusively worn by the natives, was found in a lump of lime mortar – a building material which became known in eastern Baltic only after the German immigrants arrived.

In 1237, Cēsis castle was taken over by the Teutonic Knights and it became the seat of the first Master of the Order's Livonian branch. Although subsequent masters of the Order chose the castle of Rīga as their principal place of residence, masters returned to Cēsis during the periods of danger and instability when the Order came into conflict with the town of Rīga or the Archbishopric of Rīga. Finally, at the end of the fifteenth century, the Order's administrative headquarters was relocated from Rīga to Cēsis, and it became the permanent residence of the masters.

Documentary evidence and the results of archaeological excavations show that the castle was intensively populated. The extensive faunal material indicates animals con-

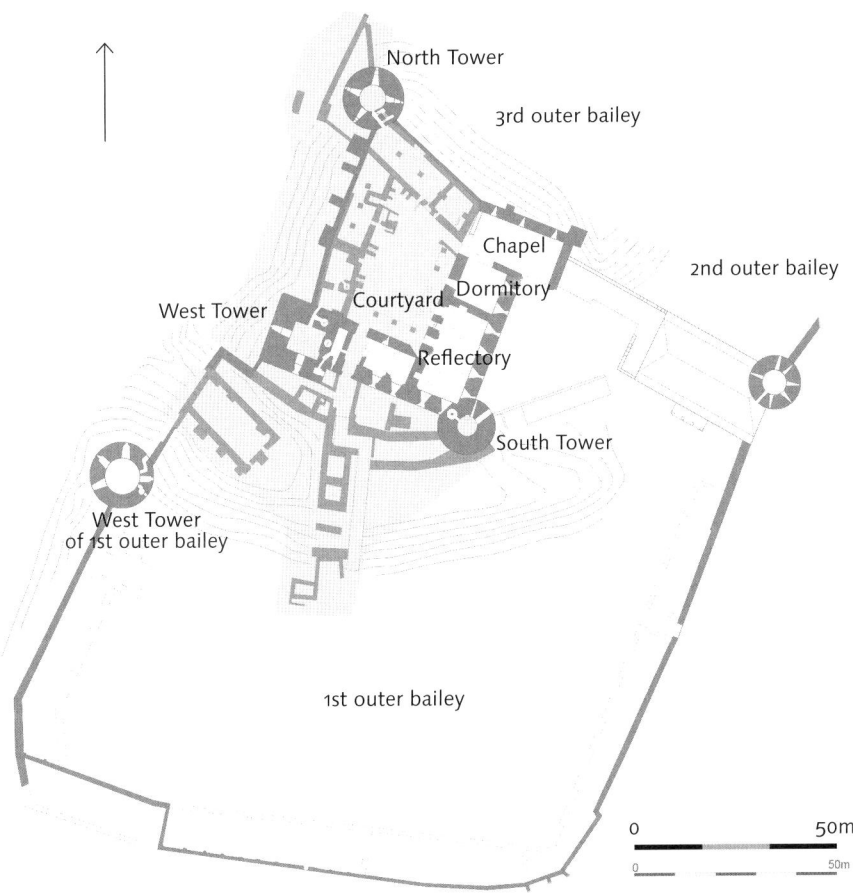

Plan of Cēsis Castle, showing areas excavated.

Fig 6.17

Archaeologies of Coercion   **267**

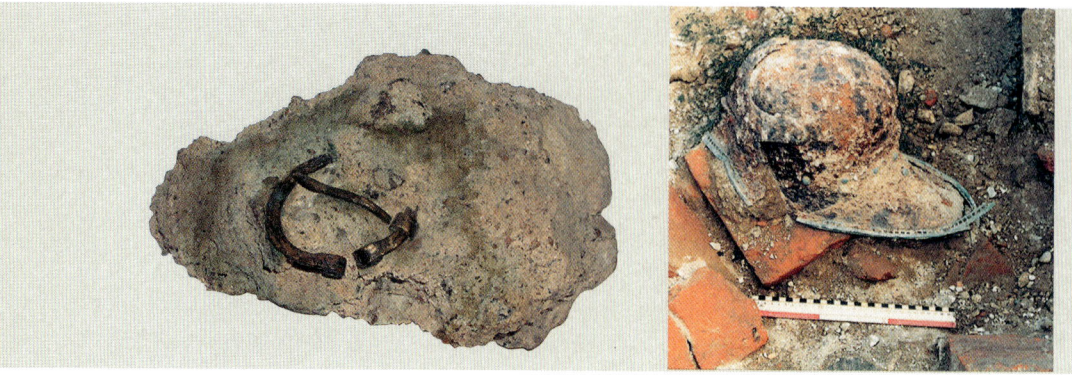

Fig 6.18   *(left) The lump of lime mortar containing a brooch owned by one of castle builders (Apala 2006).*

Fig 6.19   *(right) German-style salet (light helmet) found during the excavation of the Castle's western range (Apala 2006).*

sumed as food and can be used both for investigation of the history of consumption and the history of environment (see Ch 1, part 2). Fifteenth century visitation records refer to the vast amount of armour in the castle's armoury, while pieces of armour recovered from the castle now form the largest collection of medieval armour found in archaeological excavations in the Baltic (Apala 2006). Moreover, some luxurious pieces of armour have been found, e.g. German styled *Salet* (helmet) (Fig 6.19) embellished with brass rivets and decorative trimming, contradicting the simplicity prescribed by The Rule of the Teutonic Knights.

By the middle of the sixteenth century, the defences of Cēsis castle had assumed the extent and shape that they retain to this day and the castle formed a highly visible symbol of the Order's power over the land. The ongoing development of the castle was interrupted by the dissolution of the Order in 1561 and by devastating sieges of the castle that took place during the Livonian war (1558-1583). Excavations on the castle site have revealed not only a wide range of artefacts that illustrate the daily life of the castle's inhabitants but also reflect the most dramatic event in the castle's history, which has been described in several late sixteenth century chronicles. In 1577, when the castle of Cēsis was besieged and bombarded for five days by the army of Ivan the Terrible, 300 hundred people within the castle realized that it was impossible to defend themselves any longer and made the decision to commit mass suicide by blowing themselves up with four barrels of gunpowder (Russow 1584). In 1974, at the basement of the former west range a number of human remains of adults and children were uncovered, in association with coins consistent with a date of 1577 (Apala 2006). Chronicler Salomon Henning (1593) reports that 'all were blown up, aside from those who had hidden elsewhere in the castle' and it is likely that the human remains recovered by archaeologists belonged to those who were trying to avoid the explosion.

Claregalway Castle – an Irish tower house *by Rory Sherlock*

Located just 14km north of Galway city in the west of Ireland, Claregalway Castle is a good example of a late medieval tower house, representative of a type of building found in great numbers throughout Ireland, Scotland and northern England (Fig 6.20). In total, these three regions probably had over 4,000 tower houses between them and these were generally built between 1300 and 1650, though very few Irish examples are thought to predate 1400 (Cairns 1987).

The typical tower house is composed of a rectangular stone-built tower which stands three to five stories in height, though more complex plan forms, including L-shaped, Z-shaped and, more rarely, circular towers, are also known. Though quite unlike the larger castles of the medieval period in many respects, tower houses are undoubtedly a form of castle and were often referred to as such by those who built and occupied them. Designed as defensible (as opposed to defensive) residences, the evolution of tower houses between 1300 and 1650 represents the slow-moving transition from castle to country house and so the changing nature of the tower house reflects the changing nature of society in the British Isles in the late medieval and early modern periods.

Dating to the first half of the fifteenth century, Claregalway Castle measured 12.5m by 10m and stood on a strategic site on the northern bank of the River Clare (Fig 6.21). Many tower houses now stand alone in the landscape, but most are likely to have been surrounded by a range of residential, agricultural and defensive structures originally. Recent excavations at Claregalway have uncovered evidence for a substantial courtyard wall, which featured D-shaped corner turrets, a centrally-positioned gatehouse structure and a 6m-wide extra-mural ditch. Generally termed *barmkins* in Scotland and *bawns* in Ireland, such walled enclosures around tower houses were very common and appear to have served both as farmyards and as defensive enclosures.

Claregalway Castle is entered via a doorway at ground-floor level and this was protected by a wall-top machicolation, a portcullis and, internally over the entrance lobby, a 'murder hole' through which fire could be directed downwards upon any attackers who had succeeded in entering the main doorway. A portcullis is an unusual feature in a tower house and a *yett*, a hinged metal grille which gave extra strength to the main doorway, was more commonly employed. These were generally positioned inside the main door in Scotland, but are found outside the main door in Ireland and so were drawn closed and secured from within the building using a chain that passed through a channel in the door jamb.

A spiral stair at Claregalway gives access to the upper levels within the building. This type of stairs, often called turnpike stairs in Scotland, are a common feature of tower houses, though straight flights of stairs are also known. Most tower houses have at least one substantial stone vault within them and these features usually span the main ground- or first-floor chambers, though they can often be found at higher levels, particularly in the west and south of Ireland. At Claregalway, the vault spans the main first-floor chamber and so carries the second-floor hall above. An interesting difference between Irish and Scottish tower houses lies in the relative positions of the hall and 'private' accommodation. In Scotland, the hall is often located upon the vault at first-

Fig 6.20   *Claregalway Castle, Co. Galway, Ireland. (Rory Sherlock).*

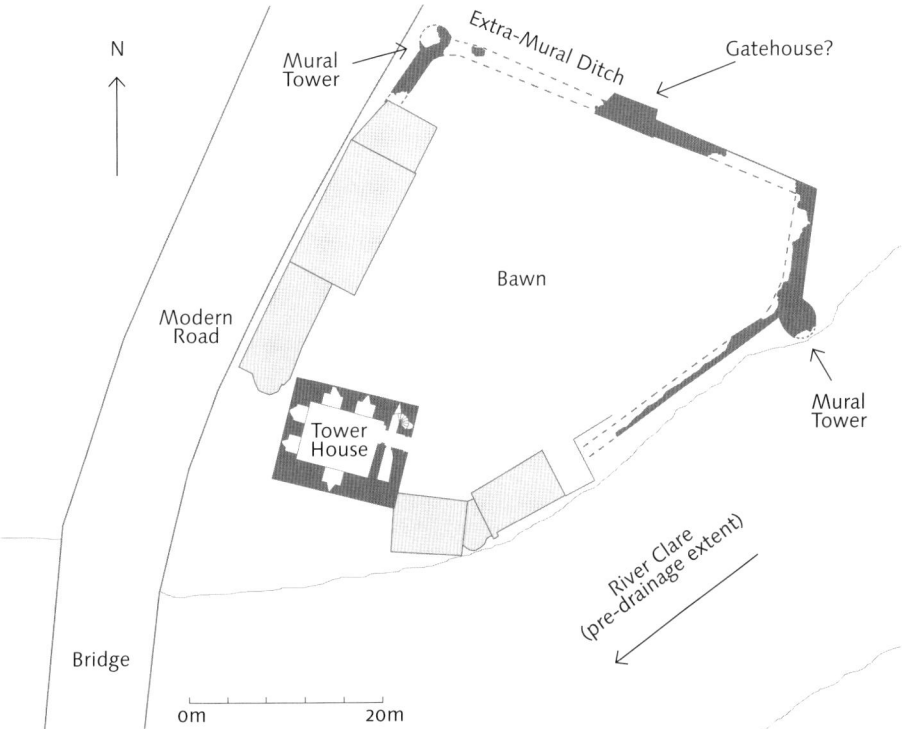

Plan of Claregalway Castle, showing the tower house and the recently excavated portions of the town wall. Note how the later buildings (in grey) follow the line of the bawn enclosure.   **Fig 6.21**

floor level and so the private accommodation within the building is positioned above the hall, whereas in Ireland it is common for the hall to be found resting upon the vault at the topmost level of the building with the lesser chambers located below it. This arrangement has an interesting outcome, in that Irish tower house halls were commonly heated by a central hearth, whereas Scottish tower house halls, having rooms above them and so having fewer options for smoke dispersal, are more likely to have had a mural fireplace.

In the late sixteenth- and early seventeenth centuries, tower house architecture underwent a number of interesting changes and the omission of certain features commonly associated with castle living may be noted. Garderobe chambers were commonly phased out, stone vaults were often omitted in favour of buildings being floored entirely with timber, and parapet wall-walks were often shortened or even omitted in order to allow gables to rise flush with the external wall faces of the building. Internal spatial arrangements became simpler too, as the tower house gradually evolved from a complex structure incorporating both public and private spaces into a simpler structure that was essentially private in nature. The privatisation of the tower house marks the decline of the castle in a social sense, as the public roles of the castle had now been stripped away from the building and what remained was, in essence, a rather anachronistic form of house.

The Bloody Battle of Towton, England *by Tim Sutherland*

In *battlefield archaeology*, multidisciplinary techniques are used to analyse the landscape of battle, including the artefacts dropped during or following a conflict, the skeletons of buried casualties and the trauma of their wounds. Most of these studies to date have been applied to post-medieval battlefields, and there are only a few examples of successful investigations carried out on sites dating from the medieval or earlier periods. Of the few studies carried out on earlier battlefields, most fail to find definitive evidence of the associated engagement in spite of intensive and large-scale archaeological prospection. An example of an elusive site is the Battle of Agincourt, in Northern France, made famous in Shakespeare's Henry V, where the outnumbered English forces defeated the French in 1415. Although large-scale metal detector surveys have been employed (Sutherland 2006) and even excavations at the acknowledged location of the 'mass graves', physical evidence for a battle is still lacking.

A more successful case of archaeological battlefield analysis, drawn from extensive physical evidence, was that of Towton, Yorkshire, England (1461) (Fig 6.22). The battle was fought during the Wars of the Roses on 29 March, 1461, between the Lancastrian forces of King Henry VI and the army of the newly established Yorkist King Edward IV. The site lies on rising agricultural ground on the edge of the Vale of York, 19km to the southwest of the medieval city. The Towton Battlefield Archaeological Survey was the first multidisciplinary battlefield archaeology survey to be carried out in Britain and revealed some of the realities of combat and combat methodology, in this case at its moment of transition from archery to gunpowder.

The project began with the discovery of a mass grave of combatants in 1996 (Fiorato *et al* 2000). Upstanding earthworks thought to be connected to the battle were then surveyed on the surface and by geophysics, and subsequently excavated. The results were surprising: enclosures and mounds supposedly containing the dead did not do so; the remains of a medieval chapel built by King Richard III to commemorate the dead were not where they were supposed to be, on Chapel Hill, and the sites of former burial tumuli, marked on Ordnance Survey maps for 150 years, were found to be fictitious (Sutherland 2003). The first results therefore altered the landscape history of the area.

It was assumed that the artefact 'signature' of the medieval battle would be ferrous metal - fragments of weapons and arrowheads lost during the conflict (Sutherland 2007). In theory, these might be located by geophysical survey, but in practice extensive surveys show that geophysical signals are masked by magnetic or ferrous debris from agricultural machinery, bonfires or other recent activity (Sutherland 2003). By contrast, sensitive metal detectors proved able to discriminate between most types of metal and other electromagnetic signals. Archaeologists have been slow to adopt metal detecting because of its association with treasure hunters, but in trained hands these instruments are unparalleled at locating even tiny fragments of metal from a buried or non-visible context (Sutherland 2000).

The Towton metal detector surveys discovered that the real archaeological 'signature' of the battle was provided by non-ferrous metal (copper alloy or lead) from clothing

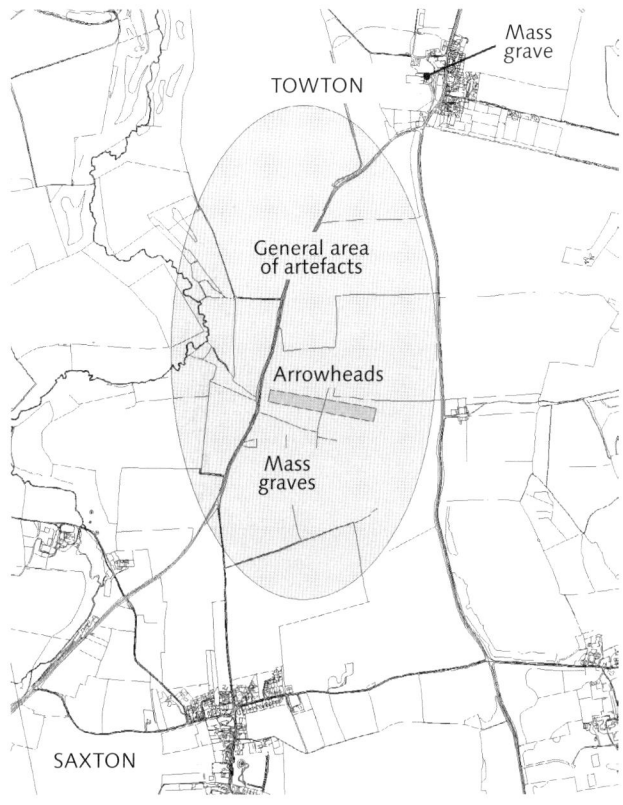

Map of the Towton area, **Fig 6.22** *showing location of the mass graves, the limits of metal detector finds, and concentrations of arrowheads.*

TOWTON

Mass grave

General area of artefacts

Arrowheads

Mass graves

SAXTON

or harness fittings such as lace ends, belt buckles, badges, brooches, purse frames and coins, and jewelry – in other words personal items lost during the conflict (Fig 6.23). Collectively, these were to prove essential as indicators of where the battle had been fought. The objects were recovered from the topsoil (the first 30cm or so), emphasizing the importance of surface layer in the medieval battlefield. The analysis of patterns within the survey led to the discovery of concentrations of hundreds of ferrous arrowheads (Fig 6.24) believed to lie in the centre of the battlefield area. Most of these arrowheads were not simply forged from a single piece of metal, but had brazed together from separate pieces, suggesting lower temperature rather than blacksmith's forges (David Starley, pers.comm.).

Human bones associated in surface deposits with arrowheads proved to mark the sites of graves, subsequently located by geophysical survey. Archaeological excavations at similar locations led to the discovery of mass graves in the centre of the battlefield (Sutherland 2007), and the graves of former combatants buried individually or in small groups (Fig 6.25). Much of the skeletal material exhibits dramatic evidence of medieval combat, including wounds received from sword blows, stabbings from knives, blows from maces and war hammers, as well as defence wounds on hands and arms (research by Malin Holst, Fig 6.26). Several of the skeletons also had healed wounds, suggesting they had survived other battles, apparently often with medical assistance. These wounds

Fig 6.23   *Late medieval personal objects, made of copper alloy, some gilded, discovered during the metal detector prospection survey of the Towton Battlefield (©Tim Sutherland: with gratitude to Simon Richardson).*

Fig 6.24   *The remains of ferrous arrowheads, some composite, found on the Towton battlefield during metal detector prospection survey (©Trustees of the Royal Armouries, Leeds: with gratitude to Simon Richardson).*

Three skeletons in a single grave discovered beneath the floor of Towton Hall, on the edge of the Towton battlefield (©Tim Sutherland).

Fig 6.25

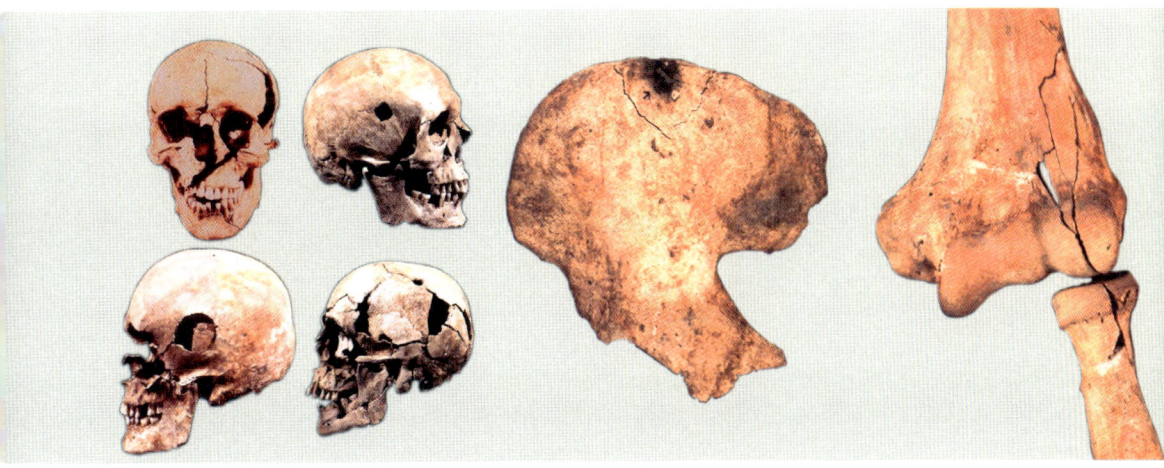

Examples of trauma. (left) Skulls with blade injuries (centre) pelvic bone marked by blunt force. (right) Stab wound to the elbow (©University of Bradford).

Fig 6.26

lacked evidence of infection, suggesting that the methods of late medieval medicine could be efficacious (Knüsel & Boylston 2000).

The Towton survey also recovered evidence for the first use of gunpowder in battle: composite lead shot (Starley pers.com.), and a fragment from a very early exploded hand cannon used in the battle and its associated lead shot (Graeme Rimer pers. comm.). These finds are currently unique in British archaeology.

The results from the Towton archaeological survey offered a reappraisal of the historical literature associated with both warfare in general and this battle in particular. The archaeology implied a highly energetic conflict focused on the same area of ground and resolved within 12 hours, in contrast with the established historical picture of three protracted skirmishes and battles - Ferrybridge, Dintingdale and Towton - over two or three days (Boardman 1996; Sutherland 2009). The procedures developed by the Towton project have been applied in the search for other medieval battlefields, for example, those of the Battles of Shrewsbury (1403), Bosworth, Leicestershire (1485), and East Stoke, Nottinghamshire (1487).

The late medieval period was a time of great changes, traditionally chronicled by documents in a manner that was not without its flaws, elements of bias, or propaganda. The archaeological investigation of the pivotal events of these turbulent times, the pitched battles of the late medieval *age of chivalry* provide extensive, wide ranging and fascinating evidence. The pioneering results from Towton show that these battles were rapid transitions from glamorous assemblies to horrendous bloodbaths. Future work can proceed in the knowledge that given the new techniques, historic battlefields can be seen as repositories of vast quantities of significant and virtually untapped archaeological information (Sutherland & Holst 2005).

CHAPTER 7

MANUFACTURE AND PRODUCTION

PART 1: CRAFT INTO INDUSTRY *by Ricardo Córdoba and Ulrich Müller*

The archaeological investigation of late medieval production invites approaches from two principal directions: the examination of production sites on the one hand, and the finished products on the other. Among our goals are the examination of the work place, the reconstruction of the manufacturing processes, the patterns of demand and distribution, and the changing relationship between production and the rest of society. This allows us to chronicle the development of crafts from a role serving a local community to their emergence as international industries (Verhaeghe 1995; Müller & Lübke 2006; Melzer 2008).

In practice, distinguishing between domestic craft and professional industry is a challenge for a single discipline. In our period we can profit from the increasing availability of written and pictorial sources to interpret methods of production, technology transfer and professionalization. This approach is also helpful in understanding the spatial and social specialisation of production, in the context of landscape and settlement geography. Although craft production took place in castles, at palaces and monasteries, and in rural industrial areas, the archaeological evidence is currently most plentiful in towns. This may be due partly to the intensity of urban excavation, but it also reflects the role of towns in gathering industries together (see Ch 9 and Table 7.1).

On production sites, finds and features can be allocated to five categories: raw materials, waste products, unfinished objects, fixed structures, tools and finished products. The amount of evidence of this kind that is won by archaeological excavation is steadily increasing. Even so, it represents only part of the late medieval production process. Multi-strand technologies, like mining, metallurgy, salt extraction and milling, encompass potentially a very wide range of activity. During the later Middle Ages we encounter important innovations in extraction techniques at the mines, hydraulic engineering, the use of wind, smelting and the diversity of fuels, including eventually coal. In these crafts we can note the arrival of a high degree of interdependence that allows us to speak about machine-assisted and professional production. Even apparently less technically complex crafts, such as textile working, begin to show signs of professional organisation, technology transfer on a large scale and developments that show a sensi-

Fig 7.1   *Crafts in the Medieval Town of Greifswald, Germany (13th-14th century).*

tivity to the market place. Taken together, the archaeological agenda can thus address the question of proto-industrialisation.

In this introductory section, we shall briefly review recent archaeological evidence for a selection of well-known crafts: pottery, glass, leather and oil. Manufacture and production are then illuminated in the body of the chapter through particular studies: coarseware and fineware pottery, the faience of the Anabaptists, and the brilliant output of pottery and glass from Al-Andalus. Two further contributions explore the major industries associated with textiles and metal extraction.

TABLE 7.1	PATTERNS OF CRAFT IN DIFFERENT TYPES OF SETTLEMENT			
	TYPE OF SETTLEMENT			
	RURAL	INDUSTRIAL	PALACE/CASTLE/MONASTERY	TOWN
Character of craft	local/ domestic	Specialised/ professional	Specialised/professional	Multiple: local, specialised, professional
Scale of production/Quality	demand-led	surplus with high quality	demand-led with high quality	Surplus; range from bulk to high quality
Demand of craft	Low	Special/ particular	Selected	high
Market	Intra-site; local	?	Local; intra-site (outer bailey?)	local and special markets

Pottery

Studies of pottery workshops have increased over the past few years thanks especially to urban archaeology (Heege 2007). Traditionally the focus was on the pottery kiln, undoubtedly the most interesting feature from a technical standpoint, but modern investigations now extend to the whole working space. Good examples have been noted at Paterna and Valladolid (Spain) and the potters' district of Marseilles (France).

The kiln used throughout the Mediterranean area was a two-tier structure, consisting of a circular fire pit sunk below ground, with a firing chamber superimposed above it in the form of a hemispherical brick vault (AME 1, Fig 7.1). The two parts were separated by a horizontal grating supported by brick arches resting on the fire pit floor. The floor of the fire pit was made with clay, and the vault above was usually furnished with a chimney. There was only one point of entry, which was at ground level and served both to add fuel and to charge and discharge the upper chamber with its load of pottery. The outside of the kiln was covered with a thick clay insulating jacket containing recycled daub.

The Paterna potteries, dating from the fourteenth and fifteenth centuries, have been studied by Amigues and Mesquida (1990), who not only examined the typology of the kilns but also the organization of the workshops and the different stages of production. The clay was settled in water in rectangular tanks in an open courtyard. Purified clay was then taken to a room containing the foot-driven potters' wheels, and the fashioned vessels were then placed in the chamber for firing in a second room and stood to cool. These three stages occupied two rooms and a courtyard in an L-shaped building, built with rubble walls and a tiled roof.

Pots were glazed by coating the surface of the vessel with a transparent vitreous film. In the Mediterranean region, from the tenth century onwards glazing was achieved by mixing lead oxide with sand and water and applying the mixture to the surface of the earthenware vessel. This could be done by immersing the pot in the mixture, or by painting it on with a brush or splashing, so that the glazing could cover the whole vessel or only part of it, such as the inside or the neck. Once the lead oxide was applied, the vessel was submitted to a second firing, during which the mixture became vitrified, forming a waterproof, transparent, shiny coating. If no other oxide was added, the vessel remained the colour that the clay had acquired during the first firing. However, if it was desired to vary that colouring or obtain different tones, it was only necessary to add another metal oxide to the mixture, which would change the transparency of the lead to the colour corresponding to; iron oxide for ochre and reddish tones, copper oxide for green tones, antimony oxide for yellow, and cobalt oxide for blue.

From the thirteenth century onwards, tin glazing gradually superseded lead. This used a mixture of sand with stannic dioxide, which gave an opaque white coating, so that coloured decoration could be painted on it once it had dried. Sometimes the decoration would be painted on first, before glazing. The new glazing system allowed ceramics to carry more detailed images and epigraphy. The adoption of tin glazing originated from the Islamic tradition, which was spread around the western Mediterranean from Spain, in white, blue, green and brown variants (see below). The so-called lustre ware was pottery with a metallic lustre which required a third firing to soften the tin glaze and fix the lustre – made by sprinkling copper sulphide, gold or silver filings, or iron oxide on the surface. This third firing required a low temperature (65°C) and a great deal of smoke, produced by adding heather or rosemary sprigs to the wood used as fuel. Although the pottery looked black and sooty when taken out of the kiln, subsequent cleaning revealed the glitter and sparkle owed to the metal in all its splendour.

Between the twelfth and sixteenth century, there were numerous other innovations in pottery production, technology transfers that are to be understood against the background of increasing Europeanisation (see below for an example from Southampton, England). In the northern and north-eastern parts of Europe, Scandinavian and Slavonic hand-made or partly wheel-turned earthenware were replaced by wheel-thrown pottery with a partial lead glaze. Special clays were required to make *stoneware*, limiting its areas of production (see below). Also required was a high firing temperature over 1200°C, to make the clay partially melt or 'sinter.' These factors, combined with an increasing shortage of wood, led to the design of special kilns and methods of stacking. The success of the product and the services of the Hanseatic trade network meant that it was distributed from its point of origin over the whole of northern Europe by the end of the Middle Ages (see Ch 8, p 340). The example of stoneware shows how technical innovations were interweaved with economical and socio-archaeological questions.

Potteries were generally located in the countryside near supplies of fuel, water and suitable clay. When their economic importance rose, potters were attracted to towns, but were generally situated in the suburbs, because of the fire risk. Only at the end of the Middle Ages do potters' workshops begin to appear in the town centres. In Part 2 we present six case-studies reflecting the industry, trade and influence of medieval potters.

Glass

As with glaze, glass is made by melting a mixture of quartz sand with a flux, generally ash, with addition of metal oxides for colouring. The mixture is heated in crucibles to a high temperature (1200°C) to form a blob of molten glass. This is worked with simple tools such as the hollow bone blowpipe with a wooden mouthpiece through which the glass was blown, pincers and scissors for cutting it; and the *pontil*, or long iron rod, to spin it into various shapes (Charleston 1991, 242; Kurzmann 2004).

Good archaeological documentation can be found on medieval glass furnaces thanks to the studies of Danièle Foy (1988) in the south of France (furnaces at La Seube and Cadrix), and those of Mendera (1991) in Italy (furnaces at Monte Leco and Germagnana) (see also the evidence for glass-making in al-Andalus below). The kilns used for the fusing of glass in the later Middle Ages were of two types, usually called the southern and the northern. Southern kilns were circular and covered by a vault, on which two or three superimposed chambers were placed: in the bottom chamber, provided with a door, combustion was produced and the firing crucibles were placed. Heat rose up through a perforated floor to the upper chambers, accessed through openings (Charleston 1991, 239). The northern kiln was rectangular in plan, and had three connected chambers at the same height but increasing distance from the heat source. However, recent archaeological investigations have found circular and rectangular kilns in the same workshop, possibly used for different stages in the process (roasting, fusion and blowing).

The production of glass, whether hollow for vessels or flat for window glass suggests a range of specialists at work. Due to its high value glass was recycled again and again. Early glass production was confined to monastic or palace sites, but due to its high consumption of wood, ash and water, later production moved into woodland. In the course of the Later Middle Ages, it appears in special industrial zones, e.g. in the Weserbergland, France and Bohemia. Instances of glass production within towns are extremely rare (but see the example from Murcia, below).

Leather: Tanneries and shoemakers' workshops

The hides of cattle, sheep, goats, deer and horse, received from the butcher, were used to make an extensive range of leather goods. In general terms, cattle hides were *tanned* a brown colour and used to make shoes, sheaths, jerkins and bottles, while those of other animals were *tawed* white, and using to make gloves, purses and parchment. Tanning required a three stage process. First the blood and offal was washed off in flowing water. Then the hide was steeped in water and lime in a tank to loosen the hair, laid over a beam and scraped off with a draw knife. The hides were then immersed in solutions of dog dung, urine or beer to remove the lime and soften them. The hides were then placed in shallow *handling* tank where they were continuously moved around in a tanning solution to acquire an even colour; and then laid in piles interleaved with oak bark in deep *layaway* pits, for at least a year, after which they would be removed and dried slowly in sheds and then oiled until ready to work (Cherry 1991b, 296-7).

Tanneries are identified archaeologically through a range of pits, deep and shallow, preferably sited next to shallow flowing water. The pits may be circular or rectangular, and lined with timber or clay. Other diagnostic finds include grindstones to crush the oak bark used in tanning solutions for the handler tanks. Of great archaeological interest are the fourteenth-fifteenth century tanneries excavated in the cities of Wroclaw (Poland), Savona (Italy) and Troyes (France) (Busko 2003; Deborde et al 2002). Tawing used alum (aluminium potassium sulphate), imported into the rest of Europe from the eastern Mediterranean until 1453, and thereafter from Italy. The skins were trampled in a mixture of alum, egg-yolk, oil and flour in large tubs, and then stretched and dried (Cherry 1991b, 299; see also Fig 2.13 for an example of the sequence of parchment manufacture.

During the twelfth-thirteenth centuries there was an increase in production using hard-wearing cowhide, probably reflecting the domination of cattle farming. It also reflects an increased demand for craftsmen making shoes and sheaths, and for those that repaired them (the cobblers). Numerous craftsmen were now working professionally, with a fine dividing line between manufacture, recycling and repair (Mould 2003; Goubitz 2007; Harjua 2005, 2008). In the twelfth and thirteenth centuries tanneries are found in town centres, coincident with demand, but because of the terrible smell and the pollution of the water supply, they were later moved to sites in the suburbs and downstream of living areas.

Bone and antler

Workshops for the production of bone and antler are easy to detect, but difficult to map as workplaces. This is because large amounts of scrap from bone and antler processing come from displaced rubbish layers in towns, although they concentrate in a way that suggests specialists at work, for example those producing combs and dice, as in London and York (MacGregor 1985, 1991). Bone processing has also been noted next to medieval churches and monasteries, which were supplied with beads for rosaries (see Ch 9.8). During the twelfth century, bone gradually overtook antler as the raw material used for the making of many items, and horn was little used to make combs after about 1300, although it remained important longer for the manufacture of cross-bow nuts (MacGregor 1991, 366). Bone and antler seem to remain for some time at the service of their town, castle or court, although by 1455, people from abroad were coming into London to buy horn, and by the seventeenth century (and arguably earlier) horners in London were exporting 2 million leaves of horn for use on the continent (MacGregor 1991, 373). Professional guilds of horners were formed in London and York in the Middle Ages, but by the end of the period, their incipient industry, and that of the bone workers, had been redistributed among the manfuacturers of composite retail goods: knives, buttons and boxes (MacGregor 1991, 376).

Oil and sugar mills

Olive oil was widely used in the Mediterranean world for lighting as well as eating from the Roman period onwards. It was (and is) extracted in a two stage process: first the olives are crushed in a stone mill and then pressed with a screw and beam, usually of wood. In the Mediterranean world, especially the Iberian Peninsula, North Africa and Syria, many olive oil mills dated to the later Middle Ages or early modern times (sixteenth to eighteenth centuries) have been documented by archaeology. The main components were the mill (in which the olives were crushed), the beam or press with its circular stone and the tanks for the collection of the oil. The mill, called in Spanish *alfarje*, from the Arabic *al-farch*, consisted of a circular stone base of variable diameter (normally between 1.50 and 2.50 m), flat or slightly tilted towards the centre, with a concave groove at its edge, 10-12 cm wide. In this groove a circular stone rolled, upright like a wheel. The axle of the wheel was fixed to a central wooden shaft that was rotated by horse-power, rolling the stone wheel in its groove and so crushing the olives that lay there. The resulting pulp was placed in straw baskets made with two round mats sewn together at the edge. The basket was stacked on a circular stone base (*regaifa*), sluiced with boiling water and then submitted to the press; the water and oil obtained from this pressing leaked out of the baskets and ran via a gutter surrounding the stone base into tanks. Pressure was applied by means of a beam 12-15m long anchored at one end and pressured at the other by adding weights or tightening with a screw jack. To heat the water used to dampen the baskets, there was a cauldron in every mill placed on top of a small furnace, which was usually located in one corner of the workshop.

Mills for extracting cane sugar were of similar form. They are called *almazaras,* the same word used for oil mills or *trapiches* from the Latin *trapetum* for the Roman oil press. In addition to the mill and the press, a sugar refinery had ovens to boil the syrup and a storage area for the moulds in which the sugar crystallized. The refinery of Couvoucle-Stavros on the island of Cyprus had one grindstone with animal traction and another indicating the use of water-power (Wartburg 1995). The pressing released a syrup (molasses), to which water was added and which was filtered through sacking and then, once clean and strained, boiled in copper cauldrons. This was done at a temperature of 100°C and, although the process was relatively simple, it was necessary to see that the mixture did not boil over and that the sugar did not burn or stick to the cauldron, and to stir it constantly until the molasses was boiled and the sugar was ready. The refinery in Stavros, Cyprus, had eight hearths to heat the cauldrons, six of which were built in adobe and two with bricks. The firing rooms had an irregular oval ground plan 3 x 2 m with the top part converging in a sort of false vault; in each room an arch divided the hearth into two spaces.

When it had been boiled, the so-called "purging" of the sugar began, in which the purified mixture (molasses) was placed in moulds, cone-shaped vessels with a hole in their apex, which was closed up during the filling process. Once full, the moulds were kept in a shady place, and the sugar crystallized for twelve or fifteen days inside the moulds, while the remaining molasses was drained through the hole and dripped into earthenware jugs or vessels placed under the cones. These moulds are present in all the refineries excavated and have been well studied in the *trapiches* excavated in Motril, on the Iberian coast of Granada.

Craft into industry

In these areas of production, as well as those of textiles and iron (see below) there is a clear trajectory, from craft to industry. While every early community had its smith, weaver and cobbler, the production of weapons, precious church plate and more luxury goods were initially dedicated to noble or monastic service. Changes came with the rise of the towns and the concentration of craftsmen with similar skills. As well as relying on continued patronage, these provided each other with commodities, and thus built up a system of close exchange that resembled a market. Craftsmen congregated in parts of towns, as can be seen from street names all over Europe (Fig 7.1). This might be due to shared resources or nuisance, as the tanners, or to protect their output. The advent of the guilds showed that different crafts were keen to maintain their monopolies – and presumably their prices, but these were weakened by the rise of specialist providers, such as the stoneware potters (below) and the Anabaptists (below). Competitive products were also achieved by combining different crafts to produce a particular desirable item – such as the bone handled knife, or rosaries, of beads and metal. Although individual craftsmen strengthened their control of the market by forming guilds (Ch 9, p 396), the material evidence strongly suggests that manufacturers would need numerous links across crafts. The ultimate suppliers to the wood-workers were farmers, and of metal smiths the miners; but the butcher would act as point of supply to twenty or more crafts, including makers of soap, combs, handles, gloves and saddles; a barker supplied tanners, and the used bark ('tan burves') could be traded on for use in metal extraction (Fig 7.2).

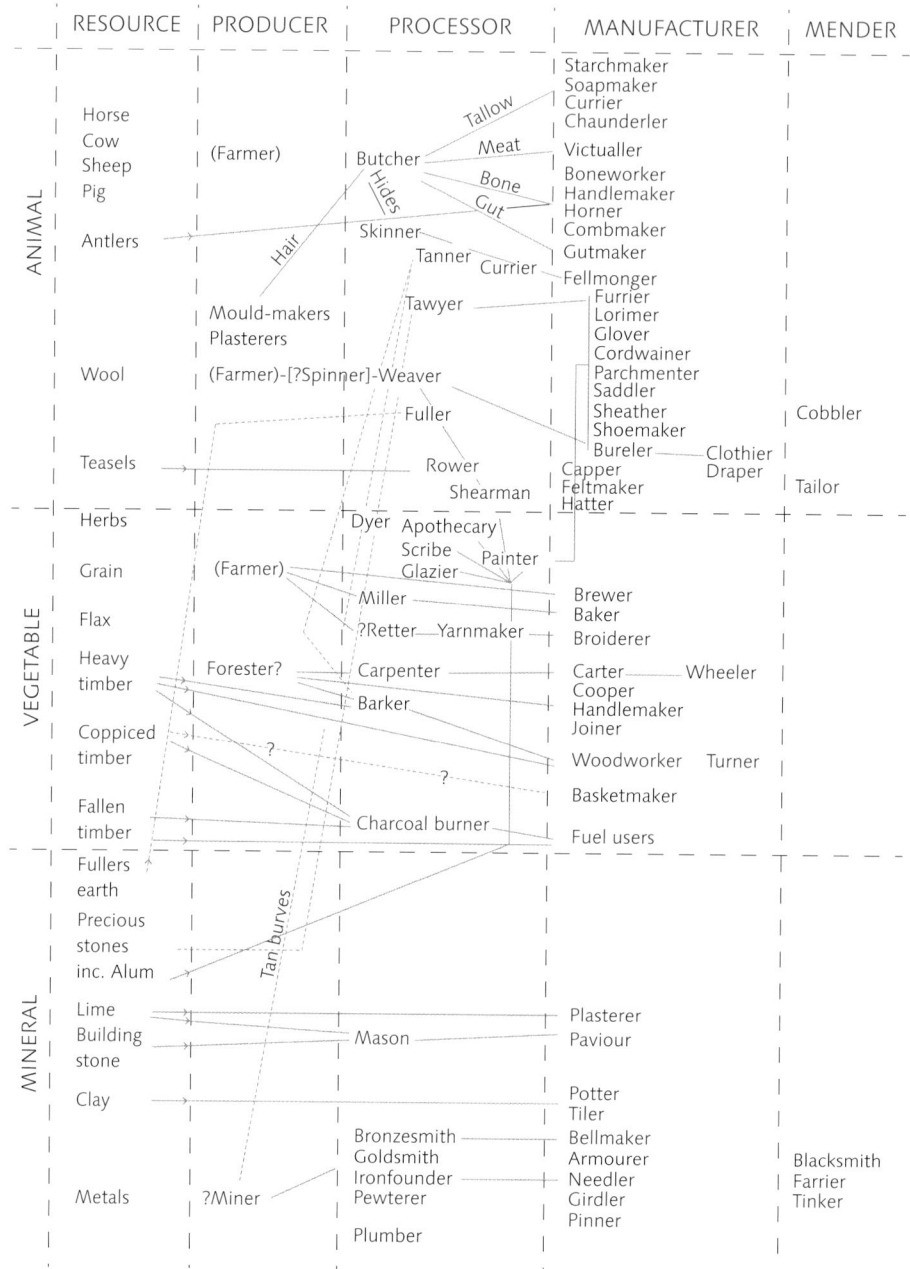

Fig 7.2   *Hypothetical interdependence of crafts (Carver 1987b, 82).*

By the later thirteenth century, urban craftsmen were people on the rise, and on their way to becoming the key economic players of the future. At Worcester, Sidbury, three craftsmen's tenements were excavated side by side (Fig 7.3). According to the archaeological evidence, mainly pits filled with debris, in the late twelfth century to fourteenth century all three tenements had been occupied by bone-workers, producing decorated bone and horn (Fig 7.4). They were superseded in the fifteenth century by bronze-workers whose debris included buckles, strips, rings, loops, rods, springs, pins, scrap and lumps. There was a stone mould, possibly for making rods, a pair of tongs and a sherd of bell-metal (Fig 7.5). Other features included a bowl furnace, a hearth

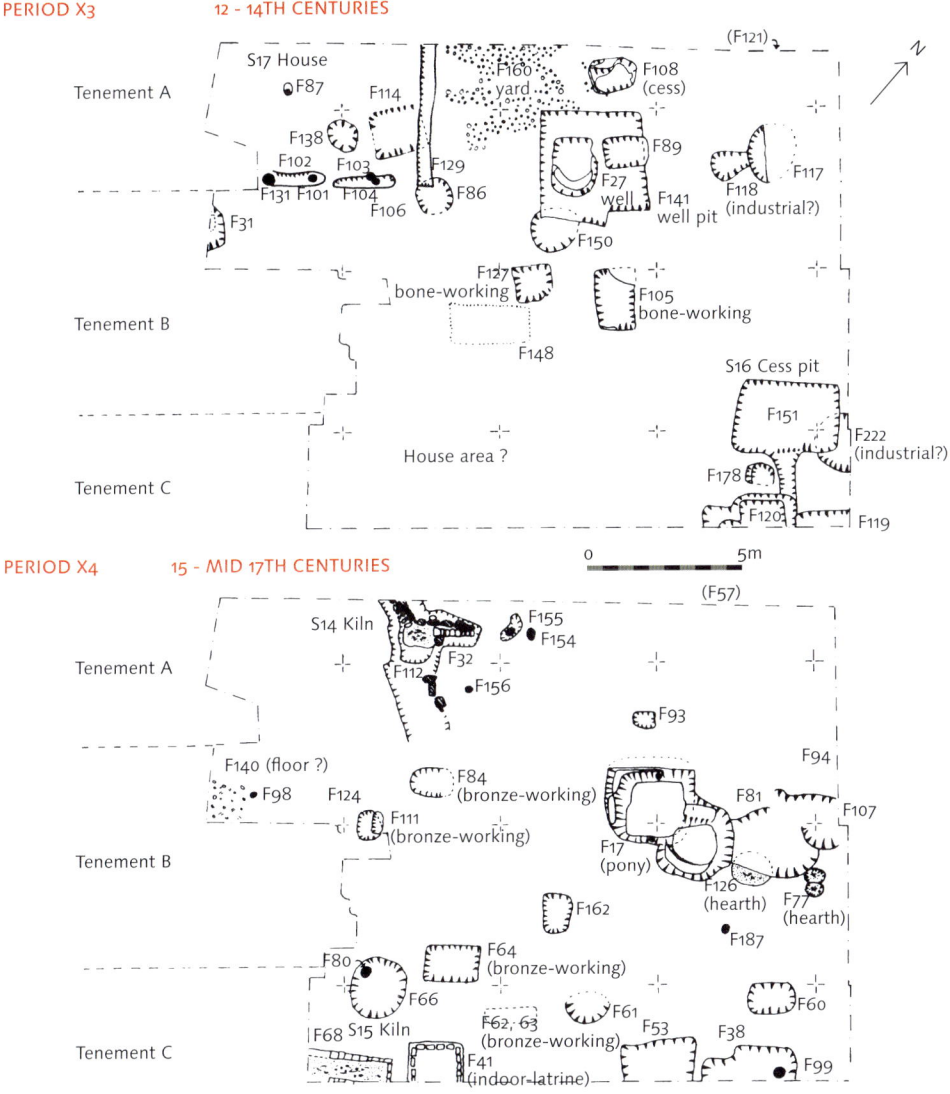

Worcester, Sidbury, England: plan of excavated tenements (above) bone-workers', 12–14th centuries; (below) *bronze-workers' (15th–17th centuries) (Carver 1980, 167).* **Fig 7.3**

and a kiln perhaps for firing moulds. Charters for the City of Worcester show that in 1359 two adjacent tenements in Sidbury were occupied, and apparently owned, by John le Belyetere (bell-maker) and William Le Goldesmyth. These craftsmen were multi-tasking but focussed in each generation on a principal industry. They were not

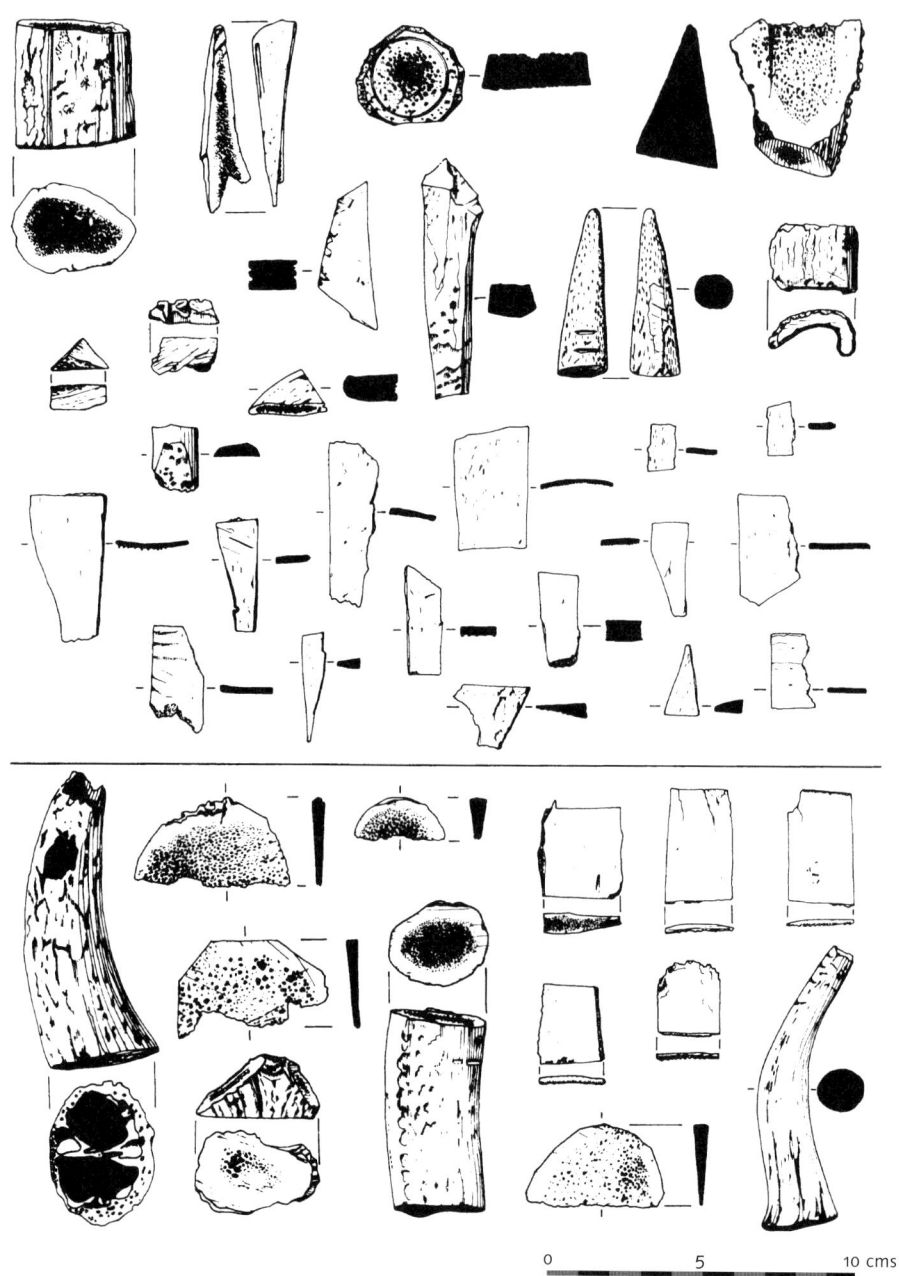

Fig 7.4   *Bone-workers' scrap from Sidbury, 13th century (Carver 1980, 194).*

impoverished. In their pits were coins, fragments of painted window glass, an Italian glass flask and a Majolica dish. A stone-lined latrine showed they had feasted on blackberries, strawberries and grapes (Carver 1980). In this way, the craftsmen's market tended to expand and lose both its upper-class controls and its local protection.

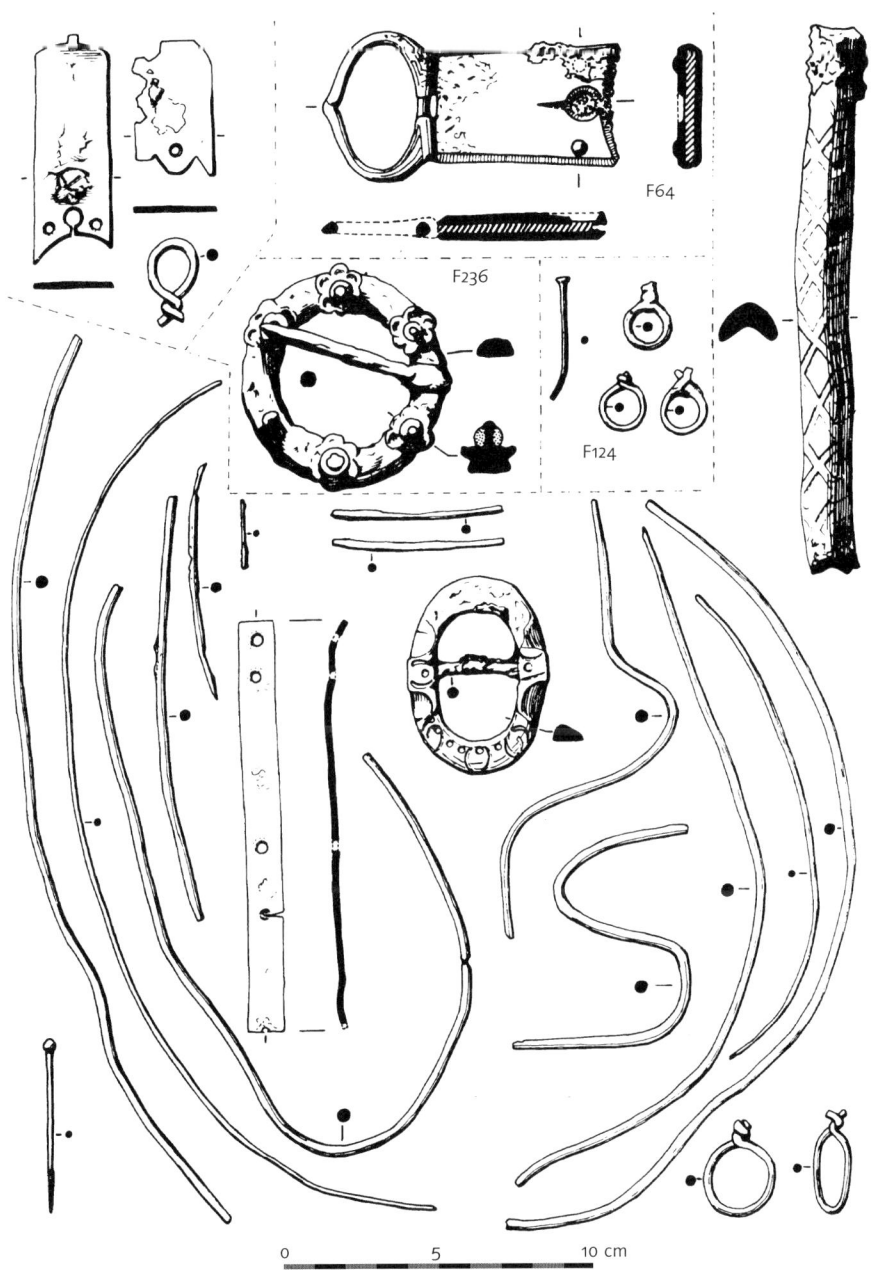

Bronze-workers' scrap from Sidbury, 14-15th centuries (Carver 1980, 198).

Fig 7.5

Supply and demand – pottery in medieval Southampton *by Duncan H. Brown*

A pot reflects the economy, cultural values, identity, social hierarchies and personal conditions. In terms of understanding human behaviour, pottery has value because our interpretations of how it was made, moved around and used reveal something of the people of the past, people who left a part of their own selves in the patterns of its design and function. In this example, we present a narrative of pottery used in a single southern English town with access to the sea: Southampton.

Pottery in Saxon Wessex mostly took the form of handbuilt, round-bottomed jars or cooking pots with high shoulders and everted rims and this tradition extended into the twelfth century (Fig 7.6a). In Southampton, the fabric of such vessels was usually tempered with flint, chalk and shell derived from local river gravels, which improved the chances of a successful firing in clamp or bonfire kilns. By the second half of the thirteenth century coarseware cooking pots were wheel-thrown but they still had high shoulders and everted rims and the base had been pushed out into a sagging profile (Fig 7.6b). The use of the wheel coincided with the adoption of multi-flue kiln structures,

Fig 7.6a   *Medieval pottery from Southampton, England. (a) cooking pot and jugs of the late 12th century.*

(b) cooking pot and jugs of the late 13th century.

Fig 7.6b

(c) pottery of the late 15th century, with plain local bowl and cooking pot and imported cooking pot, **Fig 7.6c**
bowls, jar and mugs.

making firing a more controlled process. The use of temper persisted, however, and it may be that it was culturally significant. It seems that cooking pots were supposed to have those inclusions; they always had and they always would.

It took the Black Death, war and recession to put an end to that tradition and the pottery types that emerged in the early fifteenth century represent the beginning of something new, in the form of flat-based jars with upright rims, and saucepan-like pots, or pipkins, with straight handles (Fig 7.6c).

In the medieval period it is clear that pottery was moved over substantial distances, both overseas and within a region. Studies of provenance show that pots from Lincolnshire could end up in Cornwall (Brown *et al.*, 2006) or jugs from Normandy in Southampton (Brown, 2002). Local products continued to make up most of the pottery used, but by the mid-thirteenth century even these were being produced by communities that specialised in pottery-making and directly supplied a variety of local markets (Vince 2005). By the late thirteenth century, pottery from the Saintonge area, north of Bordeaux, came into Southampton on ships carrying barrels of Gascon wine. The merchants who ran those ships were thus clearly involved in the movement of pottery, but it is unlikely that it was brought in for trade, because more often than not it remained in the port; even the principal hinterland town of Winchester has produced comparatively few finds of Saintonge. The same pattern may be observed between other English ports and their hinterlands. Late thirteenth-century merchants were thus bringing pots into Southampton to serve themselves or a very local market, rather than to make a profit by distributing them more widely.

The Gascon trade was interrupted by the advent of the Hundred Years War and more specifically by the sacking of Southampton in 1338. The events of the mid fourteenth century led to a recession: late fourteenth-century pottery assemblages contain few imported wares. But in the fifteenth century there was a revival in fortune as Genoese merchants established offices in the port to service their trade in cloth and dyestuffs. Links with the Mediterranean developed further when Venetian galley fleets became annual visitors to the port, dispensing cargoes of silks, spices and other luxuries. At the same time the rise of the North Sea ports such as Antwerp and Ghent saw local ships plying the English Channel and further north, carrying a variety of diverse cargoes (see Brown 1998 and Brown 2002; see Ch 8, p 328).

This widening of trade horizons after the earlier focus on France is reflected in the arrival of Italian and Iberian pottery, complemented by material from the Low Countries, the Rhineland and northern France. Pottery was now imported for distribution in the hinterland. Italian maiolica and Valencian lustreware were highly decorated types, and contemporary accounts record the duty payable on bringing them in or out of the town. Rhenish stoneware beer mugs (see below) were imported in consignments of as many as 3,000. Highly decorated dishes and jugs were not being made by local potterymakers and it is clear that these pots were imported in answer to an English demand.

Comparative studies have shown that a peasant household mainly utilized cooking pots or jars, while more jugs were used in the townhouses of wealthy burgesses (Brown 1997). Cooking pots were also the most commonly used vessel type in early medieval

Southampton, comprising up to 95% of many domestic assemblages but after the mid-thirteenth century jug use became more common. Medieval jugs are associated with the decanting and carrying of wine from barrels to serving areas, which would have been an activity more prevalent in the wealthier households. At the same time, potters increased their output and expanded the range of vessel types available. Curfews (for covering a hearth at night), dripping pans (for collecting meat fat), costrels (portable flasks) and lanterns represent new forms in this period. In the fifteenth century pottery production and use extended further to include mugs, pancheons (large bowls), chafing dishes (for keeping food warm), bunghole pitchers (or cisterns) and pipkins (handled cooking pots) (see MacCarthy and Brooks, 1988).

Increasing availability combined with low prices throughout the medieval period doubtless led to increased circulation of pottery but imported types concentrated in the homes of the wealthy. It is likely that further studies will provide readings of social class on the basis of pottery assemblages. Potters themselves have always been conscious of their fundamental human role, one with which archaeologists may find sympathy:

'No handycraft can with our art compare
for pots are made of what we potters are'.

(from Matthews and Green, 1969)

Stoneware production *by Hans-Georg Stephan*

Within the field of ceramic production, *Stoneware* was one of the most important innovations of the medieval period (Stephan 1988). This pottery, characterised by being fired at a very high temperature to a consistency resembling stone, was first made in the Carolingian period, as early as the eighth century in Mayen. At these early stages, there was probably no specific demand or market for this type of pottery, leaving stoneware to be once again developed and reintroduced at a much later date. It was about 1200-1250, a crucial period marked by many innovations in medieval technology, economy and society, that the time was again ripe for the production of a 'new' quality ceramic product. The two main prerequisites for the production of stoneware are high quality clays, and kilns capable of generating and maintaining temperatures of around 1200 degrees Celsius.

It appears likely that Siegburg near Cologne was the location where this innovation in earthenware was once again introduced and realised economic success (Hähnel 1987, 1992). Its development can be traced there, from proto-stoneware in the early thirteenth to near-stoneware, to stoneware with a visible quartz fabric around 1250, through to stoneware exhibiting a total fusion without visible inclusions around 1300 (Fig 7.7). Early competition with this powerful market force may have emerged from places like Mayen, Pingsdorf (with a shift to Brühl around 1280) and Brunssum (with a shift to Langerwehe also about 1280), with a somewhat older tradition in the Rhine-Meuse Region. From around 1250, the necessary technology seems to have spread rapidly in Western Germany to the Middle-Rhine to Hesse and to Lower Saxony

Fig 7.7a   *Rhenish stoneware, 1250-1450: jug with rouletteing and quartz grid (mid to late 13th century) and fully developed Siegburg stoneware with ash glaze (c. 1300-1450), jugs, beakers and Jacobakannen (photo: R. Schlotthauber, Stadtarchäologie Höxter).*

Fig 7.7b   *Stoneware from Central and Eastern Germany. Front left, painted stoneware from Zittau. Back left and centre, stoneware from Waldenburg, Igel jug on foot, Jacobakannen and regional forms. Centre and front right, highly decorated stoneware of Falke-Gruppe (Lusatia?). Back left (near-) stoneware from Bad Schmiedeberg (photo: U. Wohmann, Copyright Landesamt für Archäologie Sachsen).*

Proto- and near-stoneware from Lower Saxony and Northern Hesse, 1250-1450: jugs with collared rim **Fig 7.7c**
and applied decoration, 13th century, pitcher with red iron wash, beakers and jugs of late medieval types
with brownish surface (photo: R. Schlotthauber, Stadtarchäologie Höxter).

(Fredelsloh, Duingen) and in the fourteenth century to the Upper Rhine (Hagenau, Alsace). Generally stoneware was produced at this time only in a limited number of regions in Western, Central and Eastern Germany.

Its dense distribution is limited to these Regions and additionally to the Hanseatic market in north-west and northern Europe and around the Baltic (Stephan 1996). In Southern Germany, Austria and Switzerland as well as in the Czech lands, Slovakia and Hungary medieval stoneware is rare. Except for Siegburg, most potters produced and distributed mainly for the wider regional market and notably, only the Weserbergland seems to have conducted, to a greater degree, long distance trade to Northern Germany, Scandinavia and the Baltic from c. 1270. From about 1320, the entire Hanseatic market was overwhelmed by the Siegburg ceramic products, which caused a crisis in other production centres.

The thirteenth century is marked by a broad variation of both of technology and forms, including a large variety of jugs, pitchers and beakers, often with collared rims and, in some regions, with decoration formed by ribbons and rouletting. The surface tends to often be reddish but also brownish or iron wash or, at times, an ash-glaze as in Siegburg. Most of these ceramic products were, in a sense, mass-produced with a good technical and functional quality but rather uniform and lacking in more formal detail.

The wares from the Weserbergland, in particular, are more sophisticated in their formal design, in decoration and tend to have finer walls.

The fourteenth century highlights a further trend to uniform mass production in the Rhineland. As well as surpassing Siegburg in influence, Langerwehe took over a part of the western market including Great Britain. The production in the Eifel and the Westerwald along with Dreihausen and Dieburg (proto-stoneware) gained more importance while in the Maas Region, Bouffioulx and, to the northeast of Paris, Beauvais, emerge as new production centres for the French-speaking countries and the Benelux area after 1350. Interestingly, production in Beauvais closely resembles that of Siegburg. The formal development of Rhenish stoneware with simple straight rims and, the long slim or the bellied jugs with almost no decoration other than cordons is reflected in all minor centres and even copied in lesser earthenwares. Other centres like those in the Weserbergland were drifting into a crisis brought about by the high quality and well-organized long distance trade of Siegburg stoneware (by Cologne merchants) in the fourteenth century.

The technology of stoneware production also spread to Central and Eastern Germany. Bad Schmiedeberg in Sachsen-Anhalt near Wittenberg seems to have been established by potters from Lower Saxony in the second quarter of the fourteenth century, as evidenced by nearly identical technology and forms, while at the same time, Waldenburg achieves local forms and a regional distribution. Other minor production centres of regional importance were to be found in north-eastern Thuringia (Bürgel?). Lausitz is, as yet, not as well known, but in Zittau, from around 1300, stoneware seems to have been made for a regional market utilising forms imitating earthenware.

Lausitz stoneware in the first half of the fifteenth century generally seems to become more important and its outstanding contribution lies in the unique, highly decorated vessels with overall rouletting and richly modelled figures (*Falke-Gruppe;* Stephan & Gaimster 2003). At the same time, Loštice in Moravia develops as a new centre of a crude and uniform, but also very specific, stoneware production, helping to make stoneware more common in the south-east of central Europe. Also during this time, Waldenburg takes over large market areas, mainly east of the Elbe and Leine rivers up to Scandinavia and the Baltic States. Meanwhile in the Rhineland, Langerwehe increased its exports and new centres sprang up in Aachen and Raeren, taking over control of some of the western market of Siegburg (for the networks, see Ch 8, p 340).

Apart from the uniform common vessels of the fifteenth century, some new more elaborate forms do occur, such as face-jugs, puzzle-jugs and beakers with medallions. Around 1500, the face-jugs, which were perhaps first popular in Waldenburg about 1400, became typical for Raeren, while around 1510-20, the most ornate Bellarmines and other types of vessels with moulded reliefs were made in Köln, and from 1550, in nearby Frechen. In the second quarter of the sixteenth century, the new style of the Renaissance becomes popular in Köln and from 1560 this spread all over Central Europe leading to a fashion of highly decorated table-ware, creating a totally new style of decoration and forms. This in turn promoted the establishment of new production centres, particularly in the Westerwald, in Central and Eastern Germany while also bringing about a decline in importance of certain others such as Siegburg, which lost sway around 1600.

The Anabaptist potters of Moravia *by Jiří Pajer*

Moravian Anabaptists belonged to a special Protestant sect originating in Switzerland and Southern Germany. They came to Moravia in 1526 and by 1534 formed the largest branch of Anabaptists, called Hutterite brothers or Hutterites. At the end of the sixteenth century, about 22 000 members of this group lived in Moravia in 56 locations. Expelled from the country in 1622, they subsequently settled in what today is western Slovakia.

Hutterites became famous for their handicraft and especially for the advanced manufacture of ceramics (Fig 7.8). They produced common and fine decorated wares and

Pottery of the Moravian Anabaptists: (left) *The earliest manufacture of faience from 1593 (Museum of Applied Art Prague).* (right) *Faience tankard from 1609. Found at Vacenovice.*   **Fig 7.8**

(left) *Tazza with ribbed walls, about 1610. Found at Vacenovice.* (right) *Fragments of bowls with moralising inscriptions: Pouzdřany (top), Vacenovice (bottom).*

stove tiles, and in the sixteenth century began the manufacture of attractive faiences which were favoured by the highest social classes. Faience is pottery glazed with lead rendered white by the addition of tin oxide (see p 279 above), and then painted with patterns, usually in blue. It was known as delft in Holland, and majolica in the Mediterranean, but was in fact made in a number of different centres. The direct inspiration for the manufacture of Moravian faiences can be found in Southern Germany (not in Italy as has been generally thought until now).

Archaeological research has documented twelve centres manufacturing Anabaptist faiences in Moravia, while three other possible locations are noted in written sources. The largest was discovered in Vacenovice (District of Hodonín), which revealed the foundations of a unique large-capacity kiln and numerous examples of ceramic products. Nearly as large was the workshop at Strachotín (District of Břeclav), which appears to have served as a development centre for the production of faience wares. This workshop achieved the highest artistic levels, in its range of creative images and the excellence of its technical execution. The third-largest centre was situated at Tavíkovice (District of Znojmo), which seems to have been among the earliest workshops to experiment with faience technology.

In addition to ceramics, the Moravian Anabaptists produced metalwork of iron and copper, especially cutlery. They were also said to excel at watch-making, joinery, textiles, dress-making, footwear and other products. Their advanced technical and artistic levels, especially in faience (which was widely available elsewhere), no doubt owed something to the isolated environment and cultural focus of a competitive community determined to survive. This provoked a new style of specialist production closely associated with the economic beginnings of modern Europe (sources: Krisztinkovich 1962; Horvath & Krisztinkovich 2005; Pajer 1997, 2007, 2009).

Pottery manufacture in Al-Andalus
by Julio Navarro Palazón and Pedro Jiménez Castillo

For a map and historical framework for al-Andalus, please see Ch 1, p 19

Interest in Andalusian pottery owes much to such early pioneers of medieval archaeology in Spain as Gómez Moreno (1924), González Martí (1933, 1944), Torres Bálbas (1934), Casamar (1959), Jorge Aragoneses (1966) and Llubiá (1967). Typically, their studies focused on fine wares in museum collections, which were thus interpreted and dated stylistically without an archaeological context. The real advances in the understanding of ceramic production came with the development of modern Medieval Archaeology, between 1970s and 1990s (eg Duda 1970, Bazzana 1979/80, Rosselló Bordoy 1978, Zozaya 1980, Navarro Palazón 1986b, Torres 1987, Fernández Sotelo 1988, Varela Gomes 1988, Retuerce 1998). Naturally these first systematic studies were generally aimed at the classification of the material and the alignment of typologies with specific periods of time.

From the early 90s, however, there was a significant slowdown in enthusiasm. It had been discovered that, unlike the Roman period, the Middle Ages was characterized by a proliferation of local products, ruling out the possibility of defining a typology valid throughout al-Andalus. While settlement archaeology flourished, pottery studies were heavily criticized for being descriptive and unable to address historical questions. Add to this the tedium of creating massive inventories of sherds, and one can see why the subject was losing its vocational attraction. This was the state of affairs when Rosselló Bordoy (1991) showed that while production in the Caliphate era and the first half of the thirteenth century was becoming well defined, major questions remained about pottery production in other periods, particularly the eleventh and twelfth centuries and the Nasrid dynasty (thirteenth-fifteenth centuries).

Signs of a new agenda can be noted in publications from the 1990s. There is a greater emphasis on archaeometry, more attempts to identify centres of production and areas of distribution and marketing, more interpretation of the social and political implications of form and decoration, a greater attention to historical questions and a significant increase in synthesis.

Pottery of the Caliphate period (tenth century) initially attracted attention thanks to the excavations at Madînat Ilbîra and Madînat al-Zahrâ'. It featured a type of ornamentation, applied equally to open and closed forms, and termed *green and manganese* (verde y manganeso) or otherwise *Medina Azahara* ware (Cano Piedra 1996). It has a variety of decorative themes: vegetation, geometric, figurative and inscriptions (AME1, 240).

Unfortunately we can say little as yet about the eleventh century, as comparable settlements and ceramic assemblages have yet to be investigated, and this is also largely true of the Almoravid period (first half of twelfth century). However, recent excavations in Platería Street, Murcia, have turned up a pottery-rich midden heap of the last quarter of the eleventh century or, more likely, the first quarter of the twelfth (Jiménez & Navarro 1997). The assemblage included a group of glazed bowls with patterns realised in gold paint (lustre wares) that recall a group of those used in the facades of Italian churches dateable to the last quarter of the eleventh century. Murcia is accredited in Arab sources as one of the most prestigious centres for the production and export of gilded fine wares in the twelfth and the first third of the thirteenth centuries. The coarse wares in the same assemblage are thick-walled, made on a slow wheel and show no signs of interior glazing. The most common hollow-form table-ware is the little jar, and the predominant decoration is *cuerda seca*, already common in the eleventh century. The oil-lamps derive from those of the Caliphate period, but they are narrower (see below).

Coincident with the expansion in the Peninsula of the Almohad empire in the second half of the twelfth century, there are changes in some ceramic series, both formal and decorative, and the emergence of new types that profoundly transformed the Andalusian ceramic landscape. New forms (cooking pots, lamps, pot-stands or *reposaderos*) and decorative techniques (tin glazing, sgraffito, stamps, applied strips) reach the Peninsula already formed, so they are not the product of an evolutionary local process; some evidence points to the east – north Africa, Egypt and even Persia. By contrast

Fig 7.9a *Products of Andalucia (a) dishes of the 13th century from the excavations at the house of San. Nicolás (Murcia).*

Fig 7.9b *(b) Pitchers, jars and bowls of the 13th century from the excavations at the house of San. Nicolás (Murcia).*

(c) Ablution set of the 13th century, with water jar and stand (reposadero) and containers for unguents.   **Fig 7.9c**

Fig 7.9d *(d) Jar of the Nasrid period (13-15th century).*

with earlier periods, ceramic production of this time is now well-known, thanks to its abundant appearance in archaeological excavations (Figs 7.9 A-B). It occurs in town and country, often in contexts of destruction and desertion linked to the conquests of the Castilians, Aragonese and Portuguese in the second quarter of the thirteenth century that reduced al-Andalus to a territory from the river Tagus to the Kingdom of

Granada. Good examples of these assemblages are that discovered in 1937 in the city of Mallorca (Rosselló Pons, 1983) and that recovered from a house-site next to the church of San Nicolás in Murcia (Navarro 1991; and see p 314 below). In general, the material is characterized by the fine quality, variety and specialization of types. The cooking pots are quite different from those of previous phases (which flowed directly from the tradition of late antiquity); they are made on a fast wheel, with fine thin walls, and glaze covering the whole surface of the interior (Fernández Navarro 2008). The oil lamps, now with an open bowl and always glazed, are different to the early lamps, unglazed and with a closed body and a spout, as in Roman types. Also introduced at this time are ceramic incense burners and chafing dishes for portable warming or cooking, as well as big jars with their stands (*reposadero*), and wash-basins with water jugs (Fig 7.9C).

One of the most characteristic types of decoration of this period is *sgraffito*, which was effected by applying a coating of manganese oxide and engraving it while still fresh with a chisel or stylus. This showed up the colour of the clay fabric beneath, generally off-white or beige (Navarro 1986a). It seems indisputable that Murcia achieved prominence in this art, although there were undoubtedly other production centres: in the Balearics, Valencia and southern Spain (Rosselló Pons, 1983; Fernández Sotelo 2005; Hita Ruiz *et al.* 1997). Jars and jugs, particularly those intended to contain water, were often decorated with protective symbols. The repertoire included the *khamsa* or hand of Fatima, the seal of Solomon, the key to paradise and the tree of life flanked by confronted birds. All these signs were designed to protect the water contained in the vessels, and prevent the ingestion of a *jinn* (evil genie), reflecting an almost universal belief documented in ancient Egypt and contemporary cultures of the Fertile Crescent. Other themes, such as the lute player or banquet scenes were also of probable Fatimid inspiration and arrived in al-Andalus through lustre-ware and metalwork in the thirteenth century. This iconography reveals a powerful flow of ideas new to al-Andalus, originating in Eastern and Berber society. *Sgraffitto* appears in al-Andalus in the late twelfth century and its use in the eastern region decreases significantly after the Christian conquests of the mid-thirteenth century, and it thereupon declines to a repertoire of very basic geometric shapes (Navarro & Jimenez 1995, 211). The technique continued to be employed in north African workshops throughout the fourteenth century, but never achieved the heights of perfection reached by the workshops of Murcia.

From the mid-thirteenth century until 1492, al-Andalus was reduced to the Kingdom of Granada, which comprised roughly the present provinces of Almería, Málaga and Granada. Products of this, the Nasrid period, caught the attention of early scholars, especially ornamental tiles and the large vessels, decorated in blue and luster sometimes known as the "vases of Alhambra" (Gómez Moreno 1924, Frothingham 1951, Llubiá 1967, Martínez Caviró 1983;Flores Escobosa 1988; Flores Escobosa *et al* 1989; AAVV 2006a) (Fig 7.9D).

The influence of Islamic pottery in the Mediterranean
by Alberto García Porras

Archaeology has made one of its greatest contributions to the historical reconstruction of the Middle Ages in respect of the relationships – mostly economic – between different areas, especially between diverse civilizations like the western Christian, Islamic, Byzantine and Slavic. Ceramics, which survive well in the ground and were widely distributed provide a powerful index of context and cultural preference. Pottery was used in most domestic activities, and this also provides an indication of the local practices of daily life. Large amounts of ceramics were traded or moved as containers, thereby assisting the reconstruction of trade routes (Davey & Hodges 1983).

One of the most interesting exchanges of ceramics took place between feudal Europe and the Islamic world, defined in this case as North Africa and south-east Spain (al-Andalus). Pottery produced in the Islamic world shows similar forms, decorative patterns and the same technical procedures, the result of a wealth of shared knowledge of ceramics production. These features show up clearly if we compare, for example, the sherds recovered from Medieval layers in a variety of sites in Northern Africa, like Lixus (Habibi *et al.* 2001), Belyounech (Grenier de Cardenal 1980), Qsar el Seghir (Redman 1980), and many others, with those recovered in diverse sites in the Iberian Peninsula dating from the same period (see above, p 296). The sherds of the Almoravid and Almohad periods found in different sites or contexts show only minor differences in decoration, but the fabric varies with the place of manufacture, as may be determined by archaeometric analysis (Ch 1, p 45). The trade involved not only pottery with outstanding aesthetic qualities, like Tunisian glazed pottery decorated in blue and black on a white ground that was much appreciated in the Italian and French markets (Blake 1972; Berti 2002, Berti & Bianchi 2007), but also more ordinary wares that required the use of lower technical devices (green glazed pottery) and with plainer decorative features (stamped with or without the same glaze). Goods reached not only the farthest points in the Muslim world (Azuar Ruiz 1998), but could also be traded outside its boundaries, reaching all corners of the Mediterranean (García Porras 2000).

Three examples illustrate the process. The north Italian town of *Pisa* enjoyed a central trading role during the Central and Late Middle Ages. Research carried out on *bacini*, the ceramics used for decorating mainly religious buildings, clearly points out the economic relationships existing between Pisa and other centres, as well as the nature and intensity of this trade (Berti & Tongiorgi 1981). Merchants from Pisa sailed to Egypt, then to Tunis and objects manufactured in Morocco or in al-Andalus were usually included in the goods they collected. All the evidence analysed to date clearly indicates that these interchanges were relevant in the process of establishing the first local production of glazed pottery in Pisa (Fig 7.10). So far as we know, Pisa was the place where tin-glazed pottery was first produced in Italy, the *Maiolica Arcaica*. The technical procedures were the same as those employed in al-Andalus for making glazed pottery decorated in green and brown, products that had themselves been widely imported to Pisa. Thus, the relationship between Pisa and this part of the Islamic world (al-Anda-

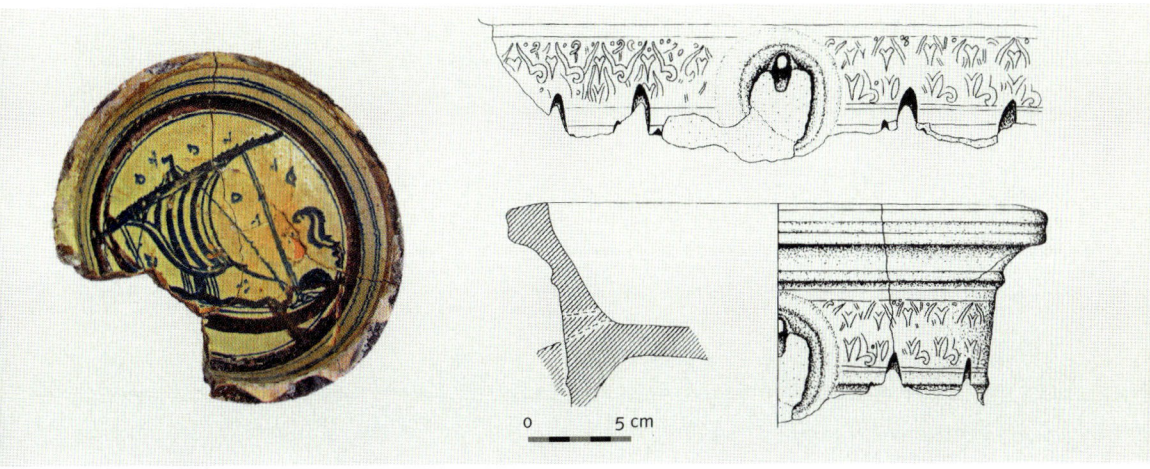

Islamic pottery in Italy. (left) Tunisian glazed pottery decorated in blue and black recovered in Sant'Antimo   **Fig 7.10**
sopra i Canali, Piombino, Italy (Berti & Bianchi 2007). (right) Islamic ceramic with stamped decorations
recovered in Piazza Santa Caterina, Finalborgo, Savona, Italy (Frondoni et al. 2001).

Distribution of ceramics imported from the Iberian Peninsula into Italy (11th–15th centuries).   **Fig 7.11**

lus), not only led to the establishment of new trade routes, but also greatly influenced the first production of tin-glazed pottery in Italy (Berti *et al.*1997) (Fig 7.11).

The case of *Marseille* is quite similar. During the first half of the thirteenth century new forms of pot and techniques of pottery-making were introduced into this French town. These included the use of tin-glazing on the outer surface of the objects (Marchesi et al. 1997). During the excavation undertaken in the area of the town known as Sante-Barbe, where potters had their workshops during the Middle Ages, kilns clearly showing Islamic features were found. This new evidence clearly pointed to the origin of the new technique employed in Marseille and confirmed the way this technique was transmitted.

The third and last case to be considered is the production in the area of *Valencia and Granada*. It has been proved that new ceramics production started in the Iberian Peninsula in the beginning of the fourteenth century (above, p 297). Cobalt oxide was introduced and used for decorating pottery over an opaque white glaze. The first production of the new blue, or blue and lustre-ware decorated pottery, was made in the area of Granada, in the newly formed Nasrid Kingdom. However, the evidence collected so far seems to indicate that the use of this new technique for decorating pottery was the result of the transmission of technical methods developed in Tunisia (Fig 7.12) and successfully traded within the Mediterranean area during the previous decades (García Porras 2003). To some extent, Nasrid potters were trying to imitate North African products, aiming at carrying on this tradition, as well as at starting to control the market. By the fourteenth century, the ceramic technology had moved from Granada to Valencia (Fig 7.13). Written sources appear to show quite clearly that entire families of potters moved from the south to establish themselves in the Valencian area (López Elum 1984, 65-66). Once there, they succeeded in producing objects that were widely

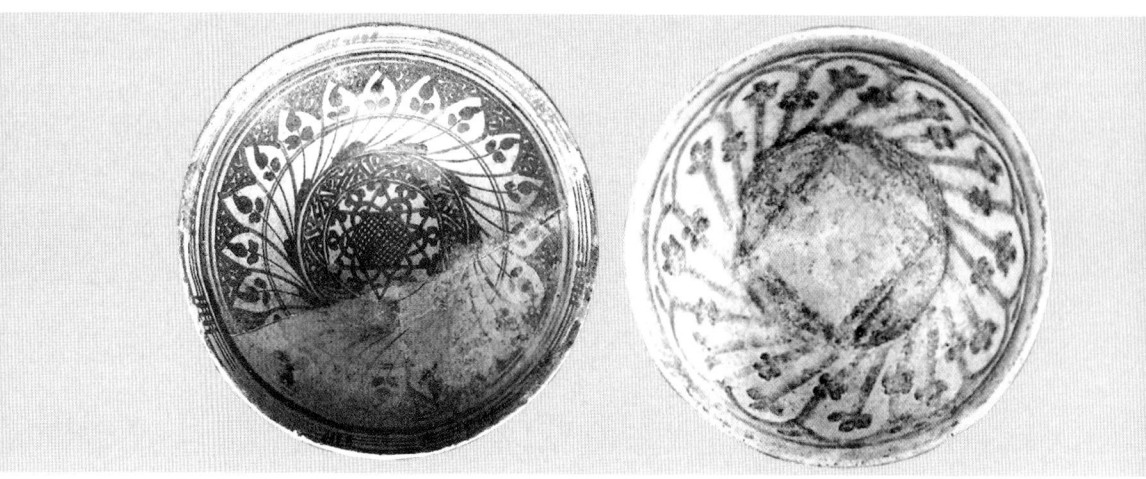

Fig 7.12   *Origins of Nasrid ceramics. (left) a dish recovered during the excavations carried out in Tunis (Kasbah) (Daoulatli 1995); (right) Bowl from the dungeon of the "Puerta del Vino" in the Alhambra, Granada (Flores Escobosa 1988).*

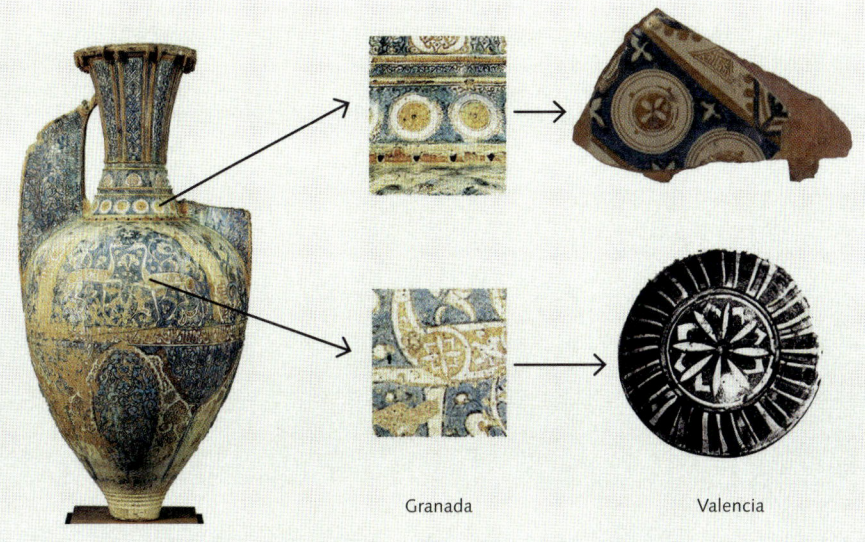

Some decorative patterns of the emblematic Nasrid Jar known as "Jarrón de las Gacelas" kept in the **Fig 7.13** *"Museo de la Alhambra" (Granada) and some examples of Valencian dishes dating to the 14th century.*

appreciated throughout the Mediterranean and as far as the North Sea (Gutiérrez 2000; Coll Conesa 2007), where they also circulated.

Thus, certain ceramic products, such as those from Tunisia, circulated within a trading system, reaching faraway harbours. Furthermore, the technique that these potters used deeply influenced later European production both in the Islamic (García Porras 2006) and in the Christian areas (Berti et al. 1997). These contacts were not only important from an economic standpoint, but had a strong cultural influence. In fact, they resulted in the establishment of new pottery workshops of Islamic type in Christian Europe, especially in the Mediterranean area, from the beginning of the thirteenth century onwards.

The versatile bote: Spanish decorated jars and their uses
by Alejandra Gutiérrez

Decorated wares from Spain, especially lustrewares produced near Málaga and Valencia, have been found in fourteenth and fifteenth century contexts on excavations across the Mediterranean and northern Europe, from Ireland, Sweden and Poland to Montenegro, Greece and as far as Acre in modern Israel. Important collections can be seen at the *Museo Nacional de Cerámicas y Artes Suntuarias González Martí* in Valencia, the Victoria and Albert Museum and the British Museum in London.

There are contemporary written references to *operis Maleche* or *Malyk* pots from the end of the thirteenth century, mostly in port books and custom accounts in their country of destination. Trade sometimes benefitted from tax exemptions, as it did in

Fig 7.14   *A lustreware bote (foreground) depicted in Crying over the dead Christ by Pedro Berruguete (c. 1450-*
1504) (Reproduced by courtesy of Palencia Cathedral (photo: Javier Marín).

306   Medieval Archaeology

Flanders and Venice in the middle of the fifteenth century, and no doubt a certain preference for this sort of pottery expressed by the European nobility also helped to boost demand. Eleanor of Castile was already importing bowls and jars into England by 1290 (Gutiérrez 2010), and lists of acquisitions could be lengthy. In 1454 Queen Mary of Aragon ordered for purchase 'dishes for serving food and for eating off, small bowls to drink broth and to make thick soup, water jugs, large mortars, little bowls and small pieces, jugs with and without spouts and containers for drinking water' (Osma 1912).

Apart from plates and bowls, a frequent find on European excavations is the *bote*, *albarello* or concave-sided jar. These vases could have been used as containers for exotic foodstuffs, such as spices, honey, syrup or sugar-preserved fruits (Gutiérrez 2000, 100–112). Such ingredients were much in demand throughout the high status kitchens of Europe and the use of ceramic containers to transport sweets and preserves is well attested in custom accounts (Childs 1995, 29). The containers would have been covered with a piece of cloth or parchment and then tied with string around the rim. As imported foreign goods, preserves of this type were exclusive and available only to those who could afford them.

Other uses for *botes* are also worth noting. Some undoubtedly travelled empty, and documents from Valencia record them as such being readied for export in the fourteenth and fifteenth century. *Botes* are also listed in contemporary Spanish inventories in apothecaries' workshops, where they were used for storing potions and medicines such as myrrh, aniseed and basil seeds (Olivar 1950, doc V). The same vessels also appear on fifteenth century paintings depicting birth scenes, usually positioned by the bed of the convalescent mother, for instance in Ghirlandaio's *Birth of John the Baptist*. In paintings of Christ's entombment a jar of this type holding embalming oils is also often represented in the scene, in some cases sealed with parchment or waxed paper (Fig 7.14). On the other hand, the *Adoration of the Shepherds* for the *Portinari Altarpiece* by Hugo Van der Goes (Uffizi Gallery, Florence) shows a lustreware *bote* holding lillies and irises. The use of the *bote* as a flower-vase here serves to illustrate that pots, especially containers, had multiple uses and were re-used to suit particular needs or situations. In this case the *bote* has a deliberate association with the qualities of the Virgin, the unbroken clay pot representing her virginity and the flowers her purity. This is a reminder that some objects found in medieval households had symbolic qualities for their users, sometimes religious, sometimes as a mark of the exotic.

The production of glass in al-Andalus
by Pedro Jiménez Castillo and Julio Navarro Palazón

Arabic texts that offer information about glass production in al-Andalus are very scanty and of unequal value. According to the historian al-Makkari, the poet Ziryab, who was exiled by the Abbasid dynasty and settled in Córdoba at the court of 'Abd al-Rahmân II, introduced glass tableware in place of goblets of precious metal at official dinners. Al-Makkari also reports that the physician Abbas ibn Firnas from Córdoba, a vassal of Muhammad ibn 'Abd al-Rahmân (852-886), discovered the secrets of glass and founded numerous workshops in al-Andalus. This information belongs to a seventeenth century compilation and so should be treated with caution as source for earlier periods, but it is not improbable that glass-working had revived in al-Andalus by the mid-ninth century (AME 1, 213).

A treatise about the management of the *souk* (market) of a Saqati, written in the first quarter of the thirteenth century, refers to the production of glass and (among other things) advises that freshly blown glass should be allowed to cool for a day and a night. Indeed, this is an essential tenet for glass-makers: a glass vessel needs to cool slowly once blown, since a sudden change in temperature will cause it to fracture. This requirement was served by intermediate chambers of gradually diminishing heat. Another contemporary reference to the production of glass comes from Ibn Sa'id al-Maghribi, a native of Granada writing in the mid-thirteenth century. In his eulogy of al-Andalus, he highlights the craftsmanship of glass, citing the most important production centres: Murcia, Málaga and Almería. Having praised the embroidered handkerchiefs, rugs and metal-work made in the first mentioned city, he continues: *"Murcia was also renowned for the manufacture of glass and ceramics, [making] great vessels of the most elegant and exquisite manufacture, likewise glazed ceramic and others bathed in gold"* (Gayangos 1840, Vol I, 51, 93, II, 311).

Archaeology

Whether in Arab or Christian sources, written or pictorial references to the production of glass in al-Andalus are perfunctory and rare. Therefore, archaeology is an essential means of study, aimed both at the objects themselves and the workshops where they were made. The study of production is still in an early stage, and we know of only two workshops so far, both excavated in Murcia (Jiménez 1996), plus a furnace found in the town of Pechina (Almería). The study of these objects has yet to produce a narrative account of the development of the forms and functions encountered. Vessels in museum collections were previously noted by Gómez Moreno (1951, 341-343) and Torres Balbás (1949a, 219-221) and later briefly by Alice Frothingham (1941, 1963). The development of Spanish medieval archaeology since the 1970s has not achieved a breakthrough in the study of glass comparable to that in ceramics (p 296, above), but this may change following publication of the proceedings of a recent conference (AAVV. 2000c), the catalogue of a later exhibition (AAVV. 2006b), organized by the Casa de Velázquez and the National Glass Centre Foundation (Fundación Nacional del Vidrio) and new analysis of glass composition (Carmona *et al* 2008 and 2009).

Workshops

First-hand archaeological information on glass manufacture has recently come to light in Murcia, endorsing the remarks of al-Maghribi (above). Two glass workshops were found in the vicinity of the ancient congregational mosque, the present cathedral, and a few metres from the main street and market of the early city, now Frenería Street. The first, discovered in 1998 on a plot in Puxmarina Street (Jiménez et al. 2000; Jiménez et

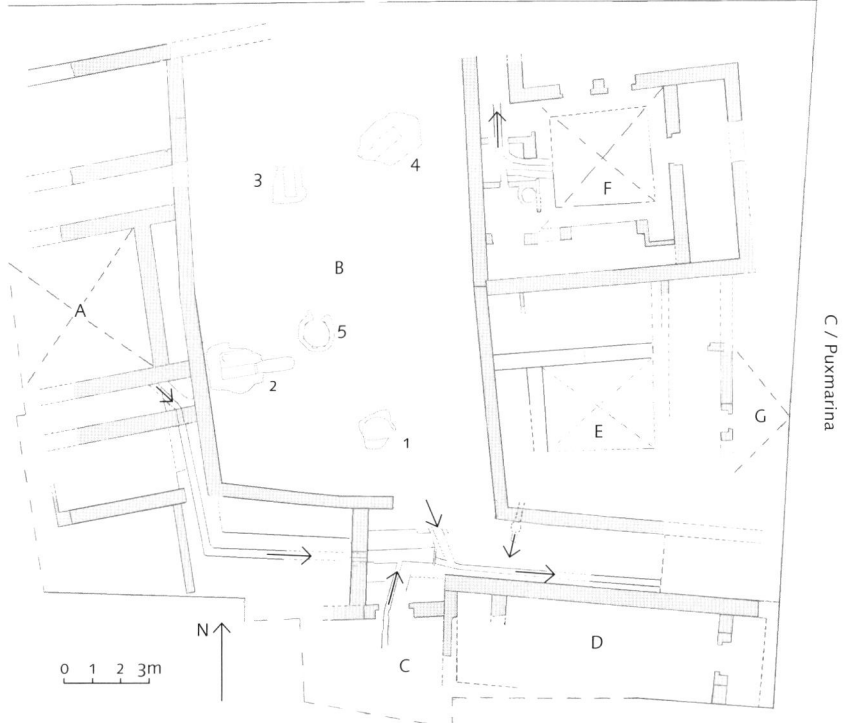

C / Puxmarina

0 1 2 3m

N

Plan of an Andalusian glass-makers' workshop excavated at Puxmarina Street, Murcia (12th century), **Fig 7.15**
showing the direction of flow of drains.

al. 2005), was dated to the twelfth century by stratigraphy and archaeometric dating (Gómez-Paccard *et al.* 2006) (Fig 7.15). Among its products were a moulded vessel, decorated with enamel and applied trail, flat glass for windows and a mirror on a lead base. Five relatively well-preserved glass furnaces were found, and remnants belonging to earlier phases indicated that the workshop had been in operation over a long period. Furnaces 1 and 4 presented similar characteristics: an elliptical plan, a ledge in the shape of a horse-shoe on which the crucibles were placed, and a central cavity in which the raw material was heated, before its transfer to the crucibles. The stoke-hole and firing chamber lay outside, though feeding heat directly to the central cavity. Furnaces 2 and 3 were similar, but smaller and simpler, having two side ledges on which crucibles were placed (Fig 7.16). Furnace 5, in the centre of the workshop, was completely different, and resembled the type of kiln used to fire ceramics. The chamber was circular in plan, divided into two parts separated by an openwork grill. It is not clear if this was designed as a chamber for cooling glass vessels or a kiln for making the ceramic crucibles.

The second workshop was located about 50 m from the first, at the junction of Polo de Medina Street with Belluga Square. The excellent state of preservation allowed for a more secure interpretation. The furnace was oblong in plan, oriented east-west, measured 4.20 m long and 3.20 m wide and had survived to a height of 1.25 m from its base

Fig 7.16 *Glass furnace no. 2 on the Puxmarina St. site.*

(AME 1, 213). The U-shaped ledge retained the imprints of crucibles and the remains of glass frit, some of it coloured. In the centre of the U was a rectangular tray where the raw material was initially melted.

The presence of ovens of different forms implies that a number of different operations were required, and some of the output may have served other craftsmen (for example potters). Given the fuel used (wood), it is unlikely that the ovens could easily reach a sufficiently high temperature to fuse glass directly. Documents of the sixteenth and seventeenth century imply a two-stage process, whereby the raw material (sand, flux and other minor components) were heated together for about six hours at a temperature of around 750 ° C, and so transformed into a glassy mass, with all the impurities ejected to the surface. The pure solidified glass was then broken up with a hammer and placed in a crucible together with any glass for recycling, and melted again ready for moulding or blowing.

Products

Although the finding of the workshops at Murcia has been a considerable advance in the knowledge of glass-making in al-Andalus, we still have little information about the products. This is partly due to the inherent fragility of the glass vessels as well as their relative scarcity compared to other materials such as ceramics. However an attempt will be made in what follows to summarise the types of glass in circulation, focusing on form and decoration.

To our knowledge, the only Andalusian assemblages that have been subject of a percentage study of the decorative technologies are those of Madînat al-Zahrâ' (tenth century) and Siyâsa (Cieza, Murcia; mostly of the twelfth-thirteenth century). These differ not only in location and period of occupation but in the type of site, the first being a city of the ruling establishment and the second a *hisn*, a large settlement that does not reach the category of *medina,* market town (Table 7.2).

TABLE 7.2 GLASS-MAKING TECHNIQUES at the palace site of Madînat al-Zahrâ' (10th century) and the town site of Siyâsa (12-13th century)		
TECHNIQUE	MADÎNAT AL-ZAHRA'	SIYÂSA
Mould-blowing	59.5%	77.9%
Carved	19.5%	0%
Stamped	9.5%	0%
Applied	3.5%	17.1%
Enamel	3.5%	0.2%
Marvering	1%	0.2%
Gold painting	4%	2.2%
Pinched	0%	0%

Mould-blowing is an ancient technology in which glass is blown into a mould with a pipe, and which may have preceded free-blowing (Fig 7.17, left). The mould came in two parts, usually made of wood or clay, and its interior surface could be incised with motifs that would appear in relief on the body of the glass vessel. At Madînat al-Zahrâ', this is the most widely used technique, amounting to 60% of all decorated glass recovered during the archaeological work. Among prominent decorative schemes is the "honeycomb" grid, consisting of a network of hexagonal or elliptical depressions that cover almost the entire surface of the glass vessel. This motif, with origins in antiquity, was widely diffused by Muslim glaziers. At Siyâsa it was even more common, occurring on 77.9% of the decorated fragments.

In *carved* cut-glass or crystal vessels, parts of a thick surface are cut away or left raised up. The technique was widespread from late antiquity to the early centuries of Islam, so it is not surprising to find it in early contexts in al-Andalus such as Pechina and Madînat al-Zahrâ'. However it is completely absent at Siyâsa and does not appear in other Murcian contexts of the twelfth century, so we are inclined to think that it was already rare in al-Andalus by the eleventh century.

Stamped decoration is achieved by pressing a die on the surface of the glass while it is still hot. It was common to use a pair of calipers, one of whose faces was engraved with the chosen ornament. This type of decoration was prevalent in the eastern Islamic world and employed for stamping an omphalos (a boss), rosettes, ovals or inscriptions. The earliest Andalusian example of this technique is from Pechina and should be dated to the ninth or tenth centuries. It was a piece of fairly thick wall of dark green glass, ornamented with a band of "eyes." In Madînat al-Zahrâ' this technique of printing or stamping is present in 20% of the decorated pieces found and their motifs are simple: circles, oval shapes, ellipses and diamonds strung horizontally. The eye-band motif was also found on a complete bottle discovered in the excavations conducted in Platería Street (Murcia), and belongs to an assemblage of the Almoravid period (some bottles from this site are shown in Fig 7.17).

Applied decoration is based on the flexibility of glass at high temperatures, which makes it possible to stretch it into threads that attach easily to the hot surface of the glass. The thread may be of the same colour or different from the body. The technique is rare at Madînat al-Zahrâ' (4%) but rises to 17.1% at Siyâsa.

Pinching is a very simple technique that consists in pinching the glass surfaces while still hot. It occurs on a bottle from Platería Street (Murcia) with a foot-ring, globular body, broad cylindrical neck and a multi-lobed rim with pouring spout. This bottle was found in a midden with an assemblage dating approximately to the end of the eleventh century or first half of the twelfth century.

Marvering involves applying glass appliqué cords (trails) on the vessel and then rolling it on a flat (marble) surface (a *marver*), so that the trails merge with the body. Usually these cords were smoothed with the help of sharp tools, which were then used to create patterns on the surface in the form of a nib or pin. This technique was used by the Egyptians in the first millennium BC and in the eastern Islamic world it occurs from the eleventh to thirteenth centuries, especially in Egypt and Syria. It was noted

Products: (left) Vase of mould-blown glass from the abandoned town of Siyâsa (Cieza, Murcia) (13th **Fig 7.17**
century). (right) Group of bottles found at Platería Street, Murcia (Almoravid period).

at Madînat al-Zahrâ' but in only 1% of the decorated specimens, while in Siyâsa the percentage drops to 0.2%.

Enamelling is one of the most characteristic techniques of medieval Islamic glass, although it too traces its origins to late antiquity. Probably such ornamentation was already practised under the Abbasids, judging by specimens discovered in Raqqah and dating to the ninth century; however, it is in the twelfth century that the production centres in Iraq and northern Syria began to establish their reputation. During the second half of the thirteenth and the fourteenth centuries, enamelled glass from the Middle East reached its peak, spreading from Western Europe to China. We have a fragment from Siyâsa having in its outer surface remains of two horizontal red stripes. A fragment from the Murcia area must have belonged to an open vessel, cylindrical or conical. Judging by the archaeological context, this seems to date to the twelfth century. This is surprisingly early, but enamelling is also seen on a piece of glass belonging to a vase retrieved from Furnace 2 in Puxmarina, firmly dated by archaeological context and archaeomagnetic analysis to the twelfth century.

The technique of *gold painting* on glass is very similar to that of lustre pottery. Most researchers believe that motifs in gold paint were first applied in Abbasid Mesopotamia to decorated pottery, although Lamm (1929) and others argue that it originated among the Copts in the fourth century. In any case, there is no doubt that it reached its maximum development, both on pottery and on glass, in Islamic territory from the Abbasid period. At the site of Madînat al-Zahrâ' fragments of blue glass decorated with golden brown paint represent only 4% of the decorated pieces, and it is not possible to determine if they were manufactured locally or whether they were Eastern imports. From Siyâsa there were about fifteen pieces of gold painted glass (2.2%), of which three are rims belonging to open forms. The painted motifs have a golden tone ranging from olive to purple forming plant motifs, with details marked by fine incised lines. The archaeological context can be dated to the twelfth and thirteenth centuries. In the current state of research we cannot be sure that the Siyâsa glass was made in Murcia, but it is not improbable since, as it has been demonstrated in relation with the lustre painted pottery, there were artisans in Murcia who knew the technique.

Stained glass

Finally, we highlight the finding in Murcia of coloured flat glass, which proves the existence of an element that is still today part of traditional Islamic architecture: coloured-glass window-grilles, in Arabic *samsiyya* or *qamariyya* (Jiménez 1991, 71-80). The discovery was made in an outhouse, perhaps a cess-pit, belonging to a large house (San Nicolás). Found with the window glass was an outstanding collection of ceramics dating back to the mid-thirteenth century (Fig 7.9). Since the house can be dated to the twelfth century and windows were part of the architectural decoration, it is probably more appropriate to date the glass as contemporary with the house, rather than the pottery. Thanks to the fragments of window glass in the workshop of Puxmarina, in a context with dates from the twelfth century, we can say that glass windows were made in Murcia at this early date.

The total number of flat glass fragments exhumed in the house at San Nicolás is forty-eight. The colours include blue, green, yellow and violet. Close examination of the pieces showed circular grooves implying manufacture by the method called 'crowning' (Charleston 1991, 242). In this process, glass was blown into a crown or hollow globe which was transferred from the blowpipe to a pontil and then flattened by reheating and spinning out the bowl-shaped piece of glass (*bullion*) into a flat disk by centrifugal force, up to 1.5 to 1.8 m in diameter. The glass was then cut to the size required. The coloured glass disc thus obtained was placed on a lattice of plaster, but unfortunately none of these has survived. Despite the degradation suffered by the glass at San Nicolás, it was also possible to detect traces of painted decoration. The decorative motifs seem to be of vegetal shapes. The presence of paint on flat glass has been documented at Qasr al-Hayr al-Sharqi (Grabar *et al.* 1978) and Samarra (Lamm 1928). In both cases, a blackish paint was employed, usually called *grisaille,* and used to draw simple geometric and vegetal patterns.

The use of stained glass was prominent in the Umayyad period, as witness buildings at both Qasr al-Hayr, Khirbet al-Mafdjar, Qusayr Amra and Mafraq. The technique travelled into North Africa in the tenth and eleventh centuries, as traces of these coloured-glass window-grilles have been found at Sabra-Mansouriya and the Qal'a of the Banu Hammad. We know very little about the use of stained glass in al-Andalus, although Torres Balbás (1949b) and Elie Lambert (1957) dedicated some of their works to its study. The earliest documentary reference is to the palace of al-Ma'mun of Toledo in the mid-eleventh century.

The window glass at San Nicolás, dated to the twelfth century, is the earliest so far found in al-Andalus. Even the windows of Santa María la Blanca (Toledo), though of uncertain date, are surely later. From the fourteenth century, artisans began to employ lead frames (*calmes*) such as those seen in the windows of the Alhambra and the *madrasas* of Fez (Lambert 1957, 107). The San Nicolás window-glass has a major significance for western Islamic architecture, not only because it is the oldest archaeological evidence for its use in al-Andalus, but also because it was found in a domestic, secular setting, not in a palace or religious centre.

PART 3: TEXTILE PRODUCTION IN WESTERN EUROPE
by Eva Andersson Strand

Sources

The production of woollen cloth in the medieval period was a major employer of labour, of capital, of technical expertise and of business skills (Clarke 1986, 129-130; Munro 2003 a, 181). Thanks to different types of evidence such as legislation and lists of textile types and their prices, it is possible to gain important insights into the textile trade and its economic influence and significance (e.g. Carus-Wilson 1962-63; Munro 2003b; Vestergård Pedersen & Nosch 2009). However, archaeological evidence is also useful, particularly for illustrating the innumerable varieties produced. Preservation on archaeological sites is assisted by anaerobic conditions where bacterial activity is inhibited, for example in wells or midden deposits in towns (Ch 1, p 21). Types of textile are determined by analysis of the fibres and the weave, and by comparing the results with information in the written sources (e.g. Crowfoot *et al.* 1992; Østergård 2004; Kirjavainen 2009; Maik 2009; Rammo 2009; Tidow & Jordan Fahrbach 2007). Textiles were not only used for clothing but for furnishing, tapestry, table-cloths, bedding, sacks, sails and tents, not to mention the use of special textiles in the church for vestments, furnishings and different liturgical rituals (e.g. Pritchard 2003). It has been suggested that a well-educated medieval merchant could differentiate between thirty and sixty types of cloth (Jahnke 2010, 76).

Production

The production of textiles was organised at a number of levels, from the household to large workshops run by guilds, the output ranging from domestic articles to speciality products. Within the household, it is plausible that all household members, even if in slightly different ways, were involved in the different steps from procurement to finished garment. Within the body of professional textile producers were weavers, dyers, fullers and tailors (see Fig 7.2).

At all levels of organisation, the basic *chaîne opératoire* of textile production was more or less the same. The raw material must be selected, cleaned, combed and spun into fibres, the fibres woven into fabric and the fabric dyed, washed, degreased (with fullers' earth), stretched and sheared. The apparatus used was closely connected with general trends in the economy and society (Dyer 1997b, 298); for example the great spinning wheel and the horizontal loom were adopted during the Later Middle Ages, reflecting the rise of mass production (e.g. Øye 1988; Walton Rogers 1997).

Our primary focus here will be upon the procurement of the most common textile fibres, wool and flax, and the production of cloth in medieval Western Europe from an archaeological perspective. This is only a general overview and it is important to note that there were numerous regional and cultural variations and specialist techniques (for more detailed treatment and techniques such as band weaving, embroidery and lacing, see e.g. Geijer 1979; Seiler-Baldinger 1994; Walton Rogers 1997; Andersson E 2003; Munro 2003a).

Wool

The most common fibre employed in Medieval Western Europe was wool (Fig 7.18). From the twelfth century onwards wool was exported on a large scale from England. In the late thirteenth and fourteenth century most Flemish cloth was made from English wool. English wool was also traded by merchants from Italy, Germany and Northern France (Carus-Wilson 1962-1963, 185-186; Munro 2009, 1, 9; Jahnke 2009, 76). Both secular and monastic estate accounts record vast flocks of up to 16,000 sheep (Carus-Wilson 1962-63, 185).

Archaeological finds of sheep bones in England suggest significant changes in animal husbandry from the twelfth to the fifteenth century. In the twelfth and thirteenth centuries, urban excavations produce many bones from juvenile animals, which suggest that the older animals were being used for wool production in the countryside (Grant 1988, 153). In the fourteenth and fifteenth centuries, older sheep were being brought into the towns, indicating that the sheep were yielding more clips than previously (Grant 1988, 154). The number of sheep also changed drastically over time, specifically when epidemics came into England in the late thirteenth and early fourteenth century when some flocks were reduced by as much as two thirds (Grant 1988, 154). The common ailments were sheep scab, sheep pox and gum disease. Pulmonary anthrax, known as the wool sorter's disease, is deadly for both animals and humans. Anthrax was associ-

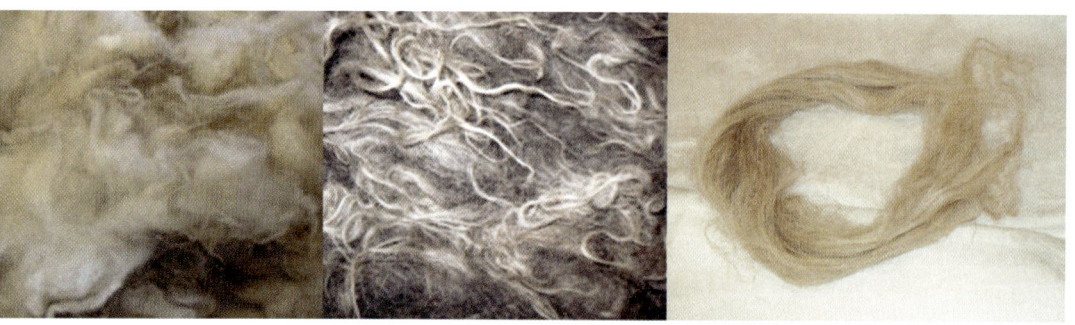

Fig 7.18 *(left and centre) Wool from two Shetland sheep; note the differences in colour and texture. (right) Flax ready for spinning.*

ated with moist soil such as rivers, valleys, swampy districts and lake regions (Laforce 1978, 957). The occupations at risk from anthrax include wool sorters, combers, carders and spinners, as well as cloth and carpet weavers (Witkowski & Parish 2002, 340).

The sorting of wool was of great importance. Different qualities are reflected in series of wool price schedules and the analyses of textiles demonstrate that different types of wool fibres were used for different types of textiles (e.g. Ryder 1981; Crowfoot *et al.* 1992, 15; Munro 2010). How much wool one sheep can yield depends on the breed of sheep, but also on whether it is a lamb, ewe, ram or wether. Differences also related to the pasture available to the sheep, to the type of climate and husbandry. Finally, there is great difference in the fineness of wool fibres depending on which part of the sheep the wool comes from. Every sheep has longer coarser hair and shorter, finer underwool. Depending on the type of yarn required these two fibre types could either be spun individually or mixed (e.g. Crowfoot *et al.* 1992, 15; Andersson 2003).

The long hair was separated from the shorter under wool by *combing*. A wool comb had a row of iron teeth and sat at an angle in a handle of wood. The use of wool combs has a long tradition, and their iron teeth are found in many places and regions such as England and the Nordic countries (e.g. Wild 1970, 25; Hoffmann 1974; Crowfoot *et al.* 1992, 16). The combing was carried out with either a pair of wool combs or a wool comb attached to an upright post. In order to separate the fibres and make the combing process easier, the combs were heated and dipped into a pot of grease (Crowfoot *et al.* 1992, 15).

Flax and hemp

Flax was the principal plant fibre used in textile production in Medieval Europe (Crowfoot *et al.* 1992, 18). During the Late Medieval period the regions south of the English Channel such as northern France became important regions for flax cultivation and linen production, whilst in England, flax and hemp were only cultivated on a small scale (Dyer 1988, 31). By the end of the period linen *damask* had become an important item of trade (Geijer 1994, 18).

The production of flax for textiles is a laborious and time-consuming task requiring special skills and tools. When flax is ripe it is pulled up by the roots and the seeds are removed by combing with a *ripple* (toothed implement). The flax then has to be *retted* placed in water or on the ground. When retted in water the stems are attacked by bacteria, a process which is extremely smelly. Retting pits have therefore in general been placed away from living areas. The next step is *breaking*, beating with a wooden club to break up the stems and separate them from the fibres. The flax is then *scutched* with a broad wooden knife, a process that scrapes away the last remains of stem and bark. Finally, the fibres are *hackled* or combed (e.g. Walton Rogers 1997; Andersson 2003). Processing the flax fibres (and also other plant fibres such as hemp) manually is dangerous work. *Byssnosis* "brown lung disease" is an occupational hazard, workers who break and scutch the stems being the most exposed (Noweir *et al.* 1975). The dangers were probably recognised and encouraged the working of flax outdoors. After this processing, the fibres are ready to be spun (Fig 7.18).

Spinning

Traditionally, spinning fibres into yarn was achieved by twisting a *spindle* carrying a *whorl* which acted like a flywheel to give the spindle its axial momentum. The fibres were drawn from a loose bunch placed on a *distaff* (Crowfoot et al. 1992, 16). Tests with different spindle whorls indicate that weight is significant, but fibre quality and the skill of spinners will also affect the outcome (e.g. Andersson E 1999, 23-25; 2003, 25-26; Andersson E *et al.* 2010). The spindle whorl is normally the only surviving part, and these have been found in numerous archaeological layers, including in rural settlements of later periods (e.g. Øye 1988, 51; Walton Rogers 1997, 1815).

During the early fourteenth century the great spinning wheel appears in England (Geijer 1979, 27; Walton Rogers 1997, 1745). It was at first primarily used to produce the weft yarn, while the warp yarn still was produced on the spindle (Munro 2009, 5). The spinning wheel theoretically produces more yarn in the same amount of time, but in other ways it is less convenient. Medieval illustrations show women standing whilst using a spindle (Crowfoot *et al.* 1992, 16), so this is a task that can be carried on while addressing other household chores.

Weaving

At the beginning of the thirteenth century, different types of loom were in use, but examples rarely survive archaeologically, being made mainly of wood. The looms presumed in use during this period are the vertical warp weighted loom, the vertical two beam loom and the horizontal loom. The horizontal treadle loom had probably been introduced into Western Europe by the beginning of the eleventh century at the latest (Hoffmann 1974; 258-60; Clarke 1986, 132) but upright (vertical) loom types were also in use. On the upright warp-weighted loom the warp threads were kept taut by weights (Fig 7.19), while on the vertical two-beam loom and the horizontal loom, the warp threads were kept in tension by being wound round a wooden beam (Fig 7.20). The vertical two-beam loom could also have been in use for tapestry weaving (Walton Rogers 1997, 1759). Vertical looms were common in Western Europe and the Nordic countries in the previous period (Hoffmann 1974, Crowfoot *et al.* 1996, 21; Walton Rogers 1997, 1760), and Helen Clarke suggests that they remained in use well into the later Middle Ages (Clarke 1986, 133). The upright loom could stand against a wall either in the dwelling-house or in a subsidiary outbuilding, and was the principal method of domestic production (for a workplace using a treadle loom, see Fig 9.9).

In the process of weaving, the weft is inserted between the warp threads; to facilitate this, the warp threads are divided into different layers so that sheds can be created. The principle is the same for a vertical and a horizontal loom. To weave a tabby on a warp-weighted loom, alternate warp threads are placed in front of or behind a heddle rod or shed bar on the loom. In a tabby weave, two rows of loom weights are generally used. One row of loom weights lies in front of the shed bar, while the other lies behind it. Depending on the size of the loom weight, a certain number of threads are attached to each individual weight (e.g. Andersson 2003, 34). The heddle bars can then be used to lift all of the warp threads in a given layer at the same time, thus creating different sheds, through which the weft threads were passed..

The most important advantage of the horizontal loom is that one can weave much longer fabrics at a much faster rate compared to the other two loom types (Walton Rogers 1997, 1827). With the more elaborate horizontal loom such as the draw-loom it is also possible to weave extremely complex patterns (Crowfoot et al. 1992, 23). It is plausible that the horizontal loom types were first used in the textile industry and only

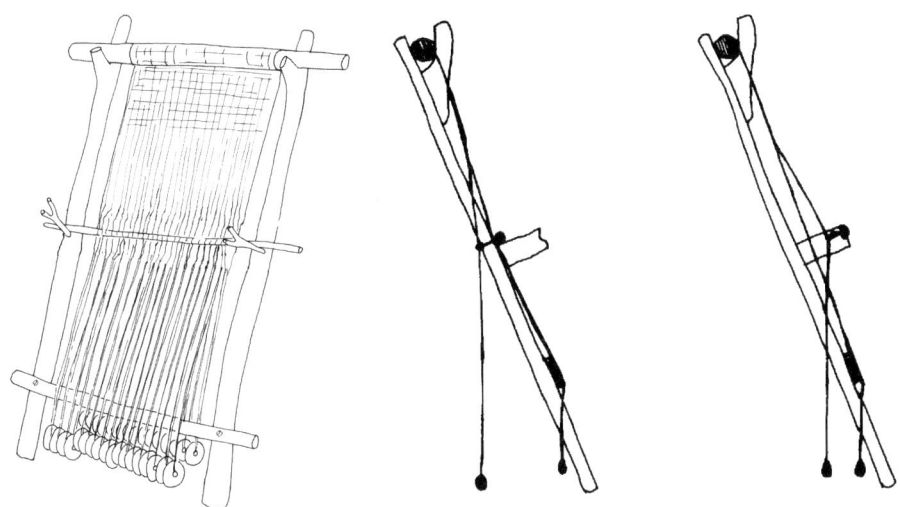

A warp-weighted upright loom, with two rows of loom weights, viewed from the front (left) (drawing: **Fig 7.19**
Annika Jepsson) and side (right) showing the two sheds for a tabby weave (drawing: Tina Borstam).

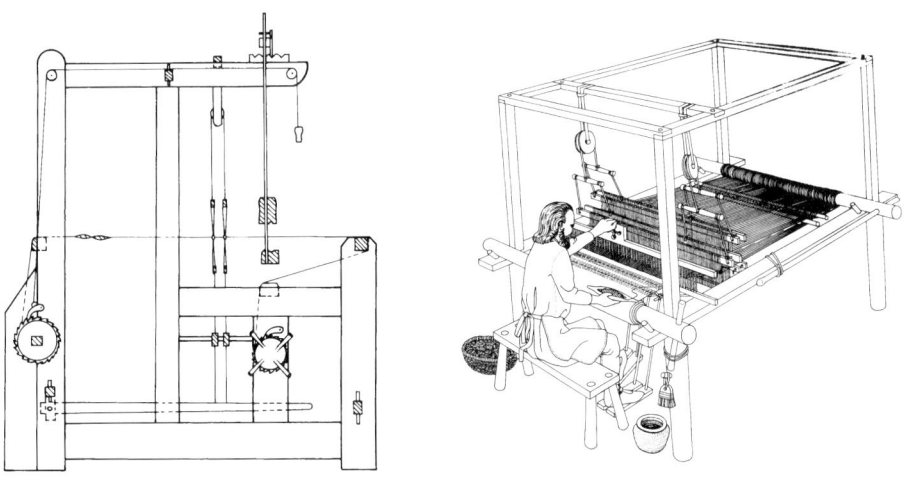

(left) A horizontal treddle loom, showing the sheds and (right) in action (Crowfoot et al. 1992, 22). **Fig 7.20**

later replaced the older loom types in household production. However, it is interesting to note that loom weights are generally absent from English domestic sites from the eleventh century onwards (Clarke 1986, 133), while the warp-weighted loom was in use, alongside the horizontal loom, until modern times on the north Atlantic islands and in the north of the Nordic countries (Hoffmann 1974).

Dyeing

Dyeing played a vital role in textile production (Crowfoot et al.1992, 19). Plant fibres, such as flax and hemp, are more difficult to dye than wool (Cardon 2007, 11). Plant fibres are generally shades of creamy white to light tan. Flax fibres can be bleached by various methods. The simplest method is to expose the linen fabric to the sun (or snow). Wool, on the other hand, comes in a variety of natural colours. The different colours can be sorted and spun separately, taking advantage of the shades in the weave. The stage at which dyeing takes place varies according to the type of textile fibre used and the desired effects, but generally the dyer can choose to dye either the fibre, the yarn or the woven fabric.

In *direct dyeing*, dye plants are boiled, or sometimes soaked, in water to prepare a dye bath. In order make the dyeing molecules adhere, different types of *mordant* are added, for example alum, urine and salts of copper and tin (e.g. Cardon 2007, 20-49). Another dyeing technique is *vat dyeing*. This is the technique used to dye with indigo (blue colours) and with molluscs such as murex (with different types of mollusc giving different colours, including red, blue and purple). The pigments in indigo and molluscs are insoluble and it is necessary to submit them to a reduction process in alkaline conditions before they can be absorbed by the textile fibres (Cardon 2007, 4).

Numerous plants were used for dyeing; for example, a blue colour can be obtained from woad (*Isatis tinctoria L.*), a red colour from dyer's madder (*Rubia tinctorum L.*) and a yellow colour from dyer's weed (*Reseda luteola L.*) or saffron (*Crocus sativus L.*) (e.g. Cardon 2007). An endless number of combinations can be used to obtain different shades of colours. If, for example, a grey yarn is dyed in a yellow dye bath, the yarn will become greenish; if one dyes an indigo-coloured yarn in a red dye bath, the yarn will become purple. Woad and madder was imported from the Continent as well as cultivated in England (Clarke 1986, 135).

Before dyeing, the fibres, yarn or textiles have to be washed. Water is also required for the dye baths, and to rinse the fibres, yarn or textiles after dyeing. The requisite equipment is a supply of fresh water and hearths for heating the dyeing vats. Dyers workshops have for example been found in Bristol, Winchester and Fountains Abbey (Clarke 1986). Grinders, pestles and mortars are used to prepare the dye material and/or mordants (e.g. Cardon 2007).

Finishing

Since wool has a tendency to form a matted surface ('*felt*') an important finishing method was that of *fulling*, that gave it a firm structure and softness. The process could differ slightly, but to remove dirt the fabric was soaked in an alkaline cleansing agent and water and subsequently processed (Crowfoot et al. 1992, 17). After fulling, the cloth was hung out to dry on *tenter frames* where it was stretched taut to achieve the correct dimensions, a necessary process as standards for cloth were laid down by law and governmental officials could pass or condemn their quality and size. Several tenter grounds have been discovered in Bristol and Winchester, where postholes in rows up to 16 m long indicated the drying racks and where characteristic implements, the *tenter hooks*, used for attaching the cloth to the wooden frames were also found. After stretching and drying, the cloth was finished by being *teased* and *sheared*. The surface of the cloth was raised with spiky heads of teasels mounted on a wooden frame and could finally be sheared off by very large-bladed nap shears to make a smooth, in some cases almost velvety surface. The cloth was then sent to the officials who would have to seal the cloth with a leaden seal if it were up to standard for sale on the open market (e.g. Clarke 1986).

Conclusion

The study of textiles has enormous potential in archaeological and historical research as it reveals social and cultural aspects of medieval society, as well as giving us a unique opportunity to come very close to the individual. A textile is not simply a binary system of spun, twisted or spliced fibres, but a result of complex interactions between resources and technology within society. The catalysts for this interaction are the need, desire and choice of the society, which in turn influence the exploitation of resources and development of technology. The totality of these interactions is expressed during textile production (Andersson E *et al.* 2010).

PART 4:   METAL WORKERS AND MINING
by Marie-Christine Bailly-Maître, Ricardo Córdoba and Ulrich Müller

A wide variety of metals was extracted and used for manufacture in the Middle Ages. Gold and silver was used for high status objects, such as rings and reliquaries, worked as solid, or inlaid, or worked as filigree decoration or as hammered leaf for ornamenting manuscripts and vessels. Mercury was used to purify gold by dissolving out other metals (as an *amalgam*); lead was employed in roofs and pipes; copper, alloyed with tin (bronze) or antimony, arsenic and zinc (brass) was used to make every kind of implement. The principal colourants of pottery and glass were the salts of lead, mercury, copper, cobalt and manganese (see above). The principal metal for all social classes was iron, the material of swords, spears, ploughshares and tools (for detailed treatment, see Bailly-Maitre 2002, 2004; Bailly Maître & Simoncl 1996; Bailly-Maître & Dhénin, 2004; Claughton 2008; Orejas & Ruiz del Árbol 2006; Pétrequin, *et al* 2000).

Processing

Metals were generally extracted from surface deposits known from Roman times and before. Gold, which does not occur in combination as an ore, was recovered from streams that carried it from underground. The other metals are found as oxides, sulphates, sulphides and carbonates (*ores*) embedded in seams of rock (*gangue*). Rich silver deposits were known in Poland and Serbia, mercury concentrations in southern Spain and Slovenia, copper in south Spain, the Balkans and Sweden, and tin in Cornwall, England.

Ores were extracted, crushed and washed or soaked to remove soluble impurities and roasted to remove volatile impurities by sublimation. The ore was then heated in a furnace until mobile (*smelted*). Where sufficiently high temperatures can be reached gold, copper, lead and tin can be liquefied in a crucible and poured into moulds (*cast*). Iron was generally not cast in Medieval Europe, but the smelt was recovered as a semi-solid *bloom*, which could be shaped by hammering and reheating (*forged*). Forging was also used to repair ploughs and tools, reshape horseshoes and make nails, all objects accessed by most communities in town and country through the services of a blacksmith (Pleiner 2000, 2006; Verna 2001).

The extraction of metals took place where they were located, creating dedicated mining communities living in the wild. The metals were transported to population and manufacturing centres where they joined the expanding network of the growing industries: initially at manors, palaces and monasteries, and later mainly in towns.

The metal-worker in the Middle Ages was a professional whose social status was good and whose skills were in demand. The smelting and forging of iron was widespread in the rural settlements, as indicated by the distribution of bloomery hearths, slag and hammerscale. Some settlements had a large number of features and slag distributed over a large area, suggesting a quasi-industrial character. In towns, iron working was mostly situated on former vacant or sparsely built-up locations in the suburbs.

Non-ferrous production had a lighter archaeological impact, consisting of small scale hearths with crucibles and moulds for casting copper and bronze, touchstones for assaying gold, cupellation dishes for refining gold and silver. Smiths working copper and other precious metals begin to appear in towns, as towns are reborn in the later tenth century (see an example from Worcester above). They are engaged in recycling and sheet metal processing and the casting of cauldrons, candlesticks or buckles. Bronze smiths also made bells, but in this case the smith generally went to the church and cast the bell on the spot. There are numerous examples of these "bell pits" in association with the building or refounding of churches. The hollow bell mould, prepared by the lost wax method, is supported upside down in a pit and the molten bronze poured into it. Once the bell has been cast, it is removed for finishing and polishing, and the pit is backfilled, with its pieces of broken mould that the archaeologists find. One piece sometimes carries a helpful inscription.

The nature of medieval mining

In the Middle Ages most metals (iron, copper, silver, lead) were extracted by open cast mining. When it became necessary to dig deeper, the method used was the "room and pillar" system, in which the miners dug out the veins in the shape of large rooms, leaving some unexcavated pillars to prop up the ceiling. During the fourteenth and fifteenth centuries, underground trenches were used, where the spoil of the new trench was backfilled into the previous one. Lead and copper ores were mined in underground networks joined by passageways.

Ore was extracted by pressure (wedge/hammer) or direct percussion (pick). The technique most employed was excavation by tiers or steps; if the vein was a hard one, excavation by fire-setting was done by making a log fire at the bottom of the rockface so that the heat would cause cracks and collapse. The tool most commonly used was a small pick, of iron and 14-15 cm long, with a forged point and blade, seven or eight of which were usually carried by each miner (Fig 7.21). The material was transported manually in baskets pulled up by ropes; the use of small wagons did not become general until the sixteenth century.

All the mines had a hearth or meeting place that served as a dining room and tool store (for baskets and picks), and a forge where the picks and other tools, which wore out very quickly, were repaired. The remains of a forge building consisting of two rooms, the main one equipped with three hearths, were found at Samson (Sainte-Croix-aux-Mines). In Pampailly, a dry stone building dating from the fifteenth century contained

Miner's pick of the 13th century from St-Laurent-le-Minier (Gard, France).

Fig 7.21

two adjacent spaces: one a room with a hearth and the remains of a chimney, and the other a forge, with the fireplace, the base of the anvil and traces of slag (Benoît 1997). Also found were hand-operated mortars in which the mineral was ground. These usually consisted of simple concave stones where the mineral was pounded with a stone hammer; large-sized grindstones, similar to those used in water mills, were only used where a mineral was too hard to crush by hand (especially in gold mines). Washing was done at the extraction site itself using a series of pipes bringing the water from rivers or wells to the circular or quadrangular pits that served as sedimentation or washing tanks. In many places, there are signs of the dumps and scatters of the waste spoil (clay, silt, sand, gravel), generally ending up at the bottom of a valley, to mingle with the natural deposits (Dillman et al 2002).

The roasting furnaces were usually rectangular and surrounded by a low dry-stone wall; the smelting furnaces were generally small circular structures around 1m in diameter and 50cm high, with a channel for tapping off the slag, lined inside with clay. The fire was worked with manually-operated bellows, their nozzles protected by clay sheaths examples of which survive in abundant numbers. Lead smelting furnaces were habitually placed on high hills, using the prevailing wind to work up the temperature of the fire, which burnt wood and eventually coal (Verna 1999).

Documentation

There are indirect references and illustrations of miners in medieval texts and works of art, but the Middle Ages left no theoretical or practical treatises on mining (Braunstein 2003). It was not until the sixteenth century that such works appeared and even then, they only deal with the area of greater Germany. However, what is illustrated and described in the Renaissance treatises represents, for the most part, what was already known and practiced in the Middle Ages. The first mining regulations appeared in the twelfth-thirteenth century. Locally, seigneurial influence weighed heavily on the miners. Silver, directly linked to coining, attracted the attention of powerful people (Fig 7.22). Although it is difficult to speak of "mining lordships", certain influential aristocratic families exercised mining rights at a very early stage. In France, the records show the king's land being "eaten away" by these families in their quest to control the ore-producing territories. This policy gave rise to the order of 1413, the first mining regulation in French law.

Miners depicted in silver mine, 1490s (Kutná Hora gradual, Czech Republic; National Bibliothek Wien, **Fig 7.22**
sign Cod. 15501).

Archaeological investigation

Archaeological interest in mining has developed rapidly in Europe in recent decades. Preliminary surveys have made use of medieval and modern archives, which name mining areas, and geological and topographical maps, ancient drawings, maps and land registers which locate them more precisely. In the field, the landscape at mining sites is often still marked by dumps of gangue (waste situated downstream of the shafts and tunnels), or by ground subsidence or upwelling of groundwater, miners' paths and the spread of slag. Site survey maps the material and features visible on the surface, and this

Fig 7.23   *Deserted mining settlement of Brandes (Huez-Isère, France), 12th-14th centuries (photo: M.-Ch. Bailly-Maître).*

allows an estimate of the intensity and extent of the mining activities. Surface cuts are used to examine pitheads, dumps, metallurgy workshops, blacksmiths' shops and other work structures, as well as installations related to the daily life of the workers.

The Brandes site (Huez-Isère) has provided information about a small community of miners, their treatment of ore for winning silver and lead, their homes, standard of living and spirituality (Fig 7.23; and see Ch 3, p 144). The archaeological data consists of the voids and hollows left by the mining of ore and gangue, the organization of space, tool marks on the rock walls and structures created inside the networks: mine draining channels, lamp recesses for lamps, timber shoring, vertical passageways (shafts) and horizontal passageways (crosscuts). Parts of the rock-face marked by soot and fine flakes show where the rock has been broken with the use of fire-setting.

Archaeological analysis makes use of metallurgy to determine the character of the rock and the minerals and metals present; the processes involved can be inferred from microscopic examination of slag and bloom. Environmental sequences recovered from pollen deposits in the vicinity should report the dated vegetation sequence and imply the impact of mining on the environment. The cemeteries of mining communities should offer an account of the lives, health and hazards of the mining life.

The metallographic study of objects found on settlement sites far from the mines will give information on the composition of alloys, but rarely indicate the original source of the metal, especially given the amount of recycling. Metallography carried out on the wedges of the Pampailly site (fifteenth century) shows the quality of the iron/steel welding, revealing the high level of mastery of the blacksmiths (Benoît 1997). Recently, there has been growing research done on metal used in construction. In France, the first work pertains to the iron components of the Palais des Papes in Avignon and the keep of the Château de Vincennes: this approach is at the crossroads of architectural archaeology, the study of texts (construction accounts) and archaeometry (nature and quality of iron parts) (Hesse 1968).

Archeology has revealed mining districts being controlled by fortifications, for example *castelli minerari* in Tuscany – Italy, fortified enclosures in the territory of Jihlava (in German Iglau – Czech Republic), a network of towers and castles surrounding the mining district of Largentière (Ardèche – France; Ancel 1998a,b; 2006). The birth, in the Middle Ages, of townships or towns such as Brandes en Oisans, Largentière en Vivarais, l'Argentière en Embrunais, St Laurent-le-Minier in the Cévennes, Jilhava in the Czech Republic, Massa Marittima or Rocca di San Silvestro in Tuscany is evidence for the impact of this activity on the use of land and the structuring of territories (Di Gangi, 2001; Francovich 1985, 1990, 1993; Francovich & Farinelli 1999). A district of the town of Huelva, in Spain, was dedicated to work on ore produced in the vicinity and in Almaden in particular.

Conclusion

The early eleventh century to mid-fourteenth century was a period of major demographic and urban expansion accompanied by the evolution of agrarian, architectural, military and craft technology. Mining too experienced an evolution from aristocratic patronage to mass production. Metal was needed everywhere. For a long time underestimated by medievalists, this study of an early industry is now winning recognition thanks to the development of mining archaeology in Europe.

There is no longer any doubt that the exploitation of mining deposits was a political and strategic, as well as an economic and technical venture. Medieval sources provide information on the evolution of the extraction method, price fluctuations and conflicts over the possession of deposits. Powerful people confronted each other, organized the search for deposits and then legislated in their own favour. The evolution toward centralized, regulated control of mining production focused on silver and differed greatly from one state to the next.

The history of mining has much to learn through archaeology and archaeometry. The scope of research is wide, encompassing all the phenomena connected to mining and metallurgical activity: the political and economic balance of power, regulation of the output, social implications (location of homes, evolution of the status of players over the centuries), the flow of skills, the main phases of technological change, the effects of natural factors on the activity (geology and metallurgy, hydrology, fuel reserves), the impact on the landscape and the environment (modification of the natural topography, pollution, deforestation). Only a cross-reading of the data provided by the texts and illustrations with archaeology, archaeometry, experimentation and ethnoarchaeology can allow the history of technology to be written and understood in its historical context.

CHAPTER 8

THE RISING TIDE
OF TRAVEL AND TRADE

PART 1: SEA TRADE. THE DEVELOPMENT OF SHIPS AND ROUTES
by Jan Bill

The maritime highways of the North Sea, the Baltic, the eastern Atlantic and the Mediterranean were fully exploited in the later Middle Ages, a period which also saw contact and trade pushing south along the coast of Africa, and eventually into the Indian Ocean (Fig 8.1). These sea routes formed a network with the major rivers and with roads, and (in the north) with the wide and free mobility provided by snow and ice (Box 8.1).

In the medieval Mediterranean, the main direction of seaborne trade was east-west, following the Continental coast and/or hopping from island to island from Cyprus in the east to Valencia in the west. In 1239, the last of the important island strongholds in the Mediterranean, the Balearics, shifted from Muslim to Christian hands, effectively pushing the maritime border between the West and the Muslim world close to the African coast. Venice, Genoa and other North-Italian city-states were in control of the luxury trade with the Levant (Fig 8.2). Ships from these towns brought spices and silks into Northern Italy from the east, for further transport to the north and west. Much of this transport followed land and river routes, but from 1277 Genoa, and from 1314 Venice, started to send merchant fleets to Northern Europe around the Iberian Peninsula, where Muslim control now was restricted to Granada. From this time onwards, Mediterranean products such as lustreware pottery from Malaga began to make an appearance in north-west Europe (see Ch 7, p 279).

Bruges, under the patronage of the counts of Flanders, developed into the main destination for Mediterranean trading ships. Together with other Flemish towns Bruges already held a central position in the wool and cloth trade between England, Scotland and the Continent. The Flemish region was favoured by its unique position at the confluence between two of the most important waterways – the Rhine and the Channel – and was to remain the centre of north European shipping and trade well into modern times, even if the individual towns in the area experienced both rise and decline. English merchants, many of them from the so-called 'Cinque ports' (royally privileged harbour towns), were especially active in the wine trade with Gascony, but traded both with the Baltic and North Atlantic markets. Towards the north-east, the Hanseatic League

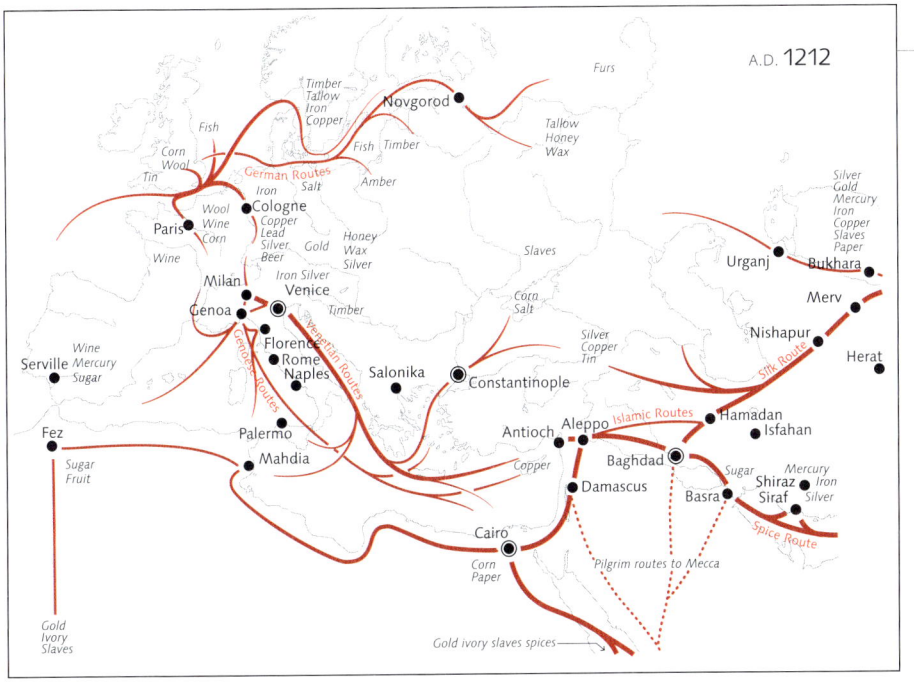

Fig 8.1a

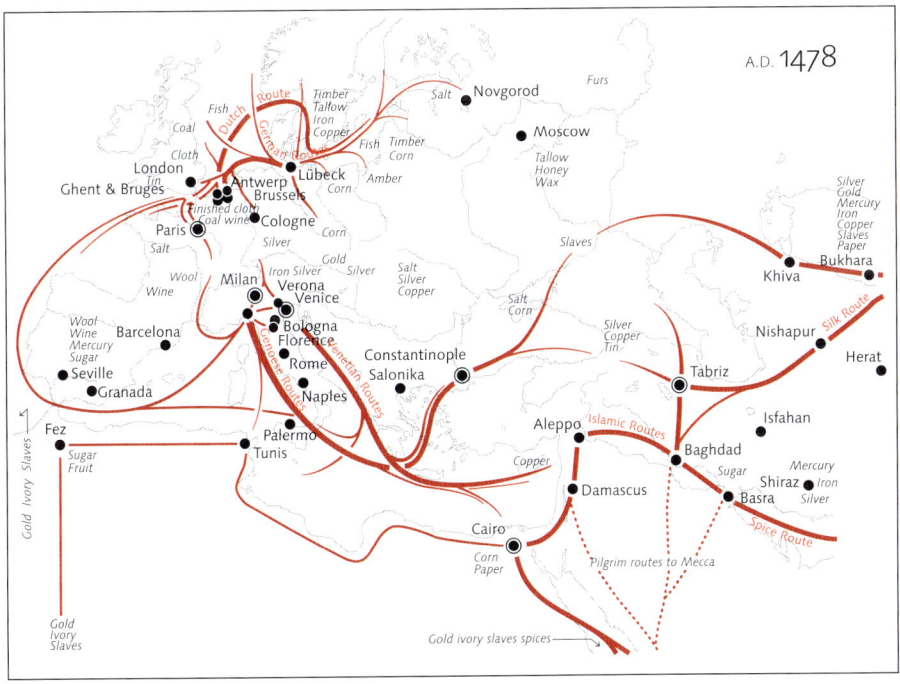

European trade routes (a) in 1212 (b) in 1478 (after McEvedy 1961).

Fig 8.1b

Fig 8.2 *Seaways: a view from Corsica, with a Genoan tower in the foreground.*

grew powerful by transporting and selling fish, grain, metals and forest products from the Baltic Sea region and Norway to the markets of central and western Europe (see below). The Hanseatic town Danzig (Gdańsk) was an especially important node in the Hanseatic trade network, as were Stockholm and Bergen, through which fish and other products from northern Sweden, Finland and Northern Norway were channelled.

Mediterranean seafaring to the fourteenth century

Around 1200 there was still very little contact between the shipbuilding traditions of Mediterranean and Northern Europe (AME 1, ch 9). Ships in the Mediterranean were, now as before, entirely carvel-built (with the planks edge to edge), but the ancient tradition of shell-first building and the use of mortise-and-tenon joints in the planking was now being entirely replaced by skeleton-construction – that is, all the frames were erected before the planking was attached. The 21 m long *Contarina* 1 ship from the Po delta, dated to around 1300, demonstrates many of the features typical to late medieval Mediterranean shipbuilding (Fig 8.3; Pryor 1994; Steffy 1993). Building skeleton-first required the frames to be constructional entities, and in the *Contarina* 1 wreck this was achieved by nailing the consecutive timbers of an individual frame to the side of the previous timber: the lower futtocks were nailed to the sides of the floor timber and the upper futtocks to the sides of the lower futtocks. The frames were so closely placed that

Excavation of the Contarina ship from the Po delta.

Fig 8.3

they lay side by side where the individual timbers were joined. Longitudinal reinforcement of the hull was provided by a system of internal and external timbers. Along the centreline, the keel, stem and stern were supported by a keelson, running on top of the floor timbers through the entire length of the vessel. Furthermore two sets of longitudinal timbers, *stringers* on the inside and *wales* on the outside, were attached to the hull in each side level with the joints in the frames. Two mast steps, one situated very far forward and one situated well behind the midship frame, were installed in the ship, which shows it had been equipped with a rigging with two lateen (triangular) sails. A large, transverse timber was found in the aft, which has been interpreted as representing a stern quarter through-beam, used for mounting two steering oars, one on each side of the ship.

With a beam of little over 5 m, the *Contarina* 1 ship was relatively slender, but still with a displacement probably well above 75 metric tonnes. Mediterranean ships could, according to written sources, be built much bigger. The largest of several ships ordered by King Louis IX of France from Marseille, Genoa and Venice for his Crusades in 1248-54 and 1270, is claimed to have had a displacement of more than 800 metric tonnes, three decks and the capacity to carry more than 1000 passengers (Pryor 1994). Other written, and pictorial sources indicate that although ships of this size were exceptions, the Mediterranean in general saw larger ships than the northern European waters.

Another important example of Mediterranean shipbuilding from around 1300 is the *Cala Culip* VI, excavated underwater on the Catalonian coast of Spain (Palou et al. 1998).

This wreck, which has been dated on the basis of its rich inventory of Islamic and Christian ceramics, has been reconstructed to a length of slightly more than 16 m, and a tonnage of *c.* 40 metric tonnes; it is thus a relatively small vessel. According to analyses of the vessel's timbers, it originated in the same region in which it was found. Analysis of its well-preserved bottom demonstrated that the ship was built by means of geometrical methods, which made it possible to define the hull-shape accurately before the ship was built. In contrast to the *Contarina* 1 the pre-erected frames were not joined simply by nailing the upper timbers to the side of the lower ones. Instead they were fastened by means of hooked scarfs, a type of joint which is resistant to pulling forces which otherwise could open the notches between the carvel-laid planks and make the ship leak.

North European shipbuilding to the fifteenth century

In the middle of the twelfth century, clinker construction was the dominant shipbuilding technology in northern Europe. It was found in Scandinavia, but also in areas where the Vikings and later the Normans had settled or achieved domination: in England, Scotland, Ireland (McGrail 1993) and, as indicated by conjecture and later finds, in Normandy itself and along the west coast of France. In the southern Baltic it was used by Slavs as well as by Germans and Danish colonizing the southern coast of that sea. Where we do not have finds of the ships, their presence is indicated by the numerous occurrences of clench nails in the harbour towns. In the Netherlands and north-western Germany, these are often found together with large numbers of *sintels*, indicative of the construction of cogs or barges (Ellmers 1992; Krause 1999).

From the twelfth to the fourteenth century, large cargo ships in Northern Europe are usually described as either 'keels', 'cogs' or 'hulcs' in the written sources, unless the generic term 'ship' is used. These terms are not used consistently – the same ship may appear as a 'cog' in one source and as a 'hulc' in another – and should not be confused with the archaeological terminology for medieval ship types. Archaeologically, only two major types seem to have played a significant role throughout this time span, namely the entirely clinker-built *keel*, and the *cog*, characterized by having a carvel-built bottom and clinker-built sides, in combination with a straight stem and stern (AME 1, Ch 9) (Fig 8.4). It is believed that the 'hulc' of the twelfth to mid-fifteenth centuries was a clinker-built ship.

Cogs and keels developed along the same lines during the twelfth to fourteenth centuries, although they remained technologically distinct. The common factor in their development was the pursuit of cheaper carrying-capacity, achieved partly by increasing ship size, partly by reducing building costs. From the mid-twelfth to the mid-fifteenth century, the capacity of the largest cargo ships in Northern Europe increased from around 100 tonnes to *c.* 450 tonnes for the largest cargo carriers (Bill 2002). Increase in size, however, was not always a competitive way to reduce transport costs – in fact only few routes could maintain shipping at a level which justified the use of very large vessels. Smaller ships had an immense role to play in the transport system, both because they could serve the numerous smaller centres through which only a limited flow of goods passed, and because they were able to navigate waterways and enter harbours

A reconstruction of a northern European cog. Fig 8.4

inaccessible to the larger ships. Lowering the building costs was therefore an efficient means for reducing the transport cost, and it was applied, with a few exceptions, in all sectors of shipbuilding in northern Europe in this period.

Building costs were primarily reduced by cutting labour-intensive elements in the building process. In Scandinavian clinker shipbuilding the smooth run of the planking, emphasised with decorative profiles – a highly appreciated quality in the twelfth century – disappeared gradually during the thirteenth and fourteenth. The complex, symmetrically-constructed framing with thwarts for every frame that had been used since the Viking Age, also disappeared in favour of a simple, more massive framing first found in the earliest cogs. In cog building – but at this point not in clinker-building – savings were also achieved by going from the use of split, hewn planks for the construction of the hull to the use of sawn planks. Since the early cogs are all from southern Scandinavia, it is possible, however, that the use of split planks in early cog building is a regional, rather than a chronological phenomenon. There were regional differences in shipbuilding and in the speed with which new techniques were accepted. It seems that urbanisation was an important factor in promoting the adoption of new ways of building, and older building traditions tended to survive in poorly urbanised areas. An example is the northern parts of Scandinavia, where local shipbuilding techniques changed little from the twelfth to the nineteenth century (Bill 2009).

The cog was used as warship for the German expansion in the Baltic, and cog builders moved into the Hanseatic towns as they were established along the southern Baltic coast (Kulessa 2000). Dendrochronological studies have demonstrated that cogs and barges were also built in Denmark and the southernmost part of Sweden in the twelfth and thirteenth centuries (Bill & Hocker 2004; Daly 2007). In the North Sea region, cogs and cog-like vessels dominated ship construction especially in the Wadden Sea region, as demonstrated by the many medieval wrecks excavated in the Zuiderzee, dating from the thirteenth century onwards. The expansion of the cog as cargo carrier was closely connected to the German Hansa. As a successful trader and warship it was certainly desired and acquired by the elite in much larger parts of Northern Europe, but the archaeological finds so far almost unanimously point to the Wadden Sea area and the southern Baltic coast – with some instances in southern Scandinavia – as the region where these ships were produced. In the rest of northern Europe, clinker technique very much seemed to continue to dominate shipbuilding. This was, however, a situation that was about to change as south and north European shipbuilding started to merge in the fourteenth century.

The merging of traditions: European shipbuilding in the late Middle Ages

The earlier phases of the joining of shipbuilding traditions in northern and southern Europe are not well known, partly because there are few archaeological discoveries from the Mediterranean and Atlantic coasts of Europe to illustrate it. Depictions and written sources do, however, illuminate some of the changes. In 1304 it is reported that Mediterranean shipbuilders started to copy Biscayan "cogs", and the term "choche" are used about some Genoese and Venetian ships between 1302 and 1312. The Biscay and Galicia had, at least since the early twelfth century, been a meeting place for northern and southern shipbuilding (Hutchinson 1994, 79-80), and it would not be surprising if this was the place where the medieval merger of the two traditions started. However, there is no archaeological evidence of construction of ships similar to the north European cogs, either in Gascony or Galicia, nor in the Mediterranean, and since Gascony was under English rule until the late thirteenth century, we may suspect the Biscayan "cogs" to be clinker-built *keels*, rather than cogs in the archaeological meaning of this word.

Changes in the depiction of Mediterranean ships indicate that the technology transfer was related to rigging and steering, rather than to hull construction. The lateen sail was replaced with a large, single square sail, and the stern rudder replaced the two large side or quarter rudders. The main advantage of the square sail was that it was easier to handle, and thus significantly reduced the crew necessary to sail a vessel – perhaps by as much as half. From the mid-fourteenth century, the first illustrations of Mediterranean ships with a rigging using both the square sail and the lateen sail occur, and a Catalonian manuscript from 1409 shows us the first three-masted ship with this combination (Friel 1994, 78; Hutchinson 1994, 63f; Fig 8.5). In northern Europe the first depiction of a two-masted ship is found on a church-bench in King's Lynn in England, and is believed to date to the early fifteenth century (Friel 1995, 161). During the fifteenth century, a rapid development of multi-masted rigging took place both in the north and in the south, and already by 1485 large warships could be four-masted and carry both sprit- and topsails.

The presence of Mediterranean ships in northern waters from the decades around 1300 seemingly left few other immediate traces in northern shipbuilding, even if such

(left) A Catalanian manuscript from 1409 showing a three-masted ship with square and lateen sails. **Fig 8.5** (right) Image of a large three-masted ship, with castles fore and aft and armed with a row of cannons, carved in a large stone relief of the 1440s. (Hôtel Jacques Cœur, Bourges, central France).

ships were indeed being constructed in Northern Europe, as demonstrated by the example of Rouen. Here the French crown, with help of Genoese shipwrights, established a galley wharf as early as in 1295, in order to produce both clinker-built and Mediterranean-type galleys for the war against the English (Rose 2002, 13-15; Rieth 1989). The wharf remained in use until it was destroyed by the English in 1417, but it appears that for extended periods of time many of its galleys were not in a state that allowed them to go to sea. The English crown at the same time was not able to maintain and make use of captured Mediterranean warships, an indication of how big the difference still was at this time between the northern and southern shipbuilding traditions (Friel 1995, 173-174).

Instead, the clinkerbuilt vessel was developed to reach sizes comparable to that of the large ships of the Mediterranean, a striking example being the *Grace Dieu*, which was built 1416-1418 by Henry V of England. This was a two-masted warship with a total length of 55 m and a beam of 15 m, and it was built with a peculiar clinker technique, which included three layers of radially split oak planking. The remains of the ship, which never came to play any important role as a warship, still lies today on the banks of the river Hamble, near Southampton (Clarke et al. 1993; Friel 1993). Another example of a large, clinker-built warship, although an imaginary one, is represented on a carving at Hotel Jacque Cœur in Bourges, central France. The three-masted ship, with castles fore and aft and armed with a row of cannons, is shown in a large stone relief which originates from 1440's and which is one of the most vivid illustrations of a large fifteenth century warship that we have (Friel 1995, 162-164, Fig 8.5). Two examples of a more commonplace nature, are the c. 25 m long (reconstructed hull length) Aber

Wrac'h ship from around 1400, found in Brittany but believed to originate from the Biscay area (L'Hour & Veyrat 1994) and the Newport ship found in 2002 in Newport in Wales. The latter, which was built between 1446 and 1465, is also believed to originate from the Biscay area, and may have had a total length close to 35 m, of which the hull constituted at least 26 m (Roberts 2004; http://www.thenewportship.com/members/newsletter.html, No. 15).

About the same time as the Newport ship was being built, the first shipwrights in northern Europe set out to construct entirely carvel-built ships. Two different approaches were chosen. In the core area of cog building – around the Zuiderzee – the existing technology stayed in use, but was modified. Carvel-built ships were built as bottom-based vessels, by the use of temporary fasteners, clamps, as cogs had been before. Study of the *B&W* 4 wreck from Copenhagen, a Dutch carvel-built ship from ca. 1595, demonstrates that the clamps served not only to secure the planks until framing timbers were inserted, but also defined the angles between the planks and thus were instrumental in controlling the shape of the hull (Lemée 2006, 108-147). If clamps were used like this already in the fifteenth century, at the transition from cog building to carvel building, this may explain the conservatism that cog-builders showed in this transitory phase.

Outside the cog-producing areas it appears that a more fundamental shift was made. The practice of shell-first, clinker-built construction was abandoned, and frame-first building was adopted along with geometrical construction methods. This took place in northern and western France, in the western part of the Netherlands, and in England during the second half of the fifteenth century. Finds from this early phase are scarce, but several wrecks from the early sixteenth century have been excavated that illustrate the similarity of these early modern vessels. They are today regarded as representing a specific, oak-based Atlantic shipbuilding tradition of the late medieval/early modern period, which can be separated from Mediterranean carvel building (Loewen 2001) and which, to a large extent, created the basis for the European expansion across the seas in the late fifteenth and sixteenth centuries.

Even if the changes that took place in shipbuilding during the Late Middle Ages are impressive and in some areas revolutionised the trade, it is important to note that these did not influence all Europe equally. Traditions from the Early Middle Ages, or the centuries before, continued to survive in small-scale shipbuilding and boatbuilding. Clinker-built boats and skiffs continued to be built in areas from the eastern Baltic in Scandinavia, England and Ireland down to the Biscay and Portugal long after carvel-building had superseded the construction of large keels.

Transport capacity

The period 1200-1500 saw very significant changes in the performance and transport capacity of European ships. In northern Europe, the increase in the size of the largest ships tripled (Bill 2002, 101-103), and probably similar developments took place in Mediterranean Europe too. The increase in the carrying capacity of the largest ships reflects an increase in the total volume of shipping during the period, and it follows several imperatives. One was the growth in trade in specialised commodities, operating between a few nodes in the transport system, sometimes facilitated by creating staple towns. Toll records from Lübeck from the closing years of the fourteenth century illustrate how the ships travelling between Lübeck and the staple towns of Bergen and Stockholm were of a completely different size to those involved in trade with other destinations in Scandinavia, including the Scania market (Bill *et al* 1997). Another imperative was the demand for increased traffic south, which presented both north European and Mediterranean shipbuilding with challenges that they had not met before.

It is important to note that increased demand for transport capacity was met not only by increasing the capacity of the largest vessels, but also simply by increasing the number of vessels. While there is certainly an efficiency gain in the use of larger ships, there are adverse factors which make their economy vulnerable: in times of economic slow-down they more easily risked sailing half-empty; there were fewer harbours with adequate facilities for ship and goods; and they were more dependent on high capital investment and specialist knowledge for their construction, maintenance and use. Thus it is likely that fluctuations in transport demand was primarily met through adjusting the number of vessels, and that an increase in ship size required a substantial pressure – either from the market or from political events, like war.

War was, then as now, a strong promoter of technological development, but the character of medieval warfare at sea – which had as its primary goal the boarding and capture of the enemy crew – itself put a premium on ship size. The larger the ship, the more soldiers could be brought on board, and the more difficult it would be to capture. Considerable developments were seen in the armament of military vessels. Castles fore and aft and top-castles at the mast head became common in the thirteenth century. With the large warships of the fifteenth century, the *carracks*, the ship castles reached their zenith, especially the fore-castle which acted as a formidable platform for shooting and throwing missiles into an enemy ship and for boarding it. The forecastle often had a huge grappling iron hanging under the bowsprit, which could be dropped down to secure the enemy vessel.

The introduction of the stern rudder, following its initial development in the twelfth century, may not have led to better manoeuvrability, but certainly to better security, since it was a more robust construction than the earlier side-rudders. What did improve manoeuvrability was, however, the introduction of the multi-masted rigging, since it allowed the sails to be used more efficiently to turn the vessel. Splitting up the sail area over several masts instead of one also reduced the strain on rigging and the need for manpower to handle the extremely large sails of the largest single-masted vessels. Speed probably did not increase significantly, if at all, since speed improvements from developments in propulsion tended to be consumed by greater resistance to movement through the water caused by increasingly bulky hull shapes.

BOX 8.1   TRAVEL ON SNOW AND ICE

Almost six months of ice and snow every year provide challenging conditions for the movement of people and goods in the far north of Europe; it could easily be imagined that the northern winter is an impediment to movement and communication. This, however, is not the case: communications and even social relations become easier to manage. In the summer, movement is restricted to particular land routes, since wheeled vehicles and draught animals require good-quality roads and countless bridges and ferries. Winter freezes the water and reinforces the soil, even solidifying large bogs. Thus in the winter months, roads become available everywhere, offering low friction surfaces facilitating the movement of heavy loads. Moreover, sledges, sleds and skis open paths that are easy for other travellers to follow.

The subsistence of farmer-peasants and hunter-gatherers of the northern Coniferous Zone was broadly based and required much movement in winter. As a result, highly varied equipment for winter transport evolved, indicating a thorough knowledge of the properties of snow and ice, and the weights they would bear. The northern Finns have more than ten words for snow conditions, and the Sámi even more. For example, the Skolt Sámi grade the weight-bearing properties of snow and ice from 'mice' to 'elk' (on life in wilderness areas see e.g. Pälsi 1944).

Similar methods of winter transport are widely shared between the Coniferous Zone and the Eurasian tundra, and most predate the Middle Ages and go back even as far as the Stone Age. The skis and *ahkio* sledges adopted by the Finnish army on independence had

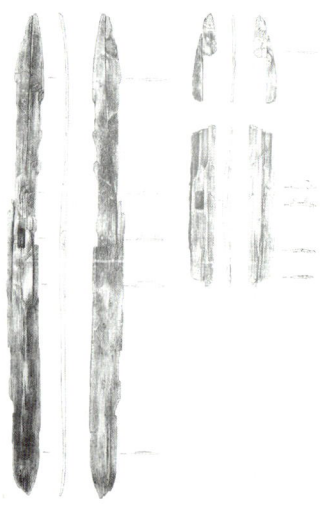

Fig 1

Pair of skis found in a bog at Hetekylä in Pudasjärvi, Northern Ostrobothnia. The 14C-date of the lyly, longer ski, and of the kalhu, shorter ski, is mid 15th century. Skis like this were used on even snow plains. The third ski in the figure, the short and broad one was found at Pohjoisniemensuo in Kuhmo, Northern Finland. Its 14C-date is 16th century (Taavitsainen et al. 2007, 73, fig. 53; drawing: S.N./National Board of Antiquities/Department of Antiquities).

Fig 2

Reconstruction of a medieval ahkio sledge based on the Taivassalo find, western Finland dated to c. 1160–1190 AD (photo Timo Kuokkanen).

Fig 3

Pavel Hatamovic Anagurici, in the district of Yamal Nenetsia, east of Gulf Ob in Siberia, driving a sled drawn by three reindeer. The team is steered with one bridle which is thrown from one side to the other when necessary and a long driving stick. The sled represents a type used in the Middle Ages. The construction does not need any nails, only wedges, which makes the type "ageless" and highly practical (photo: Janne Vilkuna 2001).

been used for centuries in the roadless regions to transport people, game and other materials. The study of the evolution of winter transport equipment is still in progress (Taavitsainen *et al* 2007; Berg 1935). The surviving material is limited and so far not well dated.

Snow shoes were meant for use in non-bearing snow conditions and for short distance. *Skis* were the fastest and most important means of personal transport, and came in many different lengths and widths to suit different tasks and users (Fig 1). Wide skis, used for walking in the manner of snow shoes, were slow but good for use in deep snow or in thickets when checking snares. Lining the undersides with animal skins made it easier to go uphill. Travelling skis were long and narrow, sometimes with one of them being shorter and having a fur-lined bottom surface, the 'kicking ski.' These were also suitable for hunting trips on crusted snow and for hunting elks, when the crust would carry

a skier but not an elk. There were also *wooden skates* for use on ice, but they were suitable only for ice without snow cover. The user of *bone skates* was propelled with a spiked staff.

Sledges were used for transporting goods and dead game (Fig 2). The *ahkio* or *pulkka* is a boat-shaped sledge with a square back end and no runners, which was pulled by people or animals. As in boats, boards were raised on the sides to improve carrying capacity. The *ahkio* was used by hunters and pulled or drawn while skiing. The *ahkio* sledges were extremely durable, flexible and adaptable to the terrain. Since the ribs were not of rigid timber but of flexible withes and the strakes were strips of wood, the size of the *ahkio* could be varied to some degree according to the load. *Ahkios* were used up to recent times. *Sleds* are defined here as sledges on two runners. They were drawn by humans, dogs or reindeer. An all-purpose runner-sled was made very easily and quickly, and was easy to use. However it did not work in deep snow, only on ice with a thin snow cover.

The range of winter travel increased in the Viking period (800-1025/1050), probably prompted by a rising international demand for furs (AME 1, 272), and it is likely that the *ahkio* sledges originated approximately in this period. While the *ahkio* sledge could be drawn by humans and dogs, reindeer could pull heavier loads in larger sledges (Fig 3). The precise period that wild reindeer were domesticated is still unclear. There are no indications of reindeer herding on a large scale until the 1700s (Aronsson 1991). The study of the evolution of winter transport equipment is still in progress (Taavitsainen et al 2007; Berg 1935).

by J.-P. Taavitsainen

The Hansa in the North Sea and Baltic: commercial and cultural networks

The Hansa formed the principal agent of trade and exchange in northern Europe and the Baltic during the medieval to early modern period; it eventually reached from London and Bruges to Tallinn, Riga and the Gulf of Finland (Fig 8.6). The origin of this confederation of German cities can be traced back to the foundation of Lübeck in 1158. In the wake of conquest by the Teutonic Order, German merchants rapidly colonised the lands to the east during the course of the following century and founded such towns as Rostock, Stralsund, Gdansk and Riga. Hanseatic trade reached its zenith during the fourteenth to fifteenth centuries with the foundation of permanent trading posts or *Kontore* at Novgorod in the east, Bergen in the north, and London and Bruges in the west. Together they formed a dynamic economic and cultural network, which stretched the length and breadth of Europe and beyond (Bracker et al 1999; Caune & Ose 2009) (Box 8.2).

The Hanseatic trading system which had emerged by the late thirteenth century drew the west, the east and the north of the Continent together by acting as an intermediary for the exchange of goods between two very different patterns of production: raw materials from the east and finished/semi-finished products from the west, and by stimulating the wider long-distance market. Despite their dispersed geographical position, a new type of ship, the *cog*, which developed around 1200, enabled the Hanseatic merchants to maintain economic superiority over the Continent for centuries. It was

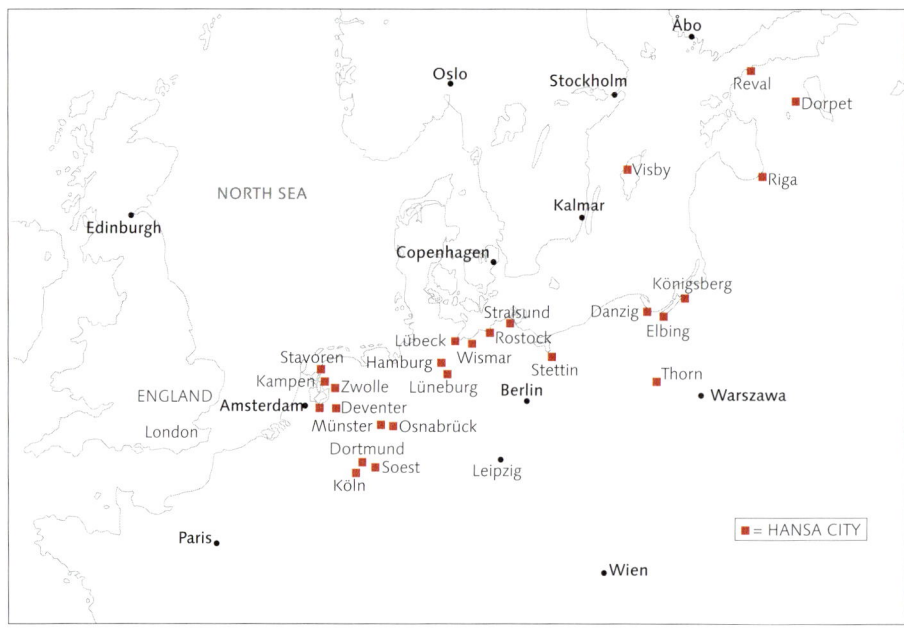

Fig 8.6   *Map showing the location of the Hansa cities.*

more capacious and more stable than previous models, and at around 200-300 tons, could carry two to three times the cargo (see above, p 332). As well as raw and processed material and finished goods the ships also carried people. Traders, wholesalers and retailers, members of the aristocracy, administrators, soldiers, churchmen and, crucially, craftsmen – shipbuilders, altarpiece-carvers and potters – all were prepared to migrate long distances, with the prospect of acquiring wealth. Thus, perhaps as influential as the growing economic and technological dominance of the Hanseatic League, were the 'horizontal' cultural networks, which developed between trading partners, towns and families the length and breadth of the Baltic region (Gaimster 2005; 2007b).

Hanseatic urban settlements in northern Europe shared many things in common, not only in their commercial function, but also in their language and in their cultural, religious and political identity. Art-historians have spoken in defining terms of a cosmopolitan Hanseatic 'signature' which was articulated physically through a shared vocabulary of town plan, public building, church layout (designed as much for business meetings as for the veneration of the Saints), a distinctive architectural style of step-gabled buildings (*Backsteingotik*), and through common design in the visual arts, particularly in the ecclesiastical and devotional spheres (Zaske and Zaske 1986; Jaacks 1989). Here carved and painted altarpieces endowed by leading merchant families or guilds, carved bench- and pew-ends, monumental grave slabs and baptismal fonts and doors in cast bronze all allude to the shared religious and social values of the urban bourgeois elite (Hasse 1979).

Archaeology of the Hansa

Archaeologists have noted that traded domestic ceramics share much of the same cultural signature across the Hanseatic commercial network. Archaeology both supports and supplements, but also amplifies, the documentary record for the period, possibly no more so than in the study of the trade in domestic goods and its cultural impact. Many of the key documents relating to trade are incomplete. For example, customs accounts were created for the purpose of taxation rather than for the purpose of rigorously recording trading activity and its value. Certain classes of traders were exempt and were therefore not recorded: a principal exemption in England was shipping trading with other English ports. Thus there is no record of any coastal traffic, and hence no data on the catches of English fishing fleets. Other classes of traders, such as the Hansa merchants, enjoyed special privileges and so were taxed in England at lower rates than others: in this case the total values of customs collected need to be treated with extreme caution. Finally, the port books list the home ports of ships and the cargo of taxable gods, but not the ports visited en route nor the private cargoes of the crews. These gaps in the record gaps obscure the real patterns of coastal trade in the Baltic and North Seas, including evidence for the transhipment of goods (Evans 1987 for discussion).

An equally perplexing aspect of the historical record for the medieval commodity trade is that most classes of material generated by archaeology seldom appear in the documents, mainly because – as in the case of pottery, for instance – they were of negligible value as a source of revenue to the Crown. Thus baskets of ceramic table ware, even though often a significant part of a ship's cargo, often went unrecorded. And lastly, our reliance on documents makes no allowance for piracy, illicit trade and smuggling, which was endemic in the late Middle Ages around the North Sea and Baltic region and only declined with the emergence of organised naval policing from the early eighteenth century (Meier D 2006).

While the documentary sources prove elusive and often misleading in their representation, the excavated material sample is equally problematic. The overwhelming bulk of trade during the Middle Ages was in perishable goods or in raw materials such as timber and foodstuffs that are usually undetectable in the archaeological record. In 500 years of trade through the port of Hull, 98-99% of its exports and perhaps as much as 95 per cent of its imports fell into this category (Evans 1999). Of the small amount of evidence generated by archaeology, by far the most common is pottery, which as we have seen was a marginal and unrepresentative element in the overall mercantile statistics. But while the excavated sample may be unrepresentative and inadequate for the reconstruction of the whole long distance commodity trade, its study as an index of consumption and of cultural transfer is considerably more valuable.

Through the excavated record we are able to assess the degree to which trade in consumer goods influenced the lifestyles of communities of varying status and function. In view of their short lifespan and long survival in the ground, imported ceramics can be cross-examined as *Kulturträger* in their own right, alongside gabled brick architecture and ecclesiastical objects (Stephan 1996; Gaimster 2005 and 2007b). Pottery assemblages show commercial or social links between trading communities and have the potential to provide a quantitative index of cultural transfer in a region over time and space. The study of luxury imports from castles and towns – such as decorated stoneware vessels, or relief-moulded stove-tiles – show elite patterns of consumption and social competition in the marketplace (Gaimster 2001). Domestic ceramic evidence also provides a physical measure of the spread and adoption of domestic practice or *habitus*, particularly in the spheres of dining rituals, heating technology and the interior environment (Verhaeghe 1998).

The Baltic ceramic market 1200-1500

The early phases of the emerging international pottery market in the North Sea and the Baltic during the thirteenth to fourteenth centuries are dominated firstly by the trade in decorated *red earthenware* and the migration of its production from western Europe to the southern Baltic zone; and secondly by the increasing competition from the more robust and functionally superior *stoneware* vessels from western and northern Germany (Gaimster 1999) (see also Ch 7, p 291).

The development of towns along the Baltic littoral during the course of the thirteenth century stimulated a demand for high quality ceramic tableware suited to the needs of urban living and social competition. Initially, imports of highly decorated lead-glazed *redwares* from the North Sea coast of Flanders and the Netherlands satisfied the demand at the expense of imports from England or western France: the Bruges kilns of *c.* 1200-1350 acting as epicentre of the industry (Verhaeghe 1989; Schäfer 1997).

But the discovery of a series of redware production centres along the Öresund (spanning the Danish islands of Funen and Zealand and the coastline of western Scania), at Lübeck and more recently at sites along the Mecklenburg coast, producing typologically and technologically indistinguishable wares to the Low Countries exports, suggests the movement of western European workshops into the southern Baltic region. Here suitable clays were ubiquitous, and could be fired through the oxidising process to emulate the red earthenware jugs and cooking utensils, such as dripping pans, so familiar to the urban populations of the North Sea littoral.

A distinguishing feature of the southern Baltic redware rod-handled jugs of the midthirteenth to mid fourteenth centuries is the plastic decoration in a white-firing clay with a copper or iron-rich lead glaze, the most common forms being notch-rouletted zones or bands and applied strips (sometimes rouletted) forming vertical panels or large chevrons filled with fish scales, leaf designs or individual pellets, rosettes or raspberry motifs. Occasionally the upper bodies and necks of these jugs are applied with anthropomorphic decoration, the so-called hooded 'monk's face' being the most common (e.g. Schäfer 1997, fig. 5b).

The distribution of western European and regionally-produced redwares stretches from the mouth of the Baltic in the south to Finland and Novgorod in Russia to the north. Their relatively low proportional representation on town sites along the Mecklenburg and Pomeranian coastline during the thirteenth century suggest that these wares enjoyed a certain social premium that made them only accessible to the Hanseatic mercantile and rural feudal elite (Rebkowski 1997; Schäfer 1997). Castle sites around the Baltic Sea region have produced some of the largest and more ornate groups of redware anthropomorphic jugs (Gaimster 2001, 54-56).

In terms of numbers, however, the late medieval international ceramic trade in the Baltic is dominated by the competition between *stoneware* producers in the Rhineland, Lower Saxony and Saxony (Gaimster 1997, Chap.3.3; 1999; and see Ch 7, p 291 for origins and production). Although outcrops of clay suitable for high temperature stoneware production were limited to Germany, its robust body enabled stoneware to be transported in bulk and over long distances (Gaimster 1997, Chap.2).

Following transhipping at major ports, recent finds of wrecks containing cargoes of medieval German stoneware in the archipelago off the Hanseatic trading town of Turku (Åbo) in south-western Finland are beginning to form a picture of coastal redistribution of stoneware in the Baltic zone (Gaimster 2000a). Continuing recording and analysis of the cargo of Lower Saxon stoneware jugs of early fourteenth century date recovered from a shallow-draught coastal trading vessel found at Nauvo is shedding new light on how the majority of domestic consumer goods (as opposed to bulk raw materials) transported in ocean going ships such as cogs, were distributed to markets (Alvik and Haggrén 2003).

Intensive workshop production resulted in a relatively low cost to the consumer and the ability to reach a wide spectrum of the population. The rapid development of the fully fused stoneware body fired to between 1200 and 1400°c (with a porosity value of 0.4%) in the Rhineland and Lower Saxony at the beginning of the fourteenth century coincides with and may even be consequential on the growth of urban populations in northern Europe. With its technically superior body, which is impervious to liquids, stainless and odour free, stoneware revolutionised many domestic activities from washing up to preserving food. In addition, its increasingly varied repertoire of forms over the fourteenth to fifteenth centuries reflects a market response to the multiple drinking, decanting, transport, storage and sanitary needs of town dwellers across the Continent.

By 1350 the highly decorated redwares had begun take a lower profile in the Baltic market due to the pressure from German stoneware exports. Despite the plain, utilitarian body, stoneware captured a niche in the popular tableware market of northern Europe, enabling the aspiring middle classes to imitate aristocratic drinking and dining practices in a less expensive medium, substituting precious or base metalware and drinking glasses with a finely potted ceramic that imitated their role (Gaimster 1997, Chap.4.4). In view of its wide penetration of the international domestic ceramics market, German stoneware may be regarded as a type-fossil of mercantile or 'Hanseatic' urban culture that linked consumers irrespective of means from London to Tallinn and beyond (Gaimster 1993; 1999).

Finds from the castle harbour (*Slottsfjärden*) at Kalmar in southern Sweden provide an instant synopsis of the competition in the Baltic stoneware market over the late medieval period (Fig 8.7). Out of the 885 German stoneware vessels of fourteenth to fifteenth-century date, 68 per cent could be sourced to Siegburg (Rhineland), 21 per cent to Lower Saxony, 9 per cent to Waldenburg (Saxony), and 3 per cent to Langerwehe and Raeren, and others in the Rhineland (Elfwendahl and Gaimster 1999). In addition to the associated social status afforded by its castle, the concentrations of German stoneware found at Kalmar, which make up around 5 per cent of the overall domestic ceramic inventory from the town, may also be explained by the relatively high numbers of alien names recorded as resident in the city. During the late fourteenth century, for instance, one third of out of a total of 2000 family names listed as resident in the city

Fig 8.7   *Medieval ceramics excavated from Kalmar Castle harbour, southern Sweden, comprising imported German stonewares and regional highly decorated redwares lost and deposited during transfer to docks or lighters, c. 1250-1400 (Kalmar Läns Museum).*

were German in origin. A similar explanation could also be made for the Stockholm stoneware sequence. Here the well-documented population of resident German merchants provides a context for the high frequency of imported stoneware finds recorded in the *Gamla Stan* (Old Town) and in neighbouring districts (Gaimster 2002a).

Among the bulk trade in German stoneware to the Baltic during the late Middle Ages there is one group of vessels, however, which, by virtue of its elaborate ornament and biased social distribution, can be discussed realistically in terms of a status indicator. According to recent trace-element analysis of the ceramic body, the Lausitz region of Saxony is the most likely source for a series of high-quality stoneware goblets and beakers of fifteenth-century date found across the study zone (Stephan & Gaimster 2002; Schwedt *et al.* 2003). These characteristically dark-bodied and thinly-potted stonewares with their ecclesiastical forms, painted anthropomorphic plastic ornament, intricate geometric rouletting and applied gold foil surfaces are found in small quantities but enjoy a widespread distribution on from the Öresund to western Finland and Estonia (Stephan & Gaimster 2002, 159-161). Apart from a limited number of finds from the mercantile waterfront and mercantile residential districts of Stockholm and Turku, Finland, the middle to northern Baltic finds of this ornate group of stoneware drinking vessels are exclusive to castle and monastic sites (Gaimster 2001a, 57-59). To name but two examples, excavations in the 1920s and in the mid-1990s in the courtyard of Stockholm castle have produced fragments of three cylindrical chequer-rouletted goblets, while in 1987 a goblet fragment with the same chequer-board surface design was recovered from the outer bailey of the Bishop of Finland's castle and residence at Kuusisto, western Finland (*c.* 1318-1528). On the eastern Baltic coast a group of goblets recovered from the 1531 destruction levels at the Dominican monastery of St Catherine in Tallinn's lower town further emphasises the social premium of this particular Hanseatic trade good.

Archaeological finds have also demonstrated the extent to which utilitarian plain stoneware vessels were valued among those expatriate communities situated on the very margins of European cultural contact. Excavations on St James's Street in the Livonian frontier town of Tartu, Estonia, have produced an example of a standard fifteenth-century Siegburg beaker inside its original moulded leather container which was incised with a frieze of forest animals and birds (Gaimster 1999, fig.2). A further discovery at Greifswald on the Mecklenburg-Lower Pomerania coast of an early fifteenth-century Siegburg stoneware beaker encased within a tooled leather cover (Schäfer 2000, fig.159) reinforces the impression that, despite the ubiquity of western European stoneware in the region, such vessels were highly prized and their value could be enhanced through embellishment with another medium more suitable for decoration, in this case moulded and tooled leather (see Ch 7, p 291 for stoneware manufacturing sites).

The shifting distributions of forms, designs and iconography in the domestic ceramic market of the Baltic over the period of study form a guide to the penetration of new technologies and fashions, into the homes of the region's urban merchant communities and residential feudal elite, many of whom were living on the very edge of the European cultural orbit. For example, the remote Hanseatic *Kontor* of Novgorod, situated on the edge of the Russian pine forest, offers a case study in the archaeology of cultural resistance (Brisbane & Gaimster 2001; Fig 8.8). Here, despite the 'Hanseatic' signature of the range of imports excavated in the centre of the city, the relatively polarised distribution of western ceramics around the alien mercantile enclave contrasts strikingly with patterns recorded in nearby trading centres on the Livonian-Russian frontier, where western imports circulated more widely amongst the host community (Gaimster 2001b; Fig 8.9). Clearly in Novgorod, with its domestic wood culture, there was entrenched resistance to the use of highly decorated ceramic tableware from the West, irrespective of its technological superiority.

Fig 8.8   *Plan showing the polarized distribution of imported German stoneware and 'European' Baltic redware vessels inside the Russian city of Novgorod, with concentrations around the residential enclaves of Hanseatic merchants (from Gaimster 2001b).*

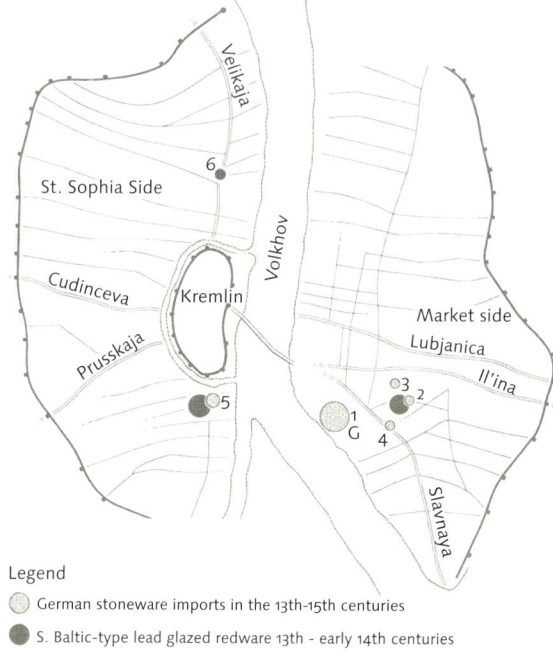

Legend
- German stoneware imports in the 13th-15th centuries
- S. Baltic-type lead glazed redware 13th - early 14th centuries

Fig 8.9   *Carved and painted wooden panel from the pew stall of the Novgorod Traders in the Church of St Nicholas, Stralsund, North Germany, c. 1400. The panel shows Russian hunters collecting pelts, pine resin and honey from the forest and delivering it to Hanseatic German merchants outside their fortified enclave within the city of Novgorod (Kulturhistorisches Museum, Stralsund).*

The smokeless ceramic tile-stove: a Hansa type-fossil

The archaeological evidence for the introduction of the smokeless ceramic tile-stove into the Baltic Sea region from central and western Europe forms a further key quantitative and qualitative measure of long distance trading connections together with cultural and technological transfer. Stove-tile finds make up just under 20 per cent of all domestic ceramics found on urban mercantile and residential feudal sites across the region and, as such, represent a key element in the Hanseatic domestic inventory and in trading activity (Gaimster 1999; 2000b; 2002b). Moulded tiles of various designs were used in the construction of large stoves of architectonic form, which were mainly erected in living spaces to form a key element of the domestic interior design (see Box 4.1). Ceramic stoves were normally fitted with stoke holes and flues which were serviced from another room or corridor so as to prevent any fumes polluting the room. Lead-glazed earthenware stoves contributed not only a technological transformation of the domestic environment but also, with the development from the mid-fifteenth century onwards of coloured glazes and moulded relief, they introduced a new visual and iconographic element into the home. Scenes from the lives of the Holy Family and the Saints based directly on the individual narrative compartments of carved wooden altar shrines of churches were replaced during the early stages of the Lutheran Reformation by the secular iconography of coats-of-arms and portrait busts of the region's temporal rulers and religious leaders. As with relief-decorated stoneware, the ceramic stove provided a symbolic medium for the introduction of new attitudes and beliefs on to the domestic scene.

Earthenware stove-tiles, in contrast to stoneware, were fragile and risky to transport over long distances. Although it is possible to identify rare instances of North or central German whiteware tiles imported into southern Scandinavia, it is clear from the number and distribution of production sites and from analysis of the fabrics that most stoves made in the Baltic region were manufactured locally, often with the use of moulds imported from northern and central Germany. Realistically, and following the model for redware manufacture in the thirteenth century, production on this scale can only be explained by the movement of specialist craftsmen or even workshops around and across the Baltic rim. The documentary evidence for German tile-makers (*pottomakare*) settling in Lund, Malmö, Kalmar in Sweden and Turku (Åbo) in Finland from the mid-sixteenth century illustrates the extent to which Continental craftsmen were attracted by the prospect of new markets opening up in the North (Gaimster 1999; 2005).

This network of demand and the migration of production are most evident in the series of rectangular pre-Reformation niche- and panel-tiles moulded in relief with biblical figures and scenes surrounded by architectural and botanical ornament derived from church altarpiece carving. A workshop assemblage of moulds and wasters, with designs including scenes from the Life of Christ, was found in the centre of Lübeck in 1939. Recent excavations in the cellar of a late fifteenth-century house on the Pläterstrasse in Rostock produced moulds and wasters contemporary with the Lübeck Fischergrube site. Both the Rostock and Lübeck assemblages contained matrix-identical moulds of the *Charity of St Martin* that suggests that the workshops were themselves linked (Burrows and Gaimster 2001). A further find of matrix-identical mould among pottery waste in the centre of Greifswald suggests the development of satellite workshops along the coast of Mecklenburg-Lower Pomerania, their advantageous location facilitating export to southern Scandinavia as finds of matrix -identical stove-tiles in Malmö indicate. The identification of matrix links and possible prototypes for the Rostock Pläterstrasse tile moulds in Hungary, Switzerland and the Upper Rhineland hints at the extent of Hanseatic commercial and cultural networks which were instrumental in the origin and movement of this Baltic craft industry. The design of several of the main Rostock moulds corresponds to tiles which form the ornate tower-stoves of the royal palace of Buda, Budapest, commissioned by the Habsburg Kings Ladislas V and Martinus Corvinus of Hungary between the 1450s and 1480s. The format of the moulds, their border ornament and their design repertoire of scenes drawn from the Life of Christ and the Lives of the Saints compare closely to the moulds found alongside production waste in the Norrmalm district on the outskirts of medieval Stockholm (Gaimster 2002a; here Fig 8.10).

In contrast to the uniform distributions of late medieval imported stoneware excavated from the town and the royal castle in Stockholm, the group of fifteenth-century stove-tiles with low-relief moulded ornament found in the cellars of the castle in the 1920s do not appear to have been distributed to any great extent amongst the urban population. The finds serve to highlight the class differential between Stockholm's royal court and mercantile households. The Stockholm castle group consists of a series

Fig 8.10 *A mould for the manufacture of stoves tiles excavated in Norrmalm district, Stockholm, Sweden, c. 1475-1500. Such moulds finds reflect the migration of redware potters and tilers from North Germany to Sweden in the 15th century (Stockholms Stadsmuseum).*

of square panel tiles, moulded in low relief with figurative, animal and mythological subjects, including St Olaf, a stag, a unicorn, a further fabulous beast, a pair of lovers in a garden, St George and the Dragon, an Imperial (double-headed) eagle (Gaimster 2001a, figs. 9-11; 2002a, 201). Outside Stockholm the form of the tiles and their iconography are unknown in Scandinavia and the northern Baltic, although a recent find of a waster moulded with the same full-length portrait of St Olaf from a redware production site in Pasewalk, Lower Pomerania, suggests that the type was being introduced into the southern Baltic region during the second half of the fifteenth century. The type represents the earliest known moulded relief stove-tiles in the Baltic region and the beginning of the transition to moulded panel relief from undecorated hollow vessel-shaped forms. The finds at Stockholm Castle suggest that the royal Swedish court was participating in the latest trends in interior design and heating technology being introduced from the central Europe. To find the closest parallels in terms of form and iconography one must look to the rich late medieval urban material culture of Bohemia and its castles, particularly in and around Prague, a centre of artistic culture linked to the Baltic through the Hanseatic commercial network.

Conclusion

Traded domestic ceramics fulfilled dual utilitarian and social roles among the medieval mercantile communities living in northern Europe. Their archaeological distributions provide a measure of the absorption and promotion of imported cultural codes and lifestyle practices, notably in the spheres of dining culture and domestic comfort. The study of individual luxury products and the composition of assemblages from high-status residential sites such as castles injects a dimension of social hierarchy into the analysis. One persistent pattern in the archaeological record is not just the evidence for long distance trade in domestic goods but, where possible and where the equivalent raw materials exist, the transplantation of their manufacture closer to the marketplace, as in the case of highly decorated red earthenware or moulded earthenware stove-tiles. Such relatively fragile ceramic products were less suited to long distance transportation, whereas stoneware, for which the appropriate raw materials were rare outside narrow seams of high-performance clays in western and central Europe, was robust enough for bulk sea-going transport.

The success of these commodities and manufacturing enterprises hints at something more than long-distance commercial transactions and the transfer of technical expertise. The patterns of consumption identified in the excavated record also reflect a brandan element of loyalty and a measure of the embedded cultural and possibly ethnic identities that characterise mercantile communities on the North Sea and Baltic rim, particularly those part of the Hanseatic trading network. The emerging material evidence points to a proto-colonial scenario comparable to early European contact sites in North America and the Caribbean where settlers asserted their cultural affiliations, ethnicity, class and religion through the active use of domestic goods and the transfer of indigenous craft production to service new markets overseas.

BOX 8.2   HANSEATIC KONTORE

Fig 1

Town plan of 1647 showing an aerial view of Stral-sund, N. Germany, with street plan and gabled brick houses typical of the Hanseatic trading town (Photo: Kulturhistorisches Museum, Stralsund, after original in National Archives, Stockholm) (D Gaimster).

Towns could be involved with the Hansa trade network in different ways (Immonen 2007). Some, mostly Northern German, were actual members of the league. The town of Lübeck, "Queen of the Hanseatic League", being the largest and politically most powerful, had a central position in the Hanseatic trade and expansion. Other German towns in the League included, among others, Greifswald, Hamburg, Kiel, Lüneburg, Rostock, Stralsund and Wismar (Fig 1). These towns also formed a major colonial force sending German colonists under Hanseatic control to the Baltic countries, where such towns as Danzig (Gdańsk), Dorpat (Tartu), Elbing (Elbląg), Reval (Tallinn), and Rīga were founded.

The Hanseatic League established *Kontore* ('counting houses') as their permanent trading posts in the most important northern European towns, among them the Steelyard in London, Brugge in Bruges, Belgium, Tyskerbryggen in Bergen, Norway, and the Kontor in Novgorod, Russia. Counting houses were enclaves of German urban culture, and for instance in London, formed a walled community with its own warehouses, weigh-house, church, offices, and living quarters. A large number of towns lacked a proper Kontor, but still had substantial communities of German merchants active in their trade and life. Hence, the Hanseatic influences not only affected the international trade routes and the urban setting of the Hanseatic towns themselves, but had fundamental effects on local economies throughout Northern Europe.

The wide geographical distribution of the Hansa as well as its supervision over trade and the prominent presence of its merchants in towns had great impact on contemporary material culture. Some art historians, like Nikolaus Zaske, maintain that *Hanseatic art* was an urban, burgher phenomenon formed under the socio-political auspices of the Hansa, and it is possible to distinguish a Hanseatic style as a special category in the European Gothic (Zaske & Zaske 1985). Jan von Bonsdorff (1990), by contrast, argues that the artefacts and architecture produced by Baltic craftsmen were simply part of the contemporary European style. Art historians have traditionally focused on such sumptuous artefacts as metalware and ecclesiastical works of art deposited in old museum collections and churches (see Ch 10, Fig 10.7). However, archaeologists examining more down to earth materials such as pottery and stove-tiles tell a more subtle story of cultural transfer and resistance.

by Visa Immonen

By the beginning of the thirteenth century, coinage was a regular, if not necessarily daily, element of the lives of most individuals. While corvées and other payments in labour or goods were still common, and some transactions on both the local and long-range level were covered by credit arrangements, many rents, wages and purchases were carried out by the exchange of minted coins. For much of the population, coins were the only physical emanation of governmental authority they came into regular contact with, and coin imagery would have become associated with the identity of the ruler (Fig 8.11).

Medieval European coins. (a) France, Philip Augustus, 1180-1223, silver denier [18 mm]. (b) Italy, Genoa, commune, 1272-1339, silver denaro [16 mm]; (c) Italy, Venice, Enrico Dandolo, 1192-1205, silver grosso [20 mm]; (d) France, Louis IX, 1266-1270, silver gros tournois [26 mm]; (e) Italy, Florence, commune, 1252-1303, gold florin [21 mm]; (f) Spain, Ferdinand and Isabella, 1474-1504, billon blanca [20 mm]; (g) France, Henri III, silver franc, 1586 [35 mm] (All coins are in the Numismatic Collection, Department of Rare Books and Special Collections, Firestone Library, Princeton University, and are illustrated with its permission). **Fig 8.11**

The Penny of the Central Middle Ages

Throughout Latin Europe, there was a single denomination in common use, the silver *penny*, known as the *denier* in French and the *Pfennig* in German. The terms of account *shilling* (*sou, Schilling*) for 12 *denarii* and *pound* (*livre, Pfund*) were used in counting and book-keeping, but only the penny existed as an actual coin. While all coins were issued by government authorities, these varied considerably according to the political situations: all of England used a single coinage produced in a dozen mints under royal control, but there were hundreds of minting authorities in the Germanic realms, including towns, bishoprics and monasteries as well as all levels of seigniorial authority.

Pennies varied widely in imagery, size, weight and purity of silver from issuer to issuer and were frequently subject to changes in standard over time, with the result that exchange above the local level often required the services of money changers. In some places (England, France, Italy) the coin imagery remained unchanged over long periods of time (even *immobilized* with the names of former rulers), while in other regions (Germany, Spain, Bohemia) coin imagery changed frequently, sometimes with the requirement that only current types were valid. Though conditions varied widely, as a rule of thumb one English sterling penny (about 1.35 grams of pure silver) equated to the daily wage of an unskilled adult male agricultural labourer.

Proliferation of denominations and means of exchange

The thirteenth century witnessed a proliferation of coinage denominations. Larger, purer silver coins were introduced as multiples of the penny; these usually took the name of *groat* (*gros, Groschen*). For the most part, these were tied into the local penny systems and often had a specific value in terms of the local *pound* of account, though often such values fluctuated over time.

Towards the end of the thirteenth century, gold coinage began to be minted in Europe for the first time since the seventh century. Several Italian communes produced gold coins on almost exactly the same standard: the *florin* of Florence and the *genovino* of Genoa, both introduced in 1252, and the *ducat* of Venice initiated in 1284 (all with about 3.53 grams of 24 carat gold). These circulated throughout Europe and became a common monetary standard, with a value floating against the various local pounds of account. Other issuers (most notably the monarchs of England and France) sought to mint gold coins whose value was tied to their silver-based currency. The inevitable changes in the relative worth of gold and silver (the bimetallic ratio) resulted in a constant manipulation of the silver and gold coins of these systems to keep them in tandem.

In the course of the fourteenth century, further denominations came into use, some intermediate between the penny and the groat and others representing fractions of the penny. The fifteenth century witnessed the first appearance of copper coinages from European mints; as the labour required to mint these coins was more expensive than the metal that went into them, their value was chiefly fiduciary. The fifteenth century also saw the introduction of *anno domini* dates onto coins, and in the sixteenth century marks of denomination became a feature of some coins.

With the proliferation of monetary metals and denominations, various coins became associated with different social and economic roles. Gold coins, especially the Italian ones of fixed standards, became the basis of international and interregional trade and taxation. The large silver coins were often used for salaries and for commerce on the regional level. The pennies and their fractions were used in local markets and for almsgiving.

By the end of the fourteenth century, Europe began to experience a shortage of bullion available for coinage, especially of silver. To some extent, this appears to have been the result of a steady drain of coins and ingots to the East in exchange for imported goods, as well as the exhaustion of traditional sources of ore. Bullion did not become plentiful again until the opening of new silver mines in Tyrol and Saxony in the late fifteenth century and the arrival of shipments of gold and silver from the New World in the sixteenth. One of the results of the replenishment of silver stocks was the appearance of the large silver dollar (*franc Thaler*) as a replacement for the medieval gold florins and ducats as the basis of monetary systems. Another was a general inflation beginning in the sixteenth century known as the Price Revolution of Early Modern Europe.

As economic systems increasingly came to depend on money, and as coinage became less available in the later Middle Ages, substitute forms of exchange came into common use. Money-changers, who had earlier been involved chiefly in the exchange of one type of coinage for another, increasingly became active in banking functions of deposit, credit and exchange. Banks of deposit offered a safe place for people to keep their wealth, as long as they did not go bankrupt. Bankers also got into the practice of advancing funds to merchants and rulers as credit; expected interest was often disguised to avoid the prohibitions on usury imposed by the medieval Church. A system of letters of credit tied together commercial centres throughout Europe; as these documents became standardized and transferrable through endorsement they came to resemble cheques and even paper money. Ultimately, however, all such bank transactions had to be settled with coinage or other forms of bullion; in the sixteenth century large currency fairs arose periodically to serve as clearing houses for such exchanges.

Coins and the archaeological record

Medieval coins enter the archaeological record in two distinct ways, as stray losses and as hoards. Stray losses, the result of unintentional loss of individual coins, are generally found either scattered in fields or by excavation. Scattered finds have until recently rarely been recorded, but in some European countries antiquities authorities are establishing databases of such finds, usually with the co-operation of metal detectorists.

Archaeological excavations, initiated either for scholarly research or on an emergency basis as a result of discovery during construction activities, allow a specific recording of where individual coins were lost, both within the context of a specific site or on a larger geographical basis. As a result of the fact that most of the coins of the central Middle

Ages (as well as the centuries immediately preceding) were relatively large silver pennies, sites from this period tend to be less plentiful in numismatic finds than those of antiquity or the later periods, when copper-based coins prevail. This is a factor both of the dull colour of copper-based coins and the less strong incentives for losers to recover them. As in classical archaeology, the stratified discovery of coins is often the excavator's best guide as to the chronology of site features (see also Ch 1, p 46).

Pennies of the central Middle Ages, as well as the higher denominations of later periods, are known chiefly as a result of the discovery of hoards. As a result of the scarcity of banks and other safe forms of wealth storage, medieval individuals often buried their valuables routinely at night or on such occasions as their departure for a trip or the feared arrival of hostile forces. As such burials were generally unmarked and frequently at a distance from habitation sites, they occasionally remained unretrieved until found in recent times, either by extended and deeper ploughing in the nineteenth century or by metal detectors in more recent times. In many cases, the find spots of such hoards have been intentionally obscured by finders and dealers, so their geographical context has been lost. In cases where the coins are kept together long enough for study and recording, they provide an internal context by documenting various coins that were available for burial at the same time. The comparison of the presence of issues in various hoards is one of the chief methods for the establishment of chronologies of coinages that do not bear dates or other key criteria for dating.

There are some useful sources to help identify and interpret coins found in archaeological investigations. One of the few comprehensive studies of money in Early Modern Europe is Braudel and Spooner 1967. For the range of coins produced, Engel and Serrure (1891-1905) is still the point of reference. The series *Medieval European Coinage* is intended as a complete guide to the subject but as of 2009, only Volume 1, *The Early Middle Ages,* and Volume 14, *Southern Italy* have appeared. An excellent summary of the development of medieval coinage is Spufford 1988, with Spufford 1986 for exchange rates. A more recent survey is Grierson 1991 and see Stahl 2000 for a detailed study one of the most important medieval mints. The most comprehensive printed bibliography on medieval coinage is Grierson 1976; a more up-to-date online bibliography will be found in Stahl 2010.

BOX 8.3 REUSED COINS IN THE ENGLISH LATER MEDIEVAL PERIOD (C1200-1600)

The study of coins should not be restricted to monetary themes such as mint output, circulation, metrology and the composition of hoards. One new direction, which is under-researched in medieval archaeology, is the adaption of coins to serve non-currency roles. A familiar method of re-using coins, for example, was to incorporate them into items of jewellery such as pendants, rings and brooches. This sort of adaption has a long tradition from the Roman period onwards, and in England from the 1050s it was silver pennies, principally those of Edward the Confessor, which were mounted with fittings to be attached to clothing as badges. Coins of this period invariably carried a stylised cross on their reverses and these were, more often than not, gilded for display. Until recently, this trend was thought to peter out by the middle of the twelfth century but metal detector finds are now beginning to have a serious impact on the known quantity and range of coin-jewellery. Among these finds are three thirteenth century coins from Lincolnshire and Norfolk which were converted into annular brooches; two pennies of Henry III and a rare Bergamese *grosso* of Emperor Frederick II. In each case the central roundel has been removed and a small hole drilled in the ring in order to take a pin. In so doing, the lifespan of the coin was no longer contingent upon the normal rules of monetary circulation – an old coin was transformed into something new and different. One suggestion is that coin jewellery may have been handed down from one generation to the next as heirlooms or mementoes of the past and the dead.

Other than badges and brooches, pendants sometimes also took the form of a gilded coin in the thirteenth to sixteenth centuries. They were usually pennies with a loop soldered at the top of the reverse cross. Two examples, a Henry III Long Cross penny from an unknown source and an Edward I penny found at New Romney, Kent, include collets for the setting of stones. The former retains three red glass inserts in the collets while the Edwardian coin shows scarring where the collets embellished the reverse cross of the coin (Fig 1 *top*) revealing the pendants as having a probable prophylactic (protective) purpose. The largest single group of converted coins from this period are those with a soldered loop and hook on the obverse and a gilded reverse, again designed to emphasise the cross (Fig 1 *bottom*). These appear at the very end of the thirteenth century using the four-penny groats of Edward I which were issued briefly between 1279-81. When the groats ceased production, similar-sized *gros* from France and the Low Countries (and the occasional English penny) were used instead. The loop was intended to be sewn onto a garment so that the hook could be secured to the opposite side. The fashion for coin-jewellery seems not to have survived beyond the 1320s and only the occasional piece, such as a gold noble of Edward IV mounted as a pendant, is known beyond this date. More humble, singly pierced, coins are a feature of the finds record throughout the period that is only now beginning to be recognised. They were likely to have served as amulets and are most common in coins minted 1464-1544.

In addition to the re-use of coins in jewellery, many more folded coins have also been recorded thanks to advances in the registering of metal detector finds in England and Wales. Previously, folded coins were known only from a handful of excavations at religious sites and from the Thames foreshore, but now there is evidence for this practice from most counties in England. A papal commission into the canonization of Thomas Cantilupe at Hereford in 1307 called the phenomenon of coin bending 'the English custom'. Whether or not the commission was correct in its assumption has yet to be established, but coins were apparently bent when making a vow to a saint to cure some illness or affliction, the folded coin being the token presented by the pilgrim at the saint's shrine in the hope of miraculous relief. Examples of successful healing come from a number of shrines, such as those of Thomas Cantilupe at Hereford, Simon de Montfort and Henry VI at Windsor (Finucane 1977, 94, 115; Spencer 1978, 243). It was not only the sick who performed such actions, pennies are recorded as being bent to cure a horse of blindness, for the health of Edward I's hawks and chargers each year and even to stop the spreading of a fire or to avoid shipwreck (Finucane 1977, 94). Silver pennies seem to have been the preferred choice for bending, but there are instances where gold coins were used.

Medieval coins may also be found in unexpected contexts, such as graves. Here they are usually placed at the shoulder of the dead person (in England and in Normandy, for example), or in the mouth and could thus play a part in funerary rites. A skeleton from Bristol had two folded pennies at the shoulders. Coins have also been found built into the fabric of excavated ships in Wales and Guernsey, usually under the main mast. In Italy, and to a lesser extent in England, coins were placed in tombs by visiting pilgrims and

there is good evidence in Italy and Germany for coins being used as foundation deposits in high-status buildings. Scandinavian churches are well-known for the quantity of coins excavated from their floors and in eastern Europe coins have been found in association with hearths (Suchodolski 1996). As these examples illustrate, coins have a contribution to make to our understanding of medieval attitudes to display, religion, healing and superstition across Europe. The fact that coins have their own discipline in numismatics has often meant that they are divorced from more general debates on medieval material culture; but that is now set to change.

by Richard Kelleher

Fig 1

Pennies of Edward I converted into jewellery. Top: pendant from New Romney, Kent (Treasure Annual Reports 2000, 151); bottom: dress hook from Urchfont, Wiltshire (Treasure Annual Reports 2008, T218; see http://finds.org.uk/treasure/reports).

The trade in exotic beasts

Throughout the course of the Middle Ages there was a growing demand for exotic (i.e. non-native) animals. Rare skeletal fragments of lions and monkeys from across Europe complement the more extensive documentary and artistic record of their place in aristocratic collections, and the houses of prosperous clerics and merchants. Raw materials derived from the bodies of exotic species were also sought after for the aristocratic market, particularly elephant and walrus ivory, as well as the furs of Scandinavian and eastern European mammals. Most interestingly, the body parts of some exotics were transformed into artefacts; a process where their zoological identity was reconfigured.

Living marvels

Strange and unfamiliar creatures from the edges of the known world were described by contemporary intellectuals as *mirabilis* or 'marvels' (Le Goff 1988: 27), and they were increasingly imported into Europe in the second millennium. Live exotics, particularly lions, are documented in royal and princely collections or 'menageries' in the twelfth and thirteenth centuries (Loisel 1912). From the fourteenth century, the ownership of such animals extended to the greater nobility and even municipal authorities. Monkeys, obtained from North Africa, appear to have been popular with gentry, merchants and clerics, and their discarded remains have been found in a handful of contexts from

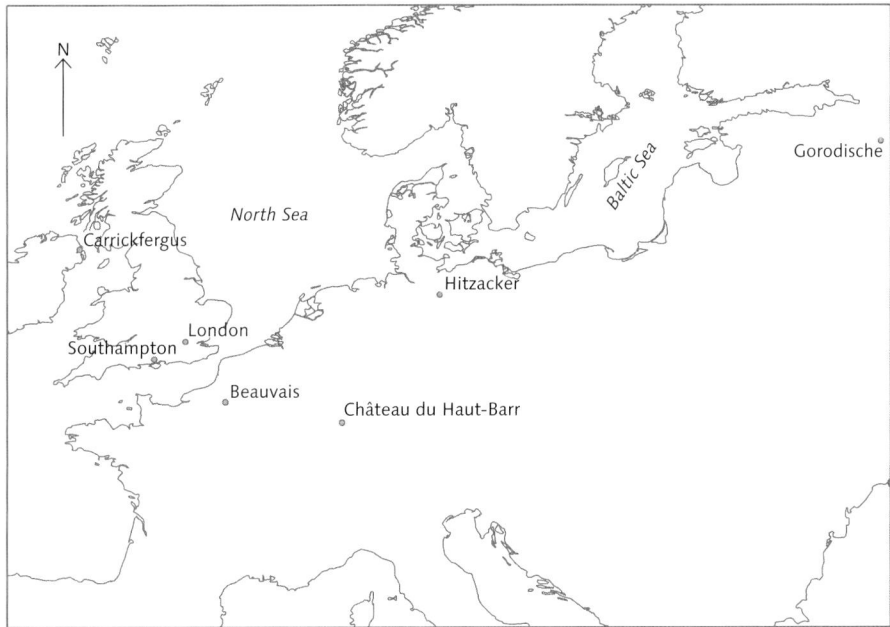

The distribution of monkey remains recovered from medieval north European archaeological contexts. **Fig 8.12**

Ireland to Russia (Fig 8.12) (Brisbane *et al* 2007). The recovery of two lion skulls (radiocarbon dated to 1280-1385 and 1420-80) (alongside the partial skull of a leopard, dated 1440-1625) from excavations in the moat of the Tower of London indicated no interest in preserving the carcass or pelt (O'Regan, Turner & Sabin 2006). After Portuguese expansion into western Africa and the Indian Ocean, and the colonisation of the New World, the trade in exotic animals exploded. At this time direct experience of the exotic began to supersede earlier, medieval constructions rooted in allegory, literature and emblematic art (Pluskowski 2009: 120-1).

Horns and claws

The body parts of exotic animals were more frequently moved around the international trade routes of later medieval Europe (Pluskowski 2009). The process of acquiring these products involved a curious transformation of identity, resulting in narwhal tusk from western Greenland being categorised as unicorn horn, and ibex horns from the Near East or bison horns from the Eastern Baltic becoming griffin claws. This transformation was not so much about duplicity as cultural relevance and re-contextualisation. Unicorn products were far more desirable than the body parts of an obscure Arctic whale. Initially incorporated into ecclesiastical paraphernalia such as crosier and processional staffs, perhaps because of the spiritual significance of the spiralling pattern, unicorn horn, either as a raw material or converted into artefacts such as jewellery was subsequently sought after by the nobility (Pluskowski 2005). Only a few medieval pieces are still extant, and suggest the spiralling pattern of the tusk came to be closely associated with representations of the unicorn in art by around 1200, perhaps in response to the importation of narwhal tusks (Gotfredsen 1999:152). By the fourteenth century, the

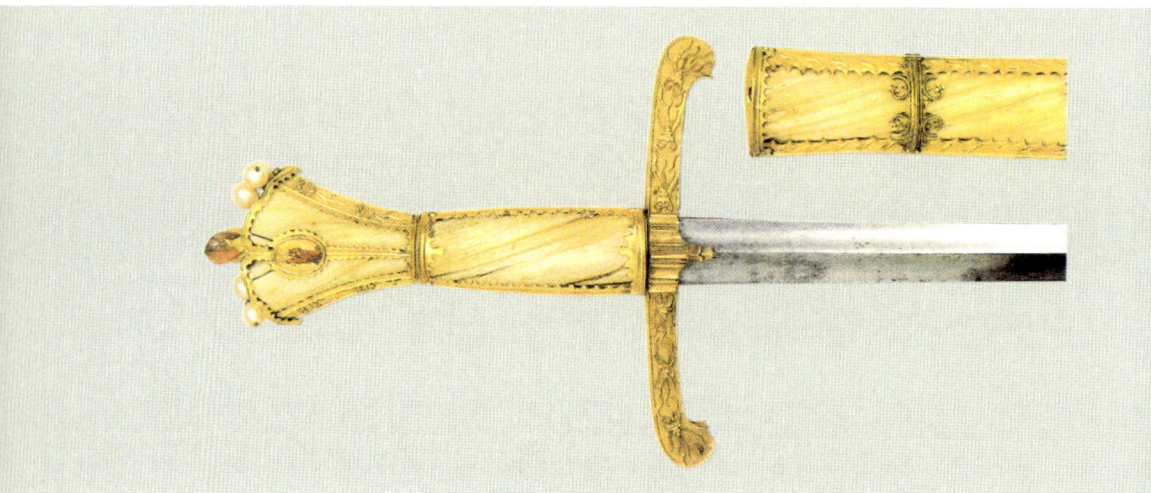

Fig 8.13   *The Ainkhürnschwert or 'unicorn sword' of Charles the Bold, Duke of Burgundy (1433-1477), now housed in the Imperial Treasury (Schatzkammer) in Vienna.*

zoological identification of narwhal tusk as unicorn horn was so firmly established that retaining its distinctive shape was no longer necessary; it could be chopped up and incorporated into a range of artefacts (Fig 8.13). The symbolism of the unicorn in Christian Europe is elaborate and multi-variant, but its horn was consistently thought to effectively ward against poison; and the unicorn hunt, a popular artistic motif especially in the later medieval period, was conceptualised as the quest for Christ and for salvation (Grössinger 1998; Gotfredsen 1999). The heraldic use of the unicorn remained limited compared to the lion and eagle, but some powerful families adopted it as their emblem, most famously the kings of Scotland, who also possessed unicorn products in their treasury at Stirling.

Ivory and fur

The movement of exotic animal products in the form of body parts that represented what we would consider to be fantastic creatures, was eclectic and limited compared to the trade in ivory and fur. These two luxury commodities, derived from a variety of species, were fundamental to the culture of the later medieval aristocracy, as well as to the economies of their source regions. Elephant ivory was obtained from Eastern Africa and India; walrus ivory from the circumpolar regions of Greenland, Iceland, Arctic Norway and the White Sea (Pluskowski 2009:122). Raw walrus ivory was exported to workshops in the British Isles (particularly Winchester), southern Scandinavia (e.g. Lund), western Russia (e.g. Novgorod) and other places, although walrus skulls may also have been used in household display. A number of examples, whole and fragmentary, some even decorated, have been found in Trondheim, Bergen, Oslo, Uppsala, Sigtuna, Lund, Schleswig, Dublin and Novgorod (Roesdahl 2003b:150; 2005, with distribution map). Elephant ivory was initially predominantly associated with production centres in north-east Africa and southern Italy, where elephant tusks were elaborately decorated and produced for an aristocratic market. Around 75 carved elephant tusks or 'oliphants' are extant in museums, private collections and church treasuries around the world, although written sources, particularly church inventories, suggest many more (Shalem 2004:152). The majority derive from south Italy, probably commissioned by Normans. During the crusades, these artefacts may have been regarded as the attribute of a valiant knight, exemplified in the *Chanson de Roland,* which was popular with the Norman elite, although the dominance of oriental motifs on oliphants suggests an additional Eastern aspect to their meaning. Their secular function was short-lived; eleventh and twelfth century inventories indicate that many of these artefacts were donated to churches soon after they were made (Shalem 1998:106-7). The most important workshops for ivory after this period were to be found in Paris from 1270-1400. Here artisans produced the majority of the 2000-3000 medieval ivory objects which are extant today and which were shipped all over Europe, representing some of the finest craftsmanship of the later medieval period (Barnet 1997).

Fur-wearing was an established aristocratic practice by the twelfth century, when the use of ermine (stoat's winter coat), miniver (stoat's unspotted coat) and vair (red squirrel) in garments and heraldry expressed a symbolic and commercial hierarchy (Delort 1978; Pluskowski 2007c, 36). By the fourteenth century, fur-wearing had proliferated amongst lower social groups such as merchants and craftsmen, prompting sumptuary legislation in many regions of Europe to restrict the use of fur to the nobility, exemplifying its function as a social marker in visual display. Sources of fur varied; Scandinavians dominated the fur trade into the high medieval period, but various regions across Europe gradually became known for producing specific types of fur (Fig 8.14). Traces of fur working are rarely encountered at medieval sites, but they tend to occur more frequently in supply regions, particularly – in the case of luxury furs – north-eastern Europe, the Scandinavian Peninsula and Russia. This reflects the ecological dimension of the fur trade, which developed in regions with abundant populations of fur-bearing species.

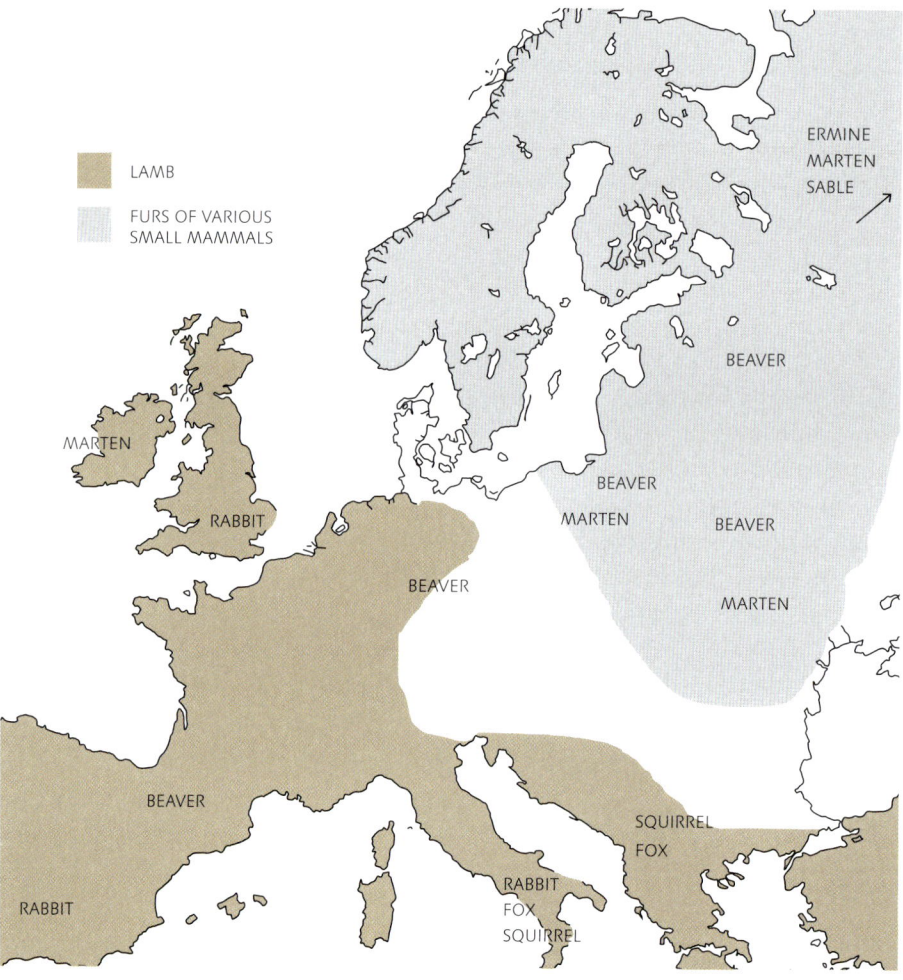

Fig 8.14   *Fur-producing regions in later medieval Europe (after Delort 1978).*

The process of Europeanisation saw the extension of an international fur trade network, involving trappers, furriers and merchants, already present in the early medieval period. In Livonia (which became known as a major exporter of furs), the exploitation of beaver pre-dates the Christian period (beginning in the thirteenth century with the crusades) and may have had a cultic aspect. Certainly faunal assemblages from castles of the Teutonic Order in the region reflect the continued trapping and working of fur from beaver, fox, marten and hare (Mugurēvičs 2002:178-179). Isolated examples of fur working most likely represent opportunistic skinning, such as a rare find of a butchered lynx skeleton in Hungary (Bartosiewicz 1993); even in Livonia where documentary sources hint at the abundance of this species, lynx remains account for less than 1% of medieval faunal assemblages (Mugurēvičs and Mugurēvičs 1999). Indeed, furs from the other large indigenous carnivores – wolves and bears – are infrequently encountered outside their source regions in documentary sources (Delort 1978); for one reason or another, there was little international market for these furs. The growing population of rabbits – exotics introduced into Western Europe and contained in warrens (see Ch 3, p 2, 91) – provided a readily exportable source of fur. In towns across Europe, feral populations of cats with mixed coats provided the cheapest source of fur, which sought to emulate the more expensive products. The most unusual fur derived from leopards, and was sought after for lining garments, or for use as a coverlet or rug. Fragments of leopard crania have been recovered in Hungary, but documentary sources indicate this was a widely traded product (Pluskowski 2007c, 43-44). By the thirteenth century, the international fur trade was dominated by the Russian principalities, especially Novgorod. However, by the end of the fifteenth century this had been eclipsed by Moscow, which came to dominate both Russian politics and the fur trade (Martin J 1986).

The rising trade with Africa *by Sam Nixon*

The period AD 1200-1600 saw an exponential growth in European contacts with Africa, and in the economic importance of Africa for Europe (Fig 8.15). In AD 1200, while trade with the North African coastal region was steady, there were as yet no European trading settlements there (Devisse and Labib 1984), and the sub-Saharan world to which the North African Muslim cities were already strongly linked by cross-Saharan trade networks was almost completely unknown to Europeans (Devisse 1988; Nixon 2009). By AD 1600, the whole of the African continent was ringed with European forts and trading stations, Africa and Africans were strongly part of the European scene (Northrup 2002; Earle and Lowe 2005), and Africa's trade goods were essential for Europe, especially its slaves for the newly discovered Americas.

Trade with North Africa and trans-Saharan connections

European trade with North Africa had maintained a steady growth after the decline of the Roman Empire, North African products such as grain, oil, dates and salted fish being exchanged for European products such as textiles, copper, timber and metalware. In

Fig 8.15 *Map of Africa illustrating the development of European trade links in the late medieval period. As well as selected sites directly associated with European contact, also shown are important centres of Islamic cross-Saharan trade where European products were sold.*

the eleventh and twelfth centuries, trade between Europe and North Africa began to increase considerably (Devisse and Labib 1984; Fernandez-Armesto 1987). The Crusades and the *Reconquista* of Iberian lands helped to spur increased knowledge of Islamic wealth and desirables. Europe was also becoming increasingly wealthy, powerful and economically expansive, creating new markets for these products. This trade was conducted by southern European coastal cities, notably Venice. North African markets offered not only Islamic products and eastern spices but African gold, slaves and ivory via the flourishing Islamic trans-Saharan trade, gold and slaves being especially important for the expanding European currency and labour force. From the thirteenth century, the increasing power of European groups enabled the creation of commercial colonies in Mallorca and the Canary Islands and permanent European quarters in North African cities (e.g. Tunis, Tripoli and Oran) (Devisse and Labib 1984). This process set in train a scramble for North African commerce, which continued even following the European discovery of sub-Saharan Africa by coastal routes in the fifteenth century.

African Islamic pottery found in Europe has enabled improved understanding of the intensification and geography of trade between Europe and North Africa in the late medieval period (above, p 302). Luxury wares show this pottery was not merely a container for the goods that are documented historically, but an important trade item in its own right, as a desirable object of display. Islamic glass from North Africa has also shown up in Europe in not inconsiderable quantities (Mack 2002), providing insights into this little discussed but historically important luxury item (see Ch 7, p 307). Islamic glass beads, while perhaps less of a high-status desirable commodity, have also been recorded in European contexts and the extent of their circulation needs to be quantified. While gold finds in Europe from this era are rare, the archaeological potential in investigating even limited museum collections is great. Chemical techniques can tell us for instance how much of the European gold coinages – struck from 1173 onwards –relied on African gold sources (Guerra *et al* 1999). Excavations in West Africa have also evidenced the ivory sent to North African markets where Europeans traded, including somewhat surprisingly hippo as well as elephant ivory (Insoll 1996: 98). And amongst exotic animal remains found in Europe (see above), DNA analysis of fourteenth-century lion remains found in London has shown that wild animals were coming to Europe through North Africa.

Comprehensive work on the site of Qasr-es-Seghir in Morocco (Redman 1986) – occupied by Portugal in the fifteenth and sixteenth centuries – demonstrates the wealth of data potentially available from the archaeology of European coastal colonies in North Africa. Not only are town structure and lifeways illuminated – showing a veritable 'Europe abroad' – a good idea of the range of European imports to these places can also be gauged. Other European colonies in North Africa can be seen, such as the spectacular remains at Mazagan, but while work is underway, significant archaeology is yet to be published. It would certainly be interesting to see how much earlier colonies resembled the picture constructed at Qasr-es-Seghir. Beyond the coast, there has been some investigation of important trading cities where Europeans are known to have traded, most notably Sijilmasa, a major trading town at the northern edge of the trans-Saharan network which supplied sub-Saharan African products to the coast (Messier 1997). But the extent of the European material presence in these towns is yet to be gauged.

While European traders were not able to infiltrate the trans-Saharan system to establish direct trade links with sub-Saharan Africa, European products were certainly traded across the Sahara by Muslim merchants. Archaeology from the trans-Saharan entrepots south of the Sahara such as Audaghust, Gao, Tadmakka (or Tadmekka) and Timbuktu (see Fig 8.15) is beginning to provide an improved sense of the European products traded on from North Africa to sub-Saharan Africa (Insoll 2003; Nixon 2009). Copper was shipped in huge quantities across the Sahara as it was the main commodity exchanged for gold, and chemical techniques are beginning to show that early trans Saharan shipments of copper were likely significantly composed of European copper (Fenn *et al* 2009). Excavations at the entrepots south of the Sahara have also recovered large quantities of glass vessels and glass beads supposedly traded from Europe. The remarkable preservation at these towns has even enabled the recovery of textiles, also recorded as having a European provenance. Instances of other individual European items found which moved across the Sahara are twelfth-thirteenth-century swords (Joire 1955), a Richard II era (late-fourteenth century) bronze ewer (Posnansky 1973), and an eleventh-century Islamic tombstone brought from Spain (Insoll 2003).

The fifteenth-century Age of Discovery

While certain trading profits were to be made in North Africa, Europeans increasingly sought to venture further south along the Atlantic coast, thereby gaining direct access to African gold and slaves, and a route to the Indies and its spices (Newitt 2004). Another motive was to find and ally with the fabled Christian king of Africa Prester John, and thereby combat the growth of Muslim economic and cultural influence. From the early fifteenth century European discovery south of the Sahara began, thanks certainly to the northern adoption of the lateen sail (see above, p 331) – necessary to successfully round Cape Bojador and return – but also due to state backing and economic readiness, led most famously by Prince Henry the Navigator of Portugal. The explorers and traders moved down along this unknown coast in stages, charting new territory and reporting back to the Portuguese crown. By the 1430s they were below the Sahara, by 1449 the Cape Verde Islands, the Guinea Islands by 1472, the River Congo by 1482, and by 1488 Port Elizabeth beyond the South African Cape. Building on this knowledge Vasco de Gama was to return in 1499 having charted the coast of East Africa and reached the Indies.

While many of the explorers' exploits and activities left no trace, they did leave *padrões*, stone crosses bearing the arms of Portugal and intended to register land claims (Fig 8.16). Historical records mention the erecting of crosses between the River Congo and the Cape by the famous explorers Diogo Cáo and Bartolomeu Dias (Ravenstein 1900; Axelson 1973). Seven *padrão* are reported – including their destruction or veneration by locals – but the records are not specific about their precise form or position. Sketches and the collection of fragments by travellers of the Victorian era led to an increase in information (Ravenstein 1900), but it was only in the 1930s that an archaeologist, Axelson, set out to document, excavate and collect as far as possible the remains of the stone crosses mentioned in texts, successfully locating six of them (Alexson 1961, 1973). The most famous is that left at Kwaaihoek, near Port Elizabeth, on the coast of South Africa's Eastern Cape province, the site marked by Dias after becoming the first European to round the South African Cape in 1488. Alexson's study firstly clarified ideas of iconography – in particular showing that Arabic was not used for inscriptions despite historical documents stating this – as well as defining formal types. His investigations gave a more accurate idea of the specific positioning of the *padrao* choice of position within the landscape, as well as clarifying a crucial debate concerning the furthest point of Dias's journey.

Fig 8.16

Padrão de São Gregorio placed near Port Elizabeth in 1488 by Bartolomeu Dias, now located at the University of Witwatersrand (photo: Victor Couto).

While it is possible that a range of monumental '*padrão*' inscriptions existed on rocks, the only series of inscriptions so far found are those on the stone of Yalala, up the Congo River (Lewis 1908: 589-591; Axelson 1973: 75-76). This completely intact and remarkable inscription, never recorded in historical documents, records the arrival of Diogo Cão's ships on the Congo in 1482, as well as later voyagers to the spot; another fascinating insight into iconography and place in the African trade.

Sub-Saharan trading settlements

The best-known early European sub-Saharan settlements are the coastal forts designed to serve as storage/supply centres for trade with the African interior and stopover points for further exploration, ultimately to the Indies. The foundation of many of these is documented in historical records. Even before the great voyages of Dias and Cão, the fort of Arguin was built off the coast of Mauretania (1441). Forts followed at Elmina in Ghana (1482) and at Sofala on the East African coast (1505). While a variety of goods were sought, including gold, increasingly these places came to serve as slave trading stations; this became the most profitable trade, especially following the discovery of the Americas. Settlement was not limited to the coast, the forts being linked to interior trading factories, Arguin for instance being linked to one at Oudane, and beyond the East African coast a network of settlements was established within the Mutapa state (Pikirayi 2009). Certain more expansive colonies developed, namely in Angola (particularly the settlements of Luanda and Benguela), and on islands off the coast, such as the Cape Verde Islands and the Guinea Islands. Throughout the sixteenth century, forts and associated settlement continued to be constructed, soon multiplying, to establish a tradition that went on for the next three centuries. Other than the island colonies and Angola, interior settlements did not expand further in the late medieval era and many were disbanded.

The sub-Saharan coastal forts offer some of the clearest archaeology of the European-African trade encounter, as their locations are well known and they have often survived later redevelopment. The early fort best known from archaeology is that of Elmina in Ghana (see Fig 8.17; and De Corse 2001). Investigations here have provided an understanding of the initial architectural design, and evidence for ways of living, such as diet and material culture. These are data only dimly visible in historical records. Additionally, the investigation has provided valuable information about the settlement created around the fort walls by Africans. Another good excavated example is Fort Jesus (1593), built right at the end of the period we are dealing with, showing the further potential of this fort archaeology (Kirkman 1974). The locations of other early forts are well known, including the earliest, Arguin (Monod 1983), and future investigations will no doubt tell us more about them.

Amongst the trading towns and networks inland, the best known archaeological example has long been a study on the seventeenth-century Hueda kingdom (in modern Benin), which amongst other things importantly showed the circumscribed lives traders lived next to the Royal palace (at Savi) and the African use of European trade goods

Excavations in the vicinity of Elmina fort, Ghana (photo courtesy of Christopher DeCorse, Department of Anthropology, Syracuse University).   **Fig 8.17**

(Kelly 1997). Less discussed, but fascinating, are the studies that have been conducted on the sixteenth-century Portuguese trading settlements in the Mutapa state, such as at Massapa (Pikirayi 2009). Also, on Gorée Island (Senegal), work has started to uncover settlements, and this has already contributed to the debate over how important a place this was (Thiaw 2008). At present, investigations are also underway at Cidade Velha in the Cape Verde Islands (Rodriguez 1997) which includes investigation of the earliest colonial church in the world, built in 1495, and also a sixteenth-century fort (Evans *et al* 2007). Not only does archaeology give us insights into European trading settlements and their immediate surroundings, it can give us insights into the wider surrounding African peoples and environments which European trade and settlement operated within, only partially seen from history and art history. African historical archaeology is a major developing area of research and offers a mine of information on this (see Swanepoel 2009).

Shipwrecks south of the Sahara

The iconic ships which enabled the sub-Saharan African trade and the passage to the Indies are the caravel and the Indiaman. Not only were these ships the technological marvel of the trade and the means of passage, they were often villages at sea, and trading places in themselves in lieu of a safe landfall. Well-known excavated vessels from this period are the mid sixteenth-century ships the Bom Jesus and the São Bento, found in Southern African waters (see Smith R 2009; Mitchell 2002). Perhaps the greatest wealth of shipwreck data being generated is by the firm Arqueonautas, who have conducted major surveys on concessions they have obtained in areas where shipwreck concentrations are believed to be, such as Cidade Velha in Cape Verde (see Arqueonautas website). Representative collections from these investigations are making their way into museums and the finds are being well documented (the Cidade Velha wrecks by Margaret Rule and Alejandro Mirabal, and the important wreck of the Espardarte (1558) from Mozambique by Mensun Bound).

The recovery of parts of ships during these excavations – including for instance a complete hull (Smith 2009) – is telling us about the shipbuilding technology of these vessels of the Africa routes, including hull design, rigging and how they evolved. The quantity of artefacts coming from these shipwrecks is immense, including ivory, gold, coins, copper, military equipment and personal possessions (see Arqueonautas website). The recovery of rare individual items such as astrolabes can shed insight on little-known navigational ideas. Reconstruction of the material culture baggage of passengers on board is hugely advanced by recovery of such items as combs, culinary materials and shoes, as well as more unexpected items such as syphilis needles (Smith 2009). We also learn of the profusion of European coinages which were held on these ships, and also Moorish coins (Smith 2009). The wreck assemblage improves understanding of how settlements were provisioned, including the recovery of 'Olive Jars' more commonly known from New World contexts. Beyond all this, the assemblages are expressive of the goods that were being traded between Europe and the African continent from the fifteenth century onwards.

The goods trade south of the Sahara

With direct contact with sub-Saharan Africa, Europe had unprecedented opportunity for goods exchange with sub-Saharan African groups (for following see Devisse and Labib 1984; DeCorse 2001; Thornton 1998; Blake J 1942; Monod 1983). One of the key products immediately sought were slaves, and already by 1441 the famous slave trading market, the Mercato des Escravos, was created in Lagos, Portugal. This slave trade became even more important with the discovery of the Americas. By the mid-sixteenth century black African districts developed in Europe, and these were significantly composed of slaves; Lisbon for instance was 10% black African by the mid-sixteenth century (Northrup 2002: 8).

Gold was also sought and was hugely important, at least until the discovery of the supply of American gold. Other prominent products were sugar, woven mats, and the pepper substitute 'Grains of Paradise'. We know from historical records and museum collections (Bassani 2000) that a range of individual items and curiosities started to come back to Europe, none more famous than the 'Afro-Portuguese ivories', the highly ornamental virtuoso ivory carvings produced by African manufacturers for Europeans (Bassani and Fagg 1988). In exchange for these African products, a profusion of European goods was offered, including the key products copper, cloth and beads. The range of other products included such things as needles and looking glasses. Also, many of the products sold were not European but Islamic and Oriental, and indeed African products purchased at other points along the coast.

One of the most significant trade items recorded historically are copper manillas, a mid-sixteenth-century record of a single order for 1,000,000 copper manillas clearly demonstrating this (see Mitchell 2005:187). Large quantities of the horseshoe-shaped copper manillas have now been found (see Fig 8.18; and Smith 2009 and Arqueonautas). Their form is remarkably similar to the copper manillas traded by Muslim traders within the trans-Saharan system and chemical/technical analysis is being used to investigate the origins and production of alloys used to produce them (Benito and Ibanez 2005). Archaeology has provided very good recovery and insight into the profusion of glass beads traded by Europeans (see e.g. De Corse 2001). Finds of pottery not only allow us to chart the movement of European wares, such as German stonewares, but we can also see that imported Oriental pottery was sold on to Africans (see Mitchell 2005). Amongst the other kinds of material evidence moving under the radar of historical documentation are brass crucifixes, offering a fascinating insight into the nature of early exported religious paraphernalia (see Fig 8.18; and see Arqueonautas). Recovery of glass alcohol bottles and Dutch bricks from later contexts (Kelly 1997) shows us the range of things likely to turn up as investigations of shipwrecks and coastal trading sites proceed.

So far the insights into African goods coming into Europe are more limited but shipwrecks are starting to show their potential. Findings of Portuguese ivory shipments featuring owners marks, large quantities of contraband gold, gold trade beads (see Fig 8.18), and peppercorns have already turned up (see Arqueonautas website), and evidence such as the 200 log cache of ebony from a later wreck (Kirkman 1974) shows the potential of these wrecks to rediscover concentrations of trade goods.

(left) Copper manilla excavated from a Cape Verde Islands shipwreck, dated mid-17th century; (centre) **Fig 8.18**
copper crucifixes excavated from a Cape Verde Islands' shipwreck, mid-17th century; (right) gold trade beads excavated from a Mozambique shipwreck, early-17th century (photos courtesy of Alejandro Mirabal).

CHAPTER 9

TOWNS

PART 1: THE DEVELOPMENT OF MEDIEVAL TOWNS *by Hans Andersson*

Definitions

In most societies there are central places, where people meet to perform duties of political, economical, social, religious and cultural character. Those in power also use such places to control the surrounding regions. What is a central place? What is a city or a town? Central places differ in their appearance from period to period and region to region, and may perform a variety of functions, but they are thought to be connected by a characteristic that we call "urban." Important considerations for research in the Later Middle Ages are the mode, degree and significance of urbanisation.

Archaeology studies the physical manifestations of a settlement and life within it, and archaeological work in old cities and towns as well as in smaller central places or market places has been intensive in Europe and beyond. It has been especially strong over the last 40 years, although coverage remains uneven from country to country (Council of Europe 1999; Schofield 2003; Schofield & Vince 2005, 1-19). But archaeology has not influenced the general urbanisation discussion to the extent it deserves. Archaeologists themselves have not always followed the important discussions that are going on in other disciplines. The study of urbanism can profit from the integration of archaeological with historical and geographical approaches.

Which are the towns? Urban criteria may be defined in three main ways: administrative, topographical and functional (Haase 1960), none of which is sufficient on its own. Historical research tends to rely on documented administrative status, as read from charters and privileges. The geographic approach describes processes of nucleation on the ground, whereby people aggregate and share tasks, resulting in a hierarchy of specialisation. The ascription of functional criteria is insufficient, since central functions can also be found in other types of places, which cannot physically be defined as towns. In Europe, there are regions where towns are entirely lacking, for example in northern Scandinavia and in Iceland, but it is still possible to find places with one or several central functions. Such "simpler" central places can of course also be found in regions with fully developed towns. Sometimes, therefore, it is more appropriate to talk about central regions than central places (Andersson H 2002).

For the archaeologist this suggests the benefits of keeping an open mind (Andersson H 2003). The places we study are part of a greater process, but the forms can be radically different, as also the economical, political and ideological contexts. If the most appropriate target for archaeological research is urban function, we must accept that these are spread to more places than the documented towns alone. This implies in turn that the towns should not be treated as isolated objects, but seen in a landscape context. Functions can be exchanged between town and country, sometimes privileging one at the expense of the other, as the politics, economy society and ideology changes (cf Carver 1993; Anglert & Larsson 2008).

Regional differences are also significant. The Roman Empire provides one enduring regional division. Inside its borders many Medieval towns and cities can be tracked to a Roman origin, even if it is often a problem to demonstrate continuity between them. Outside the Roman Empire, towns had many other diverse starting points (see Schofield & Steuer 2007).

The re-emergence of towns in the late twelfth and thirteenth century

Although post-Roman urbanisation had begun in the later first millennium (see AME 1, Ch 4), there are important qualitative and quantitative changes beginning in the later part of the twelfth century and peaking during the thirteenth century, which make this period especially important in the history of urbanisation. The existing cities and towns enlarged their areas and their population rose drastically, and all over Europe new towns were founded or rationalised, for example *poblaciones* and *villanovas* in Catalonia, *borghi nuovi* in Italy, *villeneuves* and *bastides* in France and *Gründungsstädte* in Germany. There were increased international contacts, trade and economic exchange and also an increasing tendency to organise and control society through administration, law, privileges and the church. These were the keystones of the success story of the thirteenth century. This renaissance was a part of the general economic and cultural development in Europe.

The century also meant increased contact outside of Europe. This is true for the relations to East Asia in particular, but also to Africa (Ch 8, p 361). The Italian cities played a key role as points of exchange with the eastern and southern parts of the world. This fact has been used in the great discussion about world systems. This may be a reminder that studies of urbanisation cannot only be limited to Europe (Abu-Lughod 1989 (1991), Andersson 2002).

Urban trajectories in northern and western Europe

The urban growth of the late twelfth-thirteenth centuries can be observed in a number of examples. Many existing places doubled in size. Metz (France) in the Roman period covered 71 ha, but grew to 159 ha in the thirteenth century. It meant that several villages around the original Roman city were incorporated in the city. A similar pace of development can be seen in many Roman cities in France and also in other Mediterranean countries. The increase was also typical for towns and cities that had their origin in the early Middle Ages. Montpellier got its first wall in 1091. In the second half of the twelfth century a new wall was built, to include some new suburbs. In approximately 1180 the area within the wall was 40 ha and perhaps 10,000 inhabitants lived there. During the thirteenth century the population increased four times. Montpellier is also an example of the new medieval towns in France, where many cities achieved great importance. One measure of a city's importance was the number of houses of friars it supported. In France there were 52 cities with 3 or 4 mendicant houses, and both Metz and Montpellier had four (Le Goff 1980: 403).

The urbanisation process was not only limited to the bigger cities and towns. Around 350-400 *bastides* were founded in the south-western parts of France. These were new fortified settlements mainly founded by magnates to re-settle part of the population. Like *poblaciones* or *villanovas* in Spain and their counterparts in Italy, they are seen as a major colonisation and restructuring of the medieval countryside of Europe (Higounet 1992 (1979), 17 ff)

In England rapid urban growth from the late twelfth century is seen both in the development of the bigger towns and cities, some with Roman ancestry, and in the emergence of regional centres and smaller towns. During the thirteenth century around 2500 markets and 300 boroughs were created in England. An urban hierarchy appeared, with London at the top, a series of provincial towns – York, Norwich, Lincoln, Bristol, Northampton, Canterbury, Dunwich, Exeter and Winchester – and even smaller towns below these. There were clear signs of growing self-government, the development of laws and craft regulation. At the end of the thirteenth century the urban network was at its height, and towns were now fully embedded in medieval society (Astill 2000:46 ff; Schofield & Vince 2003, 26 ff).

In Germany in the first decades of the twelfth century there were about 30 *Grosstädte* with international markets and several hundred regional towns. By 1320 there were perhaps 4000 towns. Among them were 50 with more than 5000 inhabitants; Köln was the biggest with more than 50 000 inhabitants. Mainz, Augsburg, Speyer and Erfurt had more than 20 000. To these may be added, many much smaller towns that were of only local importance (Scholkmann 2009: 67 ff).

In his study of Westphalia (North Germany) in 1960, Carl Haase did not use archaeological material (understandable because the main development of urban archaeology was yet to come) but his results are instructive. He used the year 1180 as a start point, since there were rather few places that were urban before then, but a rapid growth thereafter. In the period 1180-1240, 30 new towns were founded in Westphalia. Two of them could not be reliably dated and four of them were *Fehlgründungen* where nothing or very little happened. In the following period (1240-1290) there were another 31 new towns. Three of these were again of uncertain date, and another three Fehlgründungen. This period saw the appearance of small towns, and he named it *das Zeitalter der Klein- und Zwergstädte* (Time of the 'Dwarf towns'), which continued to the end of the Middle Ages (Haase 1960).

The northern parts of Germany can be treated together with Scandinavia and Eastern Europe. From the end of the twelfth century on, many places have both archaeological and written source material, and it is evident that both a qualitative and quantitative change occurred at this time (Fig 9.1). It happened first in Norway and Denmark, somewhat later in Sweden-Finland. The settlements became more densely built; the churches were rebuilt and enlarged, sometimes changed from wooden churches to stone. Denmark got the highest frequency of towns, while Norway only got a few but rather important towns and cities. The same was the situation in present-day Finland, while Sweden was somewhere in between (Andrén 1989). Bergen in Norway, to take only one example, developed from a local harbour to its status as the most important trading city in Norway during the Middle Ages, with a German Hansa Office (Hansen 2003). Some of the other Scandinavian towns also played a great role economically and politically, as for instance Bergen, Trondheim and Oslo in Norway, Stockholm, Visby, Tallinn and Riga in the Baltic region. The old herring markets around the Sound

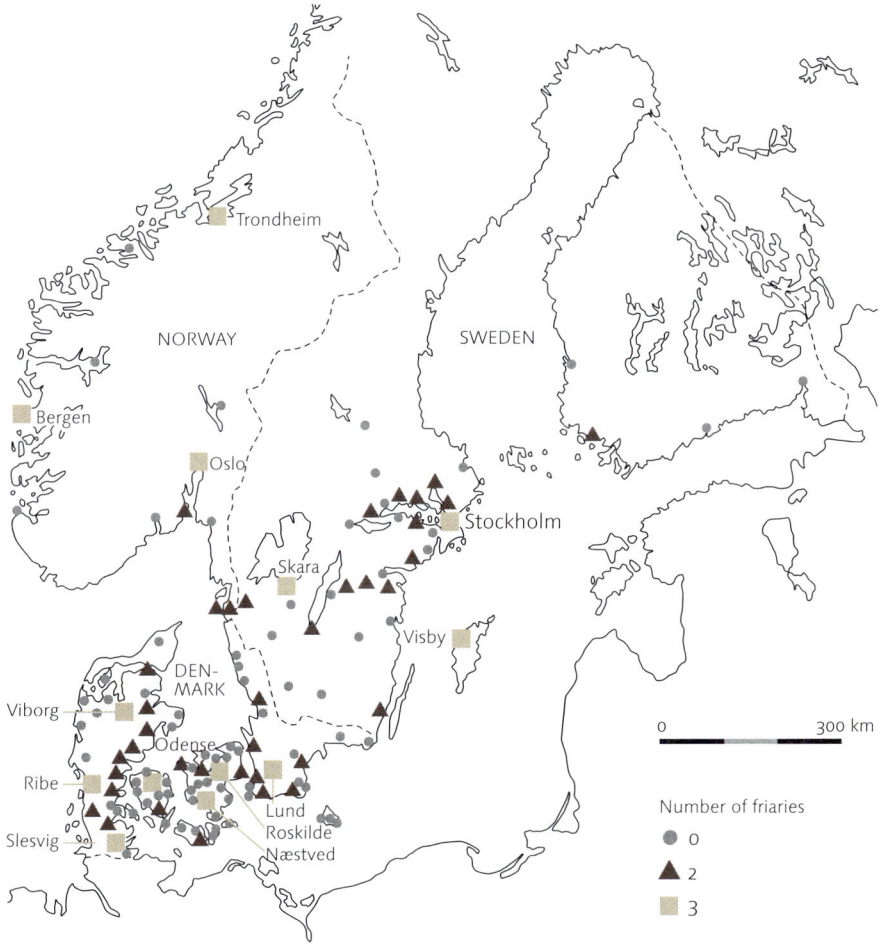

Urban growth in Scandinavia, 1150-1350, using the number of friaries as a proxy for ranking (after Andrén 1989, fig. 2).   **Fig 9.1**

Fig 9.2 *Vágar on Lofoten, Norway, located to take advantage of two landing-places. Archaeological deposits are confined to the areas by the water's edge.*

were of considerable proportions, frequented by people from cities on the southern coast of the Baltic. In the Mälar region around Stockholm the iron from the mines in Bergslagen was essential for the establishment of the towns around the lake. Stockholm established a strong position through its monopoly in the export of iron.

In the northern parts of Scandinavia, no town received privileges, but this did not mean that there were no central places. Ongoing urbanisation still influenced the area. An example was Vágar on Lofoten in Northern Norway (Fig 9.2). A headquarters for the local leader in the tenth century, the place developed into a centre for trade, especially in fish, but also for the tax enforcement of the king. As late as 1384 a royal charter tried to uphold the trade monopoly of Vágar in the region (Bertelsen & Urbanczyk 1988, Urbanczyk 1992). In Iceland, Reykjavik got its town privileges as late as 1786. In these northern regions the population was very sparse and did not encourage the imposition of towns (Andersson H 2003; Carlsson 2008; Andersson H et al. 2008).

Crisis – Fourteenth and fifteenth centuries

The peak of urbanisation was reached at the end of the thirteenth century, by which time an urban network had been established that did not change radically until the industrial revolution. But signs of crisis were already evident, and they were exacerbated by famines and plagues during the fourteenth century. The food supply sometimes failed to support the urban populations. The crisis became economic, demographic and political. In most of Europe fewer new towns were founded; in Denmark for example there were no new towns at all during the first half of fourteenth century. Such towns as were founded were mostly small and with a local range, as with the *Zwergstädte* mentioned above (Stoob 1959, Haase 1960). In many cases, they hardly differed from the villages in the region. They had very little, if any, international contact. Rather soon many of these towns disappeared totally. The houses fell into decay. Some places had privileges, but still there was nothing built. This sometimes happened also to the older towns. Winchester in England is such an example (Schofield & Vince 2005, 28 f, 57).

These changes also included a greater differentiation within the urban network. Some of the older cities and towns grew rapidly and got a stronger position, domestically as well as internationally. Bergen, Stockholm and Copenhagen can be mentioned as examples for Scandinavia. The two last-mentioned towns had also begun to be transformed into the capitals of their countries. In England, London reinforced its position as the leading city. Thus, the towns of the late Middle Ages display a contradictory picture, steep decline on the one hand and great rise in importance on the other.

The dynamics of urbanisation over time has been described in a diagram for Central Europe by H. Stoob, later corroborated for the north by Andrén (Fig 9.3; Stoob 1956, 21; Andrén 1985, 32). While there will be uncertain details in the sources used, it can be accepted that these models describe the rise and decline of the regular town with privileges in western, central and northern Europe. It is important to emphasise that this trajectory of urbanisation was a part of a common trend experienced throughout much of Europe.

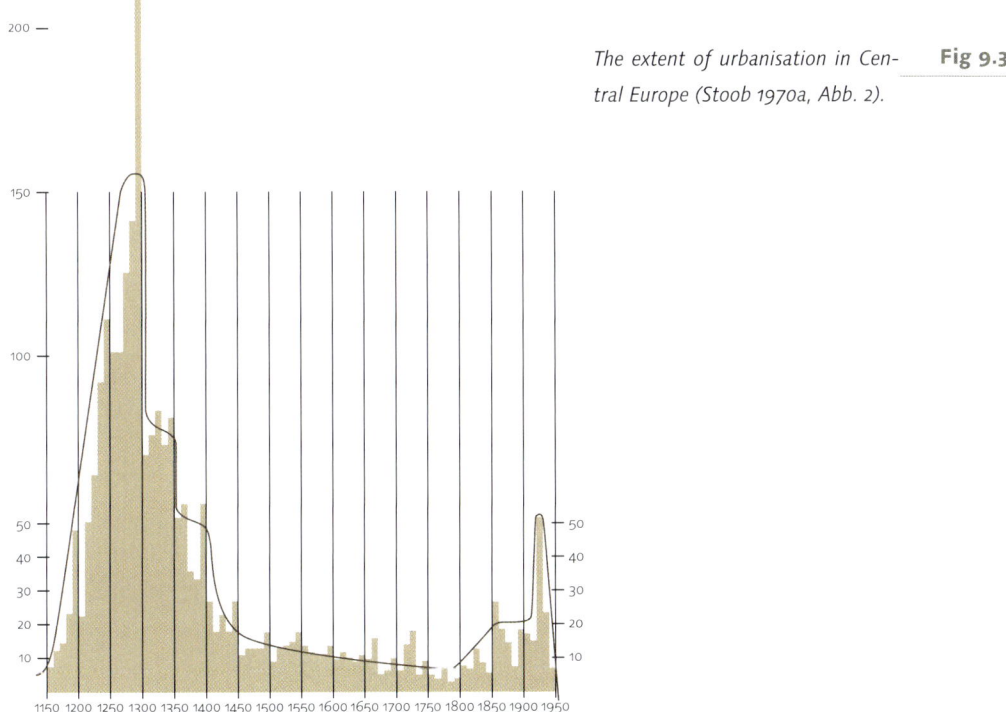

The extent of urbanisation in Central Europe (Stoob 1970a, Abb. 2). **Fig 9.3**

BOX 9.1   WROCŁAW IN THE TWELFTH-SIXTEENTH CENTURY

Urban archaeology in Wrocław, the main centre for Silesia and a major city of medieval and modern Central Europe, has furthered understanding of the origins of the town, the development of its structure and infrastructure, and the conditions of daily life (Wachowsky 1999). Wrocław lies on the Odra at a point where the river forms a number of channels and islands, a fine fording place (Fig 1). The archaeological deposit in Wrocław lies up to 3 m thick and has yielded a large quantity of organic, metal and most of all ceramic finds, an excellent basis for

studying medieval and early modern urban material culture (eg Busko 2003) (Fig 2).

During its proto-urban phase Wrocław had a polycentric structure. It consisted of a number of settlement centres that had grown up on the islands and along the river banks. There was an earth-and-timber fortified settlement with the ducal residence and cathedral, a trade settlement, two abbeys, residences of the nobility and agrarian settlements. Intensive development, especially of the trading centre on the left bank of the Odra, took place in the twelfth and early thir-

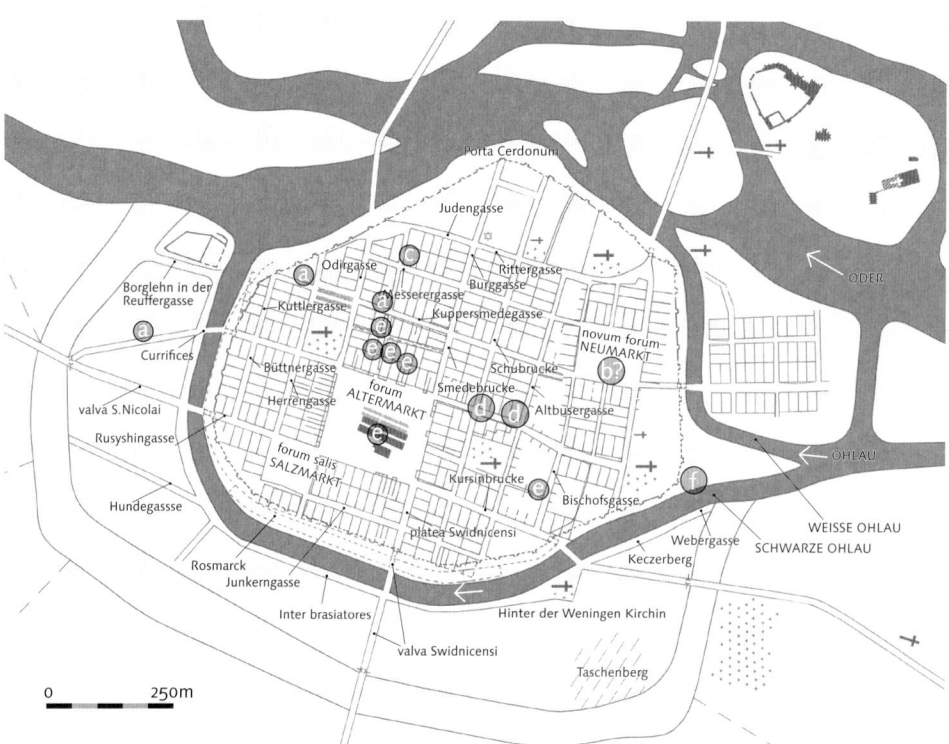

Fig 1

Wrocław around 1300. Production workshops identified by archaeological research: a – production of iron, b – smithy, c – tannery, d – shoemaking, e – bone and antlerworking, f – production of clay figurines (Bilderbaecker).

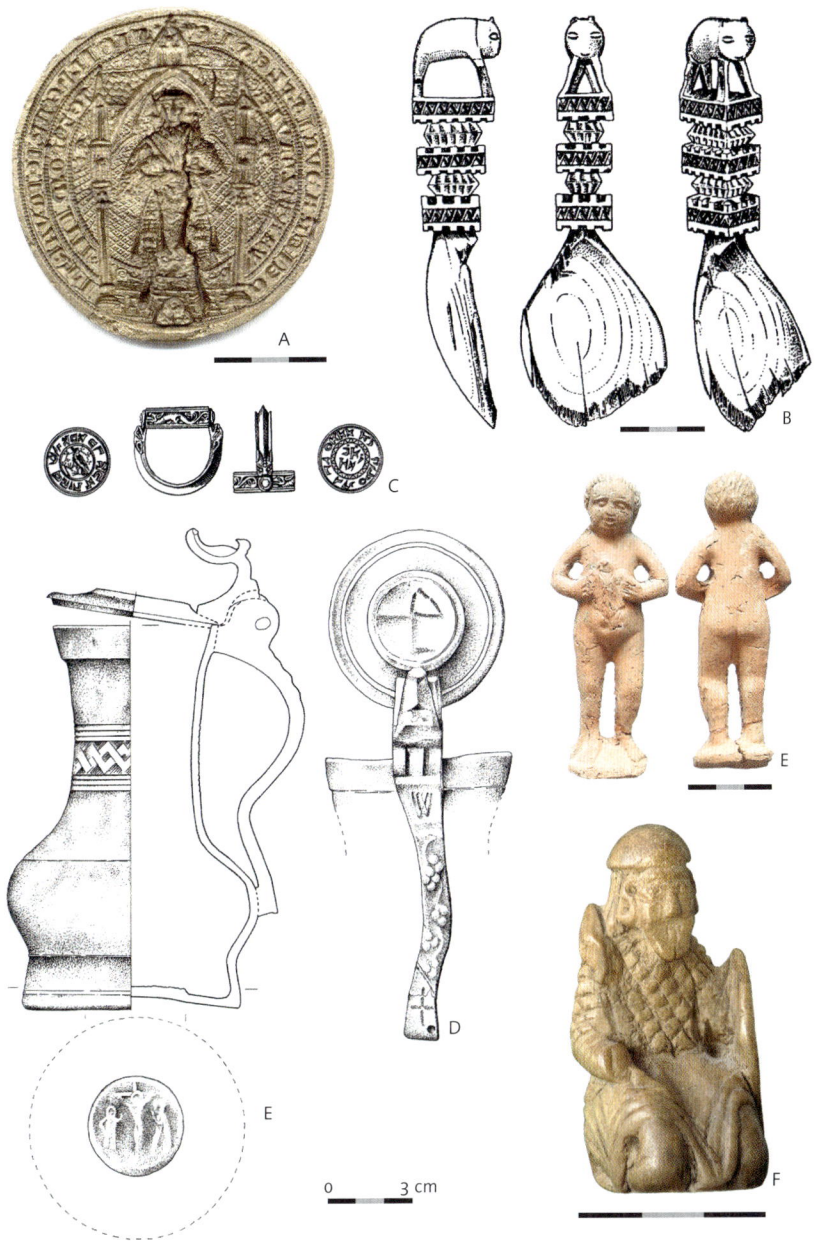

Fig 2

Medieval finds from Wrocław. A – seal of Duke Henryk IV Probus (2nd half of 13th century), B – wooden spoon (15th century), C – signet ring of a Jewish merchant (Aba son of Aba, 14th-15th century), D – tin jug (15th century), E – clay figurine of Jesus with Holy Spirit (15th century) F – chess piece made of red deer antler (13th century).

teenth century. At a later stage its community became multi-ethnic, with a Polish, German, Walloon and Jewish population. The importance of Wrocław outside the region was marked from 1150 by an annual fair of St Vincent, one of many stops on the *via regia* running from Brugge and Köln to Kiev. It became the capital city of the province of Silesia, the principality ruled by the Piast dynasty until the fourteenth century, when they were superseded by Bohemian kings.

Transition to the communal phase took place in the first half of the thirteenth century, with the establishment of a town of a new type on the periphery. Its rapid development and new legal and economic status led to the decline of the old settlement. The demographic base of the new town's commune was formed by colonists from the German Empire, using a legal model adopted from Magdeburg. The new regular street plan combined an aesthetically satisfying layout with the practical necessity of having plots with areas (and taxes) that were easy to calculate.

A central feature in the street plan of Wrocław was its large rectangular market square (Ring/Rynek). Its main function was commerce, reflected by the presence of a fine cloth hall and lines of stalls, property of the duke, but rented out to the townspeople. Commercial activity in private houses was forbidden. When the trading facilities were sold to the townspeople in the second half of the thirteenth century, they were not pulled down but remained in the city plan as a lasting distinctive feature. Research carried out in the Town Square identified traces of small-scale production, for example the making of gaming dice. In addition to its

dedication to commerce and production, the square was also the centre of administration and self-government, the judiciary, the centre of local and regional exchange of information and also the focus of recreation and festivities. Other important elements in the city plan were two smaller market places, churches and churchyards.

Town houses were built of timber in a frame construction, also of brick. From the fifteenth century, brick houses became dominant. Water was supplied by a system of ceramic water mains built in the fourteenth century. Sewage was disposed of in cesspits in the backyards, or more rarely, dumped in open drains in the street. Streets were surfaced with timber, later, increasingly with stone paving. From around 1350 waste was systematically removed from the streets which prevented further accretion of layers.

Before 1250 the regularly planned area of the city was encircled with a system of brick ramparts, complete with towers and a moat. Around the middle of the fourteenth century districts added to the city on its south and west side were fortified in a similar manner. At the turn of the early modern period the city wall was equipped with bastions as a defence against artillery. From the middle of the sixteenth century, modern bastions started to be built giving the town the character of a state fortress (see also Ch 6, p 248).

by Jerzy Piekalski

Sources

In contrast to early medieval towns, which are known to us almost entirely through archaeological research (AME 1, Ch 4), late medieval towns possess a written and pictorial documentation that increases steadily in volume and variety from the thirteenth century onwards. Charters, law books, chronicles and administrative documents provide information about the foundation of a town and the people involved, about its constitution, governance, civic law, the urban middle class, the guilds, the development of the urban administration as well as the formation and organisation of urban and ecclesiastical structures (Pervenier & de Hemptinne 2000). Townscapes and depictions of daily life on altar panels frequently provide, albeit under varied artistic influences, an idealised picture of urban buildings and urban life (Raynaud 1998; Boockmann 1986). Map evidence in the form of historic town plans generally does not go back to the Middle Ages, but appears in the modern period, in Scandinavia for example from the seventeenth century onwards, in Central Europe mainly from the nineteenth century onwards. They document the urban topography and its transformations from the time they were founded (Opll 2009).

While historical and topographic research into late medieval towns, based on documentary, map and pictorial evidence, follows a long tradition going back to the nineteenth century, archaeological evidence has only been sought over the last few decades. Of primary significance are the surviving buildings. In Germany for example, despite the destruction of the Second World War, countless buildings of the late Middle Ages survive: churches, public buildings, town houses, residences, some of the oldest going back to a period starting shortly after 1200, and sometimes entire town quarters. Though they have been frequently remodelled in the course of the centuries, they still provide high quality evidence for the late medieval town. The archaeology of still extant buildings and its connexion with the archaeological results obtained from the ground have increased in importance (Fig 9.4).

At the centre of the research agenda throughout Europe is a broad spectrum of topographical enquiries that address the process of development of individual towns and of the medieval townscape in general (Fehring 1996; Schofield & Vince 2003). The spatial requirements for town foundation at a specific location and the previously existing, abandoned or partly or wholly subsumed earlier settlement nuclei form part of this enquiry. Just as important is the investigation of the different phases in the constitution of the town plan and townscape, complete with harbour, street pattern, open spaces and organisation of plots. Seats of power and public buildings, the development of urban housing, the formation of different types of town houses and the sacred topography including churches, chapels and monasteries constitute a further area of research. The same applies to the infrastructure, above all the provision of water and the management of refuse, as well as the interaction between town and its surroundings. The archaeological evidence for artisan production and short- and long-distance trade occupies a large part of research (see Ch 7 & 8). Finally, daily life reflected in archaeological de-

Fig 9.4 *Vertical section of a medieval house in Freiburg in Breisgau in Germany showing the results of archaeological investigation. (drawing and photo: Regierungspräsidium Freiburg, Referat 26 Denkmalpflege).*

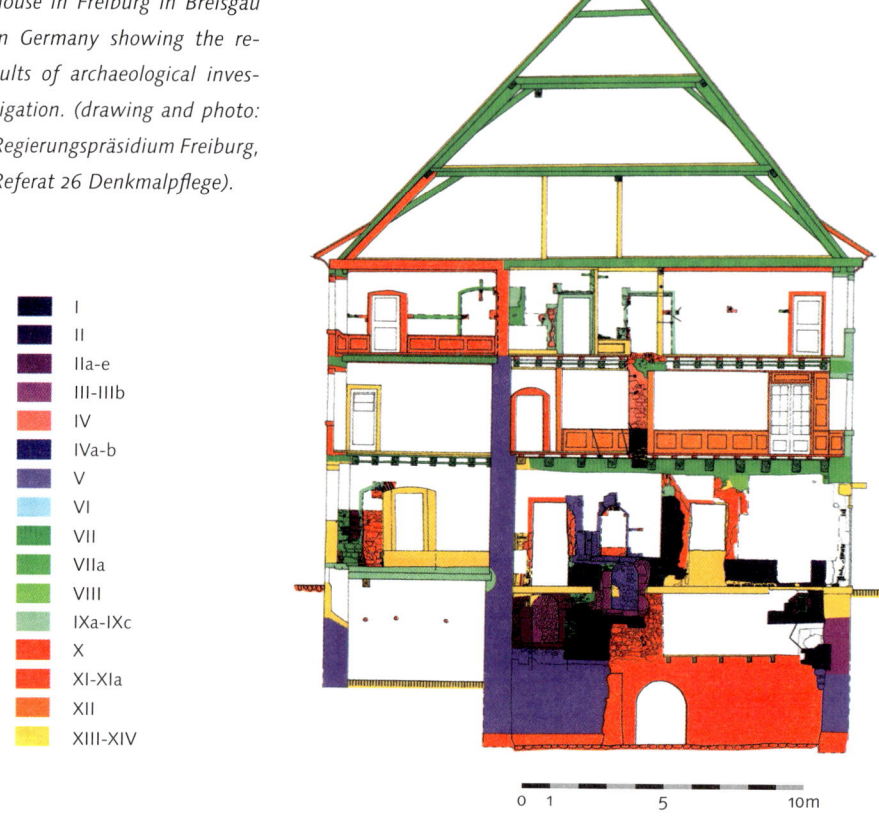

I
II
IIa-e
III-IIIb
IV
IVa-b
V
VI
VII
VIIa
VIII
IXa-IXc
X
XI-XIa
XII
XIII-XIV

0 1 5 10m

posits is a theme that concerns all settlements but is particularly well documented for the inhabitants of the late medieval towns (see Ch 4 & 5).

The results of numerous archaeological investigations in late medieval towns indicate that there are trends in the emergence and development of towns detectable all over Europe (Schofield & Vince 2003. 257 ff.; see part 1, above). This is especially true for the part of Europe located north of the limits of the Roman Empire, i.e. an area extending from Ireland to South-east Europe and from Scandinavia to the Alps. The towns possess a great variety of individual characteristics conditioned by different political, economic and cultural regional influences; but at the same time the European townscape constitutes an extremely coherent cultural sphere.

Today we have at our disposal, in greater or lesser amounts, archaeological data for many European towns (Schofield & Vince 2003, Appendix, Report 1999, Andersson H *et al.* 2008, Gläser ed. 1997). Good insights into the archaeology of town centres in individual European countries can be found in the proceedings of the Medieval Europe conferences in York in 1992 (*Medieval Europe* 1992), Bruges in 1997 (De Boe & Verhaege eds. 1997) and Basel in 2002 (Helmig *et al.* eds. 2002). Each town experienced its own evolution through the Middle Ages and this was influenced by a variety of factors. The large number of archaeological investigations in town centres nevertheless allows us to recognise common and typical traits, to compare them and to interpret them. The greatest insights, given the focus of interest in the larger and most important towns, have so far come from these towns, whereas the numerous medium-sized and small towns (which form the majority) have been investigated intensively only in some regions of Europe. What follows is a presentation of results, using examples from Central Europe and Scandinavia.

The emergence of towns

Decisive elements in the development of urban space were politics, the economy and a convenient location for transport. Pre-existing settlements might become towns through the granting of municipal law or trade privileges or a town was newly founded. A key question is therefore whether a town evolved from an earlier nucleus or was a new foundation on a previously unsettled area. The process of town emergence can be read in the surviving town plan only with caution. The layout does indeed often reflect earlier conditions, sometimes of the time of foundation, but in many cases it was re-modelled in the course of the Middle Ages; therefore only archaeological evidence can give secure indications. For example, the city of Bern in Switzerland originated around 1200 as a seigniorial castle to which a founding town was attached on a hitherto unsettled loop of the river Aare (Baeriswyl 2003, 159-92). Freiburg in Breisgau in Germany, with a foundation charter dating to 1120, was also a 'green-field' site whose earliest urban traces are dated to around 1100; a presumed earlier settlement has so far not been encountered (Untermann 1995). When previous settlement nuclei were present, town development often took place as a 'polycentric' process. Pre-existing adjacent settlements such as castles, villages, seigniorial courts or mills coalesced, partly or totally, into an integrated town. Such is the case for the planned town of Villingen in south-western Germany in the second half of the twelfth century (Jenisch 1999). It is also possible that a town 'appended' itself to an earlier settlement. Göttingen emerged in the second half of the twelfth century in this way, next to a rural settlement in existence since the early Middle Ages which was abandoned as the town developed and was part-integrated into the new city (Arndt & Ströbl 2005).

When towns were founded or re-developed the topography was remodelled, sometimes with long-lasting impact. Extensive dumping to heighten low-lying areas was undertaken for example in Braunschweig, where an estimated 2 million tons of earth was dumped to level the low lying ground of the river Oker and create building areas for the town which was established in the second half of the twelfth century (Rötting 1997, 16-20). Similar arrangements were made in the episcopal town of Konstanz, where land was gained from the twelfth century onwards from the shallow water zones of Lake Constance in the form of dumps revetted by timber; thus land reclamation enlarged the episcopal town which had hitherto been confined to a conveniently located moraine (Flüeler and Flüeler 1992, 53-68). Stockholm in Sweden was a new town founded in the mid thirteenth century, which grew rapidly from a ridge beside Lake Mälar, and soon expanded into the lake using material dumped from the shores.

Town plan and structure

The topographical layout of the late medieval town is formed by its defensive circuit, the network of streets and the plots adjoining them, one or several marketplaces, the densely built fabric of houses, and civic buildings such as an urban castle (*Stadtburg*), town hall, mercantile halls and warehouses, and ecclesiastical buildings including parish churches, urban monasteries and chapels. But it is only the well-populated, largely autonomous, economically strong and socially differentiated towns that possessed all these elements. Small towns and 'minor towns' developed only partly along these lines. This led, despite the general trend of urban investment, to a most varied topography (see Box 9.1).

Town defences are a central element of the townscape (cf Ch 6, p 248). The defensive purpose of their construction was as important as their significance as a symbol of the town *per se*. Providing security for the urban community against the outside world was the communal duty of the townsfolk. There are a number of sources for the establishment of defences in numerous European towns (Isenberg & Scholkmann 1997). Defences were generally laid out soon after the foundation of the town and, within the limitations of the local topography, as close as possible to an ideal geometric form. Freiburg in Breisgau provides an example. There, the course of the town wall was laid out apparently just a few decades after the town's foundation and this caused the abandonment of the buildings that had been erected only shortly before (Porsche 1994). In towns with earlier settlement nuclei, the latter were enclosed within the town walls and the gaps between them closed. So, for example, Zürich was provided in the thirteenth century with a new town wall with numerous towers and a ditch over 20m wide and 6m deep (Fig 9.5) (Stadt Zürich 2004). The town defences of Central Europe were generally built of stone and the few known examples of timber and earth defences were mostly soon replaced. But in Scandinavia, stone walls are rare. Only three are known from Sweden: Visby (still extant; Fig 6.1), Stockholm and Kalmar. Other towns had mostly earthen banks sometimes complemented by timber fortifications and a ditch, such as in Lund.

The development of the internal urban topography consisted of the laying out of streets and open spaces, and the establishment of plots or *tenements*. Archaeological investigations have shown that the street network or even the course of the urban drains were set up very early on in the establishment of the towns and that they, as well as the open spaces, were not altered by later development. Freiburg in Breisgau again provides a good example: shortly after the beginning of the town after 1200, the layout of the streets, the size of the plots and the building lines were determined and not altered later. In some Scandinavian towns the layout goes back to the early twelfth century. The street network, access to water - the sea or river - and the first churches were especially important when the town plan was set down; during the thirteenth century the streets were infilled and the buildings became more densely packed. An example is Lund in Skåne, where the plan was established in some parts as early as the eleventh century but developed during the twelfth and thirteenth centuries. The same situation can be found in Bergen in Norway.

The fact that the town walls delineated a finite urban area meant that, as the population increased, room could only be found for new houses by packing them more densely, so plots laid out at the time of a town's foundation had to be divided. Long

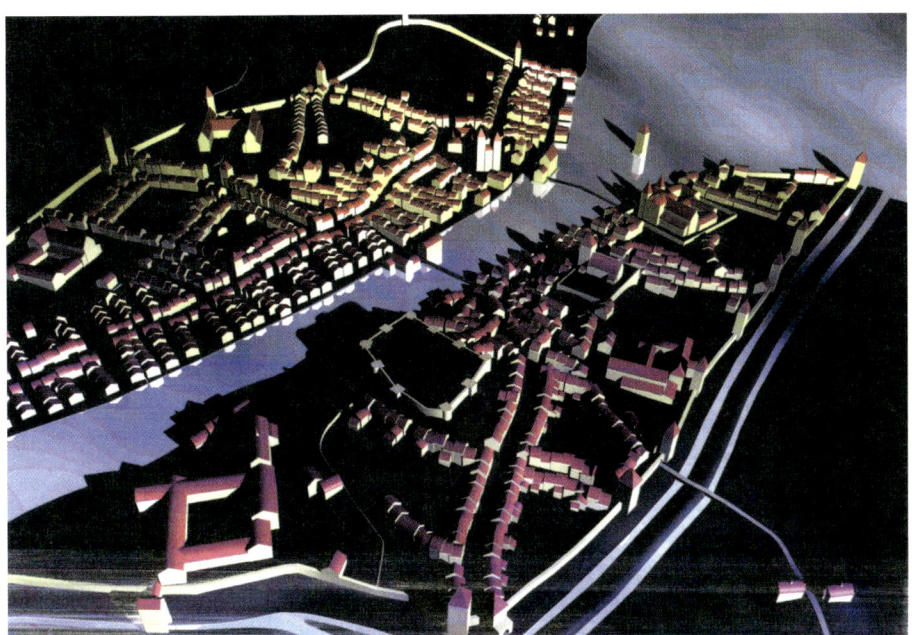

Model of the late medieval town wall of Zürich in Switzerland (Stadt Zürich. Amt für Städtebau, **Fig 9.5**
Archäologie und Denkmalpflege).

and narrow plots with their short end facing onto the street are typical of late medieval towns. During the late Middle Ages and often soon after their foundation many towns outgrew their original defences and were enlarged by planned suburbs defended by walls. These enlargements do not always prove, as archaeological investigations have demonstrated, to be a later addition to the town. More often, as has for example been shown at Burgdorf in Switzerland, they were pre-urban settlements which were incorporated as suburbs into the defensive circuit of a town (Baeriswyl 2003: 35-86). Inner city 'redevelopment measures' are also documented. New open spaces were created by demolishing houses, as happened in the small town of Laufen in Switzerland which emerged in the last quarter of the thirteenth century: There a whole row of houses which had burnt down around 1500 was not rebuilt to make space for a new market place (Pfrommer & Gutscher 1999). New churches and monasteries could also often only be established if existing buildings were given up.

The process of emergence and topographical development of a town's layout can be followed nowhere better than in Lübeck, the first German foundation on the Baltic which was soon to become a commercial hub between the North Sea and the Baltic, Central Europe and Scandinavia, and which, with other Hansa towns, is considered a prototype of a foundation town (Gläser & Mührenberg 2002). Around 130 excavations in the urban zone make it the best archaeologically investigated town in Central Europe (Fig 9.6). Lübeck grew from the site of a Slavic castle with bailey on a hill in the north part of the eventual town. The Earl of Holstein, Adolf II, took it over, enlarged it and founded a town there in 1143; in 1158 he had to hand it over to his lord, Henry the Lion. There are hardly any traces of occupation from the phase of first foundation between 1143 and 1158 and therefore no conclusions can be drawn regarding its extent or the type of buildings. After 1158 the first urban structures grew in the centre of the town and a harbour was established on the river Trave. The earliest town was surrounded by a brick wall. The western

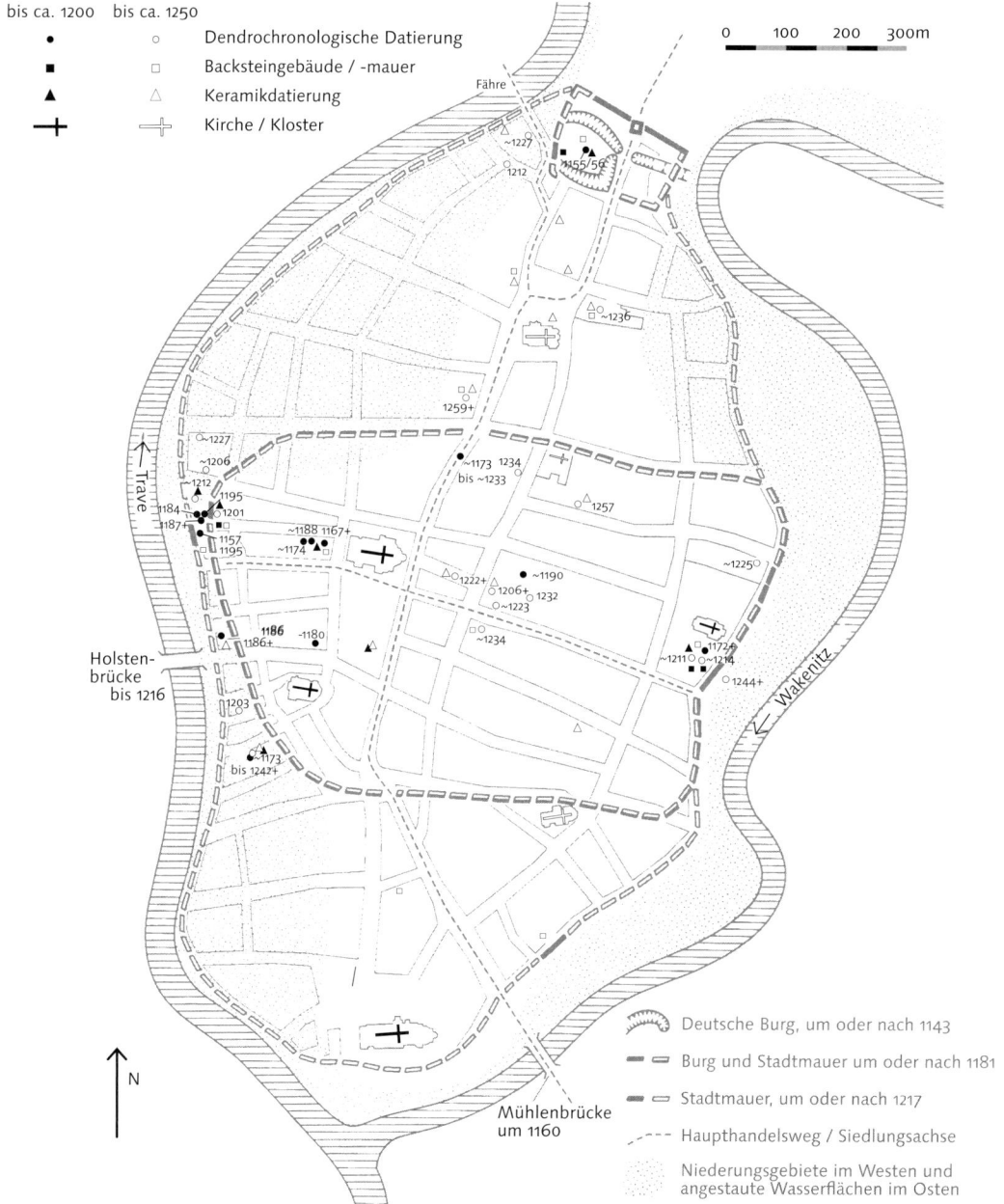

Fig 9.6 *The town plan of Lübeck in Germany: the development of the town in the 12th and 13th century (Hansestadt Lübeck. Der Bürgermeister. Bereich Archäologie).*

area, later to become the merchant quarter, also obtained already (in the twelfth century) its small narrow tenements that survive to this day (Fig 9.7). From 1217 the town was protected by a wall which also enclosed the flood-plain to the north and south, following landfill revetted by timber up to 6m deep. This extended the habitable surface by *c.* 25 per cent. After the cathedral (*Dom*) and the church of St Mary (*Marienkirche*), Lübeck's earliest stone buildings were erected already in the twelfth century, further churches and monasteries were established in the thirteenth century, as well as the new merchants' hall (later the town hall). Around the middle of the thirteenth century, the topography of the town was set and the merchant quarter was already built up, with buildings fronting onto the streets. The area occupied by the town was not enlarged later; the growth in the urban population in the following centuries resulted in an increasingly dense pattern of occupation, a subdivision of plots and in the construction of rows of small houses in backyards, the so-called *Gänge* which still characterise today's townscape.

Bergen in Norway can also be traced archaeologically through the centuries. The medieval townscape can partly still be seen in the Bergenshus castle, the churches and the timber-built settlement by the harbour, the latter a reminder of the German Hansa (see Ch 8, p 340). Activity started already before 1000 with the building of a jetty. During the first half of the eleventh century, plots were laid out according to some kind of regulation, probably a royal initiative. In the ensuing period there were many new initiatives, probably taken by king Olav Kyrre: it included the organisation and enlargement of the town's area and the building of new churches. Development continued in later periods. By the end of the twelfth century Bergen had became a centre for both internal and external trade and shipping. During the thirteenth century the town grew further and became stronger. The harbour area was enlarged and parts of the shore were

Lübeck: A model of the merchants' quarter in the first third of the 13th century (Hansestadt Lubeck, **Fig 9.7**
Bürgermeister, Bereich Archäologie).

BOX 9.2 A PRESERVED MEDIEVAL SUBURB – SEZIMOVO ÚSTÍ (CZECH REPUBLIC)

The medieval town of Sezimovo Ústí in South Bohemia was founded around the middle of the thirteenth century by one of the foremost aristocratic dynasties of the kingdom of Bohemia. On 30 March 1420 it was engulfed by fire and an urban centre of ten hectares disappeared, along with three suburbs outside the walls. The destruction was deliberate. The supporters of the Hussite

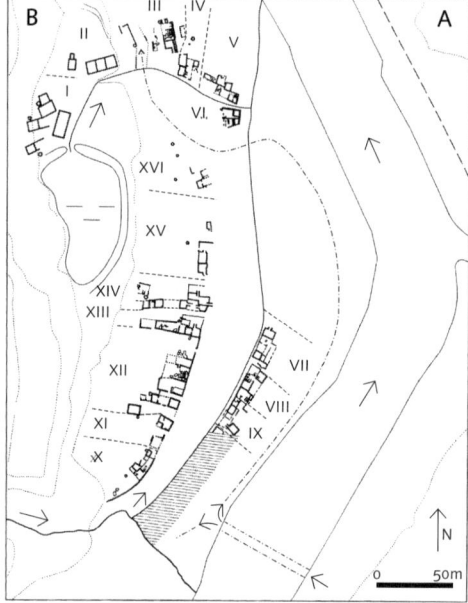

Fig 1

Sezimovo Ústí (Bohemia), the town core (A) and the suburb on the left bank of the River Lužnice (B). A generalised ground plan of the built-up area from the beginning of the 15th century, reconstructed according to the archaeological research. The allotment system of Homesteads I-XVI, a reconstruction of the water network and the likely road network have been added. The hatching denotes the settlement area indicated by the geophysical research (after M. Richter).

movement, who had seized the town shortly before, decided to transfer the inhabitants to a new foundation in a strategically more advantageous position, named after the Biblical Tabor. The whole event was part of the liquidation of the old world.

The urban renewal of the site of Sezimovo Ústí had to wait until the nineteenth century, but when it came, the newly built-up area did not cover all of the old medieval complex. One of the former suburbs, situated on the other side of the River Lužnice, was not affected. The dramatic chapter in medieval history thus provided a unique archaeological opportunity, where extensive programmed research took place from 1962 to 1988. It was here that, to a significant degree, Czech archaeology of the late Middle Ages was shaped in the 1960s, developing the scope of its activity and methods of field research. The archaeological excavations, led by Miroslav Richter, uncovered roughly 1.5 ha. and identified three stages between the mid-thirteenth century and 1420. The third and last stage, in particular, offered the prerequisites for an outstanding archaeological testimony (see Richter 1986, Richter 1994, Richter – Krajíc 2001).

In the first stage (dated to the second half of the thirteenth century), a substantial part of the area of the suburb was already settled. The buildings were of wood and clay, placed directly on the surface of the ground and anchored by earth-fast timber posts. Some rooms had sunken floors. There were several non-agrarian production activities. Blacksmithing slag was distributed over almost the entire investigated area. Clay moulds testified to the casting of small bronze artefacts. Pottery wasters were evidence of pottery manufacture on site. There was material from tanning and leather-working, and fishing weights indicating the dwelling of a fisherman. The second stage (dating to the first half of the fourteenth century) followed without interruption, but there were now signs of a more structured layout.

The third stage embraced the period between the mid-fourteenth century and the abandonment of the site in 1420. The ground plan of the suburb then comprised two rows of homesteads staked out on the lower terrace parallel to the axis of the river (Fig. 1). Twenty homesteads were identified, of which sixteen were examined by archaeological excavation. The width of the majority of the plots was between 18 and 30 m, but Homesteads I and XV stood on plots 48 m wide, and Homestead XII was located on a plot 54 m wide. Water, indispensible for the life and operation of each of the homesteads, was provided by several sources. In the immediate vicinity, the River Lužnice flowed and a brook running down from the neighbouring slopes was canalised to the centre of the suburb. On the elevated northern edge of the suburb, there was a system of reservoirs and the individual homesteads also had wells usually 3.5 to 4.5 m deep.

Although houses were still constructed mainly in timber and clay, in this final stage stone found an important application in building. It provided walls for the cellars and formed the foundation walls for elevations in wood and clay. With rare exceptions, the stonework was not bonded by lime mortar; drystone walling provided sufficient stability and durability. Stone was used also for lining the sides of wells and channels, the latter used, for example, to drain water out of the cellars. The plan and superstructure of the buildings was variable. Several houses had one room with a fireplace or oven, built directly on the surface of the ground, and another room for storage, with a cellar beneath.

Evidence for production was richly preserved. The most numerous group were potters (Homesteads VIII, X, XII, XIII and likely also IX), while brick-makers worked in two homesteads (Homesteads I and II). There was a blacksmith working in the Homestead VI (Krajíc 2003) and a tanner in Homestead VII. Food production was represented by a butcher in Homestead XIV, a maltster in Homestead III (Krajíc 1989) and perhaps also a baker in Homestead IV. In the remaining four homesteads, signs of production were lacking. Craft was not necessarily practised continually on the same plot. Whereas in Homestead III malt production took place through the fourteenth century until 1420, in a number of other cases striking changes occurred. The potters in Homestead X took the place of a tanner, and in Homesteads XII and XIII potters were new arrivals in the mid-fourteenth century. All the sixteen plots investigated lacked agricultural outbuildings and artefacts, and it is clear that none was primarily focused on agriculture. A similar conclusion was reached also by the analysis of the archaeobotanical macro-remains (Opravil 1997).

The excavation revealed details of the life style of different craftsmen. The blacksmith (Homestead VI) worked in a plot of circa 600 m². He had a house with five rooms in it, of which the largest area, roughly 38 m², was taken by the smithy, with the forge in one corner. Living space seems to have been

Fig 2

Sezimovo Ústí (Bohemia), Homestead XII. (1-3) stove tiles carved in openwork, (4) a tile with a scene from Aesop's fable, The Fox and the Stork, early 15th century (after M. Richter).

confined to a single room with an area of 14.7 m². The production space included the courtyard, from which came almost 400 kg of smithing slag. The inventory of finds includes 2,643 iron objects, comprising a wide spectrum from raw material to prepared products. The blacksmith started with bar or strap iron but also made use of a supply of obsolete artefacts prepared for recycling. The sequence of manufacture can then be tracked from sundry semi-finished products and defective objects, damaged during the production process. Finished products mark the end of the production line, these being objects undoubtedly intended for the local urban market. The value of iron to the inhabitants was here shown with unusual clarity, since the site was deserted suddenly and not subsequently pillaged. A cloth sack with nineteen coins from 1407-19 remained under the floor of one of the rooms of the smith's house. It was apparently personal cash hidden at the beginning of 1420, for which the owner never returned. Stocks of damaged iron artefacts were found in Homesteads VIII and XI, whose inhabitants were not smiths, showing that scrap too had its value.

The brick-makers worked in two homesteads (I and II) situated in the immediate vicinity of a source of brick-making clay. At the time of abandonment, the first of the brick-makers' plots covered 1,720 and the second close up 2,160 m²; in the first, there were three and in the second two kilns. The initial step of production was the preparation of air-dried bricks for firing. The second step is represented by the wasters that the brick-makers had not managed to remove from their kilns, and the third step was evident from the fired products stored under the porches and ready for sale. One of the kilns in Homestead I preserved burnt roof tiles and floor tiles, whereas in one of the kilns in Homestead II were burnt floor tiles and bricks. These were the basic products of both brickworks, which left their mark also in exceptionally abundant waste.

The potters' homesteads were of radically different sizes. While the plot of Homestead VIII occupied only about 1000 m² , Homestead XII covered 2950 m², almost three times as much, a difference reflecting the extent of the production facilities. The commencement of production required masses of potter's clay, some prepared in pits dug below the level of the water table. Supplies of sand were quarried from pits in the plots. The fir-

ing most likely began in drying kilns and continued in firing kilns. The production was concentrated in central workshops, accompanied by other buildings. The storage areas for the finished goods are likely to have been on an upper floor. In Homesteads VIII and XII, pots as well as potter's instruments had apparently fallen into cellars from a raised floor during the conflagration. The potters' output included table- and kitchen-wares and stove tiles. Evidence for the production of stove tiles was preserved in Homestead VIII, where a stock of approximately eighty vessel-shaped stove tiles stacked in columns had tumbled from an elevated floor. In Homestead XII the fallen products included as many as 150 stove tiles carved in openwork with architectural motifs (Fig. 2:a-c). The 'rotating flame' motif (Fig 2b) appeared on stove-tiles manufactured at Sezimovo Ústí roughly one generation after it had first featured in Bohemian Gothic architecture (Hazlbauer – Chotěbor 1990; see also Box 4.1). The ceramic tile with the scene from Aesop's fable, *The Fox and the Stork* (Fig. 2:d), allows us a glimpse of the intellectual context of the craftsmen's clientele.

Archaeological study has also set the suburb of Sezimovo Ústí in its wider regional context, comparing it with the culture of the adjacent town itself and with the rural hinterland. The neighbouring villages in the vicinity similarly abandoned during the Hussite period provide an invaluable resource for archaeological research into Europe of the late fourteenth and early fifteenth centuries (Smetánka 1965, Krajíc 1987).

by Jan Klápště

reclaimed from the sea for new jetties and houses up to three storeys high (Helle 1995, Hansen 2003; for the study of a well-preserved suburb, see Box 9.2).

Towns and their hinterland

The impact of the newly founded towns on their hinterland, in other words the interaction between towns and their surroundings, is a topic so far little touched by archaeology in Central Europe and Scandinavia. Yet the emergence of a town had huge repercussions. The forest clearances, drainage and dumping operations as well as the provision of building materials, particularly timber for the construction of houses, had a considerable impact on the landscape. The surroundings were also directly affected by the establishments connected with towns but located outside the town walls, such as the leper colonies that were constructed outside because of the danger of contagion. Gallows, some of which have been rediscovered and excavated in recent years (Becker *et al.* 2007), were located outside town too. Moreover, the town walls did not always constitute the outermost defences of towns: there were often obstacles constructed further out. Above all many towns protected landholdings located outside the walls or agricultural land used by the townsfolk with further defensive works, the so-called land defences *Landwehren* (Landschaftsverband Westfalen Lippe ed. 2007). They consisted of ditches, often water-filled, and banks reinforced by hedges which were as high as a person and interwoven to create a barrier that was difficult to penetrate. The roads leading into town were blocked by barriers, which were guarded. Sometimes lookout towers were also erected there. These external defences provided effective protection against attacks but it also demarcated a town quite visibly from its surroundings.

The most enduring impact was however the 'flight from the land' (Scholkmann 2009, 70) or rural exodus, which the emerging towns caused. Many people left the settlements in the surrounding countryside to settle in the newly flourishing towns. The prospect of a secure life behind the town walls and the possibility of freeing oneself from servitude to landlords by settling in towns were probably the most important reasons. As a result, many rural settlements in the vicinity of towns lost their inhabitants and were abandoned. The surroundings of the small medieval town of Rottenburg in southern Germany show the effect of these processes quite clearly. At the time of its foundation in the thirteenth century there were at least three rural settlements within close range. The largest of these was excavated: It had been established in the fourth-fifth century but was completely abandoned during the thirteenth century. Only the church remained and it became the parish church of the later town. The other two villages were abandoned during the Middle Ages. All that remains is a chapel in one instance, a farm in the other.

Urban houses

The results obtained by archaeological investigations and buildings' analysis are particularly rich in information about the development of town houses (Gläser ed. 2001). A characteristic of urban house-building in Central Europe is the fact that they are multi-storeyed. In contrast to rural settlements, the lack of space available in towns led to the combination of different functions – housing, storage, workshops, warehousing – accommodated in the vertical plane in a single building. The first step was seemingly the integration of structures which had hitherto been separate, such as the incorporation of *Grubenhäuser* as cellars dug into the ground beneath houses, which later developed into stone cellars. Such trends can be detected in towns that emerged already in the twelfth century. In Lübeck, for example, the earliest houses were timber buildings of one or two floors, whose sides measured 4-6m and which had a cellar accessed from the outside.

The town houses of Central Europe are regionally differentiated, influenced by earlier building traditions and conditioned by the availability of building materials (cf Ch 4, p 2, 66). An important influence on the townscape was the arrangement of the houses, with the house gables facing onto the streets or, as is the case in many regions of southern Germany and Switzerland, with their eaves along the street frontage. Throughout Central Europe townhouses were built of timber as well as of stone or brick and their appearance side by side marked the urban landscape from the beginning. Timber and stone buildings coexisted side by side in southern Germany (Flüeler & Flüeler eds. 1992, 225-87). In the twelfth and thirteenth centuries, two- or three-storied, rectangular or square, cellared, massive stone houses of various ground plans and elevations are documented; in most towns they existed as single buildings only. Their owners belonged to the urban elite. This is the case in important towns such as Basel, Zürich, Trier or Regensburg where such buildings are found in greater numbers and where the urban nobility's 'house-towers', which also had a defensive character, are still in part preserved. There were also towns where stone buildings were predominant in the more modest quarters, for example in Freiburg in Breisgau. But most townscapes were characterised by timber buildings, half-timbered houses on stone foundations or with a stone ground floor, which developed differentially by regions. The earliest surviving houses go back to the thirteenth century and exhibit construction types that differ from the later houses. The late medieval townhouse with its typical elements, such as heated panelled living rooms with bay window (oriel) on the first floor developed from the fourteenth century onwards. These buildings marked the late medieval townscape, while the stone buildings lost prominence.

Late medieval house building was different in northern Germany (Gläser 2001 ed. 233-472). High two-storied half-timbered buildings conceived as a hall with a super-imposed floor are known from the thirteenth century onwards. One type of early town house were tower-like massive buildings, the so-called *stoneworks* or *Kemenaten*. These square or rectangular multi-storied and mostly cellared buildings are documented from the twelfth century; they were often combined structurally with timber houses on the street frontage and are to be attributed to the urban upper classes. A second type of building found throughout northern Germany consists of brick-built timbered halls with gable-ends facing onto the street. They are known from the late thirteenth century onwards, for instance in Lübeck, where brick buildings have been recorded archaeologically from shortly after 1200. Multi-storied buildings occupying a large surface area and mostly without cellars, the positioning onto the street frontage of a heated living room (the so-called *Dornse*), and elaborate façades are characteristic elements which mark historic towns of northern Germany up to this day.

In Scandinavian countries it is possible to follow an evolution that to some extent was similar to that in Lübeck. Normally only churches and castles, and some cellars, were built in stone, although some towns had stone houses: Visby and Stockholm, and Riga and Tallinn on the other side of the Baltic; at the end of the Middle Ages also Malmö, in today's southern Sweden. Elsewhere timber building predominated, mostly of a single storey but at Lödöse in western Sweden there are archaeologically recorded examples of two-storied houses, and in Bergen they could possess up to three storeys.

Urban infrastructure

It was essential to provided the new dense population with a comprehensive access to water and a regulated way of disposing of refuse (Gläser ed. 2004). In many towns water was procured by means of private wells or cisterns in the backyards of the plots; they were constructed in different ways, such as barrel or timber-clad wells as well as stone-built ones. Public fountains were mainly fed from springs whose water was brought into town by means of water pipes. Examples in lead, clay or hollowed timber trunks are well documented. The earliest known medieval urban water pipe system is the *Wasserkunst* recorded in 1294 in Lübeck, where a water-wheel scooped water out of the river Trave and fed it into a system of wooden pipes supplying the eastern part of town. Here several breweries were established. After extending this network up to AD 1500, some 3000 households could be supplied over a pipe system measuring around 9.8km, which survived into the nineteenth century (Gläser ed. 2004, 182-90).

The accumulating refuse, i.e. organic refuse and non-reusable waste from domestic and craft activities, had to be discarded. Especially in large towns strategies for this disposal had to be developed. Solid waste was largely disposed of the rear of properties. This is documented by the many, sometimes very large and timber- or stone-clad, pits which were used as rubbish pits for discarding solid waste and as cess-pits (Fig 9.8; see also Box 4.2). Abandoned cess-pits and wells were also used. Large quantities of waste, such as waste from craft activities, could be used in land reclamation schemes or for drying out humid zones. Waste was also discarded, together with all the waste water, in the towns' rivers and streams. The waste water from households flowed from the narrow lanes between the houses onto the streets and then onto the water courses. The crafts that needed a lot of water, such as tanning and dyeing were located on the banks of rivers and the waste flowed directly back into the river (see also Ch 7, p 320).

The topography of craft and trade

There were a great many different trades exercised in the late medieval towns that produced goods for local or long-distance trade, depending on their importance, quantity or demand. While the houses of merchants were always located by preference in the vicinity of the marketplace, the workshops could be spread all over town, even crafts which involved a fire risk, such as potters' workshops or smithies and forges. Some craft activities were however tied to certain areas on the grounds of the conditions for production, especially the tanneries because of their need for water and their smell. As a result artisan quarters containing the houses and workshops of these artisans developed in many towns (for examples of shops and workshops, see Ch 4, p 169).

The processes of production and the resulting products, as well as the movement of goods are amply documented (Gläser ed. 1999, Gläser ed. 2006; see Ch 7, passim). Archaeological excavations have uncovered workshops of potters and metalworkers such as forges and the workshops where non-ferrous metals were smelted and cast. There exists also frequent indirect evidence for the work of wood-turners, coopers and wood-carvers as well as workers in bone, horn and antler. Leather is well attested archaeologically since tanning required static, excavated structures; as for the leather-workers, it is the cobblers that are best represented by their products. A technical innovation in the weaving workshops of late medieval towns, the treadle loom with horizontally arranged warp which could be lowered or lifted by pedals, led to a significant improvement in weaving techniques and to an acceleration of production. The workshops were located, as shown for example by findings from Winterthur in Switzerland (Windler 1999/2000) in the basement floor of townhouses as the damp conditions there were particularly appropriate for such work (Fig 9.9). As for the products of the building trade, they survive today in medieval buildings.

The towns became centres of organised and professional trade from the twelfth century, thanks to the market privileges bestowed upon them. In many small towns, trade was mainly local, supplying the town and hinterland with the locally or regionally-produced products necessary for daily life. The regional and supra-regional distribution of products and coinage as means of payment enables us to reconstruct the movement of goods. However, only products that survive in the archaeological record can be traced in this way. Thus trade in perishable materials such as timber, foodstuffs including meat, fish, honey, cereals, fruit, spices, wax, furs and skins are rarely found intact. Trade in wine and beer leaves indirect evidence in the form of finds of containers such as barrels or large ceramic vessels, and more direct evidence in the traces of lipids inside them (see Ch 1, p 45). The export of a given product, for example German stoneware (Gaimster 1997) can be traced through the distribution of finds outside its production area (Ch 7, p 291). In contrast 'foreign goods', i.e. goods not produced locally, tend to indicate import. The import of goods in a Hansa town, either as traded goods or for local consumption, can be documented by the example of Greifswald (Schäfer 1999). The following goods were present: timber from northern Poland, the Baltic area and southern Scandinavia, limestone from the latter for building, pottery from the Rhineland, the Low Countries, southern Lower Saxony and Saxony, crucibles from the upper Danube area, millstones from the Eifel area, glass from Bohemia and Italy as well as cloth from Flanders (see Ch 8, p 340).

Trade can be understood in part through static structures, such as marketplaces, guildhalls, warehouses and shops or stalls as well as through the instruments specific to trade such as scales and weights. The marketplace was the centre of trade in the late

Fig 9.8 *A latrine pit of 1290 in the medieval town of Greifswald (Archäologisches Landesmuseum und Landesamt für Denkmalpflege Mecklenburg-Vorpommern).*

medieval town. It was laid out at the time of a town's foundation and its surfaces were consolidated with rubble or wooden boards. Sometimes the remains of stalls have also been recorded. Large towns had several marketplaces for trade in different goods. Trade was also conducted from shops within houses. But above all, well-appointed guildhalls were built in which commercial transactions took place; sometimes specialised trade was carried out in such buildings, as indicated by their names: Salthouse (*Salzhaus*), Taylors' Hall (*Gewandhaus*) or Cloth Hall (*Tuchhaus*). Many such establishments survive today, as do the large warehouses in which the goods were stored (see Box 9.3).

Urban sacred topography

The late medieval townscape was prominently marked by parish churches, monasteries and numerous chapels that together show the great importance of the institution of the Church in medieval society (Slater & Rosser 2005; Schofield & Vince 2005, 175-211, Flüeler & Flüeler 1992, 437-93). Large towns and older foundations possessed several parish churches to which different parishes were attached (see the example of Viborg, Box 10.1). A particularity of the ecclesiastical organisation in late medieval towns was that the town churches were frequently put under the control of a pre-existing earlier parish belonging to a village in the area and that the subsidiary town church had no parish rights. The city of Ulm only acquired its own parish church when the Minster construction began in 1377. In Denmark and Sweden there are examples of parishes shared between countryside and town. But the majority were 'pure' town parishes,

Reconstruction of a weaver's workshop (end of 13th-14th century), in the medieval town of Winterthur Fig 9.9
in Switzerland (Kantonsarchäologie Zürich, Maria Szabó).

for examples at Nyköping, Arboga or Lund (the latter with several) (Andrén 1985). A number of archaeological investigations in parish churches have uncovered the original buildings and their subsequent transformations. Episodes of enlargement and enrichment in these churches provide us with a reflection of the growth and economic success of the town (see Ch 11, part 2). The cemeteries of the parish churches were sacred locations too. They provide data on the demography, the structure of the population, the pathology and the dietary habits of the urban population (see Ch 12, p 494; Arcini *et al.* 1999). The monasteries of the mendicant orders are a specific characteristic of the sacred topography of late medieval towns (see Box 11.3). These monasteries disappeared completely or partly from the regions of Europe that became Protestant after the Reformation, so that it is only through excavation that their structure and sequence can be revealed (Fig 9.10).

The late medieval townscape in many regions of Europe was also marked by the settlements and cemeteries of the Jewish communities. Synagogues and *mikva'ot* or ritual baths were at the centre of Jewish life. The cemeteries are always located at a set distance from the living quarters. However, the plots in Jewish quarters, the houses built on them and the infrastructure are no different from those found in other parts of town. The earliest building phase of the Jewish quarter in Vienna, which began around

BOX 9.3   ENGLISH GUILDHALLS

Fig 1

Trinity Hall (The Merchant Adventurers' Hall), York (©Giles).

Guilds or 'gilds' were associations of townsmen who grouped together for commercial and social purposes, and defined themselves in relation to certain claims or rights (Campbell 2000: 64; Gross C 1890; Reynolds 1977: 82-93; and see AME 1, 127, 307). In some towns, these guilds were the precursors of later councils and corporations, and by the second quarter of the thirteenth century many of these had their own meeting halls, as in York and London (Fig 1; Palliser *et al.* 2000: 177; Barron 1974: 15-18; Bowsher *et. al* 2007: 65-6). These buildings provided the models for the numerous town halls that existed in England by the end of the middle ages (Tittler 1991: 12, 29). Here, there are clear links with the kinds of guild and town halls built in the Low Countries and Italy throughout the medieval period.

However, by the fourteenth century two other kinds of 'guild' organization had emerged that also had a profound impact on medieval Europe (Farr 2000: 229; Lambrechts & Sosson 1994). The first of these were religious guilds or fraternities, dedicated to particular saints or devotional foci, and providing members with spiritual, as well as charitable benefits (Duffy 1992: 142-54; Hanawalt 1984; Hanawalt and McRee 1992; McRee 1992, 1994; Toulmin Smith 1962; Rosser 1994; Scarisbrick 1984: 22; Westlake 1919). The second group were the secular 'crafts', or 'mysteries', which were central to the organization and regulation of medieval economic life, and which often also played an important role in the political, social and cultural life of many European towns and cities (Epstein 1991: 164; Swanson 1988; Stabel 2004; Rosser 2006).

Urban councils and corporations often allied themselves closely with a particular religious fraternity, such as the close links which developed between the civic elite of Norwich and St. George's guild (McRee 1992) or the St. Christopher and St. George's guilds and the corporation in York (White E 1987). Moreover, religious fraternities also developed strong links with particular crafts, such as those between fraternities dedicated to St. John the Baptist and the Taylors (ie tailors) of London and York (Davies 2004; Dobson 2006). These associations often make it difficult to identify the specific groups or motives behind investment in buildings and other forms of guild material culture. But it is significant because it reminds us that religion underpinned every aspect of medieval European secular life. By the later middle ages, guilds had become one of the major foci for devotional and social activity. They offered their members a range of spiritual and economic benefits, including financial assistance with, and attendance at, funerals, and prayers for the souls of the deceased. Indeed, guild hospitals and almshouses func-

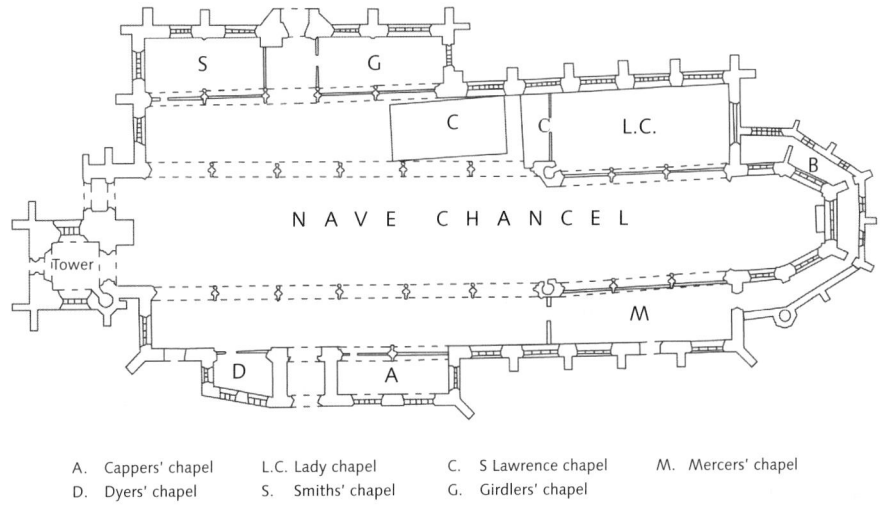

Fig 2

Guild chapels within St Michael's church, Coventry (after Cook 1954).

Legend:
A. Cappers' chapel   L.C. Lady chapel   C. S Lawrence chapel   M. Mercers' chapel
D. Dyers' chapel   S. Smiths' chapel   G. Girdlers' chapel

tioned as a species of chantry (Giles 2000a: 69-73; Rawcliffe 2008).

Given that many religious guilds and craft associations drew their members from particular parishes or occupational 'zones', it is hardly surprising that guilds began to build up portfolios of contiguous or neighbouring properties, often clustering around their church, hall or marketplace. In London, for example, the late-fourteenth century Gold-smiths Hall was newly-built north of the gold-smithy at the north end of Foster Lane, in which there were also fourteen shops also owned by the guild (Reddaway & Walker 1975: 29-30). This trend was not limited to the capital, however. In Leicester, the guild of Corpus Christi built a new hall in *c.* 1390 adjacent to the parish church of St. Martin and began to amass property either side of their hall (Courtney 1998).

English guilds invested in a wide range of buildings, but their initial focus was often the parish church, where they constructed their identity through the appropriation of space within the aisles of the nave. This is evident, for example in St. Martin's, Leicester, where the south aisle of the church and chapel dedicated to the Blessed Virgin was used in the fourteenth century by the Corpus Christi guild, then subsequently extended so that its west end could be partitioned and used by the guild of St. George (Banks 2001: 14-15). In some cases, as St. Michael's, Coventry, almost the entire nave became partitioned by guild chapels and screens (Fig 2; Cook 1954: 110-11). Surviving inventories of guilds such as that of St. Mary's, Boston reveal the breath-taking splendour and wealth of the fixtures, fittings and moveable goods of guild chapels – in this case both within the parish church (again partitioned in the south aisle of the nave) and duplicated in the guild chapel itself (Giles 2010). These inventories also reveal the rich textiles, including altar cloths, ban-

Fig 3

Corpus Christi Guildhall, Lavenham (Suffolk)
(©Giles).

ners and hangings and priests' vestments that decorated such chapels and which the guild liveries used in their ceremonies.

Throughout the medieval period, guilds met, traded, worshipped and socialized in parish churches, cathedrals, monasteries and townhouses. In York, for example, the St. Christopher guild met in the south aisle of the nave of York Minster (White E 1987), whilst the wealthy Corpus Christi guild used Trinity hall, Fossgate for its general meetings (Crouch 2000: 165). However, from the late fourteenth century and well into the early sixteenth century, many guilds also built new halls. In London, many of the Livery companies, such as the Taylors, appear to have adapted large houses bequeathed to the company, as guildhalls (Schofield 1994: 44). In large towns these halls often sat at the heart of a guild's parochial base or occupational zone. In smaller urban settlements, such as Lavenham (Suffolk) they were often located close to the parish church or in visually-prominent locations around market places (Fig 3; Alston 2004b). Guildhalls, like other buildings within the guilds' property portfolios, therefore played an important role in the

construction of 'public space' in late medieval towns and villages (Giles 2005).

The English buildings are often large, multiple-storeyed structures, with impressive and decorative facades, set within courtyards or adjacent to prominent streets or a river frontage. They appear to have drawn on both contemporary domestic and ecclesiastical architecture for inspiration. What all guildhalls had in common was the hall itself, which was organized hierarchically, with a 'low' end containing services and a high end, with a raised dais, mimicking the halls of the elite and perhaps also the east-west spatial and symbolic divisions of the parish church (Fig 4). These halls were used for business meetings, indenturing new apprentices and feasts, and were often sub-let to other guilds or organizations. Chaucer vividly evokes the use of these halls in his description of the Pilgrims' Guild:

'Wel semed eche of hem a fayre burgeis. To sitten in a gild halle, on the deis' (quoted in Toulmin Smith 1870: xxx)

Some guildhalls, such as St. Mary's Boston (Lincs) and St. George's, King's Lynn (Norfolk), also appear to have provided spaces for the storage, examination and perhaps even the sale, of goods, particularly in undercrofts with easy access to streets and river frontage (see also Ch 4, p 169). In more rural contexts, where guildhalls were much smaller, but still often two-storeyed, such as Lavenham (Suffolk), shops and workshops seem to have been accommodated within the Guildhall complex (Brown R J 1986: 190-202; Alston 2004b: 8-9). Rural guildhalls were often in close proximity to the parish church and therefore rarely accommodated a separate guild chapel. But urban examples often did so, whether

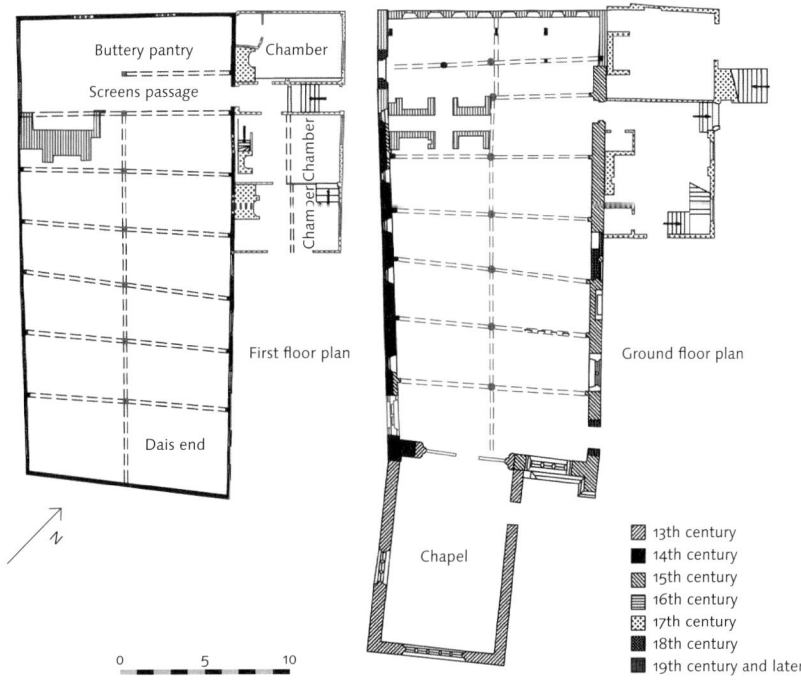

Buttery pantry

Chamber

Screens passage

Chamber

Chamber

First floor plan

Ground floor plan

Dais end

N

Chapel

13th century
14th century
15th century
16th century
17th century
18th century
19th century and later

0   5   10

Fig 4

Plan of the ground and first floor of Trinity Hall (The Merchant Adventurers' Hall), York (see fig. 1).

these were relatively small and low-key, such as that at St. Mary's Boston, or large and impressive, such as the chapel of the Holy Cross, Stratford-Upon-Avon. In urban contexts, these chapels were often located in close proximity to guild hospitals, maisons dieu or almshouses, which have recently been the focus of a major synthesis (Rawcliffe 2008). These buildings functioned almost like chantries, in which inmates were encouraged to say prayers for the souls of the fraternity or craft responsible for maintaining them.

The remarkable survival of medieval guildhalls, particularly in the provincial cities, towns and villages of England, make this an exciting and significant area for further research. Patterns are beginning to emerge from detailed archaeological investigation,

dendrochronological dating and documentary analysis of individual buildings, such as those of York, as well as Boston (Lincs) and Stratford-upon-Avon (Warwicks). These shed important light on the role of guilds in the formation and development of urban society and the creation and use of public space. Moreover, such analyses are also emphasizing the significance of these buildings in the post-Reformation period, as medieval buildings were deliberately appropriated and adapted to legitimize the authority and power of early modern corporations and communities.

by Kate Giles

Fig 9.10 *Excavations at the Carmelite monastery in the medieval town of Esslingen in Germany. The monastery was destroyed after the reformation.*

the middle of the twelfth century was characterised by timber buildings on strip plots. Stone buildings began to be built from the thirteenth century, as elsewhere in the town. The very large and vaulted stone cellars discovered in Regensburg – often several per single house – indicate an increasing need for storage (see also part 3 of Chapters 10, 11 & 12; also Wamers & Backhaus 2004).

Public health

Provision for social welfare in late medieval towns was through the hospitals (Thier 2002). These were places where orphans, the infirm, the old and the poor, but also travelling pilgrims were cared for. The sick who suffered from contagious diseases like leprosy were excluded from inner-city hospitals and were housed instead in leper hospitals (*Gutleuthäuser*) outside town. Excavations provide a graphic illustration of these hospitals and the living conditions of their inmates. The hospital's infirmary was a large communal room for all inmates, where they slept, ate, lived and were attended to. Attached, frequently without partition wall, was a chapel, as the care of the soul was deemed as important as that of the body. A large hospital like the Hospital of the Holy Spirit (*Heiligengeistspital*) in Lübeck had a communal room which could accommodate up to 200 individuals. From the fourteenth century onwards, as at the hospital on the Kornmarkt in Heidelberg, old people's homes were added; these so-called *Pfründnerhäuser* were places where lifelong care could be bought. The known household inventories of hospitals barely contain any artefacts typical for the care of the sick; instead they contain the utensils also present in ordinary urban households such as cooking and eating equipment in pottery, wood and glass. The archaeological investigation of hospital cemeteries gives insights into the living conditions and diseases of the inmates and indications as to the state of medicine. The skeletons of the inmates of the hospital at Heidelberg, buried in its cemetery between the thirteenth and fifteenth century (Flüeler & Flüeler 479-85) clearly reflect their origin in different social classes, given by the analysis of their dietary status and the examination of tooth wear. Nearly half of the buried population showed pathological symptoms in the skeleton, including caries, deformations of the spine, arthritis, badly-healed fractures,

BOX 9.4 MEDIEVAL BATH IN A ROMAN RUIN: CRYPTA BALBI

The Crypta Balbi excavations from 1981 were notable for their archaeological study of a continuous sequence from early Roman period to the twentieth century, all recorded to a high level of precision (Manacorda 1982). This excavation was the first of its kind in the city of Rome, and set a standard admired over much of Europe. To the director, Daniele Manacorda, and his team, the medieval period was thus as important as any other, and provided an opportunity to put well-known types of pottery (such as maiolica) into a stratigraphic context for the first time (Saguí 1990, 6).

Reading the stratigraphic sequence was, however, far from simple. The Roman presence consisted of a massive theatre constructed by L. Cornelius Balba in AD13. Beside the theatre was an area facing an internal courtyard (the Crypta Balbi), attached to a monumental *exedra* (semi-circular meeting area) (Fig 1).

In 1981 the strata lay 4m deep, and considerable skill was required by the excavators to distinguish the events that occurred and put them in stratigraphic order (Fig 2). The Medieval use of the area had developed within the robust hulk of a partly buried Roman building, itself surviving to different heights, which was tunnelled into, quarried and re-exploited. Its principal function from the eleventh to the fourteenth century was as a bathhouse with two baths, contrived in the corridor of the *exedra* (Fig 3). The eleventh century bathhouse had a water cistern and a furnace used to heat the hypocaust of a room

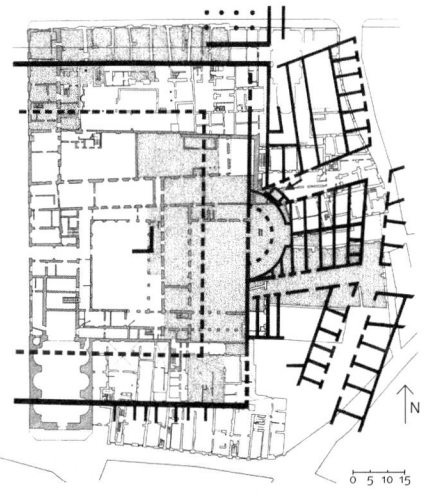

Fig 1

The Roman theatre of Balba (in black) and the convent of the Renaissance period (in grey). The excavated area is stippled, and marked with a black arrow is the part of the semicircular corridor of the Roman exedra that was recommissioned in the Middle Ages as a bathhouse (Saguí 1990, fig. 1).

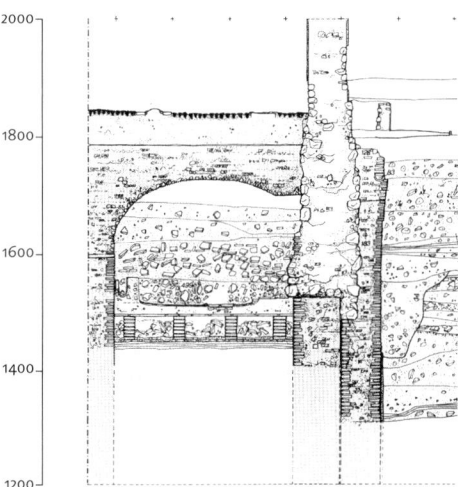

Fig 2

North-south section through the exedra, showing the hypocaust of the bathouse (left) (Saguí 1990, fig. 78).

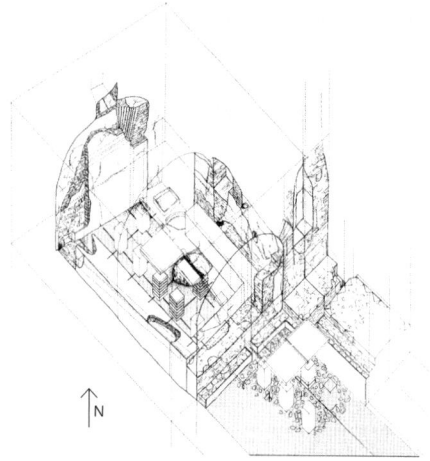

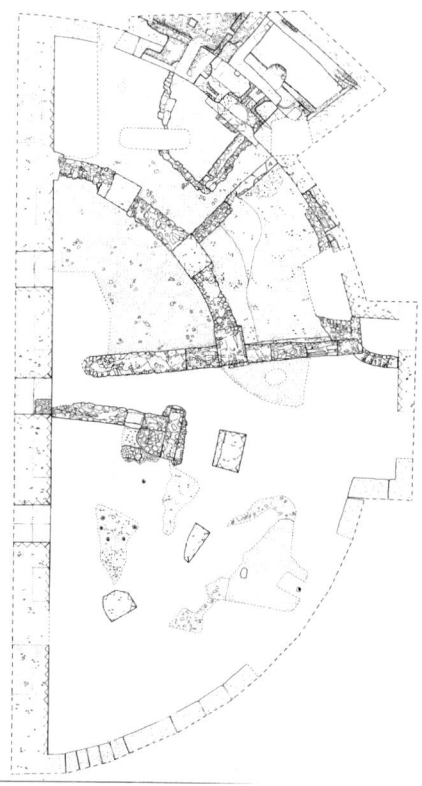

Fig 3

Axonometric reconstruction of the bathhouse in the late 13th century (Period VIIA) (Saguí 1990, fig. 65).

Fig 4

Plan of the exedra in the early 13th century (Period VI). The bath house is at the top right (Saguí 1990, fig. 58).

with a paved floor. In the late twelfth-early thirteenth century, the bathhouse was re-storcd, and a new entrance constructed. This phase was characterised by abundant coins and jetons, and the arrival of green glazed and polychrome pottery and protomaiolica. The bathhouse was enlarged and refurbished in the later thirteenth century, occupying the whole area of the ancient exedra and with an additional heated room – perhaps a sweat room (Fig 4). By the later fourteenth century, the baths were abandoned and demolished.

This example reinforces the situation that many urban excavators have confronted, namely that European towns do not nor-mally create a large dome of deposit, like the Bronze Age tell settlements of western Asia, with the latest phases at the top and the ear-liest at the bottom. Where there are robust constructions, as in many former Roman cities, the later settlement grows up around and inside them. In Poitiers, for example, the late medieval citizens tunnelled through the rubble of demolished Roman buildings and into the foundations of the town wall to make themselves a suite of cellars, later redis-covered, to their considerable astonishment, by nineteenth century antiquaries engaged in subterranean explorations of the town (Carver 1983, 361-369).

by Martin Carver (source: Manacorda 1982 and Saguí 1990)

rickets and infestation by parasites. There were probably many more diseases whose presence cannot be proved (see also Ch 12, p 479).

Care of the body, health provision and medical care were also provided in public bathhouses (Tuchen 2003; Box 9.4). Their location in the town was obviously dependent on the provision of freshwater. The bath chamber with sweat-chamber or plunge bath was on the ground floor, where there was also the oven for heating the bath chamber and dousing as well as heating arrangements for the boiler to heat the bath water. Next there were also rooms for undressing, cleaning and resting. The upper floor contained the living quarters of the bath attendant. He worked as a barber and attended to wounds and small operations. But he was mainly responsible for blood-letting, which medieval medicine considered to have a particularly beneficial effect. This was carried out through the application of bleeding cups, which, together with combs, brushes and scissors, are part of the assemblage found in bathing establishments.

Decline in the fourteenth and fifteenth centuries and the consequences of the Reformation

The economic, demographic and political crisis of the late Middle Ages meant that only a few new towns were founded during the fourteenth and fifteenth centuries and that these never developed beyond the status of small or minor towns (see above); this crisis is also noticeable in the development of established towns (Baeriswyl 2003, 270-3). The decrease in population brought the spatial expansion of towns to a halt. The suburbs were no longer occupied and inner-city areas declined as houses were abandoned, leaving larger plots of land. Yet the fifteenth century is also characterised by the fact that it was the period where topographic modifications were made in many towns, and this for the first time since their emergence. Catastrophic fires, but also economic recovery after a period of crisis were motives for restructuring the town, for instance by creating prestigious open spaces.

The Reformation had a long-lasting impact on urban development in the regions of Europe that became Protestant. It led to a comprehensive transformation of the urban topography, in a way comparable to the transformations that took place in the nineteenth century. While urban parish churches were adapted to spaces for Protestant religious services, the large monastic complexes and the chapels lost their function. They came into the possession of the towns or the town leaders or became private property and were either destroyed or given over to wholly or partly new uses (Gaimster & Gilchrist 2003, 221-324). Lund in Sweden provides an example. In the Middle Ages the town had around 20 parish churches. After the Reformation only the cathedral remained and Lund also lost its archbishop, a momentous event for the city. One nunnery church became a parish church and four monasteries disappeared. Even though these transformations did not happen overnight it was a significant change for the townscape. The newly created large open spaces in the inner-cities provided room for newly developing profane uses: town squares, new streets and buildings of different aspect. These developments had a profound effect on the physical aspect of towns lasting up to the remodeling of the nineteenth century.

BOX 9.5 THE ISLAMIC TOWN IN MEDIEVAL EUROPE

For a map and historical framework for al-Andalus, please see Ch 1, p 19

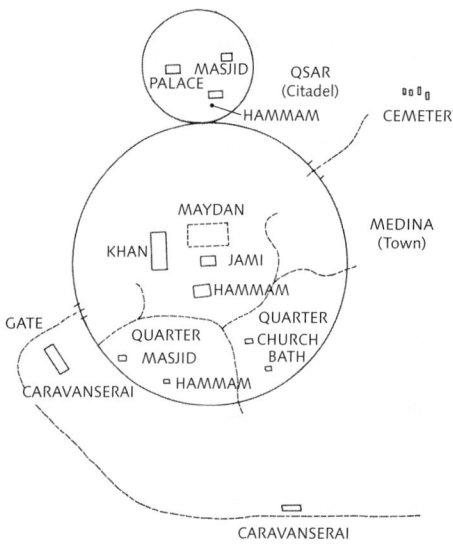

Fig 1

Schematic plan showing the elements of an Is-lamic town, with the qsar (citadel) the medina (town), jami (Friday mosque [sing.]) masjid (other mosques), hammam (baths) maydan (market hall) and a Christian quarter (Carver 1996, fig. 8.2).

Defining the nature of the city under Islam has naturally been influenced by the background of the scholars concerned, and whether they approach from a western or an eastern perspective. Explicitly or implicitly, the point of departure for most western studies has been the work of Max Weber (1864-1920), who emphasized a difference between the Western and Eastern city. While the western city was engaged in putting Europe on the road to capitalism, the agglomeration of burgesses and merchants free of military and bureaucratic control that he saw in the east, did not, in Weber's opinion, qualify as a proper city.

The Weberian legacy is present in some of the issues that have dominated the historiography of the Islamic city during most of the twentieth century. William and then Georges Marçais examined the cities of the Maghreb that were under French colonial rule (Marçais W. 1928, Marçais G 1945). Their studies, along with input from Brunschvig (1947), incorporating information from Muslim law, that of Sauvaget (1934 and 1941) on Syria and the synthesis of Von Grunebaum (1955), defined what has been called the "traditional concept" of the Muslim city, featuring a long-term continuity of use and character (see Fig 1 for a model). These inquiries, which mainly involved detailed descriptions of the *madina* (the trading and residential part of the town), must be placed in the context of colonialism. Attitudes changed as decolonisation took hold between 1945 and 1962, since from then on European scholars could hardly maintain a belief in the superiority of their own social, political and cultural system (Raymond 1995, 318).

From the middle of the twentieth century and up to end of the seventies, urban studies continued to develop a more critical, socio-economic interpretation of the role of the medina and its changing history, and since the early eighties most of the literature has been permeated by the thinking of Edward Said, whose book *Orientalism* (1978) postulated that western interpretation was based on a number of insecure ethnocentric assumptions that had acquired scientific value by virtue of their repetition in print. The influence of Said is explicit in most of the voices of the new critical current such as Brown K (1976), Ilbert (1982), Djaït (1986), Abu-

Fig 2

Courtyard house unearthed in the Islamic suburb of Zaragoza (11th century) (photo provided by J. Mª Viladés Castillo).

Lughod (1987), AlSayyad (1991) and the Japanese school (Haneda & Mihura 1995). The main thrust of the new critique is directed against the alleged immutability of the medina, exposing the city described in the colonial literature as one that was actually itself created in colonial times.

In Spain, modern investigation begins (as in so many historical fields) with the work of Leopoldo Torres Balbás (1968, 1971). He considered that the cities of al-Andalus were profoundly different from those of contemporary Christian Spain. They manifested a *"uniform urban Islamic mould"* that was *"a consequence of a way of life"* and they were *"totally different to the Christian areas"* (Torres 1968, 68, 92-93). Emphasis on the socioeconomic and administrative aspects of the city was taken up in the work of Lévy-Provençal (1950) and Pedro Chalmeta (1973). In 1992 Basilio Pavón published a monograph with the same title as that of Torres Balbás and a content indebted to it, especially with regard to the overall themes treated.

But Pavón included a descriptive catalogue of 59 Hispano-Arabic cities plus 5 Luso-Arabic examples (Islamic-Portuguese), adding 35 more in his monumental 1999 treatise. In 1996 Ch. Mazzoli-Guintard published *Villes d'Al-Andalus*, a work based largely on Arabic sources but which also included some archaeological data, especially from the excavations of the abandoned towns such as Madînat al-Zahrâ', Saltés, Siyâsa and Vascos.

Traditional studies of urbanism in al-Andalus drew principally on written sources and the surviving urban fabric in cities like Granada, Toledo and Córdoba. Early medieval archaeologists carried out some investigations at abandoned sites such as Madînat al-Zahrâ', Medina Elvira or Bobastro during the first decades of the twentieth century, but their objectives were mainly artistic or historical and the results obtained were very modest. It is from the seventies that interest in medieval archaeology in general, and al-Andalus in particular begins, accelerating in the following decade thanks to the pace of rescue archaeology in modern cities with an Andalusian past, such as Córdoba, Seville, Granada, Toledo, Málaga, Almería, Murcia, Valencia, Zaragoza, Calatayud and Albarracín. Although some *madinas* and villages were depopulated or abandoned after the Castillian conquest, most settlements have survived as archaeological deposits captured in and under the Christian towns that succeeded them.

The urban planning of the Caliphate period is represented in the splendid courtly city of Madinat al-Zahrâ', the abandoned town of Pechina which corresponds to the former Bayyana (Almería) and, of course, Córdoba. The eleventh and early twelfth centuries see the final phase of Vascos (Toledo) and

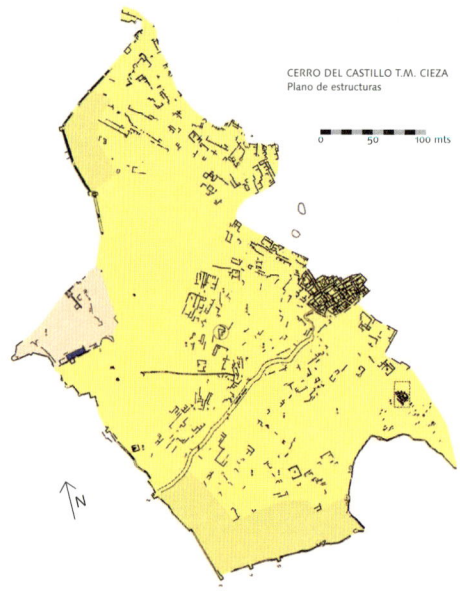

CERRO DEL CASTILLO T.M. CIEZA
Plano de estructuras

0   50   100 mts

N

Fig 3

Plan of the abandoned 12-13th century town of Siyâ-sa (Cieza, Murcia), showing the traces of walls visible on the surface, the area excavated (east), the citadel (west) and the cemetery (south) (see also fig. 4.12).

the recently unearthed urban complexes in Zaragoza (Fig 2). In the twelfth and thirteenth centuries archaeological sequences have come to light in rescue excavations at Murcia, Valencia, Xativa, Denia, Orihuela, Elche, and Lorca, and area excavations have revealed parts of abandoned sites at Bofilla, l'Almisserá, Yecla, Calasparra and especially Siyâsa (Cieza) (Fig 3; and see Fig 4.12).

The complexity of the topic and the great quantity of ongoing information coming from different disciplines, especially from archaeology and Arabic studies, mean that it is still difficult to construct an overall synthesis. This is why the work of the last few years has been mainly reported in the proceedings of scientific meetings. Some of these have

dealt with the topic in a general way (AAVV 1991; 2001), whereas others have addressed specific topics, such as the origins of the Andalusian cities (AAVV. 1998), or the information inherent in legal sources (AAVV. 2000b). There is also a large number of articles and monographs dedicated to different localities, cities and villages of Andalusian origin. Some of these study the complete medieval landscape of the town and others a certain urban element (wall, baths, fort, etc.). Some works are based exclusively on written sources, others are fully archaeological, and some combine both types of sources. Further guidance to the bibliography will be found in our monographs on the urbanism of al-Andalus (Navarro and Jiménez 2007a, 30) and on the site of Siyâsa (Navarro and Jiménez 2007b, 194-199).

At present almost all experts accept that the medina was not an unchanging entity (see above), rejecting simultaneously the idea that the traditional examples that survived into the beginning of the twentieth century need resemble their medieval antecedents. However, we have as yet seen very little tangible evidence for the origin and development of the earliest cities and how they were transformed into what survives. A recent thesis proposed the elements, relationships and basic operational rules of urban morphogenesis and then applied them to the Islamic city (García-Bellido 1999). In 2003 we published a study on the Islamic city and its evolution, which took as its basis the idea that all Islamic cities are constantly changing, and tried to define the guidelines governing the formation of the urban fabric. In effect we proceeded in the opposite way from García-Bellido, beginning with the archaeological results and ar-

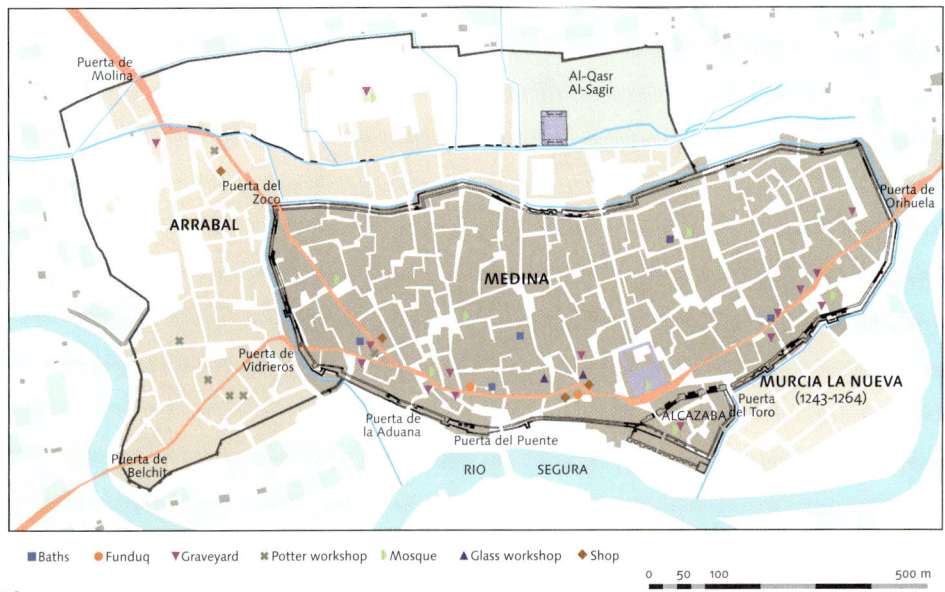

Fig 4

Archaeological plan of the city of Murcia in the 13th century, showing the town wall and the sites of excavations.

guing for the general principles that should apply. The sources used were basically three: archaeological, ethno-archaeological and textual, especially Islamic, and we focussed on two exceptional sites: the abandoned town of Siyâsa and the present city of Murcia (Fig 4) (Navarro and Jimenez 2007a).

The results of these studies show that urban agglomerations were initially much less dense within the city walls than they became in the later Andalusian era (Navarro & Jiménez 2007c). As the urban population grew, green areas disappeared, property was divided, houses acquired multiple storeys, encroached on streets and acquired jetties, and there was a proliferation of alleys and cul-de-sacs to gain access to properties behind. Religious forces were also at work. It was an obligation on all citizens to attend service on a Friday at the same congregational mosque,

which meant that there was a regular meeting of all the believers living inside the walls and in the hinterland. This had a number of consequences for urban development. First, it attracted a concentration of commercial establishments around the mosque; second, it developed a network of streets joining the mosque with the gates through the town wall and with other principal routes; and, third, it encouraged the linear development of souks on both sides of the arteries so generated (see also Ch 11, pt4). These changes gave us the town that became characterized as 'Islamic', but the true nature of the earlier, less densely occupied, Islamic cities of the Middle Ages still remains obscure.

by Julio Navarro Palazón and Pedro Jiménez Castillo

SPIRITUALITY

Introduction *by Martin Carver*

Christian practice and ethos dominated the material culture of Greater Europe between 1200 and 1600, but this domination was never total. The process of conversion from previous 'pagan' practice, which was often political and imperial in character, continued from 300 AD in the Mediterranean until at least 1300 in the Baltic where the southern and eastern Baltic countries were the subject of Europe's latest official crusades. Earlier crusades in the late eleventh-early thirteenth centuries were waged against Islam in the eastern Mediterranean, and the hostility towards Judaism, always present, erupted from time to time in the form of pogroms and expulsion. The catholic church of the Christian west, with its headquarters at Rome, held its territory jealously apart from the church of the Christian east, with its headquarters at Byzantium. Scarcely had eastern (orthodox) Christianity fallen to Islam in 1453 than western (catholic) Christianity began its struggle against the Protestant reformation that still continues here and there in Europe today. Catholic Christianity therefore triumphed on its own terms, although it never wholly won the intellectual argument, even against the 'pagans'. In this third section of the book we try to give attention to the less-studied archaeologies of Islam and Judaism (see below) while recognising that the surviving material evidence for European medieval spirituality is overwhelmingly Christian (for general surveys see Carver 2003; MacCulloch 2010).

Part 1 of Chapter 10 surveys both the Christian private scene, where a wide variation was theoretically possible, and the development of institutions - the diocese, the parish, the monasteries - where liturgical purity was continually sought and challenged. The archaeological potential for exploring private ritual practice is immense and largely untouched (but see Ch 12). Given that individual thought or dissent could invite censure or even charges of heresy, its public and overt expression was uncommon. Nevertheless, the clandestine gestures of belief that archaeology defines are indicative of strongly held ideas that were seldom recorded. Examples of how important this was to the development of societies have been deduced from documents of the Inquisition (eg Le Roy Ladurie 1978), but archaeology has the advantage of anchoring a practice in time and space, without the intervention of a clerical scribe. This kind of archaeological investigation, used for example to reveal hoodoo thinking among slave communities in America (Ruppel *et al.* 2003), detects underlying thought in settlements as well as cemeteries, and draws on archaeology's long experience of studying prehistoric religion. Thus not the least of the rewards of the study of private religious practice in the Middle Ages is the light that may be thrown on earlier prehistoric ritual, though this is by no

The west door of the Basílica de la Asunción de Nuestra Señora, Lekeitio, Basque country, Northern Spain (built between 1374-1487). (M.Carver).

means a straightforward reading. A good example is the cult of relics, whereby parts of the body of a holy person were conserved in caskets (reliquaries), from which good fortune and spiritual protection might be obtained, a practice which seems to have its roots in ancestor worship. The connections between prehistoric belief and emergent heresies, such as witchcraft, are also now being tackled by archaeologists, as well as scholars of other disciplines (Mitchell et. al 2010).

It is not assumed here that all readers in twenty-first century Europe or elsewhere will be familiar with the beliefs and ceremonies of the Christian religion, and so we provide a basic briefing on these matters and their material expression in part 2 of Chapter 10. As an individual, and within the family, the practising Christian was equipped with material reminders of belief in their household possessions (cf also Ch 5, p 190), and personal apparel – we give the example of a prayer ring (Box 10.4), as well as in the whole of their rural or urban ambience (Box 10.1, 10.3). In addition to private and congregational devotion, perhaps the greatest adventure for the individual in pursuit of piety was pilgrimage, which took travellers on long journeys in fulfilment of a vow (Box 10.2). This was a phenomenon with a large number of significant if unintended consequences – the enlightenment of travel, the entertainments of social mixing and the promotion of trade.

The institutionalised church was an elastic alliance between the Diocese, which served the lay population through a hierarchy of Bishops and priests working from Cathedrals and parish churches, and the monastic network, in which convents or colleges of monk and nuns devoted themselves to influencing the spiritual world through work, prayer and ritual performance. Each of these three spheres, private, diocesan and monastic, has much potential for the greater understanding of the medieval period through archaeological investigation. This will be our objective here; not only retailing some successes to date, but gathering some of the very much larger agenda yet to be explored.

The *cathedral* in its precinct was the headquarters of the diocese and contained the seat of its leader the bishop. As the principal monuments of belief, cathedrals were the subject of lavish and continuous endowment, and our examples hope to show something of how they were constructed, renewed and collapsed (Ch 11, part 1; Boxes 11.1, 11.2). Their buildings and furnishings encapsulate the best that could be contrived in the style of its day, and therefore act as deep artistic archives also for architectural and art historians. *Monasteries* represent some of the most successful of all Christian institutions in their own terms: the attempt to ascend to the summit of spiritual engagement by work, prayer and ceremony as an autonomous and self-governing convent, but at the same time creating their own highly lucrative agricultural and industrial estates (Ch 11, part 1; Box 11.3). Although Christianity had a spiritual executive that was all male, in these monastic orders we find women exercising power, both administrative and sacred (see also Gilchrist 1999).

Within the diocese was a network of *parish churches*, giving access on foot to every Christian in Europe. The parish church was the focus of local identity, creating a community in life and death (Ch 11, part 2). It was itself a theatre, which hosted the Mass and expressed the communal aspirations; and like other theatres the scenery changed as the relationship changed between priest and people and between classes – shown here by an example from Scotland (Box 11.4).

A medieval person saw life on earth as one aspect of their overall existence. Death was ever-present, and so were the dead. Chapter 12 part 1 reviews the life cycle, the battles for health, deployment of cures, causes of death and the farewell rituals of burial. The changing attitude to the final destination, usually the parish cemetery, can be read from the geography of the churchyard: more and more burials confined to a smaller space through time seem to describe a change from a more family-based to a more community-based allegiance (Ch 12, part 2).

Jewish and Islamic communities had similar structures of private practice and institutional worship, designed to provide spiritual sustenance and promote a moral code. The Jews were widely distributed in European towns, and interacted with urban society while maintaining a strong sense of identity (Part 3 of Chapters 10, 11, 12). Their commercial success was expressed in advanced stone buildings and investment in Synagogues and cemeteries. By contrast, only a small part of Europe was fully Islamic: most prominently south-east Spain, (al-Andalus) until 1492 (Ch 11, part 4) – and Sicily until the early thirteenth century (Box 11.5). Islam adopted or adapted aspects of the Christian infrastructure in both town and country, including the conversion of churches to mosques, a process that was sometimes later reversed. Both Jews and Muslims established separate new sites for burial that were to be subsequently reserved, respected and protected (Ch 12, part 3, Box 12.3).

The current archaeological agenda serves a considerable modern interest in detecting and explaining separatism and co-existence. Communities may theoretically be distinguished by diet – neither Jews nor Muslims ate pork (see Ch 1, p 53). But religious buildings and inscriptions provide a more reliable way of mapping religious allegiance in towns, since places of worship and cemeteries are likely to mark the residence of congregations and vice versa. In a routine that cannot have assisted the synergy between them, for Christians compulsory attendance at a church was on a Sunday, for Jews at the Synagogue on a Saturday (the Sabbath) and for Muslims on a Friday at the 'Friday mosque'. Although forming a minority with respect to Christianity in Medieval Europe, the proponents of the other two world religions followed similar strategies: the promotion of homilies, pilgrimage, prayer and investment in a professional infrastructure in pursuit of spiritual rewards. These are matters on which much comparative research remains to be done.

CHAPTER 10

ARCHAEOLOGIES OF BELIEF

PART 1:   RELIGIOUS LIFE IN PUBLIC AND PRIVATE
          (THIRTEENTH-SIXTEENTH CENTURY) *by Christina Vossler*

General overview

The transition from the early to the later Middle Ages is marked, from a religious view-point, by transformations which affect the organisation of the Church on the one hand, and the multiplicity of religious expressions on the other. The Crusades in the Mediter-ranean come to an end in the thirteenth century, after which the Church returns its focus to central Europe, the mendicant orders bring a wholly new form of monasticism, the established monasteries and the Church are constantly subjected to reformation movements and private piety increases in intensity. This finds its expression in numer-ous religious lay movements and, alongside this, pilgrimage spreads all over Europe and gifts and donations to religious establishments increase. A strong religious complexity is also reflected in the struggles of the Inquisition, first against heresy and heretics (Wal-densians, Cathars) and from the fifteenth century onwards through the persecution of witches. The increasing exclusion and displacement of the Jewish population as well as the re-conquest of the last part of Islamic Spain in the *Reconquista* belong to this context. By the end of the Middle Ages the whole of Europe is under the influence of the Christian Church; internal tensions and attempts at reform finally culminate in the split of the Church at the Reformation. This event ended a universal religious world order and was irreversible.

In Christianity, the concept of religion must be considered on two levels: one con-cerns the institution of the Church, the other is the personal, individual piety as ex-perienced and lived. The demarcation between the two is fluid and it is often difficult to pinpoint what took place out of private devotion and what was demanded by the Church. Not least is the question of what role the Christian lords played in conversion and their significance for everyday religious control, since they had the power to imple-ment, enforce or inflict the guidelines of the Church.

Institutional purity

As in the eleventh-twelfth century, continuing attempts were made to reform the institutional Church 'root and branch'. Most targeted the secularisation of the Church and demanded strict adherence to the ideals of chastity and poverty as well as an end to the purchase of offices (simony). A serious crisis was the western schism starting in 1378, which saw one Pope in Avignon and another in Rome: the authority of the papacy had reached a low point. In France, England and Bohemia in particular it was expressed in attempts to cut loose from the Church of Rome, but this was not carried through (Zschoch 2004). It was only at the Council of Constance in 1441-1418 that a new Pope was chosen for the whole Church. From then on, church-political and theological decisions were the responsibility of the Councils.

Closely connected to the problems of Church structure were the reform movements that developed on the margin or even outside the official Church. These included the new mendicant orders which emerged during the thirteenth century and which built on the strict asceticism of their founders, saints Francis of Assisi and Dominic (see Ch 11, p 466). The strength of this movement was recognised by the official Church. The orders obtained papal recognition and were subsequently integrated into the canon of the Church; above all the Dominicans had a significant part in the Inquisition and with it the persecution of witches which took place over wide parts of Europe from the second half of the fifteenth century and continued well into modern times. Other reform movements with extremist ideas such as those of the Cathars and Waldensians were however persecuted as heretic. The transition could be fluid, as numerous ecclesiastical sources from Eastern Europe intimate, where clerics were repeatedly suspected of heresy and magic (Wünsch 2006).

New religious lay movements emerged during the fourteenth century too; these did not achieve the status of orders, but lived as semi-religious or lay pious communities. They too had to fight for legitimation by the Church. Their goal was the emulation of Christ, whose life they wanted to experience through the care of the poor and infirm. The most significant of these movements was the *Devotio moderna* which originated around 1370 in the Netherlands. Faced with these initiatives the old monastic orders, such as the Benedictines and Cistercians, had to repeatedly adopt reforming measures to emulate the monastic ideals of simplicity and asceticism.

Also characteristic of late medieval religiosity were the new opportunities for a religious life for women. Personalities such as Hildegard of Bingen (died 1179) or Birgitta of Sweden (died 1373) were models for such movements. Through their own writings and through the founding of their own orders they were able to break into an aspect of life otherwise entirely determined by men. The nunneries were affiliated to the male monasteries in varying ways, ranging from a loose spiritual connexion to the foundation of twin monasteries of different types. A central element of this linkage was the spiritual accompaniment of the nuns by priests from male monasteries. The number of convents eventually grew so large that all orders greatly restricted the admission of more women in the thirteenth century or even, as the Dominicans did in 1252, temporarily gave up the spiritual guidance of nunneries. Alongside women's convents, a multiplicity of pious lay communities developed; the best known were those of the Beguines (Klueting 2006).

The Catholic Church's claim to salvation led to an increasing exclusion of other faiths, above all Judaism. What had started with the twelfth century Crusades reached its climax in the fourteenth century, during the period of the devastating Black Death epidemics of 1348-1350, in numerous pogroms; it resulted eventually, in the fifteenth century, in the quasi-total displacement of Jewish communities from Central Europe (Part 3). They moved further and further east and eventually started a new existence mainly in Poland, Lithuania and the Ottoman Empire (Haverkamp 2005).

The Islamic parts of Spain were re-conquered by Christians in the late Middle Ages. The Islamic sphere of influence had already begun to be pushed back to the south in the early thirteenth century, after cities such as Seville and Cordoba had become Christian again, until finally only a small territory around Granada remained Islamic. In 1492, the last Arab ruler was defeated and in the same year all Jews were expelled. Mosques and synagogues were destroyed; many were however simply converted into churches, as had been the reverse case after the Islamic conquest (see AME 1, 390 ff.; Ch 11, p 486).

Personal sanctity

A central element of personal religious practice was the confession, i.e. the care of the soul. Confession had been declared a common obligation at the fourth Lateran Council of 1215, and this promoted a more intensive confrontation with one's own life and therefore a more profound religious commitment. Confession required examining one's own conscience, and without confession it was impossible to obtain the forgiveness of sins and therefore salvation. Forming part of this salvation was the trade in indulgences, which bought time off from punishment in the after-life. This trade grew enormously up to the Reformation but had long been regarded critically. Tendencies towards greater piety were accelerated by a general crisis in the fourteenth century, which included failed crops and above all outbreaks of bubonic plague. Fear of death, of Satan and of purgatory (a binding dogma only since 1274) led to an increased demand for counter-measures. Such measures included founding religious convents, making pilgrimages and embracing a life in a religious community. Increased piety was expressed in art too, devoted to the altar and aumbries that contained body of Christ (the sacred wafer or host kept in a pyx, see Part 2, below). Images of holy figures became larger and more life-like. Christ was no longer represented as a king but as a sufferer and the story of the Passion of Christ was continually enriched with more detail (Dinzelbacher 2000).

The themes of religion and piety and their multifaceted expressions constitute research areas that are only just beginning to be explored in medieval archaeology. Although churches and monasteries were always on the agenda, it seems that it is only in the last few years that questions concerning the history of mentalities and the daily interaction with religion have come into focus. Religion and piety are expressed more broadly than churches and monasteries; they are reflected in the archaeology of landscape, daily life and burial, in both the ecclesiastical and the private spheres. Research into conditions at the time of the Reformation offers great potential, since it is there that questions regarding religiously-conditioned forms of expression, detectable in transformations as well as in continuity, are most acute.

Topography of religion: the town

Life in medieval towns was dominated by cathedrals, churches and monasteries. The steeples of this sacred topography characterised the urban fabric from afar: in many towns there was a church or a monastery on nearly every street (Fig 10.1; Box 10.1). To this pre-existing topography, the later Middle Ages added the churches of the mendicant orders, often located on the periphery (but see Ch 11, p 466). The growing bourgeoisie also founded many new churches and chapels. A further development of the late Middle Ages was the foundations of the Hospitallers within towns (Moritz 1983).

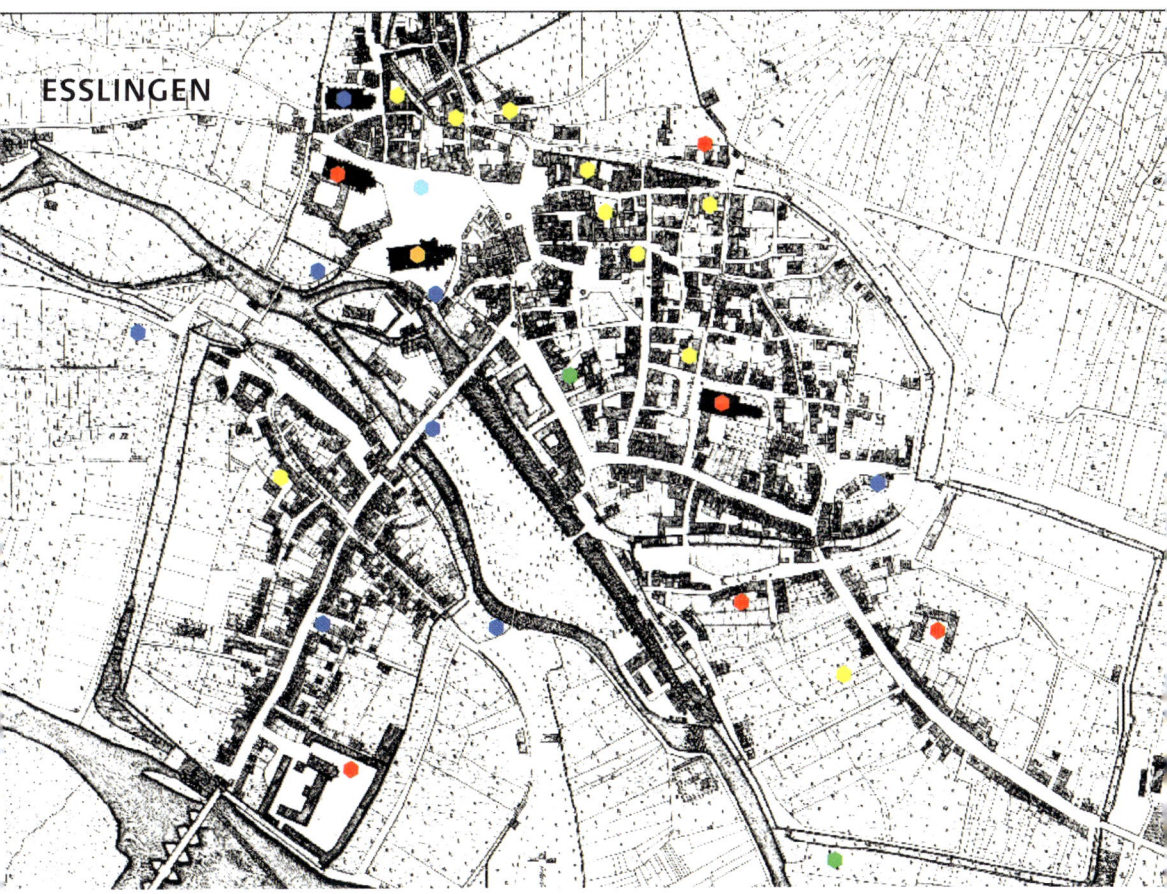

Esslingen, Germany and its churches, monasteries and chapels. red: monasteries, orange: churches, yellow: chapels, blue: hospices (Pfleghöfe), light blue: hospital, green: Jewish quarters (Vossler, after Regierungspräsidium Stuttgart, Landesamt für Denkmalpflege).

Fig 10.1

BOX 10.1 A CHRISTIAN TOPOGRAPHY: VIBORG IN DENMARK

The city of Viborg provides a useful example of Christian religious topography (Fig 1). Romanesque in origin, its cathedral was dedicated to S. Mary but also had its own saint, S. Ketillus, who was canonised in 1189. It was later modernized and supplied with chapels in the Gothic style. It had many side altars and was equipped with a large collection of relics shown to the public on feast days and at fairs in the town. The church was originally run by monks of the Augustinian order, but in the mid-fifteenth century the community was closed and the administration handed over to secular canons. The bishop of Viborg took possession of the former monastic buildings and transformed them into a large Episcopal palace.

Surrounding the cathedral in the town were twelve parish churches. Some of them were probably built in timber in the eleventh century and rebuilt in stone in the twelfth. The earliest, dedicated to S. Botulph, was probably founded under English influence at the time of Cnut the Great. The urban parish churches resembled those in the countryside, each surrounded by a small churchyard. A few were enlarged in Gothic style, while others were closed during the fifteenth century.

From before 1200 the town had two nunneries, one in the town centre and one just outside, across the lake in Asmild. In the second quarter of the thirteenth century, the Dominicans and the Franciscans established convents, both close to the cathedral. Both friaries developed into large monastic complexes (cf Ch 11, p 466). In the north-eastern part of the town, a Hospital of the Order of S. John of Jerusalem was founded at the end of the thirteenth century; its growing es-

tate prevented the development of the town in this area. Just outside the rampart to the south stood a hospital for lepers. The town centre nunnery was closed before the Reformation and the nuns transferred to Asmild.

The axial road led to the north and south gates, whence they departed in different directions. One kilometre from the town walls on the north side stood the church or chapel of S. Laurence while the chapel of Jerusalem stood a similar distance to the south. Viborg was on the pilgrimage route from Scandinavia to Rome, Santiago and Jerusalem (known from an Icelandic pilgrimage itinerary). Probably the chapels were used for prayer by pilgrims and other travellers before leaving the town. About 8 km south along the pilgrimage route (also called the Army Road), there was a small chapel dedicated to S. Margaret in a valley to the west. It was associated with a holy spring.

The countryside around Viborg was divided into parishes, and by the late twelfth century most of them had a church built of granite ashlar, giving a distance between churches of less than 5 kilometres. By the fifteenth century, most parish churches had a western bell tower and a porch. None of the churches in this region was totally rebuilt and only a few were enhanced with a sacristy or a private chapel. Some disappeared, for example Navntoft northwest of Viborg, which was probably closed after The Black Death; half the lands of the parish ended up in the hands of the inhabitants of Viborg.

Churches might be erected as memorials to important events. A chapel was founded on Grathe Hede, some 20 kilometres south of Viborg in order to commemorate king Svend who lost his life in the civil war of

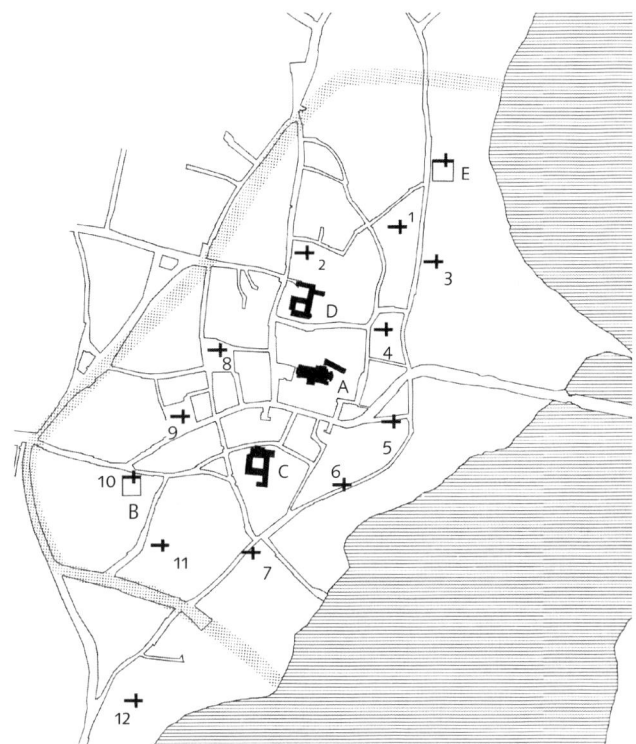

Fig 1

Religious topography of Viborg. A: The Cathedral and the major wing from the bishop's palace, former part of the Augustinian cathedral chapter. B: Nunnery by the church of S. Bothulph; C: Friary of the Dominicans; D: Friary of the Franciscans; E:Hospital of the Order of S. John of Jerusalem; 1-12 Parish churches. The dotted line indicates the location of the defences from 1150 following the terrain and leaving S. Michael's Church outside.

1157. Nine kilometres beyond the walls of Viborg, king Erik Glipping was murdered in 1286 in a small village, Finderup. Here too a memorial chapel was erected on the spot, less than 200 m from the parish church.

The huge interest in pilgrimage in the later Middle Ages resulted in building (or perhaps rebuilding) a pilgrimage church in a very small community at Karup situated on the great moors *c.* 25 km from Viborg. The cruciform church was dedicated to the Virgin and contained an effigy of the Madonna which was claimed to have wept real tears (according to later Protestant propaganda). Some hundred metres away there was a natural spring led through a paved area in front of a small chapel. It is unclear how the two destinations worked together.

Much of Viborg's Christian topography disappeared at The Reformation, leaving a legacy of legends. The beliefs of many ages sometimes resurfaced in material form. In many parishes, springs were believed to be holy, and a few were dedicated to a saint. But was their 'holiness' of Christian or pre-Christian origin? On one occasion, we hear about a cross placed on a prehistoric burial mound and provided with a collection box (Source: Krongaaard Kristensen 2004).

by Hans Krongaard Kristensen

Mostly instigated by religious communities as well as by monastic orders, but especially through the knightly orders (the Knights of St John, the Order of Saint Lazarus, the German Order, the Order of the Holy Spirit), they became a significant component of the social fabric of towns. Some medieval hospitals have by now been excavated, for example in Lübeck, Soest and London. The modest accommodation of the early days gave way to more and more complex arrangements in the late Middle Ages, involving composite buildings with a chapel, living quarters and ancillary buildings, and often a cemetery. An architecturally distinctive feature is the direct access between the infirmary and the chapel that allowed the sick to take part in religious services from their bed, as for example S. John's hospital Bruges, where aisles added to house the sick were dated by dendrochronology to 1268 and 1285 (Coomans 2007, 191; Ch 12, p 498).

The Reformation brought about the destruction, either partial or total, of many ecclesiastical establishments, especially the monasteries, so that archaeology constitutes an important source of information for the understanding of medieval sacred topography. On urban excavations the areas of formal monasteries and even entire monastic precincts have been investigated (for example Münster in Germany). The rewards offer more than just a structural sequence: the rich assemblages give precious indications about life and work in a monastery. The opportunity to compare the different orders under similar social, spatial and political conditions is of particular interest here. In large towns monastic hospices complement the sacred topography. These establishments of the Cistercian and Benedictine monasteries located outside towns were mostly places where they could trade their products. But they were also often provided with a chapel, thus representing the outlying monasteries.

The processional ways, which on certain holy days determined by the Church (Palm Sunday, Ascension) led out of the church, through town and past other churches, form another aspect of urban religious life. This is particularly well documented in Zürich, where the 'Liber Ordinarius' of 1260 describes these routes in detail (Wiener & Jezler 1992). But it has proved difficult to identify them archaeologically.

In many towns the Jewish quarter can be identified as a separate entity and in today's urban plan it survives in street names such as 'Judengasse' (Fig 10.2; see Part 3 below, and AME 1, 39ff). These quarters were however not strictly demarcated; the Jewish ghettos developed sporadically in the late fifteenth century. In many towns, especially in the Mediterranean area, Jews and Christians long lived together near the town centres. Churches and synagogues are frequently found close together, as for example in Speyer (Germany) or Gerona (Spain) (see Ch 11, p 484). The displacement of the Jewish population that began in France at the end of the thirteenth century led to the disappearance or major transformation of buildings. Their archaeological investigation has however attracted attention only in recent years: synagogues and *mikva'ot,* cemeteries and even whole Jewish quarters have been excavated, for example in Regensburg, Speyer and Lorca (see Ch 11, part 3). The Jewish sacred buildings are quite distinct from the Christian ones, but the living areas contain buildings and assemblages that are barely distinguishable from those in other quarters. This could be interpreted as a sign of good integration, but in many towns the Jewish population was forbidden to exercise

Gerona/Spain. The Jewish quarter in the middle of town next to the big cathedral (model at the Museu d'Història dels Jueus; Havercamp 2005, 30). Fig 10.2

a craft, which impeded the production of culturally distinct goods. The conception of Jews as money-lenders severely obscures understanding of the actual situation. Indeed in the southern countries of France and Spain, where the largest Jewish communities were living, there are written sources recording the most diverse occupations, such as traders, doctors, craftsmen, book printers and also farmers (Haverkamp 2005).

Private religion: religious objects of daily life

Following the canonical transformations of the early thirteenth century set down in the Lateran Councils (above), more and more places were designated as places of pilgrimage, new holy days were introduced (for example Corpus Christi in 1246), the number of saints grew steadily and obscure saints such as Christopher or the Fourteen Saints ('Nothelfer') gained prominence (Angenendt 2000; Webb 2002). There was a figure or a patron saint for every aspect of life and they could be conceived in the most diverse of forms. The mysticism of the thirteenth and fourteenth centuries gave rise to writings that expounded on the relationship between God and individuals: they spread rapidly through publications personalised by figures such as Birgitta of Sweden (above).

Central to this private piety were devotional objects and images, rosaries and pilgrimage souvenirs as well as private prayer books. Many noblemen and rich burghers built devotional rooms and chapels in their own houses. Architecturally well-docu-

BOX 10.2 PILGRIM BADGES: A CASE STUDY FROM THE NETHERLANDS

Pilgrimage

The journeys undertaken by medieval pilgrims leave their trail in the metal souvenirs subsequently found in archaeological excavations or as casual finds. The distribution patterns show us the favoured shrines often far from home, and the social and economic implications of these attractions. The patterns themselves require records of find spots and types to be systematically made, the kind of data-base being developed at the Art History department of the Radboud University in Nijmegen (the Netherlands). The data base, named *Kunera*, after a saint venerated in Rhenen, registers individual and groups of finds of badges and flasks in a Geographical Information System (http://

Fig 1

Our Lady of 's-Hertogenbosch, c. 1300, oak, 102 cm, Cathedral of St. John, 's-Hertogenbosch.

www.kunera.nl). The utility of this approach will be illustrated by considering a case-study focussed on the pilgrimage site of 's-Hertogenbosch in Brabant.

For more than six years Hein Collaert, who lived in Berghem near Oss, suffered from the falling sickness (epilepsy). Five pilgrimages to Kornelimünster where he prayed to the relic of the skull of the third-century pope Cornelius, were unable to relieve him. But when he promised to make a pilgrimage to Our Lady of 's-Hertogenbosch and to give his weight in wine and wheat as offering, he was immediately cured. On 11th May 1383 Hein came to 's-Hertogenbosch to give thanks to the statue of the Virgin there (Hens *et al* 1978, 249).

We can read this anecdote in one of the 481 reports of miracles that were registered and preserved in the *Miracle book* of Our Lady of 's-Hertogenbosch [*Bossche Mirakelboek*] of 1382-1603 that is devoted to the statue of the Virgin in the Church, now the Cathedral, of S. John in 's-Hertogenbosch (Fig. 1). In the fifteenth and sixteenth centuries, it was one of the most important pilgrimage churches in the Netherlands (Margry & Caspers 1997-2004, vol 2, 395-424). Whether they had come there to pray for something or to show their gratitude, pilgrims purchased badges (Fig. 2). The image on these religious objects served as a reminder of the shrine they had visited; in addition they had a protective function, driving away evil and bringing luck (van Heeringen *et al* 1987; van Beuningen & Koldeweij 1993, 2001, 7-10; Spencer 1998; Koldeweij 1999, 2006).

We know of pilgrims' souvenirs in the form of badges and small flasks (ampoules)

Fig 2

(left) Badge of Our Lady of 's-Hertogenbosch, Cathedral of St. John, 's-Hertogenbosch, 1400-1499, pewter alloy, 8.9 x 6.1 x 0.2 cm, found in Nieuwlande (van Heeringen et al. 1987, p. 78-9, nr. 11.2.) (right) Mirror badge of Our Lady of 's-Hertogenbosch, Cathedral of St. John, 's-Hertogenbosch, 1400-1449, pewter, 6 x 4,3 cm, found in Nieuwlande (Uden, Museum of Religious Art, inv. BM 1988.6.7.1).

than 20 types) demonstrates that there was an enormous trade in such badges in the town, and of these relatively few have come to light. Fixed elements of the various types are the image of the Virgin (crowned with Child and sceptre), John the Evangelist, a kneeling pilgrim, one or more trees (the coat of arms of the town [bos(ch) = wood]) and various ex-votos (Fig 2). Like the silver pilgrim, the ex-votos on the badges from 's-Hertogenbosch, such as a leg, crutches, chains, a model ship and a shirt, are to be found listed as gifts in the miracle book of Our Lady of 's-Hertogenbosch. The other elements – the architecture of the church and the image of John the Evangelist – also seem to be very concrete indications of the actual historical situation in the Church of St. John (van Beuningen and Koldeweij 1993, 58-63; Koldeweij J 1998).

Geographical patterns

Analysis and comparison of groups of badges and flasks offers information about the travels and behaviour of pilgrims in the late Middle Ages. Pilgrims' souvenirs that were made and sold in one place and then came to light in another give insight into the routes, the number of pilgrimages and the distances travelled to a particular shrine. In a broader context, they also give insight into the religious, economic and political networks between towns.

Distribution of badges from 's-Hertogenbosch

When all the badges originating in 's-Hertogenbosch are placed on a map it appears that most of them have been found in Zeeland and Holland (Fig 3). The miracu-

from hundreds of pilgrimage sites in medieval Western Europe. With the exception of those placed on bells, reliquaries, in manuscripts and 'Enclosed Gardens', they are found abandoned in the ground, often with the help of a metal-detector, and occasionally during the excavation of graves (see above and Ch 12, p 507). Analysis of these objects gives fascinating insights into medieval visual culture, but can also lead to new insights into the actual devotion that took place at a pilgrimage site.

The pilgrim badges from 's-Hertogenbosch were first identified and presented in 1987 by Jos Koldeweij (van Heeringen *et al.* 1987, 76-80). Up to now 47 more or less complete badges from 's-Hertogenbosch have been found (http://www.kunera.nl, accessed July 2010). The great variety (more

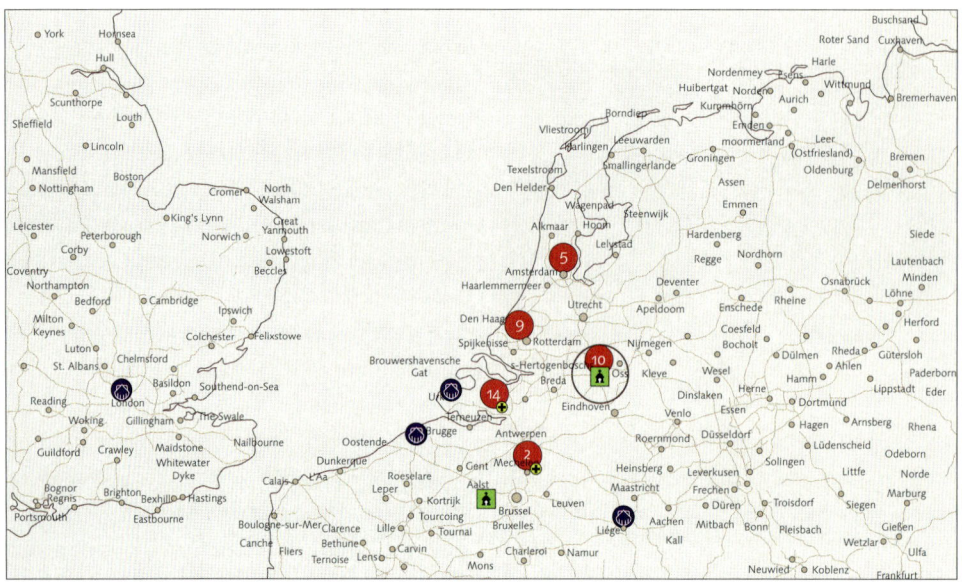

Fig 3

Distribution map of badges originating at 's-Hertogenbosch (http://www.kunera.nl, as in July 2010).

lous statue of the Virgin thus had a strong regional influence: the pilgrims came from what is now the Netherlands and Belgium. The single badge found in London seems to be an exception.

It is notable that at least 13 of the 46 badges were found in Nieuwlande. This can be explained by the favourable soil conditions of this western part of the Netherlands: in just such damp conditions the fragile – often pewter – badges were preserved from the corrosive effects of air. One of the problems in this sort of geographical- historical research into pilgrims' souvenirs is the vulnerability of the material. Even though in the Middle Ages great quantities of badges and ampoules were produced, sometimes a hundred thousand per year for just one shrine, most of them have been lost, and what has been preserved has been by chance. Nieuwlande,

in the Verdronken Land [Drowned Land] of South-Beveland, in quantitative terms, is the biggest sources of finds for badges in the Netherlands, and as such can be compared to such places as Paris and London – but with the important difference that in the Middle Ages Nieuwlande was a place without any political, economic or religious importance. There was a certain amount of shipping to and from Nieuwlande, as a wharf with slate paving shows, but even this had no particular importance either nationally or internationally. At the moment the village lies under the surface of the water and its remains can be reached for only a few hours each day when the tide is at its ebb. From the 1920s archaeological research has been carried out there and – certainly since the use of metal-detectors – more than a thousand badges have been found; since 1991 it has been a closed and protected nature reserve. The question remains as to whether the number of finds at this site can be seen as 'normal' or whether the number of badges found is due to the favourable soil conditions and the fact that the whole area of the village has been the subject of intensive research (van Heeringen 1987; van Beuningen 1993). Due to building, cost, licences and time, at the moment it is often impossible to subject a large area to systematic archaeological research. This also affects the research into pilgrims' badges and that it is often dependant on chance finds.

The current distribution suggests that most pilgrims came from the western part of the Netherlands. But two written sources demonstrate that 's-Hertogenbosch was important as a pilgrimage site within an area of 200 kilometres or so: the *Miracle Book*, already mentioned, and the *Brugse Wegwijzer* [Bruges Itinerary]. The texts of both are integrated in the data-base and accessible to users (Kruip 2010). Pilgrims mentioned in the 481 accounts of miracles in the Miracle Book did come from Zeeland, but they also came from the northern Netherlands (Groningen), from the west of present day Germany (Dortmund) and what is now Belgium (Brussels). The implication is that the area of spread of the badges of the Virgin of 's-Hertogenbosch would have been much greater than is indicated by the badges found.

Distribution of badges found in 's-Hertogenbosch

Badges have also been found in the city of 's-Hertogenbosch itself, including badges from other shrines. Until the 1990s only five, somewhat uncertain, badges of various origins had been recognised. A breakthrough

came with the extensive excavations in what was known as the old Tolbrugkwartier [Toll Bridge quarter] from 1994-1997. These excavations brought to light not only the remains of houses, a fifteenth century pottery workshop, the Saint-Elisabeth Bloemkampklooster [St. Elizabeth Flower Meadow cloister] (1459-1892) and the Toll Bridge barracks (1744-1892), but also about 250 religious badges, sixty secular badges and more than a thousand other pieces of decorative jewellery. A number of the finds were the result of the controlled archaeological research in situ, while another collection came from amateur archaeologists who searched the route of the A2 motorway with metal-detectors. The majority of these badges came from an early fifteenth century layer of rubble that had been recycled for building (Janssen and Thelen 2007). Although the original context has been displaced, the assemblage nevertheless offers valuable information.

The geographical spread of the other badges found up to now in 's-Hertogenbosch is far greater than those that were made there (see http://www.kunera.nl). Southern Brabant, Flanders and the Rhine-Moselle region were the areas most frequently visited, but Spain (scallop shells), England, France, Switzerland and eastern Germany are also represented (also Koldeweij A 2007). The badges give an indication of which destinations were popular. Ninove (27 badges), Aachen (18 badges), Maastricht (12 badges), Geraardsbergen (10 badges) and Neuss (10 badges) were clearly favoured by the citizens of 's-Hertogenbosch, their visitors, or merchants in religious and other commodities.

by Marjolijn Kruip

mented examples exist in Regensburg, where they are also mentioned in 'Schedel's World Chronicle' ('Schedelsche Weltchronik') of 1493 (Hoernes 2000). More modest forms were house altars, portable shrines or tabernacles which were used in private worship. Devotional images and figures of saints in alabaster, ivory, wood or pipe clay (Signori 2005) also belong to this realm. The figures in pipe clay are well documented archaeologically (London, Cologne; Gaimster 2007a).

Souvenirs of pilgrimages can be traced back to the twelfth century (see Box 10.2; also AME 1, 386-7); their increasingly common occurrence in the late Middle Ages reflects the importance of individual piety. At first, the destinations were the long-distance pilgrimages to Rome, Jerusalem and Santiago di Compostela. From about the middle of the fourteenth-century pilgrimages became more numerous and destinations more varied, when places where miraculous events, apparitions of saints or images of miracles were declared places of pilgrimage. Thus travelling to nearer destinations became more common, a trend documented in several European countries (Fassbinder 2009; Webb 2002). The souvenir badges were part of the pilgrims' outfits and served later as personal devotional items, deposited because of their special healing powers, in graves, reliquaries or sanctuaries, as well as in farms and stables (Köster 1983). They consisted almost exclusively of metal objects cast flat or in openwork; in Santiago jet figurines and shells could be obtained. England is an exception: there mostly pilgrims' flasks were produced, filled with holy or health-bestowing water and worn around the neck. It is only later that openwork casts were produced. In the early modern period, massive pilgrims' medallions decorated on both sides replace the pilgrims' badges. Both types of devotional objects were mass-produced and sold at the pilgrimage sites as proof of pilgrimage. The Reformation brought this movement largely to an end in many parts of Europe, since pilgrimage was held to be unnecessary for the salvation of the soul by Luther and the other reformers. In Catholic areas the practice saw a revival during the Baroque period in the seventeenth century.

Rosaries are another object of late medieval piety, found in ecclesiastical and museum collections as well as in archaeological contexts (mainly graves) (Fig 10.3; see also Fig 1.15 and Box 5.1). These prayer strings became widespread mainly from the fourteenth century onwards and served as supports for prayer, since a prayer was said at each bead (see Part 2 below). Men often wore short strings with up to 15 rings, the women had mainly long strings with up to 50 beads, the form that eventually became standard. They are shown in the hands of individuals in numerous late medieval pictures, grave covers and panels, expressing the particular devotion of the persons represented. In post-Reformation times the presence of rosaries is a clear indication of a Catholic population. The survival of other materials such as devotional images or prayer books is highly problematic and these objects are generally only documented in written sources. For the modern period there are occasional finds of books in archaeological contexts, as recently in the excavations of the monastery of Bebenhausen (Germany) (Vossler 2009).

Rosary found in a grave at the monastery of Bebenhausen, Germany (Regierungspräsidium Tübingen, Referat 25 Denkmalpflege). **Fig 10.3**

The reformation: the end of a common religious Europe

While the ecclesiastical and religious aspect of the Middle Ages has long been the subject of research in church archaeology and monastic archaeology as well as in the study of burial rites (Ch 12, p 504), it is only in recent years that questions pertaining to the history of the Reformation have become part of the archaeological agenda. The increase in pictorial and written sources from the late Middle Ages onwards apparently made archaeology superfluous. But new research and several conferences in recent years are now targeting the transition period between the late medieval and modern period and show a plethora of new initiatives, research questions and results (Gaimster & Gilchrist 2003; Jäggi & Staecker 2007). Central is the question of how far religious changes had repercussions in ecclesiastical spheres as well as in daily life. The material culture is a significant indicator here; moreover, the question of change or continuity needs to be investigated in the social and societal relationships manifested in settlements, in structures of power as well as in the economy.

The reformation, starting with Luther's posting of the Ninety-Five Theses at Wittenberg in 1517, is the culmination of a development which began in the late Middle Ages and which articulated religious tensions expressed as repeated attempts at reform and in the intensification of individual piety. These conflicts led to the split of the Church.

Since late medieval society was essentially marked by the Church, it follows that the Reformation resulted in changes in all aspects of life in all social classes.

The Reformation does not constitute an end-point for the archaeology of the Middle Ages and the post-Medieval period is also increasingly attracting archaeological investigation. By straddling the two periods, it becomes possible to study the role the Reformation played in causing cultural changes, at a time when the evidence, from numerous surviving written and pictorial sources, increases significantly. This provides new opportunities but also a whole new set of major challenges. All types of sources must be incorporated into an interdisciplinary historical research framework.

In recent years we have become increasingly conscious that changes perceived in the history of religions are linked to cultural, social and economic structures. We must ask whether and how the upheaval in the church left its traces in material culture and what influence it had on other aspects of life. We must however also consider that in the sixteenth century the Renaissance brought further spiritual and artistic developments that marked the Zeitgeist as much as the Reformation, and the boundaries between them are fluid. In many cases it is impossible to decide whether transformations are owed to religious change or to the Renaissance.

The elements where archaeological remains are particularly capable of giving insights into the cultural impact of the Reformations are the church and monastic buildings and their interior arrangements, burial rites, material culture in its manifold manifestations of daily life, as well as urban and rural forms of settlement and power. The medieval, i.e. Catholic, churches and monastic buildings and their interiors met a variety of fates, going from continued use by Protestants with slight modifications to wholesale destruction. This is particularly visible in Visby (Sweden) today where the whole town retained its ruined monastic buildings and churches (Fig 10.4).

The circumstances of the Dissolution are to be investigated from case to case as they depend on a multiplicity of factors. Thus, countless monasteries in the duchy of Württemberg were transformed into schools for Protestant children and the medieval building ranges were in part fully preserved (for example at Maulbronn). The monasteries in the Protestant towns on the other hand lost their sphere of influence, as the new faith did not require the reading of mass, the memoria for the dead or confession for the salvation of the soul. Many monks and nuns had in fact joined the Reformation, as exemplified by Luther himself.

In terms of burial customs, we can observe changes: amongst grave goods the almost compulsory inclusion of a rosary or pilgrim's badge disappears; on the other hand the church interior is again more in demand as a place of burial. The choir, which in Catholic times had been the sole preserve of clerics is now (theoretically) accessible to all believers.

The clearest signs of religious change are seen in the imagery and cultural material of the church. The origins of this change lie in the strongly symbolic 'pictorial language' of the Middle Ages from which the reformers sought to distance themselves; now the central element was the word of God. The healing effects of the saints and fathers of the Church were dismissed, which means that in Protestant contexts their representation

Visby/Sweden. The ruin of St Katharina, monastery of the Franciscans, destroyed after the reforma- tion (Markus Wolf). **Fig 10.4**

mostly disappeared. Other individuals, such as the Apostles or the Evangelists, were however of great importance to the Protestants too and thus continued to be depicted. This had a direct impact on ecclesiastical spaces, where images, figures, crosses, etc. had been abundant in the late Middle Ages. Depending on the representation, some were forcefully removed in the iconoclastic movement of the Reformation but others were simply whitewashed. The stone statues of saints were mostly re-used as rubble, as demonstrated on several occasions in Switzerland and southern Germany (Gutscher 2009). But images still had their uses in Protestant contexts in the post-Reformation period, and Luther specifically referred to their didactic function (Wünsch 2006). Yet a shift from image to writing is noticeable. The written word was used increasingly in paintings, on pulpits and panels already from the fifteenth century onwards; first it acted as complement to the images and later stood on its own (Signori 2005).

This 'media change' from image to word was accelerated by the Reformation and indicates that larger parts of the population were now literate. The burial memorials – which originally depicted the dead and in the late Middle Ages acquired surrounding inscriptions and finally exhibited text panels in the modern period – also show this development (Ch 12, p 509). The style of memorials is marked by the spirit of the times and small details reveal important information for the interpretation of the confession (Zerbe 2007).

Religious change can be detected in the secular sphere too, for example in the stove tiles (Ch 4, p 157; Ch 8, p 348). They no longer depict holy images or motifs relating to the Passion of Christ but Luther himself, or individuals connected with Protestant power, as well as Biblical images in keeping with the Lutheran theme of 'law and mercy' ('Gesetz und Gnade') (Hallenkamp-Lumpe 2007).

It is appreciated that not all our readers will be familiar with the beliefs and practices of Christianity, a faith and an intellectual regulator that formed such a basic driver for the Middle Ages; nor that its material expression, frequently encountered in architecture, excavations and collections will always be immediately recognised. The Christian infrastructure is described above and we have encountered some of the more familiar religious objects in Chapter 5 (p 212). Here the task is to introduce the basic apparatus of Christian belief in use in the later Middle Ages, from the standpoint of an ordinary parishioner.

Christianity's basic tenet, originally owed to the teaching of the Levantine prophet Jesus Christ (*c.* 5BC-30AD), was that regulated and charitable behaviour on earth ensured eternal life and the saving of the soul (*salvation*), but this was increasingly accepted as only possible with the intercession of holy men and women and controlled through the ritual of an established church. This church was proclaimed as *Catholic* (ie universal) and the eventual destiny of all nations. As an institution, the church sustained a vast number of employees at a wide range of establishments, supported by endowments, donations, tythes (tax at 10% of income) and services in kind, and deployed in a complex hierarchy aligned with the feudal system, its development reflecting the gradual transfer of its power to the rising middle class (see for example guilds, Ch 9, p 396).

At the base of the religious pyramid, all farmers and artisans and their families would expect to protect their bodies and their souls, and those of their ancestors, through the performance of daily rituals. Some of these probably derived from former pagan local practice, which varied across Europe (see Box 10.3). Other personal ceremonies were more regulated, such as the *Angelus*, a set of prayers said everyday at midday at the workplace, on hearing the Angelus bell. Greeting, swearing, and good luck gestures all employed the signs and sayings of the Christian pantheon, particularly God the Father, God the Son (Christ) and the Holy Ghost (the three persons of the Holy Trinity), the Virgin Mary mother of God, and a large and varied army of saints, some initially derived from pagan deities but mostly featuring Christian martyrs and other historical figures.

The material culture of daily domestic ritual practice, included containers for holy water, statuettes or icons in the home, particularly of the Virgin Mary and favourite saints, and the marking of amulets, jewellery, weapons and buildings with Christian aphorisms or symbols, at first the fish, the Chi-Rho and the vine scroll and later mainly the sign of the cross (for an example, see Box 10.4). Most later Christians also possessed or had access to a rosary, a set of 50 beads designed to count prayers recited as part of private devotion (see above). Each decade consisted of one *our Father*, ten *hail Marys* and one *glory be* and had a theme (for example "The Annunciation"). The five decades on the rosary added up to one *Mystery*, of which there were three (The Five Joyful, The Five Sorrowful and the Five Glorious Mysteries). Saying the rosary, together with other kinds of *penance*, such as endowment of convents or pilgrimage earned time off (*indulgence*) from Purgatory (see above). The material evidence of endowment is often archaeologically invisible even in monastic graveyards. While it is certain that not all the burials encountered are those of monks and many must be their patrons, the spiritual benefits of humility and anonymity ensure that most graves appear poor, and so rob the archaeologist of a principal window on identity (but see Ch 12, p 504 and Gilchrist 2008). The material traces of pilgrimage took the well-known form of pilgrim badges and flasks, (see Box 10.2) but the Christian, like the pagan, must always have been equipped with other souvenirs, charms and amulets: flowers pressed in a missal, the dried knotted reed from Palm Sunday.

All Christians were required to go to a church every Sunday to hear the Mass, to confess their sins monthly to a priest and to receive communion at least once a year, and that at Easter or thereabouts (the 'Easter duty'). Those who had offended the church hierarchy could be denied communion (*excommunicated*) and thus hope of eternal life. All communities, whether rural or urban, had access to a parish church, and in many European countries the distribution of churches provides a direct insight to the pattern of medieval settlement. The physical form of a medieval church was closely associated with the words and actions to be performed there (the *liturgy*), which were recorded for each day in a handbook (the *Missal)* which survived more or less intact until the reforms of Pope John Paul 23rd and the end of the universal Latin Mass (Missal 1965). The Mass was the principal ceremony, consisting of a sequence of prayers and chants culminating in the enacting of the transmutation of bread and wine into the body and blood of Christ. These were then ritually eaten and drunk, as a beneficial feast (*Eucharist*) bringing comfort and wisdom to the communicant. The Mass had variants to mark other key rites of passage, such as marriage (Nuptial Mass) and burial (Mass for the Dead).

The parish church generally took the form of two rectangles of unequal size orientated east-west, the larger being the *nave,* where the parishioners stood, and the smaller (to the east) the *chancel,* at the east end, where the priest officiated. In many European countries, the building was often extended to north and south with transepts and aisles, to give the form of a cross, with a tower at the intersect (*crossing*) or the west end, either of which could carry the church *bell* in a belfry (Fig 10.5). A hanging oil lamp (*sanctuary lamp*) was required to burn permanently in front of the altar to denote the presence of Christ.

Summoned by the bell, members of the congregation entered, often by a *south door,* dipped their fingers in holy water contained in a stone or bronze *stoup,* and blessed themselves by making the sign of the cross on their head (father), heart (son) and both shoulders (holy ghost). At the west end was the *font,* a basin in which babies were dipped in holy water and anointed with oil (*baptised*). Candles were important adjuncts of the church ceremony, creating a numinous atmosphere for services within the building and excitement in processions involving hundreds and often thousands of people. Some ceremonies, such as those of Holy Week, were conducted in the dark (*Tenebrae*), and the church year began on Easter Saturday with the kindling of the Holy Fire in the dark by means of struck flint.

BOX 10.3 PAGAN-CHRISTIAN CO-EXISTENCE IN MEDIEVAL ESTONIA

Fig 1

A 'village' cemetery at Arula Kabelimägi.

The Christianization of Estonia, on the east coast of the Baltic Sea, occurred much later than in most parts of Europe; its territory was incorporated into Christian Medieval Europe only in the course of the crusade wars of 1208-1227. The social structures that characterized it emerged not as a result of internal change, but as a result of conquest. For this reason, the leading positions in society, re-organized after the European pattern, belonged to the foreign nobility, mainly of German origin. The community remained split into the German-speaking nobility and the native lower classes until the late nineteenth and early twentieth century. This social situation is reflected in the archaeological record of the cemeteries, which provide evidence for the long persistence of pre-Christian burial rites (Valk 2001; 2003). Especially conservative were beliefs and religious practices in the peripheral Orthodox south-east corner of the country (Valk 2006a & b; 2008). Different ethno-cultural identities can be mapped from artefacts as well as burial rites. For example, in the northern part of the medieval bishopric of Tartu (Dorpat), Finnic immigrants from the Novgorod region can be noted arriving sometime in the late thirteenth century and their identity can be followed until the middle of the fifteenth century (Ligi and Valk 1993) (see also Ch 5, p 218).

After the conquest in Estonia, a dual system of burial grounds emerged, consisting of churchyards on the one hand and 'village cemeteries' on the other. Village cemeteries, situated apart from the church, number more than 2500 in Estonia and there were, on average, 20-30 local cemeteries in a parish (Fig 1). There, the practice of furnishing graves with coins, small tools, utensils and ornaments continued; folkloric data refer to

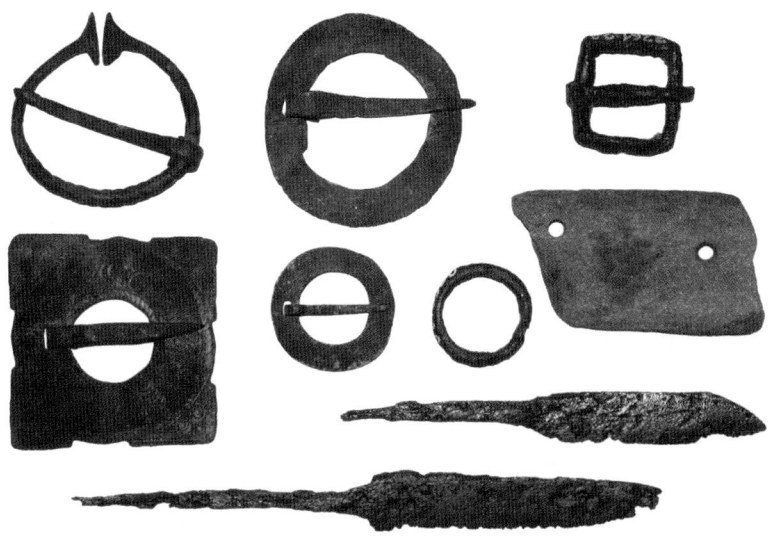

1 cm

Fig 2

Grave goods from Tilga.

its persistence until the nineteenth century and even longer (Fig 2). In southern Estonia, ornaments (brooches, rings and necklaces) occur in medieval rural graves. In peripheral areas, even the practice of cremation burial and, in inhumations, the burial of men and women with opposing orientation, endured in the village cemeteries alongside Christian practices until the sixteenth century. In the extreme eastern peripheries even weapon graves existed until the fifteenth century (Laul & Valk 2007).

In the districts where the old elite partly preserved its positions in the new power structures, a certain Europeanization of burial practices can be observed within some generations after the conquest. The acceptance of the new, European customs was mediated probably by representatives of the native nobility who adapted their positions to the new power structures. The process

remained unfinished – probably due to the increasing distance between the natives and the elite.

The persistence of pre-Christian traditions is reflected also in the long-time use of sacred natural places: sacred groves, trees, stones, hills and springs which were in active use, in parallel to Christian cult, until the nineteenth century (Valk 2003; 2004). These sites form a natural part of the network of medieval archaeological monuments in Estonia. Popular belief is reflected also in the archaeology of medieval chapel sites. i.e. in coin offerings. Votive coins appear in the fifteenth century and their number gradually increases until the mid-sixteenth century. The practice gained its peak in the second half of the seventeenth century, and lasted, probably, until the Great Northern War (1700-1721).

by Heiki Valk

Among the finds from excavations at the Cistercian monastery of São João de Tarouca, in northern Portugal, was a silver finger ring (Castro and Sebastian 2004) (Fig 1). This object was found inserted into the chapter house wall, which was constructed around the end of the twelfth century or beginning of the thirteenth century. The ring itself is inscribed with 18 capital letters separated by 7 small Greek crosses (Fig 2), each carefully made and spaced as follows: + Z + DIA + BIZ + SAB + Z + MGF + BFRS. The meaning of the inscription is at first obscure, but an eighteenth century manuscript describing 'virtue rings' reveals that each letter is in fact the beginning of a longer phrase, thus:

+

D - *Deus absconditus, dives, destructor mortis*
I - *Imago Dei, intellectus invisibilis*
A - *Alpha et Omega admirabilis*

+

B - *Bonitas Bonus Messias mediator propheta(m)*
I - *Iesu iustus procedens iudex vivoru(m) et mortuoru(m)*

+

S - *Salvator Sanctus splendor gloria(m)*

+

S - *Salvator salutaris Dei, seggregatus ab omni malo*

+

A - *Altissimus Agnus Dei qui tullis peccata mundi*
B - *Benignus spiritus animaru(m) sanctarum*
N - *Novissimus sacerdos*

+

S - *Serpens exaltatus in cruce vos q(ui) credis in ipso n(on) pereat s(e)d habeat vitam eternam*

+

H - *Homo, hostia, hostium*
C - *Candor lucis eternae, Christus, creator, consolator*
E - *Emanuel egenus*
B - *Bona radix Jesse, bonus et fidelis*
E - *Excelsior calis factus expectatio gentiu(m)*
R - *Redemptor rex regnum*

+

S - *Sancte Deus, Sancte fortis, Sancte et immortalis miserere nobis.*

It would seem that the purpose of the letters on the medieval ring is as a mnemonic to remind its wearer of specific phrases which were believed to ward off accidents and bring good health. According to one account, published in Madrid in 1630, when the Council of Trento and the city were struck by plague in 1545, the Greek archbishop Birando commended to those present a very similar letter sequence. This was said to have been used by St. Zacharias when Jerusalem was affected by the plague, with miraculous results. Apparently the letter sequences were placed 'in bracelets, rings and other possessions, carrying them on their left arms, the letters and their explanation, reading them and including them in their prayers. The effect was immediate, and the plague was gone'. In fact, similar later rings are also known. There is, for example, one of seventeenth century date from Oporto in Portugal (Vitorino 1932, 56-59) which is engraved with the sacred trigram of the name Jesus (IHS) with the following inscription inside the hoop: + DIABI + S + AB + N + S + H + C + EBE + R + S. Differences in the second half of the lettering may indicate a slightly different prayer or, quite possibly, a lack of

Fig 1

Finger ring from São João de Tarouca (Portugal) (A. Cabeço).

understanding on the part of the engraver. Similar letter sequences are also found later in printed form, once again as protection against plague and disease (Vitorino 1941). One German example dating from 1602 and entitled *Das Glückselige haus Kreüz* ('The home cross blessed with luck') depicts a central cross of complex form with letters overprinted along the arms. The sequence reads: DIA+BIZ+SAB+Z+HGF+BFRS. This paper was apparently considered protective against bad deeds, plague, fires and storms and this is confirmed by two anonymous Portuguese booklets of the eighteenth and nineteenth centuries in which the sequences are again referred to as 'the letters of St Zacharias' which acted as a 'salutary prophy-

lactic against plague and infection'. During nineteenth century plague epidemics in Portugal very similar prints were highly popular and widely distributed, either to be kept in the home or carried about the person.

The inscription on the medieval ring from Tarouca is therefore an early example of a long-lived formula that cannot have been introduced to Europe as a novelty in the mid-sixteenth century, as contemporary commentators seem to suggest. Its find-spot suggests it may have been placed in the chapter house more than 300 years earlier as part of the ritual of consecration. The individual responsible must surely have been a 'white' monk or, just possibly, one of the lay brethren. It is hard to think who else might have had access to a space like this at the heart of the monastery. Whatever the case, the ring was one of a number of objects of later medieval date that might be described as apotropaic, serving to ward off sickness and other evils. Other medieval jewellery with apotropaic powers include certain precious stones, cameos and, most commonly, the pilgrim badge which was touched against a relic or shrine (Murray Jones 2006).

by Mário Jorge Barroca

Fig 2

Inscription (S. Pereira).

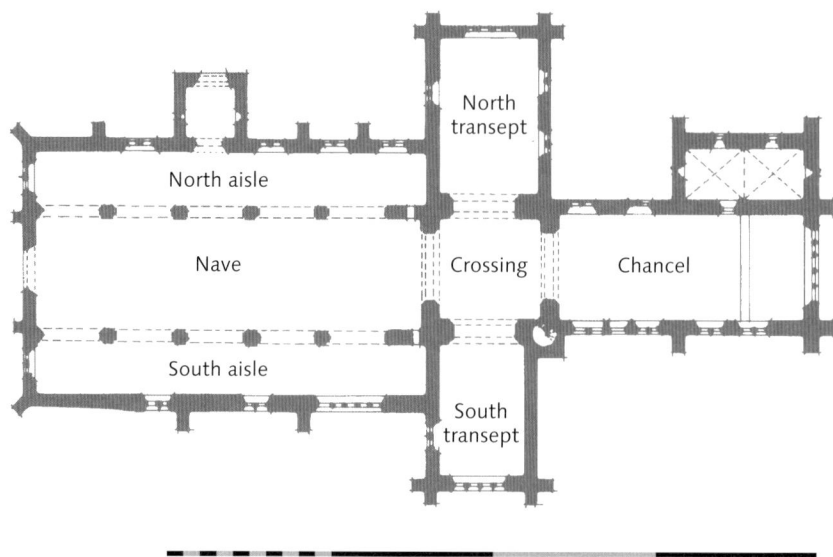

Fig 10.5   *Form of a late medieval church, showing position of chancel (for the altar, priest and choir), transepts (for devotional altars) and nave and aisles (for the congregation).*

A *chancel arch* led from the nave to the chancel where the altar stood, containing a flat altar-stone marked with five crosses and sunken space for relics, and on it the *tabernacle*, a small cubicle containing the blessed sacrament (the consecrated bread). Built into the side wall, or free-standing, was an *aumbry*, a lockable cupboard used to contain the sacred vessels and *relics*, human remains or objects attributed to the person of a saint contained in a reliquary. The priest officiated in an alb, chasuble, maniple and stole, deriving ultimately from the formal attire of a late Roman country gentleman. A server began mass by sprinkling holy water in the nave and chancel (the *Asperges*) a memory of the method of laying dust in the Roman villa. Another would then fumigate the nave and chancel with incense from an *incense boat*, sprinkled on glowing charcoal in a censer or *thurible*; this too being a memory of late Roman servants' procedure in the house of their lord (Doig 2008; Fig 10.6). The servants of the priest formed a hierarchy, rising from *torch bearer* (who carried candles), to the *thurifer* (who carried the thurible) and the *acolytes* (who served the bread and wine). In a small parish church, these were mainly boys, clad in the clerical cotta (white) and cassock (red or black) and they were overseen by a deacon, sacristan or master of ceremonies. Boys too would make up the choir, which sang the words of the mass, all in Latin and using the antiphon and response mostly following the cadences of the Gregorian chant. The performance of the defining rituals of the church was confined to males. Just as only a man could say mass, so it must also be observed that, whether as servers or singers, the principal actors in the routine rituals of the Catholic church were boys.

The Ramsey Incense boat (c. 1350) and censer (c. 1325), silver gilt; found in 1850 while fishing for eels, **Fig 10.6**
and attributed to Ramsey Abbey. The censer (i.e. thurible) is modelled on a chapter house (Victoria
and Albert Museum; Alexander & Binski 1987, plate 121-2).

The bread took the form of large circular wafers, *hosts*, kept in a *ciborium* in the tabernacle once consecrated. A measure of wine and a measure of water were put into two *cruets* that stood on a side table covered by a cloth. During Mass, the cruets would be served to the priest, who would use the water to wash his hands (the *Lavabo*) and to add to the wine. The host would be laid on a plate or *paten*. At the moment of consecration, the priest held the host aloft, and then held the *chalice* aloft with its ration of wine (a small glass-full) (Fig 10.7). At this moment the server would ring a *handbell* three times. After the consecration, the priest broke up the host and ate it and drunk the wine and polished the chalice with the cloth. Hosts of smaller diameter for the congregation to take at communion were contained in a *pyx* (a pedestalled container with a lid) and consecrated by association, by means of the lid being left off during the consecration. Ciborium, paten, chalice, pyx, collectively the church vessels (or *plate*), were natural candidates for the jewellers' art, although they could theoretically come in wood or pottery. Similarly, the priest's vestments and the altar cloths were the subjects

Fig 10.7   *The chalice and paten of St. George's Hospital Chapel in the town of Turku, Finland, were made by a local goldsmith in the 1440s, and donated by a local burgher family. These objects of silver, however, are stylistically indistinguishable from communion vessels produced in Northern Germany. The height of the chalice is 15.9 cm, and the diameter of the paten 13.3 cm (photo Visa Immonen).*

of increasingly rich and ornamental weaving and embroidery, as the parishes became more prosperous.

The Mass required a standard ritual performance daily but it varied in detail through the canonical year. The basic readings (Introit, Collect, Epistle, Gospel, Communion and Postcommunion) were specific to each day, as were the colours of the altar frontal and the priest's vestments. The walls might be decorated with murals featuring episodes from the Bible or the lives of the saints, and the sculpture would included statues of the Virgin Mary and other saints, as well as architectural carvings in wood and stone carrying a plethora of references to liturgical and vernacular meanings that are by no means all resolved. Altar boys and priest moved about the space in front of the altar, wearing a pattern of use on the floor. Each 'act' of the mass was introduced with a chant and pronouncements, with interactive responses from the congregation. The sermon, intended to reconcile the laws of god with contemporary events, brought both comfort and terror. The Mass had the force of theatre, but remembering that most of the congregation were not schooled in Latin (even if familiar with its epithets) the role of the cultural material – the stage props - was paramount.

The message of the building and its ornaments was not solely homiletic. The parish church also collected and preserved a record of the hopes and fears of the local community, its economy, the way it was structured, and its version of history. When the reformation came, focus switched from the ceremony of the mass to the preacher, and the script and layout of the church performance changed accordingly (see Ch 11, p 472 and Box 11.4). The parish church and its furnishings thus formed a material archive of a particular locality, at a time before archives were routine in written form.

Although the Church was universal in its objectives, there were considerable variations in Christian material expression all over Europe, reflecting a variation in liturgy and performance, and probably in belief too (see above). While previous archaeologists and historians tended to scrutinise this variation to determine a common original core, the modern agenda stresses the value of the variants in understanding local beliefs and loyalties (Doig 2008, 14, 124). By the period we are concerned with, the liturgy was the product of centuries of accumulated references expressed metaphorically in colours, numbers, clothing, carving, architecture and performance. Its execution was thus necessarily learned and professional – and often confused. This 'complexification' of the liturgy (Doig 2008, 81), and its consequent materiality, provides both a challenge and an opportunity for archaeological research in the later Middle Ages.

PART 3: THE ARCHAEOLOGY OF JUDAISM *by Samuel D. Gruber*

The systematic and planned archaeology of Judaism in Europe is a relatively new phenomenon that has evolved from several trends that even today are not always easily reconciled. Judaism is a religion and those who practice it are Jews, sometimes referred to as the Jewish people, or even the Jewish Nation. Jews have been traditionally defined by their adherence to religious laws and practice, but also by ancestry. European Christians have defined Jews based on broader cultural affiliation, created as much by birth and association than belief. The archaeology of Judaism uses material culture to investigate the past of the Jewish religion and the broader lives and culture of those self-defined as Jews, and those so-defined by others.

The roots of "Jewish Archaeology" lie in the nineteenth and early twentieth century German *scientific study of Judaism* (*Wissenschaft des Judentum*), an academic movement that advocated intensive study of ancient, medieval and post-medieval source material and set out to create a more nuanced history of Jewish settlement and community. The movement mostly saw traditional Judaism as an historic relic, rather than as a dynamic religion, and was thus rejected by most practising Jews. The *Wissenschaft* movement was particularly attentive to texts, but was also recognised the possibility of the new field of archaeology providing new information.

A similar movement developed in England, led by the Jewish Historical Society of England (founded 1893), which identified Jewish settlement sites in England from before the expulsion of 1290, and details about the names, occupations and wealth of many Jewish individuals. This effort has continued for more than a century and recently led to archaeological excavations in York, Guildford and London. Nearly contemporary with the Jewish Historical Society was the publication by Israel Abrahams (1858-1925) of *Jewish Life in the Middle Ages*, a work about the everyday life of Jews as much as about religion. It gave extensive coverage to material culture (Abrahams, 1896).

Along with the development of Biblical Archaeology in the Near East, Jewish scholars supported excavations in Europe. Archaeological investigation into ancient Judaism was deliberately developed in the Holy Land, first by Europeans in the 19th nineteenth century. In the early twentieth century, Jews resident in Palestine supported this work, and continued after 1948 in the new state of Israel. The Israel Exploration Society (originally Society for the Reclamation of Antiquities) was founded in 1914. Among many discoveries – which continue today – are the remains of synagogues and Jewish villages of late antiquity. Parallel to this, were accidental discoveries in Europe of signs of ancient and medieval Judaism in the form of inscriptions and synagogues. One of the earliest was the uncovering of the Jewish cemetery of the rue de la Harpe in Paris in 1847 (Max Polonovski, pers.comm.). In the second half of the nineteenth century Jewish scholars joined the study of texts and material culture by studying Jewish funerary epitaphs, including those from the catacombs in Rome, but also cemeteries dating from the twelfth through sixteenth centuries in Worms, Prague, Vienna, Lvov and many other cities.

In Palestine there was a growing interest and professionalism in "Jewish archaeology," while in Europe there was growing evidence – but not widespread interest – in the potential of archaeology to expand historical horizons. Unfortunately, many finds explicitly linked to the European Jewish past have languished in storage and the potential link to Jews and Judaism of other finds have received little scrutiny. One of the few publicly accessible collections of medieval Judaica in Europe was that of the Musée de Cluny in Paris, assembled in the mid-nineteenth century by Joseph Isaac Strauss (1806-1888) who displayed 82 items at the Universal Exhibition in the Trocadero Palace in Paris and exhibited part of the collection at the Anglo-Jewish Historical Exhibition in London in 1887. This collection, which is mostly comprised of synagogue and household ritual objects was later purchased by Baron Nathaniel de Rothschild who presented it as a gift to the French nation (van Voolen, 1986/87).

The Archaeology of Judaism in Europe as we know it today developed directly out of the destruction of European cities in the Second World War. Post-war urban renewal developed opportunities for archaeological excavation in bombed out city centres. Documentation of standing Jewish structures – mostly synagogues – had begun in earnest in Germany and Poland during the interwar years, but most of these buildings were subsequently destroyed in the Holocaust, and many of the researchers killed. After 1945, however, remains of extensive medieval Jewish settlements in German cities could be fully exposed and investigated. These sites – previously known mostly through documentary evidence – gave a new physical dimension to the medieval presence in Europe. Unfortunately, limitations of archaeological technique as well as post-War political issues, financial constraints, and pressure for urban rebuilding, restricted the results of excavation and analysis. Otto Doppelfield's work at Cologne was the most extensive; where he revealed the remains of a medieval synagogue that he dated to the eleventh century (Doppelfield a & b, 1959). An impressive multistory *mikveh* (ritual bath), a monument of early medieval engineering was also revealed (see Ch 11, p 479). New excavations carried out by the City of Cologne on the site since 2007 have confirmed much of Doppelfield's analysis, but has conclusively pushed the origin dates of synagogue and *mikveh* back to the Carolingian period and possibly – at least for the synagogue – to late antiquity (Schütte, 2004) (Fig 10.8).

The aftershocks of the destruction of Jewish communities in the Holocaust continued to influence Jewish scholarship in Europe. Two generations of scholars were lost – precisely those great teachers and their promising students who were most interested in the medieval Jewish past. Those that survived moved to American and Israel, far from the physical remains of European Jewish culture. Jewish medieval studies became again concerned almost totally with texts and movable objects. The methodology of the Center for Jewish Art at the Hebrew University, for example, emphasized iconography over physical context.

Nowhere was there any planned effort to identify Jewish sites, nor to further exploit the opportunities afford by unexpected finds. Throughout the Jewish world "Jewish archaeology" became almost synonymous with the uncovering of ancient Jewish remains, primarily in Israel, but also throughout the Mediterranean littoral, where a number of finds such as those from Ostia (Italy), Sardis (Turkey), Plovdiv (Bulgaria) and Stobi (Macedonia) attested to Judaism's widespread acceptance in the ancient world (Rutgers 1998).

Recent excavations in Cologne have explored nearly a hectare of the Jewish quarter, revealing a synagogue, bath, hospital, bakery and houses from 13th–15th century and earlier. Among 150,000 objects recovered are about 500 fragments of limestone from the Gothic bimah of the synagogue, with inscriptions carved in the form of animals and plants. These were made by English and French masons from the workshops of Cologne cathedral (courtesy of Sven Schuette). **Fig 10.8**

Medieval archaeology itself, as a serious discipline with its own rationale and methods continued to evolve, especially in Britain and in Germany and Italy (Ch 1). Many of the favoured archaeological conceptions such as urban archaeology and regional settlement surveys that should have brought more attention to the medieval Jewish component, however, tended to ignore it completely. A close reading of the archaeological literature from Europe between 1960 and 1990 would suggest that Jews were hardly present on the continent – despite their ubiquity in religious, historical, and legal sources as well as historical toponyms in many countries. Thus historians and archaeologists have different perceptions of the place and role of Jewish people in the European Middle Ages.

From the 1960s through the 1990s most identification of Jewish materials in Europe was almost entirely accidental (Gruber 2002). The most spectacular instance was the discovery of a massive Romanesque structure in Rouen, France, in 1976, that may have been a synagogue, but was more likely a *yeshiva* (Talmudic school) or possibly a scriptorium (Golb, 1998). In 2002, excavations in Lorca, Spain uncovered the entire plan of a fifteenth-century synagogue (see Ch 11, p 483) and surrounding houses.

The archaeology of Jewish sites has centred on religious and ritual sites. These were the most prominent structures of Jewish communities, especially synagogues and *mikva'ot* (ritual baths), building types that are also most likely to incorporate distinguishing features allowing them to be identified as Jewish (see Ch 11, p 479). These structures have usually been found in the course of building renovation or construction, or as part of other excavations. Recently, as in Regensburg (Germany) and Vienna (Austria), planned excavations have been carried out at sites where medieval synagogues were known have existed before they were deliberately demolished, and the remains of those buildings and adjacent structures have been exposed (Codreanu, 2004; Mitchell, 2004). In Spain, a sensitized archaeological profession is now more adept at identifying Jewish sites discovered by accident, and historians and archaeologists are also seeking Jewish remains. A rich array of documentary sources, as in Jaén, Spain, can help locate former Jewish settlements in towns and cities throughout Iberia.

For centuries, traces of many Jewish cemeteries have been found, mostly sites which Jews were forced to abandon during periods of expulsion, or which were expropriated from them by authorities (see Ch 12, p 522). Commonly, inscribed stone gravestones (*matzevot*), often in only fragmentary condition, have been found; mostly discovered in locations of re-use, incorporated in later structures, roads, city walls, river embankments, etc. where they served as ready building material.

In a few cases, such as York (England), Prague (Czech Republic) and Lucera and Tarrega (Spain) previously forgotten and long unmarked Jewish cemeteries have been discovered in the course of urban development. In the past, such cemeteries might have been destroyed without careful examination. Now, such finds are usually reported to cultural heritage authorities and they are carefully excavated by trained archaeologists. In some cases, their Jewish character was perceived when excavations began, but archaeologists did not consult with present-day Jewish communities. In almost all cases when the burials were identified as Jewish – either before or after excavation – Jewish communities and other Jewish organizations have protested about the excavation and especially the exhumation of human remains as a violation of Jewish religious practice and law. In cases where the location of medieval Jewish cemeteries is known, Jewish communities have generally encouraged non-intrusive archaeological methods as a means of investigation. Jewish communities and archaeologists are still developing procedures to lessen conflict over cemeteries (see Ch 12, p 526).

Medieval treasures have been uncovered, mostly as accidental discoveries. The two most famous medieval treasure "hoards" are those of Colmar, discovered in 1863 and one from Erfurt found only in 1996. These hoards of money and precious objects were probably hidden in time of persecution and mass murder of Jews, and not recovered. The Colmar treasure contained an elaborate early fourteenth century wedding ring. Nothing is known of the individuals or groups who hid the treasures other than their apparent wealth, but it is assumed that they died in the massacres of 1348. Similar accidental discoveries of caches of documents and many artefacts of everyday life have been found in *genizot*, (plural of *genizah*), storage spaces in synagogues used for discarded texts and ritual items. But with the exception of the famous Genizah of the Ben Ezra Synagogue in Cairo (Goitein, 1999), whose documents have helped rewrite the Jewish and economic history of the Mediterranean region in the Early Middle Ages, these *genizot* have produced materials only from the eighteenth century on (Wiesemann, 1992). In the case of *genizot*, after a series of accidental discoveries in the 1980s and 1990s in former south German synagogue buildings, more systematic investigations have been undertaken. An assessment of the excavations and the medieval Jewish presence in Worms and Speyer has been published (Engels, 2004a & b; Heberer, 2004) in connection with a major exhibition at Speyer (Historisches Museum der Pfalz, 2004).

CHAPTER 11

RELIGIOUS BUILDINGS

PART 1: CATHEDRALS AND MONASTERIES *by Martin Carver*

The practice of the Christian religion was administered within three main networks: the *Diocese* headed by a Bishop, with the Cathedral as his headquarters, the *Monastic orders* organised into Abbeys, each with their Abbot and monastic estate, and the *Parish*, each with a priest, a church and a burial ground (see Ch 10). The buildings that served the community at these different levels were of a size and grandeur proportional to their wealth and function. The Cathedral (*Dom*), containing the *cathedra*, the Bishop's symbolic throne, stood at the summit of the Christian hierarchy. Although its basic purpose, the performance of liturgy, was the same as in other churches, the scale of the activity was hugely magnified, and the investment prodigious (Fig 11.1). The cathedral

Fig 11.1   *The Christian flagship: the cathedral church of Saint-Nazaire, Béziers Cathedral, southern France. The cathedral on this site was destroyed, together with much of the town and its inhabitants, during the Albigensian massacre of 1209, and rebuilt during the 13th and 14th centuries. The Vieux Pont in the foreground, originally constructed in the 12th century, retains fabric of the 14th, 15th and 16th centuries (M. Carver).*

stood as the office of the principal authority, and not only the religious authority. Situated in towns, to which their presence allowed the term 'city' (*civitas*), they consciously evoked Roman governance.

Cathedrals: Designing and building

The basic spatial design of the north European cathedral was a pathway, not a place: worshippers entered via an atrium or collecting point at the west end, and made a journey towards the sacred east end and the beatific vision (Davies 1982, 186). In the later Middle Ages, the journey was enhanced by the application of the Gothic style launched by Abbot Suger at St Denis in *c.* 1140. While Romanesque buildings used more hefty arches to span wider spaces, Gothic spaces were spanned by clusters of ribs of an equal delicate size. The walls were punctuated by openings with tall pointed arches that thrust towards the roof line. Capitals were reduced to a minimum, and the buildings soared heavenwards, creating a flow of vertical energy like organic plants. Flying buttresses and pinnacles were added to the outside, but these too were symbolic rather than structural (Davies 1982, 168-192). In fact one could say that while the Romanesque church recalled the grandeur of a Roman official building, the northern Gothic cathedral evoked the mystery of a sacred grove, with the stained glass filtering many coloured glints of light through upper foliage.

The proportions of the plan were long and narrow in the north, sometimes making use of the Golden Section in acknowledgment of the work of God, as at Chartres. In the south, the tendency was to stress width rather than length, with the bays square, the smaller windows admitting the strong light of the Mediterranean. From the fourteenth century in Germany, cathedrals begin to smooth out the distinction between nave and chancel and came to resemble a single space, or Hall Church, creating less of a path and more of a meeting place in the lead up to reform (ibid. 188-9; Coomans 2007, 192, 198).

The foundations of these huge buildings were correspondingly massive: early examples on soft ground used close-set timber piles, and later trenches filled with rubble or large cobbles. The walls were carried up in ashlar blocks marked up by masons (Fig 11.2) and bonded with lime mortar. Piers took the place of nave walls, with access to the aisles between them. The engineering achievement of creating vaults out of clusters of ribs was sometimes defeated by inadequate appreciation of the character of load-bearing soil and lime mortar, and gradual movement in both could lead to collapse (see Box 11.1). The construction used immense quantities of cut, moulded and carved stone, lead for roofs and window glass and terracotta tiles for roof and floor. The later cathedrals were subject to detailed drawn designs (Box 11.2).

Within the cathedral, the space was carefully allocated and appointed to its diverse tasks. The chancel would contain an altar, with a tabernacle, with the choir in front of it where choristers sung the services. Alongside the nave, the aisles often featured numerous additional altars (chantry or devotional chapels) variously dedicated and endowed. Magnificent tombs, of the clerical and secular aristocracy, adorned the arcades. Upper

BOX 11.1 HOW CATHEDRALS COLLAPSE: THE CASE OF BEAUVAIS

Fig 1

Beauvais cathedral in 2008 (Marc Roussel, Creative Commons).

Work on the new cathedral of Beauvais was started in 1225, and by the end of the first series of campaigns, in 1272, the apse and three bays of the choir had been built, up to the intended transepts (Fig 1). The cathedral stood in this state until 1284; on 29 November, at the hour of curfew, the high vault collapsed. The records imply that conditions were quiet – no high wind, no earthquake – and the collapse is mysterious. Why should a cathedral stand for twelve years, and then collapse?

At the time it was believed that the size of the bays of the choir, 15 m by 9 m, was too great, and the repair work over the next fifty years included the intercalation of piers between those already built, so that the bays were halved to 4.5 m. It is true that the comparable cathedrals of Bourges, Chartres, Amiens and Cologne, all having the standard

"French Gothic" bay width of 15 m, have piers spaced at about 7 m, but the stretching of medieval rules of proportion at Beauvais does not explain the twelve-year period of stability. In the same way, the height of the Beauvais vault, 48 m, is indeed somewhat greater than the others, but Cologne has a height of 46 m. A modern twelve-storey building would fit comfortably inside Beauvais. The standard bay width of English Gothic is 12 m.

Viollet-le-Duc advanced a reason for the collapse which is certainly of the right kind, that is, a defect which develops slowly. Lime mortar is slow to dry, and in drying it shrinks; Viollet suggested that, after twelve years, shrinking mortar joints between masonry blocks forming the main piers could have thrown excessive load on adjacent monolithic colonnettes, which had not been designed to support major structural elements. Their fracture could have triggered overall collapse of the high vault. However, such a mechanism of collapse is not easily envisaged.

A clue to an alternative explanation may lie in the later history of the cathedral, which recorded settlement of the foundations. The choir had been rebuilt by about 1337, but work was interrupted for the next 150 years by the Hundred Years War and the English occupation. It was not until 1500 that a start was made on the transepts, and some fifty years later these were virtually complete together with (probably) the first bay of the nave. (This is the present state of the cathedral. Since the nave is missing, no long perspective view can be obtained as, for example, that at Amiens.) In 1564 a central crossing tower was commissioned, and completed five years later. This masonry tower rose to the enormous height of 153 m, and alarmed the Chapter from the first. Several examinations were made, and two King's Masons from Paris presented a detailed report. The four crossing piers were beginning to lean, those to the east being out of plumb by up to 4 inches, and those on the nave side by up to 11 inches. The King's Masons recommended the construction of two more bays of the nave to provide buttressing, and of temporary bracing walls between the crossing piers, together with the strengthening of the pier foundations. The chapter discussed this report for two years, and on 17 April 1573 decided to put the work in hand; thirteen days later the tower fell.

Here again there is a period (four years) of apparent stability followed by collapse, but in this case there is the revealing evidence given by the state of the crossing piers. Ma-

sonry vaults in a great church thrust horizontally – to the north / south resisted by (flying) buttresses, and to the east / west by the whole length of the fabric, terminating in massive west work and a strong east end (as the apse at Beauvais). All this was clearly understood by the King's Masons – at Beauvais the nave did not exist, and there was no path for the east / west forces, which had to be resisted by the crossing piers. The fact that these had been pushed sideways implies unequivocally that their footings had given way – some settlement had occurred in the supporting soil.

Settlement, caused by the consolidation of a soil, results from water being squeezed out from a matrix of solid particles, until those particles make sufficient contact to resist whatever compressive load is being applied. It is a matter of fact that the soil-mechanics time scale for consolidation can be up to ten or twenty years (an analogy would be ten or twenty seconds needed to depress the plunger of a cafetière); over several years the fabric of Beauvais, apparently stable, was in fact moving imperceptibly, until stages were reached, in 1284 and 1573, when the overall geometry was so altered that stable equilibrium was no longer possible. Such behaviour has been by no means uncommon; very many crossing towers, in England as well as in France, collapsed within a decade or so of their construction. At Wells Cathedral, in 1338, some twenty years after completion of the tower, failure was averted by the insertion of the spectacular strainer arches at the crossing.

by Jacques Heyman

Fig 11.2   *Masons' marks from Glasgow cathedral, with (left) a mark on an ashlar block.*

stories admitted light (clerestory), or allowed a circulation above ground (gallery or triforium). Beneath the altar was sometimes a crypt, used to house relics of particular sanctity; these could be visited and worshipped (for example on the saint's day) by large numbers of people moving down one flight of steps and returning via another. Cathedrals took a long time to construct and the projects often ran out of money. Every medieval town with any pretension had a half-finished cathedral in the process of construction or modification. For this reason, and the fact that they attracted the highest ranks of sponsors, cathedral buildings are archives of style, and have provided the basis for the chronological framework used by art historians.

The precinct

The cathedral building was managed by a Dean and Chapter, a group of high ranking clergy that convened for decision-making in the Chapter House, usually adjacent to the chancel. The community that served the cathedral might belong to monastic order (such as the Benedictines, see below), or be a community of Secular Canons, that resembled monks without necessarily belonging to one of the prominent orders. For this reason the cathedral church was often adjoined, usually on its south side, by a cloister, refectory, reredorter and other ancillary buildings in the same manner as a monastery (see below). The enclosure containing the cathedral complex (the *precinct* or *close*) also featured houses of diocesan representatives (*prebends*) and might be equipped with a piped water system as at twelfth century Canterbury (Box 4.2).

Such enclosures defined to a town within the town, and some were strongly fortified (see below).

Medieval cathedrals frequently rose on the site of previous Roman cathedrals (as at Geneva) or on former Roman administrative headquarters, as at York, where the Minster stands on the Basilica of the Roman Legionary fortress (Philips and Heywood 1995). Within a town, the site of the cathedral and its parish churches greatly influenced the developing street plan, by virtue of the ceremonial traffic that connected them (Krautheimer 1980, 249), as did the Friday mosque in Islamic towns (see Ch 9, part 5).

Cathedral archaeology

The archaeological agenda for cathedral sites draws inspiration from their sensitivity to ritual and social change over a very long period in the same place. Material changes in burial, building and the use of space can be dated and often explained by detailed documentary references in cathedral archives. Cathedral archaeology offers three main types of research opportunity provided by the strata beneath the building, the building itself and the enclosure that contains it.

A cathedral building usually stands on top of a key sequence of strata in the town centre, dating to the periods preceding its erection. However, access to this sequence is limited: outside the building the ground has been disturbed by the cutting of innumerable graves. The archaeological deposit is usually well conserved under the building itself, which has protected it from graves and from modern development. But modern opportunities for excavation are usually restricted to small holes required by engineering projects to improve the stability of the structure or to insert electricity cables or heating ducts. For example at York Minster, 53 areas cutting through up to 4m of stratification were recorded before they were filled with concrete to help consolidate the foundations and prevent them spreading (Phillips and Haywood 1995). Where architectural and engineering programmes are successfully combined with archaeological research, excavation may be on a large scale, as at Cologne (Dopplefeld & Weyres 1980; Fig 11.3, 11.4) or Münster (Kroker 2007). At Geneva, the foundations of the vast early thirteenth century cathedral rested on layers of glacial sand, gravel and clays that rose nearly 100m above the rockhead. Settlement in these layers after 750 years led to deformation and cracks in the walls. Once the movement of the building was detected, a major archaeological excavation in 1979 served not only to exposed the foundations, but the walls of eight successive cathedral buildings dating from the fourth to the eleventh century (Fig 11.5; Bonnet 1993). The restoration of the cathedral, employing many different specialist firms, proceeded in close collaboration with the archaeological campaign. The restoration programme included the underpinning of the medieval walls and piers by drilling numerous narrow piles through them, to a depth of 11m (Fig 11.5; Les Clefs de St-Pierre 1993). The excavated area was eventually covered over by an extensive undercroft in which visitors today can navigate from the present cathedral back to late Roman times with the help of conserved walls and standing earth sections.

BOX 11.2 THE BUILDING OF ST PETER'S IN ROME

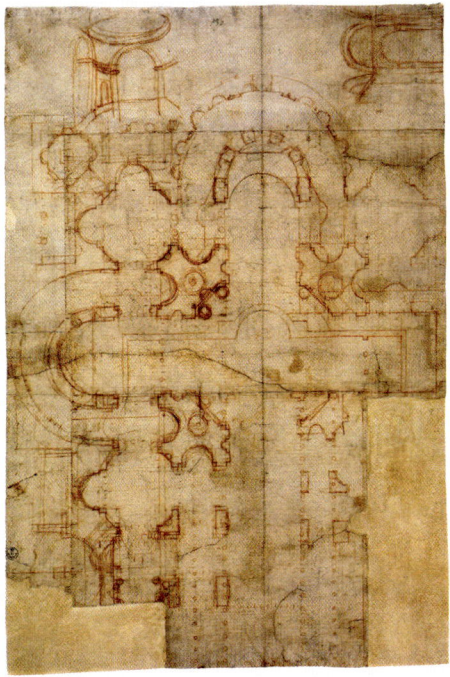

Fig 1

Bramante's first sketches for St Peter's: a ground-plan and two cross sections superimposed over a plan of the ancient basilica, identifiable by its short chancel and rows of columns (Franco Borsi, Bramante, Milan 1989, 75).

Constantine, the first Roman emperor to profess Christianity, built a great basilica over the supposed tomb of St Peter in Rome (consecrated in AD 326). Over the ensuing centuries, and particularly during the mediaeval period when the fortunes of Rome ran low and the papacy fled to Avignon, this basilica fell into poor repair. During the fifteenth century pope Nicholas V (d, 1455) commissioned the architect Rossellino to build a great choir beyond the basilica with the intention of then demolishing the basilica and adding a new nave in its place; but although the choir itself

was constructed, the whole project remained incomplete at his death, and the dilapidated basilica remained untouched.

It therefore fell to Pope Julius II (1503–1513) to address the challenge of resolving this highly unsatisfactory state of affairs. Never one to approach a task with anything less than single-minded determination, he commissioned designs for a great new church: new not only in structure but in total conception. In this Julius drew together three key strands: political supremacy, in proclaiming the authority of the Church to the weak governance of the time; cultural acumen, in uniting the ideal aspirations of Renaissance thought with the historical tradition of Christianity; and architectural patronage, in using the power of the emerging new architectural style to express his vision.

His chosen architect was Donato Bramante (Fig 1). Bramante had come to Rome from Milan in 1499 and had immediately impressed his contemporaries by his mastery of reinvented classical architecture. In 1502 he had erected, on the supposed site of the martyrdom of St Peter, perhaps the most perfect building ever to be designed in what we now recognise as the high renaissance style – a small circular domed Tempietto. Perhaps on the basis of this, Julius chose him to design the new St Peter's; and in 1506 the foundation stone was laid, in the presence of Julius, for a church as vast as the Tempietto is tiny.

As a style, classical architecture adapts well to size: both small and large buildings can conform to the same principles of proportion. But the practicalities of construction of a large building are another matter entirely. St Peter's was conceived on a huge scale, requiring enormous resources of mate-

Fig 2

St Peter's in 2007 (Chris Sloan, GNU Free).

rials and labour to construct it, and requiring an understanding of how the significant structural forces must be resolved. It is not surprising that the building was only partly complete at Julius' death in 1513. When Bramante died a year later it was not only still far from complete, but structural defects had already begun to make themselves felt.

A dome of the kind on which Bramante had set his heart puts an enormous load on the supporting structure beneath; and although Brunelleschi had spanned a similar dimensioned space with his dome in Florence, his was not of the pure circular plan and 'ideal' semicircular section which Bramante planned.

After Bramante's death the task of resolving the structural problems fell to a series of architects who altered his plans to suit their own versions of his original vision. Raphael was appointed to succeed Bramante, with Antonio da Sangallo the Younger as his assistant, later to succeeded him in his turn. The sack of Rome in 1527 brought the project to a standstill; but when work was able to begin again in 1540 the new model then constructed did scant justice to the originality of the conception.

On Sangallo's death in 1546, however, Pope Paul III summoned Michelangelo to bring his extraordinary originality to bear on the project. Instead of carrying on with the construction of the Sangallo plan, Michelangelo took a radically different approach. He demolished and rebuilt the piers constructed by Bramante to support a completely redesigned dome. Michelangelo worked on St Peter's until his death in 1564, and by then the whole project had been so invigorated by the force of his genius that the momentum carried on under his successors Vignola and Ligorio. The dome was eventually completed under della Porta and Fontana in 1590.

At last in 1605 the remains of the original basilica could be demolished (under Pope Paul V), and the way was clear for Maderno to complete the nave and new east front. In 1626 the new St Peter's was consecrated, on the 1300th anniversary of the consecration of Constantine's basilica.

The story does not end here, however. Archaeologists in 1940 investigating Roman period burials beneath the floor of the church discovered a domed tomb construction of undoubted importance, with the earliest mosaics of Christian origin. To look up from the tiny domed tomb with its representation of Christ as the sun god driving his chariot up the sky, through the small opening in the floor of the cathedral to the huge dome above is to realise the significance of the scale of the expansion of Christianity, from its small beginnings to the mighty structure represented by the Church today (Fig 2).

by Martin Stancliffe

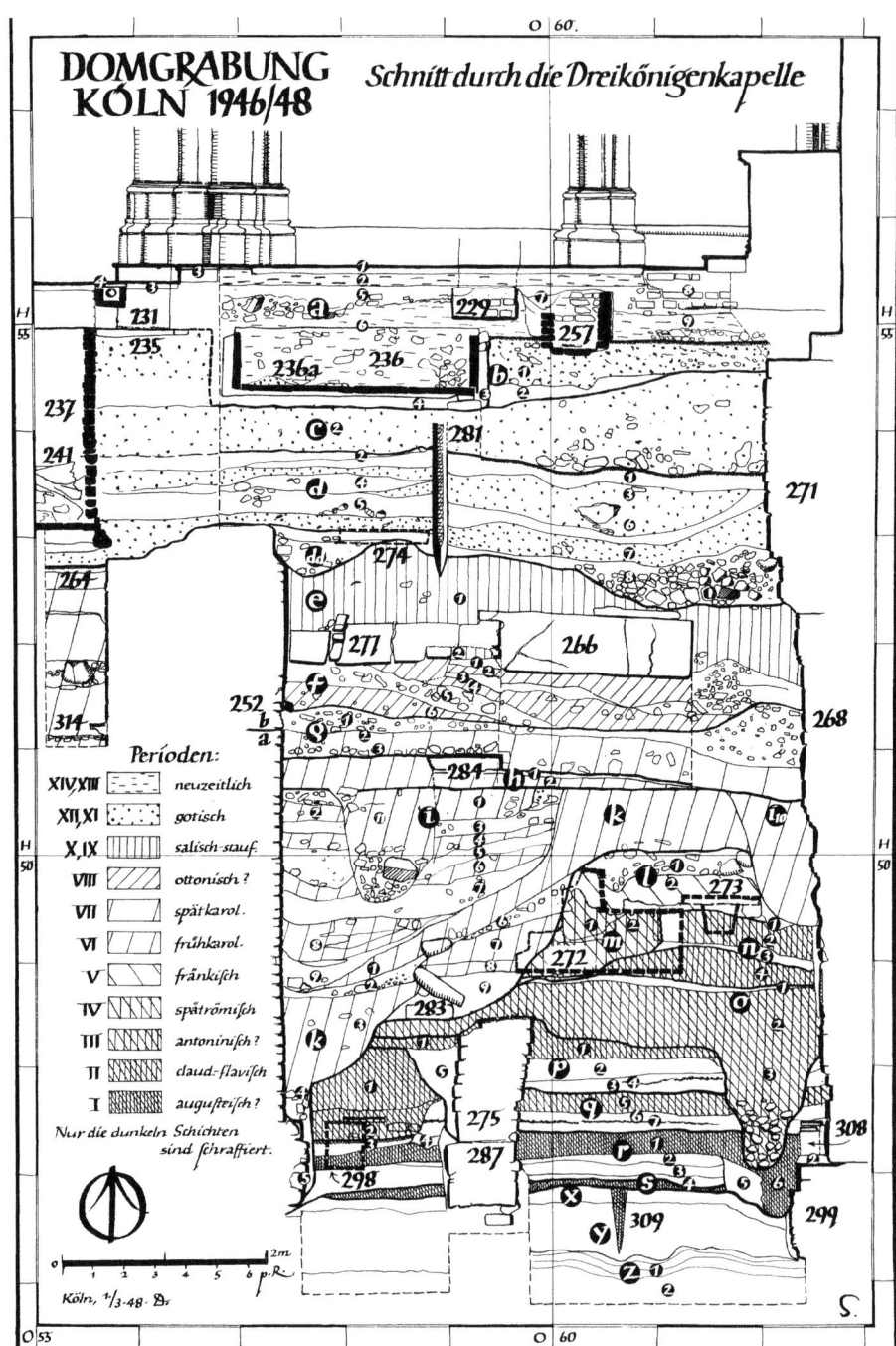

Fig 11.3 *The classic section from the excavations at the east end of Cologne cathedral, 1946-48. The Carolingian apse is labelled "252". The Gothic reconstruction (1248-1322) is represented by layers c and d and Feature 271. (Doppelfeld and Weyres 1980, 17).*

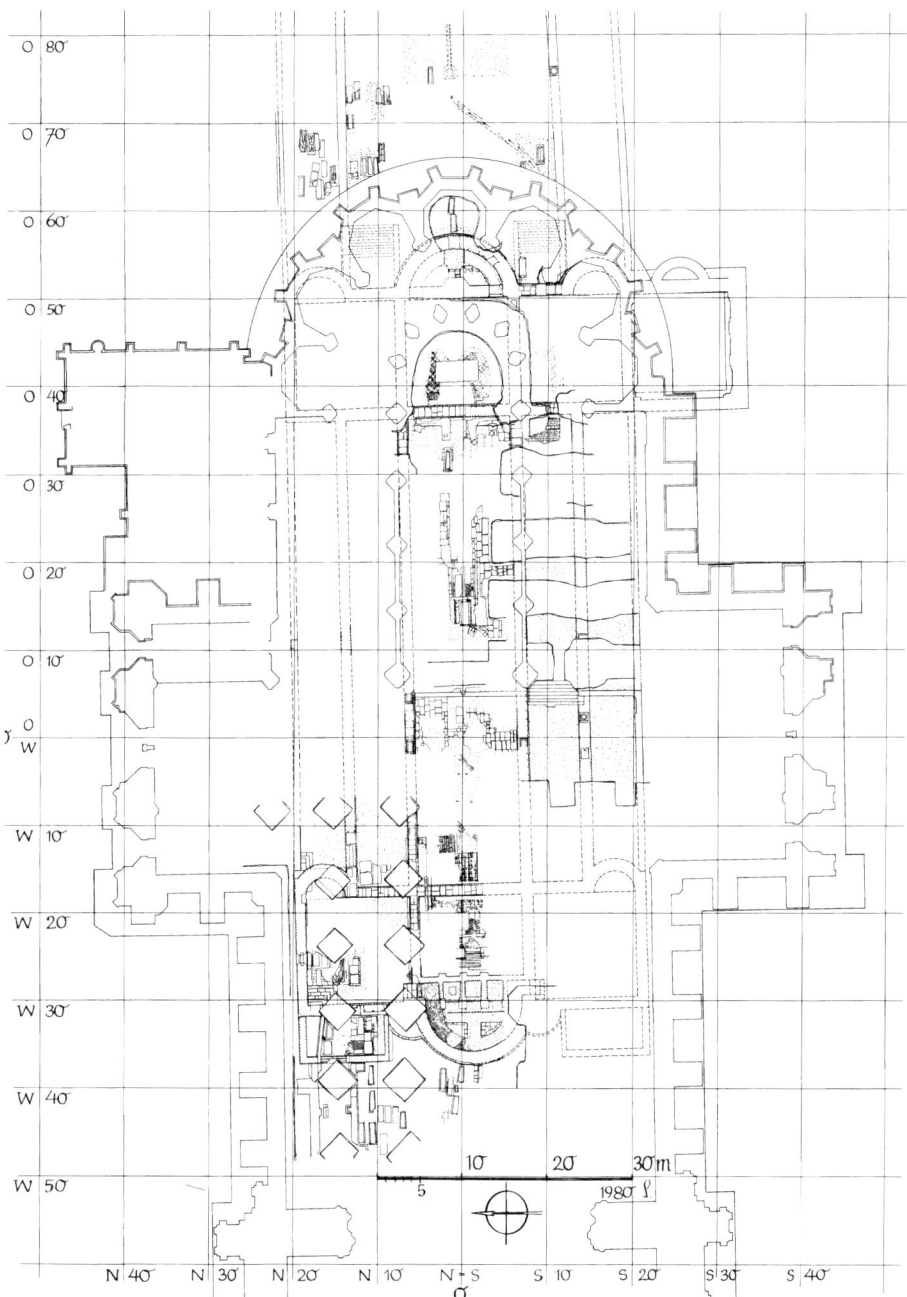

Plan of Cologne Cathedral, showing the excavated features (1946-1979), the Carolingian cathedral with **Fig 11.4**
*its east and west apses and the later Medieval cathedral (main outline) (Wilhelm Schneider in Doppelfeld
and Weyres 1980, endmap 9).*

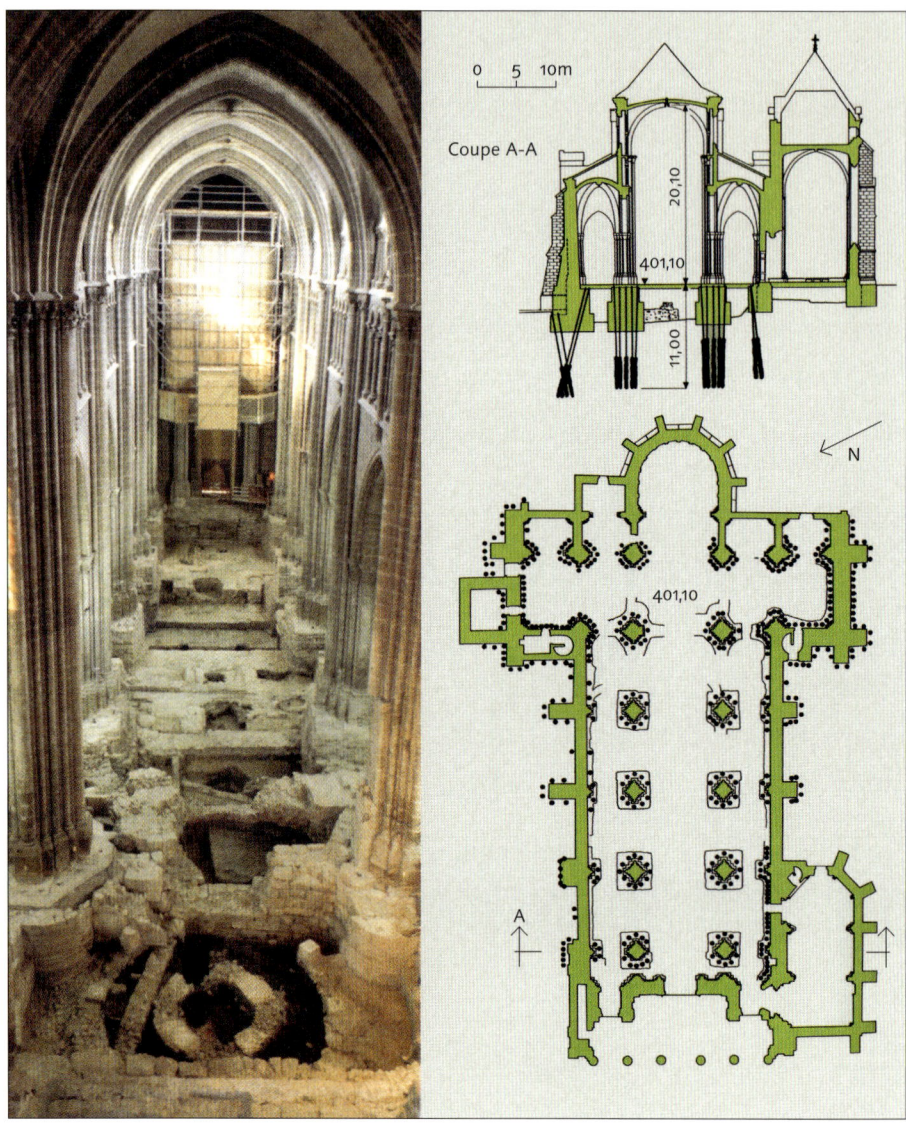

Fig 11.5 *Excavation and restoration at Geneva Cathedral (Switzerland). (left) Excavations in progress in 1979 showing the exposed bases of the 13th-century piers. (right) The reinforcement of the piers with mini-piles (by Swissboring) (Bonnet 1993; Les Clefs de St-Pierre, 1993).*

A second area of study is the building itself, its fabric, ornamentation and content, areas where archaeologists, architects and architectural historians find common cause, especially in projects of repair and restoration (see Ch 1, p 38). The archaeologist is particularly interested in the cathedral building as a 'stratified site', in which a sequence of events can be deduced from minute investigations of the fabric. Opportunities for such investigation are provided by the numerous small exposures occasioned by architec-

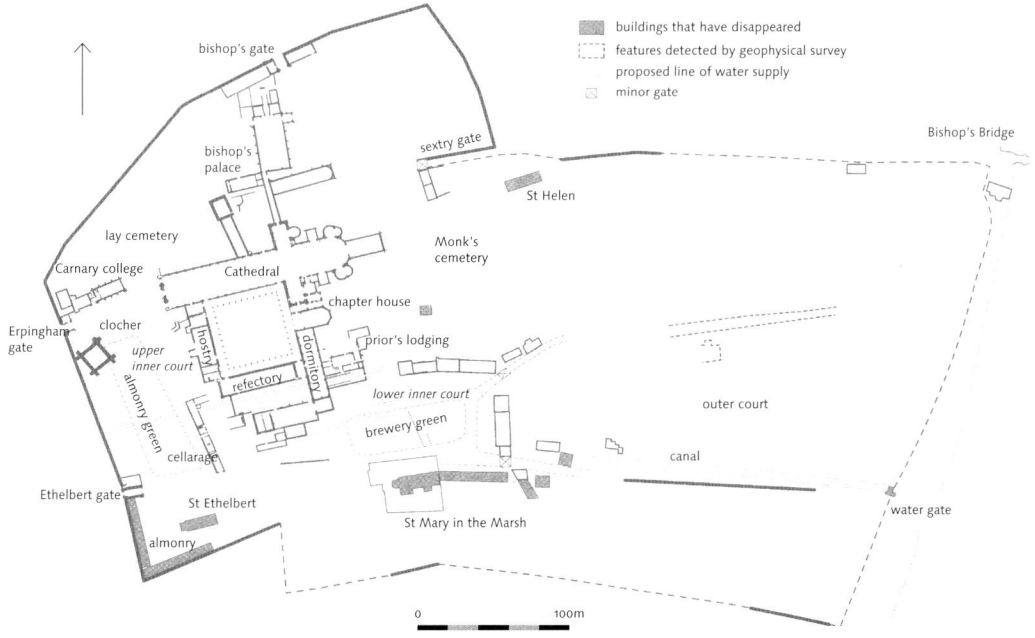

Norwich Cathedral precinct (Gilchrist 2005, 42).

Fig 11.6a

Legend:
- buildings that have disappeared
- features detected by geophysical survey
- proposed line of water supply
- minor gate

bishop's gate

bishop's palace

sextry gate

Bishop's Bridge

St Helen

lay cemetery

Carnary college

Cathedral

Monk's cemetery

Erpingham gate

clocher

chapter house

prior's lodging

upper inner court

hostry

dormitory

refectory

lower inner court

outer court

almonry green

brewery green

cellarage

canal

Ethelbert gate

St Ethelbert

St Mary in the Marsh

water gate

almonry

0   100m

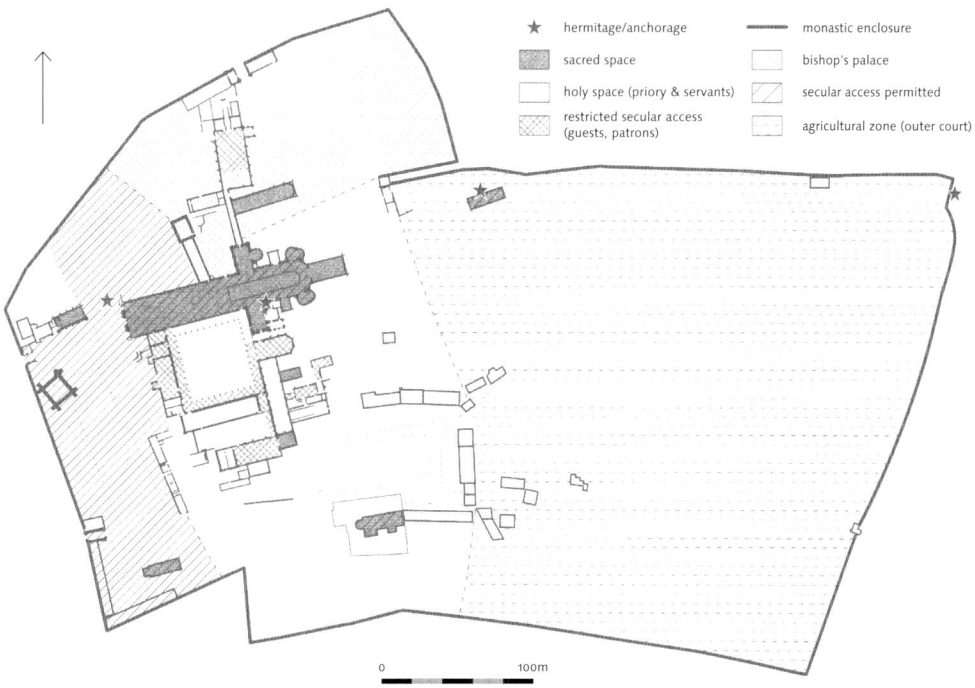

Norwich Cathedral: Sacred and social space (Gilchrist 2005, 239).

Fig 11.6b

Legend:
- hermitage/anchorage
- sacred space
- holy space (priory & servants)
- restricted secular access (guests, patrons)
- monastic enclosure
- bishop's palace
- secular access permitted
- agricultural zone (outer court)

0   100m

tural inspection, and have the potential to provide a very full narrative of the long use of the building and its social implications. Modern procedures of heritage care begin with the gathering up of all the information about the building and its context, from surviving documents and architectural and archaeological interventions. This results in a *Conservation Plan*, a document that offers an assessment of the state of knowledge (for the example of Saint Denis, France, see Wyss 1996). This plan often includes an agenda for future research as well as an assessment of the condition of the building and its future viability.

Archaeologists are also increasingly interested in studying the cathedral precinct or close, which housed a clerical community of a particularly wealthy and aristocratic nature. Although the excavation of a Deanery or a prebend's house and their rubbish is rarely available today, analysis of the existing buildings to determine the use of space (for example though access analysis) can lead to interesting hypotheses about the activities of the church hierarchy (Richardson 2003; cf Ch 4, p 153). A comprehensive study of the precinct was included in a recent in-depth assessment of Norwich (Gilchrist 2005). The cathedral archaeologist here assembled all available information on the fabric of the cathedral and the other buildings in the extant precinct, also exploring open space with geophysical survey (Fig 11.6a). The boundaries of the precinct in the eleventh and twelfth centuries could be reconstructed from documents. Bad relations between the cathedral and the town led to an incendiary attack by the citizens in 1272, with three days of pillaging that left its mark on the cathedral fabric as a pink scorching (*ibid*, 29-31). The precinct was enlarged in 1318 to provide additional space for the Bishop's palace and again attacked in 1443. These attacks provide a context for the defensive walls and gates that surrounded the cathedral; at Norwich the extended circuit was first constructed in 1276 and today still stands 5m tall. The cathedral close had to serve its devotional purpose, its provision for a cloistered community and its requirements for high status residence, and to combine these with a range of more public duties – teaching the young and welcoming the public for a range of ceremonies, including baptism, marriage, burial, the celebration of major feast days and the delivery of keynote sermons. Equilibrium between these demands was achieved through the dedicated use of space, broadly graded as ceremonial, ie the church itself (sacred), monastic (holy), invited (access restricted to guests), private (the bishop's palace) and open to the public (the cemetery next to the town gate) (Fig 11.6b). In addition, a large part of the precinct was laid out in orchards or gardens. In material terms, the form of the establishment and the richness of its accoutrements endowed the cathedral close with a prestige that emulated and challenged the highest ranks of the aristocracy (see eg Ch 4, p 147).

Monasteries

Like the cult of relics, solitary devotion to the spirit world through prayer is likely to have had deep prehistoric roots in medieval Europe. Ostensibly, however, monasticism derives most immediately from the activities of the desert fathers in the fourth-fifth centuries who escaped the Roman imperial cities to commune with god, performing as hermits in small cells (*eremitic*) or in communities (*coenobitic*). The instrument of the hermits was the inducement of visions through deprivation: hunger, cold, heat, self-beating or other forms of ascetic challenge, such as holding the arms outstretched for long periods while standing on an old Roman column (the pillar saints). In communal worship, the emphasis was on prayer and chanting. These communities aimed to be self-sufficient by growing their own food, and they developed successive sets of rules, owed initially to Benedict of Nursia (480-547) and Benedict of Aniane (*c.* 747-821), which regulated their activities 24 hours a day. In the later Middle Ages, the monastic movement became still more regulated and organised itself into orders of men and women, each with distinctive clothing and practices (see below, p 466; and for a general overview Brooke 2006). All were single sex communities dedicated to prayer, ritual performance and contemplation, supported by servants. Each establishment was also geared to the creation of wealth, by farming, mineral extraction and manufacture (see below). Monasteries often acted as the advance guard in newly converted territory, with a brief of winning the inhabitants to Christ through passive example, although conversion by force was also applied up to the sixteenth century and beyond (see eg Ch 10, p 412).

Monasticism set its sights on the most potent form of intercession with god, and as such was in receipt of massive donations, resulting in great wealth expressed in buildings, codices, church plate and tombs. The riches of the Abbot and his community periodically generated pressure for a return to devotional purity and led to the appearance of new movements. A major surge came in the thirteenth century with the creation of the friars, the *mendicant* orders, who claimed to take the vow of poverty and chastity literally (by begging), and to bring the message of salvation into the towns and directly to the people by their example. Although their example convinced no-one for long, as Boccaccio relates in numerous anecdotes in his *Decameron* (written in mid fourteenth-century Italy), every major town acquired one or more Friaries (see Box 11.3; Fig 9.1). The mission of the friars was fundamentalist, and spawned countless offshoots, dissidents and prophets demanding institutional reform and personal repentance. Some protagonists were denounced as heretics and publically tortured and burnt at the stake. Like public execution, and the dismembering of traitors, the overall aim was to induce conformity and obedience through the controlled use of terror.

Form of sites

The initial design of monastic premises (AD 400-800) was very varied and local, but from Carolingian times a pattern was set that has come down to us as the St Gall Plan (AME 1, 411). It can be seen that this takes the approximate form of a Roman villa, with a main building (the church) with a courtyard on the south side (the cloister), off which are ranges of buildings for meeting (chapter house), eating (refectory), sleeping (dormitory) and latrines (Fig 11.7). In or around the main block were kitchens, bakeries, gardens. A monastery required a parchemenerie (for making parchment) and

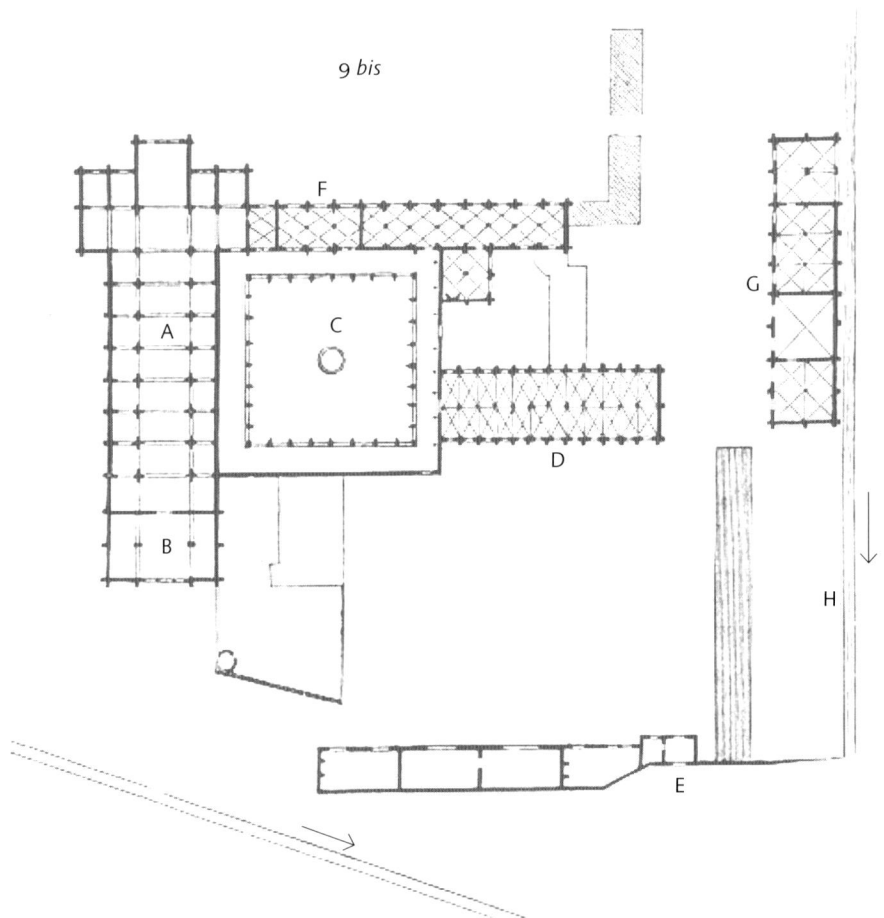

9 bis

Fig 11.7   *Plan of the extant precinct of the Abbey of Fontenay in the 15th century. A & B abbey church; C:*
cloister; D: pigeon loft; E: (left) granary and mill (right) entrance and stables; F: chapter house, with
dormitory above; G: Forge; H: stream, driving forge hammers. The gardens lie to the top of the plan
(Viollet-le-Duc 1856, fig. 9bis; for a plan of the 12th-century church and cloister see AME 1, 409).

a scriptorium (for making manuscript books, or *codices*), and workshops for making
church plate, so that it could found daughter houses and push forward the Christian
expansion.

There is some variation between the layout of monasteries and friaries, and between
the establishments of different orders, and these variants form part of the archaeological
agenda. For example, some monasteries, as at Carthusian Mount Grace in Yorkshire,
tried to combine the spirituality of the solitary hermit with the administrative convenience of a convent, by creating rows of cells in which the individual monks could be
passed food by lay brothers under their door.

There is increasing interest in how devotional attitudes varied between the sexes. Women were not allowed to officiate in the mass or preach, but they could be nuns, exercising their own governance under an Abbess, albeit requiring a 'nun's priest' to celebrate mass. Women featured prominently in the religious establishments of the Low countries and in Germany their foundations outnumbered those of the men (Brooke 2006, 235). Recent research has shown how nuns maintained their hierarchies through the use of space (Gilchrist 1994). Through its assemblages, a nunnery also has the potential to show how women varied their economy of consumption with respect to the men, and how their ability to control land and income changed during the medieval centuries.

Monastery archaeology

The establishments of the convent orders, whether monks, nuns or friars were capitalised, networked and very profitable businesses, in control of extensive areas of land and practising their own industries and agriculture. Monasteries have therefore long attracted archaeological investigations as special types of settlement, offering rich insights into the medieval economy as well as its ideology. As with cathedrals (above) the archaeological agenda should be concerned not only with the buildings, but with their wider context. Monasteries not only had enclosed precincts featuring a wide range of agricultural, horticultural and industrial activities, but large estates in which the monks were active in clearing and reclaiming land, both dry and wet (Pressouyre 1994; Bond 2004).

In many European countries, especially those most affected by the Reformation, the monastic orders were dissolved in the sixteenth century, leaving a large number of abandoned ruins in the countryside. These have provided happy hunting grounds for antiquaries admiring their weathered sculpture and secluded locations, and have supported a number of medievalist revivals in the nineteenth and twentieth century. Many of these sites, laced by antiquarian trenches, are now conserved as national heritage. Although the working of the late medieval monastic establishment is now fairly well known, there is still fruitful research to be done on the buildings (for example the source of materials), assemblages (for example well-dated pottery groups) and cemeteries (the health and mobility of the monks). But perhaps the greatest archaeological potential lies in the economy of the monastery and its estate. Two case studies follow, one an example of a monastery that has largely remained standing, and the other one that has wholly disappeared. Both are notable for their major industrial components.

Fontenay Abbey

Fontenay Abbey in Burgundy, France, is one of the best surviving and most visited of medieval monastic properties (Fig 11.8; Aynard 2008). The original church, dormitory, much of the cloister and the medieval forge building are all extant, and their setting at the end of a long valley with its chain of ponds evokes the size and local dominance

Fig 11.8   *Fontenay from the air (photo: Beaujard; Editions Gaud 77950 Moisenay).*

of what was in its day a major rural property. The foundation of Fontenay belongs to the third phase of Cistercian expansion, after Cîteaux (1098) and Clairvaux (1115). In 1119 Saint Bernard caused a dozen monks from Clairvaux to reconnoitre part of the thick forest of Grand-Jailly, in which they eventually chose a place reminiscent of Clairvaux, provided with springs (thought to have inspired the name) and began to clear the woodland. Construction of the abbey began in 1139 using limestone from a quarry at the end of the valley (now a formal garden). In spite of the idealism and the initial reality of its remote location, the venture was high-profile and well-endowed from the start. The land was owned by the family of Saint Bernard's mother, and largely funded by the English bishop of Norwich Ebrard who left his diocese and put his fortune at the disposal of the builders. Although payment of the builders was theoretically forbidden, over a hundred monks and local peasants were put to work and a large church, cloister and outbuildings were soon raised: in 1147 the church was ready for consecration by the Pope (Fig 11.9). Fontenay prospered in the thirteenth century and came under royal patronage in 1269. By this time it was thought to have 300 monks, most of whom were resident in the monastic farms of the estate, managing large flocks of sheep and cattle which will have generated considerable revenues.

Fontenay was also a prime industrial site, processing iron by means of a large hearth and a giant hammer driven by a watermill (Benoît 1988). This forge was housed in a grand stone building, nearly as large as the church and parallel to it (Fig 11.10, 11.11). It was constructed in the twelfth century and equipped with buttresses in the thirteenth.

The cloister (M. Carver).

Fig 11.9

The forge building, 12-13th century (M. Carver).

Fig 11.10

Fig 11.11 *The water-driven bellows of the forge, inside the forge building (restored 2008) (M. Carver).*

There were finds of iron slag and fifteen mine shafts in the neighbourhood whence iron ore was extracted. The size of this factory and the occurrence of local streams and of iron ore, together with good quality building stone raises the possibility that whatever its spiritual clothing this was an economic venture of considerable acumen.

Indirectly, the robustly-built forge saved the abbey site for the future. After the Revolution the buildings were sold by the government in 1791 to Claude Hugot who successfully adapted the forge as a paper-mill. By the second half of the nineteenth century the Fontenay valley had become a 'veritable industrial complex', supplying paper to Paris and employing some 200 persons. But in 1903 it became unviable, and the site was sold to a Lyon banker, Edouard Aynard. It was Aynard's ambition to restore the Cistercian Abbey to its former glory, which he achieved with some sensitivity. Still in possession of the Aynard family, the site now attracts over 100,000 visitors a year.

Bordesley Abbey

Few medieval monasteries have had such a charmed life as Fontenay, and in England where the Dissolution took effect in the mid-sixteenth century, the demolition and recycling of monastic property was vigorous until the revival of interest in things medieval in the nineteenth century. By then many sites had already disappeared. In the 1960s, the Abbey of Bordesley in the Arrow Valley, West Midlands, was a set of low-

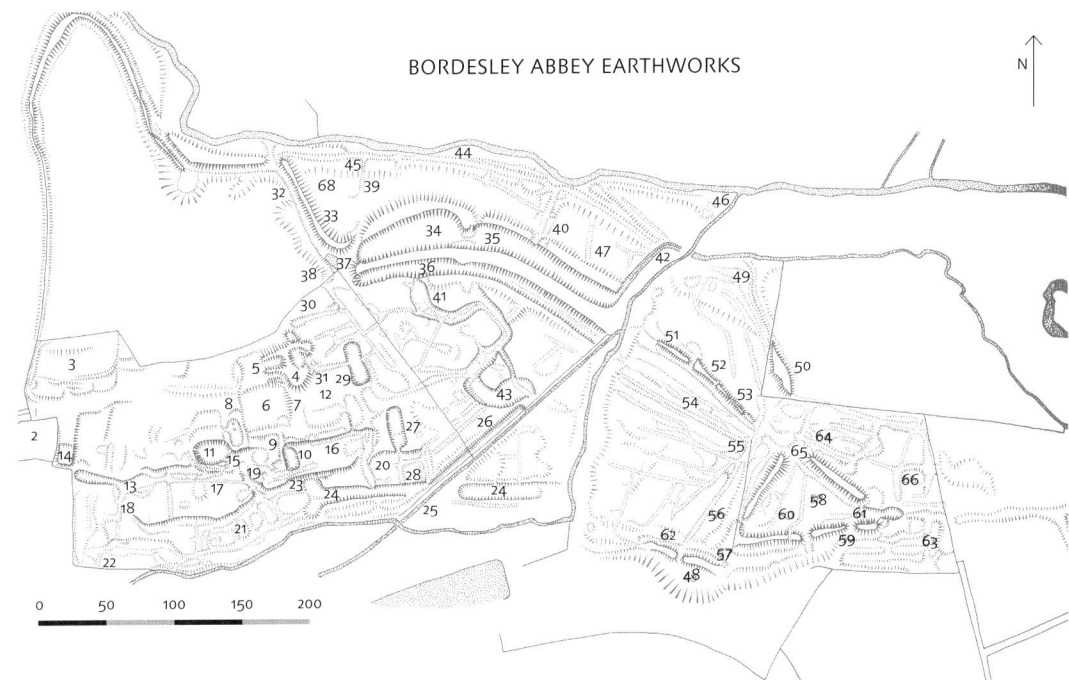

N

0   50   100   150   200

Bordesley Abbey earthwork survey, with principal features numbered (Rahtz & Hirst 1976, fig. 43).   **Fig 11.12**

lying earthworks with no standing buildings of any kind (Fig 11.12). All the same, the site was recognisable, and a topographical survey undertaken in 1968 identified the church, cloister and an extensive system of water management including a triangular mill pond. An initial project design by Mick Aston recommended fourteen locations where excavations were likely to inform the history of the abbey from its documented foundation in the 1140s to its eventual desertion (Rahtz and Hirst 1976; Fig 11.13).

The subsequent campaign by the University of Birmingham under the direction of Philip Rahtz saw the excavation of the south transept and choir of the church together with part of its neighbouring cemetery. The excavations chronicled the sequence of repair and embellishment and the changes in the use of space within the abbey church, and also gave evidence, in the form of artefact fragments, for the manufacture on site of textiles, leather goods, wooden objects (including a possible book cover) and pottery (Rahtz and Hirst 1976; Hirst et al 1983; and see Ch 1, p 36).

The focus of research then moved to the mill site with its adjoining water-works (Astill 1993). The Cistercian engineers had set out to clear the valley, canalise the water and establish a hydraulic system that functioned over some 36 ha. If one of the aims of this was to drain the land and make its meadows usable, others were to drive a mill and supply fishponds. Excavations by Grenville Astill revealed the mill pond, leet and the foundations of four successive mills. Driven by an undershot wheel, the mill was concerned with metal-working, – not the extraction and smelting of iron as at Fontenay,

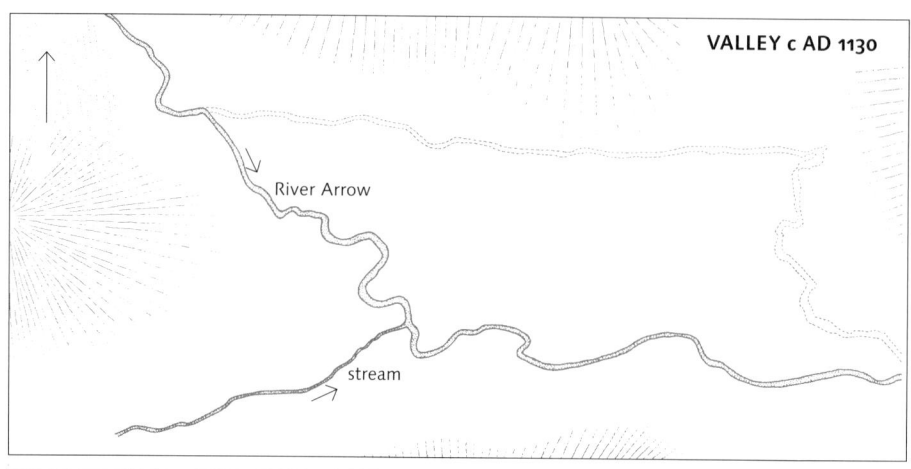

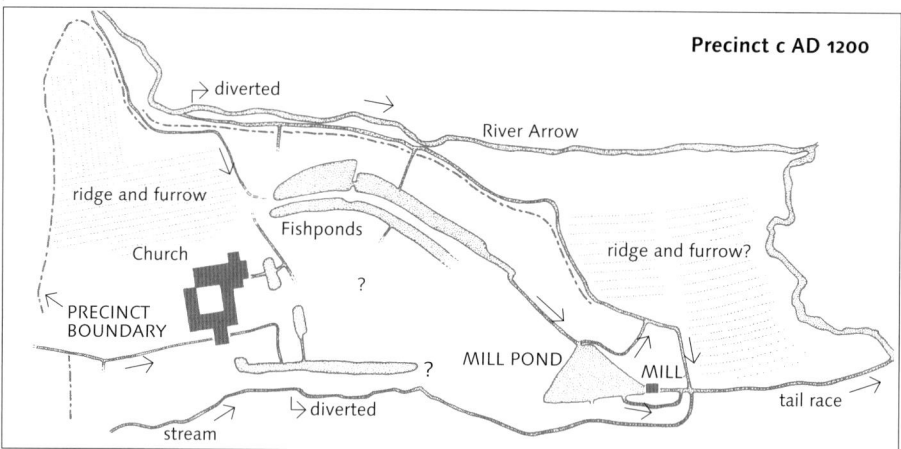

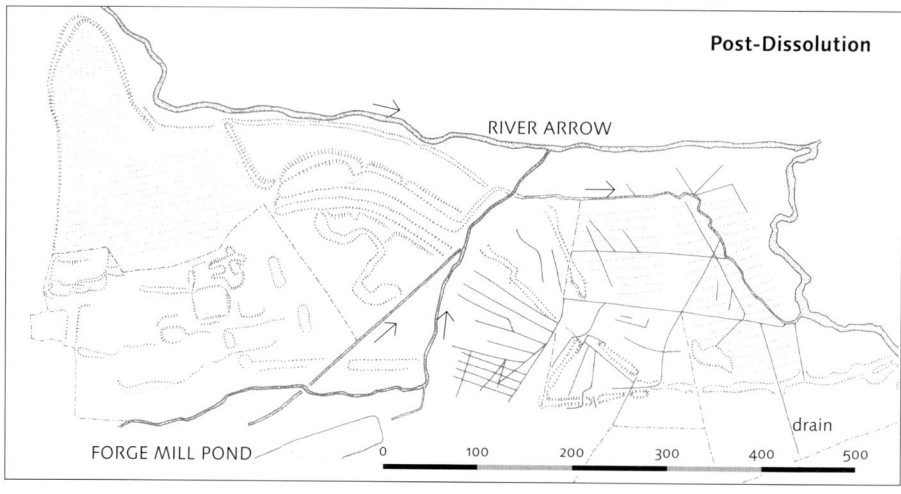

Fig 11.13 *Bordesley Abbey; the sequence (a) before the monks arrived (b) c. 1200 (c) after dissolution (Astill 1993, 106).*

but the mass production of objects of iron, bronze and lead, including nails, knives, tools and a relatively large sample of weapons and armour, including sword pommel casings and arrowheads. The water wheel drove smaller wheels that operated bellows and a hammer via a trip wheel (Fig 11.14). More than 20 dendrochronology dates from timber linings of drains and leets showed that the wheels and leet system were installed in the late twelfth century and functioned, with replacements, for over 200 years. Silting up of the channels required the reshaping of the pond banks to provide an increased head of water in the early fourteenth century.

A third phase of research turned attention to Bordesley's twenty monastic granges (Astill 1994, 2006) (Fig 11.15). These farms were created in the neighbourhood with an initial endowment in the twelfth century and then expanded over three counties in the thirteenth century. At this time, the monastery was drawing commodities from arable, pasture and forest, stored in the granges and sent for processing to the abbey precinct (Astill 1994). As well as barns for storing grain and tending animals, a grange

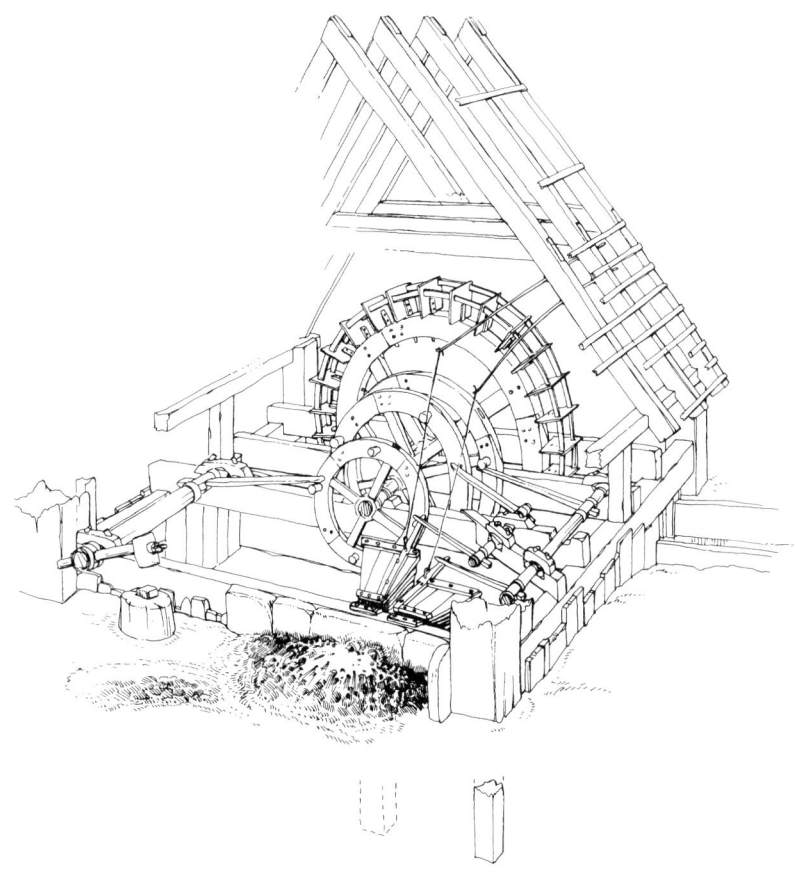

Reconstruction of metalworking mill (D. A. Walsh) (Astill 1993, 270).

Fig 11.14

Fig 11.15 *Map of the location of the recorded granges of Bordesley Abbey 12-15th century (Astill 1994, fig. 6).*

Fig 11.16 *Earthworks of New Grange (see fig. 11.15), with millpond and fishponds (Astill 1994, fig. 8).*

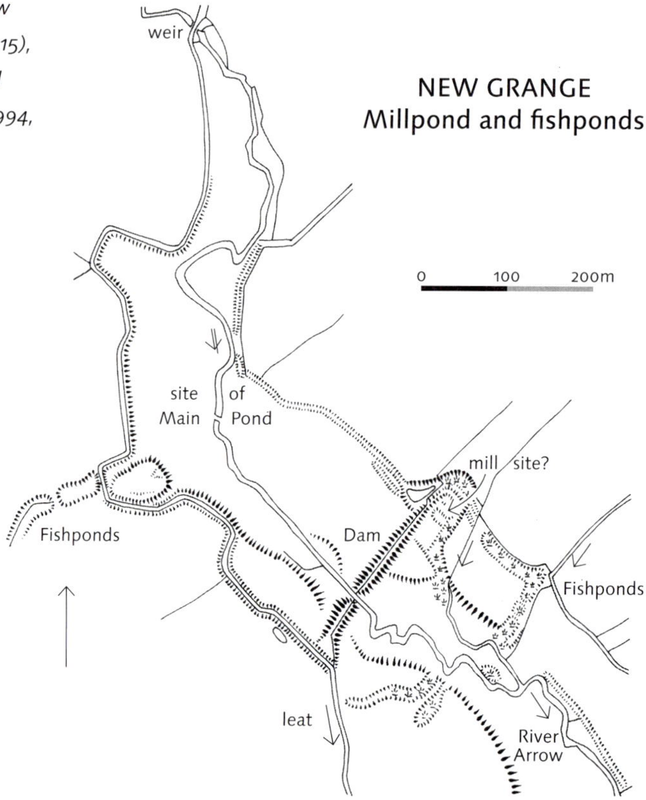

Within the map (Fig 11.15):

Stour

Kingsuch
King's Norton
Houndsfield
Forest of Arden
Avon

Chaddesley corbet *m*
New Grange
Sidnalls
m Osmerley
m Hewell
Tardebigge *m*
Sheltwood Redditch Ullenhall
m Preston Bagot
Kington
Songar *m*
Bearley Barford

Knottenhull
Holway
Forest of Feckenham

Arrow
Alne

Severn
Terne

Binton *m*
Bidford
Feldon

Vale of Evesham
Stour
Oxhill

Combe

Childs wickham

Stretton

Avon
Cotswolds

● Grange   *m* Mill owned by Bordesley Abbey   └ land over 400 ft (122m)

Within the map (Fig 11.16):

NEW GRANGE
Millpond and fishponds

weir

0 100 200m

site of Main Pond

mill site?

Fishponds

Dam

Fishponds

leat

River Arrow

could itself have a mill, fishponds and a dovecote and its own chapel and residential buildings (Fig 11.16).

There was no doubting here, as at Fontenay, the massive investment and business-like agenda of the Cistercian community. Engineering skills not seen since Roman times were employed to reclaim the valley's resources and put them to work. The community was self-sufficient, but also manufactured, and presumably sold, a wide range of products, including armour and weapons, for which the monks could have had little use themselves. By the mid fourteenth century, the granges were being leased, and the industrial energy of the abbey site diminished. The mill area was abandoned in the late fourteenth century: an inability to manage the flow of water and a slackening of the traditional weapons market being likely contributory factors. The nature of the economic operation had thus changed markedly sometime before 1538, when the monastic community was dissolved, the abbey largely demolished and its contents and building materials sold off.

Fortified cathedrals and monasteries

The self-contained character of cathedrals and monasteries, their material wealth and their symbolic dominance over people's lives meant that the convents often attracted aggression and were moved to fortify their enclosures (Harrison 2004 for what follows). Some resembled the sites of castles. Some of the earliest monasteries in Egypt and Syria were fortified (as Saint Catherine's, Sinai), and military orders castellated their churches or enclosed them in castles. For example, the Templar church at Ambel in Spain (see Ch 1, p 49), or the Crusader church of St Michael in Chastel Blanc, Safita, Syria of *c.* 1220 (Harrison 2004, 45), or the church in the thirteenth-fourteenth century castle of the Livonian Order at Cēsis, Latvia (Ch 6, p 265). Churches exposed to raiding and piracy were notable candidates for fortification or enclosure, for example those situated on the Scottish and Welsh Marches, the round tower fortress churches of Denmark, or the free-standing fortified thirteenth century church tower at Näs on Gotland, with its loops for cross-bows. The area of south-west France, contested by England over the Hundred Years War (1337-1453), was the subject of a massive programme of defence, particularly against the 'Free Companies' of English roaming warbands. Famously, the pilgrimage destination of the abbey of Mont Saint Michel (Manche), made impregnable in 1393, heroically defended by Louis D'Estouteville in 1425, and never surrendered to the English, became a symbol of French resistance (Harrison 2004, 119). On the return of the Papacy from Avignon in 1377, the Vatican itself was strongly fortified and now included the tomb of Hadrian, renamed the Castel Sant'Angelo with its dominant position overlooking the Tiber crossing. The Vatican was encircled with a new wall under Pope Nicholas V (1447-55) (*ibid.* 152).

BOX 11.3 ESTABLISHMENTS OF THE MENDICANT ORDERS

The most important mendicant (begging) orders were: the Dominicans and the Franciscans (Ch 10, p 455). The Dominicans (*ordo fratres predicatorum*) were founded by the Spaniard Dominicus Guzmán with the intention of working against heresies by preaching to the urban poor, gaining their attention through being poor themselves. The founder of the Franciscans (*ordo fratres minores*) was Saint Francis of Assisi, a rich layman who started a movement aiming at preaching and following the example of Christ by living in poverty.

At the outset the two orders lived quite differently: the Dominicans were intellectually orientated and study was important, while the Franciscans focused on emotion. But over time they grew closer. For lay people it was often difficult to distinguish between the missions of the mendicants, and the popular descriptions reflected their clearly visible clothing: grey friars (Franciscans), black friars (Dominicans) and white friars (the later order of the Carmelites).

The orders spread quickly throughout Europe. Lund in present southern Sweden, for example, had a Dominican convent already in 1222. The Franciscans had many friaries in Italy, most of them small and situated in the countryside, but some very great friaries were in cities, like Venice, Siena, Florence. North of the Alps it was normal for friaries to be placed in towns. In many parts of Europe, friaries totally outnumbered the older monasteries, and the huge mendicant churches in the Mediterranean and central Europe easily measured up to late medieval abbey churches in size – in spite of the orders' original ideals of modesty and poverty.

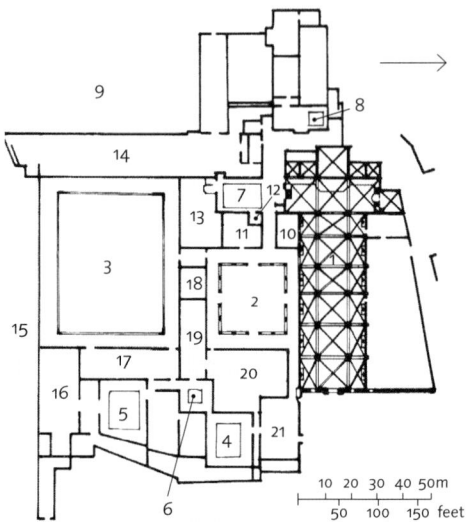

Fig 1

Plan of the Dominican friary of Santa Maria Novella in Florence around 1500 (after Braunfels 1972). Key: 1. Church. 2 Chiostro Verde. 3 Chiostro Grande. 4 Chiostro della Porta. 5 Chiostro dell' Infermeria. 6 Chiostro Dati. 7 Chiostro dei Morti. 8 Minor cloister. 9 Monastery garden. 10 Sacristy. 11 Spanish Chapel. 12 Chapel of Our Lady. 13 Dorter. 14 Dorter della Capella. 15 Guest house. 16 Chapel of St Nicholas. 17 Infirmary. 18 Capitolo del Nocentino. 19 Refectory. 20 Domestic rooms. 21 Forecourt.

There are some archaeological studies on churches of mendicant friaries, and some regional and chronological patterns appear. But being placed in towns, new buildings often cover the original plots. Friaries, especially their origins, are therefore usually more complicated to investigate and interpret than monasteries in the countryside. Sources will often include remains of standing buildings, excavations, written sources, old drawings and photos (Fig 1 and 2).

A friary was normally organized with the church bordering a busy street or square and the other monastic buildings situated in back areas. Compass directions were not important. The church required a huge nave to hold the congregation listening to the preaching of the brethren. The mendicants avoided the term *monasterium* and instead used *domus*. In the beginning, the friaries were not organized as monasteries with ranges of buildings around a cloister; the brethren rather lived according to what was possible. But in time the friaries grew into great and elaborate building complexes arranged like traditional monasteries. The grand cloister nearest to the church was probably open to citizens for conferences (in the refectory) and funerals (in the cloister walks). Only a part of the complex was a strictly closed area for the brethren; this was often arranged around a second cloister or yard.

Mendicant orders are often found in the outskirts of towns (Ch 10, p 372), but this is not a necessary rule; rather the location depended on where and in which town the founder owned land and could make it available. The mendicants could probably reject an offer, but normally they would accept it. Who were these founders? The Dominicans were favoured by the established church, and bishops and canons were therefore often involved in establishing a house. In southern Europe, with its big towns and rich bourgeoisie there were probably also many citizens among the founders, while in northern Europe the prince (duke, count) of the area was often the founder.

Fig 2

The Franciscan friary of Svendborg, Denmark. It was founded in 1236, the nave of the church was consecrated in 1361, and the west wing was built in the early 16th century. The picture was drawn in 1828 as documentation just before demolition of the friary (after Krongaard Kristensen 1994).

In the later Middle Ages, monasticism developed along different lines in different parts of Europe. In Denmark, for example, nearly a quarter of the 116 monasteries and friaries that existed at the time of the Reformation (in 1536) had been founded within the previous 100 years, and 17 of those were from after 1450. But in England the peak number of monasteries was reached shortly before the time of the Black Death. Just before the Reformation in 1530 the figure was about 15% lower, although a number of new convents had been founded in the meantime (Sources: Braunfels 1972; Krongaard Kristensen 1994; Schenkluhn 2000; Rasmussen 2002; Hillebrand 2003; Untermann 2009).

by Hans Krongaard Kristensen

Introduction

To the student of the Middle Ages, parish churches are of unparalleled value, as there are few buildings that offer such substantial insights into the material culture of religious belief, secular status and identity. The example given here – of the parish church in England – offers many aspects of research and interpretation that may be encountered throughout the Christian parts of Europe. Although local churches were never as physically imposing or aesthetically impressive as cathedrals and abbeys, their ubiquity, prominence, and accessibility ensured that they played a crucial role in the lives of all strata of society. They served as the site and space of day-to-day religious activity, a focal point for the display of secular wealth and authority, the arena in which the major milestones of life were marked, and a hub for formal and informal contact with members of the community (Ch 10, p 428). The material manifestation of these activities was already significant in the early medieval period, but it was further heightened in the late medieval economic and sociocultural climate. During these centuries, the obligation of parishioners to the upkeep of the church was formalized, patrons' contributions to the fittings and fabric of churches steadily grew, and the range of people able to exert influence on the form and use of the parish church reached its greatest medieval extent (Carpenter 1987, 66; Ford 1992, 236; Mason 1976, 28). As a result, parish churches had a social significance that far outweighed their designation as the 'minor' churches of the ecclesiastical hierarchy.

Church buildings

Church building in the late Middle Ages has been succinctly summarized as primarily a time of 'adaptation rather than origin' (Brown A 1996, 63). After the final codification of the parochial system in the twelfth century (Pounds 2000, 3; Tatton-Brown 1998, 265), patrons focused less on constructing new churches, and more on rebuilding and elaborating those that already existed. Despite considerable evidence for an economic downturn across the whole of England in the fifteenth century, investment in the church was nevertheless so widespread that there are only a very few churches in England which remain wholly untouched by late medieval building programmes (Morris 1989, 351; Postan 1973, 44-45). In the thirteenth century, the short apsidal chancels of the twelfth century were frequently rebuilt longer, larger, and with squared-off ends, probably to accommodate liturgical changes to the site of the altar and the position of the priest when celebrating mass (Davidson 1999, 76). Aisles were often added in the later Middle Ages as well, if the church had not already acquired them in the building boom of the twelfth century (Brown A 1996, 65). The addition of aisles, and their occasional subsequent demolition, was long thought of as a reflection of expanding and declining population and congregation size. Indeed, in some cases, as at Wharram Percy (North Yorkshire), the addition and loss of aisles does seem to trace the late medieval prosperity and demographic trajectory of the settlement (Beresford and Hurst 1990) (Fig 11.17).

However, recent research has argued convincingly that aisles were not merely a pragmatic response to population, but were instead meaningfully constructed social spaces, driven by both religious and secular motivations. A new aisle could impact not only on the layout of the church, but on the ways in which liturgical practice and processions moved through it. By adding an aisle, a patron laid claim to a space within the church, and could emphasize his status and significance by determining behaviour within that space (Graves 1989, 315; Graves 2000).

Piecemeal remodeling continued and intensified throughout the late medieval period, and the fourteenth and fifteenth centuries saw numerous additions, enlargements, and rebuildings of chantry chapels, towers, aisles, and porches. Compared to other fittings and fabric, church windows are mentioned relatively infrequently as bequests in medieval wills (Ford 1992, 227), but the archaeological evidence is clear that fenestration programmes were by far the most common form of late medieval adaptation. Windows were a particularly attractive investment, and in urban areas they seem to have been a favourite of the wealthy mercantile classes, as has been shown in the churches of late medieval York and Norwich (Barnett 2000, 76; Graves 1989, 313). Windows were appealing because they were a relatively rapid means of updating the church to the latest architectural style, and the stained glass within them provided an opportunity to conspicuously express patronal ambitions and commemorate the dead, while simultaneously beautifying the church, and even altering the internal ambience of the building through light and colour (Platt 1995, 127; Mattingly 2000; Barnwell 2005, 81; Giles 2007, 115) (Fig 11.18). Along with adjustments to the fabric, internal decorations and fixtures such as rood-screens, pews, sculpture, decorative cloths, and wall paintings proliferated in the late medieval period, although only a few survived the Reformation (Peters 1996) (Fig 11.19). These fittings drastically changed the internal character of the church, not only in terms of its visual character, but by restructuring the performance and experience of the mass, and redefining social relationships and hierarchies based on visibility, access, and claims over space.

St Martin, Wharram Percy, North Yorkshire. **Fig 11.17** *The south wall of the nave, with evidence of an aisle added in the twelfth century, and subsequently removed and blocked in the fifteenth/sixteenth centuries (photo by Chris Brown, used with permission of www.eriding. net/media).*

Fig 11.18   *(left) The Corporal Works of Mercy window, All Saints, North Street, York, early 15th century. The window likely commemorates Nicholas Blackburn Sr, Lord Mayor of York. It is probable that the man performing the acts of mercy is the patron himself (photo by David O'Connor, used with permission of the CVMA).*

Fig 11.19   *(right) Rood screen, St Helen, Ranworth, Norfolk, fifteenth century. Ranworth has retained its medieval chancel screen, although without the surmounting cross, and it gives some impression of how the east end of the church would be blocked from view from the nave. The door for the former rood loft is still visible high on the northeast wall (photo by John Salmon).*

As a result of the continuous addition, subtraction, and modification of subsequent generations, medieval parish churches and chapels are particularly complex palimpsests of construction, and church archaeology has contributed significantly to our understanding of how and why churches were transformed over time (for an example, Box 11.4). The use of systematic, empirical recording techniques and stratigraphic analyses of fabric has elucidated minute details of the relationships between building phases, revealing that the structural development of the parish church was even more complex than purely stylistic architectural assessments had suggested (Rodwell 2005, 65, 73). However, church archaeology's role has not been limited to implementing methodological advances. One of its most enduring contributions has been the consideration of the parish church not as an isolated building, but as an integral part of the surrounding physical, social, and built environment. Furthermore, archaeologists have recently embraced an interdisciplinary, explicitly theoretical approach to the study of parish churches, that sees architectural and decorative developments not as lifeless processes, but as the outcome of active, meaningful choices made by knowledgeable agents. This approach has encouraged exploration of a number of pertinent issues which were bound up in the material culture and use of the medieval church, including examinations of space, landscape, belief, authority, memory, perception, and identity. Recent research in church archaeology has thus not only transformed our understanding of the late medieval local church, but of late medieval society as a whole.

Churches, landscapes, and lordship

One of archaeology's most vital contributions to parish church studies is the treatment of these structures in a landscape and settlement context. The chronology of parochial formation has long been of interest to early medieval church archaeologists, but late medieval archaeology has now demonstrated that the parish network was by no means static after the twelfth century. Dependent chapels were frequently founded well into the later Middle Ages, further subdividing the parochial system, and marking sites of population growth, urban and suburban expansion, and new settlements colonizing marginal, assarted, or reclaimed land (Owen 1976, 68). Many of these dependent chapels eventually acquired the rights of burial and baptism, and some even became fully independent parish churches, thus complicating and revising the hierarchical and financial relationships between churches, settlements, and estates. New chapel foundations in the later Middle Ages could also refocus a settlement's communal and religious life and sense of identity. Gaining independence and the right to bury and commemorate often drew patronage and expenditure to the chapel, and away from the traditional hub of the parish church (Dymond 2003, 209).

Other studies of churches and the landscape have characterized churches as a physical and conceptual embodiment of secular authority, and argued that they were key material components of elite identity. The construction and location of churches in medieval settlements has been seen as indicative of feudal power, as building or rebuilding a church required wealth, human and technological resources, and control over land and materials. In this view, the permanence of the church reinforced and stabilized feudal relationships of dominance, and articulated lordly and elite authority over the lower classes (Saunders T 2000, 224). This view has been reinforced by studies demonstrating the close physical proximity of churches and manor houses. In a study of rural Lincolnshire, it has been shown that not only were manors and churches in close physical association, but at times were situated on the periphery of the settlement, apparently deliberately creating an elite enclave separate from the communal space of the village (McDonagh 2007, 199). In these cases, churches were constructed and decorated not only to reflect the status and wealth of lords and patrons, but also to provide a locale in which these attributes could be negotiated and maintained. However, others have argued that in many cases late medieval churches were not a monolithic apparatus of the elite, but were instead heavily influenced by the wider parish community (Dyer 1985, 29). In urban areas, away from the traditional manorial system, parishioners, civic organizations, and the burgeoning 'middle classes' played an even more significant role in church construction and elaboration (Rosser 1988a; Finch 2004, 70-72). In the late medieval parish churches of Coventry, which profited exceptionally from the late medieval wool trade, guild and fraternity chapels occupied nearly every space in the church apart from the chancel (Platt 1995, 115-116). In a situation such as this, high levels of competition for space and prominence amongst patrons necessitated continual investment to maintain a place in the social hierarchy. The inherent accessibility and widening range of patrons in the late medieval parish church might mean that, through the use of material culture and the occupation of religious space, the established social order could be challenged or even overturned.

Fig 1

St Colman's Church, Portmahomack, as it appears today (M. Carver).

The church of St Colman stands above a beach facing the Dornoch Firth at Portmahomack on the Tarbat peninsula, north-east Scotland (Fig 1). The isthmus, where three seaways meet, was crossed by a portage (gaelic *tairbearht*) and attracted prehistoric burials and ritual interest over more than two millennia (Fig 2). In the sixth century a Pictish monastery was founded at Portmahomack (St Colman's port), which flourished until the beginning of the ninth century when it was destroyed in a Viking raid (Carver 2008).

A Christian presence was re-established in the late eleventh or early twelfth centuries, probably in the context of the reforms of King David I who imported the practices of current European orthodoxy into Scotland, where monasteries of Benedictine and Premonstratensian orders were founded and the parish system imposed. The new stone church of the eleventh or twelfth century began a sequence of buildings that would reflect local and regional Christian thinking up to the late twentieth century (Fig 3).

The first parish church took the form of a rectangular nave (12x8m) aligned east-west, with a small rectangular chancel at the east end, both founded on beach cobbles and carried up in square blocks of local red sandstone. Large pieces of Christian Pictish sculpture, residual from the early medieval monastery, were incorporated into the foundations. This building which could scarcely accommodate 30 persons (standing) probably had a belfry, implied by the find of a fragment of contemporary bell mould.

In the thirteenth century the building experienced a major redevelopment. It was lengthened by 5m to the west and 10m to the east, for which purpose the west wall and the chancel of the twelfth-century church were demolished. The new walls were embellished at their base with an external chamfered plinth. At the west end, a belfry was raised to hang a bell, and at the east end a subterranean crypt was constructed that incorporated an old wall for the Pictish monastery as its east end. This new configuration of a church at the far north of Europe conformed to the decrees of the Lateran Council in having a nave for parishioners and a chancel for a full-time priest. Traces of the new formal ceremonies were found in the form of a pottery chafing dish to burn incense and a glazed aquamanile to pour wine or (holy) water. The crypt was probably intended to house the relics of St Colman of Lindisfarne, claimed in a sixteenth century document to have been housed at Portmahomack.

Burial inside the church was a privilege reserved to a few, mainly in coffins, and high status burials were occasionally marked by a carved memorial slab (Fig 4), though here mainly unidentified. In the late fifteenth

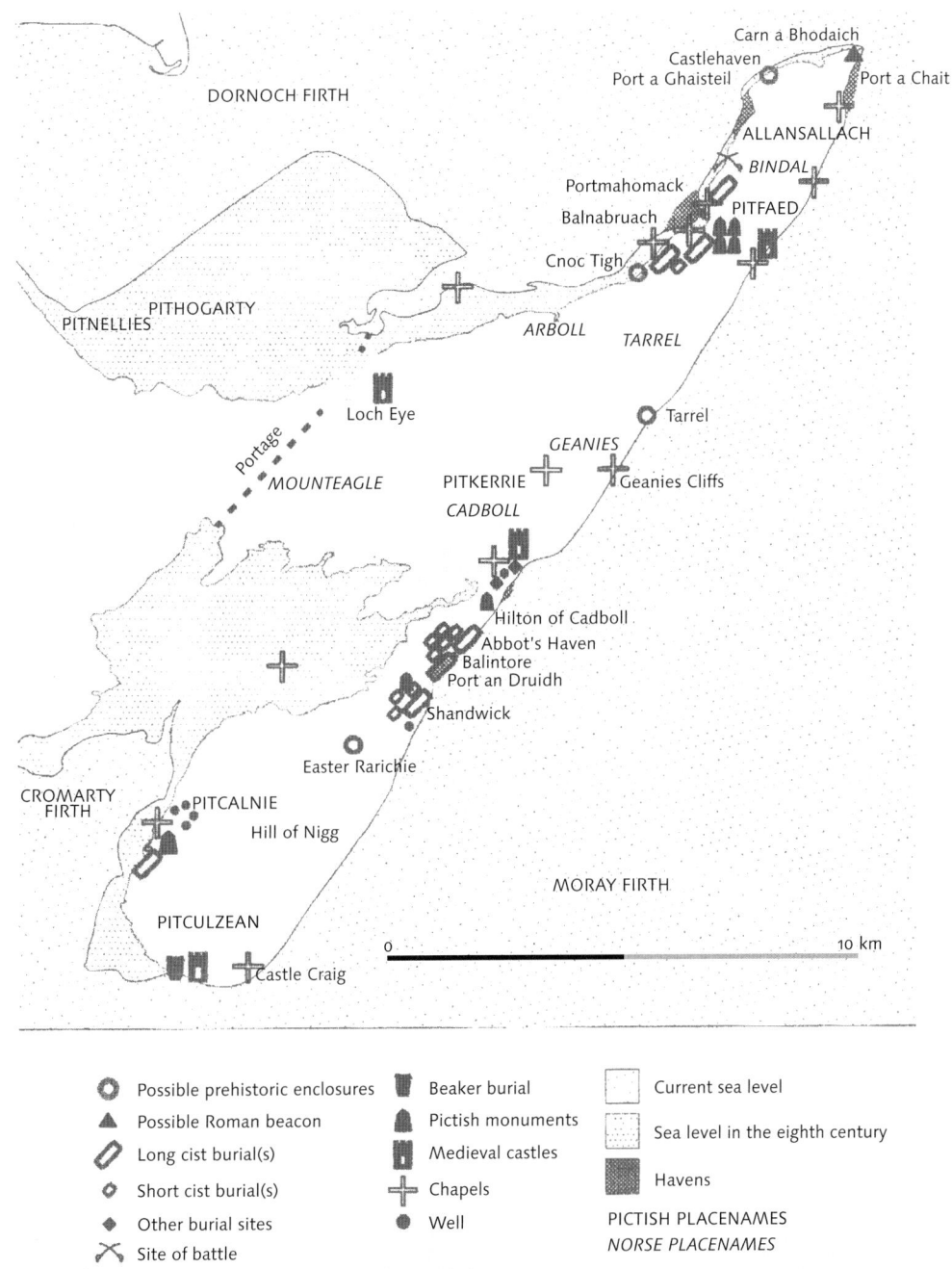

Possible prehistoric enclosures ⬤
Possible Roman beacon ▲
Long cist burial(s) ⬭
Short cist burial(s) ◇
Other burial sites ◆
Site of battle ✕

Beaker burial
Pictish monuments
Medieval castles
Chapels ✝
Well ●

Current sea level
Sea level in the eighth century
Havens

PICTISH PLACENAMES
NORSE PLACENAMES

Fig 2

Ritual landscape: the Tarbat peninsula, showing prehistoric burials, Pictish monastery and Medieval chapel sites (M. Carver).

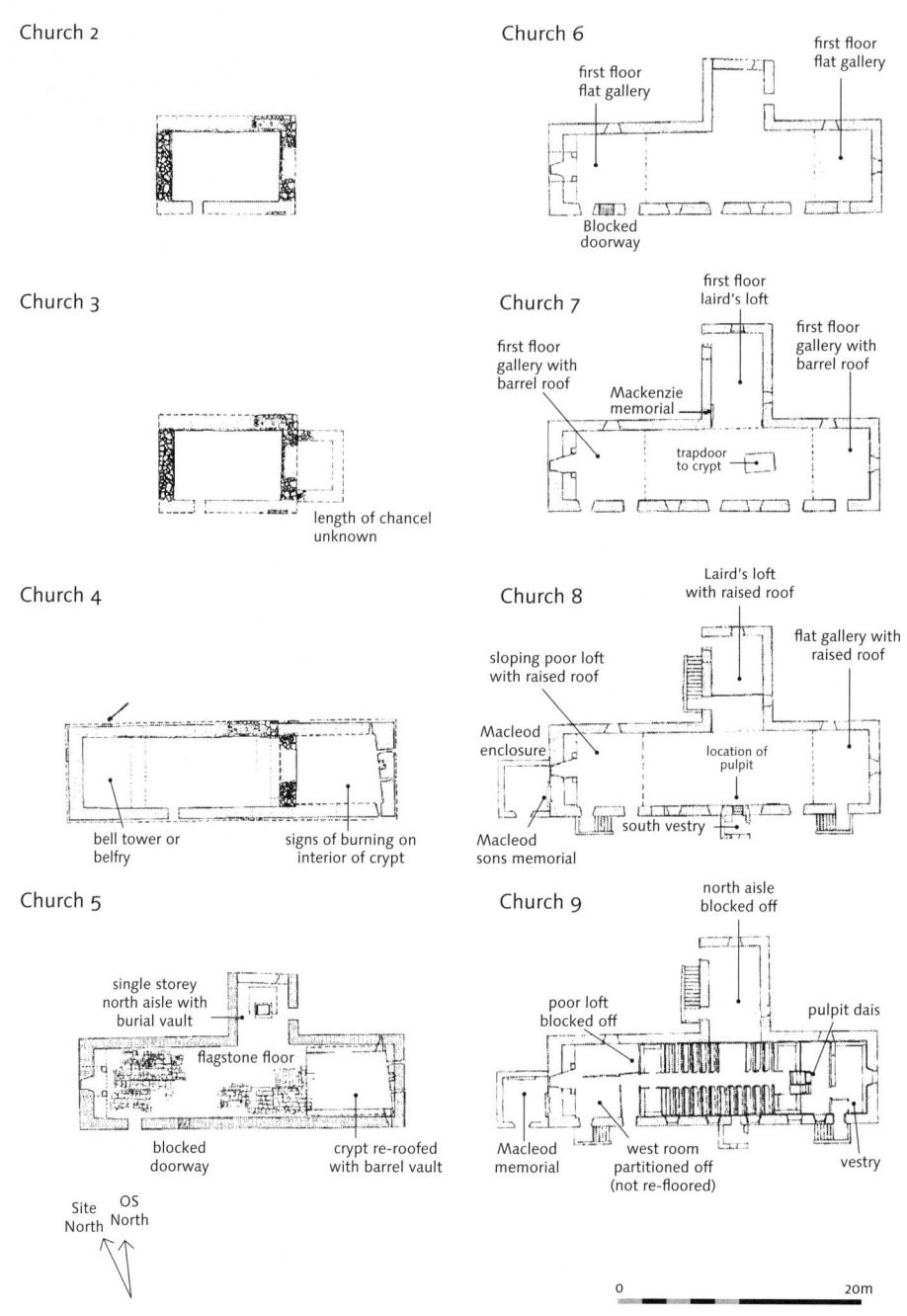

Church 2

Church 3

length of chancel unknown

Church 4

bell tower or belfry

signs of burning on interior of crypt

Church 5

single storey north aisle with burial vault

flagstone floor

blocked doorway

crypt re-roofed with barrel vault

Site North

OS North

Church 6

first floor flat gallery

first floor flat gallery

Blocked doorway

Church 7

first floor laird's loft

first floor gallery with barrel roof

first floor gallery with barrel roof

Mackenzie memorial

trapdoor to crypt

Church 8

Laird's loft with raised roof

sloping poor loft with raised roof

flat gallery with raised roof

Macleod enclosure

location of pulpit

south vestry

Macleod sons memorial

Church 9

north aisle blocked off

poor loft blocked off

pulpit dais

Macleod memorial

west room partitioned off (not re-floored)

vestry

0   20m

Fig 3

The evolution of St Colman's Church, 12-18th centuries (M. Carver).

mains showed that men averaged 1.7m and the women 1.55m in height. While 63% of those buried were children or infants, representing a high early mortality, 47% of the adults lived to be over 45 years old.

A large number of chapels and holy wells and some hermitages were known to have existed in the medieval period, reflecting local observance that went back to Pictish times (as indicated by surviving cross-slabs) and most probably into the Iron Age and beyond. They largely disappeared at the Reformation, which arrived in this part of Scotland around 1580. Its effect on the church at Portmahomack was also dramatic. The axis of worship rotated through 90 degrees, so the focus was now on a pulpit on the south wall. A rectangular annex was built facing the pulpit on the north side (the 'north aisle'), providing accommodation for the laird and his family who had assumed responsibility for the church and also, in part, for the spiritual welfare of the parishioners, through their sponsorship of their own minister. This process of secularisation and class distinction was to continue through the seventeenth and eighteenth century, the lord being soon equipped with a first floor sitting room with a fire-place (the 'laird's loft'). As indicated by inscribed headstones and cartouches, the space below the loft was reserved for the burial of his ancestors and other high ranking individuals. To accentuate the differences in social rank, four doors were cut in the walls of this tiny church, so as to provide separate entrances and sitting space for the laird, the minister, the middle class and the poor.

Fig 4

Fourteenth-century memorial slab from St Colman's Church (drawn by Trevor Pearson).

century, an inter-clan feud led to the church being damaged by fire, and following this incident the church was rebuilt, and the nave was subsequently crowded with burials, with and without coffins, inflicting much disturbance on each other. The skeletal re-

by Martin Carver

Form, space, and art

A number of studies have also considered the architectural form, interior character, and ornament of the late medieval parish church. These studies have drawn on traditional approaches from art history and buildings archaeology, but also have brought to bear sociological theories concerning people's perceptions and use of space, visuality, memory, and even sound and movement. An extremely common architectural adaptation of the late medieval church, yet one of the least studied by archaeologists, is the chantry chapel (Barnett 2000, 75-76; Roffey 2007, 7). These structures were built by a patron, usually attached to the chancel or aisles of the church, in order to provide a space for masses to be said for his soul and those of his family in perpetuity. They thus provided tangible spiritual benefits, but could serve familial, political, professional, and social motivations as well. Chantry chapels also created an area of semi-private worship for an elite family, effectively making a private claim over the public space of the church. The chapel physically and spatially distinguished the family from the remainder of the parish community, and often situated them in a privileged location, beyond the rood screen which divided nave from chancel, and closer to the high altar, the focal point of holiness in the church.

However, it has also been argued that chantry chapels were not solely individualistic private monuments, but also served the interests of the parish at large. The provision of funding for a chantry and its housing could also bring in money to embellish and enrich the parish church beyond the immediate walls of the chapel, such as the construction of a porch, vestry, or even, as at the parish church of Devizes (Wiltshire), an anchorite's cell. In addition, the divine services said in the chantry, its priest and altar, and its funerary monuments would all have been an integral visual and aural part of the standard celebration of mass. In this way, the chantry patrons would not have been perceived as isolated from the parish community, but as local exemplars of piety, who played an important, familiar, and appreciated role in the performance of the mass (Roffey 2007, 160).

In recent years, archaeologists have also begun to pay more scholarly attention to the art of the church, including wall paintings, sculpture, and stained glass. These features have been considered not only in terms of style, iconography, and technical execution, but according to the social roles they performed. Several studies have shown that art in the church was used to communicate multiple messages to a variety of audiences, such as in the chapel at Haddon Hall (Derbyshire). As a manor house chapel with parochial duties, it was an inherently private religious space with a necessary public aspect, and these dual roles were in part defined by the chapel's wall paintings. Those in the chancel were more iconographically complex, and were personalized to the Vernon family's favoured saints in order to fulfil their private devotional requirements. But those in the nave catered to the biblical knowledge of the common parishioner, with uncomplicated images of the popular saints Christopher and George. At the same time, the scheme as a whole asserted the social standing and lineage of the Vernon family to both common and elite outside audiences (Naydenova 2006, 202). The cycle of wall paintings in the nave of Pickering (North Yorkshire) parish church, which echoes the calendar of saints' feast days, may also have communicated on multiple levels (Fig 11.20). The paintings may simply reflect saints important to the parish and patron, but the placement of the saints in calendrical order may signify the laity appropriating knowledge of the liturgical framework, which was central to clerical authority. The patrons of the paintings were then ostentatiously displaying possession of that knowledge in the space of the church that was under lay control. This may suggest a lay challenge to the authority of the clergy, and also indicates the tension that could exist between conceptions of institutional and popular piety (Wright 1988; Giles 2000b, 50; Graves 2000, 167). These studies have highlighted that further research is needed to refine our understanding of medieval perceptions of secular and sacred space and behaviour, and the boundaries that lay between them. Recent work has already shown that these concepts, and their material manifestations, could become particularly blurred within the bounds of the late medieval parish church, as secular patrons used their wealth and influence to encroach ever more upon the spaces traditionally controlled by the clergy (Graves 2000, 166; Woodcock 2005, 121).

Future research into the creation, use, and meaning of social space within church buildings and ecclesiastical landscapes will undoubtedly benefit from rapidly advancing

The Martyrdom of St. Edmund, **Fig 11.20**
SS Peter and Paul, Pickering, North Yorkshire, 15th century. This painting occupies the easternmost bay of the north wall of the nave, marking a feast day of 20 November (photo by T. Marshall, used with permission of www.thepaintedchurch.org).

A 3-D rendering of a 'typical' me- **Fig 11.21**
dieval parish church of c. 1240, from a complete virtual reality model of the development of an English parish church from the 7th to the 15th century. The model emphasizes the coexistence of stylistic phases, and the recreation of light, texture, and interior decoration to model the sensory experience of the medieval parish church (created by Anthony Masinton).

technologies of spatial analysis, particularly computer-aided mapping, modeling, and 3-D visualization. Geographical Information Systems (GIS) mapping facilitates the examination and visualization of the landscape context of churches, and of their physical relationships to key political, topographical, and settlement characteristics or boundaries (e.g. McClain 2005; Stocker and Everson 2006). It also enables the systematic analysis of changes in patterns over space and time on a large scale, in a way that was time-consuming, if not impossible, to do by hand. Furthermore, 3-D architectural reconstruction programs can be used to model the form, space, decoration, and even the aural and visual experience of the medieval church and liturgy, and to demonstrate how that experience could change over time depending on formal and spatial variables (e.g. Masinton 2005; Fig 11.21).

Conclusion

The archaeological study of the late medieval church is a relatively recent development, and it has not been nearly as prominent as early medieval church archaeology, with its well-known digs of Anglo-Saxon churches. As the vast majority of England's late medieval churches are unthreatened sites that remain in use, excavation is generally an unfeasible approach. But the above discussion undoubtedly demonstrates how much can be accomplished even without access to the below-ground archaeology. Indeed, the lack of excavation opportunities on late medieval sites is perhaps in some measure responsible for the resultant innovations in the theory and method of church archaeology, which will hopefully inform future study in churches of all periods. The studies mentioned all provide a firm foundation on which to build new research directions in church archaeology. They all embrace interdisciplinarity with history, art history, geography, and sociology, and they offer interpretations which provide insight into the unique melding of the religious and the secular that characterized the medieval parish church. Given the staggering number of surviving parish churches in England, the amount of archaeological work carried out on them has been relatively small, and the study of the late medieval church, particularly, is still often ceded to historians and art historians. But archaeologists, as demonstrated above, have much to contribute to a better understanding of not only the church's material characteristics and development, but also the ways in which people used and engaged with them, and how individuals and groups acted within religious spaces. This short discussion has hopefully demonstrated not only what great strides have been made in the archaeology of the late medieval church, but also how much more there is still for future scholars to do.

Jewish communities in Europe during the Medieval and Early Modern period were generally restricted in the area in which they were allowed to reside, and in the number, type and size of buildings they were allowed to erect (see also AME 1, 391-3 for the period before 1200).

The exact rules – and the frequency with which exceptions were granted to existing laws, regulations and traditions – were dependent upon the precise circumstances of different localities and at different times. There has been little systematic excavation of former Jewish quarters to confirm or adjust the accepted views of restrictive Jewish life proffered by the documentary evidence. That evidence, however, is mostly in the form of official proclamations, edicts and statutes that may overstate the case.

Hebrew sources, especially the *responsa* literature (written rabbinic responses to queries about the application of Jewish law), as well as notarial documents and court records, suggest a more fluid situation, as well as areas that might in time be clarified by more attentive and focused archaeological investigation (Mann, 2000).

Non-Jewish documents also indicate areas of cultural interaction between Jews and Christians. Documents reveal that Jews engaged in different commercial and communal activities, amongst themselves and in contact with the wider world. Archaeological evidence, however, is mostly silent on medieval Jewish life except for religious behaviour. This reflects the fact that most cultural material of Jews is indistinguishable from that of Christians. Preconceptions and expectations of archaeologists is also a contributing factor. Most Jewish sites are found accidentally, so only sites already associated with Jews (through a document or a toponym) or that show clear Jewish attributes such as Hebrew inscriptions or Jewish symbols have been identified as Jewish.

Jewish houses, businesses and other structures and spaces may not, however, have had distinct Jewish characteristics that have survived in the archaeological record; we may assume that many other sites might also be described in some way as Jewish. Only in a few places, such as London, have archivists and archaeologists employed systematic mapping techniques to associate specific Jewish owners with specific properties (Hillaby, 1992). Such linkage alerts archaeologists, especially those involved in salvage excavation, of the possibility of a "Jewish connection," to help interpret finds. In a few places, such as Rouen, France, where a Jewish presence was accidentally revealed in the 1980s, excavations are being deliberately planned to investigate sites known from documents to have been within the Jewish quarter and to have seen extensive Jewish occupation.

Buildings used for uniquely Jewish activities, especially religious or ritual activities, are the ones most often identified as Jewish, and these seem to be the buildings that are most common and that have best survived. Remains of synagogues and ritual baths (*mikva'ot*) have been identified at scores of sites across Europe (Wamers and Backhaus, 2004). On the other hand, while we know that there were Jewish owned shops, taverns, mills, bakeries, slaughter-houses, and other types of structures which served the same communities that used the synagogues and ritual baths, few of these have been positively identified (Metzger 1982; Toaff 1998).

Synagogues

Jewish communities were established throughout Europe in the Early Middle Ages. Hundreds of towns and cities had small Jewish populations, but few had purpose-built synagogues. There is no required form for a synagogue. The Hebrew term *Beth ha-Knesset* means "house of meeting," and the Greek-derived *synagogue* means the same (Gruber, 1999). More important is the requirement for certain forms of community prayer – the presence of ten men over the age of thirteen. Any place in which they meet for prayer can be a synagogue, and most likely many early Jewish communities adapted pre-existing spaces for such use. The key architectural elements defining a synagogue are the *Aron ha Kodesh* or Holy Ark, usually some type of cabinet, either built in or free standing, in which the scrolls are the Torah are kept, and the *bimah*, a platform from which the Torah is read at set times to the congregation. These elements were essential, other parts of the synagogue including a place for women, a place for ablutions, special types of seating, and various liturgical and ceremonial objects, varied over time and from place to place (Fig 11.22).

Built-in perimeter seating might indicate a synagogue, but also could be evidence of some other type of meeting hall. For example, interpretation of an excavated room in Guildford, England, first thought to be a synagogue remains unclear (Alexander, 1997). Discovery of the foundation of a *bimah* (as in Lorca, Spain), usually in the centre of the hall, or the evidence of an Ark niche or small room on the wall facing Jerusalem (in Europe, the East or southeast wall), are usually good evidence of synagogue use.

Prohibitions against building new synagogues were intermittently in force through-out Christian Europe from as early as the fourth century. Restrictions on synagogues can be found in most medieval law codes. Still, some new synagogues were erected, but most were small in size, discreet in location, and susceptible to sudden closure by zealous Christian authorities. For most of the Middle Ages the most substantial synagogues were in Spain, Sicily (Bucaria, 1998) and Southern Italy, and in Central Europe (Paulus, 2007).

Fig 11.22 *Schematic plan of a synagogue (western Sephardi), showing components. The tebáh (bimah) is situated near the western wall, the Hekhál (Ark) at the eastern wall, and the pews face the central axis. (M. Carver).*

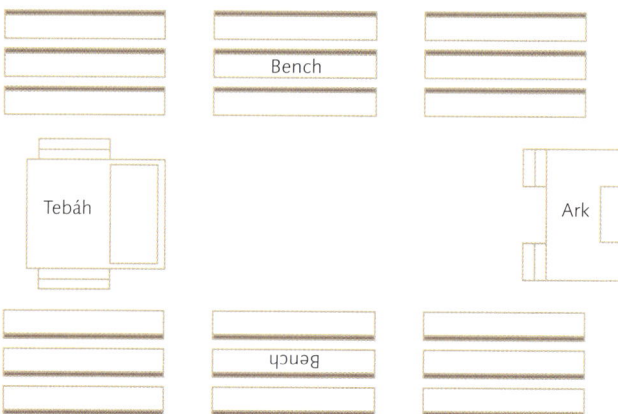

Medieval synagogues were often located in or near the house or business of the richest Jews. Scant physical traces survive since Jews were so often expelled from medieval centres, and the defining characteristics of these synagogues were their furnishings, now long gone. In Italy, a fine stone townhouse in the medieval Italian town of Sermoneta may have been a synagogue, as may the example in the Vicolo dell Atleta, Rome (Fig 11.23). Worshippers here would have met on the *piano nobile*, in a large well-lit room on the first floor (above ground level) – a space traditional reserved for the finest as rooms for the master of the house (Tetro, 1977). House synagogues of this type were once quite common, and the form continued in Europe through the eighteenth century, and has been revived in modern times with new variations.

Medieval Synagogue at the Vicolo dell Atleta, Rome.

Fig 11.23

More public and lavish medieval "hall" type synagogues existed, including two former synagogues in the southern Italian town of Trani, converted to use churches in the fifteenth century (Cassuto, 1980), and fragments of two synagogues in Sopron (Hungary) and two in Budapest. Examples of this type of synagogue can also be seen in the fifteenth century woodcuts published by the anti-Jewish apostate Johannes Pfefferkorn. The thirteenth century synagogue of Sopron has been partially reconstructed, as part of an archaeological process that extracted the earliest building elements from the later additions. It is set back from the street through a passageway between two houses. One enters the synagogue through a narrow corridor, and the sanctuary floor is three steps lower than the vestibule. The sanctuary was a vaulted space with the small Ark set permanently into the east wall and decorated with carved stone work. There would once have been a wooden door to the Ark which would lock in order to secure the Torah scrolls stored within, as these were both the most sacred and most expensive religious items in the building. The women's prayer room had a separate entrance on the south. On the synagogue plot were other structures, including a caretaker's house, a narrow building built toward the end of the fourteenth century to house travellers or the sick, and a *mikveh* (Ferenc, 1994).

In towns with larger Jewish populations and greater resources architecturally more ambitious synagogues were erected (Paulus, 2007). Among these are a series of double-nave structures built across Central Europe beginning in the twelfth century. The synagogues at Worms (Germany) and Prague (Czech Republic) are the most impressive surviving examples, but others have been excavated at Budapest (Hungary), Regensburg (Germany) and Vienna (Austria). The Worms synagogue consists of several sections built at different periods, beginning in 1170, when they rebuilt the building dating from 1034. The men's hall (1175) was divided by two columns on the east-west axis into parallel aisles of equal size. The ark stood at the east end; the bimah was between the columns. A women's annex, built at right angles to the men's section on the north side, was added in 1213. The structure was destroyed in the Second World War, but has been rebuilt, using mostly original material (Böcher, 2001).

The oldest synagogue in continuous use is Prague's Altneushul (Old-New Synagogue), built in the late thirteenth century. The Altneushul also has a double-nave plan, with two tall octagonal piers. The bimah is between the piers; its wrought iron enclosure with pointed arches probably dates from the fifteenth century. The synagogue is surrounded by a number of low annexes added throughout its history. The women's section in the west annex, dated 1732, was later extended to the north side. Narrow windows about three feet above the floor level connect the women's annexes with the main hall (Krinsky, 1985).

The twin-nave plan was probably adopted because it was commonly used in less "church-like" structures such as friaries, refectories, dormitories, and chapter houses of convents in Central Europe. A shortcoming of the twin-nave plan is that the eastern column blocked a head-on view of the Ark. This was minimized, by situating the entrance at an angle to the Ark – so some sight lines were clear. With benches around the interior perimeter much of the activity took place around the bimah, rather than along a linear axis between bimah and Ark.

In medieval Spain a separate tradition developed more dependent upon eastern Jewish authorities and Muslim cultural influences in the creation of a liturgical, linguistic and artistic tradition. There were hundreds of synagogues in Spain and Portugal before the final expulsion of Jews from Iberia at the end of the fifteenth century (Cantera y Burgos, 1984; Assis, 1992). In Toledo alone there were at least nine synagogues and five *midrashim* (small chapels). Two important synagogues from this period still survive. The older was originally the Great Synagogue, now commonly known as Santa Maria la Blanca after the church into which it was transformed after the expulsion in 1492. The exterior is modest, but inside four rows of 32 octagonal piers support horseshoe arches to create an impressive free-flowing open space. Elaborate stucco ornament in the clerestory windows gives a semblance of original decorative opulence. The *Aron ha-Kodesh* is now gone, but was once an irregularly shaped room entered from the end of the central nave. There is no women's' section or gallery, and it is not clear which spaces were open to women. A similar synagogue existed in Segovia and is now a church.

The private synagogue of fourteenth century Courtier Samuel HaLevi Abulafia was of a very different type. It was joined to HaLevi's palace on the east, and the large rectangular interior has rich stucco decoration with Hebrew inscriptions encircling the nave just below the high and richly decorated ceiling. Some inscriptions praise King Pedro I, HaLevi's patron, and others hail Abulafia as "prince among the princes of the tribe of Levi." A spacious gallery on the north side was possibly for women. A gallery along the west wall may have been the choir loft. The east wall is covered with decorative panels surrounding three arches which led to a small chamber (known through recent excavation) that served as the Ark (Palomera Plaza *et al*, 1992).

The synagogue and the surrounding eleven houses of the small hilltown of Lorca (Murcia) comprise one of the most impressive Jewish archaeological finds. The houses contained distinctly Jewish features, including ceramic Hanukah oil lamps. The synagogue included original architectural and decorative features and fragments of more than 50 glass hanging lamps – previously only known from manuscript illuminations and later similar types from North Africa. The Jewish quarter was below the fortified castle walls; the houses arranged in order to make best use of the uneven terrain. They vary in size, and most include small patios, elevated spare rooms, spaces with brick benches built against the walls (in an arrangement similar to synagogue), storage areas for large built-in ceramic jars, cabinets, cupboards, kitchens, and in at least one case, a built-in bathroom. Together, the excavated houses and the many artefacts found within them provide the most comprehensive view of Jewish domestic space ever discovered. The archaeological site in Lorca is exceptional because it lay essentially undisturbed for so many centuries, allowing one of the largest open-air excavations of any (non-cemetery) Jewish site in Europe.

The synagogue is a substantial rectangular structure set into and projecting from the hillside, facing northeast. Its short entrance end consists of a vestibule room entered from the side at the southwest corner of the building. A separate entrance and small room on the southeast probably led to a second story room above the vestibule that was reserved for women. Within the vestibule are the remains of a water source for ablutions, and an entrance into the main sanctuary on axis with the *tevah* and *Aron ha Kodesh*. The

Aron ha Kodesh wall, at the opposite end was built almost entirely above ground and is thus mostly destroyed. Still, large traces of the decoration of the *Aron* have been found in excavation including blue and white glazed pavement tiles in situ, and extensive decorative plasterwork fallen from the walls. There are significant traces of the masonry base of the *tevah*, situated in the centre of the sanctuary, as well as masonry benches built around three sides of the interior (Carrillo & González Ballesteros, 2009).

Schools

Jewish schools or academies existed in many medieval Jewish centres. There were also scriptoria where Torah scrolls and religious manuscripts were produced; these may have been attached to schools. Only one building has been excavated that is likely to have been one of these important institutions. Discovery in 1976 of a monumental Jewish building in Rouen, France (Ch 10, p 440), sparked intense debate as to its original function, and eventually led to a more attention to the history and contribution of Jews to the history and topography of that city, and to Normandy as a whole. The early twelfth-century Romanesque style building was beneath the courtyard of the Palace of Justice, on the ancient Rue aux Juifs. At first it was inferred by archaeologists that it was a medieval synagogue. Professor Norman Golb, determined, however, that the authentic monumental synagogue was located on the other south side of the Street of the Jews, approximately 75 metres west of the newly discovered building. Golb identified the new building as the "School of the Jews"– a rabbinic academy (Golb, 1998).

Baths: mikva'ot

The earliest documentary evidence of a medieval *mikveh* in the European west is from Rome (Italy), where poet and author Nathan ben Yehiel, relates that he built a ritual bath in 1088 – and a synagogue twelve years later. The *mikveh* is used for the ritual immersion and cleansing by women after menstruation or childbirth, and also for various other purification rituals. Because of their frequent below-ground location, *mikva'ot* (plural of mikveh) are frequently revealed by archaeology, or when their location is suspected, they are more easier excavated than other Jewish building types (Heuburger, 1992). *Mikva'ot* have been discovered in Sicily (Scandaliato & Mulè, 2002) but to date, most have been found north of the Alps.

Archaeology, especially from German-speaking lands informs us of two primary types of *mikva'ot*; monumental and cellar. Monumental *mikva'ot* offer remarkable evidence of the architectural resources available to Jews. All were located within the *Judenhof* (Jewish court), close by the synagogue, since women traveling to a *mikveh* needed a safe environment. Elsewhere smaller private *mikva'ot* have been discovered in the basements of houses. Two such likely examples a have been excavated in London (England) (Blair, I. *et al*, 2002).

At Speyer the stone work is similar to the part of the cathedral completed in 1109 (Stein, 1978) (Fig 11.24). These *mikva'ot* are also remarkable for their depth to water level, (up to 25 m), and for their staircases, often comprised of 30 to 40 steps. Monumental *mikva'ot* with single shafts for air and light, with access by a staircase down four sides were common. The Cologne mikvot, dated to no later than the Carolingian period when it suffered earthquake damage, may be the earliest (Schütte, 2004). Other single-shaft *mikva'ot* are at Friedberg in Hesse (ca. 1260) and Andernach on the Rhine (c. 1300). A second, mikveh type, such as Speyer (ca. 1110), Worms (ca. 1185-86) and Offenburg in Baden (not securely dated) had a vertical shaft for light and air and a diagonal one for access. Both types had large, square pools with steps continuing below water level. Offenburg had an unusual circular pool in the centre of a square chamber. *Mikvot* also have been discovered in France and in Catalonia.

In the past decade attention has begun to shift from the monumental *mikva'ot* to the simpler, cellar *mikva'ot* which are both closer to those found in Second Temple and Roman Israel, and may also have been more common in the Middle Ages and Early Modern period. An example at Würzburg may date to the early twelfth century and small *mikva'ot* have also been discovered at Erfurt, Rothenburg, Sondershausen (Thuringia), and Nuremberg. These usually had barrel-vaulted chambers with small rectangular stone or rock-cut pools with access to the water by stone steps. In Ciudad Real (Spain) in 1483 evidence of private *mikva'ot* in homes was presented to the Inquisition as evidence against Jews who were forced to convert to Christianity but who maintained Jewish customs. It is expected that more urban archaeology in Spain will reveal evidence of domestic *mikva'ot*.

Jewish ritual bath (mikveh) in Speyer, first mentioned in the year 1128. The bath was forgotten and **Fig 11.24** *built over, and only recently re-discovered and made accessible to the public (GNU Free documentation License).*

For a historical framework for al-Andalus, please see Ch 1, p 19

Sources

Study of Islamic religious architecture in Spain begins with the great mosque at Córdoba, which has survived in a form scarcely altered until the present day, and is without doubt one of the most important buildings of Islam. Of comparable importance are the minaret and much of the former courtyard of the Almohad mosque at Seville (AME 1, 400-1; Jiménez A & Almagro 1985; Jiménez A, 2002). Among other surviving buildings, all dating from before the mid-thirteenth century, the most significant are the mosques of Cristo de la Luz, Tornerías and San Salvador in Toledo ; the minarets of San Juan in Córdoba and San José in Granada, the Almohad mihrabs at San Juan in Almería and Mértola (Portugal), and the minaret at San Juan de los Reyes in Granada (see AME 1, 118; 390-1). Survivals are much rarer after the mid-thirteenth century when much of al-Andalus was Christianized (see Ch 1, p 18). The only mosques from the thirteenth to the fifteenth centuries that are relatively well preserved are found at the Alhambra, the *ermita* de San Sebastián (Granada), and the present churches of El Salvador in Granada and Fiñana (Almería).

However, medieval archaeology has revolutionised the understanding of Islamic religious buildings through the discovery and exposure of a significant number of new examples. We can pick out the mosque at Madînat al-Zahrâ, excavated by Félix Hernández and Basilio Pavón from 1964 (Pavón 1966); that of Vascos (Toledo), found close to the *alcazaba* (castle) between the year 1996 and 1997; and remains unearthed at three sites in Murcia, in the former Alcázar of the city, in the suburb of the Arrixaca close to San Esteban's church, and the three arches of a possible mosque that appeared at the monastery Nuestra Señora de las Huertas (Lorca).

Among the most spectacular discoveries of the last 25 years are two examples of the *rábita*, an Islamic analogy to the monastery, composed of a large number of small oratories provided with their corresponding *mihrabs* (the focal apsidal alcove). One *rábita* (*ribât*) was found at Guardamar (Alicante), near the mouth of the River Segura and belonged to the tenth or eleventh centuries (Azuar 2004), and the other on a peninsula called Ponta da Atalaia, six kilometres from Aljezur to the north of Cape Saint Vincent in Portugal (Varela Gomes 2007). Another surprising recent discovery was the mosque at the so-called Cortijo de las Mezquitas in the countryside at Antequera (Malaga) (Gozalbes 2006). Most of it was camouflaged in the standing fabric of a farmhouse that had been in use up to a few years ago. Its prayer-hall extended to 338 sq m and the total extent of the building, including the courtyard is 450 sq m. Most rural mosques are much smaller than this. While much of this work awaits detailed publication, interim assessments maybe found in general reviews by Calvo Capilla (2001, 2004, 2007) and Pavón Maldonado (2009).

Mosques: form and typology

The principal religious building of Islam was the mosque (sp. *mezquita*), with its defining attributes the courtyard, prayer-hall, *mimbar* (pulpit) and *mihrab* (niche), situated in the *qibla* (the long wall of the prayer hall) (Fig 11.25). The orientation of the *qibla* determined the direction in which worshippers faced, which was in principle towards Mecca. The orientation of the *qibla* in distant al-Andalus has naturally been a matter of some debate. We know that the *qibla* at Madīnat al-Zahrā' which is oriented at 109 degrees, was aligned by means of astronomical calculations, and lies within 9 degrees of the true direction of Mecca. However, that at Córdoba is oriented at 152 degrees. Rius (1999) has distinguished five principal orientations and assigned them to distinct schools or doctrinal groups. One of these was favoured by the Malikíes, the Quaranic school that held majority sway in al-Andalus, and it used the direction of sunrise at the winter solstice (at 120 degrees).

The plan of most mosques followed that of Córdoba, which in turn followed that of the al-Aqsà mosque in Jerusalem, in that the aisles were perpendicular to the *qibla*, rather than parallel as at Damascus. Recent study by Calvo (2001) has distinguished three types of mosque plan: (1) longer than they are wide, with 3-5 aisles perpendicular to the *qibla*; (2) wider than they are long, with 3-5 aisles perpendicular to the *qibla*; and (3) prayer halls with one or two aisles parallel to the *qibla*.

Type 1 appears to have been inspired by the phase 2 or 3 mosque at Córdoba, corresponding to the reign of Muhammad I (up to 886) and 'Abd al-Rahmān III (up to 961). Into this category fall the mosques at Madînat al-Zahrā', Almonaster, Niebla, Cuatrovitas, La Xara and Cortijo del Centeno. Type 2 appears to emulate the first prayer hall at Córdoba (belonging to the end of the eighth century). To this type belong the relatively well-conserved examples from Vascos (tenth or eleventh centuries) and Archidona (tenth century).

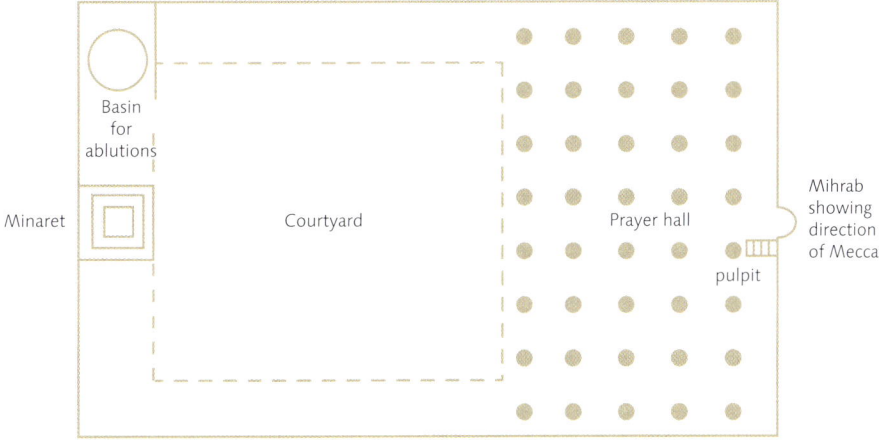

Schematic plan of a mosque showing principal components (M Carver).

Fig 11.25

Religious Buildings   **487**

Type 3 mosques, with one or two aisles parallel to the *qibla* is apparently the least sophisticated. The nearest parallels are to be found among the traditional layouts used as prayer halls by nomadic populations of North Africa and the Near East. Examples from al-Andalus are rural mosques from Guardamar (ninth-tenth centuries), the suburb of Vascos (tenth or eleventh centuries) and Marcén (eleventh century), all relatively modest in appearance and small in size (and see Box 11.5 below for an example from Sicily).

The mosque in the town

The mosque was intended as a ritual building in which to pray, and its design derives from the time of the Prophet. Arab medieval sources distinguish the ordinary mosque from the 'Friday mosque' (*masyjd al-jâmi*), where the citizens were obliged to go on Fridays to hear the sermon (*khutba*) delivered from the pulpit (*mimbar*). The sermon performed a political as well as a spiritual purpose, since it served to transmit the Caliph's policies to the people and command their allegiance. For this reason, in the first centuries of Islam there could only be one Friday mosque with a mimbar in each city. The mosque also functioned as a palace of justice and place of religious instruction until the appearance of the *madrasa* (religious school) in the eleventh century. The mosque also housed the treasury of religious assets (*waqf*). The obligation to attend the Friday service brought a large population into the town with important consequences for urban planning and development (see Ch 9, p 407).

In addition to the *jami*´, every Andalusian city had a number of neighbourhood prayer-halls. After the Christian reconquest, some of these were recommissioned as parish churches, while others were adapted to various uses by the incoming Christian population. Most of the Jamis themselves were transformed into collegiate and major churches, including the magnificent cathedrals whose Gothic fabric sometimes rose upon Islamic foundations, as happened, for example, with the Seville mosque. Famously spared from refurbishment was of course the mosque at Córdoba, which is likely to have been appreciated for its architectural values, since its vaults, arcades and façades were imitated or reproduced in churches and monasteries through the thirteenth and fourteenth centuries.

Rural mosques

The importance of praying together meant that some mosques were constructed to serve small agricultural populations living at a distance from the town. The best known examples in which some architectural elements are conserved are those at Cuatrovitas (Sevilla) and "La Xara", in Simat de Valldigna (Valencia). Numerous textual references make it clear that in some cases such establishments might also be designated to take Friday prayers and exercise the functions of a *jami*´. From a thirteenth-century document we know of three small villages on the outskirts of Murcia (Benibarrira, Tel Alquibir and Benieça) of the same size and similar wealth; but only one was designated as a Friday mosque and provided with a mimbar (Torres Fontes 1971, 83). Similarly three small settlements in Almisserà (Villajoyosa, Alicante), which were occupied between the eleventh and the mid thirteenth century, set up a mosque with a cemetery midway between the three (García J R *et al* 2004). Sometimes, but not always, the location of the communal mosque coincided with that of the communal fortress (*hisn*), where a dispersed population could congregate and take refuge in times of trouble (Angelé and Cressier 1990).

Excavations at Centeno, Lorca (Murcia) revealed a small quadrilateral rural mosque with three aisles (the centre wider than the other two) perpendicular to the *qibla* wall (Fig 11.26). The internal dimensions of the prayer hall were only 9.8 x9.30m, amounting to 91.14 sq m. A series of buttresses was added to strengthen the walls, and a square foundation for a minaret was placed at the north-west corner. An extra room of a few metres in depth had been added to the *qibla* wall with a door opening on to the street. On the floor of the prayer hall were imprints of a structure in a place suggestive of the *mimbar* from which the Friday sermon would be delivered. The *mihrab* niche was incorporated in the thickness of the *qibla* wall but projected to the exterior with a pentagonal plan, while the interior was semicircular. To its right was a second niche of rectangular plan measuring 1.24x0.66m, with a similar projection into the exterior. The positioning of this niche, together with tracks left on the floor by wheeled furniture, implied the position of the now-vanished *mimbar* – the first archaeological evidence for such a key liturgical fitting from a rural site.

It seems likely that this was the Friday mosque serving the nearby fortress of Puentes and no doubt a group of other small settlements in the neighbourhood. Although difficult to date, the mosque is likely to have been abandoned by the conquest of Lorca in 1244 (Navarro & Jiménez 2002).

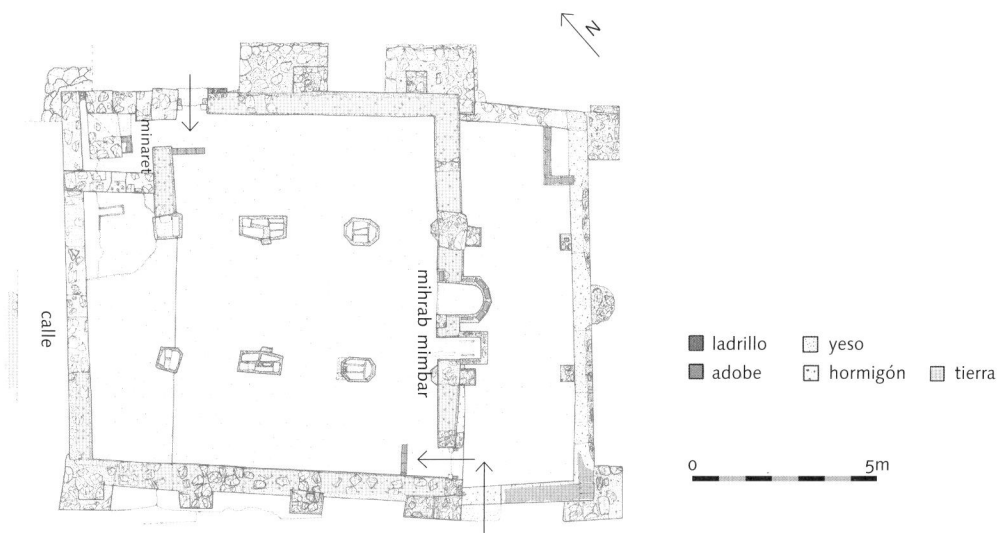

Archaeological plan of the excavated rural mosque at Cortijo del Centeno (Lorca, 12-13th century), showing the mihrab, mimbar, minaret and entrances. The extension to the south-east was probably **Fig 11.26** *intended as a room where the dead rested before burial (masyid al-yana'iz). The semicircular buttress on the exterior wall signals the location of the qibla wall, now enclosed.*

BOX 11.5 A SICILIAN RURAL MOSQUE AND ITS CONTEXT

Fig 1

Map of Sicily, showing places mentioned.

Sicily is a large fertile island in the centre of the Mediterranean Sea, so it is not surprising that it has been profitably visited, conquered or occupied by numerous peoples (Fig 1). In the early Medieval period, the successive dominant groups were Vandals and Goths (their presence on the Island is however controversial), followed by Byzantine, Muslim, Norman and finally Hohenstaufen (Swabian) authorities. Serious archaeological research of Medieval Sicily began only in the 1970s and still lacks systematic application. But its potential is very high for the study of important issues: migration, acculturation, conflict, co-existence and developments in agriculture (Molinari & Nef 2004).

The Islamic conquest of Sicily began in AD 827 but remained incomplete for centuries. Moreover archaeological evidence suggests that a large number of villages extant in the tenth century were Late Roman or Byzantine in origin. The example excavated at Villa del Casale at Piazza Armerina had an untidy plan of multi-cell buildings with courtyards, connected by blind alleys, with a ceramic assemble that fits perfectly into the Islamic material language of the western Mediterranean (Pensabene 2010). Other sites less extensively explored, like Casale di Calliata, an undefended village, were associated with burials exhibiting the Islamic rite

Fig 2

Map of the area investigated: top: the Greek theatre of the Classical period; centre, left: the churches of the 12-13th century; centre, the castle complex, 12-13th century. Bottom: the mosque (Molinari 1997).

(the body on its side facing Mecca, see Ch 12, p 514) (Castellana 1992).

While *Islamicization* no doubt progressed from the ninth century, it is a vague term that may refer to a number of different effects: the arrival of a new Arab or Berber population, the adoption of a religion by the native population, the development of tribal-type groupings or the acquisition of oriental tastes. These things may have been achieved at different rates and at different times, and driven by different imperatives: the State on the one hand or the agency of migrants on the other. All should be observable through the medium of material cul-

ture: in settlement plans, agricultural practice, diet, cuisine and burial rite.

In practice, the distinctions were more subtle. In the tenth-eleventh century, material culture in Sicily had a certain uniformity. Even so, we know that in the eastern part of the island many people were Greek-speaking and Christian. Moreover, the records of Monreale Abbey, even in the late twelfth century, do not show two distinct populations, but rather a broad spectrum from Greek Christian to Arab-Islamic, with the majority somewhere in between (Johns 2002a-b; Metcalfe 2003).

Fig 3

The mosque at Calatabarbaro, photomosaic (Molinari 1997).

The Norman invasion certainly imposed a strong military aristocracy on a population with a weak hierarchy. In one relatively well-studied area, that of Segesta-Calathamet-Calatafimi in western Sicily, we can see how the Norman knights inserted their castles and churches into the settlement network, often planting them on top of already established prominent sites (Molinari 1997). By the second half of the twelfth century, undefended villages are being abandoned and high sites settled in a more extended form. In the first half of the thirteenth century, during Hohenstaufen rule, a marked distinction emerges between western and eastern Sicily, directly reflected in the ceramic assemblages. While the east was now Latin and Christian, the west remained markedly Islamic and Arabic. The Islamic resistance of western Sicily was well organised, struck its own coins and effectively formed an independent emirate.

However the Hohenstaufen monarchy would not allow such an open rebellion to flourish for long, and Frederick II set out to crush it. The results of this campaign were decisive: a very large number of sites abandoned, a hiatus in the material culture of the whole island and the virtual disappearance of the Arab language and Islamic practice – a true case of "ethnic cleansing".

This sequence has been informed by archaeological results of the greatest interest from recent investigations at Iato, Entella and, particularly Segesta/Calatabarbaro, the last of which brought to light the first mosque to be excavated in Sicily (Di Stefano & Cadei 1994, Molinari 1997, Molinari, Nef 2004). Segesta, the site of a famous Greek temple that still stands, was a large Hellenistic and subsequently Roman city abandoned in the seventh AD. During the Byzantine and early Muslim periods, inhabitants avoided it, preferring better connected sites nearer to their crops. But in the upheavals of the twelfth century, when a Norman aristocrat established himself near Calathamet, the high point of Segesta was chosen as the site of a fortified settlement by the Muslim population of the area. There they settled and built a mosque and the site became known as Calatabarbaro, Castle of the Berbers (Fig 2).

The mosque was a rectangular building measuring 20.5 x 11.4m (234 sq m.) with white plastered stone walls (Fig 3). It had a mihrab in the qibla wall, correctly orientated to the south-east. The mihrab was visible as a rectangular projection on the exterior of the qibla wall, and in the interior was semicircular in plan, marked at its corners by two small columns. A row of three central columns suggested that the hall was divided into two aisles parallel to the qibla wall. There was no sign of a minaret. The features of the mosque suggest that it derives its closest parallels from the eastern Maghreb.

The "castle" initially took the form of a group of buildings linked by a perimeter wall around a courtyard, resembling not so much a castle as a fortified farm. This cluster of habitations was constructed, together with the mosque, in the mid-twelfth century. The size of the floor area in the mosque at Calatabarbaro (Monte Barbaro) suggests that it was intended to serve as a prayer hall, probably a Friday mosque, for the occupants of both this fortified village and perhaps a more widespread rural population (see above).

The castle proper was developed on the same site in the late twelfth- early thirteenth century. The perimeter walls were strengthened to make a curtain wall and a large square keep was implanted in the centre. At this point, the mosque was demolished and an apsidal church constructed on the opposite side of the hill (see Box 1.2, Fig 2). These events undoubtedly signal the arrival of a Christian seigniorial authority that culminated in the elimination of Islam. Around the middle of the thirteenth century, Monte Barbaro was completely abandoned and never settled again. The excavations thus provide a vivid picture of a Medieval Islamic community and its struggle for survival.

by Alessandra Molinari

CHAPTER 12

LIFE, DEATH AND MEMORY

PART 1:   LIFE, DEATH AND MEMORY
            by Andrea Augenti and Roberta Gilchrist

The medieval lifecycle

It was common by the thirteenth century for people to conceptualize their lives in comparison with cycles found in nature and episodes recounted in religious texts. The microcosm of the human life was related to the larger macrocosm of Christian cosmology and the natural world – the four seasons, the six ages of history, the seven planets, the twelve months, and so on. This approach to understanding human experience from birth to death is known as the 'ages of man', a scheme borrowed from classical models and further developed in medieval medicine and theology. One of the most common schemes divided the human lifecycle into six ages, following the classification of Isidore of Seville (d. AD 636): *infantia* (up to age seven), *pueritia* (up to fourteen), *adolescentia* (up to 28), *juventus* (up to 50), *aetus senioris* or *gravitas* (up to 70) and *senectus* (until death). These theories spread to popular culture through the preaching of sermons and by visual depictions of the ages of man in religious art and architecture – for example on the façade of Notre Dame Cathedral in Paris. Different versions of the ages of man were also pictured in the books of hours that were used by prosperous people for daily prayers, and on tapestries and wall paintings in elite houses, favoured particularly in Italy and Switzerland (Sears 1986).

The reality of the medieval life-span is reflected more accurately through a combination of historical and archaeological evidence. Documentation of chronological age was relatively rare, but life expectancy has been estimated from tax assessments, hearth surveys, manor court rolls and monastic records. Such sources are biased towards the recording of men, and a healthy working male in the town or countryside could expect to survive into his early 50s. Women might live longer, but female mortality was greater in young adult years due to the dangers of childbirth and exposure to infections while caring for the sick. Records of monastic deaths confirm that monks and nuns could achieve considerable longevity, living well into their 60s and 70s. Infant and child mortality is especially difficult to judge from historical sources. Baptismal records began only in the late fourteenth century in Italy, Germany and Spain, but not until the early sixteenth century in France and England (Youngs 2006). A broad estimate of c. 30%

child mortality has been suggested from such sources, considerably lowering the average medieval life expectancy (see for example Giovannini 2001, for Italy). The osteological study of human remains from medieval cemeteries provides essential insights to the health of ordinary medieval people. However, accurate estimates of life-expectancy based on osteology are limited by a number of factors, particularly the under-representation of infant skeletons in medieval cemeteries, and the methodological difficulties of accurately ageing the skeletons of older individuals (for discussion of anthropological methods and issues of bone taphonomy, see Meier with Graham-Campbell 2007). In many cases an age range of 46+ is given to skeletons that may be aged up to 70 years or more. Osteological evidence is therefore more useful in building up a general picture of trends in health and mortality.

Climate and catastrophes

Medieval Europe witnessed considerable climate change, with the 'medieval warm epoch' AD 1150-1300, followed by a period of climate deterioration from AD 1300-1500, and the onset of the Little Ice Age from the mid-sixteenth century (Lamb 1995). The warm epoch contributed to a peak in population growth by the early thirteenth century, followed by a trough in the later fourteenth century caused by episodes of mass death, an ageing society, and a reduction in fertility caused by poor nutrition. The combined population estimate for West and Central Europe in AD 1000 is 12 million, with a peak in 1340 of 35.5 million, down to 26.5 million by 1500; the combined population estimate for the Mediterranean is 17 million in AD 1000, 25 million in 1340, and 21.8 million by 1500 (Meier with Graham-Campbell 2007, 424). Climate change may have played a part in the rise of infections such as leprosy and plague, and the wet conditions of the fourteenth century caused an epidemic of ergotism in central and southern Europe. 'St Anthony's Fire' is a parasitic fungus (*Claviceps purpurea*) that affects rye grass and causes deadly toxins; when consumed in contaminated bread, the fungus led to convulsions, hallucinations, gangrene, and finally death (Roberts and Cox 2003, 227). But the major impact of climate change was to cause widespread famine and slow, miserable death by starvation. Wet summers led to harvest failures and famines in 1294-5, 1315-18 and 1437-40. The famines and animal murrains of the early fourteenth century were particularly vicious, no doubt weakening immunity to successive waves of the Black Death after the first outbreak in 1348-51. The plague seems to have attacked particular groups of the population, with greater numbers of young children and male adults falling victim to the pestilence, leaving isolated pockets of elderly survivors in all regions of Europe. The higher mortality rate for children was a pattern that continued in the regional outbreaks of the plague, for example in Germany in the 1380s, in Paris in 1418, and Florence in 1423-4 (Youngs 2006, 25-6, 32).

Natural disasters also played their part in the devastation of medieval Europe: ice core evidence from both poles has revealed that a massive volcanic eruption occurred in the tropics in 1257-8 (site unknown). The resulting ash blanketed Europe in thick fog and caused cold, wet summers for three years, resulting in crop failures and high mortality rates (Oppenheimer 2003). It is likely that some of the victims of this famine were interred in mass burial pits that have been excavated at the hospital priory of St Mary Spital in London. Up to 3000 people were buried in pits that contained between 25 and 42 individuals, buried in layers up to five deep (White W 2007). The pits were located at the extreme south-east of the hospital precinct, as far as possible from the main building complex. Radiocarbon dates suggest a close correlation with the famine that developed in the aftermath of the volcanic eruption. Excavations at the hospital of the Holy Ghost in Lübeck, Germany, also revealed mass burials dated c. 1260 or later: a number of mass graves each contained between 10-20 individuals. During the Black Death, the hospital at Lübeck was the site of mass burials pits containing 696 individuals, buried five or six layers deep (Prechel 1996).

Health and lifestyle

Certain diseases were characteristic of medieval Europe, developing alongside the growth of towns, trade, increased migration and changes in lifestyle. A high population density is necessary for the transmission of infectious diseases such as leprosy (Hansen's Disease), which is passed between humans by coughing and sneezing. Leprosy was a problem throughout Europe by the eleventh century, but it seems to have declined in some areas by the later Middle Ages. Urban living brought an increase in the incidence of tuberculosis, which shares the same bacteria as leprosy (*Mycobacterium*), so that an individual suffering from TB may possess immunity to leprosy. Leprosy remained more active in regions with few towns, such as Scandinavia, but had declined in England by the fourteenth century. Osteological evidence has proven that syphilis was present in medieval Europe (for example, at the Icelandic monastery of Skriðuklaustur, Kristjánsdóttir 2008), challenging the long-held view that the disease originated in the New World (e.g. MacKenzie 2008). Venereal syphilis is sexually transmitted; the associated dermatological symptoms would have resembled the early stages of leprosy (Roberts & Manchester 1995). The disfigurement of leprosy was sometimes regarded as a punishment for sexual sin, and sufferers were secluded in hospitals at the margins of medieval towns.

Medieval people also suffered disease and injury resulting from their housing conditions and occupations (Roberts & Cox 2003). For example, the use of open hearths to heat medieval houses resulted in poor air quality that caused a high level of sinusitis, an inflammation of the sinuses of the face, which leads to new bone formation. Other conditions were age-related: for example, rickets has been identified in a small number of infant remains from medieval England, perhaps resulting from the practice of swaddling infants and consequently preventing the body's production of Vitamin D (stimulated by sunlight). Osteoporosis is normally a condition of old age, but a study of medieval skeletons from Trondheim (Norway) and Wharram Percy (England) suggested that young women (aged 25-35) showed a loss of bone mineral density that may have been caused by the stresses of pregnancy and lactation, in association with poor nutrition (Turner-Walker *et al* 2001). Poor sanitation (see Box 4.2) meant that most people would have suffered from internal parasites, leading to iron deficiency anemia, recognized in skeletal remains through the presence of cribra orbitalia and porotic hyperostosis (pitting of the bones of the skull). Pulmonary infections, typhus, measles and 'sweating sickness' were also endemic, but leave no permanent signature on the skeleton. Study of fracture trauma from sites in medieval England suggests that rural agricultural workers were at greater risk of occupational injury than town dwellers. Within towns, however, there was a greater danger of injury from violence, and men were particularly vulnerable to injury by blade or blunt force. Medieval warfare required the intensive training of men to wield swords and cross-bows, resulting in occupational stress to soldiers' spines. Mass graves from battle sites such as Visby (Gotland, Sweden, 1361) and Towton (Yorkshire, England, 1461; Ch 6, p 272) give insight to the gruesome nature of medieval battle and the haphazard disposal of the war dead, still wearing their armour or clothing (Fiorato *et al* 2000).

Medieval medicine and healing magic

Only the very wealthy had access to medical physicians who had been trained in universities, but medieval cities offered a wider range of practitioners including barber-surgeons, apothecaries and midwives. Medical theories of the body drew on classical sources, particularly Hippocrates (c. 460 BC) and Galen (d. c. AD 216), and were based on the principle that the microcosm of the human body was connected to the four natural elements of fire, water, earth and air. The theory of the humours proposed that each natural element produced substances in the body, the balance of which influenced health and disposition. Fire, which was hot and dry, was believed to produce yellow bile in the body, and led to a choleric complexion. Water, which was cold and wet, was understood to produce phlegm, and the phlegmatic disposition. Earth, thought of as cold and dry, was represented by black bile in the body, and associated with the melancholy complexion. Air, hot and wet, made blood, and the sanguine temperament. A balance of humours was required for good health in each individual, but it was believed that age and sex influenced the overall humoral makeup. Women were regarded as watery and changeable, with a cold, wet humoral balance which contrasted with the hot, dry male. Infants and young children were considered to hold an excess of water and heat; in contrast, the elderly were perceived to be cold, dry and brittle. Medieval physicians made diagnoses based on the temperament and complexion of the patient, but they also examined their urine to consider its colour, clarity and consistency. The glass flasks used for this process (called jordans or urinals) are relatively common archaeological finds from medieval monasteries and hospitals (e.g. St Mary Spital, London: Thomas *et al* 1997; and Strasbourg, Fig 5.14).

Most medieval people sought spiritual succour for their ailments through prayer or pilgrimage to religious shrines, and they drew on traditional herbal medicines and popular magic to bring relief from their physical symptoms. The use of healing magic was associated particularly with the care of women in childbirth, when a combination of prayers, herbal remedies, verbal charms and amulets were employed by the midwife. Prayers and charms were written on parchment and wrapped around women in labour or placed directly on their bodies. A vivid remnant of this practice is a 'birthing kit' which survives from the French town of Aurillac in the Auvergne, consisting of a group of handwritten and printed amulets, and an array of objects associated with St Margaret. Margaret was regarded as the patron saint of women in childbirth, due to the apocryphal story that she had escaped from the belly of a dragon. The earliest in the group is a complex folding amulet dating to the thirteenth century, made up of 30 medallions laced together by parchment strips. The items were kept together in a linen sack to be used by women of a family or community, and handed down over many generations (Skemer 2006, 242). It has been suggested that traces of healing magic can be found occasionally in later medieval burials, for example the folded lead and parchment parcels that were placed near the pelvises of two adult females interred at St Mary Spital, London, and St James' priory, Bristol, in England (Gilchrist 2008).

Medieval hospitals: Christian bodies and souls

In contrast with modern hospitals, the medieval hospital seldom dispensed urgent medical treatment, and relatively few were attended by trained physicians. Instead, the medieval hospital provided residential accommodation, a healthy diet and spiritual sustenance for the needy groups in society – the sick, elderly, poor and leprous. Most hospitals were organized according to monastic principles and were staffed by canons and lay-sisters. The hospital was essentially a religious institution that provided welfare as Christian charity. Charitable giving was a kind of spiritual intercession which was believed to hasten the passage of the soul through the torments of Purgatory. The founders and patrons of hospitals gave alms to the poor inmates to cleanse their own sins, and thus reduce the period that they might spend in Purgatory. Hospitals were also linked to Christian memorial practices: they were established by wealthy families as private chantries, with the expectation that the patient-inmates would pray for the souls of the patrons in perpetuity.

Medieval hospitals have been classified into four major categories: infirmaries for the sick poor, leper hospitals, hospices for pilgrims and wayfarers, and almshouses, which sheltered the worthy Christian poor (Gilchrist 1995). In reality, however, many hospitals performed a combination of these functions, or they changed their roles over time. For example, with the decline of leprosy in the later Middle Ages, many *leprosaria* were converted to almshouses, plague hospitals or asylums. Because leper hospitals were located outside towns and usually provided accommodation in separate cells, they were ideally suited to reuse as isolation hospitals. Infirmaries were established in towns and ports, or along major routes of travel, and were set up as male or mixed communities, with both staff and inmates segregated by sex. The basic component was the infirmary hall, which was generally divided into three aisles by arcades, with a chapel attached to the east. Smaller hospitals in Britain resembled parish churches, with the layout of the hall and chapel similar to that of the nave and chancel (e.g. St Mary's Hospital, Chichester). French hospitals were constructed on a much grander scale, such as the extant Notre-Dame des Fontenilles, Tonnerre (Yonne), established by Marguerite of

12.1

Reconstruction of the interior fittings of the medieval infirmary at Tonnerre, Burgundy, including choir screen, patient alcoves and gallery, from Viollet-le-Duc 1862, Dictionnaire raisonné de l'architecture francaise de xi au xvi siècle III, Paris.

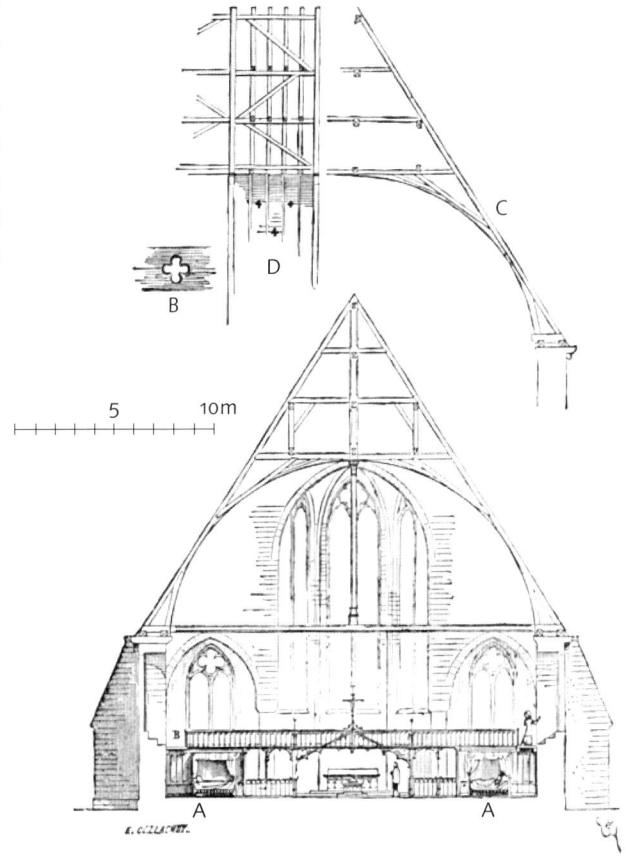

Burgundy in 1293 (Fig 12.1). The hospital shared its site with Marguerite's private chateau, which was closely connected with the massive infirmary hall (c. 100m long) that provided 40 beds for men and women, with timber screens partitioning the space into alcoves for the patients. The hall is covered with an ornate timber barrel roof and the chapel at its eastern end is vaulted in stone and was provided with lofty, traceried windows. The hospital at Tonnerre was designed within a seigneurial landscape: it was built contiguously with the city defences and the precinct was walled, crenellated and moated by chanelling the river. Natural streams were diverted to flush the waste of the latrines and domestic buildings (Courteney 2007; Lillich 1998).

The largest hospitals were organized around a number of cloisters and chapels, such as St John in Bruges (modern Belgium), where parallel halls were added to the south of the original twelfth-century infirmary until further expansion was prevented by the canal; to the north, four further courts were added. The excavation of hospitals provides unique insight to how they evolved over time. At St Mary Spital, London, a simple infirmary hall with chapel (c. 1197) was replaced by a T-shaped complex around 1235. Claustral ranges were developed to the north of the church (c. 1280-1320) and a second infirmary was built against the west side of the first infirmary (Fig 12.2). The T-shape was remodeled to

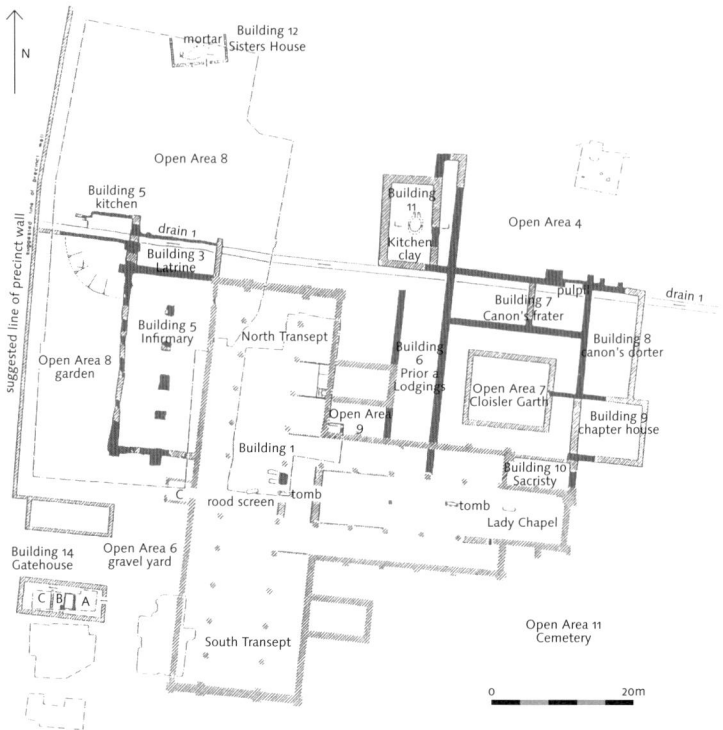

Fig 12.2 *Plan of the hospital of St Mary Spital, London, excavated by the Museum of London Archaeology Service. The T-shaped hospital plan was remodelled c. 1280-1320 to develop claustral ranges and a second infirmary (from Thomas et al. 1997) (reproduced with permission of Museum of London).*

provide a pair of transepts for the church, and later the infirmary was extended westwards with a new, two-storey structure added (c. 1320-50) (Thomas *et al* 1997). Italian hospitals were at the forefront of medical innovation and developed the cruciform hospital plan: at Santa Maria Nuova, Florence (c. 1334), four separate sick wards intersected in the shape of a cross, so that nursing staff could oversee all areas simultaneously from the centre.

In common with all religious institutions, burial of the dead was a primary function of the medieval hospital, with provision made for the interment of patients, staff and wealthy benefactors. Excavations at St Mary Spital uncovered the remains of 10,500 individuals, including 3000 buried in the mass famine graves discussed above, and over 7000 individual interments in the cemetery. Approximately one third of the skeletons showed some form of skeletal pathology resulting from disease or injury, in contrast with the figure of around 10% that would be typical of a parish cemetery. Conditions represented in the skeletal remains of patients at St Mary Spital included cleft palate, joint dislocations, joint disease and infections such as TB and syphilis. Evidence for medical treatment is revealed in a number of bones with set and healed fractures, two cases of cranial trepanation and one of below-the-knee amputation, in addition to three skeletons interred with copper-alloy plates that were used to protect and help heal joint injuries (White 2007).

Cemetery location

The archaeological study of later medieval death began in the 1950s in France, Spain, Britain and Scandinavia, while in Italy, a thematic focus on funerary archaeology has been more directed toward Late Antiquity and the early Middle Ages. Throughout Europe, however, recent decades have seen the accumulation of significant quantities of data, permitting the identification of general trends and local variations in burial practice. Cemeteries were closely associated with towns from the early Middle Ages right up to the modern period. The Roman prohibition on intramural burial broke down in the fifth century, when interments took place in cemeteries founded within town walls. From the eighth century, it became common practice to place burials in and around

Reconstruction of the chapel of Monte di Croci in the 12th century. Burials of members of the seigneu-rial family are visible around the building, where a funeral is taking place (reproduced with permission of Studio InkLink, Florence). **Fig 12.3**

ecclesiastical buildings, a pattern that persisted throughout the whole medieval period. The Muslim conquest of Spain resulted in a distinct regional trait: cemeteries were mostly located outside city walls from the ninth century (although there were many exceptions: see Box 12.2, p 514). Following the 'Reconquista' in the thirteenth century, intramural burial was established, for example at Valencia (Gonzales Villaescusa and Lerma Alegria 1996). Urban authorities insisted on the location of Jewish cemeteries outside town walls; for example, the ten Jewish cemeteries in England were established outside major towns, located near a principal gate (see part 3, below).

In the countryside, burials dating from the fifth to eighth centuries were located either around churches or in isolated row cemeteries. Parish churches gradually developed burial rights, with the pace varying according to region – by the ninth century in Italy (Settia 1982), and from the tenth to twelfth centuries in France and England (Zadora-Rio 2003; and see below). Feudal lords were buried in private churches associated with manors or castles, which were subsequently developed as the foci for communal burial. A fine example is the chapel located within the Tuscan castle of Monte di Croce (FI), a small building (16.8 x 6.5m) excavated by Riccardo Francovich. Three small cemeteries were discovered around the chapel, with two phases of burial activity (from the tenth to twelfth centuries) including substantial stone cist graves. The earliest burials were interpreted as those of the seigneurial family who owned the castle. In the mid-twelfth century the chapel was enlarged and developed as a religious place for the entire local community (Tronti 2008) (Fig 12.3). In both rural and urban areas, monasteries became the nodal points of the later medieval funerary landscape: the laity paid for interment within the monastic cemetery in return for the prayers that the monks offered up for their souls.

The topography of cemeteries

From the ninth or tenth century onwards, Christian burial took place exclusively within sanctified ground. The cemetery was consecrated by a liturgical rite of purification that involved the singing of psalms, sprinkling the ground with holy water and marking the boundaries through prayers and the erection of physical markers (Lauwers 2005; Rosenwein 1999, 178-9). The sacred space of the cemetery was bounded by masonry walls, hedges or timber fences. One of the most monumental examples is the Camposanto of Pisa, a vast rectangular cloister built to host burials in 1278, close to the cathedral. A cross was often located in the centre of the cemetery, the cross of the Hosanna (or the Calvary cross). The cross was built in wood or masonry; burial in close proximity to the cross was considered efficacious and was very much sought after (Alexandre-Bidon and Treffort 1993, 265). Excavations have revealed the clustering of graves around churchyard crosses, for example at the Cistercian monastery of St Mary Graces, London (1350-1538) (Gilchrist & Sloane 2005, 38-40; for the development of medieval cemeteries see part 2, below).

Burial within churches was limited initially to founders and senior religious personnel, but internal burial became increasingly common with the desire to be buried *ad*

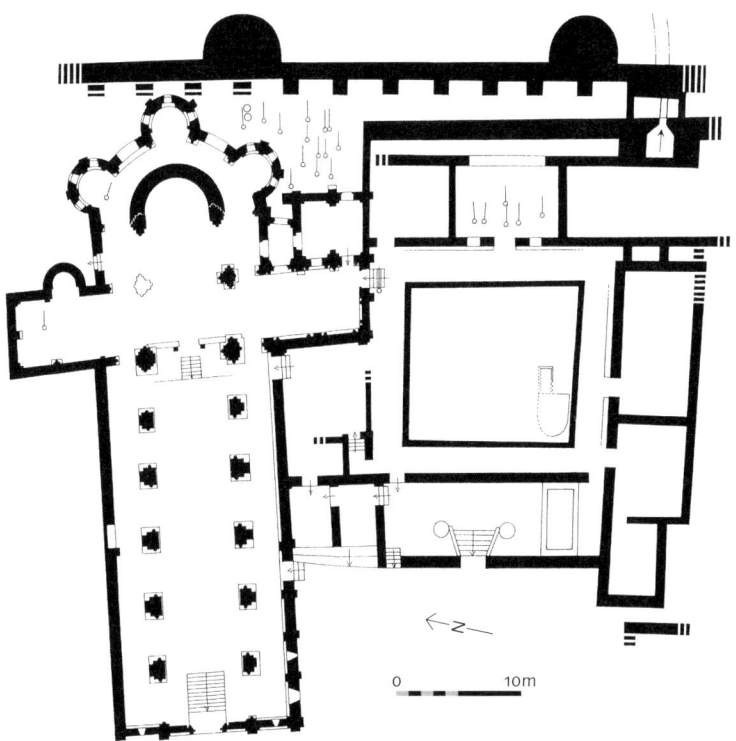

Abbey of Landevennec, Finistère: burials from the 12th to the 14th century (reproduced with permis- **Fig 12.4**
sion of the authors, from Bardel & Perennec 2004).

sanctos, close to the altar. The altar represented the most holy space of the church and was regarded as the position in which the deceased would gain greatest benefit from intercessory prayers and masses. The prohibition on internal burial resulted in the location of high status interments in satellite areas of the church such as the narthex or porch, and in the cloisters and chapter houses of monasteries (Sapin 1996; Dierkens 2002). The location of such burials was sometimes determined by the age, sex and/or social status of the deceased. It was relatively common for women to be buried within male monasteries, although their graves were usually confined to the exterior cemetery or to specific locations in the church (e.g. the south transept at the English Cistercian abbeys of Hulton, Staffordshire, and Bordesley, Worcestershire) (Gilchrist & Sloane 2005, 65-8). In Scandinavia, zoning of cemeteries seems to have been more sharply delineated according to sex, with males frequently buried to the south of the church and females to the north (Kieffer-Olsen 1993). Particular spaces were employed for the burial of children: in the cemetery of Dassargues (Languedoc) during the twelfth century, the graves of perinatal infants clustered around the apse of the Romanesque church, while older infants aged between six months and one year were buried outside the west façade of the church (Garnotel & Raynaud 1996).

It is sometimes possible to distinguish zones reserved for burial of the religious community from those developed for the laity. The chapter house was often designated for the interment of abbots, for example at the abbey of Landevennec (Finistére) between the twelfth and the fourteenth centuries. In the same phase, a group of graves discovered in the courtyard at the west front of the church, has been interpreted as a lay cemetery (Bardel & Perennec 2004) (Fig 12.4). The space to the west of the church was gradually opened up for burial of the laity, for example at the abbey of Novalesa (Piedmont). Here, excavations revealed an increase in the number of earthen graves in the zone of the Galilee chapel, between the thirteenth and fourteenth centuries, perhaps representing the extension of the privilege of burial within the monastic complex to a wider number of people (Lambert & Grilletto 1989).

The burial

Excavations have shown considerable variety in the range of medieval grave construction, but the most common type is the simple earthen grave, present throughout Europe and adopted by people of all social classes. Even members of the upper echelons sometimes selected this form of grave as a spiritual gesture of humility. Graves dug into soil or cut into rock varied in the shape of their outline: anthropomorphic (with or without head niches), rectangular, trapezoidal and oval. In south-west France, the selection of shapes has been proven to follow a chronological sequence (Colardelle *et al* 1996; for Catalunya, see Bolos i Masclans & Pages i Paretas 1982). Medieval graves were sometimes lined in a variety of materials, such as lime, clay or gravel, or constructed as stone or brick cists. In some regions the funerary *caveau* (vault) developed from the thirteenth century onwards: underground vaults constructed in masonry and covered with either horizontal slabs or barrel-vaults. The interior space was not usually decorated, with the exception of some painted examples found in Belgium. Funerary *caveaux* were usually employed as family mausolea, although one example at the cathedral of Aix-en-Provence was used by local priests (Esquieu 1996).

The vast majority of burials were oriented west-east, with the head laid to the west of the grave, and the feet to the east, ready to face Jerusalem at the moment of the resurrection. The corpse was usually placed in the grave in a supine position, with arms fully extended or crossed on the chest or over the pelvis, but many other positions are attested. It has been argued that the positioning of the body in the grave followed a chronological pattern in Scandinavia, Germany and Switzerland, with arms fully extended against the sides of the body up to c. 1250, then the hands were positioned over the pelvis or stomach up to 1450, and after 1450, hands were placed over the chest (Kieffer-Olsen 1993). It is possible that this is an important regional variation, but the dating framework behind this hypothesis needs careful re-evaluation. Where absolute dating and stratigraphic analysis of cemeteries have been undertaken in Britain, arm position seems to follow regional preference rather than chronological sequence (Gilchrist & Sloane 2005). The cadaver was usually wrapped in a linen shroud, an element that seldom survives, but is sometimes represented by the pins that were used to fasten it. Some corpses were placed in containers, with the most common being timber coffins, with stone and lead coffins reserved for burials of the highest status. In some regions the preference of container and grave construction followed a distinct chronological sequence, but there is considerable variation across Europe, and even within single cemeteries (Fig 12.5).

Ecclesiastical and royal corpses were often dressed ceremonially for the grave and displayed to the public prior to burial. Bishops and archbishops were adorned in their clothing of consecration and accompanied by their symbols of religious office: the crozier, mitre, chalice and paten, and clerical vestments. For example, Archbishop Godfrey de Ludham was buried at York Minster in 1265, laid out with his mitre, stole, pallium and leather shoes. The burials of members of royal families were similarly adorned in rich textiles of silk and gold and accompanied by insignia of royal power, such as the crown deposited by the emperor Frederic II in the grave of his wife, Constance d'Auteville, in 1220 (D'Onofrio 1994, 290; 426; 274-275). Weapons were usually prohibited from burial in consecrated ground, but exceptions were permitted for the burials of kings and nobles: the grave of the gonfalonier (standard bearer) Giovanni dei Medici (1352) in Florence Cathedral contained a sword and a couple of spurs (Buerger 1975, 208-209). Although it was less common for members of the laity to be buried in clothing, this practice has been confirmed by the presence of dress-accessories in graves (such as belt or hose buckles) and by examples where textiles have been preserved. An exceptional site is the parish cemetery of Herjolfsnes in Greenland, which was excavated in 1921; reassessment and radiocarbon dating has confirmed a fourteenth- to fifteenth-century date (Østergård 2004). The corpses were preserved in the permafrost and found wrapped in layers of clothing, including tunics, hoods, hats and hose, interpreted as the use of the personal clothing of the deceased as a shroud.

The most commonly occurring grave goods in later medieval cemeteries are the chalices (and sometimes patens) that were buried with priests, for instance those excavated in Val d'Aosta (Crosetto 1998; for chalice and paten see Ch 10, p 435). Archbishops and bishops were buried with chalices made of precious metal, while priests were buried with chalices made of pewter, or even copies moulded in pottery or beeswax (as excavated at Hulton, Staffordshire). Religious grave goods also included pottery and glass vessels used as containers for holy water and incense. According to the French liturgist Gulielmus Durandus of Mende (who wrote in the 1290s), these consecrated substances were employed to protect the corpse against demons and to prevent the stench given off by the rotting cadaver (Prigent 1996). Vessels formerly known as 'fumitory pots' (due to the occasional presence of charcoal and holes in the fabric) seem to have been linked with a rite of cleansing and demarcation of the grave site (Madsen 1983). For example, recent excavations at the Sainte-Marie-Madeleine priory in Mantes-la-Jolie (west of Paris) uncovered such pots placed on top of the coffin lids of burials dating to the thirteenth and fourteenth centuries. The pots were evidently reused from domestic contexts, but contained charcoal and were possibly used as censers placed around the coffin and bier during the funeral Mass. Now generally known by the term 'funeral pots' (céramiques funéraires), since some may have contained holy water rather than

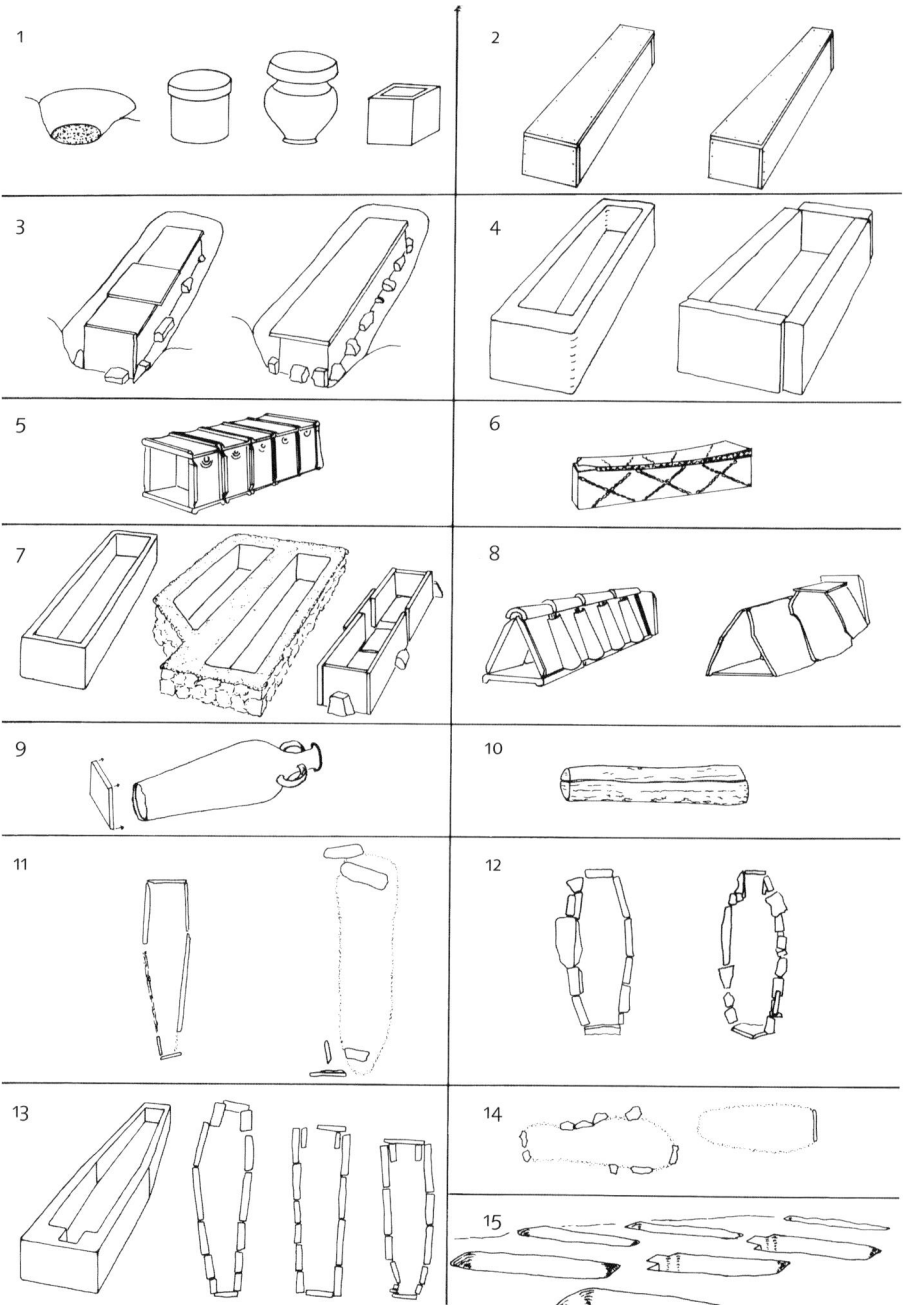

Fig 12.5 *Burial typology from the Roman to medieval period, Southern France. Types 2 and 14 were current in the Roman Imperial age, but were used also from the mid 13th century onwards. Type 15 starts in the 3rd century AD and is used until c. 1400 (reproduced with permission of M. Colardelle, G. Demians D'Archimbaud and C. Reynaud).*

charcoal, they are found all over France and in Denmark from the eleventh century onwards (Prigent 1996; pers. comm. Elizabeth Zadora-Rio).

The tradition of placing grave goods with the dead declined from the seventh to ninth centuries, although they continued to be deposited with higher-ranking clergy throughout the period. Increasing numbers of grave goods were buried with the laity from the twelfth to the thirteenth century, and a number of distinctive regional traditions can be identified. Most of the objects placed in graves are connected with religious symbolism. For example at the monastery of Skriðuklaustur in eastern Iceland, founded in 1493, approximately 120 burials have been identified including those of women, young children and infants (Kristjánsdóttir 2008). Seven graves have been excavated from inside the church, three of which were adults buried in coffins with books lying open on their chests, perhaps denoting the graves of the founding family (Fig 12.6). The books were written in Latin on parchments of goatskin, with covers made of imported wood and skin, and illustrated with Byzantine decoration (Jónsson 2008). In Scandinavia and England, it was relatively common to place timber rods or staves with the corpse, either in the coffin or more often in the grave cut, as part of a graveside rite that was used in the interment of men, women and children. The rods were made from coppiced hazel, ash or willow, and while single rods were most common, some burials were placed with several rods (Fig 12.7). The rods have sometimes been interpreted as symbolic of pilgrimage, but recently they have been discussed in terms of measuring rods that were involved in the funeral preparation (Jonsson 2007), or as objects that were used in a journeying charm performed for the dead before they embarked on their journey through Purgatory (Gilchrist 2008).

Approximately sixty papal bullae (lead seals) have been recovered from medieval graves in Europe, half of which derive from English burials of the fourteenth or fifteenth centuries (Gilchrist & Sloane 2005, 94-6). The bullae from contemporary French burials have been interpreted as being associated with priests, as 'passports to redemption' that served as proof that a deceased cleric had been absolved of his sins (Dabrowska 2005, 334-6), but the English examples are found with burials of the laity, including women. The bulla may have been attached to a papal indulgence that pertained to the deceased individual, or the lead seal itself may have served as an amulet. Medieval pilgrims sometimes took their souvenirs to the grave, and scallop shells

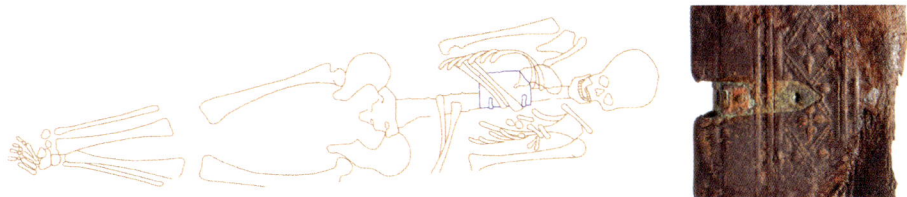

Book placed with female burial inside the monastic church at Skriðuklaustur in eastern Iceland, **Fig 12.6** *founded in 1493. Photograph copyright Graham Langford (figures reproduced with permission of S. Kristjánsdóttir).*

Fig 12.7 *Two wooden rods or staves were placed within the grave of an adult male in the church at the Cistercian abbey of St Mary Hulton, Staffordshire, England (reproduced with permission of W. Klemperer).*

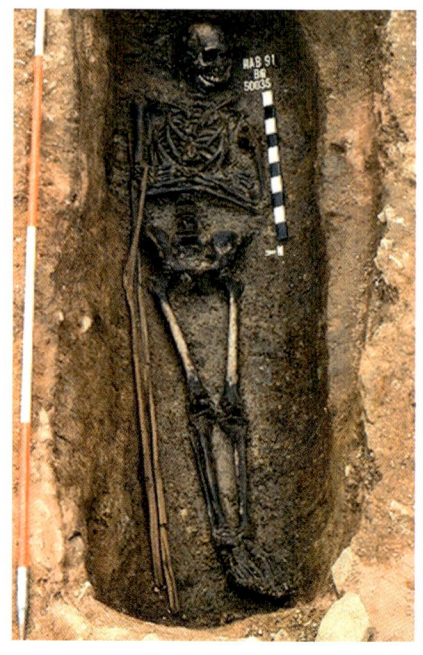

symbolic of the pilgrimage to the shrine of St James de Compostela (Spain) are found in small numbers throughout Europe (see Ch 10, p 420). They have been found more commonly in mortuary contexts in Scandinavia and in Germany (Andersson L 1989, 141-54; Haasis-Berner 1999, 274). More personal grave goods persisted especially in the Baltic, a region that was converted relatively late to Christianity in the thirteenth century. For example, Estonian burials continued to include some of the grave goods that had been used in late Iron Age rites: tools, jewellery, keys, coins and items of personal hygiene (Box 10.3). Feasts and food offerings were made in the cemetery, including regular family meals held at the graveside long after the interment (Valk 2001). In Scotland, Wales and Ireland, it remained fairly common to include white pebbles with later medieval burials, a widespread prehistoric burial rite in these regions. White pebbles were recorded in approximately two-thirds of the 1,275 inhumations excavated at the parish cemetery of Ballyshannon (co Donegal), deliberately placed in the hands of the corpses (Ó Donnchadha 2007).

Distinctive Jewish mortuary practices were uncovered by excavations at Jewbury in York (England) (Lilley *et al* 1994; and see part 3, below). Three elements at medieval Jewish cemeteries contrast with Christian rites: the prevalence of coffin use, the attention to segregation of burial by age, and the lack of intercutting of burials. It was common to mark Jewish graves with stone markers, but at York there were only traces of a few wooden grave markers. At York, 93% of inhumations were placed in coffins made from Scots pine with iron fittings; the exceptionally high rate of coffin use reflects the deeply held conviction among Jews that corpses are polluted and unclean. For this reason Jewish cemeteries were required to provide a ritual source of water, for both the hand washing of visitors to the cemetery, and for the washing of the corpse before burial. Infant burials at York were clustered in the north-east of the cemetery area. Of 476 inhumations excavated at Jewbury, there were only eight examples of earlier burials being cut by later graves (see part 3, Fig 12.14). The alignment of the graves was not the customary west-east, but rather south-south/east and north-north/east; this discrepancy in alignment was also seen in the Jewish cemetery at Worms, Germany (Maier 1984). In both cases, it seems that burials were positioned so that the resurrected corpse would rise to face an entrance in the cemetery, so that alignment was determined by local topography. In terms of burial practice, Jewish burials also utilized shrouds and shroud fasteners, including single antler toggles found positioned above the heads of two burials at Jewbury.

Memory

The widespread adoption of the doctrine of Purgatory increased the emphasis placed on the commemoration of the dead after the twelfth century. This was accomplished through prayer, written epitaphs and material practices. Collective memory was sustained by reciting the names of the deceased, performed daily in monastic churches in the Office of the Dead, and annually in parish churches in prayers associated with All Souls. The wealthy endowed anniversary and chantry masses for themselves and their families, and it was common to perform commemorative rituals at the graveside at particular intervals, usually one week, one month and one year following the funeral. Few graves were marked by substantial monuments, but ephemeral constructions such as earthen mounds or timber crosses were employed. In the vast majority of cases no archaeological trace of these crosses has survived, but occasionally it has been possible to identify their postholes, as in one of the cemeteries at the site of Nonantola in Italy (Bertoldi & Librenti 2007). Ossuaries, or charnel houses, also served to memorialize the collective dead: these ranged from simple pits to purpose-built structures located within cemeteries. They housed the disarticulated human remains that were disturbed by the cutting of new graves. Purpose-built ossuaries had arches or openings through which thousands of skulls were clearly visible, as depicted in German illuminations of the fifteenth century (Alexandre-Bidon & Treffort 1993).

Monuments for the individual dead developed from simple slabs covering the grave (inscribed with crosses and occasionally with inscriptions or effigies) to effigial tombs and brasses that depicted the deceased (Fig 12.8). The earliest example of this trend is the grave of Abbot Isarn of St Victor in Marseille (dated 1048: Favreau 1997, 71-4). Sepulchral monuments were at first employed only in the commemoration of the elite; for example, the Norman dukes developed dynastic burial places such as the abbey church of Fécamp (Normandy), and the abbey of the Holy Trinity in Venosa (Basilicata). Graves were given architectural elaboration through the addition of an arch or tympanum, such as the monument of Alberada (d. 1111) at Venosa, the wife of Robert the Guiscard, Duke of Apulia. Representational and three-dimensional monuments developed in the twelfth and thirteenth centuries, particularly through the medium of ecclesiastical tombs. Wall-monuments for popes and cardinals portrayed them sleeping in their beds, surmounted by canopies (Fig 12.9). Interesting examples survive in Rome and Viterbo, carved personally by masters such as Arnolfo di Cambio. Monumental forms particular to Italy include the 'arks' placed in urban squares, for example that of the Scaligeri family in Verona and the ark of Cangrande della Scala (1329), with an equestrian sculpture mounted on a pyramid. Similar monuments were established between the thirteenth and fourteenth centuries for university professors in towns like Bologna and Padua (among the first European universities). Here we see the extension of commemoration to the bourgeoisie, with monumentalization of the 'aristocracy of knowledge' (Petrucci 1995).

Effigial monuments were adopted throughout Western Europe in the thirteenth century and were linked to the promotion of heraldic display. Effigies of knights depicted the deceased in their military apparel and with their swords. Female effigies appeared in the second half of the thirteenth century, and their conventions were influenced by ideals of feminine beauty and depictions of the Virgin Mary. Both male and female were shown as young adults, whatever age they were when they died. This relates to the medieval idea that everyone was resurrected at the ideal age of 33, the age that Christ died on the cross. Effigies were executed in stone, timber, or alabaster, which became popular from the fourteenth century. Funerary commemoration became accessible to a much wider range of society with the development of monumental brasses in the thirteenth century. These two-dimensional representations were engraved on sheets of metal and mass produced in large workshops, notably in Flanders. Towards the end of the fourteenth century, the cadaver or 'transi' tomb developed, depicting the physical ravages of death in a realistic and gruesome manner. The shrouded body was represented in the process of decay, showing the shrivelled body, sometimes with frogs, snails, snakes and other agents of the ground. In the fifteenth and sixteenth centuries this type of funerary monument was known across Europe, although there were local variations. These tombs are usually interpreted as *memento mori*, a reminder of mortality for the living (Binski 1996).

Jewish commemorative practices are reflected in a large collection of 1508 gravestones from Würzburg (Germany), which were reused as building material after the Jewish cemetery was sold in the fifteenth century. The gravestones span the period from 1129 to 1346. In 1349, Wurzburg's Jewish community was annihilated after the townspeople accused them of causing the Black Death (Box 12.1). The Hebrew inscriptions reveal the presence of a highly esteemed centre for Talmudic learning, with frequent use of the titles *rabbi, haver* (accomplished layman of letters) and *bachur* (young man who has completed the yeshivah education). The stones indicate the migration of Jews into Würzburg from Hammelburg, Mühlhausen, Montpellier, Strasbourg, and more generally from 'France' and 'England', reflecting the reach of the medieval Jewish diaspora. The inscriptions also attest to the widespread violence against the Jews, commemorating martyrs who had been slain by Christians (Müller K 2004; and see part 3, below).

Despite the Islamic prohibition on the commemoration of the dead, memory was perpetuated through the construction of decorated mausolea and the use of inscriptions. Muslim epitaphs found in Sicily (61 in total) represent the upper strata of local society, notably the producers of precious garments, mainly resident in towns and trading with the Maghreb area (Grassi 2004; and see Box 12.2).

Incised effigial grave-slab of the architect Hugues Liber- **Fig 12.8**
gier, 13th century, Cathedral of Reims (Champagne-Ar-
denne, northeastern France) (reproduced with permis-
sion of Enciclopedia Treccani, Rome).

Funerary monument of Pope Hadrian V, 13th century, church of S. Francesco alla Rocca, Viterbo. This **Fig 12.9**
is possibly the earliest example of funerary monuments of this kind (reproduced with permission of
Enciclopedia Treccani, Rome).

BOX 12.1 THE BLACK DEATH

Fig 1

The East Smithfield Black Death cemetery, London: southward view of one of the Black Death burial trenches during excavation (photograph reproduced courtesy of Museum of London Archaeology).

Epidemics were regular occurrences in medieval Europe but one particular outbreak is infamous for its unparalleled speed of transmission, its near-complete coverage of the continent, and its unprecedented mortality rate. Medieval Europeans knew it as

the 'great mortality' or the 'pestilence', and its first outbreak killed an estimated 25m people between 1348 and 1351. Estimates of mortality in towns and villages across Europe vary widely but a likely figure is between 35% and 50%, based on chroniclers' reports, wills, administrative records and analysis of manorial and court rolls. This terrible toll was only the first strike: three more major outbreaks in 1361-2, 1368-9, and 1374-5, can be recognised as being of international dimensions; while more localised events recurred more than once per decade between 1350 and 1500. The resulting demographic slump lasted until the sixteenth century. This pestilence is of the greatest interest to a wide sphere of researchers: historians seek to understand what happened to economic systems, cultural development and spiritual values, while epidemiologists wish to understand what caused it (and whether it could happen again). Archaeological study has a crucial role to play.

Every schoolchild learns that the Black Death was bubonic plague, spread by rats and fleas carrying the bacterium *Yersinia pestis*. However, this interpretation is now being challenged. The key argument is that the characteristics of the 1348-51 pestilence are very unlike those of nineteenth- and twentieth-century outbreaks of bubonic plague. The Black Death spread much faster, it killed ten times as many people, and, it is argued, there is evidence for the development of immunity over time (something humans cannot acquire for bubonic plague). It spread as quickly in winter as summer, and affected rural and urban locations with equal ease. The described symptoms do not all sit easily with those of bubonic plague. It may instead have been anthrax, pneumonic plague, haemorrhagic plague or something similar. In support of the bubonic theory, some scientists have reported isolation of the DNA of *Y. pestis* from a number of presumed Black Death burials, although these results have been challenged (see also Ch 1, p53).

Mortality on this scale elicited a number of ritual responses, which can be seen in the archaeological record. Mass graves containing dozens or hundreds of skeletons have been identified at the Heiligen-Geist hospital, Lübeck, Germany, and in England at Hereford cathedral cemetery and East Smithfield cemetery, London. The mass graves in these plague cemeteries took the form of either long trenches or broad, deep pits. In London, two new cemeteries with their own chapels were founded to receive the corpses of the pestilence (West and East Smithfield). Archaeological excavations at East Smithfield uncovered two mass burial trenches and a mass pit, in addition to hundreds of individual interments laid out in neat rows; in total 790 burials were recorded (Fig 1). The impact on burial practice is seen particularly in the increase in the use of coffins used to contain the plague dead (by decree in Italian cities).

The skeletal evidence from the few proven Black Death cemeteries confirms that the plague did not leave any marks on bone, but an unusual demographic pattern has been detected. Study of the skeletons from East Smithfield suggests that the disease was selective by gender, and analysis of pre-existing lesions on bones from the same site suggests that it may have killed weaker individuals preferentially.

The wider archaeological record also reveals the socio-economic impact of the Black Death. Evidence from monumental brasses across Europe suggests that London workshops suffered heavily, and that a distinct and immediate reduction of the industry took place. Wider changes in pottery and tile manufacture in the south-east of England are detectable (the apparent termination of the London-type pottery; and the introduction of Penn floor tiles from Buckinghamshire). Evidence from London wills suggests significant cultural shifts in burial location, and changes in attitudes towards charity and welfare. Historians currently suggest that the plague was a catalyst, accelerating socio-economic change more than defining it (sources: Platt 1997; Raoult et al. 2000; Badham 2000; Cohn 2002; Duncan & Scott 2005; Grainger *et al.* 2008; Benedictow 2004, 2010).

by Barney Sloane

BOX 12.2 ISLAMIC BURIAL RITES

Islamic burial practice followed a distinctive set of prescriptions that was modified by Muslim communities in Western Europe. The study of Islamic cemeteries in Al-Andalus and Sicily is well advanced and has pinpointed distinctive regional variations on traditional rites (Bacqué Grammont & Tibet 1996; Bagnera & Pezzini 2004; Paz Torres Palomo & Acién Almansa 1995).

Muslim cemeteries were generally located in extramural contexts, near urban gates, as a result of the Islamic prohibition on contact between the living and the dead. For the same reason burial within mosques or houses was forbidden, but in al-Andalus several examples of these practices have been recorded archaeologically. In addition, many urban cemeteries are apparent where intramural burial has developed around mausolea (*rawda*); or more generally, where cemetery space became available with a decline in the density of urban occupation, or where town walls expanded to absorb earlier extramural necropolises. In Sicily, as much as in al-Andalus, both intramural (Palermo; Murcia) and extramural (Montevago; Zaragoza) cemeteries are attested (Fig 1). Sometimes both types are present in the same location, like in Entella, a pattern that is also evidenced in Africa. These examples demonstrate that the Islamic topography of death responded to specific conditions in the West.

A typical characteristic of European Islamic cemeteries is the frequent overcrowding of burials. The intensive use of the funerary space led to the artificial raising of ground levels, for instance at cemeteries in Palermo, Malaga (Gibralfaro) and Granada. Orientation of the corpse was a constant, with the face positioned towards Mecca (*qibla*). Providing the face was oriented appropriately, the position of the corpse within the grave varied considerably – supine, prone or placed on the side. It is not uncommon to see corpses positioned differently within the same cemetery, or even within the same phase of burial activity, as witnessed in Valencia. Grave construction was determined by the Islamic principle that the body should not be in direct contact with the soil, which was regarded as impure. A common solution was to create two grave cuts, a smaller grave-cut contained within the outline of a larger one; the interior grave-cut was lined with slabs and the corpse was placed on top of the lining, thus preventing direct contact with the ground. In the East this practice is attested from the tenth to the fifteenth century, whilst in the West it can be found from the eleventh century, and is most frequently recorded in twelfth and thirteenth century contexts. Many types of Islamic grave are documented – slab-covered, brick-constructed, rock-cut – but the most typical type is certainly the simple earthen grave, which in Sicily can be dated between the twelfth and the thirteenth century. The corpse was sometimes placed within a timber coffin before being interred in an earth grave, as seen in Segesta.

The Islamic occupation juxtaposed communities of different religions, and occasionally this coexistence led to cemeteries being used for the interment of both Christians and Muslims, for instance in Segobriga, during the seventh century. However, a situation of apartheid was more common. For example, the ancient town of Segesta was first re-occupied by the Muslims in the twelfth century, and subsequently by a group of

Fig 1

Arabic funerary inscription of Ibrahim, son of Khalaf al-Dibagi, a producer of silk-garments (1072). This is one of the earliest Arabic inscriptions found in Sicily at Palermo (reproduced with permission of Garzanti Editore, Milano).

Normans (from the end of the twelfth century) who subjugated the Islamic population. The mosque was demolished and the cemeteries of the two communities were developed in separate areas: the Christian one was located around the newly built church (Molinari 1997, and see Box 11.5).

by Andrea Augenti

Introduction: the rise of churchyard burial

Although the cemeteries of the early middle ages have long attracted the interest of archaeologists, the study of later medieval burial sites has only developed over the last twenty years - in parallel with the rise of research into rural settlement (see Ch 3, p 97). The study of the predominantely unfurnished medieval cemeteries has now benefited from advances in radiocarbon technology that facilitate the dating of graves without grave-goods. While still not plentiful, such research has already thrown new light on the changing relations of medieval communities with their dead, and challenged certain earlier preconceptions.

Up to the 1990s it was assumed that burial in unassociated open plan cemeteries in the countryside, datable by occasional grave goods to the seventh-eighth centuries AD, was closely followed by the development of churchyard burial, a move thought to signify a pivotal moment in the Christianization of western Europe. These ideas have been put into question by the discovery of small groups of burials located *within* early medieval settlement sites but without direct association with a sacred place. Over the last 15 years this type of informal scattered 'domestic' cemetery has been brought to light in many places in France and equally in England, The Netherlands, Germany and recently in Spain (Blaizot 2006 ; Pecqueur 2003 ; Zadora-Rio 2003). These informal groups comprise variable numbers of graves, from one or two to a few dozen, and include adult and immature persons; they are also frequently found in town sites, particularly in 'dark earth' strata situated between Late Roman and medieval levels (Lorans *et al.* 2007). When they were first discovered, the informal cemeteries were interpreted as the burials of outcasts, but this hypothesis no longer seems acceptable in view of the large numbers involved and also because there is nothing unusual or deviant about these graves.

These discoveries have challenged the view that Christianity caused a general or immediate change in the rite of burial, or insisted that it should take place next to a church. A re-examination of written sources has shown that for some time the Late antique Church had little interest in where the faithful were buried and saw few objections to their being interred at the side of pagans (Treffort 1996). It is not until the tenth century that we see an important move towards churchyard burial. From this period we have evidence of the consecration of cemeteries by bishops, creating a bounded sanctified space from which criminals, excommunicants, the unfaithful and the unbaptised were excluded (see above, p 502). In the same century one can also note an increase in conflicts over the right of burial, which became, from the eleventh century, a parish prerogative as important as the right to administer baptism (Zadora-Rio 2003).

It is thus only with the construction of the parish system between the tenth and twelfth centuries that the Church took control of burial places and used them as a way of drawing a line around Christian society (Lauwers 2005 ; Treffort 2001; Treffort 2010). As Philippe Ariès has shown, the main difference between the parish churchyard and previous burial-grounds is the new emphasis given to the entire communal cemetery, as opposed to the late antique concept of the tomb as a self-contained holy place (Ariès 1977: 47-49). The parish churchyard was conceived as the "bosom of the church" (*ecclesiae gremium*), in which the faithful await Resurrection.

Three case-studies of recently excavated cemeteries, briefly presented here, show how churchyard burial began and evolved, and have led to a new appreciation of this important change in the social use of death, from investment in individual tombs to the expression of belief through the communal cemetery and its association with the church building.

Raunds Furnells (Northamptonshire, England)

The cemetery at Raunds was established around a church built at the end of the ninth century within the property of a local lord. The cemetery was laid out according to a preconceived plan, a quadrilateral measuring 40x30m marked by ditches (Fig 12.10). The first burials were interred in rows alongside the church, and the cemetery grew from there until it reached the limits of the enclosure. The church was enlarged towards the end of the eleventh century, and during the twelfth it was converted into a seignio-rial residence and burial then ceased. The total excavation of the cemetery produced only 363 graves. Intercutting was rare, but the presence of reburials in pits, and of additional bones in some graves, suggests there was nevertheless some disturbance (Boddington 1996).

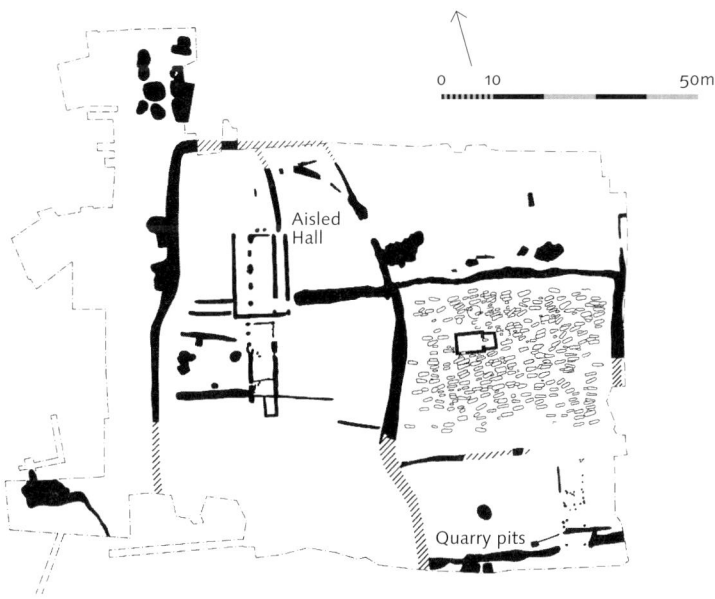

Plan of the cemetery at Raunds (after Boddington 1996), showing the enclosed cemetery of the 10-12th centuries surrounding the church. **Fig 12.10**

Raunds represents a remarkable and very early example of a dedicated but short-lived tenth-twelfth century cemetery strictly reserved for religious and funerary use, as endorsed by the absence of any domestic features and the rarity of sherds of contemporary pottery. As the next two case studies show, the development of medieval parish cemeteries was normally more complex.

Rigny, in Touraine (Indre-et-Loire, France)

Recent excavations have defined 1750 graves at Rigny, a cemetery known to have remained in use until 1865. Burial began in the middle of the eighth century around a small church constructed in the late seventh century as part of a rural property belonging to the monastery of Saint Martin of Tours (Zadora-Rio & Galinié 2001). It was in this first phase of inhumation that the cemetery spread to its maximum extent (Fig 12.11). Singly or in groups, burials colonised the ruins of earlier buildings; the church itself did not seem to exercise a particular attraction for them. The cemetery also shared space with domestic structures, hearths and rubbish deposits. In this phase, the presence of settlement activity, together with the low density and wide distribution of graves, are reminiscent of the scattered informal 'domestic' cemeteries already referred to.

Change came towards the end of the tenth century, when the church was enlarged and graves began to be focused upon it (Period b in Fig 12.11). The outer reaches to the north were abandoned, giving the cemetery a new topographical coherence, manifesting a new sense of community and corresponding with the establishment of a parish constitution. When the church was rebuilt on a grand scale in the late eleventh or early twelfth century, further reductions of the churchyard occurred, and the nucleated pattern endured in the centuries that followed. The construction of an enclosure wall in the twelfth century brought with it the erection of new buildings north of the church on land previously occupied by graves; these buildings were rebuilt several times between the twelfth and fifteenth century (Period c in Fig 12.11). However, within the enclosed churchyard, secular activity did not altogether cease, as shown by a significant assemblage of contemporary pottery. One twelfth-century building was erected astride the enclosure wall and another, in use from the mid-thirteenth to the mid-fifteenth century, was put up within the cemetery enclosure.

In the mid-fifteenth century a large presbytery was built over the previous houses to the north of the church, together with a new enclosure wall, which withdrew the boundary of the cemetery by several more metres (Period d in Fig 12.11). The newly defined space was to remain strictly reserved for the dead, and all domestic activity was excluded. No pottery has been found in the post-medieval churchyard that dates later than the sixteenth century (Period e in Fig 12.11). A roofed outbuilding, used for infant burials, was added in front of the western entrance to the church. The cemetery contracted again in the second half of the eighteenth century. New enclosure walls reduced it to the area of the Grand Cemetery to the south and the Little Cemetery to the west. The latter, which was reserved for the burial of children under the age of 7, was sup-

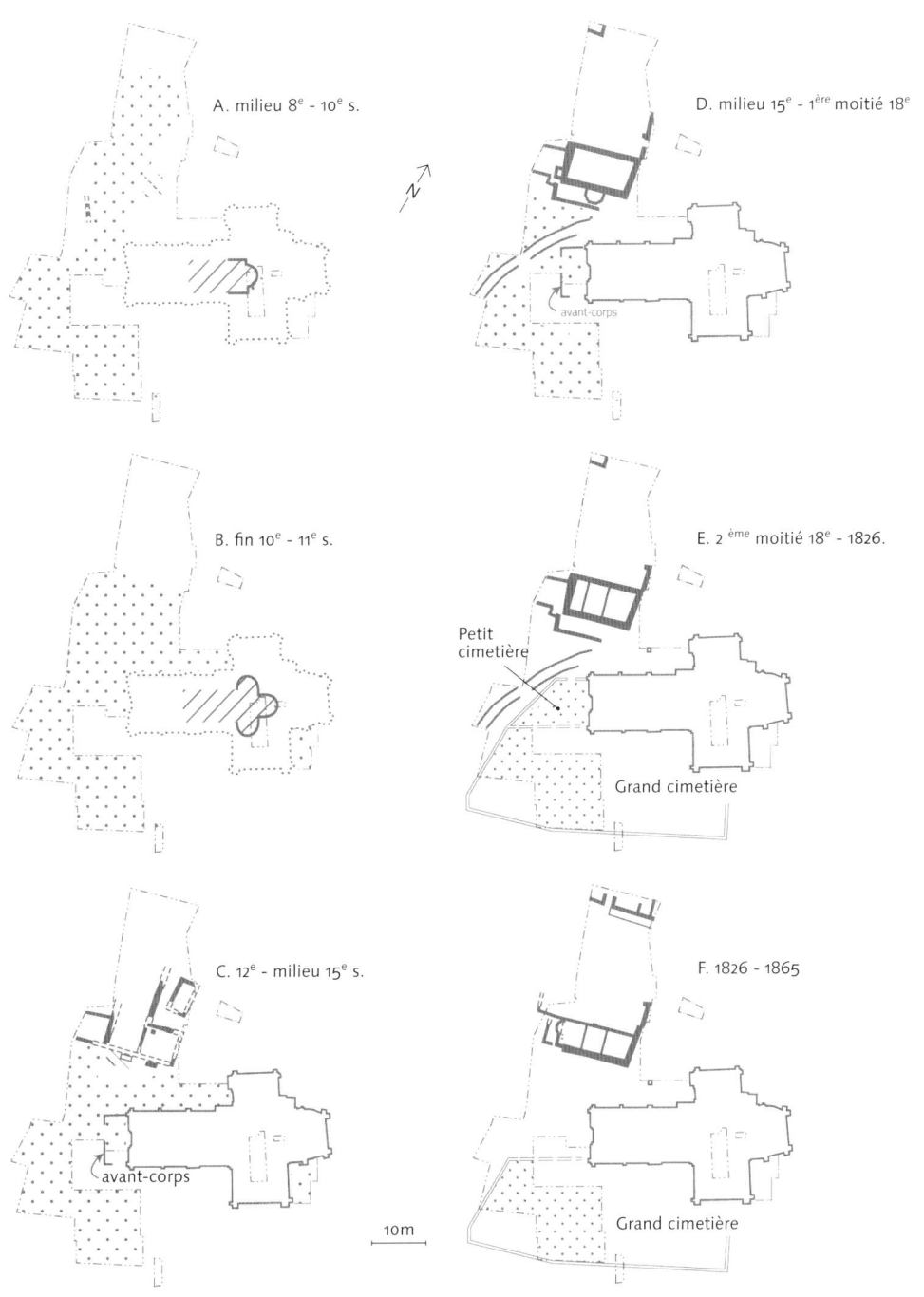

A. milieu 8e - 10e s.

D. milieu 15e - 1ère moitié 18^e

avant-corps

B. fin 10e - 11e s.

E. 2ème moitié 18e - 1826.

Petit
cimetière

Grand cimetière

C. 12e - milieu 15e s.

F. 1826 - 1865

avant-corps

10m

Grand cimetière

The evolution of the cemetery at Rigny (Indre-et-Loire) (after Zadora-Rio et al. 2001, updated in **Fig 12.11**
2010). The area of burial is marked by heavy stippling and the location of the early church by cross-hatching.

pressed in 1826, and the cemetery as a whole was superseded in 1865 by a new burial ground beside a road beyond the settlement limits (Period f in Fig 12.11)..

This excavation showed that a reduction in the size of a cemetery need not imply a decline in the size of the population it serves: the density of burial intensified with each contraction in area, and the intensive use of the smaller funerary space led to the artificial raising of ground levels in the churchyard. Rather it is linked to a growing sense of the need to separate the living and the dead. The latter are buried more and more deeply within an ever more confined space until, in the nineteenth century, they are once more exiled, as in antiquity, to the outskirts of the habitation.

Vilarnau en Roussillon (Pyrénées Orientales, France)

The cemetery at Vilarnau was excavated in almost its entirety between 1996 and 2002, producing nearly 900 graves dating from the end of the ninth to the fifteenth century (Fig 12.12) (Passarrius *et al.* 2008). Radiocarbon dating and spatial analysis show that here too the cemetery reached its greatest extent between the end of the ninth and the start of the tenth century. The density of graves was at its thinnest to the north of the church (zones 1-4 on Fig 12.12), and strongest to the south and east (zones 5-7). At the end of the tenth century or beginning of the eleventh, sunken-featured buildings,

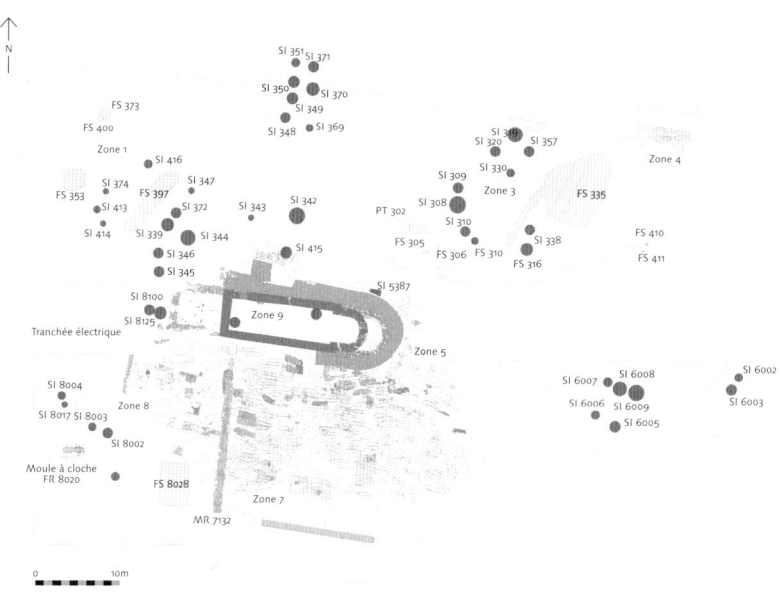

Fig 12.12 *Plan of the cemetery at Vilarnau (Pyrénées-Orientales) (after Passarrius, Donat & Catafau 2008). The 13th-century enclosure wall with a tower, embracing the east end of the church is marked in grey.*

ephemeral structures and storage pits were established at the edge of the cemetery, to be overlaid by a new phase of burials, some of which were cut in turn by rubbish and storage pits. The lack of a clear boundary between the graveyard and the inhabited area endorses a sense of interpenetration between the two. At the same time, the area available for burial was reduced: the space north of the church was abandoned for burial, while that to the south saw a great increase in the density of graves with frequent intercutting and disturbance.

Towards the middle of the thirteenth century, the erection of a new fortified enclosure wall confined the graveyard to an area that was still more reduced. As at Rigny, the recovery of large quantities of pottery and the definition of patches of occupation surface imply domestic activity within the churchyard up to the end of the fifteenth century.

Models for the development and meaning of rural cemeteries

These examples allow us to define two possible routes for the development of rural cemeteries. In the first, as in the case of Raunds, the cemetery is deliberately established within an enclosure laid out around a pre-existing church. Burial begins next to the church, subsequently expanding to limits already determined. In the second, rather more common and clearly illustrated at Rigny and Vilarnau, the churchyard is not created according to a preconceived plan. The establishment of an increasingly communal space results from the progressive nucleation of burials around the church and the contraction of the graveyard boundary. The first burials come in small groups distributed over a broad area not exclusively dedicated to funerary use. Perhaps we see here the foundation of small family cemeteries associated with dwelling places, which may precede the construction of any church. The subsequent reduction of the area of the graveyard, and its increasingly rigorous exclusion of activities other than burial, would appear to be a development of later centuries.

This pattern of cemetery shrinkage is not confined to France: similar trajectories have been noted in England at Wharram Percy, Rivenhall and Barton on Humber, where radiocarbon dating has entailed a reconsideration of earlier interpretations (Harding and Wrathmell 2007; Rodwell and Rodwell 1986, Clarke 2004; Waldron 2007), and probably also in Addingham, Brixworth, Pontefract and other places (Blair 2005, 243). As John Blair has pointed out, the known English cases are nearly all minster cemeteries, and their contraction after the mid-eleventh century may result from the increased competition for burials due to the development of local churches (Blair 2005: 467). However, some of these excavations have also provided evidence for domestic structures and significant quantities of pottery within the burial area and contemporary with the burials. It is thus possible that the process of churchyard contraction, in these cases too, may be ascribed to changing conceptions of space, resulting in smaller, more clearly bounded, more exclusive and more intensively used burial area, rather than to a diversion of burial to other local churches.

The early secular use of cemeteries is well attested in written sources too. Almost everywhere in France there are documents that cite the presence of inhabited dwellings in eleventh-twelfth century graveyards. In certain dioceses, such as Normandy, the bishops already attempted to limit domestic occupation in cemeteries to providing asylum in times of war. But elsewhere in the west of France, and in particular in the ecclesiastical province of Tours, permanent settlement was encouraged, and whole villages were sometimes constructed with the active participation of the clergy (Fixot & Zadora-Rio 1989).

By contrast, from the thirteenth century onwards one notices a change in attitude among the ecclesiastical authorities, and construction in cemeteries becomes routinely prohibited. The statutes of Bishop Eudes of Sully in Paris from around 1205 threaten excommunication to anyone rebuilding in a cemetery, and in 1220 the synod of Angers forbade the erection of new structures or the rebuilding of any house which has been left demolished for a year or more (*Nullus de novo edificare in cimiterio permittatur; nec domus aliqua si disrupta fuerit, durante per annum ruina, ibi reedificetur*). Similar injunctions were issued at Cambrai, Noyon, Soissons and Tournai, and may be found in England at Norwich in 1240-1243, and at Winchester and Exeter a little later. Statutes issued at Salisbury in 1238-1244 and those at Worcester (of 1240) require that any secular building erected in a cemetery shall be taken down, other than in time of war (Lauwers 2005, 259, n2-6). This tightening of the ecclesiastical legislation runs parallel to the ritual consecration of churchyards, which reflected a growing need to separate the sacred from the secular and led to the gradual exclusion of dwellings and domestic activities from graveyards.

The use of space, as revealed by excavations, is of the greatest value in determining how and when new ideas of community burial were put into practice. In some places, as in Raunds, the new conception of the churchyard, endowed with firm boundaries and exclusively dedicated to the dead, was imposed from its inception in the tenth-twelfth centuries, revealing seigniorial or ecclesiastical control over burials from an early date. In other places, the churchyard derived from less formal, more scattered, possibly family-based local burial-grounds, which were gradually reduced in area by the process of parochialization. This smaller area in which burial was more dense, may in turn have reflected a transformation in the allegiance between the living and the dead, from family to the wider community (Lauwers 2005, 120-132; Zadora-Rio 2003).

PART 3: JEWISH MEMORIAL PRACTICE *by Samuel D. Gruber*

The cemetery

In Hebrew a cemetery is called *Beth Kewarot* - the house or place of graves (Neh. 2:3), or more commonly *Beth ha-Chaim*, the house or garden of life, or *Beth Olam* - the house of eternity (Eccl. 12:5). In Jewish law and tradition a cemetery is a holy place, more sacred than a synagogue. A new community is obligated to designate a cemetery before building a synagogue. Traditional burial and mourning practices follow precise laws, though actual practice varies. The responsibility to erect a grave marker or monument *(mazevah)* to mark a grave and commemorate the deceased has Biblical and Talmudic precedent, and appears to have been universally practiced by Jews throughout medieval Europe for purposes of commemoration, but also to ensure standards of ritual purity were maintained. Contact with a dead body – directly or at the burial site – was strictly forbidden to men of priestly families *(Kohanim)*. In traditional Judaism, except in cases of closest relatives, even being under the same roof with a dead body or stepping over a grave causes impurity for *Kohanim*. This strict law made the visible marking of graves essential.

It is forbidden to use graves and gravestones for any other purpose. Rabbi Moshe Isserles of Krakow even forbade sitting on a gravestone. There are other rules and traditions regarding the care and use of Jewish cemeteries. One should not enter a cemetery bareheaded, pasture animals or collect grass there or run a canal through it. Also according to tradition, a ritual hand-wash is required after dealing with the dead directly and after visiting graves.

Memorials

Based on ancient and medieval finds, it is apparent that Jewish graves were marked in some way, usually with the name of the deceased. This was the norm for ancient burials in the Roman catacombs. Inscribed stone and ceramic markers have been found throughout the Mediterranean region from the Roman through Early medieval periods. The inscribed epitaphs in the Jewish catacombs of Rome were mostly in Greek, with the inclusion of few standard phrases in Hebrew. These inscriptions provide the bulk of the information known about the size, activity and location of the large Jewish community of the ancient capital. The tradition of including funerary inscriptions in languages other than Hebrew has varied through time and place. Today, it is accepted that in Chassidic or Orthodox cemeteries, funerary inscriptions can only be in Hebrew, and this was mostly true in the Middle Ages. But vernacular languages – Aramaic, Greek and Latin and later Yiddish and Ladino (Judeo-Spanish) also appear on gravestones.

In antiquity and early medieval Europe, the Jewish origin of the deceased is often deduced only by a Hebrew name. Hebrew language and Hebrew script are not employed. In other cases Jewish symbols reveal the deceased's Jewish origin, and religious practice. For example, early Jewish tombstones from the Roman province Pannonia (Western Hungary) have carvings of Menorahs and other symbols, but Hebrew letters do not appear in this period. On the other hand, the Greek words *heis theos* ('one God'), translation of the best known Hebrew Biblical prayer, often occur.

History of practice

The first Hebrew inscription in Europe (from 688 A.D.) was found in Narbonne, in southern France. It consists of three words only: *shalom al Yisrael*, peace for Israel. There are, however, few free standing Jewish grave markers from before the eleventh century. It is assumed that such markers existed made of perishable wood, or that stone markers were later pillaged and reused for other purposes. Certainly this was the case in medieval Venosa, Italy, where early medieval gravestones are incorporated into the walls of a local monastery.

Since there have been no Early Medieval Jewish cemeteries found, there is supposition that separate Jewish burial grounds may not have been the norm before Christian separation around the year 1000. For example, in 1986, the burial of an apparent Jewish child dated between the second to fifth century AD was found in a Roman-era cemetery in the region of Seewinkel, about 20 kilometres from Carnuntum in Austria.

Substantial numbers of Jewish gravestones from northern and central Europe are known from the thirteenth century on. Most of these are not in situ - they have been retrieved from other locations. In Northampton, England, a single stone fragment is the only surviving such gravestone in England (Roberts M, 1992). It dates from the twelfth century and resembles those from the Rhineland. In Worms, Germany, the oldest gravestone still legible dates from 1076. A stone from 1146 commemorates a murdered woman, perhaps one of the first victims of the pogroms that accompanied the Second Crusade. Others include a monument honouring twelve elders of whom a legend reports that, during the Crusade of 1096, they asked the town councillors for protection, and, on being refused, murdered the councillors, after which they all committed suicide in the cemetery. There are also the tombstones of Jekuthiel ben Jacob (1261); Baruch ben Meïr, father of rabbi Meïr of Rothenburg (1275); the grave of rabbi Meïr of Rothenburg himself (1307), and many others (Böcher, 1958).

In 1996, an unexpected discovery was made by an Armenian bishop who found a number of large inscribed gravestones in a river and adjoining forest near Eghegis, in the Siwniq region of southeastern Armenia. The granite stones shaped into oblong cylinders, with Hebrew and Aramaic inscriptions, are the first physical evidence of a pre-modern Jewish community in Armenia. The inscriptions are dated from the middle of the thirteenth century to 1337.

The earliest epitaph in Hungary is from 1278. The monument was erected "at the head of Pesach, son of Peter, who returned to eternity". This stone, together with two later ones, was found in Buda, at the site of the Medieval Jewish cemetery, at the junction of Alagut and Pauler Streets. In Erfurt (Germany), the oldest surviving gravestones date to the thirteenth century. Only in a few places such as Worms (Germany) and to a lesser extent Barcelona (Spain) are medieval gravestones still intact and in their original position. In the Czech Republic, Poland and Ukraine gravestones from the thirteenth century on are still fairly common despite widespread destruction during the Second World War and subsequently under Communism, when tens of thousands of gravestones – many finely carved works of art – were removed and (presumably) destroyed.

Excavations in Prague (Czech Republic) at the Jewish cemetery at Vladislavova Street and excavations at Tarrega (Spain), both showed evidence of extreme violence. In Prague archaeologists discovered a mass grave with human and animal bones that showed signs of violent executions with signs of extreme heat. In Tarrega, 159 individual graves and six mass graves were excavated and the mass graves dated through coins to the mid-fourteenth century, thus probably linked to the known pogroms of 1348. Anthropological study of the human remains, which included women, children and elderly individuals, revealed signs of violence, confirming that the identification with pogrom victims.

By 1600, Jewish gravestones were commonly carved in stone and included carefully composed epitaphs finely inscribed (Fig 12.13). The most elaborate gravestones of the period included intricate architectural and decorative borders, and beginning in the sixteenth century, the inclusion of pictorial elements, mostly symbolic, but occasionally narrative. Of course, we cannot know how many wooden markers were made and have subsequently disappeared. From later practice, we assume that markers in wood for poorer community members, or in those places where stone was rare and expensive, remained common. The opening of a new cemetery was often made necessary by minor or major epidemics. As old cemeteries were enclosed with buildings, authorities ordered the communities to found a new one, or they themselves designated its place.

Archaeological investigation

Archaeological excavation at cemeteries has focused mainly on determining the location of burials, and the process of internment of the dead. Along these lines, excavations in York (England) and Tarrega (Spain) have revealed unexpected patterns of orientation, and also some details of types of shrouds and coffins used. Against the wishes of Jewish religious communities, some archaeologists have also examined human remains for information concerning size, age, sex, nutrition, and injury of the buried population.

Little archaeological information has been gathered about the overall layout of medieval Jewish cemeteries, including how their boundaries were marked, how graves were arranged, whether there were set pathways, what kinds of structures were built, and how the cemetery was landscaped. Some information on these topics comes from literary and artistic sources, such as the desirability for a cemetery to be walled. How often cemeteries followed the preferred rules still needs to be confirmed by on site investigation.

One of the challenges to archaeologists confronting Jewish burials is the absolute prohibition of tampering with graves. Jewish law – at least as it is interpreted today – grants sanctity to graves and considers all burial inviolate for eternity. Archaeologists who knowingly excavate Jewish burials face the wrath of traditionally observant Jews. On the other hand, one of the values of archaeology – including the archaeology of cemeteries – is to demonstrate the evolution of contemporary beliefs and accepted traditions. Archaeology can indicate changes over time, or show that the behaviour that was advocated by the elite (community leaders, rabbis, scholars) was not always followed by the masses. Archaeology can be a corrective to accepted historical narrative based on selected texts, including teaching and law, or it can expand our knowledge of little known events. Archaeology can reconstruct actual behaviour as demonstrated through the discovery and analysis of material cultural remains (see above, p 494). In York, England, for example, the then Chief Rabbi of England refused at first to acknowledge that the excavated cemetery could be Jewish – since the orientation of the graves and the inclusion of iron nails (for coffins) violated contemporary (Orthodox) practice, which he accepted as historical fact (Lilley et al, 1994) (Fig 12.14).

Some cemetery excavations, as in Toledo, Spain (2007), have gone on despite complaints from Jewish groups. In Mayence, Germany, also in 2007, authorities halted excavation of a ninth-eleventh century Jewish cemetery, which had already been devastated in the Holocaust, when its many medieval gravestones were removed. Other recent excavations of Jewish cemeteries include those at Toulouse (France) in 1999, and Lucera (Spain) in 2007.

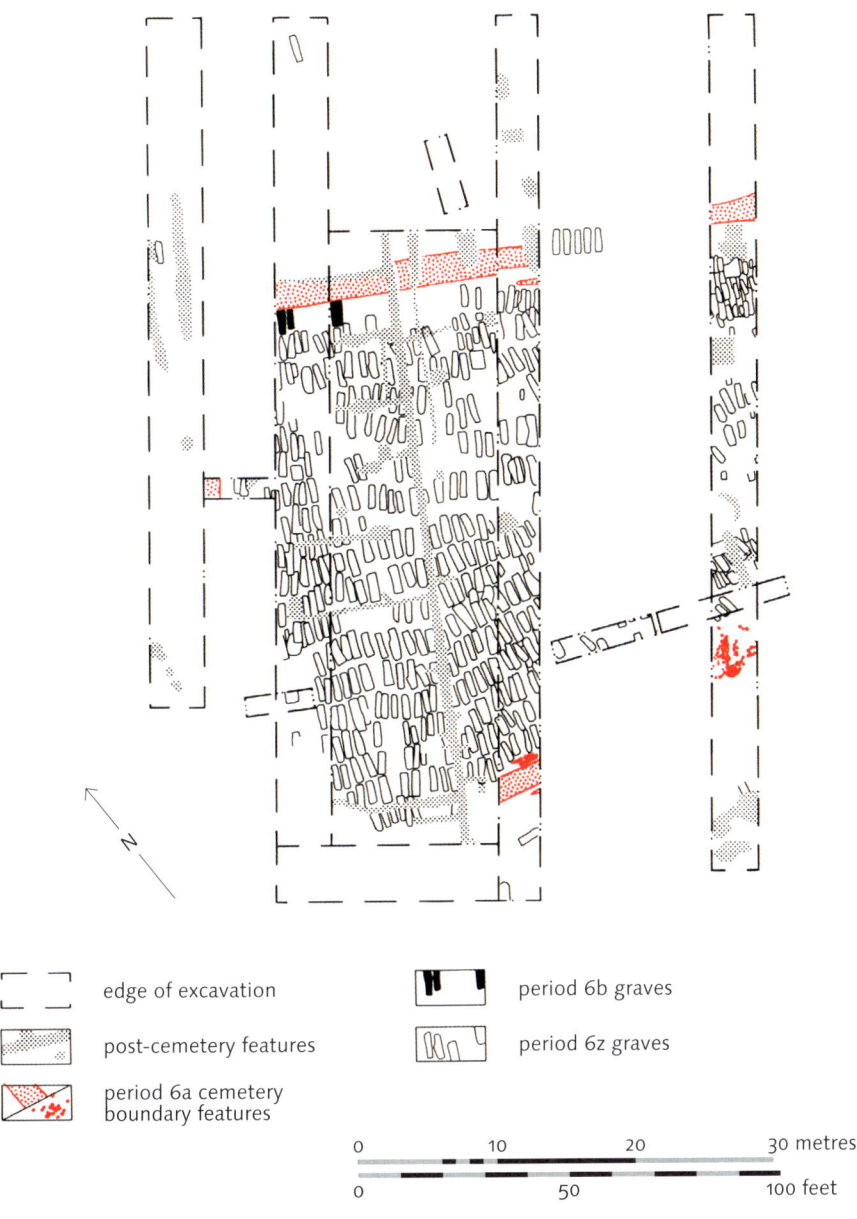

⌐ ¬ edge of excavation	▮◖▮ period 6b graves
⬚ post-cemetery features	◖◗ period 6z graves
⬚ period 6a cemetery boundary features	

0		10		20		30 metres
0			50			100 feet

Plan of excavated burials dating from late 12th to late 13th century at Jewbury, the Jewish cemetery **Fig 12.14**
*at York (Lilley et al. 1994, 322). The graves were oriented north-east/south-west, respected each other
and were probably marked – there was evidence for stakes or posts in five cases. Most burials (ibid.,
441) had nailed wooden coffins. The buried persons were reported to be 'perceptibly shorter than their
contemporaries in York' (ibid., 539). The start date of the cemetery is unknown, but the end date may
be taken as 1290, the year that the Jews were expelled from England and the burial ground sold to
Robert de Newland, a York tanner, and his wife Alice Gisburn (reproduced with the kind permission
of York Archaeological Trust).*

AME 1 See Graham-Campbell & Valor 2007

AAVV 1976 See ICOMOS (ed) 1976

AAVV 1991 See Institución Fernando el Católico (ed) 1991

AAVV 1998 See Cressier, P & García-Arenal, M (eds) 1998

AAVV 2000a See Instituto de Estudios Ceutíes (ed) 2000

AAVV 2000b See Fundación El legado andalusí (ed) 2000

AAVV 2000c See Cressier, P (ed) 2000

AAVV 2001 See Passini, J (ed) 2001

AAVV 2006a See Patronato de la Alhambra y Generalife (ed) 2006

AAVV 2006b See Museo del Vidrio La Granja (ed) 2006

Wharram III see Bell *et al.* 1987

Wharram XI see Mays *et al.* 2007

A

Abel, W 1935 *Agrarkrisen und Agrarkonjunktur in Mitteleuropa vom 13. bis zum 19. Jahrhundert*, Berlin

Abel, W 1943 *Die Wüstungen des ausgehenden Mittelalters. Ein Beitrag zur Siedlungs- und Agrargeschichte Deutschlands*, Jena

Aberg, G, Fosse, G & Stray, H 1998 'Man, nutrition and mobility: a comparison of teeth and bone from the Medieval era and the present from Pb and Sr isotopes', *The Science of the Total Environment* 224, 109-19

Abrahams, I 1896 *Jewish Life in the Middles Ages* London

Abu-Lughod, JL 1987 'The Islamic City: Historic Myth, Islamic Essence and Contemporary Relevance', *International Journal of Middle East Studies* 19, 155-77

Abu-Lughod, JL 1989 (1991) *Before European Hegemony. The World system A.D. 1250-1350*, New York & Oxford

Addy, SO 1898 *The Evolution of the English House*, London

Addyman, PV 1989 'The archaeology of public health at York, England', *World Archaeology* 21, 244-64

Ajmar-Wollheim, M & Dennis, F (eds) 2006 *At home in Renaissance Italy*, London

Ajmar-Wollheim, M, Dennis, F & Matchette, A (eds) 2007 *Approaching the Italian Renaissance Interior*, Oxford

Albarella, U 1997 'Size, power, wool and veal: zooarchaeological evidence for late medieval innovations', in *Environment and Subsistence in Medieval Europe*, York, 19-30

Albarella, U 2005 'Meat production and consumption in town and country', in Giles, K & Dyer, C (eds) *Town and Country in the Middle Ages, Contrasts, Contacts and Interconnections, 1100-1500*, Leeds, 131-48

Albarella, U 2010 'The wild boar', in O'Connor, TP & Sykes, N (eds) *Extinctions and Invasions: A Social History of the British Fauna*, Oxford, 59-67

Albrecht, T 1997 *Truhen – Kisten – Laden. Vom Mittelalter bis zur Gegenwart am Beispiel der Lünerburger Heide*, Petersberg

Alcock, NW 1981 *Cruck Construction* (CBA Research Report 42), London

Alcock, NW 1983 'The Great Rebuilding and its later stages', *Vernacular Architecture* 14, 45-9

Alcock, NW 1993 *People at Home: Living in a Warwickshire Village 1500-1800*, Chichester

Alcock, NW & Currie, CRJ 1989 'Upstairs or Downstairs', *Vernacular Architecture* 20, 21-3

Alcock, NW & Laithwaite, M 1973 'Medieval houses in Devon and their modernisation', *Medieval Archaeology* 17, 100-25

Alcock, NW & Smith, P 1972 'The long house: a plea for clarity', *Medieval Archaeology* 16, 145-6

Alexander, J & Binski, P (eds) 1987 *Age of Chivalry. Art in Plantagenet England 1200-1400*, London

Alexander, M 1997 'A possible synagogue in Guildford', in De Boe, G & Verhaeghe, F (eds) *Religion and Belief in Medieval Europe: Papers of the Medieval Europe Brugge 1997 Conference, vol. 4*, Zellik, 201-12

Alexandre-Bidon, D 2009 'Pour un "art" culinaire au Moyen Âge: le témoignage des images', in Ravoire, F & Dietrich, A (eds) *La cuisine et la table dans la France de la fin du Moyen Âge. Contenus et contenants du XIVe au XVIe siècle*, Caen, 11-23

Alexandre-Bidon, D & Closson, D 1985 *L'enfant à l'ombre des cathédrales*, Lyon

Alexandre-Bidon, D & Lorcin, M-Th 2003 *Le quotidien au temps des fabliaux. Textes, images, objets*, Paris

Alexandre-Bidon, D & Treffort, C 1993 'Un quartier pour les morts: images du cimetière médiéval', in Alexandre-Bidon, D & Treffort, C (eds) *A réveiller les morts. La mort au quotidien dans l'Occident médiéval*, Lyon, 253-73

Almagro, A, 2007 'An approach to the visual analysis of the gardens of Al-Andalus', in Conan, M (ed) *Middle East Garden Traditions: Unity and Diversity*, Washington DC, 55-73

Alper, G, Hensch, M & Kirchner, W 1994 'Ein spätmittelalterlicher Pfostenbau aus Matting', *Das archäologische Jahr in Bayern 1993*, 159-61

Alsayyad, N 1991 *Cities and Caliphs: on the Genesis of Arab Muslim Urbanism*, Wesport (CT)

Alston, L 1998 *Historic Buildings of Suffolk* 1 (Journal of the Suffolk Historic Buildings Group), Bures St Mary

Alston, L 2004a 'Late medieval workshops in East Anglia', in Barnwell, PS, Palmer, M & Airs, M (eds) *The vernacular workshop from craft to industry 1400-1900*, 38-60

Alston, L 2004b *Guildhall of Corpus Christi, Lavenham*, London

Alvik, R & Haggrén, G 2003 'Keskiakainen haaksirikkopaikka Nauvon ulkossaristossa', *Suomen keskiajan arkeologian seura* [Finnish Medieval Archaeology] 2/2003, 18-27

Ambrose, SH, 1990 'Preparation and characterisation of bone and tooth collagen for isotopic analysis', *Journal of Archaeological Science* 17, 431-51

Ambrose, SH, 2000 'Controlled diet and climate experiments on nitrogen isotope ratios of rats', in Ambrose SH & Katzenberg MA (eds) *Biogeochemical approaches to paleodietary analysis*, New York, 243-57

Ambrose, SH & Norr, L 1993 'Experimental evidence for the relationship of the carbon isotope ratios of whole diet and dietary protein to those of bone collagen and carbonate', in Lambert JB & Grupe G (eds) *Prehistoric human bone: archaeology at the molecular level*, Berlin, 1-37

Amigues, F & Bazzana, A (eds) 1990 *Fours de potiers et «testares» médiévaux en Méditerranée occidentale*, Madrid

Ancel, B 1998a 'La mine du Fournel (L'Argentière-La-Bessée, Hautes-Alpes, France): l'exploitation rationnelle aux Xème-XIVème siècles d'un filon de plomb argentifère', *Actes du Congrès Européen Civezzano-Fornace 1995*, 161-93

Ancel, B 1998b 'Techniques minières et maîtrise de l'espace dans les mines d'argent médiévales: exemples de mines de plomb argentifère des Alpes du Sud (X^e-XIVe siècles)', in *L'innovation technique au Moyen Age*, Actes du VIe congrès international d'archéologie médiévale 1-5 octobre 1996, Paris, 108-10

Ancel, B 2006 'Archéologie minière dans les Alpes du Sud et la Provence', in Barge, H (ed) *4000 ans d'histoire des mines: l'exemple de la région Provence-Alpes-Côte-d'Azur*, Marseille, 159-76

Andersen, CBH 2005 'Genstandsfund', in Kock, J & Roesdahl, E (eds) *Boringholm – en østjysk træborg fra 1300-årene*, Højbjerg (English summary and lists of artefacts 101-89), 101-89, 353-4, 358-9.

Anderson, W 1970 *Castles of Europe*, London

Andersson, E 1999 *The Common Thread. Textile Production during the Late Iron Age-Viking Age* (University of Lund, Institute of Archaeology Report 67), Lund

Andersson, E 2003 *Tools for Textile Production from Birka and Hedeby* (Birka Studies 8), Stockholm

Andersson, H 2002 'Centre-Periphery, World Systems, and Medieval Archaeology', in Helmig, G, Scholkmann, B & Untermann, M (eds) *Centre-Region-Periphery. Medieval Europe Basel 2002* (3 volumes), Hertingen, 23-34

Andersson, H 2003 'Urbanisation', in Helle, K (ed) *The Cambridge History of Scandinavia Vol. 1*, Cambridge, 312-42

Andersson, H, Ersgård, L & Svensson, E (eds) 1998 *Outland Use in Preindustrial Europe*, Stockholm

Andersson, H, Hansen, G & Øye, I (eds) 2008 *De første 200 årene – nytt blikk på 27 skandinaviske middelalderbyer* (Universitetet i Bergen Arkeologiske Skrifter 5), Bergen

Andersson, L 1989 *Pilgrimsmärken och vallfart: medeltida pilgrimskultur I Skandinavien*, Lund

Andersson, S & Svensson, E (eds) 2002 *Skramle: the true story of a deserted medieval farmstead* (Lund studies in medieval archaeology 27), Stockholm

Andersson Strand, E, Frei, K, Gleba, M, Mannering, U, Nosch, M-L & Skals, I 2010 'Old textiles – New Possibilities', *European Journal of Archaeology* 13, 149-73

Angelé, S & Cressier, P 1990 'Velefique (Almería): un example de mosquée rurale en al-Andalus', *Mélanges de la Casa de Velázquez* 26, 113-30

Angenendt, A 2000 *Geschichte der Religiösität im Mittelalter* (second edition), Darmstadt

Anglert, M & Larsson, S 2008 'Landskapets urbanitet och urbanitetens landskap', in Andersson, H, Hansen, G & Øye, I (eds) 2008 *De første 200 årene – nytt blikk på 27 skandinaviske middelalderbyer* (Universitetet i Bergen Arkeologiske Skrifter 5), Bergen, 303-22

Andrén, A 1985 *Den urbana scenen. Städer och samhälle i det medeltida Danmark*, (Acta Archaeologica Lundensia Series in 8° 13), Bonn & Malmö

Andrén, A 1989 'State and Towns in the Middle Ages. The Scandinavian experience', *Theory and Society* 18, 585-609

Apala, Z 2006 *Cēsu pils dārgumi*, Cēsis

Apala, J 2007 'Cēsis un vendi', in Rozentāle, V (ed) *Quo vadis, Cēsis?*, Cēsis

Appadurai, A 1986 *The Social life of Things: commodities in cultural perspective*, Cambridge

Arcini, C, Cinthio, M & Westrup, L 1999 *Health and disease in early Lund: osteo-pathologic studies of 3,305 individuals buried in the first cemetery area of Lund 990-1536* (Archaeologica Lundensia 8), Lund

Ariès, P 1977 *L'Homme devant la mort*, Paris

Armitage, PL 1985 'Small mammal faunas in later medieval towns: a preliminary study in British urban biogeography', *The Biologist* 32/2, 65-71

Armitage, PL & Butler, J 2005 'Medieval deerskin processing waste at the Moor House site, London EC2', *London Archaeologist*, Spring, 323-7

Arndt, B & Ströbl, A (eds) 2005 *Gutingi – Vom Dorf zur Stadt: neueste Ergebnisse der stadtarchäologischen Arbeit*, Göttingen

Arneborg, J 2003 'Norse Greenland: Reflections on Settlement and Depopulation', in Barrett, JH (ed) *Contact, Continuity, and Collapse. The Norse Colonisation of the North Atlantic* (Studies in the Early Middle Ages 5), Turnhout, 163-81

Arneborg, J 2008 'The Norse settlements in Greenland', in Brink, S & Price, N (eds) *The Viking World*, London & New York, 588-97

Aronsson, K-Å 1991 *Forest reindeer herding A.D. 1-1800: an archaeological and palaeoecological study in northern Sweden* (Archaeology and Environment 10), Umeå

Arqueonautas publications www.arq.de/

Arts, N 2001 'Het "Oude Huys": De arheologie van het eerste kasteel van Helmond, circa 1175-1375', in Arts N, Roosenboom, H & van Zalinge-Spooren, L (eds) *De kastelen van Helmond: Een machtscentrum aan de rand van de Peel,* Utrecht, 22-75

Ashby, SP 2002 'The role of archaeozoology in the interpretation of socioeconomic status – a discussion with reference to medieval Europe', *Archaeological Review from Cambridge* 18/2, 37-59

Assis, YT 1992 'Synagogues in Medieval Spain', *Jewish Art* 18, 6-29

Astill, G 1988a 'Fields', in Astill, G & Grant, A (eds) *The Countryside of Medieval England*, Oxford & New York, 62-85

Astill, G 1988b 'Rural settlement: the toft and croft', in Astill, G & Grant, A (eds) *The Countryside of Medieval England*, Oxford, 36-61

Astill, G 1993 *A Medieval Industrial complex and its landscape: the Metalworking Watermills and workshops of Bordesley Abbey* (CBA Research report 92), York

Astill, G 1994 'The Bordesley Abbey Granges Project', in Pressouyre, L (ed) *L'espace cistercien* (Comité des travaux historiques et scientifiques), Paris, 537-53

Astill, G 2000 'General Survey 600-1300', in Palliser, DM (ed) *The Cambridge Urban History of Britain 1, 600-1540*, Cambridge, 27-50

Astill, G 2006 *The Bordesley Monastic Granges monograph*, York

Astill, G 2009 'Medieval towns and urbanization', in Gilchrist, R & Reynolds, A (eds) *Reflections: 50 years of Medieval Archaeology, 1957-2007*, Leeds, 255-270

Astill, G 2010 'The long and the short', in Goddard, R, Langdon, J & Müller, M (eds) *Survival and Discord in Medieval Society. Essays in honour of Christopher Dyer*, Turhnout, 11-28

Astill, G & Davies, W 1997 *A Breton Landscape*, London

Astill, G & Langdon, J (eds) 1997 *Medieval Farming and Technology*, Leiden

Aston, MA & Gerrard, CM 1999 '"Unique, traditional and charming": the Shapwick Project, Somerset', *Antiquaries Journal* 79, 1-58

Aston, MA, Martin, MH & Jackson, AW 1998 'The potential for heavy soil analysis on low status archaeological sites at Shapwick, Somerset', *Antiquity* 72, 838-47

Atkin, M, Carter, A & Evans, DH 1985 *Excavations in Norwich 1971-1978, Part II* (East Anglian Archaeology 26), Norwich

Atkins, M & Evans D.H. 2002 *Excavations in Norwich 1971-1978, Part III* (East Anglian Archaeology 100) Norwich.

Austin, D 1985 'Dartmoor and the upland villages of the southwest of England', in Hooke, D (ed) *Medieval villages. A Review of Current Work,* Oxford, 71-9

Austin, D 1990 'The 'proper' study of medieval archaeology: a case study', in Austin, D (ed.) *From the Baltic to the Black Sea: Studies in Medieval Archaeology*, London

Axelson, E 1961 'Prince Henry the Navigator and the Discovery of the Sea Route to India', *The Geographical Journal* 127, 145-55

Axelson, E 1973 *Cape to Congo: early Portuguese explorers*, London

Aynard, F 2008 *Fontenay. L'Abbaye et son vallon* Paris

Aynsley, J & Grant, C 2006 *Imagined Interiors,* London

Ayres, J 2003 *Domestic interiors: the British tradition 1500-1850*, New York

Azuar Ruiz, R 1998 'Alfares y testares de Sharq al-Andalus (siglos XII-XIII). Producción, tipología y distribución', in Padilla Lapuente, JI & Vila Carabasa, JM (eds) *Ceràmica medieval i postmedieval. Circuits productius i seqüències culturals* (Monografies d'Arqueologia Medieval i Postmedieval 4), Barcelona, 57-71

Azuar Ruiz, R (ed) 2004, *Fouilles de la rábita de Guardamar I. El ribat califal. Excavaciones e investigaciones (1984-1992)*, Madrid

B

Backhouse, J 1989 *The Luttrell Psalter*, London

Bacqué Grammont, JL & Tibet, A (eds) 1996 *Cimetières et traditions funéraires dans le monde islamique*, Actes du Colloque International du Centre National de la Recherche Scientifique (Istambul, 1991), Ankara

Badham, S 2000 'Monumental brasses and the Black Death: a reappraisal', *Antiquaries Journal* 80, 207-47

Badham, S 2007 'Edward the Confessor's Chapel, Westminster Abbey: the origins of the Royal Mausoleum and its cosmatesque pavement', *Antiquaries Journal* 87, 197-219

Baeriswyl, A 2003 *Stadt, Vorstadt und Stadterweiterung im Mittelalter: Archäologische und historische Studien zum Wachstum der drei Zähringerstädte Burgdorf, Bern und Freiburg im Breisgau* (Schweizer Beiträge zur Kulturgeschichte und Archäologie des Mittelalters 30), Basel

Bagnera, A & Pezzini, E 2004 'I cimiteri di rito musulmano nella Sicilia medievale. Dati e problemi', *Melanges de l'École Française de Rome* 116, 231-302

Baillie, MGL 1991 *A slice through time. Dendrochronology and precision dating*, London

Bailly-Maître, M-C 1998 'Habiter la montagne au Moyen Âge', in Feller, L, Mane, P & Piponnier, F (eds) *Le village médiéval et son environnement: études offertes à Jean Marie Pesez*, Paris, 31-42

Bailly-Maître, M-C 2002 *L'argent: du minerai au pouvoir dans la France médiévale*, Paris

Bailly-Maître, M-C 2004 'Les agglomérations minières au Moyen Âge en Europe occidentale', *Naissance et développement des villes minières en Europe*, Arras, 215-26

Bailly-Maître, M-C & Bruno-Dupraz, J 1994 *Brandes-en-Oisans: la mine d'argent des Dauphins, XIIe-XIVe s, Isère* (Documents d'Archéologie en Rhône-Alpes et en Auvergne 9), Lyon

Bailly-Maître, M-C & Dhénin, M 2004 'Ateliers monétaires et mines d'argent dans les Alpes (Xe-XVe s.). Histoire, archéologie, numismatique et archéométrie', *Archéologie Médiévale* 34, 43-64

Bailly-Maître, M-C & Simonel, B 1996 'Travail et milieu. Incidences sur une population au Moyen Age', in Buchet, L & Pilet, C (eds) *L'identité des populations archéologiques*, Actes des XVIe Rencontres Internationales d'Archéologie et d'Histoire d'Antibes 1995, Sophia Antipolis, 211-44

Bailly-Maître, M-C, Martin, L, Herrscher, E & Hervieu, P 2008 'Se nourrir en haute montagne aux XIIIe et XIVe siècles. Le village de Brandes (Huez-Isère). Apports comparés de l'archéologie, des textes et de l'anthropologie', *Histoire des Alpes/Storia delle Alpi/Geschichte der Alpen* 13, 83-98

Baker, P 1993 'Le rôle de la chasse comme moyen de subsistance durant le haut Moyen Âge dans le nord de l'Italie: une comparaison des sources zooarchéologiques et historiques', in Desse, J & Audoin-Rouzeau, F (eds) *Exploitation des animaux sauvages à travers le temps*, Juan-les-Pins, 505-16

Balasse, M, Bocherens, H, Tresset, A, Marotti A & Vigne J-D 1997 'Emergence de la production laitière au néolithique ? Contribution de l'analyse isotopique d'ossements de bovins archéologiques', *Comptes Rendus à l'Académie des Sciences* 325, 1005-10

Balasse, M, Bocherens, H & Mariotti, A 1999 'Intra-bone variability of collagen and apatite isotopic composition used as evidence of a change of diet', *Journal of Archaeological Science* 26, 593-8

Banks, M 2001 *A Chronicle of Leicester Cathedral*, Leicester

Bardel, A & Perennec, R 2004 'Abbaye de Landévennec: évolution du contexte funéraire depuis le haut Moyen Âge, in Alduc-Le Bagousse, A (ed) *Inhumations et édifices religieux au Moyen Âge entre Loire et Seine*, Caen, 121-58

Barley, MW 1991 'The use of upper floors in rural houses', *Vernacular Architecture* 22, 2-23

Barnet, P (ed) 1997 *Images in Ivory: Precious Objects of the Gothic Age*, Detroit

Barnett, CM 2000 'Commemoration in the parish church: identity and social class in late medieval York,' *Yorkshire Archaeological Journal* 72, 73-92

Barnwell, P & Adams AT 1994 *The House Within: Interpreting Medieval Houses in Kent*, London

Barnwell, PS 2005 '"Four hundred masses on the four Fridays next after my decease": the care of souls in fifteenth-century All Saints, North Street, York,' in Barnwell, PS, Cross, C, & Rycraft, A (eds) *Mass and Parish in Late Medieval England: the Use of York*, Reading, 57-87

Baron, S, Carignan, J, Laurent, S & Ploquin, A 2006 'Medieval lead making on Mont-Lozère Massif (Cévennes-France): tracing ore sources using Pb isotopes', *Applied Geochemistry* 21/2, 241-52

Barrett, JH 2007 'Sea fishing and long-term socio-economic trends in North-Western Europe', in Graham-Campbell, J & Valor, M (eds) *The Archaeology of Medieval Europe, Vol. 1: Eight to Twelfth Centuries AD*, Aarhus, 201-203

Barrett, JH & Richards, M 2004 'Identity, gender, religion and economy: new isotope and radiocarbon evidence for marine resource intensification in early historic Orkney, Scotland, UK', *European Journal of Archaeology* 7/3, 249-71

Barrett, JH, Locker, AM & Roberts, CM 2004 '"Dark Age economics" revisited: the English fish bone evidence AD 600-1600', *Antiquity* 78, 618-36

Barron, C 1974 *The Medieval Guildhall of London*, London

Barry, TB 1987 *The Archaeology of Medieval Ireland*, London & New York

Barry, TB 2002 'The defensive nature of Irish moated sites', in Kenyon, J & O'Conor, K (eds) *The Medieval Castle in Ireland and Wales*, Dublin, 182-93

Barth, EK 1983 'Trapping reindeer in south Norway', *Antiquity* 57, 109-15

Bartlett, R 1994 *The Making of Europe: Conquest, Civilization and Cultural Change 950-1350*, Harmondsworth

Bartosiewicz, L 1993 'Late Medieval lynx skeleton from Hungary', in Clason, A, Payne, S & Uerpmann, H-P (eds) *Skeletons in her Cupboard*, Oxford, 5-18

Bartosiewicz, L 1999 'Animal husbandry and medieval settlement in Hungary', *Beiträge zur Mittelalterarchäologie in Österreich* 15, 139-55

Bartosiewicz, L 2003 'Eat not this fish – a matter of scaling', in Guzmán, AF, Polaco–F, OJ & Aguilar, J (eds) *Presencia de la arqueoictiología en México*, Mexico D.F, 19-26

Bassani, E 2000 *African Art and Artefacts in European Collections, 1400-1800*, London

Bassani, E & Fagg, W 1988 *Africa and the Renaissance: Art in Ivory*, New York

Baumgartner, E & Krueger, I 1988 *Phönix aus Sand und Asche. Glas des Mittelalters,* München

Bayley, Justine & Jacqui Watson 2009 Emerging from the appendices; The contribution of Scientific examination to medieval archaeology in Gilchrist, R & Reynolds, A (eds) 2009 *Reflections: 50 years of Medieval Archaeology, 1957-2007*, Leeds:363-381

Bazzana, A 1980 'Céramiques médiévales: les méthodes de la description analytique appliquées aux productions de l'Espagne orientale', *Mélanges de la Casa Velazquez* 15 (1979), 135-85; 16 (1980), 57-95

Bazzana, A & Bedia, J 2005 *Excavaciones en la Isla de Saltés (Huelva) 1988-2001*, Sevilla

Beattie, C, Maslokovic, A & Rees Jones, S (eds) 2003 *The Medieval Household in Christian Europe, c. 850-c. 1550: Managing Power, Wealth, and the Body*, Turnhout

Becker, T, Schild, W, Vogelfänger, Ulrich-Bochsler, S, Wiechmann , R & Püschel, K, 2007 'Schwerpunktthema: Spuren des Rechts', *Archäologie in Deutschland* 2007 Heft 2, 18-36

Bejenaru, L 2009 *Archaeozoological Approaches to Medieval Moldavia* (BAR International Series 1954), Oxford

Bel, V 2006 'Avant-propos', in Maufras, O (ed) *Habitats, nécropoles et paysages dans la moyenne et la basse vallée du Rhône (VIIᵉ-XVᵉ s.): contribution des travaux du TGV-Méditerranée à l'étude des sociétés rurales médiévales* (Documents d'Archéologie Française 98), Paris, 13-15

Belcredi, L 2000 'Colonization, development and desertion of the medieval village of Bystřec', in Klápště, J (ed) *Ruralia* 3 (Památky archeologické Supplementum 14), Turnhout, 187-201

Belcredi, L 2006 *Bystřec. O založení, životě a zániku středověké vsi. Archeologický výzkum zaniklé středověké vsi na Drahanské vrchovině 1975-2005* (Mittelalterliche Ortswüstung – Bystřec), Brno

Bell, LS, Lee Thorp, JA & Elkerton, A 2009 'The sinking of the Mary Rose warship: a medieval mystery solved?', *Journal of Archaeological Science* 36/1, 166-73

Bell, RD, Beresford, MW & others 1987 *Wharram:a study of settlement on the Yorkshire Wolds. Volume 3: the church of St. Martin* (Society for Medieval Archaeology Monograph 11), London.

Bencard, M 1971 'Middelalderlige stenmortere i Danmark', *Kuml,* 35-60 (with English summary)

Benedictow, OJ 2004 *The Black Death 1346-53. A Complete History*, Woodbridge

Benedictow, OJ, 2010 *What Disease was Plague? On the Controversy over the Microbiological Identity of Historical Plague Epidemics*, Leiden

Benito, A & Ibanez, M 2005 'Estudio Tipologico y Metalografico de las Manillas (Premoneda Africana) Fabricadas en Europa', *Aranzadiko Berriak* 126, 98

Benninghoven, F 1965 *Der Orden der Schwertbrüder*, Köln & Graz

Benoît, P 1988 'Une site industriel médiéval: la forge de l'abbaye de Fontenay', *Mémoires de la Commission des Antiquités du Département de Côte d'Or* 34, 219-47

Benoît, P 1997 *La mine de Pampailly – XVᵉ-XVIIIᵉ siècles – Brussieu, Rhône* (Documents d'Archéologie en Rhône-Alpes 14), Lyon

Bent, DC 1977-8 'The animal remains' in Liddle, P (ed) 'A late medieval enclosure in Donington Park', *Transactions of the Leicestershire Archaeological and Historical Society* 63, 8-29

Bentz, E 2008 '"More than a village". On the medieval countryside as an archaeological field of study', in Schlanger, N & Nordbladh, J (eds) *Archives, ancestors, practices. Archaeology in the light of its history*, Oxford & New York, 97-107

Beresford, M 1954 *The Lost Villages of England*, London

Beresford, M & Hurst, J (eds) 1971 *Deserted Medieval Villages*, London

Beresford, M & Hurst, J 1990 *Wharram Percy. Deserted Medieval Village*, London

Berg, G 1935 *Sledges and wheeled vehicles. Ethnological studies from the view-point of Sweden* (Nordiska museet handlingar 4), Stockholm

Berglund, BE 1991 *The cultural Landscape during 6000 years in southern Sweden: the Ystad project* (Ecological Bulletins 41), Copenhagen

Berglund, BE 2007 *Alstahaug på Helgeland 1000-1750*, Trondheim (summary and captions in English)

Bertelsen, R 1973 *Gårdshaugene i Harstad kommune. Et bidrag til områdets økonomiske historie i middelalderen*, dissertation, University of Bergen

Bertelsen, R & Urbanczyk, P 1988 'Two Perspectives on Vågan in Lofoten: northern perspectives on urbanism', *Acta Borealia* 1-2, 98-110

Bertelsen, R, Buko, A, Fossnes, A, Hood, J, Kobylinski, Z, Lind, K & Urbanczyk, P 1987 'The Storvågan Project 1985-86', *Norwegian Archaeological Review* 20, 51-55

Berthelot, S, Marin, J-Y & Rey-Delqué, M (eds) 2002 *Vivre au Moyen Age. Archéologie du quotidien en Normandie du XIIIe au XVe siècle*, Milan

Berti, G 2002 'La ceramica tunesiana "a cobalto e manganese" in Toscana', in *Atti del XXXV Convegno Internazionale della Ceramica*, Albisola, 89-102

Berti, G, & Bianchi, G 2007 *Piombino. La Chiesa di Sant'Antimo sopra i Canali*, Firenze

Berti, G & Tongiorgi, L 1981 *I bacini ceramici medievali delle chiese di Pisa*, Roma

Berti, G, Gelichi, S & Mannoni, T 1997 'Trasformazione tecnologiche nelle prime produzioni italiane con rivestimenti vetrificati (secc.XII-XIII)', in *La céramique médiévale en Méditerranée, Actes du VIe Congrès de l'AIECM2* (Aix en Provence, novembre 1995), Aix en Provence, 383-403

Bertoldi, F & Librenti, M 2007 *Nonantola 2. Il cimitero bassomedievale della chiesa di San Lorenzo nel borgo di Nonantola*, Firenze

Bill, J 2002 'The Cargo Vessels', in Berggren, L, Hybel, N & Landen, A (eds) *Cogs, Cargoes, and Commerce. Maritime Bulk Trade in Northern Europe 1150-1400*, Toronto, 92-112

Bill, J 2009 'From Nordic to North European. Application of multiple corresondence analysis in the study of changes in Danish shipbuilding A.D. 900-1600', in Bockius, R (ed) *Between the Seas. Transfer and Exchange in Nautrical Technology. Proceedings of the Eleventh International Symposium on Boat and Ship Archaeology, Mainz 2006*, Mainz, 429-38

Bill, J & Hocker, FM 2004 'Haithabu 4 seen in the context of contemporary shipbuilding in Southern Scandinavia', in Brandt, K & Kühn, HJ (eds) *Der Prahm aus dem Hafen von Haithabu. Beiträge zu antiken und mittelalterlichen Flachbodenschiffen*, Neumünster, 43-54

Bill, J & Roesdahl, E 2007 'Travel and Transport', in Graham-Campbell, J & Valor, M (eds) *The Archaeology of Medieval Europe, Vol. 1: Eight to Twelfth Centuries AD*, Aarhus, 261-88

Bill, J, Poulsen, B, Rieck, F & Ventegodt, O 1997 *Dansk søfarts historie 1: Indtil 1588. Fra stammebåd til skib*, København

Binski, P 1996 *Medieval Death: Ritual and Representation,* London

Binski, P 1999 'Hierarchies and orders in English royal images of power', in Denton, J (ed) *Orders and Hierarchies in Late Medieval and Renaissance Europe*, Basingstoke, 74-93

Birrell, J 1982 'Who poached the King's deer? A study in 13th-century crime', *Midland History* 7, 9-25

Birrell, J 1996 'Peasant deer poachers in the medieval forest', in Britnell, R & Hatcher, J (eds) *Progress and Problems in Medieval England: Essays in Honour of Edward Miller*, Cambridge, 68-88

Birrell, J 2006 'Procuring, preparing and serving venison in late medieval England', in Woolgar, C, Serjeantson, D & Waldron, T (eds) *Food in Medieval England: History and Archaeology*, Oxford, 176-88

Blair, J 1987 'The 12th century bishop's palace at Hereford', *Medieval Archaeology* 31, 59-72

Blair, J 1993 'Hall and chamber: English domestic planning 1000-1250', in Meirion Jones, G & Jones, M (eds) *Manorial Domestic Buildings in England and Northern France* (Society of Antiquaries Occasional Papers 15), London, 1-21

Blair, J 2005 *The Church in Anglo-Saxon society*, Oxford

Blair, J & Ramsey, N (eds) 1991 *English Medieval Industries. Craftsmen, techniques, products*, London & Rio Grande

Blair, I, Hillaby, J, Howell, I, Serman, R & Watson, B 2002 'The discovery of two medieval *mikva'ot* in London and a reinterpretation of the Bristol '*mikveh*', *Jewish Historical Studies* 37, 15-40

Blaizot, F 2006 'Ensembles funéraires isolés dans la moyenne vallée du Rhône (VIIe–XVe siècle)', in Maufras, O (ed) *Habitats, nécropoles et paysages dans la moyenne et la basse vallée du Rhône (Vie-XVe siècle). Contribution des travaux du TGV-Méditerranée à l'étude des sociétés rurales médiévales*, Paris, 281-2

Blaizot, F & Martin-Dupont, S 2006 'L'ensemble funéraire de Beaume (Châteauneuf-sur-Isère, Drôme): caractérisation et hypothèses d'interprétation', in Maufras, O (ed) *Habitats, nécropoles et paysages dans la moyenne et la basse vallée du Rhône (VIIe-XVe s.): contribution des travaux du TGV-Méditerranée à l'étude des sociétés rurales médiévales* (Documents d'Archéologie Française 98), Paris, 39-60

Blake, H 1972 'La ceramica medievale spagnola e la Liguria', *Atti V Convegno Internazionale della Ceramica*, Albisola, 55-106

Blake, H, Egan, G, Hurst, J & New, E 2003 'From popular devotion to resistance and revival in England: the cult of the Holy Name of Jesus and the Reformation' in Gaimster, D & Gilchrist, R (eds) *The Archaeology of Reformation 1480-1580* Leeds, 159-75

Blake, JW (ed) 1942 *Europeans in West Africa, 1450-1560*, London

Boardman, AW 1996 *The Battle of Towton*, Stroud

Boas, A 1999 *Crusader Archaeology*, London

Boccador, J 1988 *Le mobilier français du Moyen Age à la Renaissance*, Saint-Just-en-Chaussée

Böcher, O 1958 *Der alte Judenfriedhof in Worms: ein Führer durch seine Geschichte und Grabmäler*, Worms

Böcher, O 2001 *Die Alte Synagoge in Worms am Rhein* (DKV-Kunststätten 181/1), Munich & Berlin

Bocherens, H & Drucker, D 2003 'Trophic level isotopic enrichment of carbon and nitrogen in bone collagen: case studies from recent and ancient terrestrial ecosystems', *International Journal of Osteoarchaeology* 13, 46-53

Bocherens, H, Fizet, M, Mariotti, A, Lange-Badre, B, Vandermeersch, B, Borel, JP & Bellon, G 1991a 'Isotopic biogeochemistry (^{13}C, ^{15}N) of fossil vertebrate collagen: application to the study of past food web including Neanderthal man', *Journal of Human Evolution* 20, 481-92

Bocherens, H, Fizet, M, Mariotti A, Olive, C, Bellon, G & Billiou, D 1991b 'Application de la biogéochimie isotopique (^{13}C, ^{15}N) à la détermination du régime alimentaire des populations humaines et animales durant les périodes antique et médiévale', *Archives des Sciences de Genève* 44, 329-40

Bocherens, H, Mashkour, M, Drucker, D, Moussa, I & Billiou, D 2006 'Stable isotope evidence for palaeodiets in southern Turkmenistan during Historical period and Iron Age', *Journal of Archaeological Science* 33, 253-64

Boddington, A 1996 *Raunds Furnells. The Anglo-Saxon church and churchyard* (English Heritage Archaeological Report 7), London

Boháčová, I, Frolík, J, Hrdlička, L & Smetánka, Z 1992 'Prague and Prague castle, centre of the state of Bohemia in the ninth-thirteenth centuries', in Addyman, PV & Roskams, SJ (eds) *Urbanism: Medieval Europe 1992 Pre-Printed Papers Volume 1*, York, 89-93

Boldizsár P, Kocsis, E & Sabján, T 2007 *A diósgyőri vár középkori kályhacsempéi / Mittelalterliche Ofenkacheln der Burg von Diósgyőr*, Miskolc

Bolòs i Masclans, J & Pagès i Paretas, M 1982 'Les sepoltures excavades a la roca', in Riu, M (ed) *Necròpolis i sepultures medievals de Catalunya* (Acta Medievalia, Annex 1), Barcelona, 59-103

Bond, J 2001 'Monastic Water Management in Great Britain: A Review', in Keevill, G, Aston, M & Hall, T (eds) *Archaeology: Papers on the Study of Medieval Monasteries*, Oxford, 88-136

Bond, J 2004 *Monastic Landscapes*, Stroud

Bonde, S 1994 *Fortress-Churches of Languedoc. Architecture, Religion and Conflict in the High Middle Ages*, Cambridge

Bonnet, C 1993 *Les fouilles de l'ancien groupe épiscopal de Genève (1976-1993)* (Cahiers d'archéologie genevoise 1), Genève

Boockmann, H 1986 *Die Stadt im späten Mittelalter*, München

Borger, GJ 1992 'Draining – digging – dredging: the creation of a new landscape in the peat areas of the Low Countries', in: Verhoeven, JTA (ed) *Fens and Bogs in the Netherlands: Vegetation, History, Nutrient Dynamics and Conservation* (Geobotany 18), Dordrecht, 131-71

Boscardin, M-L 1982 *Burgen der Schweiz, Bd. 8 (Kantone Luzern und Aargau)*, Zürich

Boscardin, M-L 2005 'Production and use of soapstone vessels in the Swiss Alps', in Holm, I, Innselset, S & Øye, I (eds) *'Utmark'. The Outfield as Industry and Ideology in the Iron Age and the Middle Ages*, Bergen, 91-97

Bouby, L 2006 'Les semences carbonisées et la perception de l'économie végétale', in Maufras, O (ed) *Habitats, nécropoles et paysages dans la moyenne et la basse vallée du Rhône (VIIᵉ-XVᵉ s.): contribution des travaux du TGV-Méditerranée à l'étude des sociétés rurales médiévales* (Documents d'Archéologie Française 98), Paris, 217-39

Bowsher, D, Dyson, T, Holder, N & Howell, I 2007 *The London Guildhall: an archaeological history of a neighbourhood from early medieval to modern times*, London

Bracker, J, Henn, V & Postel, R (eds) 1999 *Die Hanse: Lebenswirklichkeit und Mythos*, Lübeck (third edition)

Brady, N & O'Conor, K 2005 'The later medieval use of crannogs in Ireland', *Ruralia* 5, 127-36

Braudel, F 1972 *The Mediterranean and the Mediterranean World in the Age of Philip II, Volume 1*, London

Braudel, F 1980 *On History*, London

Braudel, F & Spooner, F 1967 'Prices in Europe from 1450 to 1750', in Rich, EE & Wilson, CH (eds) *The Cambridge economic history of Europe Volume 4, The economy of expanding Europe in the 16th and 17th centuries*, Cambridge, 378-486

Braunfels, W 1972 (1980) *Monasteries of Western Europe. The Architecture of the Orders*, London (Princeton edition 1980)

Braunstein, P 2003 *Travail et entreprise au Moyen Âge*, Bruxelles

Bravard, J-P & Magny, M (eds) 2002 *Les fleuves ont une histoire. Paléo-environnement des rivières et des lacs français depuis 15000 ans*, Paris

Brenan, J 1998 'Furnishings', in Egan, G *The medieval household: daily living c. 1150-c. 1450*, London, 65-87

Brisbane, MA 1992 *The Archaeology of Novgorod, Russia: recent results from the town and its hinterland* (Society for *Medieval Archaeology* Monograph 13), Lincoln

Brisbane, M & Gaimster, D (eds) 2001 *Novgorod: The Archaeology of the Russian Medieval City and its Hinterland* (British Museum Occasional Paper 141), London

Brisbane, M, Hambleton, E, Maltby, M & Nosov, E 2007 'A monkey's tale: the skull of a macaque found at Ryurik Gorodishche, near Novgorod', *Medieval Archaeology* 51, 185-91

Brogiolo G.P. 1988, *Archeologia dell'Edilizia Storica. Documenti e metodi*, con contributi di Zonca A. e Zigrino L., Como

Brogiolo, GP 1997 'Dall'analisi stratigrafica degli elevati all'archeologia dell'architettura', *Archeologia dell'Architettura* 2, 181-4

Brogiolo, GP 2002 'L'archeologia dell'architettura in Italia nell'ultimo quinquennio (1997-2001), *Arqueología de la Arquitectura* 1, 19-26

Brogiolo, GP 2006 'Ha un futuro l'archeologia dell'architettura?', in Cucuzza, N & Medri, M (eds) *Archeologie. Studi in onore di Tiziano Mannoni*, Bari, 437-9

Brogiolo, GP 2007 'Dall'archeologia dell'architettura all'archeologia della complessità', *Pyrenae* 38/1, 7-38

Brooke, C 2006 *The Rise and Fall of the Medieval Monastery* London

Brothwell, DR & Pollard, AM (eds) 2001 *Handbook of Archaeological Sciences*, Chichester

Brown, A 1996 'Parish church building: the fabric,' in Blair, J & Pyrah, C (eds) *Church Archaeology: Research Directions for the Future* (CBA Research Report 104), York, 63-8

Brown, A.D. and Pluskowski, A.G. (2011) Detecting the environmental impact of the Baltic Crusades on a late medieval (13th-15th century) frontier landscape: palynological analysis from Malbork castle and hinterland, northern Poland. *Journal of Archaeological* Science 38, 1957-1966.

Brown, A, de Figueiredo, P & Grenville, J 1999 *The Rows of Chester* (English Heritage)

Brown, DH 1998 'Documentary sources as evidence for the exchange and consumption of pottery in 15th Century Southampton', in *Actas das 2as Jornadas de Cerâmica Medieval e Pós-Medieval: metodos e resultados para o seu estudo, Tondela (Portugal), 22-25 mars 1995*, Tondela, 429-38

Brown, DH 2002 *Pottery in Medieval Southampton c. 1066-1510* (Southampton Archaeology Monographs 8, CBA Research Report 133), York

Brown, DH, 1997, 'Pots from Houses', Medieval Ceramics 21, 83-94

Brown DH, Thomson RG, Vince AG with Williams DF, 2006, 'The Pottery' in Saunders A, Excavations at Launceston Castle, Cornwall (Society for Medieval Archaeology Monograph 24), 269-296

Brown, K 1976 *People of Salé: Tradition and Change in a Moroccan City, 1830-1930*, Cambridge (MA)

Brown, M 2006 *The Luttrell Psalter. A Facsimile with a commentary*, London

Brown, RJ 1986 *Timber-framed buildings of England*, London

Brun, P 2005 'From arrows to bullets: the fortification of Abdulla Khan Kala (Merv, Turkmenistan)', *Antiquity* 79, 616-24

Brunschvig, R 1947 'Urbanisme médiéval et droit musulman', *Revue des Etudes Islamiques* 15, 127-55

Brunskill, RW 1971 *Illustrated Handbook of Vernacular Architecture*, London

Brunskill, RW 2000 *Vernacular Architecture: an Illustrated Handbook*, fourth edition, London

Bucaria, N (ed) 1998 *Gli ebrei in Sicila dal tardoantico al medioevo*, Palermo

Buck, CE, Kenworthy, JB, Litton, CD & Smith, AFM 1991 'Combining archaeological and radiocarbon information: a Bayesian approach to calibration' *Antiquity* 65, 808-21

Buerger, LE 1975 'Reperti dagli scavi di Santa Reparata, Notizie preliminari', *Archeologia Medievale* 2, 191-210

Burnouf, J 2003 'La nature des médiévistes', in «Objets en crise, objets recomposés», *Études Rurales* 167/8, 215-26

Burnouf, J 2008 *Archéologie médiévale en France. Le second Moyen Âge (xiie-xvie siècle)*, Paris

Burnouf, J & Carcaud, N 2000 'L'homme et les vallées : les vals de Loire de Tours à Angers, *Annales de Bretagne et des Pays de l'Ouest* 107/1, 7-22

Burnouf, J & Leveau, P (ed) 2004 *Fleuves et marais, une histoire au croisement de la nature et de la culture*, Paris

Burnouf, J, Guilhot, J-O, Mandy, M-O & Orcel, C 1991 *Le pont de la Guillotière: franchir le Rhône à Lyon* (Documents d'Archéologie en Rhône-Alpes et en Auvergne 5), Lyon

Burnouf, J, Bravard, J-P & Chouquer, G (ed) 1997 *La dynamique des paysages protohistoriques, antiques, médiévaux et modernes* (XVIIe Rencontres internationales d'archéologie et d'histoire d'Antibes), Sophia-Antipolis

Burnouf, J, Muxart, T, Villalba, B & Vivien, F-D (eds) 2003 *Des milieux et des hommes: fragments d'histoires croisées*, Paris

Burrows, J & Gaimster, D 2001 'Ofenkachelfunde des Spätmittelalters aus der Pläterstrasse, Hansestadt Rostock', *Bodendenkmalpflege in Mecklenburg-Vorpommern Jahrbuch* 47 (1999), 279-304

Busko, C 2003 'La production de cuirs à Wroclaw pendant le bas moyen âge à la lumière des sources archéologiques', in Córdoba R (ed) *Mil años de trabajo del cuero*, Córdoba, 261-70

C

Cagnana, A 2000 *Archeologia dei materiali da costruzione,* Mantova

Cairns, C 1987 *Irish Tower Houses: a Co. Tipperary Case Study*, Athlone

Calvo Capilla, S 2001 Estudios sobre Arquitectura religiosa en al-Andalus: las pequeñas mezquitas en su contexto histórico y cultural, unpublished PhD dissertation, Universidad Autónoma de Madrid

Calvo Capilla, S 2004 'Las mezquitas de pequeñas ciudades y núcleos rurales de al-Andalus', *Ilu, Revista de Ciencias de las Religiones* 10, 39-63

Calvo Capilla, S 2007 'Las primeras mezquitas de al-Andalus a través de las fuentes árabes (92/711-170/785)', *Al-Qantara, Revista de estudios árabes* 28, 143-79

Cambon, C (ed) 1993 *Castres. Document d'évaluation du patrimoine archéologique urbain*, Tours

Cameron, E (ed) 1998 *Leather and Fur: Aspects of Early Medieval Trade and Technology*, London

Camille, M 1998 *Mirror in Parchment. The Luttrell Psalter and the Making of Medieval England*, Chicago

Camille, M 2001 '"For our devotion and pleasure": the sexual objects of Jean, Duc de Berry', *Art History* 24, 169-94

Campbell, B 1997 'Economic rent and the intensification of English agriculture 1086-1350', in Astill, G & Langdon, J (eds) *Medieval Farming and Technology*, Leiden, 225-50

Campbell, J 2000 'Power and authority 600-1300', *The Cambridge Urban History of Britain 1, 600-1540*, Cambridge, 51-78

Cano Piedra, C, 1996 *La cerámica verde-manganeso de Madinat Al-Zahra*, Granada

Cantera y Burgos, F 1984 *Sinagogas españolas* (second edition), Madrid

Caple, C 2006 *Objects: reluctant witnesses to the past*, London & New York

Cardon, D 2007 *Natural Dyes, Sources, Tradition, Technology and Science*, London

Carlsson, K 2008 'Kungahälla, Lödöse och Skara: om urbanisering i ett tidigmedeltida gränsland', in Andersson, H, Hansen, G & Øye, I (eds) *De første 200 årene – nytt blikk på 27 skandinaviske middelalderbyer* (Universitetet i Bergen Arkeologiske Skrifter 5), Bergen, 227-44

Carmona, N, García-Heras, M, Villegas, MA, Jiménez, P & Navarro, J 2008 'Study of chromophores of Islamic glasses from Al-Andalus (Murcia, Spain)', in Castillejo M, Oujja, M, Moreno, P, Radvan, R & Ruiz, J (eds) *Lasers in the Conservation of Artworks, Proceedings of the International Conference LACONA 7, Madrid, Spain, 17-21 September 2007*, Boca Raton, 73-8

Carmona, N, García-Heras, M, Villegas, MA, Jiménez, P & Navarro, J 2009 'Islamic glasses from Al-Andalus. Characterisation of materials from a Murcian workshop (12th century AD, Spain)', *Journal of Cultural Heritage* 10, 439-45

Carpenter, C 1987 'The religion of the gentry in fifteenth-century England,' in Williams, D (ed) *England in the Fifteenth Century*, Woodbridge, 53-74

Carretero, CH nd [c. 1987] *Museo de Telas Medievales. Monasterio de Santa María la Real de Huelgas*, Madrid

Carrillo, JG & González Ballesteros, JA 2009 'La Judería del Castillo de Lorca a partir de las evidencias arqueológicas', in *Lorca: Luces de Sefarad. Lights of Sepharad*, Murcia, 48-77

Carus-Wilson, E 1962-3 'The Medieval trade of the ports of the Wash', *Medieval Archaeology* 6-7, 182-201

Carver, MOH 1980 'The Excavation of three Medieval Craftsmen's Tenements in Sidbury, Worcester, 1976', in Carver, MOH (ed) *Medieval Worcester. An Archaeological Framework* (Transactions of the Worcestershire Archaeological Society third series 7), Worcester, 155-220

Carver, MOH 1983 'Forty French towns: an essay on archaeological site evaluation and historical aims', *Oxford Journal of Archaeology* 2-3, 339-78

Carver, MOH 1987 *Underneath English Towns. Interpreting urban Archaeology*, London

Carver, MOH 1990 'Digging for data: archaeological approaches to data definition, acquisition and analysis' in Francovich, R & Manacorda, D (eds) *Lo scavo archeologico: dalla diagnosi all'edizione*, Firenze, 45-120

Carver, MOH 1993 *Arguments in Stone. Archaeology and the European town in the first millennium*, Oxford

Carver, MOH 1996 'Transitions to Islam', in Christie, N & Loseby, S (eds) *Towns in Transition*, Leicester, 184-212

Carver, MOH 2002 'Marriages of true minds: archaeology with texts', in Cunliffe, B Davies, W & Renfrew, C (eds) *Archaeology: the widening debate*, Oxford, 465-96

Carver, MOH (ed) 2003 *The Cross goes North. Processes of Conversion in Northern Europe, AD 300-1300*, Woodbridge

Carver, MOH 2008 *Portmahomack. Monastery of the Picts*, Edinburgh

Carver, MOH 2009 *Archaeological Investigation*, Abingdon & New York

Carver MOH 2011 *Making archaeology happen: Design versus Dogma* Walnut Creek, California

Carver, MOH & Spall, C 2004 'Excavating a *parchmenerie*: archaeological correlates of making parchment at the Pictish monastery at Portmahomack, Easter Ross', *Proceedings of the Society of Antiquaries of Scotland* 134, 183-200

Casamar, M 1959 'Notas sobre cerámica del ajuar nazarí', *Al-Andalus* 24, 189-99

Casares Porcel, M, Tito Rojo, JY & Socorro Abreu, O 2003 'El jardín del Patio de la Acequia del Generalife II. Consideraciones a partir del análisis palinológico', *Cuadernos de la Alhambra* 39, 87-107

Cassuto, D 1980 'Edifici rituali degli ebrei nell'alto medioevo', in *Gli Ebrei nell'Alto Medioevo, Settimane di Studio del Centro Italiano di Studi sull'Alto Medioevo, 30 Marzo-5 Aprile 1978*, Spoleto, 1017-54

Castanet, C, 2008 *La Loire en Val d'Orléans. Dynamiques fluviales et socio-environnementales durant les derniers 30 000 ans: de l'hydrosystème à l'anthroposystème*, unpublished PhD dissertation, Université Paris 1 Panthéon-Sorbonne

Castellana G (ed) 1992 *Dagli scavi di Montevago e di Rocca di Entella un contributo di conoscenze per la storia dei Musulmani della Valle del Belice dal X al XIII secolo* (Atti del Convegno Nazionale Montevago 1990), Agrigento

Castro, A & Sebastian, L 2004 'Resultado preliminar da intervenção arqueológica no Mosteiro de S. João de Tarouca 1998-2002', in *Actas do Seminário Internacional Tarouca e Cister: Espaço, Espírito e Poder*, Tarouca, 163-87

Caucanas S, 1995 *Moulins et irrigation en Roussillon du IXème au XVème siècle*, Paris

Caune, A & Ose, I (eds) 2009 *The Hansa town Riga as mediator between East and West*, Riga

Cavada, E & Gentilini, G (eds) 2000 *Archeologia dei centri storici: analisi, conoscenza e conservazione* (Atti del Seminario al Palazzo Geremia, Trento, 14-21 novembre 1998), Trento

Cavada, E & Gentilini, G (eds) 2002 *Il progetto di restauro architettonico: dall'analisi all'intervento* (Atti del Seminario in archeologia dell'architettura al Palazzo Geremia, Trento, 27-28 ottobre 2000), Trento

Černý, E 1994 'Die historisch-geographische Erforschung der wüsten mittelalterlichen Dörfer und Fluren im Drahaner Hochland', *Siedlungsforschung: Archäologie-Geschichte-Geographie* 12, 125-41

Chalmeta Gendrón, P 1973 *El señor del zoco en España*, Madrid

Chapelot, S & Fossier, R 1985 *The Village and the House in the Middle Ages*, London

Chapman, HP & Fenwick, H 2002 'Contextualising previous excavation: the implications of applying GPS survey and GIS modelling technique to Watton Priory, East Yorkshire', *Medieval Archaeology* 46, 81-90

Charleston, RJ 1991 'Vessel glass', in Blair, J & Ramsey, N (eds) *English Medieval Industries. Craftsmen, techniques, products*, London & Rio Grande, 237-64

Cherry, J 1989 'Symbolism and survival: medieval horns of tenure', *Antiquaries Journal* 69, 111-18

Cherry, J 1991a *Medieval decorative art*, London

Cherry, J 1991b 'Leather', in Blair, J & Ramsey, N (eds) *English Medieval Industries. Craftsmen, techniques, products*, London & Rio Grande, 295-318

Childs, W 1995 'Documentary evidence for the import of Spanish pottery to England in the Later Middle Ages (thirteenth to early sixteenth centuries)', in Gerrard, CM, Gutiérrez, A & Vince, A (eds) *Spanish medieval ceramics in Spain and the British Isles* (British Archaeological Reports International Series 610), Oxford, 25-31

Chomel, V 1976 *Histoire de Grenoble*, Toulouse

Chouquer, G 2003 (ed) *Objets en crise, objets recomposés* (*Etudes Rurales* 167/168), Paris

Chouquer, G 2005 (ed) *Nouveaux chapitres d'histoire du paysage* (*Etudes Rurales*, 175-176), Paris

Chouquer, G 2006a 'Le paysage et l'environnement seraient-ils en train de changer l'archéologie?', *Revue Archéologique du Loiret* 29, 95-8

Chouquer, G 2006b 'Quels territoires pour les médiévistes de demain?', *Etudes Rurales* 177, 179-88

Chouquer, G 2006c 'La question de l'émergence et de la mobilité de la planimétrie rurale à l'Âge du Fer. Approches comparées en Gaule et en Italie', *Les Nouvelles de l'Archéologie* 104/105, 72-9

Choyke, AM, Lyublyanovics, K & Bartosiewicz, L 2005 'The various voices of medieval animal bones', in Jaritz, G & Choyke, AM (ed) *Animal Diversities*, Krems, 23-49

Christie, N 2008 'Of sheep and men: castles and transhumance in the upper Sangro valley and in the Cicolano, Italy', in Lock, G & Faustoferri, A (eds) *Archaeology and landscape in central Italy: papers in memory of John A. Lloyd*, Oxford, 105-20

Clark, D 2000 'The shop within: an analysis of architectural evidence for medieval shops', *Architectural History* 43, 58-87

Clark, G, Burley, D & Murray, T 2008 'Monumentality and the development of the Tongan maritime chiefdom', *Antiquity* 82, 994-1008

Clark, J (ed) 1995 *The medieval horse and its equipment, c. 1150-c. 1450 (Medieval Finds from Excavations in London 5)*, London (Second edition Woodbridge 2004)

Clarke, H 1984 (1986) *The Archaeology of Medieval England*, London

Clarke, R 2004 'Rivenhall revisited: further excavations in the churchyard of St Mary and All Saints, 1999', *Essex Archaeology and History* 35 (third series), 26-77

Clarke, R, Dean, M, Hutchinson, G, McGrail, S & Squirrell, J 1993 'Recent work on the R. Hamble wreck near Bursledon, Hampshire', *International Journal of Nautical Archaeology* 22, 21-44

Claughton, P 2008 'Coal, Ore and Metals: Coastal Mining Landscapes of South-West Britain', in Bartels, C, Ruiz del Árbol, M, van Londen, H & Orejas, A (eds) *Landmarks: Profiling Europe's Historic Landscapes*, Bochum, 163-72

Clavel, B 2001 *L'animal dans l'alimentation médiévale et moderne en France du nord (XIIe - XVIIe siècles)* (Revue Archélogique de Picardie 19), Amiens

Clifton-Taylor, A 1965 *The Pattern of English Building* (second edition), London

Codreanu, S 2004 'Das Jüdische Viertel am Neupfarrplatz in Regensburg: Jüdischer Alltag aus der Sicht der Neuesten Ausgrabungen', in Wamers, E & Backhaus, F (eds) *Synagogen, Mikwen, Siedlungen: Jüdisches Alltagsleben in Lichte Neuer Archäologischer Funde* (Schriften des Archäologischen Museums Frankfurt 19), Frankfurt am Main, 117-28

Cohn, SK Jr 2002 *The Black Death Transformed: Disease and Culture in early Renaissance Europe*, London

Colardelle, M & Verdele, E 1993 *Les habitats du lac de Paladru (Isère) dans leur environnement*, Paris

Colardelle, M, Demians d'Archimbaud, G & Raynaud, C 1996 'Typo-chronologie des sépultures du Bas-Empire à la fin du Moyen-Âge dans le Sud-Est de la Gaule', in Galinié, H & Zadora-Rio, E (eds) *Archéologie du cimetière chrétien, Actes du colloque d'Orléans (28 sept.-1er oct. 1994)* (11e Supplément à la Revue Archéologique du Centre), Tours, 271-303

Colardelle, R 2008 *La ville et la mort: 2000 ans de tradition funéraire à Grenoble: Saint-Laurent*, Turnhout

Coll Conesa, J 2007 'El comercio de la cerámcia valenciana en Flandes y el Atlántico Norte', in Mira, E & Delva A (eds) *A la Búsqueda del Toisón de Oro. La Europa de los Príncipes. La Europa de las Ciudades*, Valencia

Conan, M (ed) 2007 *Middle East Garden Traditions: Unity and Diversity*, Washington DC

Conyers, LB 2010 'Ground-penetrating radar for anthropological research', *Antiquity* 84, 175-84

Conyers, LB & Goodman, D 1997 *Ground-penetrating radar: an introduction for archaeologists*, Walnut Creek (CA)

Cook, GH 1954 *The English Mediaeval Parish Church*, London

Coomans, T 2007 'Belfries, Cloth Halls, Hospitals and Mendicant Churches: a new urban architecture in the Low Countries around 1300', in Gajewski, A & Opačič, Z (eds) *The Year 1300 and the creation of a New European Architecture*, Turnhout, 185-202

Cooper, TP 1913 'The medieval highways, streets, open ditches and sanitary conditions in the City of York', *Yorkshire Archaeological Journal* 22, 270-86

Cosmopolitiques 2002 *La nature n'est plus ce qu'elle était* (Revue Cosmopolitiques 1)

Coulson, C 1995 'Battlements and the bourgeoisie: municipal status and the apparatus of urban defence in later-medieval England', in Church, S & Harvey, R (eds) *Medieval Knighthood* 5, 119-95

Council of Europe 1999 *Report on the situation of urban archaeology in Europe*, Strasbourg

Courteney, L 2007 'The hospital of Notre-Dame des Fontenilles at Tonnerre: medicine as misericordia', in Bowers, B (ed) *The Medieval Hospital and Medical Practice*, Aldershot, 77-106

Courtney, P 1998 *Saxon and Medieval Leicester. The Making of an Urban Landscape*, Leicester

Cowgill, J, de Neergaard, M & Griffiths, N 1987 *Knives and scabbards* (Medieval Finds from Excavations in London 1), London (Reprint Woodbridge 2000)

Crane, E 1983 *The archaeology of beekeeping*, London

Crawford, DH 2007 *Deadly Companions: How Microbes Shaped Our History*, Oxford

Creighton, OH 2002 *Castles and Landscapes*, London

Creighton, OH 2007 'Contested townscapes: the walled city as world heritage', *World Archaeology* 39, 339-54

Creighton, OH 2009 *Designs upon the Land: Elite Landscapes of the Middle Ages*, Woodbridge

Creighton, OH & Higham, R 2005 *Medieval Town Walls*, Stroud

Cressier, P (ed) 2000 *Actas del seminario 'El vidrio en al-Andalus' (Madrid, 19 de febrero 1996)*, Madrid

Cressier, P & García-Arenal, M, (eds) 1998 *Actas del Seminario 'Genèse de la ville islamique en al-Andalus et au Maghreb occidental'*, Madrid

Cressier, P, Hassar-Benslimane, J & Touri, A 1986 'El urbanismo rural de Belyounech: aproximación metodológica a un yacimiento medieval islámico del norte de Marruecos', *Arqueología Espacial. Coloquio sobre el microespacio 4, Vol. 10*, Teruel, 327-49

Crosetto, A 1998 'Sepolture e usi funerari medievali', in Mercando, L & Micheletto, E (eds) *Archeologia in Piemonte, III. Il Medioevo*, Torino, 209-32

Crossley-Holland, N 1996 *Living and Dining in Medieval Paris*, Cardiff

Crouch, D 2000 *Piety, Fraternity and Power. Religious Guilds in Late Medieval Yorkshire*, Woodbridge

Crowfoot, E, Pritchard, F & Staniland, K 1992 *Textiles and clothing c. 1150-c. 1450, Medieval Finds from Excavations in London* 4), London (New edition and reprint Woodbridge 2001 & 2006)

Crubézy, E, Ricault, F-X, Martin, H, Erdenebaatar, S, Coqueugnot, H, Maureille, B & Giscard, P-H 2006 'Inhumation and cremation in medieval Mongolia: analysis and analogy', *Antiquity* 80, 894-905

Cummins, J 1988 *The Hound and the Hawk: the Art of Medieval Hunting*, London

Currie, CRJ 1988 'Time and chance: modelling the attrition of old houses', *Vernacular Architecture* 19, 1-9

Currie, CRJ 2004 'The unfulfilled potential of the documentary sources', *Vernacular Architecture* 35, 1-11

D

Dabrowska, E 2005 'Passeport pour l'au-delà. Essai sur la mentalité médiévale', *Le Moyen Age* (2005.2), 313-37

Dahm, C, Lobbedey, U & Weisgerber, G 1998 *Der Altenberg. Bergwerk und Siedlung aus dem 13. Jahrhundert im Siegerland*, Münster

Daly, A 2007 A dendrochronological analysis of structural oak timber in Northern Europe, c. AD 1000 to c. AD 1650, unpublished Ph.D dissertation, University of Southern Denmark

Daoulatli. A. (ed.) *Couleurs de Tunisie, 25 siècles de céramique, París*, 1995

Davey P & Hodges, R (eds) 1983 *Ceramics and Trade*, Sheffield

Davidson, CF 1999 'Change and change back: the development of English parish church chancels,' *Studies in Church History* 35, 65-77

Davies, JG 1982 *Temples, Churches and Mosques: a guide to the appreciation of religious architecture*, Oxford

Davies, MP & Saunders, A 2004 *The History of the Merchant Taylors' Company*, Leeds

Davison, B 1969-70 'Aldingham', *Current Archaeology* 2, 23-4

Dean, T 2001 *Crime in Medieval Europe 1200-1500*, Harlow

De Boe, G & Verhaege, F (eds) 1997 *Death and Burial in Medieval Europe. Papers of the Medieval Europe Brugge 1997 Conference*, Zellik

de Bont, C 2008 Vergeten land. Ontginning, bewoning en waterbeheer in de West-Nederlandse veengebieden (800-1350), unpublished PhD dissertation, Wageningen University & Research Centre

Deborde, G, Montembault, V & Yvinec, J 2002 'Les ateliers de tanneurs de la rue du Moulinet à Troyes (Aube)', in Audoin-Rouzeau, F & Beyries, S (eds) *Le travail du cuir de la Préhistoire à nos jours*, Antibes, 283-314

DeCorse, CR 2001 *An Archaeology of Elmina: Africans and Europeans on the Gold Coast, 1400-1900*, Washington (DC)

De Groote, K 2008 *Middeleeuws aardewerk in Vlaanderen. Techniek, typologie, chronologie en evolutievan het gebruiksgoed in de regio Oudenaardein de volle en late middeleeuwen (10de-16deeeuw)* (Relicta Monografieën 1), Brussel

De Hamel, C 1992 *Scribes and illuminators*, London

Delort, R 1978 *Le commerce des fourrures en Occident à la fin du Moyen Age (vers 1300-vers 1450)* (Bibliothèques des Ecoles Françaises d'Athènes et de Rome 236), Rome

De Meulemeester, J 2005 'Granaries and irrigation: archaeological and ethnological investigations in the Iberian peninsula and Morocco', *Antiquity* 79, 609-15

De Meulemeester, J & O'Conor, K 2007 'Fortifications', in Graham-Campbell, J & Valor, M (eds) 2007 *The Archaeology of Medieval Europe. Volume 1: Eighth to Twelfth Centuries AD*, Aarhus, 316-41

De Meulemeester, J & Poisson, J-M 2002 'La Tour d'Albon (Drôme, France) et le Dauphiné', in Helmig, G, Scholkmann, B & Untermann, M (eds) *Centre-Region-Periphery. Medieval Europe Basel 2002* (3 volumes), Hertingen, 91-5

Demians d'Archimbaud, G 1980 *Les Fouilles de Rougiers*, Paris

Denham, T, Haberle, S & Pierret, A 2009 'A multidisciplinary method for the investigation of early agriculture: learning lessons from Kuk', in Fairbairn, A, O'Connor, S & Marwick, B (eds) New Directions in Archaeological Science (Terra Australis 28), Canberra

DeNiro, MJ 1985 'Post-mortem preservation and alteration of in vivo bone collagen isotope ratios on relation to palaeodietary reconstruction', *Nature* 317, 806-9

DeNiro, MJ & Epstein, S 1978 'Influence of diet on the distribution of carbon isotopes in animals', *Geochimica et Cosmochimica Acta* 42, 495-506

DeNiro, MJ & Epstein, S 1981 'Influence of diet on the distribution of nitrogen isotopes in animals', *Geochimica et Cosmochimica Acta* 45, 341-51

Devisse, J 1988 'Trade and trade routes in West Africa', in el Fasi, M (ed) *General history of Africa Voume 3: Africa from the seventh to the eleventh century*, Berkeley, 367-435

Devisse, J & S Labib 1984 'Africa in inter-continental relations', in D Niane (ed) *UNESCO General History of Africa. Voume 4: Africa from the Twelfth to the Sixteenth Century*, Oxford, 635-72

Dickie, J 1965/66 'Notas sobre la jardinería árabe en la España musulmana', *Miscelánea de Estudios Árabes y Hebraicos* 14-15, 75-87

Dickie, J 1992 'The hispano-arab garden: notes towards a typology, in Salma Khadra Jayyusi (ed) *The legacy of Muslim Spain* (Handbuch der Orientalistik 12), Leiden, 1016-35

Dierkens, A 2002 'Avant-corps, galilées, massifs occidentaux: quelques remarques méthodologiques en guise de conclusion', in Sapin, C (ed) *Avant-nefs et espaces d'accueil dans l'église entre le IVe et le XIIe siècle, Actes du colloque international du CNRS, Auxerre 1999*, Paris, 495-503

Di Gangi, G 2001 *L'Attività mineraria e metallurgica nelle alpi occidentali Italiane nel médioevo. Piemonte e valle d'Aosta: fonti scritti e materiali* (British Archaeological Reports International Series 951), Oxford

Dillman, P, Fluzin, P & Chevallier, P 2002 'Determination of ironmaking processes using synchrotron microprobe', in Jerem, E & Biró, KT (eds) *Archaeometry 98 Proceedings of the 31st Symposium, Budapest, April 26-May 3 1998* (British Archaeological Reports International Series, 1043 II), Oxford, 327-44

Dinzelbacher, P 2000 *Handbuch der Religionsgeschichte im deutschsprachigen Raum* 2, Paderborn

Di Stefano, CA & Cadei A (eds) 1994 *Federico II e la Sicilia dalla terra alla corona. Archeologia, architettura e arti della Sicilia in età sveva,* (Catalogo della mostra (Palermo, dicembre 1994-aprile 1995), Palermo

Djaït, H 1986 *Al-Kúfa: naissance de la ville islamique*, París

Dobson, B 2006 *The Merchant Taylors of York: a history of the craft and company from the fourteenth to the twentieth century*, York

Doglioni, F (ed) 1987 *Ambienti di dimore medievali a Verona*, Verona

Doig, A 2008 *Liturgy and Architecture from the early Church to the Middle Ages* Aldershot

Donnelly, C, Logue, P, O'Neill, J & O'Neill, J 2007 'Timber castles and towers in sixteenth-century Ireland: some evidence from Ulster', *Archaeology Ireland* 21, 22-5

D'Onofrio, M 1994 *I Normanni popolo d'Europa 1030-1200*, Venezia

Doppelfeld, O 1959a 'Die Ausgrabangen im Kölner Judenviertel', in Asaria, Z (ed) *Die Juden in Köln*, Köln, 71-145

Doppelfeld, O 1959b '"Residenzen Gottes": die ältesten Synagogen von Köln', in *Schriftenreihe der Kölnischen Gesellschaft für christlich-jüdische Zusammenarbeit* 4, Köln

Dopplefeld, O & Weyres, W 1980 *Die Ausgrabungen im Dom zu Köln,* Mainz am Rhein

Douglas, M 1966 *Purity and Danger. An Analysis of Concepts of Pollution and Taboo*, London

Drancourt, M, Aboudharam, G, Signoli, M, Dutour, O & Raoult, D 1998 'Detection of 400-year old *Yersinia pestis* DNA in human dental pulp: an approach to the diagnosis of ancient septicemia', *Proceedings of the National Academy of Sciences of the United States of America* 95, 12637-40

Drancourt, M, Signoli, M, Dang, LV, Bizot, B, Roux, V, Tzortzis, S & Raoult, D 2007 '*Yersinia pestis orientalis* in remains of ancient plague patients', *Emerging Infectious Diseases* (online journal) 13/2. Available at http://www.cdc.gov/EID/content/13/2/332.htm

Drescher, H 1968 'Mittelalterliche Dreibeintöpfe aus Bronze Bericht über die Bestandsaufnahme und Versuch einer chronologischen Ordnung', in Renaud, JGN (ed) *Rotterdam Papers* 1, 23-33

Drescher, H 1969 'Mittelalterliche Dreibeintöpfe aus Bronze: Bericht über die Bestandaufnahme und Versuch einer chronologischen Ordnung', *Neue Ausgrabungen und Forschungen in Niedersachsen* 4, 287-315

Drescher, H 1982 'Zu den bronzenen Grapen des 12.–16. Jahrhunderts aus Nordwestdeutschland', in Wittstock, J (ed) *Aus dem Alltag der mittelalterlichen Stadt*, Bremen 157-74

Drewett, PL 1997 'Rich man, poor man: an archaeological comparison of the economy of a castle and a farm in East Sussex, England, c 1100-1500 AD', in Kubková, J et al. (eds) *Život v archeologii středověku – Life in the archaeology of the Middle Ages: papers in honour of Miroslav Richter & Zdeněk Smetánka,* Prague, 160-8

Driessen, H & Otto T (eds) 2000 *Perplexities of Identification. Anthropological Studies in Cultural Differentiation and the Use of Resources*, Aarhus

Drucker, D & Henry-Gambier, D 2005 'Determination of the dietary habits of a Magdalenian woman from Saint-Germain-la-Rivière in southwestern France using stable isotopes', *Journal of Human Evolution* 49, 19-35

Drummond-Murray, J, & Liddle, J 2003 'Medieval Industry in the Walbrook Valley', *London Archaeologist* 10, 87-94

Duda, D 1970 *Spanische Islamische Keramik aus Almería vom 12. bis 15. Jahrhundert*, Heidelberg

Duffy, E 1992 *The Stripping of the Altars. Traditional Religion in England 1400-1580*, New Haven (CT) & London)

D'Ulizia, A 2005 'L'archeologia dell'architettura in Italia: sintesi e bilancio degli studi, *Archeologia dell'architettura* 10, 9-41

Duncan, CJ, & Scott, S 2005 'What caused the Black Death?', *Postgraduate Medical Journal* 81, 315-20

Dunning, GC 1977 'Mortars', in Clarke, H & Carter, A (eds) *Excavations in King's Lynn, 1963-1970* (Society for Medieval Archaeology Monograph Series 7, The King's Lynn Archaeological Survey 2), London, 320-47

Durham, K 2008 *Strongholds of the Border Rievers*, Botley

Dyer, C 1985 'Power and conflict in the medieval English village,' in Hooke, D (ed) *Medieval Villages* (Oxford University Committee for Archaeology Monograph 5), Oxford, 27-32

Dyer, C 1986 'English peasant buildings in the later Middle Ages (1200-1500)', *Medieval Archaeology* 30, 19-45

Dyer, C 1988 'Documentary Evidence: Problems and Enquiries', in Astill, G & Grant, A (eds) *The countryside of medieval England*, Oxford, 12-35

Dyer, C 1997a 'Recent developments and future prospects in research into English medieval rural settlements', in De Boe, G & Verhaeghe, F (eds) *Rural settlements in Medieval Europe. Papers of the Medieval Europe Brugge 1997 Conference, Vol. 6*, Zellik, 55-61

Dyer, C 1997b 'Medieval farming and technology: conclusion', in Astill, G & Langdon, J (eds) *Medieval Farming and Technology*, Leiden, 293-312

Dyer, C 1997c 'History and vernacular architecture', *Vernacular Architecture* 28, 1-8

Dymond, D 1998 'Five building contracts from fifteenth-century Suffolk', *Antiquaries Journal* 78, 269-87

Dymond, D 2003 'The chapel of ease: symbol of local identity and ambition,' *The Ricardian* 13, 203-16

E

Eames, P 1977 *Furniture in England, France and the Netherlands from the twelfth to the fifteenth Century*, London

Earle, T & K Lowe 2005 *Black Africans in Renaissance Europe*, Cambridge

Edge, D 2002 'Scientific analysis of arms and armour at the Wallace collection, London', in Helmig, G, Scholkmann, B & Untermann, M (eds) *Centre, Region, Periphery, Medieval Europe Basel 2002*, Hertingen, 277-9

Egan, G 1998 *The medieval household: daily living c. 1150-c. 1450*, London

Egan, G 2005a *Material culture in London in an Age of Transition. Tudor and Stuart period finds c. 1450-c. 1700 from excavations at Riverside sites in Southwark*, (Museum of London Archaeology Service, Monograph Series 19), London

Egan, G 2005b 'Urban and rural finds: material culture of town and country c. 1050-1500', in Giles, K & Dyer, C (eds) *Town and country in the Middle Ages. Contrasts, contexts and interconnections 1100-1500* (Society for Medieval Archaeology, Monograph Series 22), Leeds, 197-210

Egan, G & Pritchard, S 1991 *Dress accessories c. 1150-c. 1450 (Medieval Finds from Excavations in London 3)*, London (New edition Woodbridge 2002)

Elfwendahl, M & Gaimster, D 1995 'I Dagmar Sellings fotspår: en ny granskning av keramiken från Slottsfjärden i Kalmar', in *Kalmar län 1995*, Kalmar, 95-100

Ellmers, D 1992 'Bodenfunde und andere Zeugnisse zur frühen Schiffahrt der Hansestadt Lübeck. Teil 2: Bauteile und Ausrüstungsgegenstände von Wasserfahrzeugen aus den Grabungen Alfstrasse 38 und an der Untertrave/Kaimauer', *Lübecker Schriften zur Archäologie und Kulturgeschichte* 18, 7-21

Emery, A 1996, 2000, 2006 *Greater Medieval Houses of England and Wales 1300-1500 Volumes 1-3*, Cambridge

Emery, A 2000 *Greater Medieval Houses of England and Wales 1300-1500 Volume*

Endres, W & Lichtwark, F (eds) 1995 *Zur Regionalität der Keramik des Mittelalters und der Neuzeit: Beiträge des 26. Internationalen Hafnerei-Symposiums, Soest 5.10.–9.10.1993* (Denkmalpflege und Forschung in Westfalen 32), Bonn

Engel, A & Serrure, R 1891-1905 *Traité de Numismatique du Moyen Age* (3 volumes), Paris

Engels, R 2004a 'Topography of Jewish Speyer in the Middle Ages', in Historisches Museum der Pfalz, Speyer (ed) *The Jews of Europe in the Middle Ages*, Speyer, 69-76

Engels, R 2004b 'Zur Topographie der jüdischen Kult- und Wohngebiete im Mittelalter', in Historischer Verein der Pfalz (ed) *Die Juden von Speyer, Beiträge zur Speyerer Stadtgeschichte* 9, Speyer, 93-124

English Heritage 2006 *Understanding Historic Buildings*. Available online at www.english-heritage.org.uk/publications/understanding-historic-buildings

Epstein, SA 1991. *Wage Labour and Guilds in Medieval Europe*, Chapel Hill (NC) & London

Ervynck, A 1991 '"De beer die woonde op de burg…": mens en dier ni een vroegmiddeleeuwse versterking', in De Witte, H (ed) *De Brugse Burg. Van grafelijke versterking tot moderne stadskern*, Brugge, 170-80

Ervynck, A 1992 'Medieval castles as top-predators of the feudal system: an. archaeozoological approach,' *Château Gaillard* 15, 151-9

Ervynck, A 1993 'In memoriam: de bruin beer der Benelux', *Zoogdier* 4/3, 4-11

Ervynck, A 1996 'Food rules and status: Patterns of fish consumption in a monastic community (Ename, Belgium)', *Archaeofauna* 5, 155-164

Ervynck, A 2004 'Orant, pugnant, laborant. The diet of the three orders in the feudal society of medieval north-western Europe', in O' Day, SJ, Van Neer, W & Ervynck, A (eds) *Behaviour behind Bones: the Zooarchaeology of Ritual, Religion, Status and Identity*, Oxford, 215-23

Ervynck, A, Van Neer, W, Hüster-Plogmann, H & Schibler, J 2003 'Beyond affluence: the zooarchaeology of luxury', *World Archaeology* 34/3, 428-41

Esquieu, Y 1996 'Les caveaux funéraires', in Galinié, H & Zadora-Rio, E (eds) *Archéologie du cimetière chrétien, Actes du colloque d'Orléans (28 sept.–1er oct. 1994)* (11e Supplément à la Revue Archéologique du Centre), Tours, 205-14

Eun-Joo Lee, Dong Hoon Shin, Hoo Yul Yang, Spigelman, M & Se Gweon Yim 2009 'Eung Tae's tomb: a Joseon ancestor and the letters of those that loved him', *Antiquity* 83, 145-56

Evans, C & Sorensen, MLS with Hill, JD & Richter, K 2007 Cidade Velha, Cape Verde, archaeological excavations: the 2007 season, unpublished report, Cambridge

Evans, DH 1987 'Reflections on the study of imported ceramics' in Vyner, B & Wrathmell, S (eds) *Studies in Medieval and Later Pottery in Wales*, Cardiff, 199-216

Evans, DH 1999 'The trade of Hull between 1200 and 1700', in Dunckel, R, Gläser, M & Oltmanns, U (eds) *Lübecker Kolloquium zur Stadtarchäoologie im Hanseraum 2: der Handel*, Lübeck, 59-97

Evans, J, & O'Connor, TP 1999 *Environmental Archaeology. Principles and Methods*, Stroud

Evershed, RP, Dudd, SN, Lockheart, MJ & Jim, S 2001 'Lipids in archaeology', in Brothwell, DR & Pollard, AM (eds) *Handbook of Archaeological Sciences*, Chichester, 331-50

F

Fabre-Vassas, C 1997 *The Singular Beast: Jews, Christians and the Pig*, New York

Farr, JR 2000 *Artisans in Europe 1300-1914*, Cambridge

Fassbinder, S 2009 'Umbrüche und Kontinuität: das Wallfahrtswesen vor und nach der Reformation im Spiegel der Archäologie', in Scholkmann, B, Frommer, S, Vossler, C & Wolf, M (eds) *Zwischen Tradition und Wandel: Archäologie des 15. und 16. Jahrhunderts* (Tübinger Forschungen zur historischen Archäologie 3), Büchenbach, 89-101

Faulkner, PA 1958 'Domestic planning from the twelfth to the fourteenth centuries', *Archaeological Journal* 115, 150-83

Faulkner, PA 1966 'Medieval undercrofts and town houses', *Archaeological Journal* 123, 120-35

Favreau, R 1997 *Épigraphie médiévale*, Turnhout

Fawcett, R (ed) 2005 *Royal Dunfermline* (Society of Antiquaries of Scotland Monograph 31), Edinburgh

Fay, I 2007 Health and Disease in Medieval and Tudor Norwich, unpublished PhD dissertation, University of East Anglia, Norwich

Fehring, GP 1991 *The Archaeology of Medieval Germany: an introduction*, London & New York

Fehring, GP 1996 *Stadtarchäologie in Deutschland* (Sonderheft der Zeitschrift *Archäologie in Deutschland*), Stuttgart

Felgenhauer-Schmidt, S 1993 *Die Sachkultur des Mittelalters im Lichte der archäologischen Funde*, Frankfurt am Main

Fenn, TR, Killick, DJ, Chesley, J, Magnavita, S & Ruiz, J 2009 'Contacts between West Africa and Roman North Africa: archaeometallurgical results from Kissi, northeastern Burkina Faso', in Magnavita, S, Koté, L, Breunig, P & Idé, OA (eds) *Cultural and technological Developments in First Millennium BC/AD West Africa*, Frankfurt am Main, 119-46

Fenton A 1999 *Scottish Country Life* (East Linton)

Fentz, M 1999 'Dragter', in Roesdahl, E (ed) *Dagligliv i Danmarks middelalder: en arkæologisk kulturhistorie*, København, 150-171

Ferenc, D 1994 *Sopron: Old Synagogue/Alt-Synagoge*, Budapest

Fernandez Armesto, F 1987 *Before Columbus. Exploration and Colonization from the Mediterranean to the Atlantic, 1229-1492*, Philadelphia

Fernández García R, 1995 Historia del jardín sevillano: Recopilación y edición crítica de fuentes, unpublished PhD dissertation, University of Seville

Fernandéz Navarro, E 2008 *Tradición tecnológica de la cerámica de cocina almohade-nazarí*, Granada

Fernandéz Sotelo, E 1988 *Ceuta medieval. Aportación al estudio de las cerámicas (S. X-XV)* (3 volumes), Ceuta

Fernandéz Sotelo, E 2005 *Los silos medievales en la arqueología ceutí*, Ceuta

Finan, T & O'Conor, K 2002 'The moated site at Cloonfree, Co. Roscommon', *Journal of the Galway Archaeological and Historical Society* 54, 72-87

Finch, J 2004 'The churches,' in Rawcliffe, C & Wilson, R (eds) *Medieval Norwich*, London, 49-72

Fingerlin, I 1971 *Gürtel des hohen und späten Mittelalters* (Kunstwissenschaftliche Studien 46), Munich & Berlin

Finucane, RC 1977 *Miracles and Pilgrims: popular belief in medieval England*, London

Fiorato, V, Boylston, A & Knüsel, C (eds) 2000 *Blood Red Roses: the archaeology of a mass grave from the battle of Towton, AD 1461*, Oxford

FitzPatrick, E 2009 'Native enclosed settlement and the problem of the Irish 'ring-fort' *Medieval Archaeology* 53, 271-307

Fixot, M & Zadora-Rio, E 1989 *L'Eglise, le terroir*, Paris

Flambard-Héricher, A-M 2002 *Potiers et poteries du Bessin. Histoire et archéologie d'un artisanat rural du XIe au XXe siècle en Normandie*, Caen

Flandrin, J-L & Montanari, M 1996 *Histoire de l'alimentation*, Paris

Flandrin, J-L 1984 *Familles, Parenté, Maison, Sexualité dans l'ancienne société*, Paris

Flores Escobosa, I 1988 *Estudio preliminar sobre loza azul y dorada nazarí de la Alhambra*, Madrid

Flores Escobosa, I, Muñoz Martin, M, Dominguez Bedmar, M 1989 *Cerámica hispanomusulmana en Almería: loza dorada y azul*, Almería

Flüeler, M & Flüeler, N (eds) 1992 *Stadtluft, Hirsebrei und Bettelmönch: Die Stadt um 1300*, Stuttgart & Zürich

Fogel, ML, Tuross, N & Owsley DW 1989 'Nitrogen isotope tracers of human lactation in modern and archaeological populations, *Annual Report of the Direction, Geophysical Laboratory, Carnegie Institution*, 111-117

Ford, JA 1992 'Art and identity in the parish communities of late medieval Kent,' in Wood, D (ed) *The Church and the Arts* (Studies in Church History 28), Oxford, 225-37

Forest, V 2006 'Etudes archéozoologiques', in Maufras, O (ed) *Habitats, nécropoles et paysages dans la moyenne et la basse vallée du Rhône (VIIᵉ–XVᵉ s.): contribution des travaux du TGV-Méditerranée à l'étude des sociétés rurales médiévales* (Documents d'Archéologie Française 98), 241-61

Forestier, JCN 1915 'Los jardines hispano-musulmanes y andaluces', *Bética* 43-44

Forey, A 1992 *The Military Orders from the Twelfth to the Early Fourteenth Centuries*, London

Forsyth, H with Egan, G 2005 *Toys, trifles & trinkets. Base metal miniatures from London's river foreshore, 1150-1800,* London

Fox, Sir C & Raglan, Baron FRS 1951 *Monmouthshire houses: a study of building techniques and smaller house-plans in the fifteenth to seventeenth centuries, Volume 1*, Cardiff

Foy, D 1988 *La verre médiéval et son artisanat en France méditerranéenne*, Paris

Foy, D & Sennequier, G (eds) 1989 *A travers le verre du Moyen Age à la Renaissance*, Rouen

Foy, D & Sennequier, G 1991 *Ateliers de verriers de l'antiquité à la période pré-industrielle*, Rouen

Framework Archaeology 2008 *From hunter gatherers to huntsmen. A history of the Stansted landscape* (Framework Archaeology Monograph 2), Oxford

Francovich, R 1985 'Rocca San Silvestro: an archaelogical project for the study of a mining village in Tuscany', in *Medieval iron in society: papers presented at the symposium in Norberg, May 6-10, 1985* Stockholm, 318-40

Francovich, R 1990 'Miniere e metallurgia nella Toscana preindustriale: il contributo delle fonti geo-iconografiche', *Archeologia Medievale* 17, 695-710

Francovich, R (ed) 1993 *Archeologia delle attività estrattive e metallurgiche*, Firenze

Francovich, R 2006 'Una nota su Tiziano Mannoni e l'archeologia postclassica, in Cucuzza, N & Medri, M (eds) *Archeologie. Studi in onore di Tiziano Mannoni*, Bari, 9-12

Francovich, R & Farinelli, R 1999 'I castelli minerari della Toscana', *Castrum* 6, Murcia, 467-90

Francovich, R & Parenti, R (eds) 1988 *Archeologia e restauro dei monumenti I, ciclo di lezioni sulla ricerca applicata in archeologia* (Certosa di Pontignano 1987), Firenze

Franz, R 1981 *Der Kachelofen. Entstehung und kunstgeschichtliche Entwicklung vom Mittelalter bis zum Ausgang der Klassizismus*, second edition, Graz

Friel, I 1993 'Henry V's *Grace Dieu* and the wreck in the R. Hamble near Bursledon, Hampshire', *International Journal of Nautical Archaeology* 22, 3-19

Friel, I 1994 'The Carrack: the advent of the full rigged ship', in Unger, RW (ed) *Cogs, Caravels and Galleons. The Sailing Ship 1000-1650*, London, 77-90

Friel, I 1995 *The Good Ship. Ships, shipbuilding and technology in England 1200-1520*, London

Froment, A & Ambrose, SH 1995 'Analyses tissulaires isotopiques et reconstruction du régime alimentaire en milieu tropical : implication pour l'archéologie', *Bulletins et Mémoires de Société d'Anthropologie de Paris* 7, 79-98

Frondoni, A, Murialdo, G, Palazzi, P, Paniza, M & Parodi, L 2001 'Gli scavi di Piazza Santa Caterina in Finalborgo (Savona): primi dati sui reperti ceramici, in *Atti XXXIII Convegno Internazionale della Ceramica: la ceramica come indicatore socio-economico*, Albisola, 187-94

Frothingham, AW 1941 *Hispanic Glass*, New York

Frothingham, AW 1951 *Lustreware of Spain*, New York

Frothingham, AW 1963 *Spanish Glass*, London

Fundación El legado andalusí (ed) 2000 *Actas del II Congreso Internacional 'La Ciudad en Al-Andalus y el Magreb' (Algeciras, 1999)*, Granada

G

Gabbrielli, F 1996, 'La "cronotipologia relativa" come metodo di analisi degli elevati: la facciata del Palazzo Pubblico di Siena', *Archeologia dell'Architettura* 1, 12-40

Gabbrielli, F 2000 'La chiesa dell'abbazia di San Galgano II. Stereotomia degli archi e maestranze, *Archeologia dell'Architettura* 2, 25-64

Gaborit-Chopin, D 1978 *Ivoires du Moyen Age*, Fribourg [German edition: *Elfenbeinkunst im Mittelalter*, Berlin)

Gaimster, D 1993 'Cross-Channel ceramic trade in the late Middle Ages: archaeological evidence for the spread of Hanseatic culture to Britain', in Gläser, M (ed) *Archäologie des Mittelalters und Bauforschung im Hanseraum: eine Festschrift für Günter Fehring*, Rostock, 251-60

Gaimster, D 1997 *German Stoneware 1200-1900. Archaeology and Cultural History*, London

Gaimster, D 1999 'German stoneware and stove-tiles: type-fosils of Hanseatic culture in the Baltic c. 1200-1600', in Vissak, R & Mäesalu, A (eds) *The Medieval Town in the Baltic. Hanseatic History and Archaeology*, Proceedings of the first & second seminar, Tartu, Estonia, 6-7 June 1997 and 26-27 June 1998, Tartu, 53-64

Gaimster, D 2000a 'Hansaeatic trade and cultural exchange in the Baltic c. 1200-1600: pottery from wrecks and harbours', in Schmettow, H von (ed) *Schutz des Kulturerbes unter Wasser: Veränderungen europäischer Lebenskultur durch Fluß- und Seehandel,* Lübstorf, 237-47

Gaimster, D 2000b 'Saints and Sinners. The iconography of imported ceramic stove-tiles in late medieval and Renaissance London', in Kicken, D, Koldeweij, AM & ter Molen, JR(eds) *Gevonden Voorwerpen. Lost and Found. Essays on Medieval Archaeology for H.J.E. Van Beuningen*, Rotterdam, 142-50

Gaimster, D 2001a 'Life and lifestyle in the Baltic castle: patterns in ceramic consumption c. 1200-1600', in Engberg, N, Skaarup, J, & Vesth, KB (eds) *Castella Maris Baltici* V, Rudkøbing, 51-66

Gaimster, D 2001b 'Pelts, pitch and pottery. The archaeology of Hanseatic trade in Medieval Novgorod', in Brisbane, M & Gaimster, D (eds) *Novgorod: The Archaeology of the Russian Medieval City and its Hinterland* (British Museum Occasional Paper 141), London, 67-78

Gaimster, D 2002a 'Keramik i Stockholm 1250-1600. Inflytande från Hansans handel, kultur och teknik', in Hallerdt, B (ed) *Upptaget. Arkeologi i Stockholm*, Sankt Eriks Årsbok 2002, 193-215

Gaimster, D 2002b 'Tile-stove production in the Baltic c. 1400-1600: an index of Hanseatic cultural and technological exchange', in Helmig, G, Scholkmann, B & Untermann, M (eds) *Centre-Region-Periphery. Medieval Europe Basel 2002* (3 volumes), Hertingen, 110-17

Gaimster, D 2005 'A parallel history: the archaeology of Hanseatic urban culture in the Baltic', c. 1200-1600*, World Archaeology*, 37, 408-23

Gaimster, D 2007a 'Of "idols and devils": devotional pipeclay figures from southern Britain in their European context', in Jäggi, C & Staecker, J (eds) *Archäologie der Reformation. Studien zu den Auswirkungen des Konfessionswechsels auf die materielle Kultur* (Arbeiten zur Kirchengeschichte 104), Berlin & New York, 259-83

Gaimster, D 2007b 'The Baltic ceramic market 1200-1600: measuring Hanseatic cultural transfer and resistance', in Roodenburg, H (ed) *Cultural Exchange in Early Modern Europe, Volume 4: Forging European Identities, 1400-1700*, Cambridge, 30-58

Gaimster, D & Gilchrist, R (eds) 2003 *The Archaeology of Reformation 1480-1580*, (Society for Post-Medieval Archaeology Monograph 1), Leeds

Gál, E 2005 'New data on bird bone artefacts from Hungary and Romania', in Luik, H, Choyke, AM, Batey, C & Lougas, L (eds) *From hooves to horns, from mollusc to mammoth: manufacture and use of bone artefacts from prehistoric times to the present – Proceedings of the 4th Meeting of the ICAZ Worked Bone Research Group at Tallinn, 26th-31st August 2003* (Muinasaja teadus 15), Tallinn, 325-38

García Bellido García de Diego, J 1999 Coranomía. Los universales de la urbanística. Estudio sobre las estructuras generativas en las ciencias del territorio, unpublished PhD dissertation, Universidad Politécnica de Madrid

García Gandía JR, Llorens Campello, S & Pérez Botí, G 2004 'L'Almisserà: territorio castral y espacio rural en época islámica', in Jover Maestre, FJ & Navarro Poveda, C (eds.) *De la medina a la vila. II Jornadas de Arqueología* Medieval, Alicante, 83-105

García Porras, A 2000 'La cerámica española importada en Italia durante el siglo XIV: el efecto de la demanda sobre una producción cerámica en los inicios de su despegue comercial', *Archeologia Medievale* 27, 131-44

García Porras, A 2003 'Los orígenes de la cerámica nazarí decorada en azul y dorado?, in *Atti del XXXV Convegno Internazionale Della Ceramica, Albisola*, 52-63

García Porras, A 2006 'Transmisiones tecnológicas entre el área islámica y cristiana en la Península Ibérica. El caso de la producción de cerámica esmaltada de lujo bajomedieval (ss. XIII-XV)', in *Atti della XXXVII Settimana di Studio: Relazioni economiche tra Europa e mondo islamico (Secc. XIII-XVIII)*, Prato, 827-43

García Sánchez, E & Hernández Bermejo, JE 2007 'Ornamental plants in agricultural and botanical treatises from al-Andalus', in Conan, M (ed) *Middle East Garden Traditions: Unity and Diversity*, Washington DC, 75-94

Garcin, M, Carcaud, N, Gautier, E, Burnouf, J, Castanet, C & Fouillet, N 2006 'Impacts des héritages sur un hydrosystème: l'exemple des levées en Loire moyenne et océanique', in Allée, P & Lespez, L (eds) *L'érosion, entre société, climat et paléoenvironnement. Table ronde en l'honneur du professeur Neboit-Guilhot*, Clermont-Ferrand, 225-36

Gardiner, M 2000 'Vernacular buildings and the development of the later medieval domestic plan in England', *Medieval Archaeology* 44, 159-79

Gardiner, M 2008 'Buttery and pantry and their antecedents: idea and architecture in the English medieval house', in Kowaleski, M & Goldberg, PJP (eds) *Medieval Domesticity. Home, Housing and Household in Medieval England*, Cambridge, 37-65

Garnotel, A & Raynaud, C 1996 'Groupés ou dispersés? Les morts et la société rurale en Languedoc oriental (Ive-XIIe siècles)', in Galinié, H & Zadora-Rio, E (eds) *Archéologie du cimetière chrétien, Actes du colloque d'Orléans (28 sept.-1er oct. 1994)* (11e Supplément à la Revue Archéologique du Centre), Tours, 139-52

Gauthier, M-M 1972 *Emaux du moyen âge occidental*, Fribourg

Gayangos, P de 1840 *The History of the Mohammadan Dynasties in Spain*, London (Reprint Delhi 1984)

Geijer, A 1979 *A history of textile art*, London

Genicot, L 1966 'Crisis: from the Middle Ages to Modern Times', in Postan, MM (ed) *The Cambridge Economic History of Europe, Vol. 1: The Agrarian Life of the Middle Ages*, Cambridge, 660-741

Gerrard, CM 2003a *Medieval Archaeology. Understanding traditions and contemporary approaches*, London & New York

Gerrard, CM 2003b *Paisaje y señorío: la casa conventual de Ambel (Zaragoza)*, Zaragoza. Available online at: http://ifc.dpz.es/publicaciones/index

Gerrard, CM & Aston, MA 2007 *The Shapwick Project, Somerset: a rural landscape explored* (Society for Medieval Archaeology Monograph 25), Leeds

Gerrard, CM, Gutiérrez, A & Vince, AG (eds) 1995 *Spanish medieval ceramics in Spain and the British Isles. Cerámica medieval española en España y en las Islas Británicas* (British Archaeological Reports, International Series 610), Oxford

Gilbert, TP, Cuccui, J, White, W, Lynnerup, N, Titball, RW, Cooper, A & Prentice, MB 2004 'Absence of *Yersinia pestis*-specific DNA in human teeth from five European excavations of putative plague victims', *Microbiology* 150, 341-54

Gilchrist, R 1992 'Christian bodies and souls: the archaeology of life and death in later medieval hospitals', in Bassett, S (ed) *Death in Towns: Urban Responses to the Dying and the Dead, 1000-1600*, Leicester, 101-18

Gilchrist, R 1994 *Gender and Material Culture. The Archaeology of religious women*, London & New York

Gilchrist, R 1995 *Contemplation and action: the other monasticism*, London

Gilchrist, R 2005 *Norwich Cathedral Close. The Evolution of the English Cathedral Landscape,* Woodbridge

Gilchrist, R 2008 'Magic for the Dead? The Archaeology of Magic in Later Medieval Burials', *Medieval Archaeology* 52, 119-59

Gilchrist, R 2009 'Medieval archaeology and theory: a disciplinary leap of faith', in Gilchrist, R & Reynolds, A (eds) *Reflections: 50 years of Medieval Archaeology, 1957-2007,* Leeds, 385-408

Gilchrist, R & Reynolds, A (eds) 2009 *Reflections: 50 years of Medieval Archaeology, 1957-2007,* Leeds

Gilchrist, R & Sloane, B 2005 *Requiem. The Medieval Monastic Cemetery in Britain,* London

Giles, C 1986 *Rural Houses of West Yorkshire 1400-1830,* London

Giles, K 2000a *An Archaeology of Social Identity; Guildhalls in York, c. 1350-1630* (British Archaeological Reports 315) Oxford

Giles, K 2000b 'Marking time? A 15th-century liturgical calendar in the wall paintings of Pickering parish church', *Church Archaeology* 4, 42-51

Giles, K 2005 Public space in town and village 1100-1500, in Dyer, C & Giles, K (eds) *Town and Country 1100-1500,* Leeds, 293-312

Giles, K 2007 'Seeing and believing: visuality and space in pre-modern England,' *World Archaeology* 39, 105-21

Giles, K 2010 '"A table of alabaster with the story of the Doom". The religious objects and spaces of the guild of Our Blessed Virgin, Boston (Lincs)', in Richardson, C (ed) *Everyday objects. Medieval and Early Modern Material Culture and its Meanings,* Aldershot, 267-88

Giovannini, F 2001 *Natalità, mortalità e demografia nell'Italia medieval* (British Archaeological Report International Series 90), Oxford

Girouard, M 1978 *Life in the English Country House,* New Haven & London

Giusti, MA (ed) 2000 *Temi di restauro,* Torino

Gläser, M (ed) 1997 *Lübecker Kolloquium zur Stadtarchäologie im Hanseraum 1: Stand, Aufgaben und Perspektiven,* Lübeck

Gläser, M (ed) 1999 *Lübecker Kolloquium zur Stadtarchäologie im Hanseraum 2: Der Handel,* Lübeck

Gläser, M (ed) 2001 *Lübecker Kolloquium zur Stadtarchäologie im Hanseraum 3: Der Hausbau,* Lübeck

Gläser, M (ed) 2004 *Lübecker Kolloquium zur Stadtarchäologie im Hanseraum 4: Die Infrastruktur,* Lübeck

Gläser, M (ed) 2006 *Lübecker Kolloquium zur Stadtarchäologie im Hanseraum 5: Das Handwerk,* Lübeck

Gläser, M (ed) 2008 *Lübecker Kolloquium zur Stadtarchäologie im Hanseraum 6: Luxus und Lifestyle,* Lübeck

Gläser, M & Mührenberg, D 2002 'Archäologie in den Hansestädten: das Beispiel Lübeck', in Menghin, W & Planck, D (eds) *Menschen, Zeiten, Räume: Archäologie in Deutschland,* Stuttgart, 369-75

Goitein, SD 1999 *A Mediterranean Society: an abridgement in one volume* (Lassner; J, ed), Berkeley

Golb, N 1998 *The Jews in Medieval Normandy: a social and intellectual history,* Cambridge

Goldberg, P & Macphail, RI 2006 *Practical and Theoretical Geoarchaeology,* Oxford

Goldberg, PJP 2008 'The fashioning of urban domesticity in later medieval England: a material culture perspective', in Kowaleski, M & Goldberg, PJP (eds) *Medieval Domesticity. Home, Housing and Household in Medieval England,* Cambridge, 124-44

Gómez Moreno Martínez, M 1924 *Cerámica medieval española, cursillo de ocho conferencias,* Barcelona

Gómez Moreno Martínez, M 1951 *El arte árabe español hasta los almohades. Arte mozárabe (Ars Hispaniae 3),* Madrid

Gómez-Paccard, M, Chauvin, A, Lanos, P, Thiriot, J & Jiménez Castillo, P 2006 'Archaeomagnetic study of seven contemporaneous kilns from Murcia (Spain)', *Physics of the Earth and Planetary Interiors* 157, 16-32

Gonzales Villaescusa, R & Lerma Alegria, JV 1996 'Cristianismo y ciudad, los cementerios in ambitus murorum', in Galinié, H & Zadora-Rio, E (eds) *Archéologie du cimetière chrétien, Actes du colloque d'Orléans (28 sept.-1er oct. 1994)* (11e Supplément à la Revue Archéologique du Centre), Tours, 37-44

Gonzalez Martí, M 1933 *Cerámica española,* Madrid

Gonzalez Martí, M 1944 *Cerámica del Levante español. Siglos medievales,* Barcelona

Goodman, D 1999 'Medieval cities', in Chant, C & Goodman, D (eds) *Pre-industrial Cities and Technology,* London, 115-62

Gore, A & Gore, G 1991 *The History of English Interiors,* London

Gosden, C & Marshall, Y 1999 'The cultural biography of objects', *World Archaeology* 31, 169-178

Gotfredsen, L 1999 *The Unicorn,* London

Goubitz, O 2007 *Purses in pieces. Archaeological finds of late medieval and 16th-century leather purses, pouches, bags and cases in the Netherlands,* Zwolle

Goubitz, O, van Driel-Murray, C & Groenman-van Waateringe, W 2001 *Stepping through time. Archaeological footwear from prehistoric times until 1800,* Zwolle

Gozalbes Cravioto, C 2006 *El Cortijo Las Mezquitas: una mezquita medieval en la vega de Antequera*, Granada

Grabar, O, Holod, R, Knudstad, J & Trousdale, W 1978 *City in the desert: Qasr al-Hayr East* (2 volumes), Cambridge (MA)

Graham-Campbell, J & Valor, M (eds) 2007 *The Archaeology of Medieval Europe. Volume 1: Eighth to Twelfth Centuries AD*, Aarhus Also cited as AME1

Grainger, I, Hawkins, D, Cowal, L, & Mikulski, R 2008 *The Black Death Cemetery, East Smithfield, London* (Museum of London Archaeology Service Monograph 43), London

Grant, A 1988 'Animal resources', in Astill, G & Grant, A (eds) *The countryside of medieval England*, Oxford, 149-87

Grassi, V 2004 'Le stele funerarie islamiche di Sicilia. Provenienze e problemi aperti', *Melanges de l'Ecole Française de Rome* 116, 351-65

Graves, CP 1989 'Social space in the English medieval parish church,' *Economy and Society* 18, 297-322

Graves, CP 2000 *The Form and Fabric of Belief: an Archaeology of the Lay Experience of Religion in Medieval Norfolk and Devon* (British Archaeological Reports 311), Oxford

Gravett, C 2007 *The Castles of Edward I in Wales, 1277-1307*, Oxford

Green, A 2007 'Confining the vernacular: the seventeenth-century origins of a mode of study', *Vernacular Architecture* 38, 1-7

Greig, J 1981 'The excavation of a medieval barrel-latrine from Worcester', *Journal of Archaeological Science* 8, 265-82

Grenier de Cardenal, M. 1980 'Recherches sur la céramique médiévale marocaine', in Demians d'Archimbaud, G & Picon, M (eds) *La céramique médiévale en Méditerranée occidentale, Xe-XVe siècle, Valbonne 1978*, Paris, 227-49

Grenville, J 1997 *Medieval Housing*, Leicester

Grenville, J 2008 'Urban and rural houses and households in the late Middle Ages: a case study from Yorkshire', in Kowaleski, M & Goldberg, PJP (eds) *Medieval Domesticity. Home, Housing and Household in Medieval England*, Cambridge, 92-123

Grew, F & de Neergaard, M 1988 *Shoes and Pattens. Medieval Finds from Excavations in London 2*, London (New edition Woodbridge 2001, reprint 2006)

Grierson, P 1976 'Numismatics', in Powell, JM (ed) *Medieval Studies, an introduction*, Syracuse (NY), 103-50

Grierson, P 1991 *The Coins of Medieval Europe*, London

Griffin, K 1988 'Plant remains', in Schia, E (ed) *De arkeologiske utgravninger i Gamlebyen, Oslo. Vol. 5: animal bones, moss, plant-, insect- and parasite remains*, Øvre Ervik, 15-108

Grimm, P 1939 *Hohenrode, eine mittelalterliche Siedlung im Südharz*, Halle/Saale

Grinder-Hansen, P (ed) 1997 *Margrete I. Regent of the North – the Kalmar Union 600 years*, Copenhagen (Danish version: *Margrete 1. Nordens Frue og Husbond. Kalmarunionen 600 år*, København 1996)

Groenendijk, H, & Schwarz, W 1991 'Mittelalterliche Besiedlung der Moore im Einflussbereich der Dollards: Ergebnisse und Perspektiven', *Archäologische Mitteilungen aus Nordwestdeutsland* 14, 39-68

Groenewoudt, BJ 2002 'Sieving Plaggen Soils: extracting historical information from a man-made soil', *Berichten van de Rijksdienst voor het Oudheidkundig Bodemonderzoek* 45, 125-54

Groenewoudt, BJ 2009 'An exhausted landscape. Medieval use of moors, mires and commons in the Eastern Netherlands', in Klápště, J & Sommer, P (eds) *Medieval Rural Settlement in Marginal Landscapes* (Ruralia 7), Turnhout, 149-80

Gross, C 1890 *The Guild Merchant. A Contribution to British Municipal History* (2 volumes) Oxford

Gross, U 1989 'Das Fundmaterial', in Kind, C-J (ed) *Uml-Eggingen: die Ausgrabungen 1982 bis 1985 in der bandkeramischen Siedlung und der mittelalterlichen Wüstung*, Stuttgart, 287-361

Grössinger, C 1998 'The unicorn on English misericords', in Owen-Crocker, GR & Graham, T (eds) *Medieval Art: Recent Perspectives*, Manchester, 142-58

Gruber, SD 1999 *Synagogues*, New York

Gruber, SD 2002 'Archaeological remains of Ashkenazic Jewry in Europe: a new source of pride and history' in Rutgers, L (ed) *What Athens has to do with Jerusalem: Essays on Classical, Jewish, and Early Christian Art and Archaeology in Honor of Gideon Foerster*, Paris, Louvain & Dudley (MA), 267-301

Grün, R 2001 'Trapped charge dating (ESR, TL, OSL)', in Brothwell, DR & Pollard, AM (eds) *Handbook of Archaeological Sciences*, Chichester, 47-62

Grund, A 1901 *Die Veränderung der Topographie im Wiener Walde und Wiener Becken*, Leipzig

Grupe, G, Heinrich, D & Peters, J 2009 'A brackish water aquatic foodweb: trophic levels and salinity gradients in the Schlei fjord, Northern Germany, in Viking and medieval times', *Journal of Archaeological Science* 36, 2125-44

Guerra, M, Sarthre, C, Gondonneau, A & Barrandon, J 1999 'Precious Metals and Provenance Enquiries using LA-ICP-MS', *Journal of Archaeological Science* 26, 1101-1110

Guldager, O, Stummann Hansen, S & Gleie, S 2002 'Medieval farmsteads in Greenland: the Brattahlid region 1999-2000', *Danish Polar Center Publications* 9, 1-142

Gutiérrez, A 2000 *Mediterranean Pottery in Wessex Households (13th to 17th Centuries)* (British Archaeological Reports 306), Oxford

Gutiérrez, A 2010 'Relaciones e intercambios en el Atlántico medieval: la evidencia cerámica (siglos XIII–XVI)', in *Actas del I Symposium Internacional Gentes del Mar. Historia y Arqueología en el litoral del Arco Atlántico*, Salamanca

Gutscher, D 2009 'Altäre als Baumaterial, Götzen als Füllschutt. Der Bildersturm aus archäologischer Sicht', in Scholkmann, B, Frommer, S, Vossler, C & Wolf, M (eds) *Zwischen Tradition und Wandel: Archäologie des 15. und 16. Jahrhunderts* (Tübinger Forschungen zur historischen Archäologie 3), Büchenbach, 81-7

H

Haase, C 1960 *Die Entstehung der westfälischen Städte*, Münster

Haasis-Berner A 1999 'Die pilgerzeichen des 11.-14. jahrhunderts mit einem Überblick über die Europäische Pilgerzeichenforschung', in Brather, S, Bückler, C & Hoeper, M (eds) *Archäologie als Sozialgeschichte. Studien zu Siedlung, Wirtschaft und Gesellschaft im frühgeschichtlichen Mitteleuropa: Festschrift für Heiko Steuer zum 60. Geburtstag* (Internationale Archäologie, Studia Honoraria 9), 271-7

Haastrup, U & Egevang, R (eds) 1986-1992 *Danske Kalkmalerier*, 7 volumes, København

Habibi, M, Coll Conesa, J & Carrera, JC 2001 'La ocupación medieval: las cerámicas', in Aranegui Gascó, C (ed) *Lixus. Colonia Fenicia y ciudad púnico-mauritana. Anotaciones sobre su ocupación medieval (Saguntum 4)*, Valencia

Haggerty, G & Tabraham, C 1982 'Excavation of a motte near Roberton, Clydesdale, 1979', *Transactions of the Dumfriesshire and Galloway Natural History and Antiquarian Society* 57, 51-64

Hague, DB & Warhurst, C 1966 'Excavations at Sycharth Castle, Denbighshire, 1962-3', *Archaeologia Cambrensis* 115, 108-27

Hähnel, E 1987 *Siegburger Steinzeug, Bestandskatalog Band 1* (Führer und Schriften des Rheinischen Freilichtmuseums und Landesmuseums für Volkskunde Kommern 31), Köln

Hähnel, E 1992 *Siegburger Steinzeug, Bestandskatalog Band 2* (Führer und Schriften des Rheinischen Freilichtmuseums und Landesmuseums für Volkskunde Kommern 38), Köln

Haist, M 2000 'The Lion, bloodline and kingship', in Hassig, D (ed) *The Mark of the Beast*, New York, 3-22

Hall, AR & Kenward, HK 2003 'Can we identify biological indicator groups for craft, industry and other activities?', in Murphy, P & Wiltshire, PEJ (eds) *The Environmental Archaeology of Industry.* (Symposia of the Association for Environmental Archaeology 20), Oxford, 114-30

Hall, L 1983 *The Rural Houses of North Avon and South Gloucestershire 1400-1720* (City of Bristol Museum and Art Gallery Monograph 6), Bristol

Hall, MA 2009 'Making the past present: cinematic narratives of the Middle Ages', in Gilchrist, R & Reynolds, A (eds) *Reflections: 50 years of Medieval Archaeology, 1957-2007*, Leeds, 489-511

Hallenkamp-Lumpe, J 2007 'Das Bekenntnis am Kachelofen? Überlegungen zu den sogenannten 'Reformationskacheln', in Jäggi, C & Staecker, J (eds) *Archäologie der Reformation. Studien zu den Auswirkungen des Konfessionswechsels auf die materielle Kultur* (Arbeiten zur Kirchengeschichte 104), Berlin & New York, 323-43

Hanawalt, B 1984 'Keepers of the lights: late medieval parish guilds', *Journal of Medieval and Renaissance Studies* 14, 21-38

Hanawalt, B & McRee, BR 1992 'The guilds of homo prudens in late medieval England', *Continuity and Change* 7, 163-70

Haneda, M & Muira T (eds) 1995 *Islamic urban studies. Historical review and perspectives*, London & New York

Hansen, G 2003 *Bergen c. 800-c. 1170. The Emergence of a Town*, Bergen

Harbottle, B & Ellison, M 1981 'An excavation in the Castle Ditch, Newcastle upon Tyne, 1974-6', *Archaeologia Aeliana* fifth series 9, 75-250

Harding, C & Wrathmell, S 2007 'Conclusions', in *Mays, S, Harding, C & Heighway, C 2007 Wharram*: a study of settlement on the Yorkshire Wolds. Volume 11: The Churchyard (York University Archaeological Publications 13), York, 327-36

Harjula, J 2005 *Sheaths, scabbards and grip coverings. The use of leather for portable personal objects in 14th-16th century Turku* (Archaeologia Medii Aevi Finlandiae 10), Saarijärvi

Harjula, J 2008 *Before the Heels. Footwear and Shoemaking in Turku in the Middle Ages and at the beginning of the Early Modern Period* (Archaeologia Medii Aevi Finlandiae 15), Turku

Harris, EC 1989 *Principles of Archaeological Stratigraphy*, London

Harris, EC 2003 'The stratigraphy of standing structures', *Archeologia dell'architettura* 8, 9-14

Harris, R 1978 *Discovering Timber-framed Buildings*, Princes Risborough

Harris, R 1989 'The grammar of carpentry', *Vernacular Architecture* 20, 1-8

Harris, R 1994 *The origins and development of English medieval townhouses operating commercially on two storeys*, unpublished DPhil thesis, University of Oxford

Harrison, B & Hutton, B 1984 *Vernacular Houses of North Yorkshire and Cleveland*, Edinburgh

Harrison, B 1991 'Longhouses in the Vale of York', *Vernacular Architecture* 22, 31-9

Harrison, P 2004 *Castles of God. Fortified Religious Buildings of the World*, Woodbridge

Hasse, M 1979 'Neues Hausgerät, neue Kleider: eine Betrachtung der städtischen Kultur im 13. und 14. Jahrhundert sowie ein Katalog der metallenen Hausgeräte', *Zeitschrift für Archäologie des Mittelalters* 7, 7-83

Hastorf, CA & Popper, VS 1988 *Current paleoethnobotany. Analytical methods and cultural interpretations of archaeological plant remains,* Chicago

Hatting, T 1998 'Dyreknogler', in Hjermind, J, Iversen, M & Kristensen, HK (eds) *Viborg Søndersø 1000-1300* (Jysk Arkæologisk Selskabs Skrifter 34), Aarhus, 301-308

Haverkamp, A 2005 'Europas Juden im Mittelalter: Streifzüge', in Historisches Museum der Pfalz, Speyer (ed) *Europas Juden im Mittelalter* (exhibition catalogue), Speyer, 17-36

Hayes-McCoy, GA 1964 *Ulster and Other Irish Maps, c. 1600*, Dublin

Hazlbauer, Z & Chotěbor, Z 1990 'Stavební rekonstrukce dvou vrcholně gotických kamen ze Sezimova Ústí [Ensembles hochmittelalterlicher Töpferkacheln aus Sezimovo Ústí], *Archaeologia historica* 15, 361-83

Heberer, P 2004 'The Medieval Synagogue in Speyer: Historical Building Research and Reconstruction', in Historisches Museum der Pfalz, Speyer (ed) *The Jews of Europe in the Middle Ages*, Speyer, 77-82

Hebsgaard, MB, Thomas, M, Gilbert, P, Arneborg, J, Heyn, P, Allentoft, ME, Bunce, M, Munch, K, Schweger, C & Willerslev, E 2009 'The Farm Beneath the Sand – an archaeological case study on ancient "dirt" DNA', *Antiquity* 83, 430-44

Hedges, REM & Reynard, LM 2007 'Nitrogen isotopes and the trophic level of humans in archaeology', *Journal of Archaeological Science* 34, 1240-51

Hedges, REM, Clement, JG, Thomas, CDL & O'Connell TC 2007 'Collagen turnover in the adult femoral mid-shaft: modeled from anthropogenic radiocarbon tracer measurements', *American Journal of Physical Anthropology* 133, 808-16

Heege, A 2007 *Töpferöfen – Pottery kilns – Fours de potiers. Die Erforschung frühmittelalterlicher bis neuzeitlicher Töpferöfen (6.-20. Jh.) in Belgien, den Niederlanden, Deutschland, Österreich und der Schweiz – A study of pottery kilns from early medieval to modern times (6th to 20th centuries) in Belgium, the Netherlands, Germany, Austria and Switzerland – Etude des fours de potiers du Haut Moyen Age à l'époque moderne (6e-20e s.) en Belgique, dans les Pays-Bas, en Allemagne, en Autriche et en Suisse* (Basler Hefte zur Archäologie 4), Basel

Heidinga, HA, 1987 *Medieval settlement and economy north of the Lower Rhine: Archaeology and history of Kootwijk and the Veluwe (the Netherlands),* Assen/Maastricht

Helle, K 199) *Kongssete og kjøpstad. Fra opphavet til 1536 Bergen bys historie 1*, Bergen

Hellmuth Andersen, H 2001 'Danevirke', in Crabtree, P (ed) *Medieval Archaeology: an Encyclopaedia*, New York & London, 71-4

Helmig, G, Scholkmann, B & Untermann, M (eds) 2002 *Centre – Region – Periphery. Papers of the Medieval Europe Basel 2002 Conference*, Hertingen

Hendrikx, PA, 1989 'Die mittelalterliche Kultivierung der Moore im Rhein-Maas-Delta (10.-13. Jahrhundert), *Siedlungsforschung: Archäologie-Geschichte-Geographie* 7, 67-87

Henkes, HE 1994 *Glas zonder glans. Vijf eeuwen gebruiksglas uit de bodem van de Lage Landen. 1300-1800 [Glass without gloss. Utility glass from five centuries excavated in the Low Countries. 1300-1800]* (Rotterdam Papers 9), Rotterdam

Henning, Salomon 1593 *Salomon Henning's Chronicle of Courland and Livonia* trans. 1992 by Smith, JC, Ward Jones, J & Urban, W, Madison (WI)

Henricus Lettus *The Chronicle of Henry of Livonia*, trans. 2003 by Brundage, JA, New York

Hens, H, van Bavel, H, van Dijck, GCM & Frantzen, JHM 1978 *Mirakelen van Onze Lieve Vrouw te 's-Hertogenbosch 1381-1603. Transcriptie, annotatie en inleiding* (Bijdragen tot de geschiedenis van het zuiden van Nederland 42), Tilburg

Herrscher, E 2003 'Alimentation d'une population historique. Analyse des données isotopiques de la nécropole Saint-Laurent de Grenoble (XIIIe-XVe siècles, France)', *Bulletins et Mémoires de Société d'Anthropologie de Paris* 15, 149-269

Herrscher E. Le Bras-Goude G. 2010. Southern French Neolithic populations: Isotopic evidence for regional specificities in environment and diet. *American Journal of Anthropology* 141.2, 259-271.

Herrscher, E & Valentin, F 2005 'Biométrie de la croissance et état nutritionnel à Saint-Laurent de Grenoble (13e-15e siècles, France)', in Ardagna, Y, Boëtsch, G, Dutour, O, Lalys, L & Signoli, M (ed) *L'Homme et ses images, mesures, représentations, constructions* (Actes du Colloque International du Groupe des Anthropologues de Langue Française, Marseille, 16-18 juillet 2001), Marseille, 73-86

Herrscher, E, Bocherens, H & Valentin, F 2002 'Reconstitution des comportements alimentaires aux époques historiques en Europe à partir de l'analyse isotopique d'ossements humains', *Revue Belge de Philologie et d'Histoire* 80, 1403-22

Herrscher, E, Colardelle, R & Valentin, F 2006 'Meulières et pathologies humaines : un rapport effectif ? Analyse d'une documentation bucco-dentaire entre le XIIIᵉ et le XVIIIᵉ siècle à Grenoble', in Belmont, A & Mangartz, F (ed) *Les meulières. Recherche, protection et mise en valeur d'un patrimoine industriel européen (Antiquité-XXIe siècle)* (Actes du Colloque International Grenoble, 22-25 septembre 2005), Mainz, 99-108

Herrscher, E, Valentin, F, Bocherens, H & Colardelle, R 2007 'Les squelettes de St-Laurent de Grenoble, des témoins de l'alimentation et de la santé au Moyen Age (XIIIᵉᵐᵉ-XVᵉᵐᵉ siècles, France)' in Audouin-Rouzeau, F & Saban, F (ed) *Un aliment sain dans un corps sain* (Collection A boire et à manger 1), Paris, 123-38

Hesse, P-J 1968 *La mine et les mineurs en France de 1300 à 1500*, Paris

Heuburger, G (ed) 1992 *Mikwe: Geschichte und Architektur jüdischer Ritualbäden in Deutschland*, Frankfurt am Main

Higham, R 2004 'Timber castles in Great Britain', in Hofrichter, H (ed) *Holz in der Burgenarchitektur*, Braubach, 199-204

Higham, R & Barker, P 1992 *Timber Castles*, London

Higham, R & Barker, P 2000 *Hen Domen, Montgomery, a timber castle on the English-Welsh border: a final report*, Exeter

Higounet, C 1992 (1979) 'Les bastides en question', in Higounet, C (ed) *Ville, sociétés et économies médiévales : recueil d'articles de Charles Higounet*, Bordeaux, 17-29

Hillaby, J 1992 'London; the 13ᵗʰ-century Jewry revisited', *Jewish Historical Studies* 32, 89-158

Hillaby, J 1993 'Beth Miqdash Me'at: the Synagogues of Medieval England', Journal of Ecclsiastical History 44, 182-98

Hillebrand, K 2003 *Das Dominikanerkloster zu Prenzlau. Untersuchungen zur mittelalterlichen Baugeschichte*, München & Berlin

Hinton, DA 1982 *Medieval jewellery from the eleventh to the fifteenth century*, Princes Risborough

Hinton, DA 2005 *Gold and Gilt, Pots and Pins. Possesions and People in Medieval Britain*, Oxford

Hirst, SM, Walsh, DA & Wright SM 1983 *Bordesley Abbey II. Second Report on Excavations at Bordesley Abbey, Redditch, Hereford and Worcester* (British Archaeological Reports 111), Oxford

Historisches Museum der Pfalz, Speyer (ed) 2004 *The Jews of Europe in the Middle Ages* (exhibition catalogue), Speyer

Hita Ruiz, JM & Villada Paredes, F 1996 'Unas casas meriníes en el arrabal de Enmedio de Ceuta', *Caetaria* 1, 67-91

Hita Ruiz, JM & Villada Paredes, F 2000 *Un aspecto de la sociedad ceutí en el siglo XIV: los espacios domésticos*, Ceuta

Hita Ruiz, JM, Posac, C & Villada Paredes, F 1997 'La cerámica esgrafiada y pintada del museo de Ceuta', in *Transferencies i comerç de cerámica a l'Europa mediterránea (segles XIV-XVII)*, Palma, 53-74

Hjulstro, B & Isaksson, S 2009 'Identification of activity area signatures in a reconstructed Iron Age house by combining element and lipid analyses of sediments', *Journal of Archaeological Science* 36, 174-83

Høegsberg, MS 2009 *Materiel kultur og kulturel identitet i det norrøne Grønland*, unpublished PhD dissertation, Faculty of Humanities, Aarhus University (with English summary)

Hoernes, M 2000 'Die Hauskapellen des Regensburger Patriziats. Studien zu Bestand, Überlieferung und Funktion', *Regensburger Studien und Quellen zur Kulturgeschichte* 8, Regensburg

Hoffmann, M 1974 (first edition 1964) *The warp-weighted loom: Studies in the history and technology of an ancient implement* (Studia Norvegica 14), Oslo

Holl, I & Parádi, N 1982 *Das mittelalterliche Dorf Sarvaly*, Budapest

Homo-Lechner, C 1996 *Sons et instruments de musique au Moyen Age. Archéologie musicale dans l'Europe du VIIe au XIVe siècle*, Paris

Horden, P 2000 'Ritual and public health in the Early Medieval city', in Sheard, S & Power, H (eds) *Body and City: Histories of Public Health*, Aldershot, 17-40,

Horrox, R. 1994 *The Black Death*, Manchester

Horvath, JE & Krisztinkovich, MH 2005 *A History of Haban Ceramics. A Private View*, Vancouver

Hoskins, J 1998 *Biographical objects: how things tell the stories of people's lives*, New York & London

Hoskins, WG 1953 'The rebuilding of rural England, 1570-1640', *Past and Present* 4, 44-59

Hoskins, WG 1967 *Fieldwork in Local History*, London

Hütt, M 1993 *"Quem lavat unda foris…". Aquamanilien. Gebrauch und Form*, Mainz

Hundsbichler, H, Jaritz, G & Kühtreiber, T (eds) 1998 *Die Vielfalt der Dinge. Neue Wege zur Analyse mittelalterlicher Sachkultur* (Forschungen des Instituts für Realienkunde des Mittelalters und der frühen Neuzeit. Diskussionen und Materialien 3), Vienna

Hurst, JG 1977 'Spanish Pottery Imported into Medieval Britain', *Medieval Archaeology* 21, 68-105

Hurst, JG 1984 'The Wharram Research Project: results to 1983', *Medieval Archaeology* 28, 77-111

Hurst, JG 1985 'The Wharram Research Project: problem orientation and strategy 1950-1990', in Hooke, D (ed) *Medieval Villages. A Review of Current Work* (Oxford University Committee for Archaeology Monograph 5), Oxford, 201-4

Hutchinson, G 1994 *Medieval Ships and Shipping*, London

I

ICOMOS (ed) 1976 *Les jardins de l'Islam / Islamic gardens* (2nd International Symposium on protection and restoration of historical gardens, organized by ICOMOS and IFLA), Paris

Ilbert, R 1982 'La ville islamique: réalité et abstraction', *Cahiers de la Recherche Architecturale*, 10-11, 6-13

Immonen, V 2007 'Defining a culture: the meaning of Hanseatic in Medieval Turku', *Antiquity* 81, 720-32

Innocent, CF 1916 *The development of English building construction*, Cambridge

Insoll, T 1996 *Islam, Archaeology and History: Gao Region (Mali) ca. AD 900-1250* (British Archaeological Reports International Series 647), Oxford

Insoll, T 2003 *The Archaeology of Islam in Sub-Saharan Africa*, Cambridge

Institución Fernando el Católico (ed) 1991 *Actas del simposio internacional sobre la ciudad islámica. Ponencias y comunicaciones*, Zaragoza

Instituto de Estudios Ceutíes (ed) 2000 *Cerámica Nazarí y Mariní. Transfretana (Revista del Instituto de Estudios Ceutíes)*, Ceuta

Isenberg, G & Scholkmann, B (eds) 1997 *Die Befestigung der mittelalterlichen Stadt* (Städteforschung A 45), Köln

J

Jaacks, G 1989 'Repräsentation durch Kunst', in Bracker, J (ed) *Die Hanse: Lebenswirklichkeit und Mythos*, Hamburg, 372-84

Jäggi, C & Staecker, J (eds) 2007 *Archäologie der Reformation. Studien zu den Auswirkungen des Konfessionswechsels auf die materielle Kultur* (Arbeiten zur Kirchengeschichte 104), Berlin & New York

Jahnke, C 2009 'Some aspects of Medieval Cloth Trade in the Baltic Sea Area', in Vestergård Pedersen, K & M-LB Nosch (eds) *The Medieval Broadcloth, Changing Trends in Fashions, Manufacturing and Consumption*, Oxford, 4-89

James, TB & Robinson, AM 1988 *Clarendon Palace. The History and Archaeology of a Medieval Palace and Hunting Lodge near Salisbury, Wiltshire* (Reports of the Research Committee of the Society of Antiquaries of London 45), London

Janssen, HL 1985 'De materiële cultuur van de middeleeuwse stedelijke kloosters in Nederland als probleem van de historische interpretatie van archeologische gegevens', in Andriessen, J, Bange, P & Weiler, AG (eds) *Geert Grote en de Moderne Devotie,* Utrecht, 201-31

Janssen, HL 1990 'Medieval material culture and the problem of the historical interpretation of archaeological evidence: the example of the town of 's-Hertogenbosch', in Jaritz, G (ed) *Mensch und Objekt im Mittelalter und in der Frühen Neuzeit. Leben – Alltag – Kultur. Internationaler Kongreß Krems an der Donau, 27. bis 30. September 1988* (Veröffentlichungen des Instituts für mittelalterliche Realienkunde Österreichs, 13), Vienna, 397-438

Janssen, HL 2002 'Patrician and aristocratic town residences in s'Hertogenbosch c. 1250-c. 1550: the archaeological evidence', in Helmig, G, Scholkmann, B & Untermann, M (eds) *Centre-Region-Periphery. Medieval Europe Basel 2002* (3 volumes), Hertingen, 140-8

Janssen, HL & Thelen, AAJ (eds) 2007 *Tekens van leven. Opgravingen en vondsten in het Tolbrugkwartier in 's-Hertogenbosch*, Utrecht

Janssen, W 1965 *Königshagen. Ein archäologisch-historischer Beitrag zur Siedlungsgeschichte des südwestlichen Harzvorlandes* (Quellen und Darstellungen zur Geschichte Niedersachsens 64), Hildesheim

Janssen, W 1968 'Mittelalterliche Dorfsiedlungen als archäologisches Problem', *Frühmittelalterliche Studien* 2, 305-67

Janssen, W 1975 *Studien zur Wüstungsfrage im fränkischen Altsiedelland zwischen Rhein, Mosel und Eifelnordland* (Beihefte der Bonner Jahrbücher 35), Köln

Janssen, W 1983 'Gewerbliche Produktion des Mittelalters als Wirtschaftsfaktor im ländlichen Raum', in *Das Handwerk in vor- und frühgeschichtlicher Zeit* 2 (Abhandlungen der Akademie der Wissenschaften in Göttingen, Philologisch-historische Klasse, Dritte Folge 123), Göttingen, 317-94

Jenisch, B 1999 *Die Entstehung der Stadt Villingen: Archäologische Zeugnisse und Quellenüberlieferung* (Forschungen und Berichte der Archäologie des Mittelalters in Baden-Württemberg 22), Stuttgart

Jensen, JS, Bendixen, K, Liebgott, N-K & Lindahl, F 1992 *Danmarks middelalderlige skattefund c. 1050-c. 1550* volumes 1-2, København (with English summaries)

Jeute, G 2007 *Ländliches Handwerk und Gewerbe im Mittelalter: Untersuchungen zur nichtagrarischen Produktion im westlichen Brandenburg*, Bonn

Jiménez Castillo, P 1991 'El Vidrio', in Navarro Palazón, J *Una casa islámica en Murcia: estudio de su ajuar (siglo XIII)*, Murcia, 71-86

Jiménez Castillo, P 1996 'El vidrio islámico en Murcia', *Proceedings of the Seminar Al-Andalus: Centuries of Vicissitudes and Accompliments (Ryadh, noviembre de 1993), Volume 3: Civilization, Architecture and Arts*, Ryadh, 113-61

Jiménez Castillo, P & Navarro Palazón, J 1997 *Platería 14. Sobre cuatro casas andalusíes y su evolución (siglos X-XIII)*, Murcia

Jiménez Castillo, P, Muñoz López, F & Thiriot, J 2000 'Les ateliers urbains de verriers de Murcia au XIIe s. (C. Puxmarina et Pl. Belluga)', in Pétrequin, P, Fluzin, P, Thiriot, J & Benoit, P (eds) *Arts du feu et productions artisanales. XXèmes Rencontres internationales d'Antibes*, Antibes, 433-52

Jiménez Castillo, P, Navarro Palazón, J & Thiriot, J 2005 'Taller de vidrio y casas andalusíes en Murcia. La excavación arqueológica del Cáson de Puxmarina', *Memorias de Arqueología, Región de Murcia* 13, 1998 (2005), 419-58 (available at http://digital.csic.es/bitstream/10261/3655/1/memo13-25.pdf)

Jiménez Martín, A (ed.) 2002 *Magna hispalensis I. Recuperación de la Aljama Almohade*, Granada

Jímenez Martín, A & Almagro Gorbea, A 1985 *La Giralda*, Madrid

Johansen, P, & Mühlen, H von zur 1973 *Deutsch und Undeutsch im mittelalterlichen und frühneuzeitlichen Reval*, Köln & Wien

Johns, J 2002a *Arabic Administration in Norman Sicily: the Royal Dîwân*, Cambridge

Johns J 2002b 'Sulla condizione dei musulmani di Corleone sotto il dominio normanno nel XII secolo', in Carra Bonacasa RM (ed) *Bizantino sicula* IV, Palermo, 275-94

Johnson, MH 1993a *Housing Culture*, London

Johnson, MH 1993b 'Rethinking the great rebuilding', *Oxford Journal of Archaeology* 12, 117-25

Johnson, MH 1994 'Houses and history', *Archaeological Journal* 151, 435-9

Johnson, MH 1997 'Vernacular Architecture: the loss of innocence', *Vernacular Architecture* 28 13-19

Johnson, MH 1999 *Archaeological Theory. An Introduction*, Oxford

Joire, J 1955 'Découvertes archéologiques dans la région de Rao (Bas-Sénégal)', *Bulletin de l'Institut Fondamental d'Afrique Noire (IFAN)* série B, 17, 249-333

Jones, PD & Mann, ME 2004 'Climate over past millennia', *Review of Geophysics* 42, 1-42

Jones, PN 1992 'The metallography and relative effectiveness of arrowheads and armor during the Middle Ages', *Materials Characterization* 29/2, 111-17

Jöns, H, Lüth, H & Schäfer H (eds) 2005 *Archäologie unter dem Strassenpflaster. 15 Jahre Stadtkernarchäologie in Mecklenburg-Vorpommern*, Schwerin

Jonsson, K 2007 'Burial rods and charcoal graves: new light on old burial customs', *Viking and Medieval Scandinavia* 3, 43-73

Jónsson, M 2008 'Íslensk skinnhandrit og Austrfirðir', in Lárusson, J (ed) *Skriðuklaustur. evrópskt miðaldaklaustur í Flótsdal*, Skriðuklaustur, 83-91

Jope, M 1961-2 'The animal bones', in Biddle, M (ed.) 'The medieval village of Seacourt, Berkshire', *Oxoniensia* 26-27, 70-210

Jorge Aragoneses, M 1966 *Museo de la muralla árabe de Murcia*, Madrid

Jørgensen, DM 2008 'Cooperative sanitation: managing streets and gutters in late Medieval England and Scandinavia', *Technology and Culture* 49, 547-67

K

Karlson, W 1928 *Studier i Sveriges Medeltida Möbelkunst*, Lund

Keene, D 1982 'Rubbish in Medieval Towns', in Hall, AR & Kenward, HK (eds) *Environmental Archaeology in the Urban Context* (CBA Research Report 43), York, 26-30

Kelly, K 1997 'The archaeology of African-European interaction: investigating the social roles of trade, traders and the use of space in the 17th and 18th century Hueda kingdom, Republic of Benin', *World Archaeology* 28, 351-69

Kelly, RS 1982 'The Excavation of a medieval site at Cefn Graeanog, Clynnog, Gwynedd, *Bulletin of the Board of Celtic Studies* 29, 859-907

Kenyon, JR 1990 *Medieval Fortifications*, Leicester

Kerrigan, PM 1995 *Castles and Fortifications in Ireland, 1485-1945*, Cork

Kieffer-Olsen, J 1993 *Grav og gravskik i det middelalderlige Danmark: 8 kirkegårdsudgravninger*, Aarhus

King, DC 1988 *The Castle in England and Wales*, London & Sydney

Kirchner, W & Kirchner, W 1998 'Mittelalterlicher Steinbau in Matting', in Bedal, K, Fechter, S & Heidrich, H (eds) *Haus und Kultur im Spätmittelalter* (Quellen und Materialien zur Hausforschung in Bayern 10), Bad Windsheim, 213-21

Kirjavainen, H 2009 'A Finnish Archaeological Perspective on Medieval Broadcloth', in Vestergård Pedersen, K & M-LB Nosch (eds) *The Medieval Broadcloth, Changing Trends in Fashions, Manufacturing and Consumption*, Oxford, 90-98

Kirkman, J 1974 *Fort Jesus. A Portuguese Fortress on the East African Coast*, Oxford

Klápště, J 1998 'Les outils de la préparation du sol au Moyen Age (à propos des fouilles archéologiques tchèques), in Feller, I, Mane, P & Piponnier, F (eds) *Le village médiéval et son environnement: études offertés à Jean-Marie Pesez*, Paris, 359-65

Klápště, J & Nissen Jaubert, A 2007 'Rural Settlement', in Graham-Campbell, J & Valor, M (eds) *The Archaeology of Medieval Europe, Vol. 1: Eight to Twelfth Centuries AD*, Aarhus, 76-110

Kļaviņš, K 2009 'The significance of local Baltic peoples in the defence of Livonia from the end of the thirteenth to the sixteenth century', in Murray AV (ed) *The Clash of Cultures on the Medieval Baltic Frontier*, Farnham

Klueting, E (ed) 2006 *Fromme Frauen, unbequeme Frauen? Weibliches Religiosentum im Mittelalter* (Hildesheimer Forschungen 3), Hildesheim, Zürich & New York

Knüsel, C & Boylston, A 2000 'How has the Towton project contributed to our knowledge of medieval and later warfare?', in Fiorato, V, Boylston, A & Knüsel, C (eds) *Blood Red Roses: the archaeology of a mass grave from the battle of Towton, AD 1461*, Oxford, 169-88

Kock, J & Roesdahl, E (eds) 2005 *Boringholm – en østjysk træborg fra 1300-årene*, Højbjerg (English summary and lists of artefacts)

Kock, J & Sode, T 2002 'Medieval glass mirrors in southern Scandinavia and their technique, as still practised in India', *Journal of Glass Studies* 44, 79-94

Koldeweij, AM 1997 'Sacred and profane: medieval mass-produced badges', in De Boe, G & Verhaeghe, F (eds) *Art and symbolism in medieval Europe. Papers of the Medieval Europe Brugge 1997 Conference* (IAP Rapporten 5), Zellik, 135-7

Koldeweij, AM 2007 'Opgespeld geloof en bijgeloof. Geloof en magie' in Janssen, HL & Thelen, AAJ (eds) *Tekens van leven. Opgravingen en vondsten in het Tolbrugkwartier in 's-Hertogenbosch*, Utrecht, 152-71

Koldeweij, J 1998 'Vroomheid in tin en lood. Bossche pelgrimsinsignes als historische bron', *Brabants Heem* 50, 52-61

Koldeweij, J 1999 'The wearing of significative badges, religious and secular: the social meaning of a behavioural pattern', in Blockmans, W & Janse, A (eds) *Showing status: representation of social positions in the late Middle Ages*, Turnhout, 308-28

Koldeweij, J 2006 *Geloof & Geluk. Sieraad en Devotie in middeleeuws Vlaanderen* (exhibition at Bruggemuseum Gruuthuse, 22 September 2006-4 February 2007, catalogue), Arnhem

Koster, EA 1978 *De stuifzanden van de Veluwe: een fysisch geografische studie* (Eolian drift sands of the Veluwe, Central Netherlands), Amsterdam

Köster, K 1983 *Pilgerzeichen und Pilgermuscheln von mittelalterlichen Santiagostraßen* (Ausgrabungen in Schleswig, Berichte und Studien 2), Neumünster

Kovács, E 2004 *L'Âge d'or de l'orfevrerie parisienne au temps des princes de Valois*, Dijon

Kowaleski, M & Goldberg, PJP (ed) 2008 *Medieval Domesticity. Home, housing & household in medieval England*, Cambridge

Krabath, S 2001 *Die hoch- und spätmittelalterlichen Buntmetallfunde nördlich der Alpen: eine archäologisch-kunsthistorische Untersuchung zur ihrer Herstellungstechnik, funktionalen und zeitlichen Bestimmung*, Rahden

Krajíc, R 1987 'Vesnice husitského období na Táborsku ve světle archeologických výzkumů' [Das Dorf des hussitischen Zeitalters der Gegend Tábor im Licht archäologischer Untersuchungen], *Archaeologia historica* 12, 85-95

Krajíc, R 1989, 'Středověká sladovna v Sezimově Ústí' [Eine mittelalterliche Malzdarre in Sezimovo Ústí], *Památky archeologické* 80, Prague, 159-87

Krajíc, R 2001 *Sezimovo Ústí: archeologie středověkého poddanského města 4. Středověké cihlářství* [Sezimovo Ústí: Archaeology of a Medieval Servile Town 4. Medieval Brickmaking], České Budějovice & Tábor

Krajíc, R 2003 *Sezimovo Ústí: archeologie středověkého poddanského města 3. Kovárna v Sezimově Ústí a analýza výrobků ze železa* [Sezimovo Ústí: Archäologie der mittelalterlichen Untertanenstadt 3. Die Schmiede in Sezimovo Ústí und Analyse der Produkte aus Eisen], Prague, Sezimovo Ústí & Tábor

Krause, G 1999 'Duisburg, Lower Rhineland. The harbour and the topography of the town from the Merovingian period to c. 1600', in Bill, J & Clausen, B (eds) *Maritime Topography and the Medieval Town*, Copenhagen, 99-108

Krauskopf, C 1995 '…davon nur noch wenige Rutera zu sehen seyn sollen…' *Archäologische Ausgrabungen in der Burgruine Schnellerts* (Kultur- und Lebensformen in Mittelalter und Neuzeit 1), Bamberg

Krauskopf, C 2005 *Tric-Trac, Trense, Treichel: Untersuchungen zur Sachkultur des Adels im 13. und 14. Jahrhundert* (Veröffentlichungen der Deutschen Burgvereinigung, Reihe A, Forschungen 11), Braubach (with English summary)

Krautheimer R 1980 *Rome. Profile of a City 312-1308*, Princeton (NJ)

Krebs, RE 2004 *Groundbreaking scientific experiments, inventions, and discoveries of the Middle Ages and the Renaissance*, Westport (CT)

Kreisel, H 1981 *Die Kunst des deutschen Möbels. I: von den Anfängen bis zum Hochbarock*, München

Kremenetski, KV, Boettger, T, MacDonald, GM, Vaschalova, T, Sulerzhitsky, L & Hiller, A 2004 'Medieval climate warming and aridity as indicated by multiproxy evidence from the Kola Peninsula, Russia', *Palaeogeography, Palaeoclimatology, Palaeoecology* 209/1-4, 113-25

Krinsky, CH 1985 *The Synagogues of Europe: Architecture, History, Meaning*, New York & Cambridge (MA)

Kristjánsdóttir, S 2008 'Skriðuklaustur monastery. Medical centre of medieval east Iceland?', *Acta Archaeologica* 79, 208-15

Krisztinkovich, B 1962 *Haban Pottery*, Budapest

Kroker, M 2007 *Der Dom von Münster. Die Domburg: Archäologische Ergebnisse zur Geschichte der Domimmunität vom 8.-18. Jahrhundert* (Denkmalpflege und Forschung in Westfalen 26), Mainz

Krongaard Kristensen, H 1994 *The Franciscan Friary of Svendborg* (The Archaeology of Svendborg, Denmark, vol. 6), Svendborg

Krongaard Kristensen, H 2004 'Faser af Viborgs topografiske udvikling 1000-1500', in Bitsch Christensen, S (ed) *Middelalderbyen* (Danske Bystudier 1), Århus, 79-96

Krueger, I 1993 'Glass-mirrors in medieval times', in *Annales du 12e congrès de l'Association Internationale pour l'Histoire du Verre. Vienne-Wien, 26-31 août 1991*, Amsterdam, 319-32

Krüger, J. Schumacher, D, Lorenz, S & Zotz, T (eds) 2001 *Spätmittelalter am Oberrhein 2: Alltag, Handwerk und Handel 1350-1525* (2 volumes), Stuttgart

Kruip, M 2010 'Het Bossche mirakelboek in kaart gebracht', *Brabant, tijdschrift voor Brabants heem en erfgoed* 1, 4-20

Kulessa, B 2000 'Handwerke in der Stralsunder Hafenvorstadt' in Müller, U (ed) *Handwerk - Stadt - Hanse. Ergebnisse der Archäologie zum mittelalterlichen Handwerk im südlichen* Ostseeraum, Greifswald, 175-89

Kuniholm, PI 2001 'Dendrochronology and other applications of tree-ring studies in archaeology', in Brothwell, DR & Pollard, AM (eds) *Handbook of Archaeological Sciences*, Chichester, 35-46

Kurzmann, P 2004 *Technologie des mittelalterlichen Glases. Archäologie – Schriftquellen – Archäochemie – Experimente*, Frankfurt

L

Laforce, MF 1978 'Woolsorters' disease in England', *Bulletin of the New York Academy of Medicine* 54, 956-63 (Retrieved 1 February 2010 from http://www.ncbi.nlm.nih.gov/pmc/articles/PMC1807561/pdf/bullnyacadmed00135-0058.pdf

Lamb, HH 1995 *Climate, History and the Modern World*, London

Lambert, C & Grilletto, P 1989 'Le sepolture e il cimitero della chiesa abbaziale della Novalesa', *Archeologia Medievale* 16, 329-56

Lambert, E 1957 'Vitraux de couleur dans l'Art Musulman du Moyen-âge', *Mélanges Georges Marçais* 2, Argel, 107-109

Lambrechts, P & Sosson, JP (eds) 1994 *Les Métiers au Moyen Age* (Publications de l'Institut d'Etudes Médiévales 15), Louvain-la-Neuve

Lamm, CJ 1928 *Das Glas von Samarra*, Berlín

Lamm, CJ 1929 *Mittelalterliche Gläser und Steinschnittarbeiten aus dem Nahen Osten*, Berlín

Landesdenkmalamt Baden-Württemberg & Stadt Zürich (eds) 1992 See Flüeler, M & Flüeler, N (eds) 1992

Landschaftsverband Westfalen-Lippe 2007 *Landwehren: von der mittelalterlichen Wehranlage zum Biotop*, Münster

Lapins, A & Dirveiks, I 2009 'Construction of the Order's Castle in Cesis, Latvia', in *Proceedings of the Third International Congress on Construction History, Cottbus, May 2009*, 935-41

Laul, S & Valk, H 2007 *Siksälä: a community at the frontiers. Iron Age and Medieval* (CCC Papers 10), Tallinn & Tartu

Laurioux, B 1988 'Le lièvre lubrique et la bête sanglante: réflexions sur quelques interdits alimentaires du Haut Moyen Âge', *Anthropozoologica* special number 2, 127-32

Laurioux, B 2002 *Manger au Moyen Age: pratiques et discours alimentaires en Europe aux XIVe et XVe siècles*, Paris

Lauwers, M 2005 *Naissance du cimetière chrétien. Lieux sacrés et terre des morts dans l'Occident médiéval*, Paris

Leaf, H 2008 *English Medieval Bone Flutes c. 450 to c. 1550 AD*, unpublished PhD dissertation, University of London

Le Goff, J 1980 'L'apogée de la France urbaine médiévale 1150-1330', in Duby, G (ed) *La ville médiévale des Carolingiens à la Renaissance* (*Histoire de la France urbaine* 2), Paris, 190-407

Le Goff, J 1988 *The Medieval Imagination*, Chicago

Lemée, C 2006 *The Renaissance Shipwrecks from Christianshavn: an archaeological and architectural study of large carvel vessels in Danish waters, 1580-1640*, Roskilde

Lepage, JD 2002 *Castles and fortified cities of Medieval Europe: an illustrated history*, Jefferson (NC) & London

Le Patourel, HEJ 1991 'Rural building in England', in Miller, E (ed) *The Agrarian History of England and Wales*, vol. 3, Cambridge, 1348-1500

Le Roy Ladurie, E 1978 *Montaillou: village Occitan de 1294 à 1324*, Paris

Le Roy-Ladurie, E 1983 *Histoire du climat depuis l'an Mil*, 2 volumes, Paris

Les Clefs de St-Pierre 1993 *Cathédrale Saint-Pierre Genève 1973-1993. Rapport de. Restauration*, Geneva

Lévêque, C & Van der Leeuw, S (ed) 2003 *Quelles natures voulons-nous? Pour une approche socio-écologique du champ de l'environnement*, Paris

Lever, Jill & John Harris 1993 *Illustrated Dictionary of Architecture 800-1914* (London and Boston)

Levine, LI 2000 *The Ancient Synagogue. The First Thousand Years*, New Haven (CT)

Lévy-Provençal, E 1950 *Las ciudades y las instituciones urbanas del occidente musulmán en la Edad Media*, Tetuán

Lewis, M 2002 *Urbanisation and Child Health in Medieval and Post-Medieval England. An Assessment of the Morbidity and Mortality of Non-Adult Skeletons from the Cemeteries of two Urban and two Rural Sites in England (AD 850-1859)* (British Archaeological Report British Series 339), Oxford

Lewis, T 1908 'The Old Kingdom of Kongo', *The Geographical Journal* 31, 589-611

L'Hour, M & Veyrat, E 1994 'The French Medieval Clinker Wreck from Aber Wrac'h', in Westerdahl, C (ed) *Crossroads in Ancient Shipbuilding. Proceedings of the Sixth International Symposium on Boat and Ship Archaeology, Roskilde 1991*, Oxford, 165-80

Liddiard, R 2000 *Landscapes of Lordship: Norman Castles and the Countryside in Medieval Norfolk* (British Archaeological Reports 309), Oxford

Lie, R 1988 'Animal bones' in Schia, E (ed) *De arkeologiske utgravninger i Gamlebyen, Oslo. Vol. 5: animal bones, moss, plant-, insect- and parasite remains*, Øvre Ervik, 153-195

Lightbown, RW 1978 *Secular goldsmiths' work in medieval France: a history*, (Reports of the Research Committee of the Society of Antiquaries of London 36), London

Lightbown, RW 1992 *Medieval European Jewellery*, London

Ligi, P & Valk, H 1993 'Vadjapärased kalmed Tartumaal (13.-15. sajand). Vadjapärased kalmed Eestis 9.-16. sajandil, *Muinasaja Teadus* 2, 176-214

Lilley, JM, Stroud, G, Brothwell, DR & Williamson, MH 1994 *The Jewish burial ground at Jewbury, York* (*The Archaeology of York* 12/3), York

Lillich, M 1998 *The Hospital of Tonnerre and the Queen of Sicily*, Philadelphia (PA)

Lindahl, F 2003 *Symboler i guld og sølv. Nationalmuseets fingerringe 1000-1700 årene*, København (English summary: Symbols of Gold and Silver. Rings in the Danish National Museum 11th-18th century)

Linnard, W 1982 *Welsh woods and forests: history and utilization*, Cardiff

Linzey, R 1999 *The Castles of Pendennis and St Mawes*, London

Llubiá Munné, M 1967 *Cerámica medieval española*, Barcelona

Locker, A 1994 'Animal bones' in Papworth, M (ed) 'Lodge Farm, Kingston Lacy estate, Dorset', *Journal of the British Archaeological Association* 147, 57-121

Loewen, B 2001 'The structures of Atlantic shipbuilding in the 16th century: an archaeological perspective', in Alves, F (ed) *Proceedings of the International Symposium on Archaeology of Medieval and Modern Ships of Iberian-Atlantic Tradition. Hull remains, manuscripts and ethnographic sources: a comparative approach*, Lisbon, 241-58

Loisel, G 1912 *Histoire des ménageries de l'Antiquité à nos jours, Volume 1*, Paris

Lokuruka, MNI 2006 'Meat is the meal and status is by meat: recognition of rank, wealth and respect through meat in Turkana culture', *Food and Foodways* 14, 201-29

Longcroft, A 2002 'Plan forms in smaller post-medieval houses: a case study from Norfolk', *Vernacular Architecture* 33, 34-56

Longin, R 1971 'New method of collagen extraction for radiocarbon dating', *Nature* 230, 241-2

López Elum, P 1984 *Los orígenes de la cerámica de Manises y de Paterna (1285-1335)*, Valencia

Lorans, E, Joly, S & Trébuchet, E 2007 'Les vivants et leurs morts du 1er au 12e siècle: de l'éloignement à l'insertion', in Galinié, H (ed) *Tours antique et médiéval. Lieux de vie, temps de la ville. 40 ans d'archéologie urbaine* (30e Supplément à la Revue Archéologique du Centre de la France), Tours, 373-5

Lossius, SM 1977 *Kleberkarmaterialet fra Borgund, Sunnmøre*, Bergen

Loux, F 1978 *Le jeune enfant et son corps dans la médecine traditionnelle, la tradition et le quotidien*, Paris, 173-4

Loveluck, C 2005 'Rural settlement hierarchy in the age of Charlemagne', in Story, J (ed) *Charlemagne: Empire and Society*, Manchester, 230-58

Lucas, G 2006 'Historical archaeology and time', in Hicks, D & Beaudry, M (eds) *The Cambridge Companion to Historical Archaeology*, Cambridge, 34-47

Luckhart, J. & Niehoff, F (eds) 1995 *Heinrich der Löwe und seine Zeit: Herrschaft und Repräsentation der Welfen 1125-1235. Katalog der Ausstellung Braunschweig 1995* (3 volumes), Munich

Lüdtke, H & Schietzel, K (eds) 2001 *Handbuch zur mittelalterlichen Keramik in Nordeuropa* (3 volumes), Neumünster

Luff, R & Moreno-Garcia, M 1995 'Killing cats in the medieval period: an unusual episode in the history of Cambridge, England', *Archaeofauna* 4, 93-114

Lyons, MA 2003 'Pale, or English Pale', in Lalor, B (ed) *The Encyclopaedia of Ireland*, Dublin, 852-3

Mac, Mc

McCarthy, MR & Brooks, CM 1988 *Medieval Pottery in Britain AD 900-1600*, Leicester

McClain, A.N. 2005. *Power, Patronage, and Identity: the Social Use of Local Churches and Commemorative Monuments in Tenth to Twelfth-Century North Yorkshire*, unpublished PhD thesis, Department of Archaeology, University of York

MacCulloch, Diarmaid 2010 *A History of Christianity* Penguin Books

McDonagh, B 2007 '"Powerhouses" of the Wolds landscape: manor houses and churches in late medieval and early modern England,' in Gardiner, M. & Rippon, S. (eds) *Medieval Landscapes* (Landscape History After Hoskins 2), Macclesfield, 185-200

McEvedy, C 1961 *The Penguin Atlas of Medieval History*, Harmondsworth

McGrail, S 1993 *Medieval Boat and Ship Timbers from Dublin*, Dublin

MacGregor, Arthur 1985 *Bone, Antler, Ivory and Horn* (Oxford)

MacGregor, Arthur 1991 Antler, Bone and Horn in Blair, J & Ramsey, N (eds) 1991 *English Medieval Industries. Craftsmen, techniques, products*, London & Rio Grande: 355-378

MacKenzie, D 2008 'Columbus blamed for spread of syphilis', *NewScientist* 15 January 2008

McNeal, RA 1991 'Archaeology and the destruction of the later Athenian Acropolis', *Antiquity* 65, 49-63

McNeill, TE 1997 *Castles in Ireland. Feudal Power in a Gaelic World*, London & New York

McNeill, TE 2001 'Castles', in Crabtree, P (ed), *Medieval Archaeology: an Encyclopaedia*, New York & London, 43-6

McQuitty, A 2005 'The rural landscape of Jordan in the seventh–nineteenth centuries AD: the Kerak plateau', *Antiquity* 79, 327-38

McRee, BR 1992 'Religious gilds and civic order: the case of Norwich in the later middle ages', *Speculum* 67, 69-97

McRee, BR 1994 'Unity or division? The social meaning of guild ceremonies in urban communities', in Hanawalt, B & Reyerson, KL (eds) *City and Spectacle in Medieval Europe*, Minneapolis & London, 189-207

McSparron, C & Williams, B 2009 'The excavation of an Early Christian rath with later medieval occupation at Drumadoon, Co. Antrim', *Proceedings of the Royal Irish Academy* 109C, 105-64

M

Machin, R 1977a 'The Great Rebuilding: a reassessment', *Past and Present* 77, 33-56

Machin, R 1977b 'The Mechanism of the Pre-Industrial Building Cycle', *Vernacular Architecture* 8, 819-24

Macías S. 1996, *Mértola Islâmica*, Mértola.

Mack, RE 2002 *Bazaar to Piazza. Islamic trade and Italian art, 1300-1600,* Berkeley & London

Madsen, PK 1983 'A French connection: Danish funerary pots: a group of medieval pottery', *Journal of Danish Archaeology* 2, 171-83

Mägi, M 2002 *At the Crossroads of Space and Time. Graves, Changing Society and Ideology on Saaremaa (Ösel), 9th-13th Centuries AD* (CCC Papers 6), Tallinn

Magny, M 1995 *Une histoire du climat. Des derniers mammouths au siècle de l'automobile,* Paris

Maier, M 1984 (1988) *The Jewish Cemetery of Worms* (trans. by Theobald-Maier, C), Worms

Maik, J 2009 'The influence of Hanseatic Trade on textile Production in Medieval Poland', in Vestergård Pedersen, K & M-LB Nosch (eds) *The Medieval Broadcloth, Changing Trends in Fashions, Manufacturing and Consumption*, Oxford, 109-21

Makepeace, GA 2001 'Report on the excavations of a medieval farm at Hill Top Farm, Alswark, near Bassington, Derbyshire 1992-95', *Derbyshire Archaeological Journal* 121, 162-89

Makowiecki, D 2001 'Some remarks on medieval fishing in Poland', in Buitenhuis, H & Prummel, W (eds) *Animals and Man in the Past*, Groningen, 236-41

Malmros, C & Daly, A 2005 'Anvendelse af træ til redskaber – træartsbestemmelser og håndværk', in Kock, J & Roesdahl, E (eds) 2005 *Boringholm – en østjysk træborg fra 1300-årene*, Højbjerg, 245-59 (English summary and lists of artefacts)

Maltby, M. Pluskowski, A. G. and Seetah, K. 2009. 'Animal bones from an industrial quarter at Malbork, Poland: towards an ecology of a castle built in Prussia by the Teutonic Order', *Crusades*, 8: 191-212.

Manacorda, D 1982 *Archeologia Urbana a Roma: il progetto della Crypta Balbi*, Firenze

Mane, P 2001 *L'outil et le geste: iconographie de l'agriculture dans l'Occident médiéval (IXe-XVe siècles),* Lille

Mane, P 2006 *Le travail à la campagne au Moyen Âge: étude iconographique*, Paris

Mann, VB (ed) 2000 *Jewish Texts on the Visual Arts.* Cambridge & New York

Manning, RB 1993 *Hunters and Poachers. A Cultural and Social History of Unlawful Hunting in England 1485-1640*, Oxford

Mannoni, T 1976 'L'analisi delle tecniche murarie medievali in Liguria, in *Atti del colloquio internazionale di Archeologia Medievale, Erice 1974,* Palermo, 291-300

Mannoni, T 1994 *Archeologia dell'urbanistica*, Genova

Mannoni, T & Boato, A 2002 'Archeologia e storia del cantiere di costruzione', *Arqueología de la Arquitectura* 1, 39-53

Marçais, G 1945 'La conception des villes dans l'Islam', *Revue d'Alger* 2, 517-33

Marçais, G 1957 'Les Jardins de l'Islam', *Mélanges d'Histoire et d'Archéologie de l'Occident Musulman*, Alger, 233-44

Marçais, W 1928 'L'Islamisme et la vie urbaine', *Comptes Rendus de l'Académie des Inscriptions et Belles-Létres*, janvier-mars, 86-100

Marchesi, H, Thiriot, J & Vallauri, A (eds) 1997 *Marseille, les ateliers de potiers du XIIIe s. et le quartier Sainte-Barbe (Ve-XVIe s.),* Paris

Margry, PJ & Caspers, C (eds) 1997-2004 *Bedevaartplaatsen in Nederland* (4 volumes), Amsterdam & Hilversum (online databank at http://www.meertens.knaw.nl/bedevaart)

Märkle, T 2005 'Nutrition, aspects of land use and environment in medieval times in southern Germany: plant macro-remain analysis from latrines (late 11th-13th century AD) at the town of Überlingen, Lake Constance', *Vegetation History and Archaeobotany* 14/4, 427-41

Marks, R & Williamson, P (eds) 2003 *Gothic art for England 1400-1547*, London

Martin, D 2000 'End reversal during the conversion of medieval houses in Sussex', *Vernacular Architecture* 31, 26-31

Martin, D 2003 'The configuration of inner rooms and chambers in the transitional houses of Eastern Sussex', *Vernacular Architecture* 34, 35-71

Martin, D & Martin, B 1987 *Historic Buildings in Eastern Sussex* 4, Robertsbridge

Martin, D & Martin, B 1999 'Adapting houses to changing needs: multi-phased medieval and transitional houses in Eastern Sussex', *Sussex Archaeological Collections* 137, 121-32

Martin, J 1986 *Treasure of the Land of Darkness. The Fur Trade and its Significance for Medieval Russia*, Cambridge

Martínez Caviró, B 1983 *La loza dorada*, Madrid

Martinón-Torres, M & Rehren, T 2005 'Alchemy, chemistry and metallurgy in Renaissance Europe: a wider context for fire-assay remains', *Historical Metallurgy* 39, 14-28

Masinton, AW 2006 *Sacred Space: Priorities, Perception and the Presence of God in Late Medieval Yorkshire Parish Churches*, unpublished PhD thesis, Centre for Medieval Studies, University of York

Mason, E 1976 'The role of the English parishioner, 1100-1500', *Journal of Ecclesiastical History* 27, 17-29

Matthews, LG & Green, HJM 1969 'Post-medieval Pottery of the Inns of Court', *Post-Medieval Archaeology* 3, 1-17

Mattingly, J 2000 'Stories in the glass: reconstructing the St Neot pre-Reformation glazing scheme', *Journal of the Royal Institution of Cornwall* ns 2, 3/3-4, 9-55

Maufras, O (ed) 2006 *Habitats, nécropoles et paysages dans la moyenne et la basse vallée du Rhône (VIIe-XVe s.): contribution des travaux du TGV-Méditerranée à l'étude des sociétés rurales médiévales* (Documents d'Archéologie Française 98), Paris

Maxwell, R, Lore, A, Holmes, L & Harbottle, G 2005 'The dispersed sculpture of Parthenay and the contributions of nuclear science', *Medieval Archaeology* 49, 247-80

Mayewski, PA & 15 authors 2004 'Holocene climate variability', *Quaternary Research* 62, 243-55

Mays, S 1997 'Carbon stable isotope ratios in medieval and later human skeletons from northern England', *Journal of Archaeological Science* 24, 561-7

Mays, S, Harding, C & Heighway, C 2007 *Wharram: a study of settlement on the Yorkshire Wolds. Volume 11: The Churchyard* (York University Archaeological Publications 13), York

Mazzanti, MB, Bosi, G, Mercuri, AM, Accorsi, CA & Guarnieri, C 2005 'Plant use in a city in Northern Italy during the late Mediaeval and Renaissance periods: results of the archaeobotanical investigation of "The Mirror Pit" (14th-15th century AD) in Ferrara', *Vegetation History and Archaeobotany*, 14, 442-52

Mazzoli-Guindard, Ch 1996 *Villes d'al-Andalus: l'Espagne et le Portugal à l'époque musulmane (VIIIᵉ-XVᵉ siècles)*, Rennes

Měchurová, Z 1997 *Konůvky – zaniklá středověká ves ve Ždánickém lese (Konůvky – eine mittelalterliche Ortswüstung in dem Hügelland Ždánický les)* (Studie Archeologického ústavu Československé akademie věd v Brně 17/1), Brno

Meckseper, C (ed) 1985 *Stadt im Wandel: Kunst und Kultur des Bürgertums in Norddeutschland 1150-1650. Ausstellungskatalog* (4 volumes) (exhibition catalogue, Braunschweig 1985), Stuttgart & Bad Cannstatt

Medieval Europe 1992 *A Conference on Medieval Archaeology in Europe, 21-24 September 1992 at the University of York Pre-Printed Papers* 1-8, York

Meeson, B 2001 'Archaeological evidence and analysis: a case study from Staffordshire', *Vernacular Architecture* 32, 1-15

Mehl, J-M 1990 *Les jeux au royaume de France du XIIIe au début du XVIe siècle,* Paris

Meier, D 2006 *Seafarers, Merchants and Pirates in the Middle Ages*, Woodbridge

Meier, T 2002 'The ambivalent space; where to bury a king', in Helmig, G, Scholkmann, B & Untermann, M (eds) *Centre-Region-Periphery. Medieval Europe Basel 2002* (3 volumes), Hertingen, 179-84

Meier, T with Graham-Campbell, J 2007 'Life, Death and Memory', in Graham-Campbell, J & Valor, M (eds), *The Archaeology of Medieval Europe. Eighth to Twelfth Centuries AD,* Aarhus, 420-49

Meirion-Jones, G 1973 'The Long-house: a definition', *Medieval Archaeology* 17, 135-7

Melzer, W (ed) 2008 *Archäologie und mittelalterliches Handwerk. Eine Standortbestimmung,* Soest

Mendera, M (ed) 1991 *Archeologia e storia della produzione del vetro preindustriale*, Firenze

Mengel, O 1909 *Notice de la carte géologique de Prades*, Orléans

Mennim, AM 2000 *The Merchant Taylors' Hall*, York

Mercer, E 1969 *Furniture 700-1700*, London

Mercer, E 1972 '"Domus longa" and "long house"', *Vernacular Architecture* 3, 9-10

Mercer, E 1975 *English Vernacular Houses*, London

Mercer, E 1997 'The unfulfilled implications of vernacular architecture studies', *Vernacular Architecture* 28, 9-12

Merrifield, R 1987 *The Archaeology of Ritual and Magic*, London

Messier, R 1997 'Sijilmasa: five seasons of archaeological inquiry by a joint Moroccan-American mission', *Archéologie Islamique* 7, 61-92

Metcalfe A 2003 *Muslims and Christians in Norman Sicily. Arabic speakers and the end of Islam*, London & New York

Metzger, T 1982 *Jewish Life in the Middle Ages: Illuminated Hebrew Manuscripts of the Thirteenth to the Sixteenth Centuries*, New York

Meyer, W 1974 *Die Burgruine Alt-Wartburg im Kanton Aargau: Bericht über die Forschungen 1966/67* (Schweizer Beiträge zur Kulturgeschichte und Archäologie des Mittelalter 1), Olten

Miller, E (ed) 1991 *The Agrarian History of England and Wales, Volume 3 1348-1500*, London

Minagawa, M 1992 'Reconstruction of human diet from δ¹³C and δ¹⁵N in contemporary Japanese hair: a stochastic method for estimating multi-source contribution by double isotopic tracers', *Applied Geochemistry* 7, 145-58

Minagawa, M & Wada, E 1984 'Stepwise enrichment of ¹⁵N along food chain: further evidence and the relation between δ¹⁵N and animal age' *Geochimica et Cosmochimica Acta* 48, 1135-40

Misāns, I 2006 'Cēsis Vācu ordeņa un Hanzas vēsturē', in Rozentāle, V (ed) *Quo vadis, Cēsis?*, Cēsis

Missal 1965 *The New Small Missal. The proper of the Mass for all Sundays and the principal feasts, with the text to be used in the Mass*, London

Mitchell, P 2002 *The Archaeology of Southern Africa*, Cambridge

Mitchell, P 2004 'Synagoge und Jüdisches Viertel im Mittelalterlich Wien', in Wamers, E & Backhaus, F (eds) *Synagogen, Mikwen, Siedlungen: Jüdisches Alltagsleben in Lichte Neuer Archäologischer Funde* (Schriften des Archäologischen Museums Frankfurt 19), Frankfurt am Main, 139-50

Mitchell, P 2005 *African Connections. Archaeological Perspectives on Africa and the Wider World*, Walnut Creek (CA)

Mitchell, S, Price, N, Hutton, R, Purkiss, D, Patton, K, Raudvere, C, Severi, C, Aldhouse-Green, M, Semple, S, Pluskowski, A, Carver, M & Ginzburg, C 2010 'Witchcraft and deep time: a debate at Harvard', *Antiquity* 84, 864-79

Mittelstraß, T 2004 'Die Rekonstruktion eines hölzernen Wohnturmes des 13. Jahrhunderts in Stabbauweise in Kanzach, Landkreis Biberach', in Hofrichter, H (ed) *Holz in der Burgenarchitektur*, Braubach, 117-24

Mogren, M 1998 'The village, the forest and the archaeology of Ängersjö', in Andersson, H, Ersgård, L & Svensson, E (eds) *Outland Use in Preindustrial Europe*, Stockholm, 219-36

Møhl, U 1971 'Et knoglemateriale fra vikingtid og middelalder i Århus' in Andersen, H, Crabb, PJ & Madsen, HJ (eds) *Århus Søndervold. En byarkæologisk undersøgelse* (Jysk Arkæologisk Selskabs Skrifter 9), Copenhagen, 321-9

Molinari, A 1997 *Segesta II. Il castello e la moschea (scavi 1989-95)*, Palermo

Molinari, A & Nef, A (eds) 2004 *La Sicile à l'Époque islamique. Questions de méthodes et renouvellement récent des problématiques* (Atti del Convegno in *Mélanges de L'Ecole française de Rome, Moyen Âge* 116), Rome

Monod, T 1983 *L'Ile D'Arguin (Mauritanie). Essai Historique,* Lisbon

Mook, R, Bertelsen, R & Nielssen, AR 2008 'Om vilkårene for tørrfiskproduksjon', in Paulsen, C & Michelsen, HD (eds) *Símunarbók: heiðursrit til Símun V. Arge á 60 ára degnum,* Thorshavn, 151-65

Moran, M 2003 *Vernacular Buildings of Shropshire*, Almeley

Moreno Garcia, M 1997 'The zooarchaeological evidence for transhumance in medieval Spain', in De Boe, G & Verhaeghe, F, (ed) *Environment and subsistence in medieval Europe. Papers of the Medieval Europe Brugge 1997 Conference,* Zellik, 45-54

Moritz, W (ed) 1983 *Das Hospital im späten Mittelalter*, Marburg

Morris, R. 1989 *Churches in the Landscape*, London

Morrison, I 1985 *Landscape with Lake Dwellings*, Edinburgh

Mould, Q, Carlisle, I & Cameron, E 2003 *Craft, industry and everyday life. Leather and leatherworking in Anglo-Scandinavian and medieval York, (The Archaeology of York* 17/16), York

Müldner, G & Richards, MP 2005 'Fast or feast: reconstructing diet in later medieval England by stable isotope analysis' *Journal of Archaeological Science* 32, 39-48

Müldner, G & Richards, MP 2007 'Diet and diversity at later medieval Fishergate: the isotopic evidence', *American Journal of Physical Anthropology* 134, 162-74

Müller, K 2004 'Wurzburg: the world's largest find from a medieval Jewish cemetery', in Cluse, C (ed) *The Jews of Europe in the Middle Ages*, Turnhout, 379-89

Müller, U 1992 'Tischgerät aus Holz', in Flüeler, M & N (eds) *Stadtluft, Hirsebrei und Bettelmönch: die Stadt um 1300*, Stuttgart & Zürich, 311-319

Müller, U 1996 *Holzfunde aus Freiburg/Augustinereremitenkloster und Konstanz. Herstellung und Funktion einer Materialgruppe aus dem späten Mittelalter* (Forschungen und Berichte der Archäologie des Mittelalters in Baden-Württemberg 21), Stuttgart

Müller, U 2006 *Zwischen Gebrauch und Bedeutung: Studien zur Funktion von Sachkultur am Beispiel mittelalterlichen Handwaschgeschirrs (5./6. Bis 15./16. Jahrhundert)* (Zeitschrift für Archäologie des Mittelalters Beiheft 20), Bonn

Müller, U & Lübke, C 2006 'Innovation, Professionalisierung und Technologietransfer im mittelalterlichen Handwerk', *Zeitschrift für Archäologie des Mittelalters* 34, 1-146

Müller-Wille, M (ed) 1991 *Starigard-Oldenburg: ein slawischer Herrschersitz des frühen Mittelalters in Ostholstein*, Neumünster

Mugurēvičs, E 2002 'Forest animals and hunting in medieval Livonia', in Helmig, G, Scholkmann, B & Untermann, M (eds) *Centre, Region, Periphery, Medieval Europe Basel 2002*, Hertingen, 177-181

Mugurēvičs, Ē & Mugurēvičs, A 1999 'Meža dzīvnieki Latvijā', in Strods, H (ed) *Latvijas mežu vēsture lidz 1940 gadam*, Rīga, 207-47

Mundee, M 2009 'An isotopic approach to diet in Medieval Spain', in Baker, S, Gray, A, Lakin, K, Madgwick, R, Poole, K & Sandias, M (eds), *Food and Drink in Archaeology Volume 2* (University of Nottingham Postgraduate Conference 2008), Totnes, 64-72

Munro, JH 2003a 'Medieval woollen textiles, textile technology and industrial, c. 800-1500', in Jenkins, D (ed) *The Cambridge history of western textiles 2. Part 2: the Medieval period*, Cambridge, 181-227

Munro, JH 2003b 'Medieval woollens: the western European woollen industries and their struggles for international markets, c. 1000-15000', in Jenkins, D (ed) *The Cambridge history of western textiles 2. Part 2: the Medieval period*, Cambridge, 228-324

Munro, JH 2009 'Three Centuries of Luxury Textile Consumption in the Low Countries and England, 1330-1570: Trends and Comparison of Real Values of Woollen Broadcloths (Then and Now)', in Vestergård Pedersen, K & M-LB Nosch (eds) *The Medieval Broadcloth, Changing Trends in Fashions, Manufacturing and Consumption*, Oxford, 1-73

Murphy, JC, 1815 *The Arabian Antiquities of Spain*, London

Murphy, M & O'Conor, K 2008 *Roscommon Castle*, Roscommon

Murray, HJR 1913 (reprint 2002) *A history of chess*, Oxford

Murray, HJR 1952 (reprint 2002) *A history of board-games other than chess*, Oxford

Murray, J 2003 '17 Dean's Yard, Westminster: archaeological investigations', *Medieval Archaeology* 47, 41-52

Murray Jones, P 1994 'Information and Science', in Horrox, R (ed) *Fifteenth Century Attitudes. Perceptions of Society in Late Medieval England*, Cambridge, 97-111

Murray Jones, P 1998 *Medieval Medicine in Illuminated Manuscripts*, London

Murray Jones, P 2006 'Image, word and medicine in the Middle Ages', in Givens, JA, Reeds, KM & A Touwaide, A (eds) *Visualizing Medieval Medicine and Natural History, 1200-1550*, Aldershot, 1-24

Museo del Vidrio La Granja (ed) 2006 *Vidrio islámico en al-Andalus. Catálogo de la exposición del mismo título celebrada en la Real Fábrica de Cristales de La Granja entre noviembre de 2006 y abril de 2007*, Cuenca

Mynors, RAB & Dalzell, A 1992 *The Correspondence of Erasmus 1523-4* (The Collected Works of Erasmus 10), Toronto

N

Narkiss, B 1992 'The Heikhal, Minah, and Teivah in Sephardi Synagogues', *Jewish Art* 18, 30-47

Navarro Palazón, J 1986a *La cerámica esgrafiada andalusí de Murcia / La céramique hispano-arabe à décor esgrafié de Murcie* (Publications de la Casa de Velázquez, Serie Études et Documents 2), Madrid

Navarro Palazón, J 1986b *La cerámica islámica en Murcia. I Catálogo*, Murcia

Navarro Palazón, J 1991 *Una casa islámica en Murcia. Estudio de su ajuar (siglo XIII)*, Murcia

Navarro Palazón, J (ed) 1995 *Casas y Palacios de Al-Andalus. Siglos XII–XIII*, Barcelona-Madrid

Navarro Palazón, J 2002 'The andalusi house in Siyasa: attempt at a typological classification', *Patterns of Everyday life* (*The formation of the classical Islamic world* vol. 10), Trowbridge, 43-65

Navarro Palazón, J, 2005 'Sobre palacios andalusíes (Siglos XII-XIV)', *Vivir en palacio en la Edad Media. Siglos XII-XV*, Segovia, 111-44

Navarro Palazón, J & Jiménez Castillo, P 1995 'La producción cerámica medieval de Murcia', in Gerrard, CM, Gutiérrez, A & Vince, A (eds) *Spanish medieval ceramics in Spain and the British Isles* (British Archaeological Reports International Series 610), Oxford, 183-212

Navarro Palazón, J & Jiménez Castillo P 2002 'Religiosidad y creencias en la Murcia musulmana. Testimonios arqueológicos de una cultura oriental', in *Huellas. Catedral de Murcia. Exposición 2002 (23 de enero-22 de julio)*, Murcia, 58-87

Navarro Palazón, J & Jiménez Castillo, P 2003 'Sobre la ciudad islámica y su evolución', *Estudios de arqueología dedicados a la profesora Ana María Muñoz Amilibia*, Murcia, 319-81

Navarro Palazón, J & Jiménez Castillo, P 2007a *Las ciudades de Alandalús. Nuevas perspectivas*, Zaragoza

Navarro Palazón, J & Jiménez Castillo, P 2007b *Siyâsa. Estudio arqueológico del despoblado andalusí (ss. XI-XIII)*, Murcia

Navarro Palazón, J & Jiménez Castillo, P 2007c 'Evolution of the Andalusi urban landscape: from the dispersed to the saturated medina', in Anderson, GD & Rosser-Owen, M (eds) *Revisiting Al-Andalus: Perspectives on the Material Culture of Islamic Spain and Beyond,* Leiden & Boston, 115-142

Naydenova, M 2006 'Public and private: the late medieval wall paintings of Haddon Hall chapel, Derbyshire,' *Antiquaries Journal* 86, 179-205

Nekuda, V 1975 *Pfaffenschlag. Zaniklá středověká ves u Slavonic (Pfaffenschlag. Mittelalterliche Ortswüstung bei Slavonice),* Brno

Newitt, M 2004 *A History of Portuguese Overseas Expansion, 1400-1668,* Oxford

Nightingale, P 1995 *A Medieval Mercantile Community. The Grocers' Company and the Politics and Trade of London 1000-1485,* New Haven (CT) & London

Nixon, S 2009 'Excavating Essouk-Tadmakka (Mali): new archaeological investigations of early Islamic trans-Saharan trade', *Azania: Archaeological Research in Africa* 44, 217-55

Nockert, M 1997a 'Textiles and costume 1350-1450', in Grinder-Hansen, P (ed) *Margrete I. Regent of the North – the Kalmar Union 600 years,* Copenhagen, 200-211 & cat. nos. 250-62, 273, 357

Nockert, M 1997b *Bockstenmannen och hans dräkt,* second edition, Varberg (with English summary)

Northrup, D 2002 *Africa's discovery of Europe, 1450-1850,* New York

Noweir, HM, El-Sadik, MY, El-Dakhakhny, AA & Osman, AH 1975 'Dust exposure in manual flax processing in Egypt', *British Journal of Industrial Medicine* 32, 147-54 (Retrieved 28 January 28 2010 from http://www.ncbi.nlm.nih.gov/pmc/articles/PMC1008040/pdf/brjindmed00086-0055.pdf

Nybo Rasmussen, J 2002 *Die Franziskaner in den nordischen Ländern im Mittelalter,* Kevelaer

Ó

Ó Donnchadha, B 2007 'The oldest church in Ireland's "oldest town"', *Archaeology Ireland* 21, 8-10

O'Connell, TC & Hedges, REM 1999 'Investigations into the effect of diet on modern human hair isotopic values', *American Journal of Physical Anthropology* 108, 409-25

O'Connell, TC, Hedges, REM, Healey, MA & Simpson, AH 2001 'Isotopic comparison of hair, nail and bone: modern analyses', *Journal of Archaeological Science* 28: 1247-55

O'Connor, TP 1989 'What shall we have for dinner? Food remains from urban sites', in Serjeantson, D & Waldron, T (eds) *Diet and Crafts in Towns: the Evidence of Animal Remains from the Roman to the Post-medieval Periods,* Oxford, 13-23

O'Connor, TP 2000a (2005) *The archaeology of animal bones,* Stroud (second edition 2005)

O'Connor, TP 2000b 'Human refuse as a major ecological factor in medieval urban vertebrate communities', *Human Ecodynamics. Symposia of the Association for Environmental Archaeology* 19, Oxford, 15-20

O'Conor, K 1996 'Dunamase Castle', *Journal of Irish Archaeology* 7, 107-25

O'Conor, K 1998 *The Archaeology of Medieval Rural Settlement in Ireland,* Dublin

O'Conor, K 2002 'Motte castles in Ireland'; permanent fortresses, residences and manorial castles, *Château Gaillard* 20, 173-82

O'Conor, K 2008 'Castle studies in Ireland : the way forward', *Château Gaillard* 23, 329-39

O'Regan, H, Turner, A & Sabin, R 2006 'Medieval big cat remains from the Royal Menagerie at the Tower of London', *International Journal of Osteoarchaeology* 16, 385-94

O

Oexle, J 1992 'Konstanz', in Flüeler, M & Flüeler, N (eds) 1992 *Stadtluft, Hirsebrei und Bettelmönch: die Stadt um 1300,* Stuttgart & Zürich 53-68

Ogilvie, AEJ & Jónsson, T, 2001 '"Little Ice Age" research: a perspective from Iceland', *Climatic Change* 48, 9-52

Olivar, M 1950 *La vajilla de madera y la cerámica de uso en Valencia y Cataluña durante el siglo XIV (según los inventarios de la época)* (Anales del Centro de Cultura Valenciana Anejo 2), Valencia

Olrik, J 1909 *Drikkehorn og Sølvtøj fra Middelalder og Renæssance,* København (with French summary)

Olson, RJM, Reilly, PL & Shepherd, R (eds) 2006 *The Biography of the Object in Late Medieval & Renaissance Italy,* Oxford

Oman, CC 1963 *Medieval silver nefs* (Victoria and Albert Museum Monograph 15), London

Oman, CC 1974 *British rings, 800-1914,* London

Oonk S, Slomp, CP, Huisman, DJ & Vriend, SP 2009 'Effects of site lithology on geochemical signatures of human occupation in archaeological house plans in the Netherlands', *Journal of Archaeological Science* 36/6: 1215-28

Opll, F 2009 *Publication of historical atlases,* coordinated by the International Commission for the History of Towns, Vienna (available at http://www.wien.gv.at/kultur/archiv/kooperationen/lbi/staedteatlas/bibliographie/index.html

Oppenheimer, C 2003 'Ice core and palaeoclimatic evidence for the timing and nature of the great mid-13th century volcanic eruption', *International Journal of Climatology* 23, 417-26

Opravil, E 1997 'Vegetační poměry Sezimova Ústí a jeho okolí ve středověku' [Die Vegetationsverhältnisse von Sezimovo Ústí und seiner Umgebung im Mittelalter], in *Život v archeologii středověku. Sborník příspěvků věnovaných Miroslavu Richterovi a Zdeňku Smetánkovi*, Prague, 498-506

Oram, RD 2008 'Royal and lordly residence in Scotland *c.* 1050 to *c.* 1250: an historiographical review and critical revision', *Antiquaries Journal* 88, 165-89

Orejas, A & Ruiz del Árbol, M 2006 'Habiter et exploiter le paysage : autour des mines d'or de Las Medulas', in Lévêque, L (ed) *Paysages de mémoire, mémoire du paysage*, Paris, 211-35

Orihuela Uzal, A 1996 *Casas y Palacios nazaríes. Siglos XIII-XV*, Barcelona

Orser, C 2006 'Symbolic violence and landscape pedagogy: an illustration from the Irish countryside', *Historical Archaeology* 40, 28-44

Orton, C, Tyers, P & Vince, A 1993 *Pottery in archaeology*, Cambridge

Osma, G J de 1912 *La loza dorada de Manises en el año 1454* (Textos y Documentos Valencianos 1), Madrid (Second edition)

Østergård, E 2004 *Woven into the Earth. Textile finds in Norse Greenland*, Aarhus

Ottaway, P 2002 *Craft, industry and everyday life: finds from Medieval York (The Archaeology of York 17/15, The Small Finds)*, York

Otto, T & Pedersen, P (eds) 2005 *Tradition and agency. Tracing cultural continuity and invention*, Aarhus

Oudhof, J.W.M., J. Dijkstra & A.A.A. Verhoeven (eds) 2000 Huis Malburg van spoor tot spoor. Een Middeleeuwse nederzetting in Kerk-Avezaath *Rapportage Archeologische Monumentenzorg* 81, Amersfoort, 45-77.

Owen, DM 1976 'Chapelries and rural settlement: an examination of some of the Kesteven evidence', in Sawyer, PH (ed) *Medieval Settlement: Continuity and Change*, London, 66-71

Øye, I 1988 *Textile equipment and its working environment, Bryggen in Bergen c. 1150-1500* (The Bryggen Papers, Main Series 2), Bergen

P

Pajer, J 1997 'Origins of Anabaptist ceramics in Moravia: archaeological perspectives', in Mayer, CE *The Potter's Art: Contribution to the Study of the Koerner Collection of European Ceramics*, Vancouver, 87-107

Pajer, J 2007 'Archaeological excavations of Anabaptist ceramics in Moravia', in Žegklitz, J (ed) *Studies in Post-Medieval Archaeology* 2, 227-50

Pajer, J 2011 *Anabaptist Faiences from Moravia 1593-1620. Catalogue of Documents from Institutional and Private Collections*, Strážnice

Palliser, DM 1990 'Civic Mentality and the Environment in Tudor York', in Barry, J (ed) *The Tudor and Stuart Tow. A Reader in Urban History, 1530-1688*, London & New York, 216-42

Palliser, DM, Slater, TR & Dennison, E 2000 'The topography of towns 600-1300', in Palliser, D (ed) *The Cambridge Urban History of Britain, Vol. 1 600-1540*, Cambridge, 153-87

Palomera Plaza, S, Lopez Alvarez, AM & Alvarez Delgado, Y 1992 'Excavation around the Samuel Halevi Synagogue (del Transito) in Toledo', *Jewish Art* 18, 48-57

Palou, H, Rieth, E, Izaguirre, M, Jover, A, Nieto, X, Pujol, M, Raurich, X & Apestegui, C 1998 *Excavations arqueològiques subaquàtiques a Cala Culip 2 Culip IV*, Girona

Pälsi, S 1944 *Eräelämän perinteitä*, Helsinki & Porvoo

Pantin, WA 1962-3 'Medieval English town-house plans', *Medieval Archaeology* 6-7, 202-39

Parenti, R 1985 'La lettura stratigrafica delle murature in contesti archeologici e di restauro architettonico', *Restauro e Città* 1, 55-68

Park, RB & Epstein, S 1960 'Carbon isotope fractionation during photosynthesis', *Geochimica et Cosmochimica Acta* 21, 110-26

Parry, S 2006 *Raunds Area Survey. An archaeological study of the landscape of Raunds, Northamptonshire 1985-94*, Oxford

Passarrius, O, Donat, R & Catafau A 2008 *Vilarnau. Un village du Moyen Age en Roussillon*, Perpignan

Passini, J (ed) 2001 *La ciudad medieval: de la casa al tejido urbano: actas del primer curso de historia y urbanismo medieval organizado por la Universidad de Castilla-La Mancha*, Cuenca

Patronato de la Alhambra y Generalife (ed) 2006 *Catálogo de la exposición Los jarrones de la Alhambra. Simbología y poder*, Granada

Pattison, IR, Pattison, DS & Alcock, NW 1992 *A Bibliography of Vernacular Architecture vol. 3, 1977-1989*, Aberystwyth

Pattison, IR, Pattison, DS & Alcock, NW 1999 *A Bibliography of Vernacular Architecture vol. 4, 1990-1994*, Aberystwyth

Paulus, S 2007 *Die Architektur der Synagoge im Mittelalter: Überlieferung und Bestand*, Petersberg

Pavón Maldonado, B 1966 *Memoria de la mezquita de Madinat al-Zahra*, (Dirección General de Bellas Artes (Excavaciones Arqueológicas en España 50), Madrid

Pavón Maldonado, B 1992 *Ciudades hispanomusulmanas*, Madrid

Pavón Maldonado, B 1999 *Tratado de arquitectura hispanomusulmana II. Ciudades y fortalezas*, Madrid

Pavón Maldonado, B 2009 *Tratado de arquitectura hispanomusulmana IV. Mezquitas*, Madrid

Paz Torres Palomo, M & Acién Almansa, M (eds) 1995 *Estudios sobre cementerios islàmicos andalusies*, Malaga

Pearson, S 1994 *The Medieval Houses of Kent. An Historical Analysis,* London

Pearson, S 1997 'Tree-ring dating: a review', *Vernacular Architecture* 28, 25-39

Pearson, S 2001 'The chronological distribution of tree-ring dates 1980-2001: an update', *Vernacular Architecture* 32, 68-9

Pearson, S 2005 'Rural and urban houses 1100-1500', in Dyer, C & Giles, K (eds) *Town and Country 1100-1500*, Leeds, 40-60

Pearson, S 2009 'Medieval Houses in English Towns: form and location', *Vernacular Architecture* 40, 1-22

Pecqueur, L 2003 'Des morts chez les vivants. Les inhumations dans les habitats ruraux du haut Moyen Age en Ile-de-France', *Archéologie Médiévale*, 33, 1-31

Pederson, DC, Peteet, DM, Kurdyla, D & Guilderson, T 2005 'Medieval Warming, Little Ice Age, and European impact on the environment during the last millennium in the lower Hudson Valley, New York, USA', *Quaternary Research* 63, 238-49

Pegg, M. G. 2008. *A Most Holy War: The Albigensian Crusade and the Battle for Christendom*. Oxford: Oxford University Press

Pensabene, P (ed) 2010 *Piazza Armerina. Villa del Casale e la Sicilia tra tardoantico e medioevo*, Roma

Perdikaris, S 1999 *From chiefly provisioning to state capital ventures: the transition from natural to market economy and the commercialization of cod fisheries in Medieval Arctic Norway* (dissertation, City University of New York, Ann Arbor UMI No 9912610), Ann Arbor

Pertot, G & Treccani, GP 2002 'Mentalità stratigrafica e progetti per la conoscenza e per la conservazione', *Arqueología de la Arquitectura* 1, 131-44

Pesez, J-M (ed) 1985 *Brucato: histoire et archéologie d´un habitat médiéval en Sicile*, Rome

Pesez, J-M 1991 'Outils et techniques agricoles du monde médiéval', in Guilaine, J (ed) *Pour une archéologie agraire: à la croisée des sciences de l'homme et de la nature*, Paris, 131-64

Peters, C 1996 'Interior and furnishings,' in Blair, J & Pyrah, C (eds) *Church Archaeology: Research Directions for the Future* (CBA Research Report 104), York, 68-75

Pétrequin, P, Fluzin, P, Thiriot, J & Benoit, P (eds) 2000 *Arts du feu et productions artisanales. XXèmes Rencontres internationales d'Antibes*, Antibes

Petrucci, A 1995 *Le scritture ultime, Ideologia della morte e strategie dello scrivere nella tradizione occidentale,* Torino

Petruccioli, A (ed) 1994 *Il giardino islamico. Architettura, natura, paesaggio*, Milano

Pfrommer, G & Gutscher, D 1999 *Laufen Rathausplatz. Eine hölzerne Häuserzeile in einer mittelalterlichen Kleinstadt: Hausbau, Sachkultur und Alltag. Ergebnisse der Grabungskampagnen 1988 und 1989*, Bern

Phillips, D & B Heywood 1995 *Excavations at York Minster, Vol 1: From Roman Fortress to Norman Cathedral* (Royal Commission on the Historical Monuments of England)

Phillips, K 2005 'The invisible man: body and ritual in a fifteenth-century noble household', *Journal of Medieval History* 31, 143-62

Pieters, M 2002 *Aspecten van de materiële leefwereld in een laatmiddeleeuws vissersmilieu in het zuidelijk Noordzeegebied. Een bijdrage tot de middeleeuwse rurale archeologie, inzonderheid naar aanleiding van de opgravingen te Raversijde (stad Oostende, provincie West-Vlaanderen, België)*, unpublished PhD dissertation, Vrije Universiteit Brussel

Pieters, M & Verhaeghe, F 2009 'Medieval fishing communities in coastal Flanders, Belgium, and western Mediterranean commodities', *Medieval Ceramics* 30, 2006-8, 101-16

Pikirayi, I 2009 'Palaces, Feiras & Prazos: An Historical Archaeological Perspective of African-Portuguese Contact in Northern Zimbabwe', *African Archaeological Review* 26, 163-85

Piponnier, F & Mane, P 2000 *Dress in the Middle Ages*, Yale (translation of the 1995 French publication)

Planchon, J, Bois, M & Connjard-Rethore, P 2010 *La Drôme* (Carte archéologique de la Gaule 26), Paris

Platt, C 1995 *The Parish Churches of Medieval England* (second edition), London

Platt, C 1997 *King Death: the Black Death and its aftermath in late-medieval England*, London

Platt, C & Coleman-Smith, R 1975 *Excavations in Medieval Southampton 1953-1969. Volume 1: The Excavation Report,* Leicester

Pleiner, R 2000 *Iron in Archaeology. Early European Bloomery Smelters* Prague

Pleiner, R 2006 *Iron in Archaeology. Early European Blacksmiths,* Prague

Pluskowski, AG 2005 'Narwhals or unicorns? Exotic animals as material culture in medieval Europe', *European Journal of Archaeology* 7, 291-313

Pluskowski, AG 2006 *Wolves and the Wilderness in the Middle Ages,* Woodbridge

Pluskowski, AG 2007a 'The social construction of medieval park ecosystems: an interdisciplinary perspective', in Liddiard, R (ed) *The Medieval Park: New Perspectives,* Macclesfield, 63-78

Pluskowski, AG (ed) 2007b Breaking and Shaping *Beastly Bodies: Animals as Material Culture in the Middle Ages,* Oxford

Pluskowski, AG 2007c 'Communicating through skin and bone: the appropriation of animal bodies in medieval western seigneurial culture', in Pluskowski, AG (ed) 2007 Breaking and Shaping *Beastly Bodies: Animals as Material Culture in the Middle Ages,* Oxford, 32-51

Pluskowski, AG 2009 'What is exotic? Sources of animals and animal products from the edges of the medieval world', in Jaritz, G & Kreem, J (eds) *The Edges of the Medieval World,* Krems, 113-29

Pluskowski, AG & Seetah, K 2006 'The animal bones from the 2004 excavations at Stari Bar, Montenegro', in Gelichi, S (ed) *The Archaeology of a Deserted Town,* Florence, 97-111

Polet, C & Katzenberg, MA 2003 'Reconstruction of the diet in a mediaeval monastic community from the coast of Belgium', *Journal of Archaeological Science* 30, 525-33

Postan, MM 1973 Essays on Medieval Agriculture and General Problems of the Medieval Economy, Cambridge

Porsche, M 1994 *Die mittelalterliche Stadtbefestigung von Freiburg im Breisgau* (Materialhefte zur Archäologie in Baden-Württemberg 22), Stuttgart

Posnansky, M 1973 'Aspects of early West African trade', *World Archaeology* 5, 149-62

Pounds, NJG 2000 *A History of the English Parish,* Cambridge

Pozo Martínez, I, 2000 'La alquería islámica de Villa Vieja (Calasparra, Murcia)', *Castrum 6: Maisons et espaces domestiques dans le monde Méditerranéen au Moyen Âge,* Rome & Madrid, 165-75

Prechel, M 1996 'Anthropologische Untersuchungen der Skelettreste aus einem Pestmassengrab am Heiligen-Geist-Hospital zu Lübeck', *Lübecker Schriften zur Archäologie und Kulturgesschichte* 24, 323-39

Pressouyre, L (ed) 1994 *L'espace cistercien* (Comité des travaux historiques et scientifiques), Paris

Prevenier, W & de Hemptinne, T (eds) 2000 *La diplomatique urbaine en Europe au moyen âge* (Actes du congrès de la Commission internationale de Diplomatique, Gand 25-29 août 1998; Studies in Urban Social, Economic and Political History of the Medieval and Early Modern Low Countries 9), Leuven & Apeldoorn

Prieto Moreno, F 1952 *Los jardines de Granada,* Madrid

Prigent, D 1996 'Les céramiques funéraires (XIe–XVIIIe siècle)', in Galinié, H & Zadora-Rio, E (eds) *Archéologie du cimetière chrétien, Actes du colloque d'Orléans (28 sept.-1er oct. 1994)* (11e Supplément à la Revue Archéologique du Centre), Tours 215-24

Pringle, H 2007 'Medieval DNA, modern medicine', *Archaeology* 60/6 (www.archaeology.org/0711/abstracts/blackdeath.html)

Pritchard, F 2003 'The uses of textiles, c. 1000-1500', in Jenkins, D (ed) *The Cambridge history of western textiles 2. Part 2: the Medieval period,* Cambridge, 255-377

Privat, KL, O'Connell, TC & Richards, MP 2002 'Stable isotope analysis of human and faunal remains from the Anglo-Saxon cemetery at Berinsfield Oxfordshire: dietary and social implications', *Journal of Archaeological Science* 29, 779-90

Prowse, T, Schwarcz, HP, Saunders, RS, Macchiarelli, R, & Bondioli, L 2005 'Isotopic evidence for age related variation in diet from Isola Sacra', *American Journal of Physical Anthropology* 128, 2-13

Pryor, JH 1994 'The Mediterranean Round Ship', in Unger, RW (ed) *Cogs, Caravels and Galleons. The Sailing Ship 1000-1650,* London, 59-76

Q

Quiney, A 1999 'Hall or Chamber? That is the Question. The use of rooms in post-Conquest Houses', *Architectural History* 42, 24-46

Quiney, A 2003 *Town Houses of Medieval Britain,* New Haven (CT) & London

R

Rackham, DJ 2004 'Physical remains of horses', in Clark, J (ed) *The Medieval Horse and its Equipment,* Woodbridge, 19-22

Rahtz, PA & Hirst, SM 1976 *Bordesley Abbey, Red-ditch, Hereford-Worcestershire. First report on excavations 1969-1973* (British Archaeological Reports 23), Oxford

Rammo, R 2009 'Searching for Broadcloth in Tartu (14th-15th century)', in Vestergård Pedersen, K & M-LB Nosch (eds) *The Medieval Broadcloth, Changing Trends in Fashions, Manufacturing and Consumption*, Oxford, 99-108

Raoult, D, Aboudharam, G, Crubézy, E, Larrouy, G, Ludes, B & Drancourt, M 2000 'Molecular identification by "Suicide PCR" of *Yersinia pestis* as the agent of medieval Black Death', *Proceedings of the National Academy of Sciences of the United States of America* 97, 12800-803

Rasmussen, JN 2002 *Die Franziskaner in den nordishen Ländern im Mittelalter*, Kevelaer

Ravenstein, E 1900 'The Voyages of Diogo Cão and Bartholomeu Dias, 1482-88', *The Geographical Journal* 16, 625-55

Rawcliffe, C 2004 'Sickness and Health', in Rawcliffe, C & Wilson, R (eds) *Medieval Norwich*, Hambledon, 301-26

Rawcliffe, C 2008 'Dives Redeemed? The guild almshouses of later medieval England', *The Fifteenth Century* 8 1-27

Raymond, A 1995 'Ville musulmane, ville arabe: mythes orientalistes et recherches récentes', in Biget, J-L & Hervé, (eds) *Panoramas urbains: situation de l'histoire des villes*, Fontenay-aux-Roses, 309-36

Raynaud, C 1998 *Le commentaire de document figuré en histoire médiévale*, Paris

RCHM(E) (Royal Commission on the Historical Monuments of England) 1968 *An Inventory of the Historical Monuments in the county of Cambridge, Vol 1: West Cambridgeshire*, London

RCHM(E) (Royal Commission on the Historical Monuments of England) 1985 *Rural Houses of the Lancashire Pennines 1560-1760,* London

Rebkowski, M 1997 'Medieval glazed pottery imported into Pomerania. A survey of the present state of research', in Buko, A & Pela, W (eds) *Imported and Locally Produced Pottery: Methods of Identification and Analysis*, Warsaw, 97-109

Reddaway, TF & Walker, LEM 1975 *The early history of the Goldsmiths' Company*, London, 1327-1509

Redman, CL 1980 'Late medieval ceramics from Qsar-es-Seghir', in Demians d'Archimbaud, G & Picon, M (eds) *La céramique médiévale en Méditerranée occidentale, Xe-XVe siècle*, Valbonne 1978, 251-63

Redman, CL 1986 *Qsar es-Seghir. An Archaeological View of Medieval Life*, Orlando

Regnéll, J & Olsson, M 1998 'The land-use history of summer farms (sätrar) in northern Värmland, Sweden: a pilot study using palaeoecological methods', in Andersson, H, Ersgård, L & Svensson, E (eds) *Outland Use in Preindustrial Europe*, Stockholm, 63-71

Rehren, T 1997 'Metal analysis in the Middle Ages', in De Boe, G & Verhaeghe, F (eds) *Material Culture in Medieval Europe. Papers of the Medieval Europe Brugge 1997 Conference*, Zellik, 9-15

Reid, I 1982 'Noen funn av middelhavskeramikk i Midt-Norge', *Hikuin* 8, 191-196

Reilly, BF 1993 *The Medieval Spains*, Cambridge

Retuerce Velasco, M 1998 *La cerámica andalusí de la Meseta*, Madrid

Reynolds, S 1977 *An Introduction to the History of English Medieval Towns*, Oxford

Reynolds, S 1994 *Fiefs and Vassals: the medieval evidence reinterpreted*, Oxford

Richardson, A 2003a 'Corridors of power: a case study in access analysis from medieval England', *Antiquity* 77, 373-84

Richardson, A 2003b 'Gender and space in English royal palaces c. 1160-c. 1547: a study in access analysis and imagery', *Medieval Archaeology* 47, 131-65

Richardson, C 2003c 'Household Objects and Domestic Ties', in Beattie, C, Maslakovic, A & Rees Jones, S (eds) *The Medieval Household in Christian Europe, c. 850-c. 1550: Managing Power, Wealth, and the Body*, Turnhout, 433-48

Richter, M 1986 'Sezimovo Ústí: a part of the project of investigations of Bohemian urban settlements', in *Archaeology in Bohemia 1981-1985*, Prague, 229-36

Richter, M 1994 'Sezimovo Ústí', in *25 Years of Archaeological Research in Bohemia* (Památky archeologické Supplementum 1), Prague, 201-206

Richter, M & Krajíc, R 2001 *Sezimovo Ústí: archeologie středověkého poddanského města 2. Levobřežní předměstí: archeologický výzkum 1962-1988* [Sezimovo Ústí: Archäologie der mittelalterlichen Untertanenstadt 2. Vorstadt am linken Flussufer: Archäologische Untersuchung 1962-1988], Prague, Sezimovo Ústí & Tábor

Rieth, E 1989 'Le Clos des Galées de Rouen, lieu de construction navale à clin et à carvel (1293-1419)', in Villain-Gandossi, C (ed) *Medieval Ships and the Birth of Technological Societies*1, Malta, 71-77

Rippon, S 2004 'Making the most of a bad situation? Glastonbury Abbey, Meare and the medieval exploitation of wetland resources in the Somerset levels', *Medieval Archaeology* 48, 91-130

Rius, M 1999 (2000) *La alqibla en al-Andalus y al-Magrib al-Aqsa*, Barcelona

Rizzi, A 2001 *I leoni di San Marco. Il simbolo della Republica Veneta nella scupltura e nella pittura*, two volumes, Venice

Röber, R 1999 *Von Schmieden, Würflern und Schreinern. Städtisches Handwerk im Mittelalter*, Stuttgart

Roberts, BK & Wrathmell, S 2000 *An atlas of rural settlement in England*, London

Roberts, CA 2009a 'Health and welfare in medieval England: the human skeletal remains contextualized,' in Gilchrist, R & Reynolds, A (eds) *Reflections: 50 years of Medieval Archaeology, 1957-2007*, Leeds, 307-25

Roberts, CA 2009b *Human remains in archaeology: a handbook*, York

Roberts, CA & Cox, M 2003 *Health and Disease in Britain: from prehistory to the present day*, Stroud

Roberts, CA & Manchester, K 1995 *The Archaeology of Disease* (second edition), Stroud

Roberts, E 1995 'Overton Court Farm and the late-medieval farmhouses of demesne lessees in Hampshire', *Proceedings of the Hampshire Field Club Archaeology Society* 51, 89-106

Roberts, E 2003 *Hampshire Houses 1250-1700*, Southampton

Roberts, M 1992 'A Northampton Jewish Tombstone, c. 1259 to 1290 recently rediscovered in Northampton Central Museum' *Medieval Archaeology* 36, 173-8, also available on-line at: http://ads.ahds.ac.uk/catalogue/adsdata/arch-769-1/ahds/dissemination/pdf/vol36/36_173_178.pdf

Roberts, OTP 2004 'Llong Casnewydd: the Newport Ship, a personal view', *International Journal of Nautical Archaeology* 33, 158-63

Robinson, M 2001 'Insects as palaeoenvironmental indicators', in Brothwell DR & Pollard AM (eds) 2001 *Handbook of Archaeological Sciences*, Chichester, 121-34

Rockwell, P 1989 *Lavorare la pietra: manuale per l'archeologo, lo storico dell'arte, il restauratore*, Milano

Rodriguez, N 1997 'Cape Verde. Site and Archaeological Heritage Conservation at Cidade Velha', in Arduin, C (ed) *Museums and Archaeology in West Africa*, Washington (DC), 98-104

Rodwell, W 2005 *The Archaeology of Churches*, Stroud

Rodwell, WJ & Rodwell, KA 1986 *Rivenhall: investigations of a villa, church and village 1950-1977* (CBA Research Report 55), London

Roesdahl, E 1999a 'Boligernes indretning og udstyr', in Roesdahl, E (ed) *Dagligliv i Danmarks middelalder: en arkæologisk kulturhistorie*, København, 82-109

Roesdahl, E (ed) 1999b *Dagligliv i Danmarks middelalder: en arkæologisk kulturhistorie*, København (second ed. 2004, Aarhus)

Roesdahl, E 2003a 'Møbler og indretning', in Roesdahl, E (ed) *Bolig og familie i Danmarks middelalder*, Aarhus, 223-46 (with English summary)

Roesdahl, E 2003b 'Walrus ivory and other northern luxuries: their importance for Norse voyages and settlements in Greenland and America', in Lewis-Simpson, S (ed) *Vinland Revisited: the Norse World at the turn of the First Millennium*, St. John's, 145-52

Roesdahl, E 2005 'Walrus ivory: demand, supply, workshops and Greenland', in Mortensen, A & Arge, SV (eds) *Viking and Norse in the North Atlantic. Select Papers from the Proceedings of the fourteenth Viking Congress, Tórshavn, 19-30 July 2001*, Tórshavn, 182-91

Roesdahl, E 2009 'Housing culture – Scandinavian perspectives', in Gilchrist, R & Reynolds, A (eds) *Reflections: 50 years of Medieval Archaeology, 1957-2007*, Leeds, 271-88

Roffey, S 2007 *The Medieval Chantry Chapel. An Archaeology*, Woodbridge

Rogers, JD, Ulambayar, E & Gallon, M 2005 'Urban centres and the emergence of empires in Eastern Inner Asia', *Antiquity* 79, 801-19

Rose, S 2002 *Medieval naval warfare*, London

Rosenwein, B 1999 *Negotiating Space. Power, Restraint and Privileges of Immunity in Early Medieval Europe*, Ithaca (NY)

Rosselló Bordoy, G 1978 *Ensayo de sistematización de la cerámica árabe en Mallorca*, Palma de Mallorca

Rosselló Bordoy, G 1991 *El nombre de las cosas en Al-Andalus: una propuesta de terminología cerámica*, Palma de Mallorca

Rosselló Pons, M 1983 *Les céramiques almohades del carrer de Zavellá. Ciutat de Mallorca*, Palma de Mallorca

Rosser, G 1988a 'Communities of parish and guild in the late Middle Ages', in Rutgers, LV *The Hidden Heritage of Diaspora Judaism. Essays on Jewish Cultural Identity in the Roman World*, Leuven, 125-35

Rosser, G 1988b 'The Anglo-Saxon guilds', in Blair, J (ed) *Minsters and Parish Churches: the Local Church in Transition 950-1200* (Oxford University Commission for Archaeology Monographs 17), Oxford, 31-4

Rosser, G 1994 'Going to the fraternity feast: commensality and social relations in late medieval England', *Journal of British Studies* 33, 430-46

Rosser, G 1998 'Conflict and political community in the medieval town', in Slater, T & Rosser, G (eds) *The Church in the Medieval Town*, Aldershot, 20-42

Rosser, G 2006 'Big brotherhood: guilds in urban politics in late medieval England', in Gadd, IA & Wallis, P (eds) *Guilds and Association in Europe 900-1900*, London, 27-42

Rötting, H 1997 *Stadtarchäologie in Braunschweig: ein fachübergreifender Arbeitsbericht zu den Grabungen 1976-1992* (Forschungen der Denkmalpflege in Niedersachsen 3), Hannover

Roussell, A 1936 '*Sandnes and the neighbouring farms* (Meddelelser om Grønland 88/2) København

Ruas, M-P 2002 *Productions agricoles, stockage and finage en Montagne Noire médiévale. Le grenier castral de Durfort (Tarn)*, Paris

Ruggles, FD, 2000 *Garden, Landscape and Vision in the Palaces of Islamic Spain*, Pennsylvania

Ruiz Molina, L, 2000 *Hisn Yakka. Un castillo rural de Sarq AL-Andalus. Siglos XI al XIII. Excavaciones arqueológicas en el Cerro del Castillo de Yecla (1990-1999)* (Yakka, Revista de Estudios Yeclanos 10), Yecla

Ruppel, T, Neuwirth, J, Leone, MP & Fry, G-M 2003 'Hidden in view: African spiritual spaces in North American landscapes', *Antiquity* 77, 321-35

Ruralia 1-7 1996, 1998, 2000, 2002, 2005, 2007, 2009 (Památky archeologické supplementum, Prague 1-5;), Turnhout, 6 onwards

Russow, Balthasar 1584 *The Chronicle of Balthasar Russow* trans. 1988 by Smith, JC, Eichhoff, J & Urban, W, Madison (WI)

Rutgers, LV 1998 'The Diaspora Synagogue: Notes on Distribution and Methodology', in Rutgers, LV *The Hidden Heritage of Diaspora Judaism. Essays on Jewish Cultural Identity in the Roman World*, Leuven, 125-35

Ryder, ML 1981 'British Medieval sheep and their wool types', in Crossley, DW (ed) *Medieval Industry* (CBA Research Report 40), London, 16-20

S

Sabine EL 1933 'Butchering in Mediaeval London', *Speculum* 8, 335-53

Sabine EL 1934 'Latrines and Cesspools of Mediaeval London', *Speculum* 9, 303-21

Sabine EL 1937 'City Cleaning in Mediaeval London', *Speculum* 12, 19-43

Sabján, T 2007 'Hungarian vernacular stoves of the late Middle Ages in regional context', in Sommer, P & Klápště, J (eds) *Arts and Crafts in Medieval Rural Environment* (*Ruralia* 6), Turnhout, 135-62

Saguí, L (ed) 1990 *L'esedra della Crypta Balbi nel medio-evo (XI-XV secolo)* (Archeologia urbana a Roma: il progetto della Crypta Balbi 5), Firenze

Said, Edward 1978 *Orientalism*, New York

Salamon, M, Coppa, A, McCormick, M, Rubini, M, Vargiu, R & Tuross, N 2008 'The consilience of historical and isotopic approaches in reconstructing the medieval Mediterranean diet', *Journal of Archaeological Science* 35, 1667-72

Salisbury, JE 1994 *The Beast Within: Animals in the Middle Ages*, London

Samojlik, T 2006 'Łowy i inne pobyty królów polskich i wielkich książąt litewskich w Puszczy Białowieskiej w XV-XVI wieku', *Kwartalnik Historii Kultury Materialnej* 3/4, 293-305

Sapin, C 1996 'Dans l'église ou hors l'église, quel choix pour l'inhumé?', in Galinié, H & Zadora-Rio, E (eds) *Archéologie du cimetière chrétien, Actes du colloque d'Orléans (28 sept.-1er oct. 1994)* (11e Supplément à la Revue Archéologique du Centre), Tours, 65-78

Sarfatij, H 1990 'Dutch towns in the formative period (AD 1000-1400): the archaeology of settlement and building', in Besteman, JC, Bos, JM & Heidinga, HA (eds) *Medieval Archaeology in the Netherlands. Studies presented to H.H. van Regteren-Altena,* Assen/Maastricht, 183-98

Saunders, A 1989 *Fortress Britain: artillery fortification in the British Isles and Ireland*, Liphook

Saunders, T 2000 'Class, space, and "feudal" identities in early medieval England,' in Frazer, WO & Tyrrell, A (eds) *Social Identity in Early Medieval Britain*, London, 209-24

Sauvaget, J 1934 'Equisse d'une histoire de la ville de Damas', *Revue des Etudes Islamiques* 4, 421-80

Sauvaget, J 1941 *Alep. Essai sur le développement d'une grande ville syrienne des origines au milieu du XIXe siècle*, París

Scandaliato, A & Mulè, N 2002 *La sinagoga e il bagno rituale degli ebrei di Siracusa, con una nota epigrafica di Cesare Colafemmina*, Firenze

Scarisbrisk, JJ 1984 *The Reformation and the English People*, Oxford

Schäfer, H 1997 'Zur Keramik des 13. und 15. Jahrhunderts in Mecklenburg-Vorpommern', *Bodendenkmalpflege in Mecklenburg-Vorpommern, Jahrbuch 1996*, 297-335

Schäfer, H 1999 'Archäologische Erkenntnisse zu Handel und Fremdgütern im mittelalterlichen Greifswald', in Gläser, M (ed) *Lübecker Kolloquium zur Stadtarchäologie im Hanseraum 2: der Handel*, Lübeck, 349-55

Schäfer, H 2000 'Greifswald, Hansestadt, Fpl. 96', in 'Kurze Fundberichte: Mittelalter und Neuzeit', *Bodendenkmalpflege in Mecklenburg-Vorpommern, Jahrbuch* 47 (1999), 502-505

Schenkluhn, W 2000 *Architectur der Bettelorden: die Baukunst der Dominikaner und Franziskaner in Europa*, Darmstadt

Schmidtchen, V 1990 'Castles, cannon and casemates', *Fortress* 6, 3-10

Schnack, C 1992 *Die mittelalterlichen Schuhe aus Schleswig. Ausgrabung Schild 1971-1975 (Ausgrabungen in Schleswig: Berichte und Studien* 10), Neumünster

Schnitzler, B (ed.) 1990 *Vivre au Moyen Age: 30 ans d'archéologie médiévale en Alsace*, Strasbourg

Schoeninger, MJ & DeNiro, MJ 1984 'Nitrogen and carbon isotopic composition of bone collagen from marine and terrestrial animals', *Geochimica et Cosmochimica Acta* 48, 625-39

Schöfbeck, T & Heussner, K-U 2005 'Bauforschung und Dendrochronologie in der mittelalterlichen Siedlungsgeschichte Nordostdeutschlands', in Bierman, F & Mangelsdorf, G (eds) *Die bäuerliche Ostsiedlung des Mittelalters in Nordostdeutschland: Untersuchungen zum Landesausbau des 12. bis 14. Jahrhunderts im ländlichen Raum* (Greifswalder Mitteilungen, Beiträge zur Ur- und Frühgeschichte und Mittelalterarchäologie 7), Greifswald

Schofield, J 1994 *Medieval London Houses*, New Haven (CT) & London

Schofield, J 2003 *Medieval Towns*, second edition, London & New York

Schofield, J & Steuer, H 2007 'Urban Settlement', in Graham-Campbell, J & Valor, M (eds) *The Archaeology of Medieval Europe Vol. 1. Eighth to Twelfth Centuries AD,* 111-53

Schofield, J & Vince, A 2003 *Medieval Towns. The Archaeology of British towns in their European setting*, second edition, London

Scholkmann, B 2009 *Das Mittelalter im Fokus der Archäologie*, Stuttgart

Schütte, S 2004 'Die Juden in Köln von der Antike bis zum Hochmittelalter: Beiträge zur Diskussion zum Früh-Judentum nördlich der Alpen', in Wamers, E & Backhaus, F (eds) *Synagogen, Mikwen, Siedlungen: Jüdisches Alltagsleben in Lichte neuer archäologischer Funde* (Schriften des Archäologischen Museums Frankfurt 19), Frankfurt am Main, 73-116

Schwedt, A, Mommsen, H, Stephan, H-G & Gaimster, D 2003 'Neutron activation of "Falke-Group" stoneware', *Archaeometry* 45, 233-50

Schweizer, B 1983 *Le abitazioni dei coloni cimbri*, Verona

Scott, T 2002 *Society and Economy in Germany, 1300-1600*, New York

Scriptores minores historiæ Danicæ medii ævi 1-2 1917-20 (edited by Gerts, MC), København

Sears, E 1986 *The Ages of Man. Medieval Interpretations of the Lifecycle*, Princeton (NJ)

Seiler-Baldinger, A-M 1994 *Textiles, a classification of techniques*, Bathurst

Seipel, W (ed.) 1998 *Spielwelten der Kunst*, Wien

Sessa, VM 2000, 'La Carta del Rischio del patrimonio culturale: l'esperienza della Lombardia', *Aedon* 3 (online journal: www.aedon.it)

Settia, AA 1982 'Pievi e cappelle nella dinamica del popolamento rurale', in *Cristianizzazione delle campagne nell'alto Medioevo: espansione e resistenze, Settimane di studio del Centro italiano di studi sull'alto medioevo, 28 (Spoleto, 1981)*, Spoleto, 445-89

Shalem, A 1998 *Islam Christianized: Islamic Portable Objects in the Medieval Church Treasuries of the Latin West*, Frankfurt am Main

Shalem, A 2004 *The Oliphant: Islamic Objects in Historic Context*, Leiden

Signoli, M, Séguy, I, Biraben, J-N & Dutour, O 2002 'Paleodemography and historical demograpy in the context of an epidemic: plague in Provence in the eighteenth century', *Population* 57, 829-54

Signori, G 2005 *Räume, Gesten, Andachtsformen. Geschlecht, Konflikt und religiöse Kultur im europäischen Mittelalter*, Ostfildern

Skemer, D 2006 *Binding Words. Textual Amulets in the Middle Ages*, University Park (PA)

Slater, TR & Rosser, G (eds) 2005 *The Church in the Medieval Town*, Aldershot

Smetánka, Z 1965 'Povrchový průzkum zaniklých osad v okolí Sezimova Ústí' [The Deserted Medieval Villages near Sezimovo Ústí], *Archeologické rozhledy* 17, 668-74

Smetánka, Z 1988 *Život středověké vesnice. Zaniklá Svídna (The life of medieval village. Deserted Village Svídna)*, Prague

Smith, C 1998 'Dogs, cats and horses in the Scottish medieval town', *Proceedings of the Society of Antiquaries of Scotland* 128, 859-85

Smith, JT 1965 'Timber-framed building in England: its development and regional differences', *Archaeological Journal* 122, 133-58

Smith, JT 1992 *English Houses 1200-1800. The Hertfordshire Evidence,* London

Smith, R 2009 'Shipwreck in the Forbidden Zone', *National Geographic* 216, 116-27

Smith, V 2007 *Clean. A History of Personal Hygiene and Purity,* Oxford

Söderberg, B 1997 'The development of the farmstead in Filborna village, c. 1000-1800. Traditional building technique in Scanian scrub country', in Andersson, H, Carelli, P & Ersgard, L (eds) *Visions of the Past. Trends and Traditions in Swedish Medieval Archaeology* (Lund Studies in Medieval Archaeology 19), Stockholm, 91-127

Spek, T 2004 *Het Drentse esdorpenlandschap. Een historisch-geografische studie,* Utrecht

Spek, T 2006 'Entstehung und Entwicklung historischer Ackerkomplexe und Plaggenböden in den Eschlandschaften der nordöstlichen Niederlande (Provinz Drenthe). Ein Überblick über die Ergebnisse interdisziplinärer Forschung aus neuester Zeit', *Siedlungsforschung: Archäologie-Geschichte-Geographie* 24, 219-50

Spencer, B 1978 'King Henry of Windsor and the London Pilgrim', in Bird, J, Chapman, H & Clark, J (eds) *Collectanea Londiniensia: Studies in London Archaeology and History Presented to Ralph Merrifield* (LMAS Special Publication 2), London, 235-64

Spencer, B 1998 (2004) *Pilgrim Souvenirs and Secular Badges: Medieval finds from excavations in London* (Museum of London Catalogue 7), London (new edition 2004, Woodbridge)

Sponheimer, M, Robinson, T, Ayliffe, L, Roeder, B, Hammer, J, Passey, BH, West, A, Cerling, TE, Dearing, MD & Ehleringer, JR 2003 ,Nitrogen isotopes in mammalian herbivores: hair $\delta^{15}N$ values from a controlled feeding study', *International Journal of Osteoarchaeology* 13, 80-7

Spufford, P 1986 *Handbook of Medieval Exchange* (Royal Historical Society Guides & Handbooks 13), London

Spufford, P 1988 *Money an its Use in Medieval Europe,* Cambridge

Spufford, P 2002 *Power and Profit. The Merchant in Medieval Europe,* London

Stabel, P 2004 'Guilds in medieval Flanders: myths and realities of guild life in an export-orientated environment', *Journal of Medieval History* 30, 187-212

Stadt Zürich, Hochbaudepartment, Amt für Städtebau, Archäologie und Denkmalpflege (ed) 2004 *Stadtmauern. Ein neues Bild der Stadtbefestigungen Zürichs,* Zürich

Stahl, AM 2000 *Zecca. The Mint of Venice in the Middle Ages,* Baltimore

Stahl, AM 2010 'Coins,' *Oxford Bibliographies Online: Medieval Studies* (2010).
http://www.oxfordbibliographiesonline.com .

Stallibrass, S 2007 'Taphonomy or transfiguration? Do we need to change the subject?', in Pluskowski, AG (ed) *Breaking and Shaping Beastly Bodies: Animals as Material Culture in the Middle Ages,* Oxford, 52-65

Steffy, JR 1993 *Wooden Shipbuilding and the Interpretation of Shipwrecks,* College Station (TX)

Stein, G 1978 *Judenhof und Judenbad in Speyer am Rhein,* Berlin

Stenning, D 1985 'Timber-framed shops 1300-1600: comparative plans', *Vernacular Architecture* 16, 35-9

Stephan, H-G 1978 *Archäologische Studien zur Wüstungsforschung im südlichen Weserbergland* (Münstersche Beiträge zur Ur- und Frühgeschichte 10-11), Hildesheim

Stephan, H-G 1988 'Steinzeug und Irdenware. Diskussionsbeiträge zur Abgrenzung und Definition des mittelalterlichen deutschen Steinzeuges', in Gaimster, D, Redknap, M & Wegener H-H (eds) *Zur Keramik des Mittelalters und der beginnenden Neuzeit im Rheinland* (British Archaeological Reports, International Series 440), 81-117

Stephan, H-G 1996 'Deutsche Keramik im Handelsraum der Hanse', in Wiegelmann, G & Mohrmann, R-E (eds) *Nahrung und Tischkultur im Hanseraum,* Münster & New York, 95-123

Stephan, H-G & Gaimster, D 2002 'Die "Falke-Gruppe". Das reich verzierte Lausitzer Steinzeug der Gotik und sein archäologisch-historisches Umfeld', *Zeitschrift für Archäologie des Mittelalters* 30 (2002), 107-63

Stiaffini, D 1999 *Il vetro nel Medioevo. Tecniche, strutture, manufatti.,* Roma

Stinson, T 2009 'Knowledge of the flesh: using DNA analysis to unlock bibliographical secrets of medieval parchment', *Papers of the Bibliographical Society of America* 103/4, 435-53

Stocker, D and P Everson 2003, The Straight and narrow Way: Fenland Causeways and the Conversion of the Landscape in the Witham Valley, Lincolnshire, in M O H Carver (ed.) *The Cross goes North. Processes of Conversion in Northern Europe 300-1300AD* (Woodbridge): 271-288

Stocker, D and Everson, P 2006 Summoning St Michael: Early Romanesque Towers in Lincolnshire, Oxford

Stoob, H 1956 [1970] 'Kartographische Möglichkeiten zur Darstellung der Stadtentstehung in Mitteleuropa, besonders zwischen 1450 und 1800', in Stoob, H (ed) *Forschungen zum Städtewesen in Europa, Band 1: Räume, Formen und Schichten der mitteleuropäischen Städte. Eine Aufsatzfolge,* Köln & Wien, 15-42

Stoob, H 1959 [1970] 'Minderstädte. Formen der Stadtentstehung im Spätmittelalter', in Stoob, H (ed) *Forschungen zum Städtewesen in Europa, Band 1: Räume, Formen und Schichten der mitteleuropäischen Städte. Eine Aufsatsfolge*, Köln & Wien, 225-45

Stouff, L 1986 *Arles à la fin du Moyen Âge*, Aix-en-Provence

Suchodolski, S 1996 'Absence of mind or magic? A few remarks on the so-called small or single coin finds', *Quaderni Ticinesi di Numismatica e Antichita Classiche* 25, 317-27

Sutherland, TL 2000 'The archaeological investigation of the Towton Battlefield', in Fiorato, V, Boylston, A & Knüsel, C (eds) *Blood Red Roses: the Archaeology of a Mass Grave from the Battle of Towton AD1461*, Oxford, 155-168

Sutherland, TL 2003 'The Towton Battlefield Archaeological Survey Project: an integrated approach to battlefield archaeology', *Landscapes* 4, 15-25

Sutherland, TL 2006 'The Battle of Agincourt: an alternative location?', *Journal of Conflict Archaeology* 1, 245-65

Sutherland, TL 2007 'Arrows point to mass graves: finding the dead from the Battle of Towton, 1461 AD', in Scott, DD, Babits, L& Haeker, C (eds) *Fields of Conflict: Battlefield Archaeology from the Roman Empire to the Korean War*, Westport (CT), 16073

Sutherland, TL 2009 'Killing time: challenging the common perceptions of three medieval conflicts – Ferrybridge, Dintingdale and Towton, *Journal of Conflict Archaeology* 5, 1-25

Sutherland, TL & Holst, MR 2005 *Battlefield Archaeology. A Guide to the Archaeology of Conflict* (available at http://cairnworld.free.fr/guideindex.php)

Svart Kristiansen, M (ed) 2005 *Tårnby. Gård og landsby gennem 1000 år* (JyskArkæologisk Selskabs Skrifter 54), Højberg (Summary and captions in English)

Svensson, E 2008 *The Medieval Household. Daily Life in Castles and Farmsteads. Scandinavian Examples in their European Context* (The Medieval Countryside 2), Turnhout

Svetikas, E 2008 'XIV a. Pabaigos-XV a. amuletai iš apkaustyto okio nago lietuvos didžiojoje kunigaikštystėje ir kaimyniniuose kraštuose', *Lietuvos Archeologija* 34, 171-210

Swanepoel, N 2009 'The Practice and Substance of Historical Archaeology in Sub-Saharan Africa', in Madjewski, T & Gaimster, D (eds) *International Handbook of Historical Archaeology*, New York, 565-81

Swann, LM 2007 'Economic and ideological roles of copper ingots in prehistoric Zimbabwe', *Antiquity* 81, 999-1012

Swanson, H 1988 'The illusion of economic structure: craft guilds in late medieval English towns', *Past and Present* 71, 29-48

Sweetman, D 1999 *The medieval castles of Ireland*, Cork

Sykes, N 2007a *The Norman Conquest: a Zooarchaeological Perspective* (British Archaeological Reports International Series 1656), Oxford

Sykes, N 2007b 'Taking sides: the social life of venison in medieval England', in Pluskowski, AG (ed) *Breaking and Shaping Beastly Bodies: Animals as Material Culture in the Middle Ages*, Oxford, 149-60

Sykes, N 2009 'Animals, the bones of medieval society,' in Gilchrist, R & Reynold, A (eds) *Reflections: 50 Years of Medieval Archaeology, 1957-2007*, Leeds, 347-61

Symons, M 2002 'Cutting up cultures', *Journal of Historical Sociology*, 15, 431-50

T

Taavitsainen, J-P, Vilkuna, J & Forssell, H 2007 *Suojoki at Keuruu: a mid-14th century site of wilderness culture in Central Finland* (Suomalaisen Tiedeakatemian toimituksia Humaniora 346, Annales Academiae Scientarium Fennicae), Helsinki

Taburet-Delahaye, E & Drake Boehm, B (eds) 1995 *L'œuvre de Limoges. Emaux limousins du Moyen Age,* Paris

Tagliabue, R 1993 *Architetto e Archeologo. Confronto tra campi disciplinari*, Milano

Tamla, T 1998 'Zum Grabraub in vor- und frühgeschichtlichen Gräbern Estlands', in Wesse, A (ed) *Studien zur Archäologie des Ostseeraumes. Von der Eisenzeit zum Mittelalter: Festschrift für Michael Müller-Wille*, Neumünster, 291-7

Tatton-Brown, T 1998 'Medieval parishes and parish churches in Canterbury,' in Slater, TR & Rosser, G. (eds) *The Church in the Medieval Town*, Aldershot, 236-71

Taylor, A 1998 *Conwy Castle and Town Walls*, fourth edition, Cardiff

Taylor, CC 1975 *Fields in the English Landscape*, London

Taylor, RE 2001 'Radiocarbon dating', in Brothwell, DR & Pollard, AM (eds) *Handbook of Archaeological Sciences*, Chichester, 23-34

Tegnér, G 1996 'Smyckekonsten', in Agustsson, J-E & Ullén, M (eds) *Den Gotiska konsten* (Signums svenska konsthistoria 4), Lund, 458-85

Telfer, A 2003 'Medieval Drainage near Smithfield Market: excavations at Hosier Lane, EC1', *London Archaeologist* 10, 115-20

Tetro, T 1977 'Gli ebrei a Sermoneta XIII-XIV sec', *Economia Pontina* 15, 13

Thackray, D 1991 *Bodiam Castle*, London

The Livonian Rhymed Chronicle 2001 trans. Smith, JC & Urban, W, Chicago (IL)

Theuws, F 1990 'Centre and periphery in Northern Austrasia (6th-8th centuries): an archaeological perspective, in Besteman, JC, Bos, JM & Heidinga, HA (eds) *Medieval Archaeology in the Netherlands. Studies presented to H.H. van Regteren-Altena,* Assen/Maastricht, 41-69

Theuws, F 2008 'Settlement research and the process of manorialization in Northern Austrasia', in Gasparri, S (ed) *774 Ipotesisuuna transizione. Atti del Seminario di Poggibonsi, 16-18 febbraio 2006,* 199-220

Thiaw, I 2008 'Every house has a story: the archaeology of Gorée Island, Sénégal', in Sansone, L, Soumonmi, E & Barry, B (eds) Africa, Brazil and the Construction of trans-Atlantic Black Identities, Trenton (NJ), 45-62

Thier, B 2002 'Das Hospital im Mittelalter: Pflege für Alte und Kranke', in Menghin, W & Planck, D (eds) *Menschen, Zeiten, Räume: Archäologie in Deutschland*, Berlin, 376-9

Thirion, J 1998 *Le mobilier du Moyen Age et de la Renaissance en France*, Dijon

Thomas, C, Sloane, B & Phillpotts, C 1997 *Excavations at the Priory and Hospital of St Mary Spital, London* (Medieval Monasteries Series 1), London

Thomas, R 2006 'Of books and bones: the integration of historical and zooarchaeological evidence in the study of medieval animal husbandry', in Maltby, M (ed) *Integrating Zooarchaeology*, Oxford, 17-26

Thompson, M 1995 *The Medieval Hall. The basis of secular domestic life 600-1600 AD*, Aldershot

Thorndike, L 1928 'Sanitation, Baths and Street Cleaning in the Middle Ages and Renaissance', *Speculum* 3, 192-203

Thornton, J 1998 *Africa and Africans in the Making of the Atlantic world, 1400-1800*, Cambridge

Thurley, S 1999 'Whitehall palace and Westminster 1400-1600: a royal seat in transition', in Gaimster, D & Stamper, P (eds) *The Age of Transition. The archaeology of English culture 1400-1600* (Society for Medieval Archaeology Monograph 15), Oxford, 93-104

Tidow, K & Jordan Farbach, E 2007 'Woollen Textiles in Archaeological Finds and Descriptions in Written Sources of the 14th to 18th Centuries', in Gillis, C & Nosch, M-LB (eds) *Ancient textiles, Production, Craft and Society*, Oxford, 97-101

Tito Rojo, J 2001 'Caractteristiche dei giardini ispano-musulmani', in Matteini, M & Petruccioli, A (eds) *Giardini islamici: architettura, ecologia* (Atti del Convegno di Genova, 8-9 novembre 2001), Genova, 27-52

Tito Rojo, J & Casares Porcel, M 2007 'From the Andalusí Garden to the Andalusian Garden: Remants and Re-Creation', in Conan, M (ed) *Middle East Garden Traditions: Unity and Diversity*, Washington DC, 287-306

Tittler, R 1991 *Architecture and Power. The Town Hall and the English Urban Community c. 1500-1640*, Oxford

Tjion Sie Fat, L & De Jong, E (eds) 1991 *The Authentic Garden. A Symposium on Gardens*, Leiden

Toaff, A 1998 *Love, Work, and Death: Jewish Life in Medieval Umbria* (trans. Landry, J), London

Torres, C 1987 *Cerâmica islâmica portuguesa*, Mértola

Torres Balbás, L 1934 'Cerámica doméstica de la Alhambra', *Al-Andalus* 2, 387-88

Torres Balbás, L 1939 'De cerámica hispano-musulmana', *Al-Andalus* 4, 412-32

Torres Balbás, L 1949a *Arte almohade, arte nazarí, arte mudéjar* (*Ars Hispaniae* 4), Madrid

Torres Balbás, L 1949b 'Ventanas con vidrios de colores en los edificios hispanomusulmanes', *Al-Andalus* 18, 197-201

Torres Balbás, L 1968 'La Edad Media', in *Resumen histórico del urbanismo en España*, Madrid

Torres Balbás, L 1971 *Ciudades hispano-musulmanas*, Madrid

Torres Fontes, J 1971 *Repartimiento de la Huerta y Campo de Murcia en el S. XIII*, Murcia

Toulmin Smith, L 1962 (1870) *English Guilds: the original ordinances of more than one hundred early English guilds* (Early English Text Society Series 40), Oxford

Tracy, C 1988 *English medieval furniture and woodwork*, London

Treffort, C 1996 'Du *cimiterium christianorum* au cimetière paroissial: évolution des espaces funéraires en Gaule du VIIe au Xe siècle', in Galinié, H & Zadora-Rio, E (eds) *Archéologie du cimetière chrétien, Actes du colloque d'Orléans (28 sept.-1er oct. 1994)* (11e Supplément à la Revue Archéologique du Centre), Tours, 55-63

Treffort, C 2001 'Consécration de cimetière et contrôle épiscopal des lieux d'inhumation au Xᵉ siècle', in Kaplan M (ed.), *Le Sacré et son inscription dans l'espace à Byzance et en Occident*, Paris, 285-99

Treffort, C 2010 'Une archéologie très "humaine": regards sur trente ans d'études des sépultures médiévales en France', in Chapelot, J (ed) *Trente ans d'archéologie médiévale en France. Un bilan pour un avenir* (IXe congrès international de la Société d'archéologie médiévale, Vincennes, 16-18 juin 2006), 213-26

Tronti, C 2008 'Famiglie signorili, cappelle private e insediamenti fortificati in Val di Sieve tra X e XII secolo: i casi di Monte di Croce e Montefiesole (Pontassieve, Firenze)', in Campana, S, Felici, C, Francovich, R & Gabbrielli, F (eds) *Chiese e insediamenti nei secoli di formazione dei paesaggi medievali della Toscana (V-X secolo), Atti del Seminario di San Giovanni d'Asso-Montisi, 2006)*, Firenze, 199-224

Tuchen, B 2003 *Öffentliche Badhäuser in Deutschland und in der Schweiz im Mittelalter und der Frühen Neuzeit*, Petersberg

Turnbull, S 2004 *Crusader Castles of the Teutonic Knights, Vol. 2: The Stone Castles of Latvia and Estonia, 1185-1560*, Oxford

Turner, R 2000 'St David's Bishop's Palace, Pembrokeshire', *Antiquaries Journal* 80, 87-194

Turner, TH & Parker, JH 1851, 1853, 1859 *Some Account of Domestic Architecture in England* (3 volumes), Oxford

Turner-Walker, G, Syversen, U & Mays, S 2001 'The archaeology of osteoporosis', *European Journal of Archaeology* 4, 263-9

Tyson, R 2000 *Medieval glass vessels found in England c. AD 1200-1500* (CBA Research Report 121), York

U

Ubelaker, H 1989 *Human skeletal remains: excavation, analysis, interpretation* (second edition), Washington DC

Unger, J 1994 *Kovalov. Šlechtické sídlo z 13. století na jižní Moravě (Ein Adelssitz aus dem 13. bis 14. Jh. in der Ortswüstung Kovalov bei Žabčice /Bez. Brno-Land/)*, Brno

Unger, J 1999 *Život na lelekovickém hradě ve 14. století. Antropologická sociokulturní studie (Das Leben auf der Burg Lelekovice im 14. Jahrhundert: Anthropologische soziokulturelle Studie)*, Brno

Untermann, M 1995 'Archäologische Befunde zur Frühgeschichte der Stadt Freiburg', in Schadek, H & Zotz, T (eds) *Freiburg 1091-1120: neue Forschungen zu den Anfängen der Stadt* (Archäologie und Geschichte 7), Sigmaringen, 195-230

Untermann, M 2009 'Öffentlichkeit und Klausur: Beobachtungen zur franziskanischen Klosterbaukunst in der Provinz Saxonia', in Auge, O, Biermann, F & Herrmann, C (eds) *Glaube, Macht und Pracht. Geistliche Gemeinschaften des Ostseeraums im Zeitalter der Backsteingotik*, Rahden, 199-208

Urbańczyk, P 1992 *Medieval Arctic Norway*, Institute of the History of Material Culture, Polish Academy of Sciences, Warsaw

V

Valenti, M & Salvadori, F 2007 'Animal bones: synchronous and diachronous distribution as patterns of socially determined meat consumption in the early and high Middle Ages in Central and Northern Italy', in Pluskowski, AG (ed) *Breaking and Shaping Beastly Bodies: Animals as Material Culture in the Middle Ages*, Oxford, 171-88

Valk, H 2001 *Rural Cemeteries of Southern Estonia AD 1225-1800* (Culture Clash or Compromise [CCC] Papers 3), Visby & Tartu

Valk, H 2003 'Christianisation in Estonia: a Process of Dual-Faith and Syncretism' in Carver, MOH (ed) *The Cross goes North. Processes of Conversion in Northern Europe, AD 300-1300*, Woodbridge, 571-9

Valk, H 2004 'Christian and Non-Christian Holy Sites in Medieval Estonia. A Reflection of Ecclesiastical Attitudes Towards Popular Religion', in *The European Frontier. Clashes and Compromises in the Middle Ages. International Symposium of the Culture Clash or Compromise (CCC) Project and the Department of Archaeology, Lund University, held in Lund October 13-15 2000* (CCC Papers 7, Lund Studies in Medieval Archaeology 33), Lund, 299-310

Valk, H 2006a 'Medieval and post-medieval archaeology of the native rural population. Archaeological Research in Estonia 1865-2005, *Estonian Archaeology* 1, 205-21

Valk, H 2006b 'Cemeteries and Ritual Meals. Rites and their Meaning in the traditional Seto Worldview', in Andrén, A, Jennbert, K & Raudvere, C (eds) *Old Norse Religion in long-term perspectives. Origins, Changes and Interactions* (Vägar till Midgård 8), Lund, 141-6

Valk, H 2008 'Pre-Christian and Christian: rites at two holy stones in Setomaa, south-eastern Estonia', in Falk, AB & Kyritz, DM (eds) *Folk Beliefs and Practice in Medieval Lives* (British Archaeological Reports International Series 1757), Oxford, 67-78

Valour, N, Mokaddem, K, Brochier, J-L, Fabre, L, Jeannet, M & Cecillon, C 2006 'L'évolution d'un hameau rural du XIIe au XVe s.: Beaume (Châteauneuf-sur-Isère, Drôme)', in Maufras, O (ed) *Habitats, nécropoles et paysages dans la moyenne et la basse vallée du Rhône (VIIe-XVe s.): contribution des travaux du TGV-Méditerranée à l'étude des sociétés rurales médiévales* (Documents d'Archéologie Française 98), 23-37

van Beek, R 2009 Reliëf in tijd en ruimte Interdisciplinair onderzoek naar bewoning en landschap van Oost Nederland tussen vroege prehistorie en middeleeuwen, unpublished PhD dissertation, Wageningen University & Research Centre

van Beuningen, HJE 1993 'Nieuwlande' in van Beuningen, HJE & Koldeweij, AM (eds) *Heilig en Profaan: 1000 Laatmiddeleeuwse insignes uit de collectie H.J.E. van Beuningen* (Rotterdam Papers 8), Cothen, 26-32

van Beuningen, HJE & Koldeweij, AM (eds) 1993 *Heilig en Profaan: 1000 Laatmiddeleeuwse insignes uit de collectie H.J.E. van Beuningen* (Rotterdam Papers 8), Cothen

van Beuningen, HJE, Koldeweij, AM & Kicken, D (eds) 2001 *Heilig en Profaan 2: 1200 Laatmiddeleeuwse insignes uit openbare en particuliere collecties* (Rotterdam Papers 12), Cothen

Van Damme, D & Ervynck, A 1988 'Medieval ferrets and rabbits in the castle of Laarne (East-Flanders, Belgium): a contribution to the history of a predator and its prey', *Helinium*, 28, 278-84

van der Leeuw, S (ed) 1995 *L'homme et la dégradation de l'environnement, XVe Rencontres internationales d'archéologie et d'histoire d'Antibes*, Sophia-Antipolis

van der Linden, H 1984 'Die Besiedlung der Moorgebiete in der holländisch-utrechter Tiefebene und die Nachahmung im nordwerstdeutschen Raum, *Siedlungsforschung: Archäologie-Geschichte-Geographie* 2, 77-99

van der Sanden, WAB 2004 'Een 16de-eeuwse tinnen papkom uit Orvelterveen. Naar een archeologie van de toverij, *Nieuwe Drentse Volksalmanak* 121, 184-203

van der Ven, GP (ed) 2004 *Man-made lowlands. History of water management and land reclamation in the Netherlands*, Utrecht

van Doesburg, J 2009 'Fighting against wind and sand. Settlement development in the coastal dunes and the cover sand area of the Central Netherlands in the Middle Ages', in Klápště, J & Sommer, P (eds) *Medieval Rural Settlement in Marginal Landscapes* (Ruralia 7), Turnhout, 181-204

van Heeringen, RM, Koldeweij, AM & Gaalman, AAG, 1987 *Heiligen uit de modder. In Zeeland gevonden pelgrimstekens* (Clavis Kunsthistorische Monografieën 4), Utrecht & Zutphen

Van Hoof, TB, Bunnik, FPM, Waucomont, JGM, Kürschner, WM & Visscher, H 2006 'Forest re-growth on medieval farmland after the Black Death pandemic – implications for atmospheric CO_2 levels', *Palaeogeography, Palaeoclimatology, Palaeoecology* 237, 396-409

van Klinken, GJ 1999 'Bone collagen quality indicators for palaeodietary and radiocarbon measurements', *Journal of Archaeological Science* 26, 687-95

van Klinken, GJ, Richards, MP & Hedges, REM 2000 'An overview of causes for stable isotopic variations in past European human populations: environmental ecophysiological and cultural effects', in Ambrose, SH & Katzenberg MA(ed) *Biogeochimical approaches to paleodietary analysis. Advances in Archaeological and Museum Science*, New York, 39-58

van Nie, M 1995 'Three Iron Production Areas in the Netherlands', in Magnusson, G (ed) *The Importance of Iron Making. Technical Innovation and Social Change,* (Papers presented at the Norberg Conference on May 8-13, 1995), Stockholm, 100-106

Van Ossel, P 1998 *Les Jardins du Carrousel (Paris)* (Documents d'Archéologie Française 73), Paris

van Voolen, E 1986-7 'Jewish Museums in Europe', *Encyclopaedia Judaica Yearbook*, 182-8

Varela Gomes, R 1988 *Cerâmicas muçulmanas do Castelo de Silves*, Silves

Varela Gomes, R (ed) 2007 *Ribat da Arrifana. Cultura material e espiritualidade*, Aljezur

Varela Gomes, R & Varela Gomes, M 2001 *Palacio Almohada da Alcáçova de Silves,* Lisboa

Varty, K 1999 *Reynard, Renart, Reinaert and Other Foxes in Medieval England: the Iconographic Evidence*, Amsterdam

Varty, K (ed) 2000 *Reynard the Fox: Social Engagement and Cultural Metamorphoses in the Beast Epic from the Middle Ages to the Present*, New York

Vecchiattini, R 2001 'La mappatura culturale della città vecchia di Genova: un metodo per una lettura nuova della città', in De Marchi, M & Zavaglia, A (eds) *Lo spessore storico in urbanistica*, Mantova, 129-42

Veeckman, J, with Jennings, S, Dumortier, C, Whitehouse, D & Verhaeghe, F (eds) 2002 *Majolica and glass from Italy to Antwerp and beyond: the transfer of technology in the 16th-early 17th century*, Antwerpen

Vellev, J 1998 'Eine mittelalterliche Bronzegiesser-
werkstatt in Odense – und etwas über Glocken
und Grapen des Mittelalters', *Hammaburg* Neue
Folge 12, 195-224

Verhaeghe, F 1987 'La céramique en Flandre (XIIIe-
XVe siècle): quelques aspects de l'évolution et
de la concurrence', in Chapelot, J, Galinié, H &
Pilet-Lemière, J (eds) *La céramique (Ve-XIXe s.):
fabrication – commercialisation – utilisation (Actes
du premier colloque international d'archéologie
médiévale, Paris, 4-6 octobre 1985)*, Paris, 203-25

Verhaeghe, F 1989 'La céramique très décorée du Bas
Moyen Age en Flandre', in Blieck, G (ed) *Actes
du colloque de Lille (26-27 mars 1989) du Groupe
de Recherches et d'Etudes sur la Céramique dans le
Nord-Pas-de-Calais* (Nord-Ouest Archéologie hors-
série), 19-113

Verhaeghe, F 1995 'Industry in medieval towns: the
archaeological problem. An essay', in Duvosquel,
JM & Thoen, E (eds) *Peasants and Townsmen in
Medieval Europe*, Gent, 271-93

Verhaeghe, F 1996 'Aspects sociaux et économiques
de la céramique très décorée', in Piton, D (ed) *La
céramique très décorée dans l'Europe du Nord-Ouest
(Xème-XVème siècles). Actes du Colloque de Douai
(7-8 avril 1995) du Groupe de Recherches et d'Etudes
sur la Céramique dans le Nord-Pas de Calais*, Lille
& Berck-sur-Mer, 233-47

Verhaeghe, F 1998 'Medieval and later social
networks: the contribution of archaeology', in
Hundsbichler, H, Jaritz, G & Kühtreiber, T (eds)
1998 *Die Vielfalt der Dinge. Neue Wege zur Analyse
mittelalterlicher Sachkultur* (Forschungen des Instituts für Realienkunde des Mittelalters und der
frühen Neuzeit. Diskussionen und Materialien 3),
Vienna, 263-312

Verhaeghe, F 1999 'Trade in ceramics in the North
Sea region, 12th to 15th centuries: a methodologi-
cal problem and a few pointers', in Gläser, M (ed)
*Lübecker Kolloquium zur Stadtarchäologie im
Hanseraum 2: der Handel*, Lübeck, 139-67

Verna, C 1999 'Medieval coalmining in the seigneury
of Boussagues (Hérault-France)', in Benoit, P &
Verna, C (eds) *Le charbon de terre en Europe occidentale avant l'usage industriel du coke. Proceedings
of the XXth International Congress of History of Science*, Turnhout, 31-9

Verna, C 2001 *Le temps des moulines. Fer, technique et
société dans les Pyrénées centrales (XIVe-XVIe siècles)*,
Paris

Vestergård Pedersen, K & M-LB Nosch (eds) 2009
*The Medieval Broadcloth, Changing Trends in Fash-
ions, Manufacturing and Consumption*, Oxford

Vigarello, G 1988 *Concepts of Cleanlines. Changing Attitudes in France since the Middle Ages*, Cambridge

Vince, A 2005 'Ceramic petrology and the study of
Anglo-Saxon and later Medieval ceramics', *Medieval Archaeology* 49, 219-45

Viollet-le-Duc, EE 1856 *Dictionnaire raisonné de
l'architecture française du XIe au XVIe siècle. Tome
1, Architecture monastique*, Paris

Viollet-le-Duc, EE 1862 *Dictionnaire raisonné de
l'architecture française du XIe au XVIe siècle. Tome
3*, Paris

Viollet-le-Duc, EE 1888 *La Cité de Carcassonne
(Aude)*, Paris

Virginia, RA & Delwiche, CC 1982 'Natural ^{15}N
abundance of presumed N_2-fixing and non N_2-
fixing plants from selected ecosystems', *Oecologia*
57, 317-25

Vitorino, P 1932 'Dois anéis com inscrições', *Revista
de Arqueologia* 1, 56-9

Vitorino, P 1941 'As Cruzes da Peste', *Jornal do Mé-
dico* 25, 12-13

von Bonsdorff, J 1990 'Hansakonsten – finns den?',
in Bohn, R (ed) *Gotlandia irredenta: Festschrift
für Gunnar Svahnström zu seinem 75. Geburtstag*,
Sigmaringen, 47-57

Von Grunebaum, G 1955 (1961) 'The Structure of
Muslim Town', in *Islam: Essays in the Nature and
Growth of a Cultural Tradition* (The American Anthropological Association Memoir 81), Ann Arbor
1955 & London, second edition 1961, 141-58

Vossler, C 2009 '"Ecclesia Beatae Mariae Virginis":
erste archäologische Untersuchungen in der Kirche
des ehemaligen Zisterzienserklosters Bebenhausen,
Stadt Tübingen', *Archäologische Ausgrabungen in
Baden-Württemberg* 2008, 249-52

Vretemark, M 1990 'Medeltida kammakerier i Skara
– en råvaruanalys', *Västermanlands fornminnesföre-
nings tidskrift*, 1989-1990, 133-44

W

Wachowski, K (ed), 1999- *Wratislavia Antiqua* [series]
Wrocław

Waldron, T with Rodwell, W 2007 *St Peter's, Barton-
Upon-Humber, Lincolnshire, a Parish Church and
its Community, Volume 2: The Human Remains*,
Oxford

Walton Rogers, P 1997 *Textile Production at 16-22
Coppergate* (The Archaeology of York 17/11), York

Wamers, E & Backhaus, F (eds) 2004 *Synagogen, Mikwen, Siedlungen. Jüdisches Alltagsleben im Lichte
neuer archäologischer Funde* (Schriften des Archäologischen Museums Frankfurt 19), Frankfurt am
Main

Ward-Perkins, J 1967 *London Museum Medieval Catalogue* (1940, reprint 1954, 1967), London

Wartburg, ML 1995 'Design and Technology of the Medieval Refineries of the Sugar Cane in Cyprus. A Case of Study in Industrial Archaeology', in Malpica, A (ed) *Paisajes del Azúcar*, Granada, 81-116

Wear, A 2000 *Knowledge and Practice in English Medicine, 1550-1680*, Cambridge

Webb, D 2002 *Medieval European Pilgrimage, c. 700-c. 1500*, Basingstoke

Weimer, C 1999 *Luther, Cranach und die Bilder. Gesetz und Evangelium: Schlüssel zum reformatorischen Bildgebrauch* (Arbeiten zur Theologie 89), Stuttgart

Westlake, EH 1919 *The Parish Guilds of Medieval England*, London

White, E 1987 *The St. Christopher and St. George Guild of York* (Borthwick Papers 72), York

White, W 2007 'Excavations at St Mary Spital: burial of the 'sick poore' of medieval London, the evidence of illness and hospital treatment', in Bowers, B (ed) *The Medieval Hospital and Medical Practice*, Aldershot, 59-64

Whitney, E 2004 *Medieval science and technology*, Westport (CT)

Wichmann, H & Wichmann, S 1964 *Chess: a story of chesspieces from antiquity to modern times*, London (German ed 1960: *Schach: Ursprung und Wandlung der Spielfigur in Zwölf Jahrhunderte*, München)

Wiener, CB & Jezler, P 1992 'In der Festprozession durch die Stadt: Stadttopographie und Herrschaftsansprüche im Liber Ordinarius des Zürcher Grossmünsters', in Flüeler, M & Flüeler, N (eds) *Stadtluft, Hirsebrei und Bettelmönch: die Stadt um 1300*, Stuttgart & Zürich, 463-7

Wiesemann, F 1992 *Genizah. Hidden Legacies of the German Village Jews*, Vienna

Wild, J-P 1970 *Textile Manufacture in the Northern Roman Provinces*, Cambridge

Wilkins, S 2002 *Sports and games of medieval cultures*, Westport (CT) & London

Williams, A 2003 *The Knight and the Blast Furnace: a History of the Metallurgy of Armour in the Middle Ages and the Early Modern Period*, Leiden

Wilson, CA, Davidson, DA & Cresser, MS 2009 'An evaluation of the site specificity of soil elemental signatures for identifying and interpreting former functional areas' *Journal of Archaeological Science* 36, 2327-34

Wilson, D 1985 *Moated Sites*, Princes Risborough

Windisch-Graetz, F 1982 *Möbel Europas. Von der Romanik bis zur Spätgotik, mit einem Rückblick auf Antike und Spätantike*, München

Windisch-Graetz, F 1983 *Möbel Europas. Renaissance und Manierismus. Vom 15. Jahrhundert bis in die erste Hälfte des 17. Jahrhunderts*, München

Windler, R 1999-2000 'Spätmittelalterliche Weberwerkstätten in der Winterthurer Altstadt', *Zeitschrift für Archäologie des Mittelalters* 27-28, 3-84

Witkowski, AJ & Parish, LC 2002 'The story of anthrax from Antiquity to present: a biological weapon of nature and of humans', *Clinics in Dermatology* 20, 336-42 (retrieved 1 February 2010 from http://www.science.direct.com/science)

Wittstock, J (ed) 1983 *Aus dem Alltag der mittelalterlichen Stadt. Handbuch zur Sonderaustellung vom 5. Dezember 1982 bis 24. April 1983 im Bremer Landesmuseum* (Hefte des Focke Museums 62), Bremen

Wood, J (ed) 1994 *Buildings Archaeology. Applications in Practice* (Oxbow Monograph 43), Oxford

Wood, M 1950 '13th century Domestic Architecture in England', *Archaeological Journal* 105 Supplement, 74-6

Wood, M 1965 *The English Medieval House*, London

Woodcock, A 2005 *Liminal Images: Aspects of Medieval Architectural Sculpture in the South of England from the Eleventh to the Sixteenth Centuries* (British Archaeological Reports 386), Oxford

Woolgar, CM 1999 *The Great Household in Late Medieval England*, London & New Haven (CT)

Woolgar, CM, Serjeantson, D & Waldron, T (eds) 2006 *Food in medieval England: diet and nutrition*, Oxford

Wrathmell, S 1989 *Domestic Settlement 2: Medieval Peasant Farmsteads* (Wharram, a Study of Settlement on the Yorkshire Wolds 6), York

Wright, SJ (ed) 1988 *Parish, Church, and People: Local Studies in Lay Religion, 1350-1750*, London

Wünsch, T (ed) 2006 *Religion und Magie in Ostmitteleuropa. Spielräume theologischer Normierungsprozesse in Spätmittelalter und Früher Neuzeit* (Religions- und Kulturgeschichte in Ostmittel- und Südosteuropa 8), Berlin

Wynne-Jones, S 2007 'Creating urban communities at Kliwa Kisiwani, Tanzania, AD 800-1300', *Antiquity* 81, 368-80

Wyss, M (ed) 1996 *Atlas historique de Saint-Denis. Des origines au XVIIIè siècle*, Paris

Y

Yeloff, D & Van Geel, B 2007 'Abandonment of farmland and vegetation succession following the Eurasian plague pandemic of AD 1347-52', *Journal of Biogeography*, 34, 575-82

Yeoman, P 1995 *Medieval Scotland*, Edinburgh

Youngs, D 2006 *The Lifecycle in Western Europe*, Manchester

Yvinec, J-H 1993 'La part du gibier dans l'alimentation du haut Moyen Âge', in Desse, J & Audoin-Rouzeau, F (eds) *Exploitation des animaux sauvages a travers le temps*, Juan-les-Pins, 491-504

Z

Zachrisson, I & Iregren, E 1974 *Lappish Bear Graves in Northern Sweden: An Archaeological and Osteological Study*, Stockholm

Zadora-Rio, E 2003 'The making of churchyards and parish territories in the Early Medieval landscape of France and England in the 7th-12th centuries: a reconsideration', *Medieval Archaeology* 47, 1-19

Zadora-Rio, E & Galinié, H with Husi, P, Liard, M, Rodier, X & Theureau, C 2001 'La fouille du site de Rigny, 7e-19e s.: l'habitat, les églises, le cimetière. Troisième et dernier rapport préliminaire (1995-1999)', *Revue Archéologique du Centre de la France* 40, 167-242

Zakharov, S 2002 'Below-zero town: an urban centre on the periphery', in Helmig, G, Scholkmann, B & Untermann, M (eds) *Centre-Region-Periphery. Medieval Europe Basel 2002* (3 volumes), Hertingen, 120-25

Zangheri, L, Lorenzi, B & Rahmati, NM (eds) 2006 *Il giardino islamico*, Firenze

Zangs, C & Holländer, H 1994 *Mit Glück und Verstand*, Aachen

Zaske, N & Zaske, R 1986 *Kunst in Hansestädten*, Köln

Zerbe, D 2007 'Memorialkunst im Wandel: die Ausbildung eines lutherischen Typus des Grab- und Gedächtnismals im 16. Jahrhundert', in Jäggi, C & Staecker, J (eds) *Archäologie der Reformation. Studien zu den Auswirkungen des Konfessionswechsels auf die materielle Kultur* (Arbeiten zur Kirchengeschichte 104), Berlin & New York, 117-63

Zimmermann, WH 1991 'Die früh- bis hochmittelalterliche Wüstung Dalem, Gem. Langen-Neuenwalde, Kr. Cuxhaven. Archäologische Untersuchungen in einem Dorf des 7.-14. Jahrhunderts', in Böhme, HW(ed) *Die Salier: Siedlung und Landesausbau zur Salierzeit Vol. 1*, Sigmaringen, 37-46

Zimmermann, WH 1998 'Pfosten, Ständer und Schwelle und der Übergang vom Pfosten- zum Ständerbau. Eine Studie zu Innovation und Beharrung im Hausbau. Zu Konstruktion und Haltbarkeit prähistorischer bis neuzeitlicher Holzbauten von den Nord- und Ostseeländern bis zu den Alpen', *Probleme der Küstenforschung im südlichen Nordseegebiet* 25, 9-241

Zozaya, J 1980 'Aperçu général sur la céramique espagnole', in Demians d'Archimbaud, G & Picon, M (eds) *La céramique médiévale en Méditerranée occidentale, Xe-XVe siècle, Valbonne 1978*, Paris, 265-96

Zschoch, H 2004 *Die Christenheit im Hoch- und Spätmittelalter: von der Kirchenreform des 11. Jahrhunderts zu den Reformbestrebungen des 15. Jahrhunderts* (Zugänge zur Kirchengeschichte 5), Göttingen

LIST OF CONTRIBUTORS

Hans Andersson
<hans.andersson-bjarred@telia.com>

Jette Arneborg
<jette.arneborg@natmus.dk>

Andrea Augenti
<AAugenti@libero.it>

Marie-Christine Bailly-Maître
<baillymaitre@wanadoo.fr>

Reidar Bertelsen
<Reidar.Bertelsen@sv.uit.no>

Jan Bill
<jan.bill@khm.uio.no>

Maria-Letizia Boscardin (Heyer)
<letizia.heyer@unibas.ch>

Gian-Pietro Brogiolo
<gpbrogiolo@unipd.it>

Duncan Brown
<dhb@bethere.co.uk>

Joelle Burnouf
<joelleburnouf@orange.fr>

Jean-Michel Carozza
<jmcarozza@yahoo.fr>

Martin Carver
<martincarver@yahoo.co.uk>

Cyril Castanet
<cyrilcastanet@hotmail.com>

O H Creighton
<o.h.creighton@exeter.ac.uk>

Ricardo Córdoba
<ca1collr@uco.es>

Jan van Doesburg
<J.van.Doesburg@cultureelerfgoed.nl>

Isla Fay
<isla.fay@cardolan.com>

David Gaimster
<david.gaimster@glasgow.ac.uk>

Sauro Gelichi
<gelichi@unive.it>

Chris Gerrard
<c.m.gerrard@durham.ac.uk>

Roberta Gilchrist
<r.l.gilchrist@reading.ac.uk>

Kate Giles
<kfg103@york.ac.uk>

Bert Groenewoudt
<B.Groenewoudt@cultureelerfgoed.nl>

Samuel Gruber
<samuelgruber@gmail.com>

Alejandra Gutierrez
<alejandra.gutierrez@durham.ac.uk>

Estelle Herrscher
<estelle.herrscher@univmed.fr>

Jacques Heyman

David A. Hinton
<dah5@soton.ac.uk>

Visa Immonen
<vialim@utu.fi>

Pedro Jiménez Castillo
<pedro@eea.csic.es>

Kaspars Klavins
<klavinskaspars@gmail.com>

Gundars Kalniņš
<gundars.kalnins@ccsis.lv>

Jan Klapste
<klapste@arup.cas.cz>

Mette Svart Kristiansen
<markmsk@hum.au.dk>

Hans Krongaard Kristensen
<markhkk@moes.hum.au.dk>

Marjolijn Kruip
<m.kruip@chello.nl>

Odile Maufras
<odile.maufras@inrap.fr>

Aleksandra McClain
<anm102@york.ac.uk>

Werner Meyer
<werner-h.meyer@unibas.ch>

Historisches Seminar der Universität Basel,
Hirschgässlein 21, CH-4051 Basel
<Letizia.Heyer@unibas.ch>

Alessandra Molinari
<alemoli@fastwebnet.it>

Ulrich Müller
<umueller@ufg.uni-kiel.de>

Sam Nixon
<samnixon77@yahoo.co.uk>

Kieran O'Connor
<kieran.d.oconor@nuigalway.ie>

Ingvild Øye
<ingvild.oye@ark.uib.no>

Julio Navarro Palazón
<julionavarro@eea.csic.es>

Jiří Pajer
<pajer.jiri@seznam.cz>

Jerzy Piekalski
<jerzy.piekalski@archeo.uni.wroc.pl>

Aleks Pluskowski
<a.g.pluskowski@reading.ac.uk>

Alberto García Porras
<agporras@ugr.es>

Carole Puig
<c.puig@free.fr>

Else Roesdahl
<marker@hum.au.dk>

Tibor Sabján †

Barbara Scholkmann
<barbara.scholkmann@uni-tuebingen.de>

Rory Sherlock
<rory.sherlock@nuigalway.ie>

Barney Sloane
<barney.sloane@english-heritage.org.uk>;

Martin Stancliffe

Alan Stahl
<amstahl@optonline.net>

Hans-Georg Stephan
<hans.stephan@praehist.uni-halle.de>

Eva Andersson Strand
<evaandersson@hum.ku.dk>

Tim Sutherland
<tim@sutherland6579.freeserve.co.uk>

Eva Svensson
<Eva.Svensson@kau.se>

Naomi Sykes
<naomi.sykes@nottingham.ac.uk>

Jussi-Pekka Taavitsainen
<justaa@utu.fi>

Heiki Valk
<heiki.valk@ut.ee>

Frans Verhaeghe
<frans.verhaeghe@skynet.be>

Christina Vossler
<ihlefix@web.de>

Elizabeth Zadora-Rio
<zadora-rio@univ-tours.fr>

Translations were made by

Madeleine Hummler, from the French, of contributions by Joëlle Burnouf, Cyril Castanet, Jean-Michel Carozza, Carole Puig and Estelle Herrscher; from the German, of contributions by Maria-Letizia Boscardin, Werner Meyer, Barbara Scholkmann and Christina Vossler.

Martin Carver, from the French, of contributions by Odile Maufras and Elizabeth Zadora-Rio; from the Italian, of the contribution by Alessandra Molinari.

Isabel Casellas and *Martin Carver*, from the Spanish, of the contributions by Julio Navarro Palazón and Pedro Jiménez Castillo.

Marta Caroscio, from the Spanish, of the contribution by Alberto García Porras.

Alejandra Gutiérrez, from the Portuguese, of the contribution by Mário Jorge Barroca.

Jill Bradley, from the Dutch, of the contribution by Marjolijn Kruip.

A page number **in bold** indicates an illustration

Cattle 38, 52, 54, 58, 78, 83, 85-7, 91, **98**, 101, 111-3, 119, 123, 127, 141, 144, 164, 205, 238, 250, 281, 458

Cats 83, 131, 173, 361

Cauldrons **197, 203**

Cellars **148, 153**, 154, 173-4, 235, 238, 347-8, 387,389, 391-2, 400, 402, 484-5

Cemeteries (& graveyards) Chapter 12; location of, 152, 156, 220, 326, 395, 400, 407, 409, 411, 418, 429, 501-2; development of, 430-1, 438, 440-1, 516-522; examples of, **431, 501, 503, 517, 519, 520**; see also Islam, Jewish

Censer, see thurible

Ceramics, see pottery, tiles

Cess-pits, see latrines

Chain-mail **50**

Chairs 150, 204-5

Chalices 435, **436**, 505

Chancel 429, **434**, 443, 448, 468, 470-2, 476, 498

Chapels 30, 36, 39, 44, 144, 152, 168, **228**, 235-6, 238-9, **267**, 272, 379, 382, 390, 394, 400, 403, 415-9, 431, **466**, 469, 470-1, 473, 475; Chantry chapels, 152, 443, 476, 483, 498-513; Guild chapels, **397**, 398-9; and see church buildings

Chapter House 432, 433, **435**, 446, **453**, 455-6, 482, **500**, 503-4

Cheese 47, 128

Cherries 131, 139

Chess 210, **377**

Chests 154, 201, **204**, 216

Chickpeas 139

Childbirth 484, 494, 497-8

Children 39, 46, 125, 142-3, **155**, 156, 172, **201**, 202, **206**, 207, 268, 426, 475, 494-7, 503, 507, 518, 524-5

Christianity, practice of 412-437; landscape, **473**; urban topography, **415**, 416-9

Chronology 46-7

Church buildings Chapter 11; **228**, **501**; parts of, **434**; 468-478; **469**, **472**; development of ritual space, **474**; chapel of Monte di Croci, **501**

Churchyards 516-522

Ciborium 435

Cider-press 30

Cistercians 91, 120, 125, 233, 413, 418, 432, 458-465, 502-3, 508

Clearance cairns **117**

Climate (& climate change) 27, 33, 52, 60-7, 74-5, 79, 85, 118, 120, 145, 178, 317, 495-6

Cloister 141-2, 423, 446, 454-8, **459**, 461, 466-7, 499, 502-3

Clothing 125, 155, 205-10, 221; **203, 206**

Coffins 20, 125, 472, 475, 505, 507-8, 513-4, 526-7

Cogs (ships) **332**

Coins 351, **356**, 351-6; for dating, 125, 197, 220, 268, 354; in graves, 356

Combs **212**

Contarina ship 330, **331**

Context, stratigraphic 35

Conversion (& Christianisation) 409, 412, 455

Cooking (& dining) 190-**203**

Conservation plan 454

Cope (reclaimed land) 76

Copper (& copper-alloy) 20, 67, 193, 196-8, 200, 210-1, 223-4, 272, 274, 279, 280, 283, 296, 320-3, 343, 352, 354, 361, 363, 368-9, 500

Coulter **99**, 100

cow, see cattle

cradle **201**

crafts and industries Chapter 7; rural industry, 101; urban crafts 392-4;

craft-networks, **82, 284**

cranberries 131

Crannogs (artificial islands) 252, 260, **261**

Crocodile 94

Crop-mark 28

Crucifix **306, 369**

Cruets 435

Crusades 18, 82, 90, 221, 240, 331, 359, 361-2, 409, 412, 414

Culture history 20

Cupboards 181, 201, 204, 483; see also aumbry

Curfew 291

Cutlery 199

D

Dagger **203**, 208, 265

Dates (food) 361

Dating, see chronology

Deer 31, 88, 91, 116, 132-7, 281, **377**; deer-parks, 252; see also venison, reindeer

Defences Chapter 6; and see town walls, fortifications

Forge (& forging)   **114**, 273, 322-4, 387, 393; water-powered, **456-460**, **462**

Formation processes   105-6; and see archaeological resource

Fortification, Chapter 6: 19, 147, 244-271; **188**, 217, 243-272, 327; in Africa, **367**; of churches, 50, **51**, 465; and see castles

Franciscans   416, **417**, **427**, 466, **467**

Friaries   372-3, 455, 457, **466-7**

Franc, see coins

Fuel   30, 77, 213, 277, 280, 311

Fulling   321

'fumitory pots'   505

Funerals   396, 467, 501, 505, 507, 509

Fur   64, 78, 83, 90, 113-4, 131, 155-6, 173, 207, 217, 221, 339, 357, 359, **360**, 361, 393

Furnace   glass 280, 308-13; oil, 282; metal, 285, 322, 324; bath, 401

Furniture (& furnishings)   24, 59, 112, 115, 120, 122, 125, 171, 190, 200-**201**, 202, **204**-5, 212-3, 216, 220, 222-3, 238, 279, 315, 410, 430, 437, 481, 489

Furrow, see rig and furrow

Futhark   110

G

Games   87, 194, 202, 210, 238

Game animals, see hunting

Gangue (source of ore)   322-6

Genizot (stores in synagogues)   441

Gardens   30, 182-8 **185**, **187**, **188**

Gatehouse   **153**, 168, **244**, 245-6, 250, 255-7, **259**, 269, **271**

Genovino, see coins

Geoarchaeology   65, 75

Geochemical survey,   29

Geophysical survey   29, 30, 33, 46, 65, 109, 272-3, 276, 386, 453-4

GIS (Geographic Information System)   33, 42, 46

Glass   85, 101, 131, 154, 174, 199, **191**, 202, 213, 217, **219**, 221-4, 229, 265, 344, 369, 393, 400, 497, 505; manufacture, 280-1, 307-314, 321; urinals, **211**; window (stained) glass, 67, 178, 223, 287, 314-5, 443, 469, **470**, 476; glass paste, 208; beads, 363-4, 369; reading-glasses, 212; lamps, 483; and see Islam

Goat   55, 85,141, 144-5, 205, 281, 507

Gold (gilt & gilded)   **124**, 154, 156, 199, 200, 206, 208, 210, 221, 229, 280, 297, 308, 311, 313, 321-2, 324, 345, 351-3, 355-6, 362-6, 328, 368-9, **435**, 505

Gothic art   23, 147, **157-8**, **192**, 223, 236-7, 350, 389, 416, 439, 443-4, 450, 488

GPS (Global Positioning System)   33, 46

Grace Dieu ship   335

Grain (trade)   **54**, 83, 330, 361

Graddaning   119

Graffiti   49, 50, 194

Granaries   30, **137-8**, 238, **456**

Granges   120, 126, 259, 463, **464**, 465

Grapes   125, 138-9, 189, 287; and see vines

Grave-goods   424-6, 430-1, 505, 507-8

Graves, see burials

Graveyards, see cemeteries

Griffin   95, 358; see also ibex

Groat, see coins

Guilds, guildhalls   59, 213, 229, 282-3, 315, 341, 379, 393-4, **396-399**, 428, 471; guild chapels, **397**

Gunpowder, effect of   19, 217, 229, 260, 272, 276; suicide by means of, 268

H

Habitus   222, 342

Halls, see houses

Hamlets, at Skramle   110-114, **112**; at Beaume 119-126; **122-4**;

Hanseatic League   216, **340**, **346**, 340-350

Harbours (landing places, ports & anchorages)   **129**, 225, **251**, 305, 328, 332, 337, 344, 373, **374**, 379, 384-5

Harrow   **99**, 100

Hay   100, 113, 154, 174

Hazel (nuts)   130, 139, 507

Hearths   30, 110-2, 122, **123**, 157, 162, 164, 181, 238-9, 271, 356, 496; for boiling sugar, 283; for firing moulds, 285; for heating vats, 320; bloomery hearths, 322; for casting, 322; at mines, 323-4; at a forge, 458; hearth surveys, 494; in cemeteries, 518.

Heating   157, 167, 189, 200, **201**, 216, 239, 342, 349, 403; and see stoves, hearths

Hedgerow counting   28

Helmets   268

HLC (Historic Landscape Characterisation)   27, **32**

layers, stratigraphic 25

leather 24, 81, 85, **86**, 88, 173-4, 199, 207-9, 212, 229, **278**, 281, 345, 387,393, 461, 505

leopard **95**, 116, 156, 358, 361

leprosy 400, 495-6, 498

levées (see river management)

Lidar 26, 109

Life-cycle 411, 425

Life-expectancy 495

Lighting (oil lamps, lanterns) 194, 282, 291, 297, 301, 326, 483; and see candles

Lion 80, 95, 156, 357-8, 363

Lipids (residues) 45, 393

Little Ice Age 67, 69, 85, 495; and see climate

Liturgy 429, 437, 442, 478

Liripipe hood **79**, 205-7

Looms 316, 318, **319**, 320, 393, **395**

longue durée 27, 56, 61, 65, 93

Lord of the Rings 23

Lustreware 279-80, 290, 297, 301, 304-5, **306**, 307, 313-4, 328

Lyly, see travel on ice and snow

Lynchets 100

Lynx 87, 361.

M

Machicolation 240, 246, 256-7, 269

Magic 413, 497-8.

Manilla (bracelet) **369**

Manure 27, 81, 101, 118, 173

Manuscripts 23, 46, **89**, **98**, 99, 202, 210, 246, 321, 334, **335**, 421, 432, 456; Jewish, 483-4; provenance, 55; and see parchment

Maps **110**

Marriage 149, 171, 205, **214**, 429

Marten 131, **360**, 361

Marxism 40

Masons' marks 42, 443, **446**

Mattocks **99**, 100

Meadows **31-2**, **62**, 64, 91, 100, 111, 116, 154, 186, 423, 461

Medicine 276, 307, 400, 403, 494, 497

Medieval archaeology, agenda and objectives 20-1, 48; and science, 48, 52-7; in Italy, 40-43; and see design, theory, method, buildings

Medieval Europe, geography 17-18; Fig 1.1, 1.2

Medievalism 23

Medlar 139

Memorials 341, 440, **475**, 509, 510, **511**, **515**, 523, **525**

Mendicant orders, see friaries

Merchant Adventurers **399**

Metallurgy 55-6, 101, 277, 326-7

Metal vessels 196-7

Metals, extraction, 322; mining, 323-7; see gold, silver, copper, tin, bronze, lead, pewter, iron

Methods in Medieval Archaeology, see design

Middle Ages, definition of 16-17

Mihrab (mosque) 486-7, **489**, 493

Mikveh (ritual bath); see Jews

Military orders 49-51, 417, 418

Milk 86, 119, 127, 128, 142

Millet 138, 139

Mills, watermills 31, 51, 77, 86, 120, 324, 458, 461-2, 464-5, 479; Windmills, 32, 47; oil and sugar 282-3; metalworking mill, 461, **462-3**

Mimbar 487-9

Mines and miners, 323-7; silver mine **325**; at Brandes, **326**; diet, **144**

Miniver, minever (fur) 155, 359

Mints, see coins

Mirrors 211

Missal 429

Mitigation archaeology 15, 20, 61, 137

Moats 29, 30, 76, 149, 232, **257**, 262, 358, 378, 499; Moated sites 252, 257-**259**, 260

Mobility, of people 55, 328; of livestock, 55

Monasteries 76, 86, 278, 410, 412-24, 454-465; investigation of, 457-465; **456**, **458**, **459**, **460**, **462**, **463**, **464**, **503**; at Santa Giulia, 40; at Esslingen, **400**, **415**; at Visby, **427**; at Bordesley Abbey, **36-7**, **460-464**, 465; at Fontenay, 456-460; Pictish monastery, 472; bone-working at, 282; book found at 424; silver ring found at, 432; syphilis at, 496; monastic cemeteries, 502-3; and see friaries, forge, mills

Monkeys 210, **357**

Mons Meg **247**

Mortar (for building) 233-5; lime mortar, failure of, 443-4; brooch found in, 267

Mortars (for grinding) 119, 198, **199**, 320, 324

Mosques 43, 308, 411, 414, 447, 486-8, **489**, 490-491, **492**, 493; in towns, 404-7; burial at, 514; and see Islam

Murals, see wall painting

Music (& musical instruments)   210, 238

Myrrh   307

N

NAA (Neutron Activation Analysis)   45

Nano-excavation   35

Narwhal,   78, 90, 95, 358-9; and see unicorn

Nasrid kingdom   19, 177, 186-7, 297, **300**, 301, 304-5

Nave   429, **434**

Navigation   79, 368

Necklace   208-9, **219**, 220

Nef (tableware)   200, 223

O

Oats   113, 119, 125, 127, 131, 138, 139

Olives (oil & cultivation)   120, 221, 282-3, 368; and see mills

Orchards, see gardens

OSL (Optically Stimulated Luminescence)   47

'organic crescent'   24

ovens, domestic   112; sugar, 283; glass,   311; and see kilns, stoves, furnaces

ox-house   30

P

Padrão (monument)   **362, 365**

Paganism (& witches)   75, 218-220, 409, 412-3, 428, 430-1, 516

Palaces   147-156, 237; and gender, 150; investigation at St David's, 38-39, **44**; Clarendon Palace, **148**; The Louvre, **149**; Westminster, **151**; Kennington, **153**; gardens at, **182-7**; in Africa, 197; at Buda, 348; glass at, 311, 314; at Viborg, 416-7; in Norwich, 453-4; in Toledo, 483

Paper   189, 212, 217, 307; paper money, 353

Parchment making   35, 55, **86**, 212, 217, 281, 307, 455, 497-8, 507

Parish system   472, 516

Parks (for restricted hunting)   90-1, 133-4, 136, 154, 252

Pastoral, see farming

Paten (plate)   435, **436**

Paternoster, see rosaries

Patten (shoe)   209

Peaches   139

Peacock   31

Pendants   156, 208-9, 219, 220; pendant crosses, 212; pendant coins, 355, **356**

Penny, see coins

Pepper   368-9

Pew   **346**

Pewter   196, **226, 421**, 422, 505

Pfennig, see coins

Phytoliths (plant remains)   64-5

Pick   **323**

Pictures, use of   202-3

Pigs   83, 85, 93, 127

Pilgrims, pilgrimage, pilgrim tokens; 23, 27, 168, 208, 212, 216, 223, 356, 400, 410-19, **420-2**, 423, 424, 426, 428-9, 433, 497-8, 507; in graves, 424, 507-8; Pilgrim's Guild, 398; see Santiago di Compostella, Mont Saint Michel

Pitfalls   113-4

Plaggen (soils)   76, 101

Plague   53-4, 80, 110, 256, 374, 414, 432-3, 495, 498, 512-3; see Black Death, Bubonic Plague

Plans, archaeological   **25**, 34, **37, 44**, 104, 107, **112**, **115**, **122-3, 137-8, 148, 177**

Plant remains, study of, 27, 46, 52, 58, 63; at Durfort, 137-9; and see seeds

Plots, see tenements, tofts

Ploughs   47-8, **98**, **99**, 100, 321-2; see fields

Plums   139

Pollen analysis   27, 30, 62, 64-5, 113, 128, 183, 326

Ponds   66, 73, 183, 463; and see fishponds, water mills

Porringer   **155**

Portcullis   244, 246, 255-6, 259, 269

Positivism   40

Post-processualism   20

Pottage   119

Pottery, archaeological uses of, 27, 28, **30**, 33, 35, 101, 109, 191; analysis: 45, 213; Medieval use of, 154, 174, 190, **191-193**, 194, 222-3, **288-9**; manufacture, 279-80; contents of, 45; trade in, 194, 288-291; in the Hansa towns, 342-346, **344**; lead-glazed: 192, **193**; tin-glazed (maiolica), 191, **192**; see also stonewares; faience, Islam, *bote*

Poultry   83

Pound, see coins

Prayer, inscribed   **432-3**

Preceptory   **49**

Predators   87-90

Processualism   20

Project design, see design in field research

Property boundaries   73; and see fences

Publication, see design

Pulkka, see *ahkio*

Purse   **203**, 208, 281; lost on battlefield, 273

Pyx   435

Q

qibla   487-8, **489**, **493**, 514

Quarry (prey)   88, 91, 133-4

Quarries (for stone)   113-4, 458

Querns   119

R

Rabbits   31, 47, 91, 116, 221, 360-1; and see warrens

Reclamation, in the Netherlands   73-77; **76-7**; see also river management

Radar (ground penetrating)   33, 39

Radiocarbon dating (examples and caveats)   46-7, 66, 74, 110, 233, 358, 496, 505, 516, 520-1; and see Bayesian analysis

Reflexivity   20

Reindeer   90, 128, 131, **339**

Relics (& reliquaries)   223, 321, 410, 416, 421, 424, 434, 446, 454, 472

Religious practice, Chapter 10; artefacts, 212; and see Christianity, Islam, Jews and paganism

Reposadero (water-jug stand)   **299**

Rescue archaeology, see mitigation archaeology

Research agenda   21

Retrogressive analysis   28

Ribat, see Islam

Rig and furrow   **26**, **31**, 100, **104**, 116, **117**, 118, **462**

Rivers, management of, 62, 66, **69-73**; in the Loire valley, 68-70; in Roussilon, 71-5;

Roads   59, 65, 75, 115, **116**, 119, 125, 328, 338, 386, 390, 416; silk road, 19, 217

Rood screen   469, **470**, 476

Roman legacy   19, 23, 30, 72; in roads, 119; heating, 157; landowning, 243, 249; fortification, 255; at Carcassonne, 261-2; olive oil, 282-3; in pottery, 297, 301; in mining, 322; in coinage, 355; in trade, 361; in towns, 371-2, 401-2, 443; in ritual, 434; in cathedrals, 447-9; in monasticism, 455; in engineering, 465; in Sicily, 490-3; in burial, 501, 506, 516, 523-4.

Romanesque art   23, 216, 236-7, 416, 440, 443, 447, 484

Rosaries   **52**, **203**, **425**; saying of, 428

Rural settlement, Chapter 3; in Greenland, 78-9; see villages, farming

Rye   113, 125, 127, 138-9, 495

S

Sable   155, 360

Sails, see ships

Salet (helmet)   **268**

Salt   35, **54**, 77, 192, 223, 277, 361, 394

Sanctuary lamp   429

Scales (balance)   393

Schnitt method   35

Scythe   100, 238

Seals (animal)   78-9, 92, 128, 131

Seals (signature)   212, 301, 321, **377**, 507

Section, archaeological   35, **36**, **37**, **116**

Sediments   61-3, 66, 69-71, 137, 173, 324

Seeds   45, 100-1, 183, 307, 317; at Ferrara, 52; at Durfort, 137-9

Selions (plough furrows)   24, **116**

Sequence diagram, see stratigraphy

Sequin   **124**

Sex (& gender)   21, 46, 53, 141, 152, 205, 207-8, 216, 497-8, 513, 526; segregation in burial, 503; sin, 496; sexually transmitted disease, 496; sexual relations, with animals, 93; single sex communities, see monasteries,

Sheep (or goat)   33, 38, 55; farming, 58, 76, 78, 83, 85, 94, **98**, 101, 120, 123, 127, 238, 458; hides, 281; wool, 316-7; dairy products, 119

Shields   49, **50**

Ships   328-337, **331-2**, **335**, 369; sail, see lateen; crew of Mary Rose, 55

Shilling, see coins

Shoes, see footwear

Shops   **22**, 168, **169**, 170, 326, 393-4, 397-8, 479; and see workshops

Shovel testing   28

Sickle   **124**

Sieges, see warfare

Signet ring   **377**

Silk   155, 207, 217, 229, 290, 328, 505, 515; and see silk road

In this index, Å has the alphabetical position of A and Æ as AE; Ö and Ø are treated as O.

M